Christendom Destroyed

THE PENGUIN HISTORY OF EUROPE

General Editor: David Cannadine

MARK GREENGRASS

Christendom Destroyed

Europe 1517–1648

VIKING

VIKING
Published by the Penguin Group
Penguin Group (USA) LLC
375 Hudson Street
New York, New York 10014

USA I Canada I UK I Ireland I Australia I New Zealand I India I South Africa I China
penguin.com
A Penguin Random House Company

Published by Viking Penguin, a member of Penguin Group (USA) LLC, 2014

First published in Great Britain by Allen Lane, an imprint of Penguin Books Ltd.

Illustration credits appear on pages x–xiii.

ISBN 978-0-670-02456-8

Printed in the United States of America
1   3   5   7   9   10   8   6   4   2

Set in Sabon LT Std

For Emily

Contents

Christian States in Disarray

List of Maps

List of Illustrations

List of Genealogies

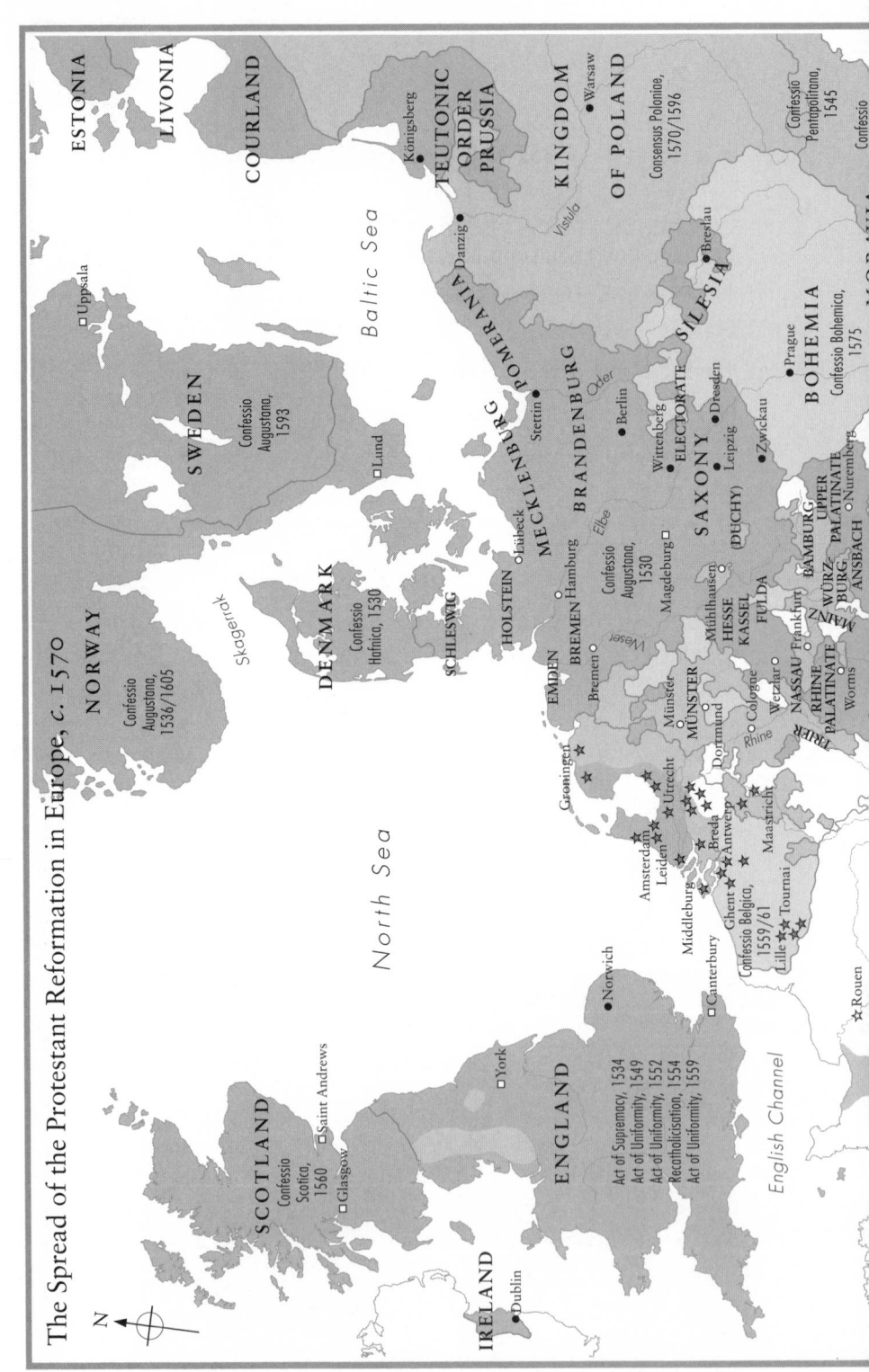

The Spread of the Protestant Reformation in Europe, *c.* 1570

N

ESTONIA

LIVONIA

COURLAND

□ Uppsala

☐ Königsberg

TEUTONIC ORDER PRUSSIA

● Warsaw

KINGDOM

OF POLAND

Consensus Poloniae, 1570/1596

Baltic Sea

● Danzig

Confessio Pentopolitana, 1545

Confessio

● Breslau

SILESIA

● Prague

BOHEMIA

Confessio Bohemica, 1575

NORWAY

Confessio Augustana, 1536/1605

SWEDEN

Confessio Augustana, 1593

Vistula

POMERANIA

MECKLENBURG

○ Stettin

Oder

BRANDENBURG

● Berlin

● Wittenberg

ELECTORATE

● Dresden

SAXONY

● Leipzig

● Zwickau

(DUCHY)

□ Lund

Skagerrak

DENMARK

Confessio Hafnica, 1530

SCHLESWIG

HOLSTEIN

○ Lübeck

Hamburg

Confessio Augustana, 1530

BREMEN

Elbe

Magdeburg □

○ Bremen

Weser

Mühlhausen ○

HESSE

KASSEL

FULDA

BAMBERG· ○ Nuremberg

UPPER PALATINATE

ANSBACH

WÜRZ-BURG·

North Sea

EMDEN

Groningen ☆

Utrecht ☆☆

Amsterdam ☆

Leiden ☆

○ Münster

○ Dortmund

MÜNSTER

Wetzlar ○

NASSAU· Frankfurt

MAINZ

RHINE PALATINATE

Worms ○

TRIER

RHINE PALATINATE

Middleburg ☆

Ghent ☆☆ Antwerp ☆

Breda ☆☆

Maastricht ☆

Confessio Belgica, 1559/61

Lille ☆☆ Tournai ☆

○ Cologne

Rhine

● Norwich

SCOTLAND

Confessio Scotica, 1560

☐ Saint Andrews

☐ Glasgow

☐ York

ENGLAND

Act of Supremacy, 1534
Act of Uniformity, 1549
Act of Uniformity, 1552
Recatholicisation, 1554
Act of Uniformity, 1559

IRELAND

● Dublin

□ Canterbury

English Channel

☆ Rouen

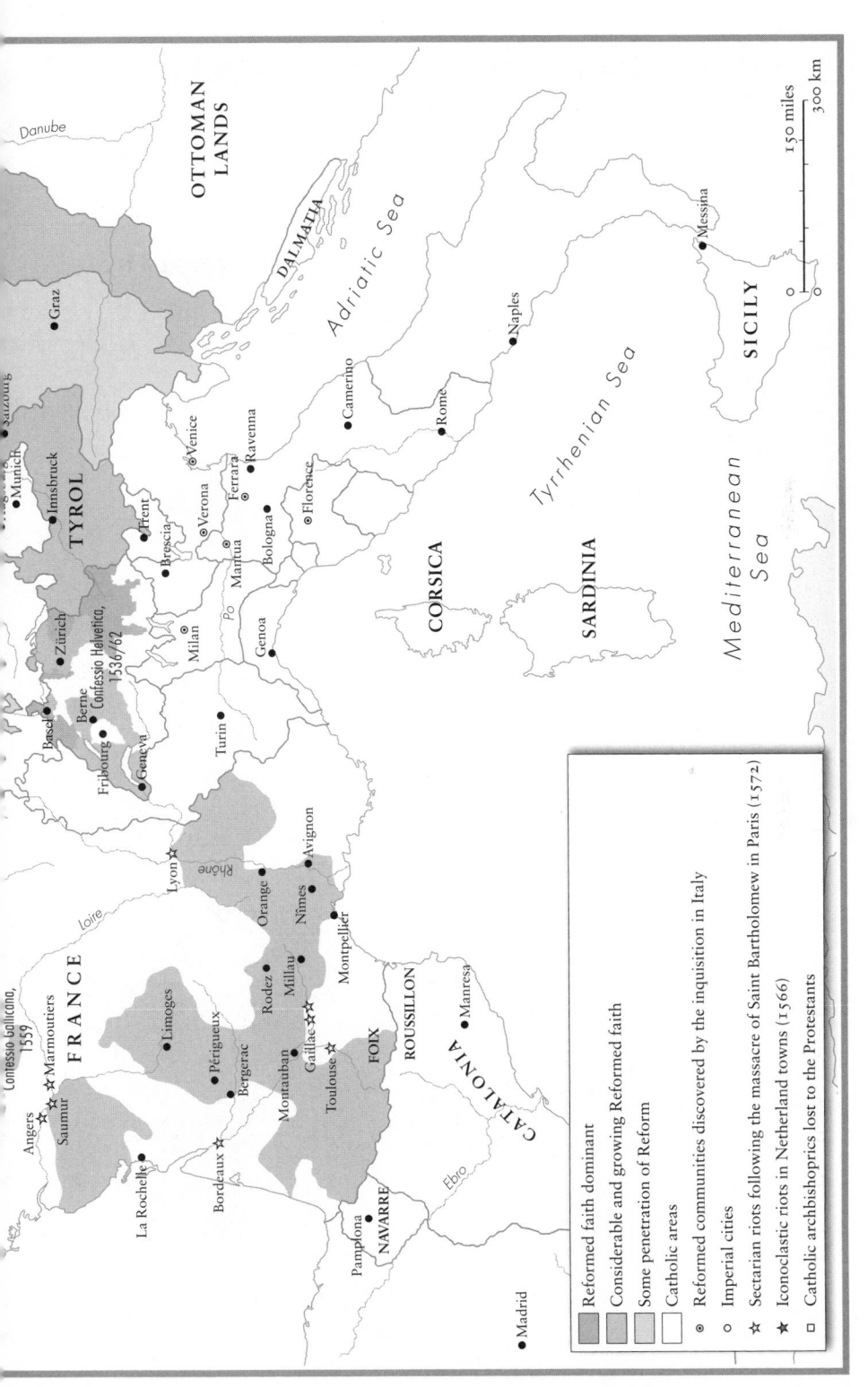

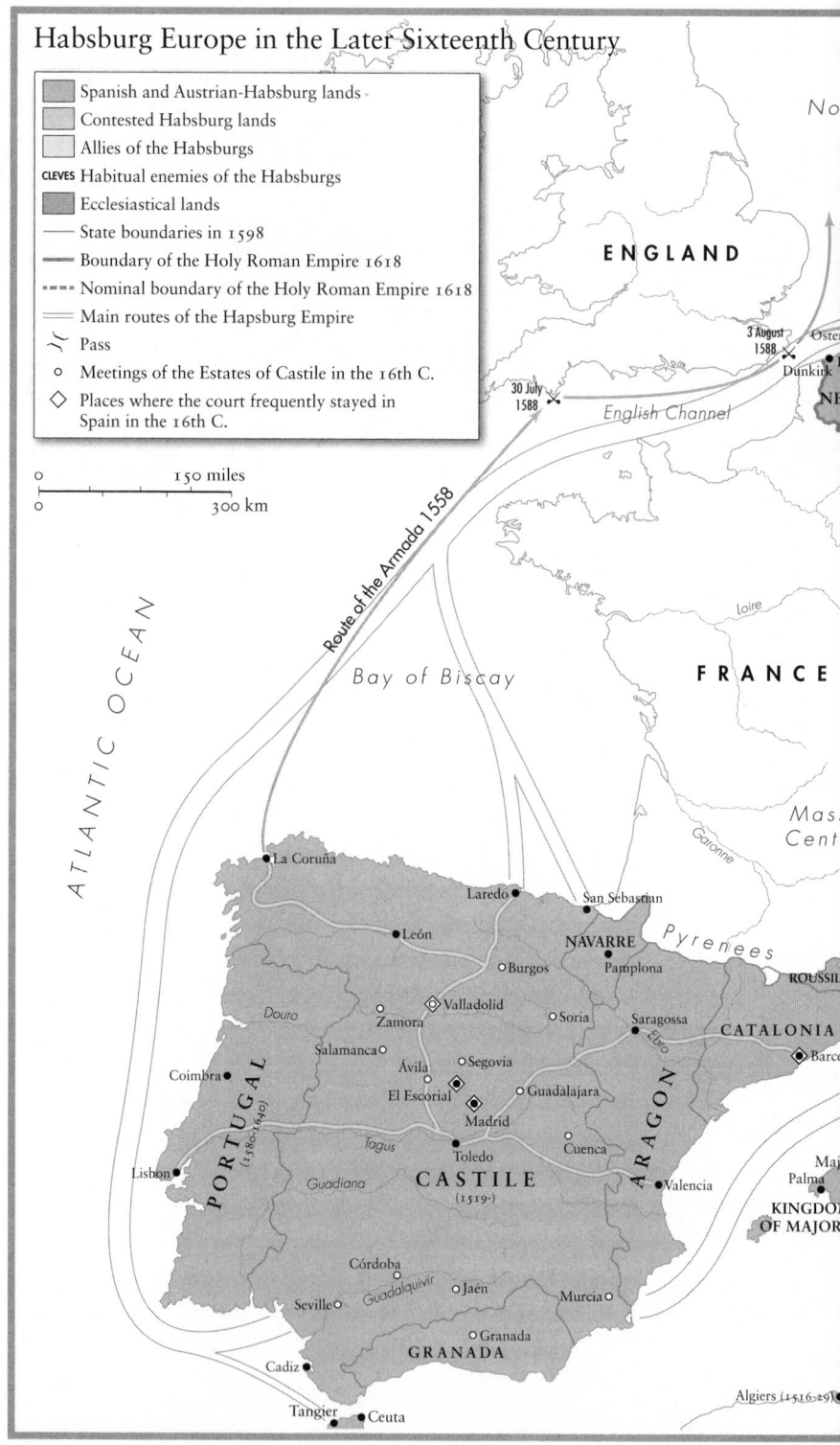

Habsburg Europe in the Later Sixteenth Century

■ Spanish and Austrian-Habsburg lands
■ Contested Habsburg lands
■ Allies of the Habsburgs
CLEVES Habitual enemies of the Habsburgs
■ Ecclesiastical lands
— State boundaries in 1598
━ Boundary of the Holy Roman Empire 1618
╍╍╍ Nominal boundary of the Holy Roman Empire 1618
═ Main routes of the Hapsburg Empire
〕⟨ Pass
○ Meetings of the Estates of Castile in the 16th C.
◇ Places where the court frequently stayed in Spain in the 16th C.

0 ___ 150 miles
0 ___ 300 km

ENGLAND

No

3 August 1588 ✕ Oster
Dunkirk
NE

30 July 1588 ✕

English Channel

Route of the Armada 1558

ATLANTIC OCEAN

Bay of Biscay

FRANCE

Loire

Mass
Cent

Garonne

• La Coruña
Laredo • • San Sebastián
• León
NAVARRE
○ Burgos • Pamplona
Pyrenees
ROUSSIL
Douro ○ Valladolid ◇
Zamora ○ Soria Saragossa
CATALONIA
Salamanca ○ Ávila ○ Segovia
Coimbra • El Escorial ◇ ○ Guadalajara • Barce
Madrid ◇
Tagus
Lisbon • Toledo ○ Cuenca Maj
Guadiana CASTILE Valencia • Palma
(1519-) KINGDON
OF MAJOR
Córdoba ○
Seville ○ Guadalquivir ○ Jaén Murcia ○
○ Granada
GRANADA
Cadiz •
Algiers (1516-29)•
Tangier • Ceuta

PORTUGAL (1580-1640)
ARAGON

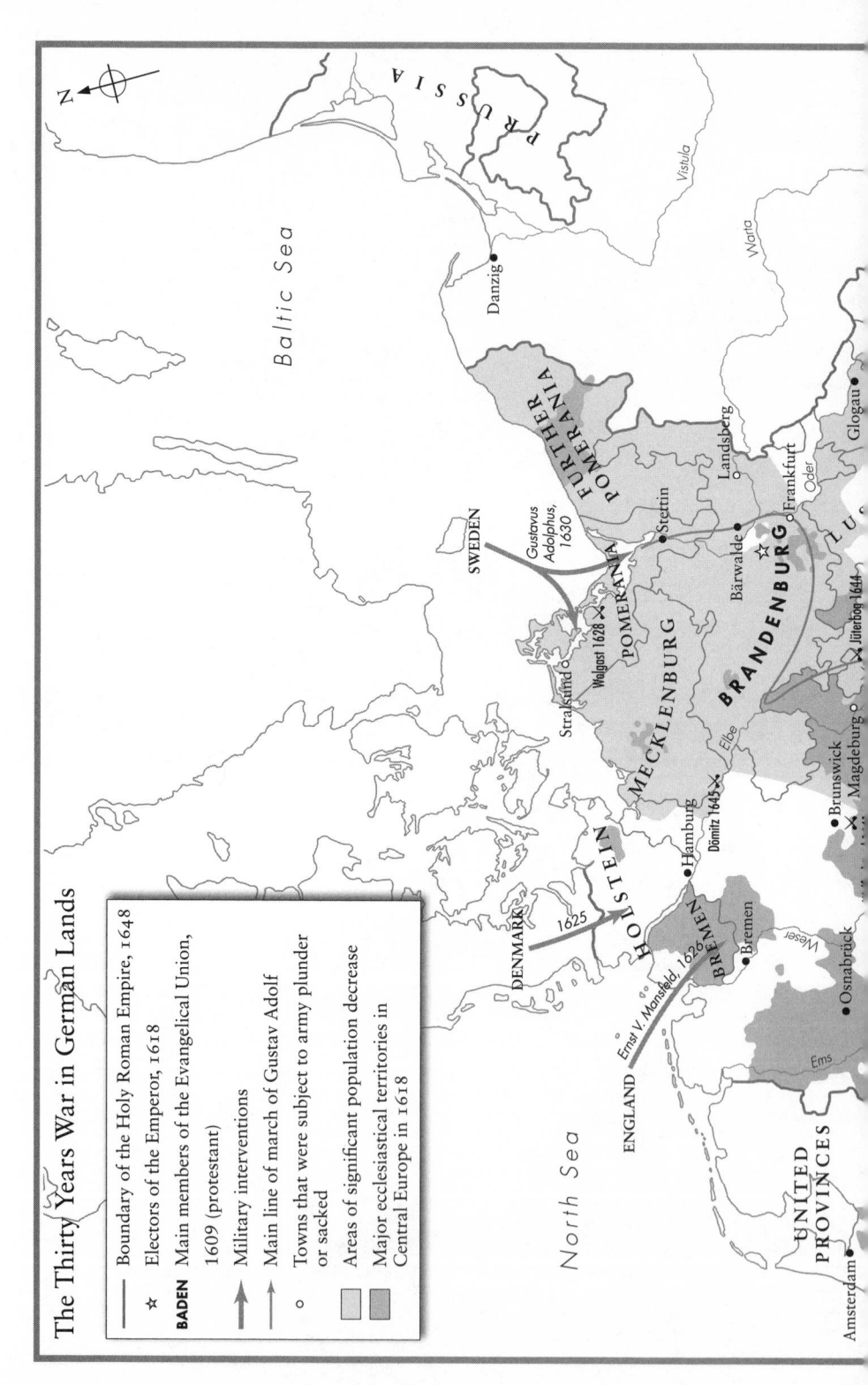

The Thirty Years War in German Lands

- Boundary of the Holy Roman Empire, 1648
- ☆ Electors of the Emperor, 1618
- **BADEN** Main members of the Evangelical Union, 1609 (protestant)
- ⬆ Military interventions
- ⬆ Main line of march of Gustav Adolf
- ○ Towns that were subject to army plunder or sacked
- Areas of significant population decrease
- Major ecclesiastical territories in Central Europe in 1618

Baltic Sea

North Sea

PRUSSIA

Vistula

Warta

Danzig ●

FURTHERIA
POMERANIA

POMERANIA

Landsberg ○

Glogau ●

Oder

Gustavus Adolphus, 1630

SWEDEN

Stettin ●

Frankfurt ○

LU...

Wolgast 1628 ✕

Bärwalde ●

☆ BRANDENBURG

Stralsund ○

POMERANIA

MECKLENBURG

Jüterbog 1644 ✕

Elbe

Magdeburg ○
✕

DENMARK

1625

HOLSTEIN

Hamburg ●

Dömitz 1645 ✕

Brunswick ●

BREMEN

Bremen ●

Weser

Ernst V. Mansfeld, 1626

ENGLAND

Osnabrück ●

Ems

UNITED
PROVINCES

Amsterdam ●

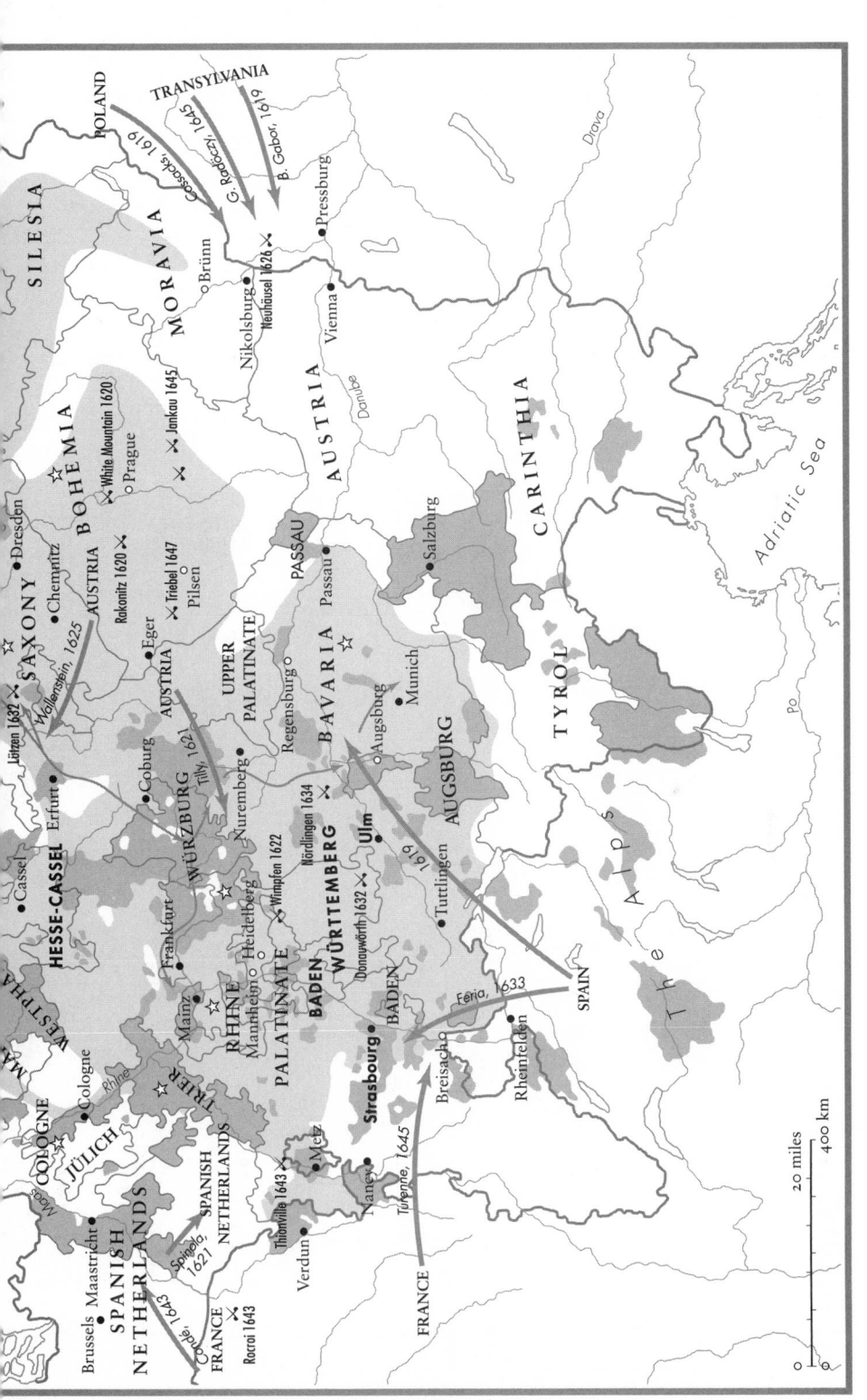

SILESIA

POLAND

TRANSYLVANIA

Cossacks, 1619

G. Rakóczy, 1645

B. Gabor, 1619

Drava

MORAVIA

Brünn

Pressburg

Nikolsburg

Neuhäusel 1626 ✕

Vienna

BOHEMIA

SAXONY

Dresden

Chemnitz

Wallenstein, 1625

Lützen 1632 ✕

AUSTRIA

Rakonitz 1620 ✕

White Mountain 1620 ✕

Jankau 1645 ✕

Prague

Triebel 1647 ✕

Pilsen

CARINTHIA

Adriatic Sea

Erfurt

Cassel

HESSE-CASSEL

Eger

AUSTRIA

Coburg

WÜRZBURG

Tilly, 1621

Nuremberg

Salzburg

PASSAU

Passau

UPPER PALATINATE

Regensburg

BAVARIA

Munich

Augsburg

AUGSBURG

TYROL

Po

The Alps

Frankfurt

Mainz

RHINE

Mannheim

Heidelberg

Wimpfen 1622 ✕

Nördlingen 1634 ✕

Ulm

WÜRTTEMBERG

Donauwörth 1632 ✕

BADEN

1619

Tuttlingen

PALATINATE

Cologne

Rhine

TRIER

Strasbourg

BADEN

Feria, 1633

SPAIN

Breisach

Rheinfelden

WESTPHALIA

JÜLICH

COLOGNE

Maas

Brussels

Maastricht

SPANISH NETHERLANDS

Spinola, 1621

SPANISH NETHERLANDS

Thionville 1643 ✕

Metz

FRANCE

Rocroi 1643 ✕

Corbie, 1643

Verdun

Nancy

Turenne, 1645

FRANCE

20 miles

400 km

0

0

Europe's Frontiers in 1648

Legend:
- —— Boundary of the Holy Roman Empire
- Ecclesiastical territories
- Spanish lands
- French lands

300 miles
400 km

Shetland Is.

Orkney Is.

Sä

Bergen

Christiania

North Sea

DENMARK – NORWAY

S

Göteb

Hebrides

SCOTLAND

Edinburgh

Aalborg

IRELAND

Durham

Copenhagen

M

Dublin

I. OF MAN

York

Bor

ENGLAND

Lübeck

Hamburg

Ste

WALES

Oxford

Cambridge

DUTCH REPUBLIC

Bremen

BRANDEN

T H E

Bristol

London

Amsterdam

Brunswick

Magdebur

SAXON

Dresden

ATLANTIC OCEAN

Cálais

Brussels

Aachen

Cologne

BO

Prag

Channel Is.

SPANISH NETH.

Mainz

Frankfurt

English Channel

NORMANDY

Trier

E M P I R

Nüremberg

BRITTANY

Paris

Verdun

Metz

Seine

Strasbourg

Danub

BAVARIA

Orléans

Munich

Nantes

Loire

Tours

Basle

Salz

FRANCHE COMTÉ

SWISS

TYROL

Charolais

Berne

CONFEDERATION

F R A N C E

Geneva

Lyon

SAVOY

Milan

Venice

Bordeaux

Turin

Garonne

Rhône

Genoa

Ferrara

San Mar

Toulouse

Avignon

Florence

PAPAL STATES

La Coruña

NAVARRE

Pamplona

Marseille

Corsica

Rome

Oporto

Valladolid

Andorra

Duero

ARAGON

Benev

Lisbon

Saragossa

Barcelona

Napl

PORTUGAL

S P A I N

Madrid

Tagus

Toledo

CASTILE

Guadiana

Valencia

Sardinia

Cagliari

Seville

Ebro

Granada

GRANADA

Mediterranean Sea

Palermo

Tangier

Ceuta

Si

(Portuguese)

Bona

Biserta

MOROCCO

Melilla

Oran

Algiers

Bejaia

Tunis

ALGIERS

TUNIS

Ma

Introduction

David de Vries was proud of having seen the world. The travel account which he published in his native Dutch in 1655 recounted the six voyages which had taken him to the Mediterranean, the Far East, Newfoundland, the Caribbean, and South and North America. Born in La Rochelle to Dutch parents in 1593, he became a trained artillery master, fluent in several European languages, a skilled navigator, a shrewd man of business, an autodidact with an observant eye. It was not his fault that his colonial enterprises – on the 'South' (Delaware) river (1633), Oyapock river in Guyana (1634) and Staten Island (1638–43) – all failed. Sponsors let him down, the local populations were difficult to manage, and competing ventures were hostile. De Vries knew where his loyalties lay. His homeland was in the Low Countries, the town of Hoorn his *patria*. If he had succeeded in establishing a colonial 'patroonship', he would have modelled it on the estates of the landed gentry of Holland as a part of the 'New Netherland' to which he often referred. He was a Calvinist Protestant who had a hand in building the first Christian church on Staten Island. De Vries understood Europe in a wider world. Landing at St John's, Newfoundland in 1620, after marvelling at the monumental icebergs he saw en route, he recounted the Dutch, Basque, Portuguese and English vessels that he had met, fishing and trading in those waters. With an eye already acclimatized by his reading of other travelogues, he accommodated himself to local Indian customs. Visiting the governor of the new English colonies along the James river in 1640, he was welcomed with a glass of Venetian wine and sat down with another English colonist who had also been in the East Indies in the late 1620s. 'I looked at him well, and he at me,' says de Vries. And he heard the colonist say 'that mountains could not meet one another, but men who go and see the world can'.

By their clothes, their food and their demeanour, these were Europeans, aware that they were on another continent, having (as de Vries said) 'steered the earth's four corners'. De Vries's career reflected the wider geographical horizons of his generation, the possibilities and challenges which they opened up, an extraordinary pluralism of contact and communication that challenged old loyalties and senses of belonging. This new sense of Europe as a geographical entity, fashioned in a reflection of the wider world, would not have existed a century before. This eclipse of the older notion of 'Christendom' by 'Europe' in the sixteenth and early seventeenth centuries, and the extraordinary changes that went with it, is the subject of this book.

Christendom conjures up – like Camelot – an imagined past. In the Middle Ages, the Latin terms for Christendom (*Christianitas* or *Corpus Christianorum*) delineated something else: an imagined present and future for a world united by its beliefs and aspirations. That belief-community emerged along with the fall of the Roman empire in the west. The Christianity that took root amid what remained of that empire was initially only the western fringe of a much wider Christian world whose heartland lay further east, towards the Middle East and in the still-active eastern (Byzantine) Roman empire. Gradually, however, and by a process of mutual estrangement, eastern and western Christianity drew apart until, in 1054, the pope in Rome and the patriarch in Constantinople mutually excommunicated one other. Following that big divide, Latin Christians were henceforth separated from Orthodox Christians in the Greek archipelago, the Balkans and Russia to form western Christendom.

In the first millennium of western Christianity, Christendom developed without any elaborate notion of where its centre lay, and therefore where its peripheries were to be found. It existed (to borrow the phrases of a distinguished medievalist) as a series of 'micro-Christendoms' held together like a 'geodesic dome', composed of self-contained segments. The traffic of 'symbolic goods' (holy relics, but also holy people, such as missionaries and saints) carried the charisma of holy power from one place to another and, with it, the values and aspirations of the belief-community from one segment to another. Then, in the Central Middle Ages, and following the rupture with the East, western Christendom developed a more elaborate sense of centre and periphery with the full emergence of two geographical and ideological units: the papacy and the Holy Roman Empire. Their claims to authority were forged competitively by theologians, lawyers, political theorists and intellectuals in an atmosphere of confident universalism. That ideal was supported by the economic transformations of the period, the impressive growth of markets and inter-regional and international trade, and by the marriages and diplomatic alliances of the aristocracy. 'Christendom' was how learned contemporaries in the twelfth and thirteenth centuries understood the world of Latin Christians in western Europe.

The Roman Catholic Church was the central pillar of the belief-community in Latin Christianity. The intellectual élites of the latter were formed around an international language (Latin, as opposed to Greek) as well as a common curriculum (centred in matters of philosophy and logic on the works of Aristotle) and ways of study (scholasticism). Papal envoys shared with princely advisers common theocratic and bureaucratic conceptions of how power was derived, exercised and legitimated. The Crusades became western Christendom's most ambitious project. Above all, Latin Christianity was expressed in inherited and practised beliefs, mapped onto that pre-existent multi-dimensional sacred landscape of shrines, pilgrimage sites, saint cults and festivals. Baptism was a universal rite of initiation. Those who were not baptized Christians (Jews, Muslims) were a significant presence in western Christendom's margins in the Central Middle Ages, tolerated precisely because they were *not* part of the belief-community. But, as Christian kingdoms pushed the frontiers of Latin Christianity southwards in Spain and southern Italy, their significance as exemplifying alien forces from those who did not belong to Christendom seemed to increase.

Christendom was a reflexive construction that felt easily threatened. In reality, its most dangerous enemy was not non-Christians. Its power-brokers were most vulnerable from a different and disparate constituency – from those with particular, local loyalties to whom the overarching aspirations of Christendom meant little or nothing. Across the landmass of western Europe, over and against the mechanisms of the universal order of the Holy Roman Empire (the dominion located in central Europe whose title indicated its claims to continuity with the Roman empire and a temporal form of universal dominion) and Church lay thousands of villages and parishes, their inhabitants often carrying burdens of obligation to their manorial lords which made them serfs. These communities were joined by towns, benefiting from the economic transformations of the Central Middle Ages. Suspicions were fostered towards the cosmopolitan ambitions and bureaucracy of the international order.

The more the sense of centre and periphery within Christendom was enhanced, the more people locally begrudged the time spent in getting permissions from above. Many resented the levies to sustain the universal Church and mistrusted the overblown supranational project of the Crusades. These sentiments spilled over into contentiousness, or heresy – the latter being a serious epidemic problem – and still more threatening in the minds of those to whom the ideals projected by Christendom mattered most – from the twelfth century onwards.

The confidence in these ideals waned as the European economy contracted in the wake of the Black Death. Serfdom and manorial obligations became matters of contention as local people asserted what they claimed were their customary rights. Although the beliefs and practices which Christendom had represented continued, and its sacred landscape flourished as never before, its local credibility diminished as it became the object of competing claims to represent a traditional social order. The Great Schism (1378–1417), too, undermined the claims to universal obedience. The existence of two lines of popes divided Christians between those loyal to Rome, and those supporting the Avignonese papacy, stigmatized by its enemies as a puppet in the hands of a disruptive French monarchy. The dispute ended in a compromise, but its legacy was lasting damage to the moral authority of the papacy. It also pointed up the dangers of an alliance between discontented localism and the new forces of secular, but non-imperial, authority. For the compromise was achieved through the authority of an ecumenical council. A council sustained the assertion (troubling for theocrats and bureaucrats), already debated two centuries previously but now presented with greater force, that a council was superior to the pope. That proposition was a radical way of putting it, and most 'Conciliarists' were moderates. They saw a council as a neat way out of a mess, not an engine to destroy universal papal monarchy, and still less a way of deriving doctrinal authority via unorthodox ways. Yet that was what the implicit successor to the Conciliar Movement, the Protestant Reformation, achieved.

So the central issue in the history of Europe in the sixteenth and first half of the seventeenth centuries was: what was to happen to Christendom – the institutions which defined its centres of gravity and, still more, the belief-community which underlay it? If Christendom was destroyed, what, if anything, was to take its place? The process was one of a progressive eclipse of Christendom by Europe (defined as a geographical notion in a relationship of distance with other parts of the world). The two entities differed fundamentally. Christendom claimed the loyalties of those who were baptized into the belief-community and who related to the outside world accordingly. Europe, on the other hand, claimed no unity beyond the geographical landmass that it represented and an emerging sense of the moral and civilizing superiority of the different states and peoples which occupied it. Western Christendom was a great project about European unity, over a millennium in the making. Its destruction, by contrast, was rapid and total. In little over a century, there was nothing left but the dream of it. Huge forces accomplished its destruction and transformed Europe. Their interaction with one another is the focus of the first chapter.

1. The Fall of Western Christendom

When Thomas Cockson published his engraving entitled *The Revells of Christendome* in the wake of the controversial truce between Catholic Spain and the newly emergent Dutch Republic in 1609, he drew on well-known satirical modes to make fun of Christendom. At the head of the table stands Pope Paul V with, to his left, other crowned heads of Europe (Henry IV of France, James I of England and King Christian IV of Denmark) facing us. Opposite, three Catholic monks play backgammon, dice and cards with them for the future of Europe. A dog urinates on the foot of one of them. The implication of the print was clear. The fate of Christendom was out of anyone's hands. It had become a joke. Many of the elements which contributed to the fall of western Christendom were already at work in Europe before 1500. But it was only when they were all in place, interacting with one another, that Christendom's eclipse became total.

THE IMPACT OF THE RENAISSANCE

The revival of classical texts and ideas had begun well before 1517 in the urban cultures of northern Italy, Flanders and the Rhineland. It challenged scholasticism as the accepted way of defining the philosophical concerns of Europe's élites, and with it the dominance of Aristotelian philosophy. Humanist scholars saw it as their task to recover the texts of classical Antiquity in their purity, and to enter into a dialogue with the thought of those who wrote them, subjecting it to cross-examination and scrutiny. Humanist teachers emphasized 'persuasion', learning how to marshal and deploy arguments that would win other people over to one's point of view. Their pupils, brought up on a diet of Latin (especially Ciceronian) texts, absorbed a new language and set of preoccupations about the proper conduct of citizens. That led to different conceptions of the relationship between ruler and ruled, the political and the social, and a different universalism (the 'public') from that afforded by 'Christendom'.

The 'public' was the largest conceivable *universitas*, a fictive person in the eyes of Roman law, distinct from those who created it, an entity which could mimic a living person, take on rights and responsibilities, and delegate others to carry them out in its name. The *universitas* of a republic embodied the will of its members. There could be a pluralism of republics, some more virtual than others. The 'republic of letters', for example, took advantage of changing modes of communication and was energetically promoted by humanist scholars of the age. It also, however, reflected the history of Europe's 'intellectual capital', which was increasingly out of the hands of a small clerical and bureaucratic élite and vested in a more complex and cosmopolitan market of producers and consumers, in which patrons, printers, engravers, librarians and readers of varying sorts all had a stake. How that market functioned depended upon the local environment, which explains why the Renaissance had a variable intellectual and social geometry, its impact differing across Europe, the distinctive contours sharpened by religious divisions. One of its important components would be the princely courts, and the Renaissance readily migrated and transmuted into a court culture, adapting itself to their needs and aspirations. Like the great scientific discoveries of the twentieth century, the Renaissance had the power to transform, and to destroy. It could cement ecclesiastical and political authority but also undermine it. It could challenge fundamental ideas about God's providence in the world, and also reinforce them. Its new pedagogies introduced fresh ways of understanding how one learned about oneself, the world and its creator.

Humanist scholars discovered, among other things, that ancient philosophy had a history to it. To understand Aristotle you had to place him in the context of those whose thought he was engaging with. He ceased to be a unique authority upon which to construct truth and legitimacy. The process had begun with the editing, translating and popularization of the Greek text of Diogenes Laertius's *Lives of the Philosophers*. This provided a genealogy for the competing 'sects' of Greek philosophers, giving lustre to views which had been marginal in the Middle Ages. Contemporaries presented Aristotle to their students within this more complex lineage, and took the arguments and debates of the Greek world seriously. Some philosophers in the sixteenth and early seventeenth centuries were disciples of the Epicureans, Stoics, Platonists and Pyrrhonists. The result was that ancient philosophy ceased to be the handmaiden of Christian truth and the instrument by which a universal order could be constructed. That did not stop philosophers of the period seeking to discern an underlying set of truths. Some thought that, as in any genealogy, you could trace the line back to an ancestral primacy, of which all the descendants would contain perennial, genetic traces. Francesco Patrizi, for example, in his *New Philosophy of Universals* traced what Aristotle wrote, back through what Plato had told him, through Solon and Orpheus, to the Mosaic account of the creation of the world and the mysticism of the Egyptians, as hinted at in the works of Hermes Trismegistus (these latter, he said, contained more wisdom than 'Aristotle's philosophy entire'), written originally over 1,100 years before Plato. Others preferred to highlight the points of agreement between Plato and Aristotle as the signs of an underlying 'symphony' in ancient thought, despite the apparent disagreements.

Just as this syncretic agenda might have been consolidated, however, there emerged the radically sceptical voices of those who read the works of the Greek philosopher Sextus Empiricus. He had used the disagreements among his fellow philosophers in Greece to disparage Aristotle's and others' efforts to attain the truth at all. If you took his works seriously (and some heavyweight thinkers of the period, notably the French magistrate Michel de Montaigne, did), then classical philosophy was full of error. Gianfrancesco Pico della Mirandola, the Martin Luther of sixteenth-century philosophy, wrote in his *Examination of the vain doctrines of the Gentiles* (1520): 'the entire learning of the Gentiles [i.e. pagan Antiquity] totters with superstition, uncertainty and falsehood'. It would take the genius of the French philosopher René Descartes to build a universal philosophy, capable of supporting a new experientially based physics, on the foundations of such Pyrrhonism. But, by then, no one could seriously imagine Christendom being patched together on the basis of radical doubt.

Humanist geographers, physicians and natural philosophers shared an emerging sense of the importance of direct practical experience and the value of experiment. That changed the picture of the natural world. Europe's geographical discoveries in the wider world contributed to the gathering perception that the natural world was a cornucopia of rich and rare phenomena, a treasure-store of secrets, waiting to be interpreted by those who held the key to decoding nature. Astrologers, alchemists, cosmographers, natural magicians and unorthodox practitioners of medicine rivalled one another to offer explanations as to how that immense variety in nature might be reducible to ordered, physical principles, or at least to demonstrate that it was conducive to empirical enquiry. Some of them sought these principles in forces higher than nature itself – magical power immanent in nature like a spirit hidden in earthly processes, or conveyed by celestial warmth and movement. They, too, like many philosophers, were vocal in their criticism of Aristotle, mainly on the grounds that his ideas about matter were too abstract. They enveloped their learning and insight in an aura of arcane mystery to protect them from their numerous critics and enhance their reputation for exceptional wisdom and power. But there was a contrary recognition that human knowledge had its limits, which implied that penetrating the secrets of nature could never be the work of a single individual. It had to be achieved through a collaborative effort of many enquirers, attentive to the practical aspects of knowledge and to the varying possibilities for its interpretation.

The impact of such changes upon the notion of Christendom was nowhere more profound than in cosmology. The Copernican heliocentric universe owed a great deal to the revival of alternative cosmologies from classical Antiquity which challenged the Aristotelian consensus. But, if the earth was simply another planet, revolving around the sun, then the universe became dramatically large in comparison to the earth – 'immense', as Copernicus conceded. That was because it was necessary to envisage an enormous distance between the orbit of Saturn and the sphere of the stars. Once the earth became one of the planets, all the processes of generation and corruption which had been explained by Aristotle as based on what happened in the natural world and on earth, could more plausibly be explained in terms of the influence of the sun, or the earth's motion and position with respect to the sun and the other planets. Christendom was most comfortable when it was cocooned within the concentric circles of a geocentric and anthropomorphic universe. Placed in a heliocentric universe, it ceased to be at the heart of the created order of things.

The brilliantly self-publicizing chemical physician Paracelsus (Theophrastus Bombastus von Hohenheim), the magician and astrologer John Dee, the theologian and cosmographer Giordano Bruno, the natural philosophers Francesco Patrizi and Galileo Galilei were among those who found themselves, in varying degrees, held in suspicion for heliocentric views by the remaining 'gate-keepers' of Christendom, the Inquisition and the papacy. In February 1600, Bruno was burned at the stake in Rome. A year later, the Dominican friar Tommaso Campanella was brutally tortured for forty hours in the Castel Nuovo in Naples for his involvement in a popular rebellion. He spent the next quarter of a century a prisoner there, raging against the 'infected roots' of pagan Aristotelian philosophy. He dreamed of a radical transformation of a world in which he now no longer truly belonged. The problem for radical thinkers in this period was that the circumstances of the moment, as well as the accident of where they happened to live, determined in what ways and how their ideas came to be seen as challenging – which is why there was no 'end' to the Renaissance, but rather a continuing renegotiation of its potential for demolishing old certainties in new contexts.

THE PROTESTANT REFORMATION

At the heart of the movement for religious change was the Protestant Reformation, a rift in Roman Christianity as spectacular and as permanent as that which had occurred between the eastern and western Churches in the eleventh century. What made it the more painfully complicated was that western Christianity splintered violently. Martin Luther became convinced that Christendom was going to wrack and ruin because of the 'louts and whores' in Rome. In May 1520, a Leipzig Franciscan, Augustin Alveld, published a pamphlet in German defending the proposition that the pope in Rome had authority over Christendom by divine right. Luther replied to 'the ass of Leipzig' and his 'rotten arguments' saying that the pope and his 'Romanists' had turned the papacy into the 'scarlet whore of Babylon', and that this papal Antichrist was at the heart of Christendom's woes. By then, his study of Scripture and Church history had led him to a contentious sense of what God's truth was, and how it was proved. 'By faith alone' (*sola fide*) was Luther's redefinition, and 'Scripture alone' (*sola scriptura*) was his way of validating it. Papal authority was human, and not divine, in origin, and ultimate authority rested not with popes or councils or church fathers, but with the Bible. That was the way by which Luther claimed that Christianity could return to its roots – the gospel of Christ. The Bible was the record of God's promise to mankind from the beginning of the world, renewed in the Old Testament and fulfilled in Christ. Nothing was more 'literally' true than this promise since God himself is to be trusted in faith.

From this reductionist and stark truth-claim, so much else descended, including an irrecoverable breach with the Roman Church and a monumental Protestant division of theological opinion as to how literally it was to be taken. Luther used the term 'Christendom' interchangeably with 'Church' and 'Christian community'. They all meant a virtual commonwealth, the communion of saints to which Christ referred when he said: 'my kingdom is not of this world'. It was a 'stinking lie' to say that Christendom was in Rome, or anywhere else for that matter. The true Church had no external forms, no vestments, special prayers, bishops or buildings. The sacred landscape dramatically shrank. According to Luther, it was faith alone which makes true priests of all believers, and turns the world in which they happen to dwell into a Christian order.

Luther succeeded brilliantly in mobilizing pre-existing and disparate local resentments, especially in Germany, against the Roman Church. If the latter was the root of Christendom's canker, then it was up to others to step in and remove the rot. Christian people should act like children whose parents had gone mad, or like an individual who, seeing a building on fire, has a public duty to raise the alarm and put the flames out. That, in particular, was the responsibility of kings, princes and nobles. Their job was to 'prevent blasphemy and the disgrace of the divine name'. Luther's purpose was to reinforce Christendom, not to destroy or replace it. But, by radically transposing the sources for authority and legitimation within Christendom, he opened the door to the decay of the united belief-community at its heart. In 1520, Luther was unequivocal. No universal authority was vested in anyone. The truth was that all Christians were members in equal standing in a Christian order, with one baptism, one gospel and one faith. These things alone created 'a spiritual and a Christian people'. There was no difference between laymen and priests, or between princes and people, in their status as Christians. Spectacularly reductive as that was, it begged more questions in practice than it resolved. How, in reality, should Christian people organize themselves? What should they do to provide themselves with suitable pastors, and what were the duties and responsibilities of the latter? How should people act if their pastors or rulers failed in their Christian duties? What was the role of the ruler in those circumstances? What should Christians do if the prince or magistrate failed to carry out his Christian responsibilities? To whom did it fall to declare and enforce a unity of true belief? Whose job was it to defend Christendom?

Beneath the theological divisions which opened up within the Protestant Reformation lay a transformation in the nature and manifestation of holy power. One of the most fundamental changes was in the relationship between ecclesiastical and state institutions. Luther and the other Protestant reformers ostensibly retained the bicephalous and notionally separate civil and ecclesiastical jurisdictions of Christendom. In reality, however, the pressures of religious change altered the relationship, accentuating an uneasy friction between the two. While affecting to maintain the 'two regimes' of Church and state, Luther enlarged the scope of the latter and emasculated the former. That renegotiation of power contributed to a different sense of what religious truth was in Protestant Europe. It became a truth declared by God, as guaranteed by the Scriptures, embodied in creeds, statements to which people subscribed, and lived out in confessionally configured communities where the instruments of public authority structured and monitored people's lives and behaviours. Attenuated was the sense of humankind as a participant in God's work of redeeming his creation. God had established a world of nature in which the sins of humankind were a fact of life, to be regulated, controlled and limited. Those limits were policed by state power, itself constructed around a theo-political imagination in which God's power was the model of that of the state itself – both almighty and irresistible.

THE ROMAN CATHOLIC CHURCH

Where did that leave the Roman Church? It did not surrender its claims to be the spiritual leader of what was left of Christendom. But what that meant when Protestant Europe had rejected those claims remained to be decided. Initially, its efforts were concentrated in the heartland of Latin

Europe. Although those efforts eventually produced a systematic rebuttal of Protestantism at the Council of Trent (1545–63), and became closely identified with the might of the Spanish Habsburg monarchy and its conflicts (especially those with the Ottomans), they never lost their ancestry in a spiritual and religious revival that re-engaged the Roman Church with the local roots from which Protestant rhetoric had sought to detach it. Catholic unity became expressed, like Protestantism, in confessional terms. Its organization remained theocratic and bureaucratic, although that reality was occluded by the renaissance of religious orders, both new foundations (Jesuits, Capuchins . . .) and the revival of older orders (Franciscans, Dominicans . . .), newly energized by the challenges confronting Christianity. That organizational unity became the basis for its polemic against Protestant theological divisions and what its defenders perceived as Protestant incoherence over the issue of authority.

Ultimately, the revival of the Roman Church was dependent on a renegotiation of the relationship between the Church hierarchy and local worshipping communities. At the heart of that renegotiation lay the objective of helping human beings to access holy power and redemption, while seeking to remove what the hierarchy regarded as the 'superstitious' excrescences introduced into the sacral landscape in earlier centuries or the residue of 'pagan' cults and beliefs among those recently converted to Christianity in the wider world. The latter became the focus for the remarkable missionary and ecclesiastical endeavour in an emerging colonial 'spiritual acreage' overseas, through which the old-fashioned universal values of Christendom were refashioned into a global Christianity.

THE SURVIVAL OF CHRISTENDOM

Both the champions of Reformation and the defenders of the old order believed, in fundamental ways, that they were protecting Christendom from destruction, proclaiming their truths as self-evident in a way that implied that it was only when they completely prevailed over the other that its defence would be complete. Christendom equally continued to mean something to ordinary folk. A devout citizen of Milan in 1565, brought up on the sermons of preachers who had emphasized the

Ottoman threat towards Christianity, could pray that God keep his family 'in perfect union and love, us and all of Christendom'. Contemporary travellers still wrote of 'embarking for', 'arriving in' or 'departing out of' Christendom. Very few of them, however, were bound for Jerusalem. Protestant reformers undermined pilgrimage to the Holy Places. To the English cleric Samuel Purchas, Jerusalem had migrated westwards: 'Jesus Christ, who is the way, the truth and the life, has long since given the Bill of Divorce to ungrateful Asia where he was born, and of Africa, the place of his flight and refuge, and has come almost wholly over to Europe,' he wrote in *Purchas his Pilgrimage* (1613), a collection of travel accounts, published to show the geographical diversity of God's creation. Even for Catholics, a pilgrimage could be undertaken in the comfort of one's own sitting room by reading one of the many published narratives which satisfied the desires of the curious as well as the pious.

When it suited, however, even the most ardent Protestant could also appeal to a sense that the peoples of Christendom were essentially one. Francis Bacon would not have followed Thomas More, his one-time predecessor as England's chancellor, to the block for the belief that Christendom was a 'common corps', but he could still appeal to that same sense, advocating in 1617 the establishment of an international tribunal to adjudicate disputes between countries to prevent the 'effusion of Christian blood'. The desire to 'see Christendom reconciled' was earnestly expressed by his contemporary Edwin Sandys in his *Europae Speculum* (1605). The sentiment was, as he wrote, in the process of being elevated to a political aspiration by his master, King James I. None of the successors of Erasmus invested quite so much history and meaning in the term *Christianitas* as he had, but they continued to see wars between its states as, in some sense, 'civil wars', and to find ways of living with religious diversity.

THE WANING OF CRUSADE

Christendom seemed most afflicted in the sixteenth and early seventeenth centuries by the rising power of Islam on its southeastern and southern flanks. Ottoman military and naval power had been resurgent from the fall of Constantinople (1453). By 1520, the Ottoman empire had absorbed Greece, the Aegean archipelago, the Dalmatian coast of the Adriatic in Bosnia, and established its overlordship in the Balkans. The Ottoman triumph over the Hungarian army at the battle of Mohács (1526) consolidated their influence in the central Hungarian plain and around the Carpathians, with Ottoman client-states in Transylvania and Moldavia. They thus created a long, exposed and vulnerable frontier with western Christianity, uncomfortably close to Vienna. By the death of Suleiman I in 1566, probably over 15 million people were under Ottoman rule, a great Eurasian land empire centred on Istanbul (Constantinople). Intelligent European observers admired the structure and magnificence of the Ottoman state and feared the discipline and scale of the Ottoman army. Istanbul itself became the showcase of empire, a great city of over a quarter of a million inhabitants by 1566, resplendent with the Great Bazaar, Imperial Palace (the *Topkapı Sarayı*), and mosques with their adjoining schools, hospitals and public baths.

The Ottomans also turned themselves into a naval power, establishing supremacy in the eastern Mediterranean lasting throughout the sixteenth century. The Ottoman conquest of Egypt and Syria (1517) and the capture of Rhodes (1522) were the prelude to Ottoman attempts to establish their predominance over the African coast dominating the narrows in the middle of the Mediterranean. The Ottomans worked through intermediaries – Muslim pirates, licensed by the Ottoman state, and local governors, who were given military ranks. The seas off the southern Mediterranean coast remained hostile to European ships well into the seventeenth century.

Did this Ottoman expansion revive the myth of Crusade? Did the Mediterranean in the second half of the sixteenth century witness a seaborne 'clash of civilizations'? The papacy often seemed more preoccupied by the Turkish Infidel than the Protestant heretic in the first half of the sixteenth century. The focus of its diplomatic initiatives was towards constructing a 'Holy League' against the Infidel, ultimately brought to fruition by Pope Pius V. Before the last two decades of the sixteenth century, the papacy put more of its resources into fighting the Ottomans than it did into combating Protestantism, drawing not only from its own coffers but also from the grant of indulgences from the faithful to others willing to take up the cause. Its rhetoric, too, echoed the mobilization for Crusade which had preoccupied its predecessors in the

Middle Ages. For Emperor Charles V, as for his son Philip II, the Ottoman threat served as a *de facto* justification of their claims to princely
pre-eminence. Anti-Ottoman mobilization remained the means by
which Christendom was sustained through this period, despite the
divisions at its heart.

The image of the Turkish Infidel certainly remained central to western
Christian antagonism towards Islam, a latent anxiety that retained its
capacity to crystallize fears and inspire loyalties, especially in those areas
most directly exposed to Ottoman expansion. That antagonism was no
longer expressed, however, in terms of a concrete project (the conquest
of the Holy Land). 'Crusade' had mutated into 'Holy War', where the
objective was a less defined and more defensive 'protection' of the Christian world from an aggressive enemy, 'common' to all. The most pervasive
fear was that Christendom would be overwhelmed. In the wake of the
attempted Ottoman conquest of Vienna (1529), the ambassador of
Charles V there (Roberto Niño), who served as a Habsburg listening-post
to the goings-on in the Ottoman world, reported on Suleiman the Magnificent's naval preparations to invade Italy and march on Rome:
'Soleiman dreams of that city and repeats endlessly: "To Rome, to
Rome!",' he said. In 1566, the Venetian cosmographer Jeronimo Ruscelli
published a collection of emblems for contemporary rulers, each designed
to reveal their secret ambitions. Suleiman was represented by four can-
dlesticks, in which only one had a lit candle. Ruscelli's interpretation of
the device was straightforward: the four candles represented the continents of the world. The Ottomans already had a stake in three of them,
and their appearance in the fourth (the newly discovered Americas)
could not be long delayed. Suleiman's design was to light the lamp of
Islam in all four through the exercise of world empire.

The existence of Christian 'renegades', those who 'turned Turk' –
much discussed in pamphlets of the time – was, for contemporaries, a
further anxiety. They had not all done so as a result of force of circumstances. Had not those on the Aegean islands of Naxos and Scarpanto,
for example, welcomed the Ottomans in the early years of the sixteenth
century, as 'liberators' from Christian oppression? Had not the consolidation of Ottoman power on the Hungarian plain been assisted by tacit
acceptance of their rule in a rural world that longed for an alleviation
of the seigneurial burdens of Christian rule and the imposition of order,
represented by Ottoman justice?

Yet the anxiety about being overrun by the Turks was interpreted in different ways by contemporaries. Desiderius Erasmus, for example, took the dangers of Ottoman expansion seriously, but initially argued that the only possible response was to strengthen Christendom by a reform from within. Later, however, in the wake of the Ottoman siege of Vienna (1529), he changed tack. Pointing the finger implicitly at Lutherans, he now said Christians had an individual and collective duty to come to arms in defence of those suffering on the front line. Luther, however, like the Protestant reformer in Geneva Jean Calvin in the next generation, interpreted the Ottoman threat as a warning sign from God about the urgent need for reform within, and continued to resist the call to arms to the challenge from without.

For others, the traditional figure of the Turkish Infidel modulated in the course of the sixteenth and early seventeenth centuries to a more complex, less religiously exclusive representation of the alien 'other', whose 'barbarity' and 'despotism' were to be compared with those of the wider world in which Europeans increasingly understood themselves. In due course, the underlying conception of an enduring and permanent hostility between Christianity and the Ottoman empire gave way to a reluctant coexistence which gave the lie to anti-Turkish intransigence. Christendom decayed along with Crusade. Europe emerged, as in a mirror, reflected geographically and culturally in comparison not just with America, but also the Levant.

THE HOLY ROMAN EMPEROR

In October 1520, Charles of Habsburg, duke of Burgundy and newly acceded to the thrones of Castile and Aragon, was crowned Holy Roman Emperor at Aachen. He processed through the huge bronze doors of the cathedral to an exquisitely choreographed ceremony. He was given the sword and ring of his predecessor and namesake Charlemagne, crowned with the imperial crown of Otto the Great, and entrusted with the imperial sceptre, orb and star-strewn mantle, as well as religious relics which included the holy lance which had pierced Christ's side. These were the emblems of the sacral heritage of universal monarchy. The octagonal crown, like Aachen's cathedral, recalled the heavenly Jerusalem. The orb represented the globe, and the star-covered mantle implied that he ruled over the cosmos as Christ's secular vicar on earth, the protector of Christendom. Technically, however, he was 'emperor-elect', his title *Romanorum rex semper Augustus* until he was invested in a further coronation by the pope – empire and papacy being the twin pillars of Christendom. That event took place a decade later at Bologna on his thirtieth birthday in February 1530. Charles V was the last emperor in Europe on whose behalf these claims to universal monarchy were made, and about whom they would have any meaning. He was also the last emperor to be invested by the papacy and to be crowned at Aachen. By the time of his abdication in 1556, the Holy Roman Empire had ceased to be one of the twin pillars of Christendom. It had shrunk to become a Habsburg dynastic instrument, for use in German lands.

Charles V had won the dynastic jackpot. By the time he was twenty-five years of age, he had inherited claims to seventy-two separate dynastic titles, twenty-seven kingdoms, thirteen duchies, twenty-two counties and other seigneurial overlordships that stretched from the Mediterranean to the Baltic, and over the New World. That meant that something approaching 28 million people owed him some kind of allegiance, or not far short of 40 per cent of western Europe. His chancellor, Mercurino Gattinara, reminded him: 'God has been very merciful to you. He has raised you above all Kings and princes in Christendom to a power such as no sovereign has enjoyed since your ancestor Charlemagne. He has set you on the way towards a world monarchy, towards the uniting of all Christendom under a single shepherd.' Gattinara set about constructing a credible image of the emperor as its secular leader.

Charles himself never seriously contemplated creating a unified, autonomous political realm, and rarely evoked the legacy of Charlemagne. Concerned to respect the rights and privileges of those who were the guardians of local identity, he almost invariably thought about universal rule only in terms of the guardianship of the faith. Yet his image-makers projected an amalgam of Christian and classical *imperium*, a reminder of the political implications of humanist powers of persuasion, especially when conjoined to new mechanical forms of reproduction and dissemination (typography, engravings, coins and medallions, tapestries). No political leader in medieval Christendom had been so deliberately fabricated, in so many different media, and to so many disparate audiences and objectives as Charles V. The Aachen coronation was the shape of things to come, detailed representations of the ceremony circulating in different languages with woodcuts, medallions and engravings of the emperor, his beard square and his hair long after the German fashion. A decade later, the engravings and woodcuts depicted a Roman emperor, his hair and beard cut short, an impresario of military victory and imposer of peace upon Europe. The accounts of the procession reported his throwing the specially minted coins with the twin columns of the demigod emperor Hercules and Charles V's personal tag *Plus Ultra* ('Yet Further') upon them, crying '*Largesse! Largesse!*', the streets ringing out to the chant of '*Imperio! Imperio!*'

Even those sympathetic to Charles V's cause recognized that this vision had an increasingly slim chance of realization. The claim to be the guardian of Christendom was compromised when imperial troops ran rampage through Rome in 1527. The Protestant Reformation gave the lie to any vision of a united Christian *res publica* in Germany, still less in Europe. Charles V's military victories, like his diplomatic initiatives, increasingly reflected Habsburg dynastic imperatives. They had become a kind of indirect imperialism, universal monarchy being a back door to hegemony by a fortunate princely family. German princes, Protestant and Catholic alike, regarded Charles V's claims to sacral *imperium* as a threat to the liberties of the German nation. In Italy, where Charles V's dynastic inheritance included the kingdom of Naples and Sicily as well as a string of territories north of the Papal States, the claims to universal monarchy were the most vigorously projected, and the most seriously contested. Charles V's French opponent, Francis I, sought to undermine the imperial pretensions at every turn. French humanists responded with counter-projections of a providential, even messianic monarchy, whose destiny was to protect the liberties and privileges of Europe's political order against Habsburg dynastic hegemony.

DYNASTIC PRINCES

If the emperor no longer protected Christendom, who did? Magistracy – the power of the sword – lay mainly in the hands of dynastic princes. Dynasticism (rulership based upon inheritance) was destined to be the dominant political order. Its attractiveness lay in legitimacy determined by descent. Especially when reinforced with claims to absolute authority, dynastic rule mobilized resources around the aristocratic and patrimonial world of princely courts. The introverted culture of favour and the competitive instincts inherent in their honour codes were the levers at the princes' disposition in the informal power structures that prevailed at princely courts. Dynasts readily understood and shared the selfish desires of those in their midst to have and to hold offices for themselves, their friends and their relatives. As a way of imposing political order, dynasticism was never more convincing than when it seemed to offer an alternative to the religious divisions and social disorder of the Post-Reformation. That said, the politico-religious violence that particularly marked the second half of the sixteenth century was concentrated in western Europe, which is also where state power was most precocious. The greatest acts of violence in the sixteenth century were either instigated by vulnerable dynasts, or they were strongly implicated in them. Dynastic monarchy was involved in the post-Reformation religious-based contentions which it then played a part in attenuating.

The dynastic state was reinforced, above all, because the ability to raise and deploy military power at increased distances grew significantly in this period. The power to levy taxes, and the confidence to survey, control and raise revenues from economic activities of all sorts, also changed, often dramatically. Above all, the authority to borrow money on the basis of this accretion of power altered the nature of state power in relation to other sorts of power in society. Europe's first generation of colonial endeavour would have been impossible without state backing. That sounds like a ringing endorsement for the older picture of this period as the rise of the 'modern state'. In reality, it was something rather different. Beyond the officials, the tax-farms, the military muster-rolls and colonial courts, the collective imagination was of a Christian commonwealth, with a moral relationship between ruler and ruled. For practical purposes, state administrative mechanisms were local, distributive and weak. At the centre, state power was too readily the focus for court rivalry, faction and division. At the locality it still often lay in the hands of power-brokers, aristocratic grandees and their clients. Behind the forward-looking statesmen and women of this period it is difficult to detect a coherent vision of an ordering state, demanding the obedience and loyalty of all its citizens. Far easier is to discover their games of disgracing their opponents and monopolizing authority in their own hands. When it came to summoning the loyalty and obedience of their subjects, early-modern non-military power was principally 'performative', the projection of power being a contrived ventriloquism for the benefit of a public gallery. Europe's enduring localism, which had been the weak link in Christendom, became in turn the Achilles heel of the dynastic state.

That was because dynasticism obeyed the logic of genealogy and the accidents of birth and death. It disregarded local cultural identities and cut across privileges and jurisdictions. Its composite states created implausible units with different legal and religious traditions, especially vulnerable to the confessional divisions of the post-Reformation world. The competitive instincts at the heart of dynasticism destroyed the possibilities for cooperation around an ideal. Internationally, it was a perpetual force for instability and warfare. The capacity of Europe's dynasts to mobilize power came at an escalating price of destructive internal conflict. Eurasian power structures, with which Europe's dynasts were now in competition, did not have to pay anything like the same price. A succession of regional tornadoes of conflict sapped Christendom's capacity to devote resources and energy to its colonial expansion. Indeed, the reverse occurred. The wealth of the New World financed the dynastic ambitions of the Old which, in due course, generated the maelstrom which afflicted Europe in the Thirty Years War (1618–48). By contrast, aristocrats, sometimes in league with representative institutions, were often better placed to understand and reflect local wishes, and to exploit the attachment to provincial institutions and customs against the centralizing aspirations of dynastic princes.

The fundamental problem was that the loyalties created by dynasticism were inherently weak. If dynastic states succeeded in aligning themselves with the stronger identities of religious truth or *patria* it was largely fortuitous. More generally, they had to accept the limits to the extent of political integration which was possible under their rule – and, with it, the perpetual swirl of factions, lobbies and networks of their court, and the reality of local autonomy, most evidently in the governing of Europe's peripheries and colonies. The attempt to build wider loyalties around the strengthening of dynastic absolute monarchy tended to expose how barren such claims were underneath. The dynastic state lacked a convincing ideology. Its political model had nothing to say about that essential part of the Christian commonwealth, the reinforcement of the public good and the right relation between political authority and the people. In the context of the Protestant Reformation those ideals broadened into an understanding that people were answerable first and foremost to God for what they did. The resulting invitations – to contribute to the public good and do God's will on earth – altered the ground rules governing the conduct of politics in the later sixteenth century, not least because they were readily adapted to the new forces of pluralized information diffusion in the transformation of public media in the sixteenth and early seventeenth centuries. The result brought different models of political association and engagement, and at all sorts of levels. It was not just in small, distinctive and somewhat vulnerable independent cities and republics that godly and well-meaning notables became convinced that they had a stake and a role in making decisions that were too important to be left entirely in the hands of rulers. Dynastic states had little by way of a reply to the demands of those who expected to be involved in the destiny of the state. The tension between ruler and ruled was fundamental in post-Reformation politics.

CHRISTIAN COMMONWEALTHS AND POST-REFORMATION RELIGIOUS CONFLICT

Humanists had popularized the notion of a 'commonwealth' (*res publica*). Any form of legitimate rulership could be a commonwealth. That was important, since the public face of the governing entities of the European landmass was varied. Besides the Holy Roman Empire and dynastic rulers, there were also elective monarchies, city-states and republics. Christian commonwealths were legitimated by the relationship between rulers and ruled, a mutual obligation in which the obedience of the people was natural and divinely ordained, but made right by the commitment of the Christian prince or 'magistrate' to obey God's laws and to rule justly in the interests of the people. A ruler who did none of those things was a tyrant. The role of the Christian magistrate was to defend right religion, dispense justice and promote peace. In the wake of the Protestant Reformation, the fundamental problem was how to square the conflicting objectives created for political rulers by religious pluralism. If they did not defend right religion, that seemed to threaten the *raison d'être* and unity of the Christian commonwealth. To do so, however, ran the risk of the commonwealth being pulled apart by religious divisions, destroying the values of concord, peace and harmony which were equally fundamental to its existence. An unanswerable conundrum confronted rulers, especially in the middle latitudes of the European landmass, where religious loyalties were mostly in doubt through to 1648. That region was where the risks of sectarian violence were greatest, and where religious-related tensions spilled over into every aspect of public and private life. Unpredictable and polymorphous, those tensions infected other, existing divisions. They manifested themselves at all social levels and proved exceptionally difficult for magistrates in a Christian commonwealth to manage. Religious divisions compromised rulers by making them a party to the conflict on one side or another. They strained the mutual obligation (and trust) between rulers and the people.

The justification for Christendom had been that it provided a set of ideals and institutions by which to encourage and realize peace within the belief-community. In the post-Reformation world, conflict over religious beliefs lay where once had been the focus for Christendom's unity. What had been a means of reconciliation now became an instrument for discord. The world grew more dangerous and divided as a new jagged-edged set of frontiers of faith emerged. Unlike the previous frontiers of Christendom, these were not at the periphery of the belief-community, facing the outside world, but in the midst of it. The new frontiers of faith divided varieties of Protestantism to the north and Catholicism to the south, setting Christian commonwealths at each other's throats, and sharpening divisions in people's minds as conflicting religious identities emerged from the oppositional processes of the Reformation itself.

For Christian commonwealths, there were other changes, too, which made the religious conflicts of the post-Reformation world difficult to contain. Firstly, the nature of religion itself was changing. The Protestant Reformation created a plurality of beliefs, argued for with conviction on all sides, each claiming its legitimation on the basis of a supposed continuity with the past. Christendom became, in the process, a contested legacy, part of what humanists had already begun to dismiss as a 'Middle Age' of decay and corruption. In the new landscape of plurality, 'religion' (qualified as 'right', 'reformed', 'Catholic') became a way of determining true beliefs from false ones. Moreover, religion became further consolidated around what people 'believed', detached from the religious observances that they performed. That detachment was most evidently manifest in the increasingly 'confessionalized' nature of religion in the Post-Reformation. Religious confessions (Lutheran, Calvinist, Anabaptist, Anglican) attempted to define what people should believe – and became the basis for a mammoth investment in education and persuasion by churches and states. For both these, however, it was harder to enforce conformity around a confessional notion of belief than it had been around a belief-community in which observances (whose performance could easily be measured, and by those who were not theologians) reflected the beliefs of the individuals and communities concerned.

There were plenty of places where, in the wake of the Protestant Reformation, religious conformity proved unrealizable. Christian princes found reasons to argue the case to make domestic peace a more immediate priority than religious uniformity, and to deploy the resources of law to resolve religious disputes. But, in the eyes of their confessional critics, such attempts to live with confessional diversity were the clearest sign that Christendom was in terminal decay. Such religious pluralism was destined, they argued, to end in tears. By fudging the issue and failing to fulfil their responsibilities, rulers who permitted religious pluralism were not only risking God's wrath, but making the inevitable and ultimate confrontation that much more violent and destructive. Such views tended to be self-fulfilling prophecies. There were no lessons in religious toleration in this period which could not be unlearned. Each generation had to discover afresh the dangerous simplicities of believing that the imposition of religious conformity would be a straightforward solution to the problems of religious dissent.

The religious-based conflicts of the post-Reformation period made conformity to a confessionalized sense of belief seem important as never before. Christian commonwealths were expected to uphold and enforce confessional conformity as an essential precondition to political unity. The ecclesiastical changes associated with the Protestant Reformation (and the Catholic response to it) changed the relationship between churches and rulers. The geometry of the relationship differed widely. In parts of Protestant Europe, there were state-based churches; in others, there were official churches, with which the state had a looser, even independent, relationship. In Catholic Europe, Church and state were a partnership in which there was plenty of room for mutual misunderstanding and frustration. In general, however, states acquired more authority over ecclesiastical affairs. With that authority came greater responsibility for the maintenance of right religion. Rulers faced more vocal appeals from their clergy. Clerical voices demanded that Christian rulers carry out their duties of promoting the true faith. They sought the arbitration of their rulers over contested issues of ecclesiastical structure, discipline and even beliefs while, at the same time, upbraiding them for interfering with rights and property that belonged to the Church. In Post-Reformed conflicts, it was not merely the mutual obligation between rulers and ruled which became strained. So too did that between magistrates and clerics.

Such increased tensions occurred in the context of broader changes in the authority of states. Christian commonwealths were becoming more extensive and intrusive locally in the justice undertaken in their name. Rulers expected more by way of taxation from their lands and subjects. Military changes meant that the magistrate's 'power of the sword' was more in evidence to the civilian population. Public authority required greater access to specialist skills and advice to undertake the more complex legal and administrative tasks of policing economic, social and public life. From different quarters came the demands to broaden fiscality over a wider range of products and services, for greater economic competition between states, and for an intensification of social discipline and moral conformity by both state and Church. At the same time, weakening social cohesion in communities compromised the loyalties of local magistrates, among whom the notion of a mutual obligation between ruler and ruled had been the most strongly rooted.

By 1600, Europe's Christian commonwealths were the political remnant of Christendom's ideal of a belief-community, but they were battered from without and undermined from within by the divisions created by the Reformation. They proved vulnerable to the explosive cocktail of religion and politics. Even in those polities which achieved a degree of religious pluralism, the results were unstable, dependent on balances of forces between different religions that were liable to change, and vulnerable to the arguments and strategies of those who had never accepted that religious diversity could be a good thing. Where the cocktail of religious and political dissent resulted in war and conflict, it exposed the weakening bonds of trust between Europe's peoples and their rulers. The first signs of demographic and economic weakness as the 'silver age' began to recede only heightened the fragility of that trust.

The recovery of a degree of stability in the early years of the seventeenth century served as a moment of respite, encouraging people to imagine that, even though the underlying problems of post-Reformation politics could not be resolved, they might be contained. Some rulers sought consciously to distance themselves from the central proposition of a Christian commonwealth – of a mutual relationship of obligation in the name of the common good between rulers and the people they ruled. Building on the traditional formulations of theocratic monarchy – that monarchs' responsibilities were solely towards God and not open to scrutiny by others – 'absolute' rulers posed as the embodiment of the destiny of the 'state', the latter being a confessionally neutral language to describe political entities. Absolute monarchs (and the French Bourbon dynasty, which ruled a French kingdom gradually reunited after its 'wars of religion', served as the exemplar to others) proclaimed themselves separate from, and above, the fundamental tensions of post-Reformation politics. They could legislate for religious uniformity or decree religious pluralism, form diplomatic alliances between or across religious divides – all as seemed fit to them, justifying their actions as for the good of the state. Absolute princely rule sat strangely at odds with those polities – generally in those parts which had not experienced the most destructive forces of post-Reformation tension – where the notion of a Christian commonwealth still survived, and where rulers and ruled were still regarded as in a relationship of mutual obligation.

EUROPE'S PAROXYSM

In the 1550s, 1590s and then again from the 1620s, military activity in Europe rose to unprecedented levels. The signs of respite in the early years of the new century were nothing more than a false dawn. Europe was plunged into a widening vortex of interconnected and destructive struggles, culminating in the later 1640s. These conflicts exacerbated Europe's economic divergences and weakening social cohesion. The 1590s became the avatar of later and longer strife. The Thirty Years War comprises three concomitant and related conflicts, of which only the first lasted thirty years. The first was a war in Germany (1618–1648) that sucked in those around it. The second was a renewed struggle between the Spanish Habsburgs and the Dutch Republic (1621–48). The third was a bitter struggle between France and Spain (1635–59). The first two had their origins deep in post-Reformation disputes whereas the latter was something different and fundamentally new in the degree to which it was openly a fight for hegemony in Europe. Each of these conflicts overlapped with the others, drawing most of western Europe into their orbit.

The burden of raising the unparalleled resources for these conflicts brought Europe's states to the brink of their call on the loyalties of their subjects. The constellation of European kingdoms of the Spanish Habsburg monarchy imploded in a series of revolts in which local stakeholders sought an alternative future for themselves and their people, aided and abetted by Spain's enemies. They began in Catalonia (1640–59) and Portugal (1640–59), but spread to the Italian peninsula in Naples (1647–8) and Palermo (1647). The more united French kingdom suffered profound strains too. They appeared first in a widespread and potentially damaging sequence of local and regional popular revolts and aristocrat-led rebellions which were contained with a mixture of repression and concessions. After 1643, its absolute monarchy was weakened by the minority of Louis XIV, who had come to the throne as a boy-king, not yet five years of age. The unparalleled effort of fighting a major international war on several fronts during a period of royal minority not only stretched the military and financial resources of the state to its breaking-point, but also tested the loyalties of those who had hitherto been the pillars of the French state, its senior magistrates and office-holders. They led the revolt known as the 'Frondes' (1648–53), a period of profound monarchical instability which included two brief episodes of open civil war.

Framing the conflicts and instabilities associated with the Thirty Years War lay two other parallel political implosions, each with its attendant devastations. In both cases, their origins lay back in post-Reformation religious settlements which came unstuck. In both cases too, the central issue was the survival, or not, of the Christian commonwealth as against the newer conceptions of absolute rule. In the British Isles, what was referred to by a contemporary as the 'falling out in the three Kingdoms' began with a rebellion against the Stuart monarchy in Scotland in 1639, enlarged with the Irish Rebellion that broke out in 1641, and culminated in the Great Rebellion of England in 1642. Charles I's military defeat in the first English Civil War in 1646, coupled with his subsequent attempts to recover the situation from a position of dangerous weakness, led to his execution in January 1649. The victorious Parliamentary forces, now commanded by Oliver Cromwell, invaded Ireland and brutally crushed a Royalist–Confederate alliance there in 1649. And, when the Scots crowned Charles I's son and heir as their king (Charles II), renewed hostilities with England resulted in Cromwell's conquest of Scotland in 1650–51. By the end of 1651, the Three Kingdoms were set to emerge as a new state, proclaiming itself a 'Commonwealth' and ostensibly a republic.

Meanwhile, to the east, a major Cossack insurrection in the Ukraine in 1648 undermined another Christian commonwealth, the Polish-Lithuanian Commonwealth (*Rzeczpospolita*). The Polish state had seen off many threats from Muscovites, Tatars and Turks on its eastern and southeastern borders, and faced down numerous previous revolts by Ruthenian Cossacks, increasingly alienated by the political and social contempt shown towards them by Polish aristocrats, who had established huge landed estates in Ruthenia (Ukraine). But nothing prepared the Polish state for the Cossack Rebellion (1648–57) led by Hetman Bohdan Khmelnytsky. With Tartar assistance, and then with the support of the Muscovites, the rebels eradicated the Polish nobility (*szlachta*) and their estates from Ruthenia, and dismantled the ecclesiastical authority of the Latin Rite Catholics there. Already weakened by a Swedish incursion in the 1620s, the military and political collapse of the once powerful Polish state after 1648 was dramatic, destabilizing eastern Europe.

Despite their different specificities, what all these rebellions, movements of protest and insurrections had in common was a breakdown of trust between Europe's rulers and the people whom they ruled. Many contemporaries interpreted these near simultaneous troubles, about which they were informed as never before by regular printed newsletters, as the fruits of divine wrath, justly earned by human sinfulness. That was a way of registering something else about the mid-century paroxysm: that Europe had lost everything that Christendom had stood for. In its place was a nakedly divided Europe. Across its landmass lay a religious frontier, reflecting a fracture of belief. Its political systems depended on states which did not seem to obey the rules of conventional morality, and whose relations with their people were openly in contention. Its leading states were engaged in a battle for hegemony and the Peace of Westphalia failed to construct a new international order to contain it. Europe was disunited in itself, and exported its divisions to the rest of the world. The social cohesion of its communities had weakened. Economic change created greater disparities of wealth and widened the gap between regions that did well and those which did badly. Meteorological change had also disrupted settled agriculture across the planet. Even Europe's understanding of the natural world and the universe had become conjectural, contingent and disputed. The Protestant Reformation was the last crisis of Christendom. The paroxysm of the mid-seventeenth century was the first crisis of what was now Europe.

THE WORLD AND THE DISCOVERY OF EUROPE

Cross-cultural interactions among the Eurasian civilizations had existed for centuries. Yet the sixteenth and early seventeenth centuries brought the peoples, not just of Eurasia but of the eastern and western hemispheres more generally, into much more intensive and sustained interaction with one another. Although that occurred as a result of a largely European-led effort to put in place long-distance trading relationships, the processes that brought it to pass were on a global scale and interactive in a double sense. They interacted with one another in a complex fashion, and they were the result of the interchange with other civilizations, especially those of Eurasia. Only an extreme Eurocentric myopia could persuade anyone that its expansion is explicable solely in terms of Europe's internal dynamics. The processes depended on the creation of global sea-lanes, potentially giving access to the world's shorelines. Measuring the latter is a hazardous enterprise. Europe's seafarers 'knew' (but to very varying degrees) about 15 per cent of that shoreline in the middle of the fifteenth century. By the same token, perhaps getting on for 50 per cent of that shoreline was 'known' by their successors in 1650. Dramatic though that expansion certainly is, it was mainly in the world's middle latitudes, and dependent on a small number of well-known sea-passages, much of the knowledge being still indirect, unverified and vague. By 1650 it is evident that Europe's overseas expansion had reinforced its maritime technologies, its navigational and cartographic expertise, shipbuilding skills and naval armaments in comparison with other Eurasian civilizations.

A second, consequential global process was the biological transfer which resulted from those interactions, now widely known as the 'Columbian Exchange'. Unforeseen and unplanned, it involved a hemispheric displacement of agricultural crops and wild plants, especially to and from the American continent to Eurasia. From the New World came major staple crops that had begun to influence European diets and agricultural practices by 1650 (maize; manioc; kidney, lima and pinto beans; potatoes). There were new salad crops and fruits (courgettes, cranberries, pineapples, pumpkins). But the process went both ways. From the Old World to the American continent came hitherto unknown staples (wheat, oats, barley, millet), and fruits and salads (figs, lettuces, peaches, pears, peas, carrots). The same was also true for domestic animals and feral species. Turkeys, llamas, guinea pigs, alpacas and Muscovy ducks moved from the New World to the Old; domestic cats, cows, sheep, chickens, donkeys, ferrets, honey bees and silkworms went in the reverse direction. The introduction of new food crops and livestock fuelled population growth, not just in Europe but in East Asia and probably in North Africa too. The most tragic evidence for the importance of these biological transfers was in epidemic disease. The Old World exported bubonic plague, chicken pox, cholera, smallpox and typhus to the New World – diseases to which Eurasians and, to a degree, Africans had developed resistance, but which decimated the indigenous American populations. This time, however, the return traffic was asymmetric. Nothing from America significantly damaged the European host population.

The Columbian Exchange became an essential part of a precocious capitalist global economy. Biological transfer lay at the heart of some of the emerging patterns of production, distribution and consumption, not to mention changes in social organization. By 1620, for example, up to 20,000 tons of sugar (a newly imported plant into America) was probably being produced for European consumption by a slave workforce, transported across the Atlantic from Africa. Raw and processed materials circulated globally in substantial quantities, satisfying new markets. The canvases which Johannes Vermeer painted in Delft represent, at first sight, an ordered and inward-looking, provincial world. Study them more carefully, however, and the objects in them – that lavish black felt hat from Canadian beaver; this Chinese porcelain dish; those silver coins, the raw material from Peru; those vermilion and scarlet red cloths (from cochineal, produced by the Indians of Central and South America) – tell a different story. Like the silk from China, the spices from Southeast Asia, the pepper and cotton from the Indian subcontinent and the tobacco from the Americas, they were all products which were traded and consumed globally in unprecedented quantities in this period. In some cases, the demands of the new market could be met by simply scaling up existing practices. That was the case for Indian cotton weavers, or Chinese porcelain factories. In others, however, it involved major social change, and the brutalizing coercion of labour forces – like the mining operations in Mexico and Peru or the slave-labour on the Brazilian sugar plantations.

In the global perspective the significance of the immense, sophisticated and monetarized economies of China and India is evident – which is why the East remained an enduring objective for Europe's overseas expansion throughout this period. The dynamism of the Chinese economy is at the heart of the explanation for Europe's overseas expansion. The market value of silver in Ming territories was roughly double its contemporary value elsewhere in the world. In that perspective, the discovery and exploitation of South American silver takes on a different dimension. Europe produced few goods that eastern hemisphere markets wanted. Silver was the one commodity with which Europe's merchants could trade in Asia. Still more importantly, on that basis Europeans became the dominant intermediaries in the global silver trade, the majority of which never reached Europe's shores. Perhaps over fifty tons of silver annually was transported by Europeans from Acapulco on the Pacific coast in the first half of the seventeenth century across to Manila in the Philippines. That is roughly the equivalent to the overall value of Europe's overseas trade per annum during the same period with the East Indies. From the Philippines, the silver was traded on to the Chinese mainland in return for silks and other goods. Spanish galleons were the middlemen in the trade, just as Portuguese ships were the carriers of Japanese silver to the Chinese mainland until they were expelled from the country in 1637.

There were immense profits to be made by those who controlled the centres of silver production – especially Habsburg Spain and Tokugawa Japan. But there were rich pickings for all the individuals and institutions involved in the trade along the way – from the mines in the Andes to the marketplaces of China. Those returns made possible the investment in Europe's first colonial projects in America. They oiled the wheels of its trade with the Far East, the beneficiaries being its merchants, especially after the organization of chartered trading companies such as the English and Dutch East India Companies (founded in 1600 and 1602 respectively). A shallow globalization was in the process of formation.

Europe's population growth in this period – partly on the basis of the Columbian Exchange of food crops – was only one facet of a more general rise in world populations, especially marked in Eurasia. Increasing state power in Europe was mirrored by the consolidation of states in Asia too. Ming China, Mughal India and the Ottoman empire were, like the Spaniards or the Portuguese and Dutch in the Far East, 'gunpowder empires'. These global phenomena were subject, however, to equally global constraints. The dramatic increase in human population in the course of the sixteenth century resulted in unprecedented pressures on natural resources. These were especially evident on the environmental frontiers – with a retreat of the steppe before the sown, an expansion into marginal cultivable land, and an explosion of commercial hunting. It was not just in Europe that those pressures were in evidence from the end of the sixteenth century onwards. They were the more marked because of global climate change – the cooling of the planet that began to be recorded from around 1580 onwards, and whose effects became more pronounced towards 1650. Europe's mid-seventeenth-century crisis belongs in a global context, even though most of its constituent elements were home-grown.

IMAGINING EUROPE

The paradox was that Europe's overseas expansion was the result of Europeans who barely knew, or spoke of 'Europe'. It was America which enabled them to reconfigure Christendom as a geographical entity, a space they increasingly knew as 'Europe'. If it had not been for the discovery of America, 'Europe' would not have existed. Mythology provided Europe's poets and artists with ways of representing the ambiguities of the world around them. The humanist revival of the ancient world opened up the veins of classical mythology, the antics of Greek and Roman gods becoming ways of holding a mirror up to power, pandering to the sexual licence of its courts but taking the viewer and the reader into a parallel universe in which fortune, virtue, human passions, danger and the all-important divine protection could all be represented, without necessarily compromising Christian morality or the conventional Christian understanding of the world and humanity's place within it. 'Europe' was part of a myth which Renaissance humanists cultivated from the ancients about the disposition of the inhabited landmass into three zones: Asia (the most important), Africa (the next) and Europe (the least), each mapped onto the story of Noah's successors. With a wider diffusion of world maps and globes, that myth began its metamorphosis into more geographically defined continents. The discovery of a fourth continent in America was an essential part of that change.

It did not happen quickly. The ideas of 'America' and 'Europe' were slow to penetrate the European imagination. Spanish administrators, for example, persisted in regarding its American colonies as 'the Indies', and the word 'America' was scarcely used in official papers at all. Shakespeare and Montaigne almost never used the word 'Europe' in their writings, although when the latter referred to 'us' he evidently had in mind a shared space that went without a name. 'Europe', however, became increasingly envisaged as a set of values, an identity given geographical extension by its humanist-educated élites. The French philosopher Louis Le Roy wrote of 'our mother Europe', using the term to describe a whole civilization with a complex history, a dynamic present and a positive future. Francis Bacon, too, grandly referred to 'we Europeans' in 1605. America was essential in defining what those values, and that identity, were. For those who were not from the Spanish peninsula, or who did not acknowledge allegiance to the papacy, the rights of trade, conquest and settlement in the New World, initially accorded in the early sixteenth century by the papacy and ratified by the emperor, were fiercely contested on the grounds of something larger, a law of nature, shared with other human beings in a world which had expanded in time and space. That law of nature could be used, in turn, to define ways of behaving that were 'human' as opposed to 'savage' and 'barbarian' – terms which became another way of understanding 'Europe' – as values that marked it out from the savage world beyond.

The word 'Europe' became utilized instead of 'Christendom' by Protestants, especially when they wanted to demonstrate that the cruelties which occurred in Europe's confessional conflicts were as great, if not greater, than those of supposed 'savages'. Europe's settlers in the New World defined themselves in terms of the values of the places from which they had come, in the process idealizing the mother country ('New Spain', 'New France', 'New England'), and gradually discovering their own identity. Some of them could not wait to get back. Manuel de Nóbrega, the first Jesuit provincial and author of an influential early history of Brazil, wrote of his compatriots: 'They do not love the land and all their affection is for Portugal. The first thing which they teach their parrot is: "Parrot royal, back to Portugal".' For others, colonialism was about making something new, in the image of the old. Indigenous Indian peoples became an example of all that colonists were not, or should not be – barbarians, pagans, profligate, undependable, lacking industry and purpose, and irrational. Protestant and Catholic missionaries alike identified an attitude towards 'freedom' in the indigenous populations that was very different from that which was accorded to Europeans by their laws of nature – careless towards responsibility and constituted authority, unconcerned about the future. America gradually became, too, a utopia for all the values that Europe should uphold, but failed to. For Domenico Scandella, a self-taught miller from Friuli, the term 'New World' evoked a world of happiness through which to see Europe, as though in a reflection. Those who sought exile on religious grounds from Europe's religious conflicts also imagined a New Jerusalem on another continent and, in so doing, invented an alien Europe which had rejected them, and which they had left behind. Through the existence of America in the European imagination, it was possible to imagine that Old World space in new ways.

Mythology played its part in that metamorphosis. On 19 June 1559, Tiziano Vecelli (Titian) wrote from Venice to the most potent ruler of Christendom, Philip II of Spain, to say that he was at work on the last of six great canvases on the *Loves of the Gods*, a commission that they had discussed when he had met the young prince eight years previously in Augsburg. The subject was the *Rape of Europa*. What he finally despatched to his patron in the spring of 1562 was a dramatic seascape under a threatening sky in which a duped and dishevelled Europa is about to lose her clothing and virginity. Being transported away and out of the picture, she hangs on for dear life to the horns of the bull which she has just realized is no bull at all, but mighty Zeus in disguise. Titian's knowledge of the myth of Europa came from Book II of the Roman poet Ovid's *Metamorphoses*. Ovid was the most studied, and certainly the most translated and commented upon, of the ancient poets in the Renaissance. Titian could not read the Latin himself, but no matter – the illustrated Ovid of his friend, the Paduan-trained man of letters Ludovico Dolce, had just appeared on the bookstalls of Venice.

Titian's brilliant painting had multiple meanings. He described the series of which it was the climax as a 'poesie' – poetry in paint. Since the subject had been chosen by Arachne in her contest with the goddess Athena as to who was to weave the best tapestry, Titian was making a claim to be the Apelles (the renowned painter of ancient Greece) of the modern world. But, as his Venetian friend Pietro Aretino remarked shortly before he died (and Aretino had published, perhaps even defined, hard-core pornography), Titian's 'poesie' was an erotic painting to titillate a princely patron, reminding him of sexual attraction and omnipotence in all its guises. It had a political message too. Rape was associated with the Turks, and with the atrocities of war. The young King Philip II was also being told that his inheritance was vulnerable to attack from without and within, the prey to its own passions and the predations of others. In a roundabout way, this 'Europe' was also about values.

Above all, Europe became geographical space. 'Queen' Europe was famously anthropomorphized into a woman by Emperor Ferdinand's cartographer, Johannes Bucius Aenicola. The graphic conceit was popularized when it was incorporated into later editions of Sebastian Münster's famous *Cosmographia* (1544). Not surprisingly, given its origins in Habsburg lands, Spain forms her crowned head and Italy her right arm, her cloak flowing out vaguely towards the east. The crown was important. Cesare Ripa, Europe's leading interpreter of the palette of iconic emblems available to its poets, painters and writers, instructed his readers in his *Iconologia* of 1603 to depict Europe with a crown 'to show that Europe has always been the leader and queen' of the four continents. That was a reversal of the inherited hierarchy, in which Europe hung onto the coat-tails of Asia and Africa, and a reflection of the emerging sense of superiority that accompanied a Europe conceived as a set of values, mapped onto a geographical space.

There was a problem, however, about such a conception of Europe. Given the lack of any defining natural frontiers to the Eurasian land-mass, where did it end? Christendom had faced no such difficulty, since its boundaries were determined by the faith community which it repre-sented. But where were the boundaries of this geographically based Europe of values? The draughtsmen of Europe as a virgin fudged the issue, running her skirts out over a vast region to the east, and scattering names around the hem of the garment ('Scythia', 'Muscovy', 'Tartary'). Was Muscovy part of Europe? The question was the more complicated since, less celebrated than Europe's maritime empires but equally important, was Russian expansion east and south down the Volga and beyond the Urals into the huge Asian landmass. The answers to the question increasingly depended on the European observer's construc-tion of an alien 'other' in terms of values, which the historians and philosophers of the eighteenth-century Enlightenment rationalized as a 'civilization', based on a particular interpretation of their political, reli-gious and cultural European inheritance.

Europe could be conceived as a geographical entity in this period because of changing senses of space. 'Cartography' was a way of understanding space as geometric quantity, abstracted from other qualities of meaning and experience. What mattered was the 'relation of distances', as Ptolemy had said. The discovery of his *Geography* in Constantinople in the early fifteenth century, long known in the Islamic world but new to Latin Chris-tendom, established the theoretical principles of cartography, introducing what amounted to latitude and longitude, providing a method of projec-tion and stressing empirical observation. European mapmakers measured and conceptualized space along those lines, the results being represented in printed maps and globes. Europe's 'age of discovery' was not simply of far-away new worlds. It was also that of its own spatial identity.

EUROPE'S INFORMATION DYNAMICS

That geographical sense of European space epitomized the changes to the sense of what was 'local' in sixteenth- and early seventeenth-century Europe. Spices, dyes, skins, furs, silks, sugar were among the traded goods which linked Europe's markets to one another and to a wider world. In addition, there was a shift in the communication and information dynamics of Europe. In other words, the impact of print technology was part of a wider transformation, embracing handwritten letters, postal services, oral transmission, travel and encounter, scientific enquiry and the structuring of knowledge. The organizational and structural means of functioning at a distance deepened. Persuasion (moral and otherwise) as a constituency for political action, religious beliefs and social behaviour became more important. Spatial limits and temporal constraints, defining who you were and how you could behave, weakened. There was greater awareness, direct and indirect, of a wider world and its pluralism and complexity. Wider, too, became the gap between those whose literacy and numeracy enabled them to access directly that dynamic, and those who were dependent on others to do so. The newsletters and pamphlets of the Thirty Years War and the conflicts which surrounded it turned its generals – those whose icy stares, curls of hair and blackened armour greet the visitor to the art galleries of Europe – into household names. Pamphlet accounts of slaughters, famine and plague became object lessons of God's wrath, experienced vicariously across Europe. The sense of shared crisis, so evident towards the middle of the seventeenth century, is the most telling evidence for what had changed in Europe's information dynamics in the previous century and a half.

It is difficult to overestimate the significance of Europe's transformed habits of communication. Had Europe not, for example, found the lexicon and shared the examples which demonstrated that a polity and social order could live with religious division and pluralism in its midst, its seventeenth-century paroxysm would have been even more profound and damaging. Had Europe not changed the political and organizational frameworks of the state to accommodate information plurality and manage its power relationships, the risks of systemic state collapse would have been greater, and the damaging death-wish rivalries of its aristocratic and dynastic élites would have been uncontrollable. Had it not used its increasingly plural and dispersed communities of wealth and power, linked by increasingly elaborate networks of economic obligation and variegated skeins of knowledge transfer, its colonialism would not have had the enduring and transformative impact that it did, both inside Europe and beyond. Had its diplomatic channels and protocols of communication and negotiation not evolved, the unprecedentedly elaborate Peace of Westphalia (1648), which brought the German Thirty Years War to a close, would have been impossible.

THE 'SILVER AGE' AND ITS AFTERMATH

By 1650, over 180 tons of gold had been exported from the Indies, and 16,000 tons of silver from the New World. This was the 'Silver Age'. Whether you had some of it, or none, became of increasing importance. Even if you had none, you could not escape its influence, because of the unprecedented spell of European inflation that continued through the majority of this period, and extended in some parts of Europe well into the seventeenth century. The 'European price revolution' was in reality a time of sustained economic growth and expansion, whether measured in monetary terms or demographic growth. French historians summarize it as the 'beautiful sixteenth century', though it came to a premature end in France as a result of war, and it was 'beautiful' for some, but emphatically not for others. It deepened the divisions between the 'haves' and 'have nots', between those who benefited from price inflation and those who lost out. Among the latter were those on fixed incomes, expressed in money (rents and many other forms of investment, but also taxation). That included those in Europe's élite – its princes, landed nobility and clergy. Inflation and economic expansion depressed their fixed incomes. But they could mostly adjust by exploiting other, frequently contested ways of raising revenues from their assets – new forms of taxation by princes of their subjects, or new burdens by landowners on their tenants. The result was more aggressive domain landlordism, higher entry-fines for tenants in some places, expropriation of woodland and commons to which the local community hitherto had use-rights in others. There was a marked deepening of seigneurial labour burdens placed upon the peasantry to the east of the Elbe and north of the Saale.

Inflation and economic expansion also increased the variety and density of social groups with assets to their name and accrued social status, and who demanded to be recognized as notables in the established social order. At the same time, the numbers of those who lost out grew – the mass of semi-landless peasant owners of tiny plots of marginal viability, the peasants in chronic debt who sold out to their creditors or became renters rather than owners, their holdings reduced to tiny farms, the swelling ranks of the urban poor. The result was a heavier social burden upon communities. Europe did not experience a profound social transformation in this period, but social cohesion was weakened. The decay of local solidarity was masked by sixteenth-century economic expansion, but it was correspondingly more exposed by the recession which followed it in most parts of Europe and which was intensified by the dislocations of the Thirty Years War.

Weakening social cohesion put pressure on Europe's enduring localism. To a degree, the sense of identity in Europe's villages and towns had always been an artificial construction by which local notables – peasant proprietors in rural environments who so often became the leading figures in village society, local nobles, or the merchants and leading guild-members who ran towns as a corporate élite – projected local solidarity as a defence of peace, justice, good order and their own interests. But increasingly those local notables found it harder to present their perception of the good of the common weal as consonant with the interests of everyone in divided communities. Religious differences made their task still harder, and the engines of the state seemed correspondingly more remote and alien, less willing to listen to their concerns, or respond to their petitions.

Relationships between the local urban and rural worlds were changing as well, with towns exercising a greater dominance over their surrounding countryside, peasants cautiously engaging in their markets (and thereby becoming partially dependent upon them) and urban notables investing in the countryside (and foreclosing on tenants who did not pay their debts). Local protest and revolt were such a sustained and important feature of this period that the question is not the degree to which they existed but the extent to which localized dissatisfaction and dissension, in the circumstances of a transformed ability to communicate more broadly, were able to find common cause within and across communities in order to make their voices of protest heard. The diminishing sense of local cohesion and the corresponding social tensions had their impact on local notables. They reached for explanations to account for the vulnerable and uncontrollable world in which they found themselves. Many drew reassurance from the order and authority of the Counter-Reformed Catholic Church. Others sought explanations in a

theology of God's inscrutable providence, or in the millennial expectations of those for whom it was a sign of living in the Last Days; others
again in the actively malign presence and sinister potential of the Devil
in the world around, or in the science of astrology to provide an explanatory framework and predictive component to it. What is interesting
about these explanations is their universality and the degree to which
they were appropriated by notables at a local level.

Metamorphosis was a way of understanding change in this period.
When Lucas Cranach the Elder, the artist-friend of Martin Luther in
Wittenberg, painted *'The End of the Silver Age'*, he turned it into an
Ovidian allegory for his own day. Each time he painted the scene, he
showed vulnerable nude women and children huddling in small groups
as aggressive and jealous men engage in fratricidal conflict around them.
Hesiod had described this metamorphosis, when 'men refused to worship the gods' and engaged in strife with one another. For Ovid it was
the harbinger of the 'Brazen [i.e. 'Bronze'] Age', when men were 'worse
natur'd, prompt to horrid warre, and rage', the prelude to the 'Iron
Age'. To Cranach, this scene was a warning-piece that had parallels
with Adam and Eve's expulsion from the Garden of Eden. It was a
reminder of how easily the cycle of human decline and decay could
occur unless one obeyed the gods.

Europe's 'Silver Age' became tarnished towards the end of the century, beginning in the 1580s and 90s, precisely at the moment when the
imports of silver from the New World were at their peak. The cycle of
economic growth and prosperity that had marked sixteenth-century
Europe started to evaporate. While the most damaging phases of the
civil wars in France and the Netherlands were played out, an underlying
economic crisis left its anxieties everywhere, but most notably in those
areas which found their population growth faltering. These regions,
especially in southern Europe, were forced to contemplate the reality
of economic stagnation, or even contraction. In some places epidemic
disease, famine and rural depopulation appeared on a scale that contemporaries had not hitherto experienced, and then continued into the
next century. Nor was it evident that there were mechanisms for adjusting the layers of political, social and ecclesiastical obligation which had
grown up in the good times, and which now constituted a burden on
these societies and an impediment to their adapting to the new reality.
Seigneurial obligations, share-cropping, serfdom – these were all ways

by which the capstone of élites bore more heavily in this period on the rural world. Meanwhile, in other parts of northern Europe societies managed to reconstitute their economies, to weather the storm and to profit from the misfortunes of others. On the northwest Atlantic seaboard, it led to the building of overseas empires and economic systems, emulating their predecessors but also introducing new elements. The differential patterns of Europe's development were among the most striking features of its metamorphosis.

Europe's communication dynamics informed its notables that the impact of the watershed of the 1580s and 90s had not been generalized across the continent, but that it was variegated. Learning from the more successful, emulating them where possible, stealing a march upon one's competitors, became an important feature of Europe's tensions. So too did wistful glances back to what became idealized as a 'golden age' in the past. The economic rivalries which underlay the succession of conflagrations that afflicted Europe after 1618 provoked social tensions that had been briefly glimpsed, but successfully negotiated away and buried in the years after the Reformation. Now, however, the margins for negotiated and mediated settlement were smaller, with the prospects of economic growth and expansion less certain. The state – and especially its subcontractors (tax-farmers, military enterprisers, office-holders, and others) – made its presence felt in a more coercive way, and drove harder bargains. If millennial convictions or mercantilist prospects still conjured up a positive picture of the future for some, for others the fortune of the gods dictated a rosy future that was in heaven rather than on earth. 'Happy the age, happy the time', says Cervantes's Don Quixote when he met some goatherds, still living the pastoral life 'to which the ancients gave the name of golden'. Their life was in contrast to 'this our iron age', against whose harsh reality the deluded knight errant set out to fight the good fight.

The Tuscan Duke Ferdinando de' Medici commissioned Pietro da Cortona in the later 1630s to decorate the walls of the small 'Sala della Stufa' in the Pitti Palace in Florence with the four ages of history. The subject had been suggested to him by Michelangelo Buonarroti, the poet grand-nephew of the artist Michelangelo. The eventual fresco for that of the 'Iron Age', finished in 1640, is a hyper-realistic evocation of human bloodshed. Against the trappings of civil society, soldiers in the foreground massacre a defenceless family while, behind them, their companions fight it out among themselves despite the implorations of an impotent priest. The scene is more violent, intense and frightening than Cranach's picture of betrayed innocence a century previously. It conjures up the colliding squadrons and murderous sieges, the destroyed landscapes and threatened populations of the Thirty Years War, the divided British Isles and wrecked Poland. 'Then, blushlesse Crimes, which all degrees surpast, the World Surround. Shame, Truth, & Faith departe, Fraud enters, ignorant in no bad Art; Force, Treason, & the wicked loue of gayne . . .' – George Sandys's popular English translation of Ovid's poem, this part published in 1621, exemplifies how contemporaries understood what afflicted Europe towards the middle of the seventeenth century – a crisis which threatened to, but did not become a metamorphosis. It was a paroxysm from which Europe's *ancien régime* recovered, and on foundations already laid.

From the 'Silver Age' to
the 'Iron Century'

2. Human Replenishment

CHRISTENDOM'S MATERIAL FOUNDATIONS

When officials in sixteenth-century Europe counted and taxed their population, they often did so by the 'hearth'. The term conjures up a family huddled around an open fire, venting through a hole in the roof, dwelling in a couple of rooms, a foyer (where cooking, eating and domestic work took place) and space for sleeping. Storage was everything; human comfort and privacy slight. Prosperity was determined by the existence of a cellar, storeroom and barn. In Europe's cold winter nights, animals were close by (inside the 'long house') for warmth.

That is a stereotype. In reality, Christendom's material foundations were regionally diverse. Different styles of housing reflected local variations in building materials as well as social and cultural distinctions. Dwellings dictated the evolution of Europe's demography. By the early sixteenth century one of the changes in their construction had become quite widespread in towns and more substantial rural dwellings: the fireplace, built into a side wall. Chimneys generated much more heat (thanks to improved draught for the fire), which they also largely wasted, but they guaranteed less smoke inside. Better still were closed stoves, built of clay and tiles. An Italian travelling in Poland in the early sixteenth century recounted how whole families slept, wrapped in furs, on benches around the stove. Descartes alluded to a famous insight which became the prelude to his search for a new method of organizing and validating human knowledge as taking place at night in a 'stove' (*poêle*, or heated inn) outside Ulm in 1619. A contemporary chronicler said that there were seventy-four in the palace at Český Krumlov. Their moulded contours and coloured lead-glazed surfaces introduced an additional visual aspect to the home. Tile craftsmen miniaturized figurative scriptural scenes from altars and books of hours and transformed them into fireside religion. Changes to the hearth implied transformations in how people lived – their space, privacy, clothing, beliefs and the proximity of rodents.

Wood, stone, brick – building materials vied with social status to determine housing construction. Construction was a motor of local economies – more important than textiles. It is difficult to evaluate how much it cost to put up a house, still less to maintain it. So much of the effort was human and paid for in kind. Even humble cottages were made of stone where it was plentiful (Cornwall, Brittany, Burgundy, the Paris basin). In Mediterranean regions (Catalonia, Languedoc, Provence) the extended family dwellings were often impressive in scale – up to 500 tons in stone-weight and three floors high. The ground floor was where grapes and olives were pressed and wine and oil were stored, with the family living above. The floor under the pantiles (widespread in the Mediterranean) stored grain. The emphasis was on ventilation, appropriate for a Mediterranean climate, with heating in winter provided by fires in braziers. These dwellings were built to last for 300 years or more with only minimal expenses in maintenance. But they cost up to fifteen times as much to build as a house made of wood. That was the preferred material in the towns and countryside in more heavily forested northern Europe. Even then, only in parts of Alpine Europe were houses built entirely from logs. Most were half-timbered – hewn wood forming the weight-bearing frame with wattle and daub in-fill. Wood was cheap, had good thermic properties and was easily replaced piecemeal. These dwellings ranged from the most common house in Poland – a wood frame on stone foundations, with a clay floor, a roof of thatch or shingle, and earth and straw built up around outside for insulation – to the more substantial half-timbered houses of central and northern Europe, with upper storeys for living and farm quarters. Brick was the preferred building material along the coasts and rivers of northern Europe and in the larger cities of the south. Brick-making, however, required transport, plant, skilled labour and investment. Limestone, essential for a durable mortar, was expensive. So, although brick was widely adopted for urban housing, where it was appropriate for stable tall structures and provided excellent insulation without great weight, one did not need to go far outside the town before encountering mixtures of brick and half-timbered buildings or wood.

Social status and function dictated the variety of habitations. Dwellings for day-labourers – cottagers and shack-dwellers – were little more than a refuge from the worst of the elements. Marginal landless tenants in Germany lived in hovels adjacent to the buildings of the farmer on whose land they squatted. Miners in the Auvergne made do with one-room huts. Agricultural day-labourers in Sicily put up with tofts. In Hungary, and on light, well-drained soil in central and eastern Europe, country folk could be found living half-underground in houses constructed of peat and grass turfs. At Pescara, an Adriatic port, about three quarters of its inhabitants (migrant workers) lived in tannery shacks according to an enquiry of 1564. For farming families, their houses were an essential part of their livelihood. Space for processing and storing grain, olives and grapes took precedence over human habitation. If the houses of day-labourers were no more than a refuge, those of more prosperous country people were, as the surviving inscriptions on wooden buildings from the period in central and Alpine Europe suggest, a status symbol as well as an investment. Surviving buildings reveal the intuitive understanding of materials by craftsmen and the elaborate improvisation that went into distributing the weight of upper storeys evenly. 'Architects' began to appear in sixteenth-century Italy and France. The humanist Charles Estienne's *La Maison rustique* (1564) provided a pattern-book for the farmstead which French master craftsmen followed for almost two centuries. Europe's demographic vitality sustained remarkable fixed capital investment in its housing stock.

Christendom's material life is revealed in post-mortem inventories, conducted by auctioneers, notaries and rural scriveners who knew how to value objects at a glance. An inventory was a first move in inheritance from one generation to another, and it was worth undertaking only when there was something to inherit. But that included country people of modest means. Like wills, these documents were not limited to the wealthy. On the contrary, they were important to all those who wanted to secure the inheritance of infant children. In the fenland parish of Willingham in East Anglia, villagers carefully disposed of their cattle and cheese-making equipment. That of 1593 from William Pardye, a waterman, left his only son John two cows, 'all my lodge as it standith . . . with the fodder that is upon the same lodge, my boat in the fen, my boots, and a pair of high shoes'. In Burgundy, the most common objects were the fireside trivets, stew-pots, cooking utensils and bread-boards. There was often a lockable coffer, a wooden bed and a mattress. Sleeping on straw done up in a sack and laid on the ground or on planks had begun to decline in the fifteenth century. Beds – wooden frames with leather or rope cross-straps – were a significant gift upon marriage. Four poster beds from this period were enormous pieces of furniture, ostentatious signs of family wealth. In his will (25 March 1616) Shakespeare left his wife Anne his 'second best bed'. Mattresses (stuffed with feathers or wool – straw was a cheap substitute) could be elaborately covered with velvet, braids and silks. But poverty meant most people had little. In *La Chanson à boire*, the Dutch painter Adriaen Brouwer portrays the inside of a cottage, possibly on the dunes north of Antwerp. Four peasants sit on makeshift furniture (cut out of old barrels) around a table. Apart from the old clothes they are wearing, there is nothing other than a rag, a pitcher and a loaf of bread.

Europe's settlement patterns were determined by a complex mix of historical and social geography. In the mind's eye, it is the nucleated village which predominates, the settlement with its church surrounded by open fields and common pasture. That was typical of the plains and river basins, and also the dominant pattern around the shores of the Mediterranean and wherever Europe had recolonized land on its margins – on the Meseta in central Spain or on the Hungarian plain. More disparate settlement was the order of the day in Europe's animal husbandry regions, on its heathlands and marshes, its forests, woodlands and mountain uplands. Across eastern and central Europe the settlement type was the 'street village' – straggling communities built along a road. Around the Atlantic shores of northern Europe the equivalent was the coastal village, clustering around a beach or loading station.

Such settlement patterns can be traced in detail through surviving estate maps. Surveying became widely diffused in this period. One of the earliest vernacular printed surveying manuals, the *Geometria* (Frankfurt, 1531) of Jacob Köbel, explained: 'Take sixteen men, large and small' as they come out of the church, and line them up, each with one foot along a rod. Marked at both ends, this created the surveyor's 16-*Schuh* staff (the cousin of the English 'rod, pole, or perch', about 16.5 feet long) to measure fields. By the end of the sixteenth century, surveyors were expected to use geometry and a compass to triangulate surface areas that were irregular polygons. New instruments helped them: Philippe Danfrie's *graphomètre* (advertised in a Paris publication of 1597) and 'waywisers' to measure distance. Even so, it was hard to create accurate maps. Paul Pfinzing's surveying manual, published in Nuremberg in 1598, recommended cutting up pieces of cardboard to the right shapes and weighing them in order to arrive at a collective land area of an estate. His surviving estate maps reveal settlement and land use in remarkable detail. The one for his native village (Hennenfeld) from 1592, for example, enumerates the fields and plots of its seventy-nine inhabitants. Further south, Johann Rauch, a surveyor from the Vorarlberg, prepared a sequence of estate maps for the eastern shore of Lake Constance and Upper Swabia. On his plot of the village of Rickenbach, prepared in about 1628, each house is numbered and the owner's name and the corresponding fields identified. In Bavaria, Peter Zweidler mapped the estates of the bishop of Bamberg at the end of the sixteenth century, detailing the roads and villages, fishponds and even the stones which marked the edges of the properties in question.

Europe's patterns of settlement did not change dramatically in this period. The equivalents to the 'lost villages' of the Middle Ages (following the Black Death) were to be found in Mediterranean lands after 1600, especially in Spain where rural depopulation became serious in its more arid upland central regions. Count-Duke Olivares left money in his 1642 will for eight pious foundations to help repopulate such deserted communities. Those villages and hamlets which disappeared from Christendom after 1500 did so because of social engineering (emparkment by ambitious aristocrats), revenge (the erasure of the Waldensian communities in the Luberon mountains of Provence in 1545 or in Calabria in 1558), depredations (southern Slovakia and parts of Hungary in the wake of the Turkish offensive in the early sixteenth century) or as a result of climatic change. By contrast, as the marshes and fens of western and southern Europe were reclaimed, new communities sprang up. Fresh villages of miners, salt-workers, quarrymen and fishers took root. Virgin forest and untamed lands still lay to the north and east. The number of farms in Norway began to match those of *c.* 1300 – there were around 57,000 by 1665. In Norrland (North Sweden) and Savolax (East Finland) new colonization was noticeable by 1570 although there was still vast countryside where habitation was rare. Germans and Slavs colonized central eastern Europe. Further south, in Bohemia and Moravia, villages abandoned in the fifteenth century were resettled. The dominant rural reality was human replenishment.

NAMES ON A PAGE

Modern-style population censuses do not exist in Europe before the French Revolution. Instead, there are census-like documents, especially in Europe's cities and more urbanized environments. Their purposes were not demographic. Europe's rulers wanted to tax their populations, enlist them into military service or target new immigrants. Humanist wisdom favoured censuses, albeit for different reasons. Niccolò Machiavelli supported the Florentine property tax, introduced in 1427, because he felt it followed Roman precedents and prevented tyranny. His contemporary Francesco Guicciardini disliked property taxes as an attack upon the notables, but supported other progressive taxes which relied on censuses. The French humanist Jean Bodin advocated a census in his *Six Books of the Republic* (1576), seeing it as the basis for a tax system that would reflect the geometric proportions ('harmonies') in the world at large. In spite of this desire to measure, there was a profound underlying conviction that population had declined since Antiquity and was still diminishing. In the utopian writings of the period (Thomas More's *Utopia*, 1516; Francis Bacon's *New Atlantis*, 1624; Tommaso Campanella's *La Città del Sole*, 'City of the Sun', 1602), the state had a role in promoting the number of those who are born its citizens. 'We must never believe that there are too many subjects, too many citizens,' said Bodin, 'seeing that there are no riches and no forces beyond people.'

With the advent of the tax-state, population enumeration became more frequent. Italian polities were precocious in this respect – Venice, Milan, Tuscany, Genoa, Rome, the kingdom of Naples and Sicily. In the southern Low Countries, taxation depended on the enumeration of hearths. In Languedoc, it was based on an evaluation of wealth which was then recorded in land and wealth surveys. Not before the early seventeenth century was there anything approaching a civil registration of the population. Then, following Pope Paul V's *Rituale Romanum* (1614), various Italian dioceses started to keep annual congregational lists recording the age and family of each recipient of the Easter communion. To the north, the Lutheran clergy of Sweden were required from 1628 to keep annual registers, noting the literacy and religious instruction of their parishioners.

These documents are sometimes no more than names on pages. Fiscal records enumerate hearths; church documents list communicants. They require interpretation. Demography in this period is a black art. Everyone agrees that there was a 'pronounced secular upswing' in population, but when it began and when it ended is unclear. Very hesitant in the late fifteenth century, it was not significant in many places before 1520. In England, growth started to be registered only around 1510 and then nearly doubled over the next century. In the Low Countries, it was more precocious. In the northern provinces of the Netherlands, it continued towards 1650, but it faltered in the south.

In German lands increases appeared early on – more vigorous in the west than in the east. Whether they slowed down by 1618 is debatable, but they were certainly wiped out by the Thirty Years War. In France, the growth rhythms emerged strongly and evenly from 1500 to 1545, unsteadily from 1545 to 1560; renewed, and then uncertain to 1580. They then declined to coincide with the worst of the civil wars through to the end of the century. Population increase resumed unsteadily in the early seventeenth century but petered out from 1630 onwards, with different regions revealing contrasting trends. The plagues of 1628–32 and 1636–9 often wiped out what the previous generation had replenished. In parts of northern Italy, growth started before 1500 and in most places it continued through to the second half of the sixteenth century, and in some into the seventeenth century. Plagues in the first half of the seventeenth century (in Lombardy, those of 1628–32, 1635 and 1649), however, eliminated most of the increases of the previous century.

In the Spanish peninsula, Castile's population increased through the sixteenth century, with perhaps the fastest growth occurring in the 1530s. Then, as in Italy and France, epidemic disease (and possibly dearth-related mortality) swept away the gains of a generation in a sequence of bad years. The epidemic of 1599–1600 was frightening in its intensity. Up to 750,000 Spaniards – a tenth of the population – probably fell victim to pestilence in the period from 1596 to 1614. Some places do not seem to have recovered their demographic buoyancy thereafter. Others did, only to find it succumbing to later attacks, especially in 1647 and 1650. A study that concentrates on the number of baptisms in sixty-four parishes from across Castile suggests steep declines in the interior of the peninsula (in Extremadura and Old Castile). Elsewhere, the expulsion of the Moriscos (converted Muslims) in 1609 had a catastrophic impact. Some 275,000 were expatriated, meaning Valencia lost a quarter of its population. The impact in Castile and Andalusia was less, but no doubt important, especially in towns. The real difficulty is to make sense of the general upswing of the sixteenth century in the context of the evidence for stagnation in the first half of the seventeenth century. The latter was not a general crisis on the scale of the Black Death. But it raises questions about the systemic weaknesses that underlay the growth in the century before.

Converting these trends into overall figures requires a deep breath. The numbers, tentative as they are, put the population growth of the 'long sixteenth century' into perspective. By some time towards 1600, Europe's population was about 75–80 million. That is towards the *lower* end of the estimates for its population in the early fourteenth century on the eve of the Black Death. Europe replenished its countryside in the sixteenth century; it did not transform it. In 1340, Europe's population might have been around 17 per cent of the world's total (74 million out of 442 million). By 1650, it was no more than 15 per cent of that total. By 1600, China's population, which probably grew at a faster rate than Europe's in the sixteenth century, may have been between 175 and 200 million. Despite losses in the period to 1650, it remained much more than double that of Europe. Europe's demographic advance in the 'long sixteenth century' was not dramatic in world terms. By modern standards, it was modest (1 per cent per annum) and uneven – sluggish in the Mediterranean, more dynamic on the northwestern flanks. France dominated Europe's heartland, accounting for something like a quarter of Europe's population: approaching 20 million.

This was the first age of parish registers. Some dioceses, especially in Italy and Spain, were precocious. The bishop of the diocese of Nantes enjoined his parish clergy to keep baptismal registers from 1406 and that is a region with some of the earliest surviving examples. The motives were religious, not demographic – to prevent 'spiritual incest' (that is, to stop people marrying into the families of their godparents). Gradually such local initiatives were enshrined in religious and state decrees. The final session of the Council of Trent (24 November 1563) pronounced that parish priests had to keep registers of births and marriages. Secular authorities, too, wanted the means to prove that people had been born, married and buried at a particular place, and on a particular date. In France, the Ordinance of Blois (1579) justified such record-keeping as a way to avoid fraud. The Protestant Reformation's redrafting of boundaries between Church and state resulted in parochial registration in parts of Switzerland (from the later 1520s), England (from 1538) and elsewhere. In Zürich, parish registers were introduced in 1526 in order to control the spread of Anabaptism. Jean Calvin insisted upon the introduction of registers in Geneva in 1541 as part of his vision of a well-ordered polity.

Approximately 100,000 folios of parish registers survive from the sixteenth century just for one French department (Loire-Atlantique): thousands of 'Jean'-s (one boy in four) and 'Jeanne'-s (one girl in five). In theory, by using 'family reconstitution' (reconstructing the genealogy of a sufficient number of families over a long period of time) a demographic projection can be generated. In reality, the process is complicated, especially for the period before 1650. Early baptismal registers only irregularly recorded the births of those who died before baptism. In some parts of Europe (for instance, the Basque country and Estonia), the use of a patronym was by no means established. In Holland, those in the lower classes tended not to use their family names in baptismal records, though they might in others. Names were written as they sounded, and people were known by what others chose to call them. Above all, migration makes the problem of family reconstitution a jigsaw puzzle in which some of the vital pieces are missing, and some of the rest belong to another picture altogether.

Once reconstituted, however, the results are like listening through a stethoscope to a breathing organism, in which living is the systole and dying the diastole. The latter was dominated by numbing rates of perinatal and post-natal mortality. In most places, a quarter of the children born did not survive until their first birthday, and only a half lived to celebrate their tenth. The diary of Jean Le Coullon from the countryside around Metz tells an all too familiar story. He was from a family of thirteen children, ten of whom died before they were married. He himself married in January 1545, and his wife bore him his first son, Collignon, the following year, his second son two years later, his third son, Jean, in 1549, and his fourth in 1552. In 1553 his wife died of plague, by which time two children had already died. Jean remarried eleven months later and went on to have other children by his second marriage, but of all the nineteen children of his and his surrounding family mentioned in the diary, only six lived to be twenty years old. He recounts these deaths in his diary alongside details of the weather and the state of the crops. One might imagine that he did not care very much, were it not for the moment when his first namesake son, Jean, died in 1549. Then he writes: 'It was of such great displeasure to me that I became inconsolable.'

Large surviving families were not common. Life expectancy at birth was low (say, twenty-five years) and, although it improved if you survived to adulthood, you would be lucky to see the age of fifty-five. Those surviving that long tended not to know how old they were. In 1566, Wiriot Guérin, local provost from the village of Gondreville on the river Moselle, declared that he was forty-four years of age. A decade later, he equally solemnly told the officials of the duke of Lorraine that he was 'sixty years old or more'. Epidemics of killer disease – bubonic plague, but also typhus, scarlet fever and influenza – could wipe away whole families and have a serious impact on local communities. Our demographic stethoscope registers the spasm of the demographic organism as it tries to cope with death rates that suddenly spiral to 6–10 per cent and, on occasion, 30–40 per cent. An important part of the spasm was the primal, or rather social, urge to replenish. Baptismal rates stutter, then recover fast as the organism worked to restore equilibrium; mini baby-booms were a familiar response to demographic catastrophe. Marriage registers reflect the widows and widowers reconstituting their families and consolidating their inheritances.

How, then, was Europe's population replenishment sustained? The longer series of surviving parish registers pick out cycles of local and regional growth, periodically arrested by a major mortality crisis, each crisis creating its own peaks and troughs in the family and age cohorts of the future. Most of all this lay outside people's power to control. So the answer to this question lies not in those elements that prevented demographic growth but in how it was that Europe's population managed to secure relatively high levels of fertility despite all the constraints that prevented it from doing so. Here is where the demographic evidence is (literally) pregnant with as many questions as answers. How many men and women chose not to get married at all remains unknown, though it may have been as high as 10–20 per cent of the population. For those who married, the pattern of marital fertility corresponded to the modern biological clock, highest for women aged between twenty and twenty-four, and declining thereafter, gently at first, but more rapidly the closer the mother reached forty, by which time most women had conceived for the last time in their lives. Illegitimacy rates, however, were at levels that modern advocates of family values could only dream of. Somewhere between 4 and 10 per cent of brides plighting their troth were already pregnant – but over half of them were in the early months and legitimating their condition. Illegitimate children were rarely more than 4 per cent of the total births, and often under 2 per cent. They were also a declining percentage. Was this a sign of the greater emphasis upon social and sexual discipline that resulted from the religious reformations of the sixteenth century? Perhaps, but illegitimacy rates tended to move in sequence with trends in nuptiality. In early-modern Europe, illegitimate births complemented births within marriage; they were not an alternative to them.

Human fertility across Europe varied widely. Before 1650 there is no evidence for widespread, artificial birth control. Religious strictures and social norms worked together to outlaw it. They did not, however, preclude couples deciding to stop having sex in order to avoid further conceptions, although that does not seem to have been widespread. So the explanation for Europe's population growth is embedded in that complex social institution, marriage.

MARRIAGE AND FAMILY

The social foundation of Christendom rested on the family. What changed in the relationships between women and men in this period? The continuing subordination of women to men inside and outside marriage is no surprise. The more strident voices in favour of patriarchy that emerge in the wake of the religious changes of the Reformation are. They hint at a fear of possible change. Subordination could mean very different things, depending on the context. Arranged marriages were common but they still involved courtship and negotiation. Widows were not generally forced to remarry by their families and if they had an inheritance it gave them a certain power. Many offspring lived away from home after puberty so that parental authority was not an ongoing reality in their lives. Women's educational opportunities were very restricted but they had employment possibilities and the Church tried to protect their freedom of conscience. The constraints on women's behaviour were, above all, social. In the wake of the Reformation, Church and secular courts took an even closer interest in controlling sexual behaviour. Prenuptial pregnancy was widely regarded with fear precisely because it threatened to turn a patriarchal domestic world on its head. In Europe's rural world especially, women's lot was not a happy one. They could not hold offices. They generally could not be tenants of land without guardianship. And there was hideous routine male violence directed at women, documented through their attempts at legal redress, risking their honour and reputation, and the counter-charge of being a 'shrew'.

What stands out most is the variety in Europe's marriage patterns. There were late marriages and a significant number of celibate individuals (mainly servants) in the family reconstitutions for England and the northwestern urbanized regions from the second half of the sixteenth century onwards. Both help explain how parts of Europe weathered the economic adversity of the later sixteenth and seventeenth centuries. Late marriages were a form of natural contraception. The age of marriage followed the inverse of real wages; as the latter fell, the former rose. The pool of 'life-cycle servants' (sexually mature people, waiting their turn to be married) was a reservoir of demographic replenishment. Parts of urbanized Europe were demographically resilient in the seventeenth century because of this elasticity.

Beyond this more urbanized region, east of the Elbe and in Denmark for example, marriage choices were determined by the realities of serfdom where landlords could impose a marriage and refuse a household with a female head. In the Baltic countries, Hungary, southern France or central and southern Italy, different family structures reflected a mixture of pressures: the ways of exploiting the land, the relationship of population to resource, the customary laws of inheritance and modes of taxation. In southern Italy – and wherever cereal production was concentrated in the hands of large estates (*latifundia*) employing day-labourers – marriage patterns reflect a hard life where men did not last long. Marriage came early for both men and women – between sixteen and twenty years old for the latter. Celibacy was almost unheard of outside the monastery or convent. Women did not work outside their home and strongly held notions of family honour prevented its occurring. Widows remarried almost immediately and men queued to take the place of those who had died.

In Calabria, the Campagnia, Sicily and elsewhere, wherever farming was more mixed or specialized (vineyards, olive groves, fruit trees) and where there were small peasant proprietors, girls married later (between twenty-two and twenty-six years of age), and boys who did not want to stay on the farm were encouraged to move away. In Sardinia, marriages were very late and there were lots of live-in servants – male and female, milkmaids and farmhands. Sardinian children were expected to accumulate their own dowries before marriage by working outside the home, and Sardinian women had a share in the paternal estate. In Umbria, Tuscany and the Romagna, and especially in those regions which practised share-cropping (sharing the farming risk between a farmer and a proprietor), day-labourers lived in nuclear families alongside peasant proprietors whose households included several generations of their own family as well as share-croppers and day-labourers. Where Roman law required the nomination of a single heir, the father generally chose his eldest son, but it could also be the first son to marry. Upon marriage, he handed over control of the farm to the heir and became what in Elizabethan England was known as a 'sojourner' in his own home, with arrangements already in hand for the elderly parents to be looked after in their declining years. Family complexity was a function of status. Families with wealth and notability had extended possessions and interests whose preservation and enhancement by marriage and inheritance led to complex domestic and family arrangements. Family formation was an individual and collective way of trying to secure the best conditions of living in a world where recurrent economic and demographic crisis threatened the survival of the whole family unit, and there was no one recipe for all.

Custom played a large part in who inherited what. Negotiation determined the levels of dowries for women and the marriage portions for men. Even more so, customary law dictated what was supposed to happen to a succession after death. When people attended seigneurial courts, notaries reminded them of what the customary law allowed. But there was a bewildering array of customary laws in northern Europe and, as jurists set about 'codifying' them in the sixteenth century, they became perplexed by the discrepancies they uncovered. In southern France, northeastern Spain and the hereditary domains of the Holy

Roman Emperor, Roman law determined successions. The result favoured the pater familias, who could decide how to order the succession of his property and could hand it on to whomsoever he chose, using preferential legacies and donations to favour a particular individual. Children could choose to stay at home, in which case they retained their interest in the succession. If they chose to leave, however, they had the right to a dowry, but nothing more, and they were cut out of the inheritance. In Baltic lands and the British Isles common law also favoured male primogeniture (inheritance by the eldest son). Elsewhere – in Spain, Italy, northern France and the Low Countries – the customary law was more careful to protect the rights of all the heirs in a succession. It dictated 'partible inheritance'. So, for example, in Normandy and western France, even individuals who had received property in the form of a dowry were obliged to return it to the family estate when the parents died so that it could all be collectively redistributed on an equal basis around the heirs. These patterns mattered, not least because a dowry created a 'charge' on a family – most often acquitted in this period in the form of a rent, thus expanding rural credit and debt arrangements.

Partible inheritance offended jurists because it led to property subdivision and the weakening of patriarchal authority. A chorus of legal treatises demonstrated that, whatever customary law said, the experience of the Hebrews and the accumulated wisdom of the ancients favoured male primogeniture. In a dialogue, probably written in Italy in the early 1530s, the English humanist Thomas Starkey tried to represent both sides of the argument. It was cruel 'utterly to exclude [younger sons] from all as though they had commit[ted] some great offence and crime against their parents'. It was against reason and natural equity and 'seemeth to diminish the natural love betwixt them which nature hath so bounden together'. Yet partible inheritance was a slippery slope to the dissolution of wealth: 'If the lands in every great family were distributed equally betwixt the brethren, in a small process of years the head families would decay and by little and little vanish away. And so the people should be without rulers and heads . . . you shall take away the foundation and ground of all our civility.'

So the great change in this period was the triumph of male primogeniture among Europe's élites. With it, the science of genealogy enjoyed heightened legal and social respectability, as primogeniture became retrospectively validated by antiquarian researches into noble families and state-sponsored investigations into claims of nobility. Primogeniture became widespread in England among the gentry and merchant élites. The French nobility had long been constrained to practise male primogeniture, while commoners aspiring to join its ranks attempted to bypass customary law in order to concentrate their wealth and estates in the hands of the eldest son. The Italian nobilities practised functional unigeniture – either leaving their estates to a single heir or undivided to a collectivity of brothers, only one of whom would eventually marry. Only among German princes and the landed nobility of eastern Europe and Russia did partible inheritance survive, reflected most dramatically in the bewildering chequerboard of divided domains in Germany.

To what extent did customary law make a difference when it came to family formation? Twenty per cent of all couples had no surviving children at all; a further 20 per cent would have only daughters. That constrained the degree of planning for the future. In any case, there were ways round the customary law and these were increasingly exploited in this period as families adapted the law to their own needs. The growing proportions of wealth in non-landed forms made inheritances more flexible. In two respects, laws of succession seem to have had an important impact, however, on family formation – thus affecting the way that different parts of Europe responded to demographic growth. By comparing two areas in Lower Saxony one can detect both of them. Around Calemberg, impartible inheritance was enforced by the customary seigneurial law and the state. The result was the maintenance and reinforcement of large rural holdings in the hands of wealthy farmers, often living in complex households with more than one generation under the same roof. To deal with the problem of those members of the family who cut loose, the farmers gave them dowries and marriage portions which were paid for by loans on the strength of their property. At the other end of the scale, there was a growth in the numbers of cottage labourers (called *Brinkkötter* in German lands because they lived on the brink, the common land outside the village), dependent upon others for work. By contrast, fifty miles to the south around Göttingen land tenure permitted partible inheritance. The result was a growing number of smallholders living in nuclear families, sometimes adapting the sheds and stalls attached to the family house as living accommodation. The result was property subdivision especially when sixteenth-century demographic growth turned into a question of economic survival for those who had inherited patches of land which gave them no margin to live on in hard times. Partially disinherited young people, longer periods of domestic service or increasing servitude, peasant debts, smaller property holdings, contested inheritances – these were what linked succession to the broader history of what was happening to Christendom.

THE RED HORSE, THE DARK HORSE AND THE PALE HORSE

In 1498 Albrecht Dürer produced fifteen graphic illustrations for an edition of the Book of Revelation. The apocalyptic vision of John had an undeniable fascination for Europe in the sixteenth and seventeenth centuries. Between 1498 and 1650, over 750 editions of the text or commentaries on it were published, many of them in cheap print formats. Of Dürer's illustrations, none became more celebrated than that of the Four Horsemen of the Apocalypse. Where earlier illustrators had depicted them one by one, he presented them as a posse, riding across a brooding sky, slaying everything in their path, while the monster of hell below devoured the rich and powerful. In the Book of Revelation, the second horseman rides a red horse representing war. The third horseman rides a dark horse, the herald of famine, while the fourth is mounted on a pale horse, the omen of disease and death.

The impact of war is difficult to measure but it was more prominent in the century and a half to 1650. The size of Europe's armies changed and warfare became more attritional. The Spanish siege and capture of Maastricht in 1579 resulted in a third of the city's inhabitants losing their life. The population of La Rochelle was reduced from 27,000 to a mere 5,000 as a result of the famine and disease of fourteen months of siege in 1627–8. When Magdeburg fell to imperial troops, perhaps as many as 25,000 people (85 per cent of the population) perished amid the flames of the burning city. The cumulative military casualties from the Thirty Years War may have been in excess of 400,000 although, if we take disease into account, the losses may well have been four times that number. The impact of warfare on the local population was greater. Destruction of civilian livelihood to delay an enemy advance became an accepted military practice. Mercenary contingents in the

Italian peninsula in the first half of the sixteenth century regularly included 'devastators', who not merely built fortifications but destroyed crops and uprooted vines and olive trees in order to cripple a region's agriculture for years to come. Constable Anne de Montmorency employed just these tactics in Provence to delay the imperial invasion in 1536, as did the troops which invaded the duchy of Lorraine in the early 1630s and the Swedish forces in Bavaria in 1632 (and again in 1646). Unpaid and badly provisioned soldiers were especially dangerous to civilians, as those towns in the Netherlands occupied by mutinying troops during the Dutch Revolt experienced to their cost. In the engraving *Peasant Sorrow (Boereverdriet)* the Dutch artist David Vinckboons (1576–1632) depicted peasants brutally abused by soldiers. But he followed it up with another piece, showing peasants getting their own back on them. Armies on the move were held in real hatred and fear. Peasants outside Nuremberg massacred straggling Spanish and Italian contingents in the Bavarian army in 1622; stray Swedish units were slaughtered after their defeat at Bamberg in 1631.

Fleeing to the relative protection of a fortified town meant the abandonment of farmsteads and the loss of the harvest. Such migration, however, increased the risk among ill-nourished people of spreading still further the epidemic disease of which armies were often the carriers. The documentary record is fragmentary but warfare probably reversed population growth in the Netherlands and France in the later sixteenth century. Post 1600, the civilian and military deaths, those directly and indirectly related to conflict, during the Civil Wars of the British Isles as well as the Thirty Years War in Germany, were (as a proportion of the overall population) worse than those of the First World War. In Russia, the disastrous Livonian War (1558–83) provoked internal political and financial collapse that led to the Time of Troubles (1598–1613). As tax burdens doubled, peasants fled to the black-soil forest-steppe, leaving (by some accounts) over half the farmsteads deserted. The resulting famine which gripped Muscovy between 1601 and 1603 was intensified by civil war, peasant uprisings and foreign interventions. By 1620, the depopulation in many regions exceeded the disastrous levels of the 1580s. The Russian heartland took longer to repopulate than Germany in the wake of the Thirty Years War. Among the Eurasian civilizations of this period, Europe was unique in the human cost of its conflicts.

Bubonic plague was still capable of wiping out Europe's population in pandemics, Europe's interlinked urban regions acting as its conductor. In the period from 1493 and 1649, Amsterdam witnessed twenty-four outbreaks, Leiden twenty-seven, Rotterdam twenty, Dordrecht eighteen. In fourteen English towns during a similar period (1485–1666), plague occurred one year in every sixteen and was a regular London visitor. Large conurbations were most at risk. Plague aetiology required, if rats were its carrier (as seems irrefutable), regular re-infection to take place, something that was sustained by the more marked degrees of European contact and mobility. By the first half of the seventeenth century, however, civil authorities implemented quarantines – not on the basis of agreed medical science but on pragmatic grounds that it controlled the spread of disease. Following the advice of physicians they monitored the causes of mortality, established arrangements for early warning of plague elsewhere and limited contact accordingly, building temporary immunity hospitals to control outbreaks when they occurred.

Plague was rightly feared. A high number of those infected died quickly from it. It was painful and showed no consideration for social class. The French surgeon Ambroise Paré described it as an enemy entering the 'Fortress or Castle of Life' and taking it by storm. There was no cure. The best that Paré could offer was a palliative antidote, a mixture of treacle and mithridatum (an old 'sovereign' remedy) along with a cream to 'draw' the poison out of the body. That did not stop medical practitioners from rivalling one another with explanations, the favoured being 'miasma', a corruption in the air. The best antidote was flight – which, of course, further spread the disease.

Plague was joined by other contagious infections (such as smallpox, typhus and influenza), reinforcing the perception of the increasing interdependence of one region with another. Outbreaks of typhus, for example, may have claimed a million Russian peasant lives in the period from 1580 to 1620. It was called 'typhus' by physicians from the migraine 'stupor' that often accompanied it. No one could remember it appearing much before the last campaign against the Moors in Granada in 1489–92. More commonly it was known as 'camp-fever' because of its prevalence in armies. It afflicted the military forces in the Italian Wars and decimated the armies of both Christendom and the Ottomans fighting in Hungary at the end of the sixteenth century. The troops of Count Mansfeld which fled from the battle of the White Mountain (1620) to the Lower Palatine, and then to Alsace and the Netherlands (1621), carried typhus with them; 4,000 died of the disease in Strasbourg alone as a result. French troops returning from the Mantuan campaign in 1629–30 infected over a million people in southern France.

Europe's soldiers also spread syphilis. Its first major outbreak had occurred in the French armies invading Italy in 1494, who called it the 'Neapolitan disease'. Elsewhere in Europe it became known as the 'French (or German, or Polish, or Spanish) Pox'. In 1527 a physician in Rouen, Jacques de Béthencourt, proposed an alternative to the pejorative *Morbus Gallicus*. He suggested 'Malady of Venus' (*Morbus Venereus*) and three years later, a Venetian medical practitioner in Verona, Girolamo Fracastoro, wrote a Virgilian epic about a shepherd called 'Syphilus'. With Columbus's voyage to America in mind, he described how a flotilla reached a new land to the west where the explorers offended the gods by destroying exotic fauna. The natives explained that their ancestors had once ceased to worship the gods and been punished for it with a disease. The shepherd Syphilus was the first to be afflicted. The story perpetuated the myth that syphilis had originated in America. It was a disease 'by Traffic brought' (as Nahum Tate's verse translation of Fracastoro put it), a reminder that international commerce came with a cost.

Hunger was frequent and famine not unknown. Chronic food shortage – when foodstuffs became in short supply and impossibly dear – often occurred. In England, there were significant food scarcities in 1527–8, 1550–52, 1555–9 and 1596–8 (the 'Great Hunger'). In Paris, there were periods of dearth in 1520–21, 1523, 1528–34, 1548, 1556 and 1560. The Mediterranean lands experienced widespread shortages in 1521–4; the Baltic and Poland in 1570 and 1588, and many parts of Europe in the 1590s. In Mediterranean lands after 1600, significant shortage of food occurred so regularly that it was no longer a subject of report. But did people die from famine? There is only a complicated and provisional answer to that question. Major infections did not need malnutrition in order to kill. But severe malnutrition reduced immunity and opened the door to illness. King James I's physician, Théodore Turquet de Mayerne, advised the English Privy Council that it should control food supplies, since famine was 'almost inevitable to breede the Plague'. In parts of northern England, there is evidence for the distinctive footprint of dearth-related mortality (a sudden crescendo in the late winter months) in surviving parish registers, especially in the 1590s and 1630s. That same marker has been found in parts of inland Castile, northern Italy, the Papal States and Naples in the 1590s. There are credible reports of itinerant people dying from hunger and cold in winter months following bad harvests, with particular years marked out as killers: 1635, 1649 and 1655. Such dearth-related mortality was not an age-old problem. It was a late sixteenth-century creation, a reflection of the razor-sharp impact of economic change in this period on the traditional patterns of resilience.

Food shortage was a localized problem. Grain markets, especially in the rural world, remained autonomous, prices in them moving independently of one another. In major cities, conscious of the anger that high prices generated (magistrates feared grain riots, by all accounts significant occurrences), there were determined efforts to smooth out high prices by creating municipal granaries. Cities on the Mediterranean littoral stockpiled Polish rye, supplied by Dutch merchants, who consolidated their hold on the long-distance bulk grain trade there from the 1590s. In Dutch towns public authorities almost never interfered in the grain trade, so conflicting were the interests of its traders and its magistrates. Not so elsewhere, where stricter controls upon the grain trade became a staple of mercantilist political economy. Overall, it is as though there were two different sorts of Europe emerging: one which could get by in periods of dearth, and one which could not. Both knew of the other's existence, and their fates impacted on one another.

EUROPE'S REPLENISHMENT AND GLOBAL COOLING

Was there a pattern to crop failures? Europe's weather system is complex and a minor change creates excessively cold springs and wet summers which damage crop yields. Paleoclimatologists have databases in which climate and environmental evidence at different dates from across Europe and the globe is collated. Europe already had climatologists in this period. David Fabricius kept a weather diary in Emden from 1585 to 1612, recording evidence for the large number of late frosts and cold summers in that period. The Danish astronomer Tycho Brahe left a detailed account from the island of Hven in the Danish Sound, confirming Fabricius's account. Renward Cysat, a notable from Lucerne, summarized more detailed observations in monthly reckonings while also reporting on conversations with herdsmen whom he met when botanizing in the mountains. This 'human archive', when combined with the 'natural archive' (the changing dates of the wine harvest and opening of communal pastures; dendrochronological, palynological, glaciological and ice-core evidence) has enabled a tentative reconstruction of weather patterns and an impact analysis of weather events upon grain, dairy and wine production. It indicates that European (and global) climate changed quite rapidly, and with significant results at this time. There was a period of warming from the mid-fifteenth century through to around 1560. Thereafter, there was a period of notable weather events, typified by the early onset of winter, very wet winters, cold and wet springs, low temperatures in summer and excessive rainfall during the harvest months (July and August). Its severity is noticeable from around 1560 through to the 1640s.

The worst times were when cold springs and wet harvest months occurred in two successive years. These correlated with the years of highest food-grain prices – 1569–74, 1586–9, 1593–7, 1626–9 and 1647–9. In parts of Europe, climate change may well have lowered food production significantly. The impact of the 'Little Ice Age' culminated in the 1640s; 1641 was the third-coldest summer on record in Europe's history. Scandinavia recorded its coldest winter in 1641–2. In the Alps, fields and houses disappeared as glaciers advanced; 1647–9 also witnessed serious climatic anomalies. On the other side of the world, prolonged cold and drought contributed to the demographic crisis of the mid-century and the rebellions that led to the fall of the Ming dynasty.

Explanations centre on very low solar activity (the lowest recorded level in two millennia) and major volcanic eruptions (twelve around the Pacific between 1638 and 1644, the highest number ever registered). Telescopes enabled observers to enumerate sunspots with unprecedented precision. A good number appeared between 1612 and 1614, but almost none in 1617 and 1618, and very few in 1625–6, and then again in 1637–9. Between 1642 and 1644, the astronomer Johannes Hevelius made daily drawings of the sun, recording the location of all spots. They were rare and, after 1645, they almost disappeared until the eighteenth century. The aurora borealis also vanished from the northern hemisphere's skies. Equally, the known volcanic eruptions produced dust clouds which also served to cool the atmosphere and create unstable weather conditions around the world, including Europe. A Seville shopkeeper noted that, during the first half of 1649, 'the sun did not shine once . . . and if it came out, it was pale and yellow, or else much too red, which caused greater fear'.

There were some summers that never came, and some exceptional weather events (hailstorms, summer snowfalls, long rainy spells) which contemporaries interpreted as the hand of God and possibly the work of witches. The Spanish agronomist Lope de Dexa advocated a government ministry of astrologers to predict bad weather. The changes were small by modern climate change standards – a fluctuation of not more than 2 per cent over annual mean temperatures and 10 per cent in overall rainfall. But they may have been a significant element in destabilizing farming routines, causing dearth and contributing to a sense of crisis. By 1650, Europe was more dependent on the bulk transportation of grain-stuffs than ever before to feed its urban populations. Europe's communication systems informed the latter more about their vulnerability and amplified their anxiety.

It would be easier to explain the impact of food shortages if more was known about what people ate. In reality, the diet of all but the rich is largely a matter of inference from the records of what was purchased to feed those in institutional care – the sick in hospital or students, lodging in colleges. What mattered most was the grain to make bread. It was a staple to a monotonous degree, accompanying every meal as loaves, piecrusts, and starch in soups and gravies. It gave people the strength to work and it was the most calorific and least expensive foodstuff. Cereals produced six times more edible calories than milk, as well as more protein per hectare than grazing livestock. Christendom was defined by its dependence on wheat, and dry cultivation, less productive than the irrigation agricultures on which over 60 per cent of the world's population relied by 1600.

For those on day-wages, bread cost them half what they earned. Wheat was the most prized for making bread and pasta. But it was expensive because it was a 'winter corn' (sown in the autumn and reaped the following summer) which drained good soils of their nutrients, and needed a fallow one year in three or four, or some form of marling or liming to enable poorer soils to yield a crop. For the mass of the population, wheat was grown for sale or mixed with rye to provide bread flour. Rye was more widespread than wheat, and the two were sometimes sown together since the rye might survive a cold, wet spring when the wheat did not. Harvested together, they provided a bread flour known as 'maslin' which was mostly rye with a little wheat added. Spelt, barley and oats were 'summer corn', sown in the spring and harvested that same year. Spelt was widely grown in Switzerland, the Tyrol and Germany where it tolerated short summers. Barley was 'drinking corn', widely used in northern Europe for making ale and beer, while oats served as provender for horses except in places such as Scotland and Scandinavia where it was also the human staple.

The Columbian Exchange introduced more calorific staples into the European diet, bolstering Europe's demographic resilience. In the region around Valencia in southern Spain, rice became important (imported from North Africa), and this 'marsh corn' was increasingly part of the diet in parts of northern Italy and southern France. Maize ('Indian corn') was introduced from the Americas into the Spanish peninsula in the 1490s and increasingly grown in Mediterranean Europe. Fed to cattle initially, it could be turned into corn-bread, while in Italy it was refined into a ground meal (polenta). In the Cévennes, ground chestnuts furnished the 'nut-bread' of the poor. But the attitude to food remained conservative. Henry Best, a farmer from Elmswell in Yorkshire, recorded who ate what in his household during the year 1641: wheat for the family, maslin for the servants, and brown bread from rye, peas and barley for the workers on the farm.

Grain mattered because it could be stored for comparatively long periods of time. Most other foodstuffs were perishable. Despite the emphasis on food which could be stored, more vegetables appeared on people's tables. Parsnips, carrots, cabbages and turnips either made their appearance for the first time, or did so in significant quantities in this period. Many of these were the result of cultural exchange with the Near East, a more significant influence on Europe's diet than the New World. Pumpkins, melons, cucumbers and courgettes were also cultivated in Europe's kitchen gardens for the first time. Lettuces and artichokes, grown for the tables of the rich in Rome, conquered France and spread to irrigated gardens around Valencia in Spain. Calabria and Catalonia served as greenhouses for new varieties of almond, fig, pear and damson trees. Dried pulses were a convenient way of overcoming seasonality, though they attracted hostility: 'more meet for hogs and savage beasts to feed upon than mankind' reported William Harrison in 1587. In southern Europe, however, haricots, an import from Peru, alleviated food shortages. Annibale Carracci's painting of *The Bean Eater* (*Il Mangiafagioli*), *c.* 1580, depicts a rural labourer tucking into his bowl of haricots accompanied by onions, a bread roll, vegetables and a glass of wine. Fermenting, for instance cabbage, in salt water was another method of preserving vegetables, much developed in Germany and eastern Europe. When stored in butter-barrels or stone-crocks, sealed with wet muslin and a weighted wooden top, they offered an additional staple through the winter months. Butter, cheese and olive oil could easily be stored.

Meat and fish, however, remained more local and seasonal. Freshly slaughtered meat was mostly to be found on Europe's tables in spring and autumn, although a proportion was also preserved by pickling in brine, or salting, smoking, spicing and drying it. The resulting raw or cooked sausages had a rich variety of shapes, colours, flavours and names. For François Rabelais, they were the height of cuisine and a subject of ribald fun. Fish became second only to grain as a commercialized foodstuff. Fishing was a great source of employment and an even more important 'ghost acreage' of food reserve. White cod (from the Atlantic) was salted. Red cod (from the Mediterranean and Atlantic) was smoked. Herring was fished from the northern Atlantic. Eels, caught around the sluices of the newly drained marshland in the Netherlands, were sold in bulk in the fish markets of Amsterdam and London. If, as seems possible, global cooling brought the migratory shoals of herring southward, it made their commercial fishing that much easier. Europe's northwest Atlantic marine calorific reservoir was more important than its American 'ghost acreage' in the years up to 1650 in making up the dietary shortfalls that resulted from population growth and climatic uncertainty.

There are no entirely convincing and comprehensive explanations for the patterns of human mortality in this period. The devastating impact of demographic crises is evident. But no one can be sure about the relationship between epidemic disease and under-nourishment even though there clearly was one. That is because there is insufficient evidence about people's diets and about the changing relationship of man to microbe, flea and rat. There is no explanation for why some communities escaped major demographic crises from one generation to another, whereas others did not. Much must have depended on the most vulnerable members of communities, those least able to feed and fend for themselves, or those who were the most mobile and the most likely to carry infectious disease from one locality to another. The aetiology of epidemic disease remains uncertain, and the impact of harvest failure was localized. Europe's demographic growth was vulnerable to the inveterate forces of nature, but also to those of human conflict. In southern and central Europe, the gains of the sixteenth century were mostly wiped out in the first half of the seventeenth. The resilience in other regions, especially the economically advanced northwestern Europe, accentuated the regional divergences which pulled Christendom in different directions.

3. Urban and Rural Worlds

More people lived in cities in 1650 than was the case in 1500. This period saw the emergence of a more populous North Italian–Rhineland corridor, an axis of economic strength. The prosperity of that region was as much based on transformations in its rural hinterland as in its urban centres. Globally, such a development was not unique. In China, regions of advanced economic development and urbanization existed before they emerged in Europe. By 1650, the dynamism of Europe's urbanized corridor became more focused in northwestern Europe, in the lower Rhineland and across the North Sea in eastern England. By some estimates, the proportion of Europe's population living in towns had surpassed that of China by 1650. The consolidation of this more densely populated and urbanized economic region and other economic changes weakened the social cohesion which underpinned Christendom. This social cohesion is the subject of this chapter.

URBAN SPACES

Towns made an impact on contemporaries in various ways: as military strongholds, places where justice was administered, centres of commerce, locations for élites and points for cultural exchange. They were competitive nodes of concentrated presence that made their mark on the world around them. Their impact was ambiguous and paradoxical. On the one hand, they had an energizing effect upon their environment. On the other, they grew at others' expense. They increased inequality and risk.

That Europe's urban space was seen in a new light is evident from the emerging genre of 'chorography' or imagined representations of the city. Oblique views conveying an urban 'presence' to the contemporary eye were initially preferable to city plans. Sebastian Münster's *Cosmography* (1544) and Guillaume Guéroult's *Epitome of Europe's Chorography* (1552–3) contain townscapes depicting public buildings, fortifications and ecclesiastical foundations. The viewer could visualize their surroundings. It was like taking a visitor up the tallest building in a city and looking *Chorography* over it – which is what the Florentine humanist Anton Francesco Doni recommended as the best way of introducing people to his own town. Cityscapes were part of the art of travel to which humanists initiated their readers.

In 1567, Lodovico Guicciardini published his influential *Description of All the Low Countries* – the inhabitant of one highly urbanized environment commenting on another. His work was a masterpiece of sixteenth-century urban geography, illustrated by chorographic engravings. Five years later the first volume of *The Cities of the World* (*Civitates Orbis Terrarum*) appeared, envisaged as an accompanying volume to the world atlas of Ortelius. The initial volume of 132 town engravings was followed by five further volumes, published mainly in Cologne, so that by 1619 the eventual collection totalled some 546 magnificent bird's eye views and accompanying text. Many of them were drawn by the project's creator, the engraver Frans Hogenberg. It became a status symbol for a city to have its plan in the collection. The views were enlivened with human figures and heraldic crests around the margins. These served a double purpose: besides illustrating customs, these figures were believed in Europe to dissuade the Turks from using the engravings, on the grounds that their religion forbade them from studying portrayals of human beings.

The growth in urban space was not, however, uniform. In the Italian peninsula, Milan was a big city of 91,000 inhabitants in 1500, but it shrank by a third after a terrible demographic crisis in 1542, recovering slowly to its former size only by the end of the century. Florence did not match until 1650 the population of 70,000 inhabitants that it enjoyed in 1520. Bologna (55,000 inhabitants in 1493, 36,000 in 1597), Brescia (48,500 inhabitants in 1493, under 37,000 in 1597) and Cremona (40,000 in 1502 and again in 1600) found it hard to compete with smaller neighbours (Padua, Verona, Vicenza) who expanded faster. By contrast, Venice grew by 50 per cent (105,000 in 1509, 168,000 in 1563, 150,000 in 1600). Naples almost doubled in size to rival Paris as Europe's largest city (150,000 in 1500, 275,000 in 1599). Sicily's towns (Palermo and Messina) grew at an extraordinary rate. Rome was a modest regional capital of 55,000 inhabitants on the eve of its sack by imperial forces in 1527 but by 1607 it had a population of 109,000.

North of the Alps, the picture was similarly varied. Paris was Christendom's great metropolis, the only place with over 200,000 inhabitants in 1500. It continued to expand, perhaps reaching 300,000 by 1560. Thereafter, the impact of the French civil wars undermined the fortunes of the great city, its growth resuming only after 1600. London, by contrast, grew no matter what demographic misfortune (the Great Plague of 1665 lies ahead) befell it, a key element in England's political economy. Lyon may have doubled its population in the years from 1500 to 1560 (40,000 to 80,000), but it struggled to maintain that size thereafter. That was the pattern for other French cities (such as Rouen and Toulouse), although Marseille managed to triple its inhabitants between 1520 and 1600 (15,000 to 45,000). In the Low Countries, the great conurbations (Bruges, Ghent and Brussels) struggled to grow against smaller locations (Liège, Namur and Amsterdam). Antwerp, by contrast, tripled in size between 1490 and 1568, by which date it had over 100,000 inhabitants. But the conflicts of the Dutch Revolt – it was ransacked by mutinying troops (1576, 1583) and besieged (1584) – halved its population, and it only slowly recovered.

Some larger cities in central Europe (Cologne, Lübeck) barely held their own while others (Gdańsk, Hamburg) grew. Nuremberg became the largest city in Christendom east of the Rhine. In the Spanish peninsula, Lisbon and Seville more than doubled their populations. Other Spanish cities saw significant growth (Valencia, Toledo, Granada). Madrid expanded from being a small town of 5,000 inhabitants in 1500 to over 35,000 by 1600. The population of cities with at least 10,000 inhabitants has become a classic way of representing how the overall balance of urban Europe tilted from the Mediterranean to the northwest.

Yet a traveller was five times as likely to spend the night in a small town (under 10,000) than in a metropolis. England had over 700 small towns, France over 2,000, the Holy Roman Empire over 3,000 and Poland over 800. The densities varied widely too. In southern and western Germany the average was one every 2.5 square miles. To the cosmographer Sebastian Münster, the towns in the Vosges foothills were so close 'that you could fire a harquebus from one to the next'. Functional diversity and urban aspirations defined small towns better than population density. In those of Sweden and Finland, there was generally a shoemaker, tailor, blacksmith and carpenter. Urban pretension was reflected in infrastructure – walls, gates, a town hall, fountains and marketplace.

New towns flourished as nobles maximized the value of their estates and princes fostered urban investment; 270 new baronial burghs (incorporated towns) were founded in Scotland after 1500. In Lithuania, almost 400 seigneurial or 'private' towns were created in the late sixteenth century to capitalize on the growth of commercialized agriculture around the Baltic. The Vasa dynasty in Sweden granted thirty new charters for towns in the century after 1580 as part of its colonization of space. Meanwhile, the newly chartered towns in Ireland – Philipstown (Daingean) and Maryborough (Portlaoise) for example – became flagships for English plantation under the Tudor and Stuart monarchies. In Spain, there was a new incorporated town almost every year as local communities purchased a privilege that a cash-strapped monarchy was only too willing to sell.

Small towns depended for their viability on the economic landscape around them, and they did not all survive. Ambleside and Shap in the English Lake District, for example, could not sustain their town markets and sunk back to being villages. About three quarters of the new burghs in Scotland and new chartered towns in Norway ended up as 'shadow towns', villages in all but name. Hondschoote, a small commune to the east of Dunkirk, blossomed suddenly into a town with more than 15,000 inhabitants, thanks to the manufacture of lighter cloth made of wool mixed with linen. With the conflict in Flanders during the second half of the sixteenth century, however, its prosperity vanished. Oudenaarde, to the south of Ghent, doubled its population in the first half of the sixteenth century. By 1600, however, it had shrunk to under half its earlier size as the population emigrated en masse during the troubles. Urbanization was not a measure of ever-continuing European growth.

The economic relations between town and country acted as widening circles of influence around an urban nexus. Most intense was the space dominated by the weekly market, no more than a day's journey away, where perishable products were sold in quantities; 75–90 per cent of local production was generally confined within this space. The monthly or quarterly fair represented a more extensive circle of influence. That was where grain and livestock were taken to market, often from places two or three days' journey away. As with the inner zone, the scale depended upon the size of the city in question. The catchment area that supplied grain to Nuremberg was around 1,930 square miles, and its town council had its factors operating over a radius of 62 miles. That space corresponded to a definable economic region or 'country' and it was no coincidence that it also often mapped onto local judicial and administrative space. In economic terms, this region counted for the majority of the remaining 10–25 per cent of local production, the proportion being dictated by the marginal costs of bringing bulk goods to market. To carry the grain to the market of Valladolid in 1559 added 2 per cent to the price for every league (the distance traversed by a cart in an hour – less than four miles) that the sack travelled. That left the most extensive third sphere, represented by the annual market, in which wool, cloth and yarn were traded, often at distances exceeding 25 miles. These circles of influence were particularly significant in the case of large cities, which tended to asphyxiate the smaller communities around them. Rural protest might find an echo inside capital cities, but their patrician oligarchs deployed their authority to close off and patrol their walls and gates. The mutual suspicions between citizens and peasants were too great for them to make common cause for long.

MIGRATION AND MOBILITY

Population was mobile, especially in these zones of higher urban pressure. Hospital registers, apprenticeship indentures, ecclesiastical court books, probate inventories, army muster-rolls, student matriculations, registers of new townsmen and lists of 'strangers' reveal complex migration patterns. They were not new but their significance was greater. Demographic mobility explains how overseas empires were peopled. A quarter of a million migrants left Castile for the New World in the sixteenth century, the majority of the early settlers being young men.

Unlike those travelling to the New World, most migrants moved quite short distances, often proceeding as if by a ladder, step-by-step, from the countryside to the neighbouring small town, and then onwards to a larger metropolis. Their movements can occasionally be reconstructed. So, for example, the lives of 155 living-in servants in the parish of Romford, 14 miles east of London in the second half of 1562: most of them were from local families, but a proportion had come from much further afield. One rural farmhand came down from Cumbria at the age of twenty (he became a yeoman in nearby Hornchurch), while another female domestic had arrived aged fourteen from Kent (she later married a Romford tailor). Among the deponents before the Church court at Canterbury, less than 10 per cent declared themselves to be born and bred there. Just over 40 per cent were born elsewhere in Kent while a further 28.5 per cent were from outside the county. Outside urbanized zones such high levels of mobility become rarer. In the market town of Vézelise in Lorraine, half the spouses in a sample taken between 1578 and 1633 came from places that were over 6 miles distant from the town, and one in six of the brides would marry someone who had been born over 15 miles away.

Immigration into towns is easier to document than the countervailing streams of emigration. Yet wherever land was reclaimed there was population movement, drawing from towns and villages. It can be traced in the non-native nomenclatures in Finland and around the Baltic or in eastern Europe. The expansion of the coastal fishing industry of Norway would not have taken place without Scottish and Danish immigrants. Even in the wood-pasture regions in England, in the Forest of Arden or in the Shropshire village of Myddle (where a local antiquary from the seventeenth century recorded its population in detail) new people arrived, built a cottage, and made themselves a living. At the same time, there were temporary circular and seasonal migrations, essential to Europe's economic fortunes. Each spring saw the arrival of cohorts of part-time labour from inland villages to the Atlantic ports to sail the boats fishing for cod. Almost 60 per cent of the crew on board vessels sailing out of Amsterdam in the seventeenth century originated from outside the Dutch Republic. Harvesting the grain on the plains would have been impossible without migrant labour. Mountain regions served as reservoirs of labour and skill, drawn to the plains to build the walls, clean the ditches, accompany the mule-trains, and serve in the armies. In some Swiss mountain villages there were almost no menfolk about in the summer months.

Migration was a determining element in urban demography, making up the demographic deficit created by high levels of urban mortality. That was a particularly European phenomenon – in the urban environments in China and Japan, mortality rates were not significantly different from those in the surrounding countryside, partly as a result of the greater attention to urban water supplies, sanitation and food contamination. In Europe, by contrast, inward migration replenished population loss from mortality crises. Even in 'normal' years, migrants were probably needed to make up a deficit in births among indigenous city populations. Urban notables rightly regarded their environment as dangerous, nauseous, even noxious – a corporate dung-heap. City legislation is full of references to insalubrity, especially (to quote from London's) the 'stinking ordure', 'putrid smells', 'stinking filth' and 'odious and infectious stench'. Medical opinion thought that a good smell could drive away a bad one and offered civet, musk and ambergris as antidotes to contagion.

Humanist-inspired magistrates proposed projects for the common good – public fountains of clean water from outside the city, dedicated sewers and publicly funded scavengers. The Paris city provost organized scavengers to sweep the streets and carry the night soil out beyond the city walls to Montfaucon. In Rome, Pope Clement VII appointed an Office of Rubbish but inhabitants refused to pay for it. The same impediment thwarted many efforts to bring fresh water into the cities. It was expensive to the civic purse; everyone recognized the necessity but no one wanted to foot the bill.

PLOUGH AND SPADE

Producing food from the land was hard work. It occupied the overwhelming majority of the population. Agricultural technologies were rudimentary, yields were low, and everything depended on the weather. Exploiting the land meant making a living without increasing the already high risks that it entailed. That resulted in an inveterate caution towards change as well as an ecological concern for what was sustainable in the longer term. Such caution was systemic – hard-wired into the fabric of the rural world through its communal agricultural practices and legal frameworks.

Looking down on the landscape of Europe from a satellite, one would see the great European plain, the champagne lands that stretch through Poland, northern Germany, southern Denmark and Sweden, across into northern France and into the English Midlands. The dominant image would be that of open country, broken up into large fields in which each farming community had plots. The principal colours in summer would have been yellow and brown, for over 90 per cent of the cultivatable surface was devoted to cereal production. The cultivation of grain took place in a system of crop rotation that avoided depleting the mineral content of the soil. In much of northern Europe this was based on three large fields (or multiples thereof). A peasant could reckon to spend at least twenty-five days a year preparing each furlong for the crops and a further three to five days on harvesting the same area.

Agrarian practices were maintained by village custom. There was plenty to discuss each year, from the dates for planting and harvesting to the maintenance of ploughs, the size of plots, the rights of gleaning or the numbers of animals that each community could pasture ('fold') on the fallow. Decisions were not lightly taken for they could lead to tensions – and rural economic life was as much directed towards mediating disputes as it was to managing ecological hazard. Getting along with people was vital since it determined the outcome of back-breaking work. Our knowledge about overall grain yields is partial, estimated and derived. Fallowing would take between a third and a half of the arable land out of cultivation each year. Harvesting was inefficient. Further losses occurred in threshing and storage. Once a farmer had put aside the seed corn for the following year he was lucky to net a wheat-yield of more than 4:1. That was what the producers on the lands of the cathedral chapter of Cracow at Rzgów-Gospodarz managed in 1553. They bettered that only twice in eight years of accounts through to 1573. Further west, the producers at Wolfenbüttel would do better (6.5:1 in 1540). The basic picture, however, changed, if at all, only slowly.

With a wider-angle lens, the imagined satellite picture would record greater variety. Within the champagne country there were areas that saw more stock rearing or dairying. In the Netherlands, on the Frisian marshes, or in Mecklenburg between the Elbe and the Oder, the impact of animal husbandry on the cereal yields was significant through animals dunging the land and turning topsoil humus during pasturage.

Cattle were pastured with temporary fencing so there was no need for an enclosure of the fields. By bridging the crucial manure-gap, these lands delivered handsome yields: 10:1 was the average at Hitzum in Friesland in the years 1570–73. There, the farmer could even afford to abandon the fallow and crop rotation and simply grow a field of rye everywhere each year. Meanwhile, in parts of England and western France, rationalization of land exploitation with the grouping of fields into enclosures around the farmstead had begun. The construction of ditched hedges – the equivalent of barbed wire in our security-obsessed age – cut poorer people off from customary resources upon which they often depended: rights to commons, to gleaning on harvested fields and to woodland. The change should not be overestimated. Between 1455 and 1637, only 750,000 acres of England were enclosed and not more than 35,000 labourers uprooted from the soil. Sensitive to the social unrest it might cause, the English Parliament conducted commissions of inquiry and passed acts to limit its impact in 1517, 1548, 1566 and 1607.

The fear of social unrest may, in part, explain why agrarian change did not happen more widely. Far more important, however, was the reality that agricultural exploitation was based on trade-offs. Farmers understood the importance of recycling nutrients back to the soil. They had an instinctive appreciation of the importance of preventing the build-up of acid in the soil from too much arable husbandry. But spreading marl (clay, lime-rich soil) to counteract it was possible only in places where transport was readily available. Extend the arable too much, cut down the fallow, and you risked compromising the biomass feedback to the soil. Extend the arable areas into woodland and onto less good soils, and the long-term yields might not make it worthwhile. Increase the number of animals that you were grazing and there might not be enough hay to over-winter them. Too much livestock would compromise the spring growth in the meadows and hay for the next winter season. Europe's farmers were not lazy, ignorant or stupid. On the contrary, they made sensible decisions within tight constraints.

Besides, changes were taking place quietly in other ways. Rienck Hettes van Hemmema, a farmer at Hitsum in Friesland, experimented with planting peas and beans on the fallow – reducing the amount of land without crops on his estate to just 12 per cent. In Leicestershire, a survey of fourteen farms in 1558 suggests that winter wheat was being reduced, spring wheat increased and peas and beans were being planted most years on the fallow. A farming contract for land at Montrouge near Paris in 1548 stipulates that the farmer plough the land straight after harvest and plant root-crops. Like other farmers in the Paris region, he was taking advantage of proximity to the capital, fattening livestock on their way to the capital's markets and stabling horses. Such changes happened around other cities too. But agricultural innovation was slow, dispersed, and occurred only as and where local ecological and market conditions were right.

Outside Europe's champagne lands, three-field rotation had never been the norm. Instead, there were combinations of two-field and three-field rotations, some of which were in response to more intensive cereal cultivation or the planting of industrial crops (hemp, madder, etc.). On the heathlands of the Landes in Gascony or the high Meseta Central (Central Plain) in Spain, farmers had to make do with two fallows for every one year of cultivation. East of the Elbe lay pastureland in eastern Poland, Moldavia and the Hungarian plain where extensive livestock husbandry developed. South of the champagne country lay the valleys with the greatest agricultural diversity in middle Europe. In the soft climates of the valley floors, the conditions were ideal for growing grain. On the tops, the conditions were good for pasturing sheep. In between, on the sheltered southerly and easterly slopes, there were vines. On other slopes, woodland provided yet another agrarian system to exploit and one that was (like wood, vines, walnuts, olives and chestnuts) open to commercial exploitation. Common lands (pasture, woodland, uncultivated areas) were a managed and exploitable resource, complementing other, more intensively cultivated terrains.

Such diverse agricultural systems would show up in a satellite picture by the division of open fields into smaller, irregular, sometimes enclosed plots. In northern England, Wales, western and southern France, parts of Lower Saxony, Westphalia and much of southwestern Germany, the landscape was dominated by hedges or stone walls. Around the Mediterranean, there was further variety. On the Tierra de Campos in northern Castile and in parts of inland Sicily, grain predominated. But elsewhere cereals counted for less. There was irrigated rice cultivation, mixed grain and commercial arboriculture (chestnuts, olives, mulberry for silk production, walnuts) as well as the ubiquitous vineyards. Sarrasin (or buckwheat), the 'black grain' which is not a grain at all but a plant of the sorrel family, began its conquest of the poorer soils of

Brittany at the beginning of the sixteenth century, introduced there from North Africa. The Office of St George, the bank-like institution that ran Corsica for the Genoese republic, required local communities to plant chestnuts to provide a cash crop and flour for the poor. Stone walls and terraces spread up the hillsides as the quest to bring new land into cultivation stretched agrarian systems to their limits.

Land was everywhere being pressed into cultivatable use. In northern Norway, rye was sown for the first time in over 200 years. In Baltic Russia and Poland, monastic and noble estates increased the size of their demesne farms. The enterprising magnate Antoine Perrenot de Granvelle, one of the great statesmen of the century, used the profits of office to establish new villages in the Ardennes Forest and the Jura. Forest-keepers reported fighting illegal encroachment. The land surveys of Lower Languedoc reveal a picture of every scrap of land being put to use. This responsiveness to change was most evident, however, in the regions of agricultural diversity that were proximate to urbanized space. It was not always towns imposing their demands upon their hinterlands so much as a series of complementary forces creating economic regions in which agricultural product became more commercialized. The market impact upon the production (and price) of grain supplies was considerable. By 1600, Rome consumed 60,000 cartloads of grain a year.

The impact of this demand can be measured in terms of reclaimed land, improved waterways and irrigation networks, which is where urban capital investment in the countryside was most substantial. In Lombardy, irrigation work in the sixteenth century completed what had been begun a century previously. From Milan to the Ticino river ran the 'Naviglio Grande' (31 miles long), a triumph of hydraulic technology. One of its engineers was Leonardo da Vinci, and the drawings of the Codex Atlanticus include his design for a mitred lock-gate to be installed at the San Marco lock in Milan. Compared to the portcullis lock-gates, mitre-gated locks could open wider and more efficiently. By 1530, a network of ancillary canals and waterways covered the Lombardy plain from Milan to Pavia, a land of plenty, at least if you were a rich Milanese notable.

Bologna used hydraulic technology imaginatively. Two new canals provided the mechanical power for flour mills, fulling works and hydraulic saws, fed by underground conduits. The irrigated gardens around Valencia and the sluices of the Vinalopó river increased rice cultivation there. In Provence, the French engineer Adam de Craponne headed up a consortium (including the astrologer Nostradamus) to channel the Durance river to irrigate 50,000 acres of the Plain of Crau. Smaller-scale ventures led to the floating of water-meadows to increase spring forage. Not all these efforts, of course, were successful. Venice gave up its attempts to drain the lower valleys of the Po and the Adige. Ferdinand, grand duke of Tuscany, had only modest success with his great scheme to drain the lakes of the Val di Chiana. Pope Pius IV had high hopes of draining the Pontine Marshes and chose Ferdinand's engineer (Rafael Bombelli) for the purpose. Although the scheme was initially unsuccessful, Pope Sixtus V reactivated it, but died of malaria after visiting the worksite.

North of the Alps, reclamation was most extensive in the marshland deltas of the Netherlands, the most dramatic human change to Europe's coastline before 1650. In reality, coastal reclamation was a global phenomenon, probably linked to climate change. In Southeast Asia, the deltas of Burma, Siam, southern China, Cambodia and Vietnam were also transformed into populated regions where new strains of rice were cultivated, supported by inter-regional trade. In the Netherlands, hydraulic technologies permitted over 1,400 hectares of additional land to be recovered each year for agricultural use by drainage in the 1540s–60s. The investment stopped with the onset of the religious and political troubles in the 1560s but then resumed in the 1590s.

The story is heading in a well-known direction: the triumph of capital-intensive agriculture, the large independent farm, owned and run by market-sensitive agriculturalists, high per-acre yield 'convertible' husbandry, enclosure and the high road to the 'agricultural revolution'. Behind it lies the shadow of an even bigger story: that Europe's northwestern Atlantic seaboard was predestined to be its locomotive to modernity. It is hard not to read the script backwards. Yet the history of Europe's economy in this period is a reminder of the misconceptions that result when the past is telescoped by seeking the earliest genesis of future 'success'. Succeeding in the rural world was a difficult business in this period. It involved sharing and minimizing risks, feeding families and relatives year on year, and retaining the longer-term sustainability of the soil, especially when cultivating land which was only marginally capable of bearing arable crops. Is not the evidence of the terraces of cultivatable acreage creeping up the slopes of Lower Languedoc towards the stony upland plateau in fact a sign of a Malthusian crisis in the making?

There is evidence to support that view. Rural smallholdings were becoming smaller as a result of partible inheritance, increasing the temptations upon them to increase risk and place unsustainable burdens on the productivity of the soil. In the Tyneside community of Wickham, for example, the exploitation of coal attracted a small army of workers, some living in hovels around the workings, others in small cottages. Their lifestyle increased their risk and dependency on the market for food. In 1596–7, they starved for lack of it. In some of the uplands in northern England, it was perhaps the choice to concentrate on pastoral husbandry and maximize the profits it seemed to afford, partially abandoning arable cultivation in the process, which explains why dearth-related mortality occurred there in exceptional years. In the unforgiving uplands of Castile, contemporaries noted that the land was becoming exhausted and that the fields were not as productive as they had once been, an impression partially confirmed by tithe and estate records. Such declining yields were partly the result of a stand-off between sheep and arable farmers who (in reality) needed one another. It is possible, too, that the bad weather and crippling effects of epidemic disease in the 1590s meant that peasants were tempted by very high grain prices not to farm responsibly. By the 1620s, it was acknowledged that farming on the high plateau in Spain had become unprofitable for many because of high overheads and low returns. But some communities continued to flourish, so the picture is mixed. Spain would sustain a larger population in the eighteenth century with little by way of agricultural change. If Malthusian crises existed in this period they were limited to specific periods and places.

The impact of urban growth was felt in the countryside. Increases in agricultural production were not achieved by and large through capital-intensive agronomy or spectacular increases in yield per acre. They happened through local change, principally in the cultivated arable area, driven by indigenous population growth and the market prices in foodstuffs. How much of it was through the latter is impossible to say. The rural exposure to the market was always variable – sensitive to price, risk and reward, and often mediated through others. Those who had a plough had the chance to be among the winners; those with a spade would be among the losers. The majority of Europe's rural population did not have a plough; they had sickles, scythes and spades. These latter were the vulnerable ones. How they fared would depend in part upon other aspects of the rural and urban economy – its systems of exploitation, and its pastoral and manufacturing sectors.

LAND AND EXPLOITATION

Even for institutions like towns, hospitals or monasteries, the outright possession of land was unusual. In 1515, an Italian Dominican theologian Silvestro Mazzolini da Prierio (Sylvester Prierias), encapsulated a long-running debate over the relationship between *ius* ('right') and *dominium* ('property'). He wrote that people wrongly thought that these two were one and the same thing, and that anyone who had the *ius* should have the *dominium* which accompanied it, and vice versa. Ideally, he admitted, that was how it should be, but the world was not so simple. It was possible for someone to have a *ius* who did not have a *dominium*. He cited the example of a father and under-age son. The father had the *dominium* over the son but the son had the *ius*, the right to be fed in his father's household. The legal distinction between having the ownership of a property (*dominium directum*, as Roman lawyers termed it) and use-rights to it (*dominium utile*) was universally understood because it was based in the real world.

What mattered to most people were the uses to which the exploitable resources of the land were put. More often than not, these were not vested in the direct ownership of the soil. The rights to fish in a river, to walk over a land, to cut wood from a forest – these were all subject to different property rights, separable from the direct ownership of the soil itself, and among the most frequent and legally contentious issues before law courts. Many use-rights were still vested in communities where a premium was placed on the regulation of access to economic assets. Common land still existed in much of Europe and local communities had to decide on its management, decisions taken in order to mitigate risk to the farming community, to minimize organizational complexity and strife among participants, and to reflect the organization of the society of which they were part.

In many regions of Europe, rural society was still predominantly dominated by manorial estates. Even where they had leased out most of the land to peasants (i.e. smallholding agriculturalists), seigneurs often maintained a role in determining disputed use-rights through the operation of manorial courts. But overlords took an increasingly hard-nosed attitude towards the fees and duties that peasants were obliged to render. These included enfeoffment fees, payable on the death of a peasant or a lord, and comprising 5–15 per cent of the value of a peasant holding (though in some Swabian territories it became a punitive 50 per cent). In some parts of southwest Germany, landlords shortened leases in order to increase the revenues from transfer fees, payable when a new lease was signed. Such burdens multiplied when a peasant was subject to a variety of overlords for different parts of land or to multiple lords for the same piece of land. Landlords also took the offensive in restricting use-rights to woods, streams, lakes and common grazing lands as part of a pattern of agricultural intensification.

For their part, groups of smallholders were shrewd and organized enough to mobilize their village institutions. Village assemblies had representative, organizational and sometimes even a limited jurisdictional role. In much of western Europe, leading farmers became their mainstay, though in Germany and perhaps elsewhere, the headman was at the approval of, or even appointed by, a local lord. Even so, such assemblies took advantage of the law to seek protection against perceived infringements to their local use-rights. Although overlords sought to limit the power of these institutions they often came up against local smallholders whose wealth and influence were cemented in the course of this period by the role that they played as receivers of tax and as local officials, as well as by the growing disparities of wealth between themselves and other smallholders. This rural notability, sometimes assisted by the villages' priests and notaries, was in a position (if so minded) to mobilize local resistance and determine how it should be deployed. The politics of the rural world revolved around these people and their perception of the law and their responsibilities. Their role was crucial in negotiations with authorities (landlords, ecclesiastical and civil authorities) and, if those negotiations failed, in organizing passive resistance or open revolt. Rural rebellion was most likely to occur in this period where there was a conjunction of smallholders or other economically independent producers, strong traditions of communal organization and representation, and new exactions from landlords, Church and state.

Peasants were vulnerable to the impact of monetary inflation. They were excessively dependent on offering a limited range of products into a market where they often had to pay to participate, and where it was difficult for them to know whether, in cash terms, they would end up with a good deal. The products that were theirs to sell were also those upon which their households depended for food through the year and capacity to sow for the next. A large-scale survey of individual household grain reserves from the duchy of Württemberg in 1622 reveals the dynamics in a period when the Thirty Years War created anxieties about food supplies. Except for a minority of larger farmers, smallholders held on tightly to their harvest of spelt, trading it among themselves in kind. By contrast, they went to market with their oats, a cheaper product, heavily in demand for feeding horses, other animals and the poor, where prices looked too good to miss and the deal did not compromise their own security. The interaction of peasant smallholders and market was like that, varying from year to year and product to product. Peasants needed strong incentives to bring their products to market in order not to feel compromised in their wellbeing.

Rural debt was ubiquitous, even when money was hard to find. Lines of credit were furnished by prosperous townspeople, ecclesiastical institutions and Jews, groups who in turn became targets for peasant unrest. Debts were registered by notaries who often, with merchants and larger landholders, were the principal creditors – thus creating another interaction between town and country. Unpaid debts destabilized peasant security, leading to downsizing a holding, or moving to the increasingly widespread practice of share-cropping, whereby landlord and tenants shared the costs and rewards of agricultural exploitation.

For the unlucky, insolvency meant selling up completely. In almost every region of France, merchants, lawyers and nobles were buying up land from debt-ridden peasants – land transfer on a massive scale. Recorded in hundreds of thousands of notarial transactions, it was obvious enough to be noted by contemporaries. The chronicler of the town of Lyon, Guillaume Paradin, for example, described in 1573 how the city's wealthy merchants bought land from peasants at bargain prices. Where the land transfer was not to merchants, royal officers and nobles, it went to richer peasants in the same community to consolidate their holdings. The trends were towards an élite of rural smallholders, and an impoverished, dependent underclass of rural cottagers and landless labourers. These underlying tendencies created tensions in communities and, at the same time, weakened their ways of resolving them.

Virtually landless labourers existed in much greater numbers by 1650, living on the margins, dependent on earning most of what they ate, and making do the best they could. Their resilience was remarkable. In Altopascio (near Lucca in Tuscany), a village on the estates of the Medici, the poor built their huts on the swampy land near the river, from which they derived some livelihood. In Ossuccio, a village over-looking Lake Como in northern Lombardy, the landless carried wood down on their backs to Domodossola. But, in times of dearth, their vulnerability was cruelly exposed. Their only escape route was to move to a town and hope for the best. The pressures from greater rural impov-erishment are reflected in complaints from city authorities about the poor who invaded their midst. The community of Codogno near Lodi, situated in the midst of wealthy Lombardy petitioned the duke of Milan in 1591: 'The village . . . lies so close to the territory of Piacenza that it serves almost as an open door to those who come from there. At pre-sent, such is the crowd of wretched beggars who, driven by hunger, daily descend from their mountains and find refuge . . . that it looks as if, in a short time, the village itself will overflow with people.'

For many peasants, therefore, an overlord was no bad thing. A sei-gneur guaranteed social cohesion, mediated local disputes, protected a community against outsiders, ensured a local clerical presence and interacted with the larger, alien world of the state. When smallholders in the Cremona countryside were asked the question in the 1640s, whether they wanted to live under a feudal lord, one reply was: 'Yes, sir, we would, for we have suffered so much destruction, and a lord would help us in our needs.' That is the context in which to evaluate the growth and consolidation of domain exploitation in central and eastern Europe in this period, and the increase of serfdom.

Domain serfdom was already partly in place by the beginning of the sixteenth century east of the Elbe, north of the Saale, and in Bohemia and Hungary. In the processes of colonizing new agricultural land, the nobility acquired extensive judicial and economic rights over those who worked their estates. Those processes were reinforced by buoyant prices for agri-cultural products in the sixteenth century – in local markets, but also in the demands for cattle to supply the markets of central Europe, and cere-als, shipped out from Baltic ports. Entrepreneurial lordship in the hands of noble landlords and the administrators of ecclesiastical or princely domains aimed at operating large domain estates, worked by unpaid village labour. It was a model that seemed to offer something to all parties. Those who owned large amounts of land lacked the capital to invest in plough-teams and the labour to work them. Peasants had the labour and plough-teams, but neither were intensively utilized all the year round. Farm rents were rising, so peasants were prepared to commute rent into labour. Economic lordship, in any case, was only an extension of the local juridical powers which the nobility already possessed. Even when peasants were required to build the substantial manor houses and immense barns which were the characteristic landscape features of domain lordship, they had the consolation that strong lordship offered protection from the outside world and social cohesion within. Before 1600, village farms under seigneurial authority were treated as under the subjection of lords, capable of being transferred (along with the domain) to another lord, but the peasants working them were not themselves personally unfree.

How burdensome labour services were depended on how large peasant plots were, how much tenure security they had and the degree to which the peasantry was able to hold labour services within manageable limits. In Brandenburg, peasant plots were large (often 60 acres or more) and the peasantry still worked the majority of the land before the Thirty Years War. They might have to provide two or three days of weekly domain labour with their plough and team of oxen, but they could send a son, or hire someone in their place to do the work. Unmarried sons and daughters might be conscripted for domestic or other work on the farm, but they all had a share in the buoyant market prices for agricultural produce through collaborating with the domain operation for its transhipment and sale. They belonged to village communes, recognized in law, and they could take their lord to court. They had a stake in the local economy and were reluctant to move.

In Schleswig-Holstein, Mecklenburg and Pomerania, by contrast, where the demands from the markets for cattle and cereals were particularly strong, and where public authority was in the hands of the most entrepreneurial lords, villagers' hereditary tenures were converted into leaseholds. For contemporary jurists, that excluded them from the Roman law category of freeholders (*emphyteutae*). They became tenants at will (*colonii*) and tied to the land (*ad glebam adscriptus*). They were not slaves (*homini proprii*), but they were serfs (*servii*) and they were personally unfree. Village communities had few recognized rights of representation, petition or pursuit of legal redress.

Further east, in Poland, peasant plot sizes were smaller and labour service burdens greater. Some villagers, however, managed to negotiate fixed quotas, and to retain some security of tenure. Although Polish villagers lost their rights to appeal against seigneurial lords in royal courts in 1518, they held on to their rights to buy and sell things. If they were dispossessed or abused, they could up sticks and find protection under another lord. There were plenty of opportunities to do so in the Ukraine and Lithuania. In Lithuania, twenty magnate families (the Radziwiłł, the Sapieha and others) controlled a quarter of all peasant households. The peasants who settled on their estates, however, did so on favourable terms. The Polish crown encouraged the development of domain landlording by reforms on its own estates. The model farmstead became a 45-acre farm, laid out on rational lines with peasant obligations established in accordance with the size of the farmstead. Those who possessed one of these units lived well enough. About 130 days a year were spent on the domain, but the rest of the time was theirs to cultivate their plot. But then, as settlements built up, so labour dues as well as money rents increased as part of a strategy of maximizing returns. The conquest of space and the gradual enserfment of the peasantry were, in that sense, like Europe's colonization in the New World.

Further south in Bohemia and Hungary, large agricultural domains often existed alongside independent villagers with their own landed holdings. Many of these estates were part of the royal domains of the Bohemian and Hungarian monarchies, but were leased out to noble contractors or ecclesiastical foundations ('lien lordship'). Royal domain administrators required estates to be returned in the condition in which they had been originally leased out. So the Austrian Habsburgs became engaged in establishing norms for the labour services, obligations and status of peasants on their leased-out estates. The numerous peasant protests and uprisings in these regions had as their objective to persuade the emperor and his officials to intervene in cases of abuse by domain landlords. In 1515, a major uprising began with the murder of a seigneur. In 1523, the peasants of the Tyrol revolted against the newly installed seigneurs of Archduke Ferdinand. When the Great Peasant War of 1524–6 spread into the Tyrol, Salzburg and Upper Austria, peasant demands included the abolition of leased domains to nobles and the removal of Maximilian of Bavaria, a leading territorial lord. In the wake of the war, Ferdinand (by then king in Bohemia) agreed in 1527 to the registration of all peasant leasehold tenancies so that their tenancies had a legal existence. Following uprisings in Lower and Upper Austria in 1594–7 against labour dues and other impositions, Emperor Rudolf II issued the Interim Resolution (1597), which limited domain service and affirmed the right of the peasantry to seek redress when those limits were exceeded. Domain serfdom proceeded in Habsburg lands but with state oversight, and without attenuating village solidarity.

The main drivers for harsher enserfment in eastern Europe were not economic landlordism and the lure of the market but the twin evils of war and depopulation. In Russia, the dislocations of the Livonian War and the subsequent Time of Troubles were huge, resulting in a flight from the land. In 1580, Tsar Ivan IV forbade peasants from moving. From 1603, every year was a 'forbidden year' until 1649, when the Law Code formally bound peasants and their families to the land in perpetuity. If they chose flight, the lord had the right to demand their return. The number of rural dwellers who had perhaps once held a farmstead but who became dependent cottagers and farmworkers grew dramatically. The numbers of landless labourers in the region around Novgorod rose sixfold from 1560 to 1620 to become more than a quarter of the population. In the Russian heartland they became about 40 per cent of the population. The roots of Russian serfdom lay in the first half of the seventeenth century. In East Elbian Germany and Poland, the Thirty Years and Polish wars had a similar impact. Peasants fled from the conflict zones and domain landlordism temporarily collapsed. With the return of peace, landlords rebuilt their authority and recovered their losses, pushing the Brandenburg dukes and Polish Commonwealth to legalize personal serfdom. The most significant long-term impact of the mid-seventeenth-century crisis in Europe was incontrovertibly the growth of harsh personal serfdom in the East.

SHUTTLING BETWEEN TOWN AND COUNTRY

The shuttle in question was essential to the cloth industry. It was the tool that threaded the weft yarn through the warp strands, held in a trestle ('shed') to weave fabric. The textile industry gave employment to thousands of people in town and countryside. Manufacture was often undertaken outside the towns in a domestic environment by rural families for whom it constituted an important by-product, but it was almost always urban merchant drapers who controlled the process and sale. Factories were not unknown either – in reality a concentration of weaving and dyeing shops in urban locations such as Venice, Augsburg, Florence, Norwich or Armentières. Cloth remained the staple of Europe's long-distance trades, even after a century of expansion in the New World. Bedclothes, table coverings, hangings, towels and napkins were registers of social standing. The bridal trousseau embodied familial virtue in embroidered gowns, veils and underblouses. Almost everything that needed transporting (even bodies for burial) made use of cloth. Drapery, however, was the queen of cloth, displayed ostentatiously in the luminous Cloths of Honour, swags and curtains behind the Madonnas in High Renaissance religious art.

Fine drapery was, like that art, an Italian speciality in the early sixteenth century. There were significant centres of production at Milan, Como, Bergamo, Pavia, Brescia and Florence. The finishing of fine drapery was an expensive business; customers were discerning and quality control was essential to the value of the finished product. So it was vulnerable to competition and disruption. Both assailed Italian drapery production in the first half of the sixteenth century. The Italian Wars disrupted cloth-working at Brescia, Milan, Florence and elsewhere. Some of the centres managed to recover their former glory, but others stepped into their place. They included the Venetians, whose drapery production blossomed greatly in the second half of the sixteenth century. And, north of the Alps, lay the fine drapery centres of the Netherlands at Ghent, Bruges and Courtrai. But they also suffered from competition, this time from a 'new drapery'.

There was no new technology to new drapery. It was a straightforward imitation of old-fashioned wool using cheaper wools, and mixing them with other yarns such as linen or cotton. The result was known as 'says' or serge: lighter, brighter and cheaper. This rejuvenated old cloth-working towns in the southern Netherlands like Lille and its hinterland. It also made the fortunes of places where there was no old merchant corporation to stand in the way: Tournai, Hondschoote, Bailleul, Valenciennes, Armentières. Cloth-workers were hard-pressed, vulnerable to economic depression, and open to new ways of valorizing themselves and their families. Competition lay just across the North Sea in England from worsteds (cloths from East Anglia) and the broadcloth draperies of Suffolk and Essex.

The bulk of the cloth industry, however, took place in the countryside, producing cloth for everyday use. Linen, canvas, woollen mixtures – the variety was considerable, the quality variable, and the role of merchants in commercializing it different from region to region. There were plenty of places (Genoa, Lille, Ulm, Regensburg, Norwich) where cloth production still lay in the hands of independent hand-weavers who brought their pieces to market each week, and purchased their spun yarn for the following week's work with the proceeds. The individuals concerned were dependent on the market, week by week. If they did not sell their wares, they could not purchase the wherewithal to continue working. They had no control over the costs of their raw materials or the price for their semi-finished goods, and they were subject to detailed quality control. The inclination among independent weavers was to blame merchant clothiers when times were hard. When the latter failed to buy semi-finished goods, they were the target for criticism. Cloth production intensified the dynamics of the rural–urban relationships and sharpened the social contrasts within towns. It made some wealthy and others poor. Cloth production and social protest went hand in hand.

POVERTY AND SOCIAL CONSCIENCE

Being poor was a fact of life for most people. Poverty, on the other hand, was a social construct, existing in the social conscience of the rich. The poor congregated where the rich were, and between 1520 and 1560, city magistrates expressed their consciences through new ordinances for the relief and regulation of the poor. From Nuremberg (1522) to Strasbourg (1523–4), from Mons and Ypres (1525) to Ghent (1529), from Lyon (1531) to Geneva (1535) and on to Paris, Madrid, Toledo and London, cities copied best practice from one another. Their example was then generalized by laws (the Netherlands, 1531; England, 1531 and 1536). Magistrates' social consciences were framed by humanist ideals of an ordered commonwealth of virtue. When they looked at the streets in their own cities in that light, much needed to be done. There were many charitable foundations, often in Church hands, but they were not well run. They did not diminish the number of visible poor, jostling people in the public squares and entrances to churches, sleeping in doorways and wandering the streets, crying out for alms and making claims on the conscience of the virtuous citizen. And since (it was widely believed) they spread the miasma of disease, reform meant bringing health to the commonwealth.

That was how the Spanish humanist Juan Luis Vives saw it. In his *On the Succour of the Poor* (1526) he drew on his experience as a voluntary exile from Spain (partly because of his Jewish blood) in Bruges, his treatise being dedicated to its magistrates. It was, he declared, 'a shameful and disgraceful thing for Christians . . . to find so many needy persons and beggars on our streets'. Citizens had a moral duty to help them because poverty fostered uncivil behaviour. Vives found beggars offensive to the senses. They were a sign that a community was diseased. His solution was to categorize the problem as a prelude to providing a solution to it. He recognized widows, orphans, the maimed, blind and sick as needing help, possibly on a permanent basis, though he thought they could often do more to help themselves. Shelter, food, schooling, beds and charitable aid should be provided institutionally. He also acknowledged that there were those who had fallen on hard times and who needed assistance at home (the 'shame-faced' poor in contemporary parlance). He recommended that they be given succour by parish deputies, whose task it would be to assess their need and administer it. That left those who begged on the streets, 'sturdy rogues' whom city authorities should round up and send packing. It sounded simple enough.

Vives's treatise was emblematic of the mindset of a virtuous magistrate. It probably did not have much direct impact on policy. The mindset, however, did, and most immediately in Protestant Europe, where giving to the poor was no longer seen as a way of earning God's grace, and the begging of the friars was regarded as an encouragement to knavery. Protestant city councils forbade public begging. The dissolution of religious houses offered the opportunity of turning the buildings into hospitals and schools, which is what happened in Zürich, Geneva and elsewhere. In Catholic Europe, it was more complex. The institutional inheritance, with its ecclesiastical associations and avowed ministry to the souls of both giver and receiver, was retained.

In Venice, the *Scuoli Grandi* (religious confraternities) remained sumptuously maintained foundations for the charitable impulses and consciences of the wealthy in that city, whose money came in useful to the state when it was short of funds. In Florence, its numerous hospitals offered citizens medical attention from competent physicians in establishments that ministered to their souls as well as their bodies. Elsewhere, however, Catholic cities followed the lead of Lyon in 1534 and reorganized their charitable corporations into a hospital, responsible for ministering to all the poor and involving both laymen and clerics in its administration. And, like their Protestant counterparts, Catholic magistrates (and Tridentine clerics) increasingly regulated begging, responding to the reality of poverty with institutional initiatives (particularly for orphans and reformed prostitutes, and loan banks for the poor – *Monti di Pietà*). But the distinction between deserving poor and idle rogue always broke down, and expelling the 'undeserving' poor from cities was never more than a temporary fix, especially as the fundamental dislocations of Europe's growth were borne by those who were paid in wages and had to buy their bread with them.

Pioneering research in the 1930s by an international committee for price history assembled data on the daily wages of workers. Economic historians collated the evidence for unskilled and skilled building workers' wages and compared them in terms of the silver content of local currencies (known as the 'silver wage'), the volume of grain (the 'grain wage') and the amount of bread (the 'bread wage') and other consumer essentials that what they earned could purchase. The results confirm the picture of an emerging economic region in northwest Europe where silver wages were high and skilled labour plentiful. In southern and eastern Europe, by contrast, the trend towards higher wages (in terms of the silver they represented) was less pronounced and skilled labour in shorter supply. Wages were up to 100 per cent higher for skilled building workers outside the zone of advanced economic growth, where they were only 50 per cent higher. When one measures wages in terms of what they would purchase, the result is a mirror image. The purchasing power of those who were dependent on money wages fell dramatically in this period, and especially for non-skilled labourers. The gap between northwestern Europe, where those of skilled workers fell least, and the less developed parts of southern, central and eastern Europe, where real wages, especially for unskilled workmen, collapsed, was dramatic.

That is why Europe's towns also had a significant proportion (from 15 to 30 per cent) of households in regular receipt of charity: by definition, the poor. They could not be disaggregated from the vagrants ('dangerous poor'), who moved from countryside to town, and who could not be stopped. In Naples, the Papal States, Catalonia and even Venice, vagrants provided the human capital for gangs of outlawed bandits. Tolerated in rural societies, cut-purses and hired killers gave the slip to the most determined of local magistrates. Well-meaning gentry and parochial officials administered the Elizabethan Poor Law (1601) in England. They did their best to distinguish, as required, between the deserving poor and the thriftless 'vagabound that will abide nowhere'. In 1630–31 the Books of Orders (printed ordinances about food supplies, vagrancy, etc. for local administrators to follow) gave them more detailed advice, but it was to no avail. Similarly defeated were the administrators of Dutch workhouses who aimed to discipline those groups in society which magistrates regarded as idle, disorderly and an affront to a society embarrassed by its riches.

Urban expenditure on public poor relief was never, in any case, more than a tiny fraction of urban wealth as a whole, and municipally channelled poor relief was only one, and not the most important, method of relieving poverty. The most important remained private philanthropy. Protestant preachers emphasized the mutual obligations of rich and poor. People who neglected charity and who wasted their money were 'poor-makers'. In his *Treatise of Christian Beneficence* (1600), Robert Allen admitted that some poor people belonged to the 'monstrous and sottish multitude', but that was not an argument for stopping being charitable: 'their evil in no whit diminishes thy goodness'. For both Protestant and Catholic moralists, charity to the poor was about the conquest of souls and, in places where the religions lived side by side, there was straightforward competition. In Brussels in the 1580s, as later in Lyon and Nîmes, hospitals and almonries became contested spaces, and charity one of the ways of rallying the faithful and winning converts. Saving souls proved easier than reconstructing poor people's lives.

POPULAR PROTEST

The power of localism in Christendom was clearly demonstrated in its patterns of protest. The corporate loyalties and political autonomy of cities had created a tradition (christened a 'Great Tradition') among patricians who stood up for their urban rights and negotiated with princes for the maintenance of their privileges, inscribed in laws and charters. When city magistrates bargained with other authorities, they claimed to represent the urban community even though they generally had no explicit mandate to do so. The city walls, town halls, and seals and robes of office were embodiments of a community's history. That history often included protest and revolt, but it was chronicled in such a way that it was integrated into an ongoing bargaining process between those who claimed authority and those over whom it extended.

Alongside this Great Tradition, however, there was also a 'little tradition' of protest, one which included urban artisans and labourers and extended into rural communities. This little tradition did not have the benefit of being chronicled in history or charters or of being institutionalized. It was enshrined in local political culture – the 'commons', 'people' and 'community' being among the ways in which, with differing local and regional accents, that culture sought to express itself. It had its own targets of resentment (the 'rich', the 'traitors', the 'bloodsuckers' of the common weal), its own rituals (based around patronal festivals, parishes, processions) and its folk heroes (local Robin Hoods), as well as ways of assembling and expressing its grievances. Its representatives (the 'better sort of people' or the 'middling sort of people', as they were sometimes known in sixteenth-century England) were expected to defend the locality against intrusions upon established customs and traditions. They did so by negotiation and mediation but, when that failed, they found themselves leading popular protest.

In *Henry VI Part 2*, Shakespeare depicted Jack Cade, the leader of the 1450 Kentish rebellion. Drawing on Holinshed's *Chronicles*, Shakespeare's Cade vocalizes the hopes and fears of the little tradition. The ordinary folk, he said, were ignored and held in contempt. Cade had to do business with the gentry, but they were not to be trusted. Strangers and foreigners, too, were regarded with suspicion. Back in the mythical past lay a golden age when (says Cade) 'there shall be in England seven half-penny loaves sold for a penny; and the three-hoop'd pot shall have ten hoops; and I will make it a felony to drink small beer. All the realm shall be in common.' The little tradition made itself felt through petitions, bargaining and mediation, but also through staged insurrection. Political authorities in Christendom had learned to live with it.

Most protest before 1500 was limited, held in check by notions of order and respect for authority. In the sixteenth and early seventeenth centuries, however, the scale on which it occurred was transformed. Fire-arms were increasingly dispersed among local populations, and so the violence which accompanied protest increased. Its incidence is difficult to analyse in this period because it was so frequent and multifaceted. Any effort to tabulate such uprisings cannot be complete, for many occurred that went unnoticed on the larger stage. In Provence alone, by one estimate, there were 108 (2.4 per annum) incidents of popular pro-test between 1590 and 1634, rising to 156 (6.3 per annum) from 1635 to 1660. Rebellion was similarly endemic in Stuart Ireland, the inevitable consequence of the collapse of Gaelic lordship which followed the destruction of the Fitzgerald clan in the Kildare rebellion of 1534 and the attempts to build an English ascendancy on the basis of colonial plantation and a Protestant state. The organized rebellions in Ireland of the later sixteenth century (Desmond, Kildare, O'Neill, O'Doherty) required an English army of occupation that was larger than ones sent to fight in France and the Netherlands in the same period.

The most effective protests were, in any case, passive – the refusal to pay taxes and dues, for example – and unreported. Disorder short of full-scale revolt was widespread – especially if one includes soldiers' mutinies, brigandage and organized criminality. Brigands were more in evidence, partly as a reaction to the more intensive farming of landed domains in Naples and the Papal States and Catalonia from the late 1580s onwards. Brigands exploited the pastoral regions of the moun-tains, and flourished on their notoriety and acceptance among local communities. Marco Sciarra, a native of Castiglione in the Abruzzi, became a folk hero for several years in the Romagna during the later 1580s. He proclaimed himself 'the Lord's scourge, sent by God against usurers and all who possess unproductive wealth', said that he was sent to rob the rich to benefit the poor, and played on local hostility to the Spanish. Prior to his assassination in 1593, it was rumoured in Naples that 'he would soon come and make himself king'. There was more revolt talked about than actually occurred. The English authorities rightly feared a rebellion in the Midlands in 1596. In fact, it did not happen, although there were those like the miller from Hampton Gay Roger Ibill, who thought it would ('there must be a rising soon, because of the high price of corn').

Even the incomplete tabulation of unrest, however, indicates that uprising and revolt were broadly dispersed across western, central and northern Europe. There were periods when they affected several regions concomitantly (1530s, 1560s, 1590s, 1640s). Many revolts proved persistent, based on locally rooted opposition and situated in border or inaccessible regions which allowed them to last several years. The Great Tradition of urban revolt (the *comuneros* in Castile, 1520; Ghent, 1539) became assimilated into the broader sweep of urban and rural conflict which tended to engulf much larger areas than just a town, wrapped up in the bigger politico-religious conflicts of the Reformation. By contrast, the little tradition matured into a major, ongoing dynamic for popular unrest. Ordinary folk continued to believe that they were the 'people' whose 'community' should defend itself at times when its natural defenders failed to do so.

The scale of protest dwarfed the popular rebellions of the later Middle Ages. The Great Peasant War in Germany (1524–6) was the broadest mobilization of ordinary people into protest in German lands before the nineteenth century. At its height, perhaps 300,000 peasants were under arms. In Württemberg, up to 70 per cent of those capable of bearing arms joined the rebels in 1525. It had a major impact on the course of the Lutheran Reformation. In 1536 20,000 people marched south to Doncaster under the banners of the Five Wounds of Christ, the crusading symbol of the Pilgrimage of Grace. The Croquants' rebellion in southwest France in 1636–7 was the largest peasant revolt in France after the 'Jacquerie' of 1351, with 60,000 reportedly in arms in August 1636. It forced the government into talks. Peasants formed federated bands, negotiated agreements among themselves and with those in nearby towns, and found people to lead them. Their deliberative assemblies broadcast their grievances, mobilized and coerced others to join them, and tried to negotiate with authorities. Although they had different aetiologies, rural and urban protest became intermingled, both caught up in wider movements of protest and change. The coalition of forces behind protest was, however, unstable, reflecting the unpredictable politics of unrest.

The unprecedented scale of popular unrest was a function of its diversity. To some extent it was a consequence of the economic changes and the diminishing social cohesion of the period. That was particularly noticeable in the numerous enclosure riots of sixteenth- and early seventeenth-century England. It was equally evident in the anti-seigneurial and anti-serfdom elements of the Great Peasant War, or the major peasant insurrections in Upper and Lower Austria in the later sixteenth and early seventeenth centuries. As in the somewhat less numerous examples of food riots in the cities of western Europe in this period, these were confrontations where material things mattered most – rights to land, resources, space, food. But even in these instances, the grievances of protesters were expressed in ways that were not reducible to an economic equation. They presented themselves as on the side of the 'common weal' against 'rich men' and those who 'starve the poor'. They sought to recover 'ancient rights' through an appeal to the 'old law'. The famous Twelve Articles of Memmingen (March 1525), the most widely distributed peasant grievances of the Great Peasant War, included an important demand against serfdom. But it did so in terms of traditional demands for social justice, expressed within the language of Lutheran evangelism, respectful of authority: 'It has until now been the custom for the lords to own us as their property. This is deplorable, for Christ has redeemed us and bought us all with his precious blood, the lowliest shepherd as well as the greatest lord, with no exceptions. Thus the Bible proves that we are free and want to be free – not that we want to be utterly free and subject to no authority at all.'

The most pervasive context for popular unrest was military conflict and its consequences for the civilian population. Compulsory requisitioning and billeting of soldiers, the menacing depredation of troops on the move, and the activities of local opportunists who exploited the breakdown in order were the grievances which surfaced in the popular unrest which punctuated the last decade of the civil wars in sixteenth-century France (the Gautiers of Normandy, the Croquants of Périgord, the Campanelle of the region to the south of Toulouse).

Popular unrest was also fomented by the politico-religious changes of the Protestant Reformation. They affected rituals that were an integral part of local communities. They altered who owned and exploited the land. It is unsurprising that popular unrest was frequently mobilized and vocal against the Reformation (the Pilgrimage of Grace, 1536; the 'Prayer-Book Rebellion', 1549). But unrest could work the other way as well. One of the most widespread targets for protest in this period was the tithe, the ecclesiastical equivalent of seigneurial dues upon producers from the land. Beyond the passive refusal to pay which became widespread among Protestants in southern France in the 1560s and in the Netherlands during the early years of the Dutch Revolt, it was an element in the uprisings in Hungary (1562, 1569–70), Slovenia (1571–3) and Upper Austria (1593–5, 1626–7). In the novel circumstances of sixteenth-century religious pluralism, whether to be Protestant or Catholic went beyond the monarch, the magistrate or the magnate. The choice split towns and communities within and among people and their leaders.

When those divisions turned into extreme violence, they were regarded as a demonstration of what those with a humanist education already knew: that 'the people' was synonymous with a savage, barbarous and unpredictable mob. Following years of civil and religious contention, the people of the small town of Romans decided during the Carnival season, on the eve of Mardi Gras (15 February 1580), to join in the peasant insurrection that had infected the countryside around (the League of the Commoners – 'Villains'). Artisans and peasants danced in the streets, threatening the rich and crying: 'Before three days, Christian flesh will be sold at sixpence a pound!' Their elected leader, Jehan Serve ('Captain Paumier'), sat in the mayor's parlour, dressed in a bearskin, eating delicacies which passed for human flesh, while his followers dressed up as Christian dignitaries and cried 'Christian flesh for sixpence'. The town's rich, horrified by this cannibalistic prospect, descended on their opponents and massacred them in a slaughter which lasted for three days. In Naples in 1585, the angry mob, protesting against the high price of bread, lynched the local magistrate, Giovan Vincenzo Starace, for failing to control prices. His body was mutilated, and pieces of his flesh offered for sale before the remains were dragged through the street and his house destroyed. In the 1626–7 insurrection in Upper Austria, a woman removed the eyes of one of the noble victims and took them home in her handkerchief. Another cut off his genitals and fed them to her dog.

The state and political authority were implicated in popular protest because it seemed to threaten both. The senior nobility tried to turn unrest to its own advantage, one element in their efforts to protect themselves against over-mighty princes, and to influence political change. The French nobles were not alone in believing that they had a 'right of revolt', by which they meant a legitimate duty to lead protests against a tyrannical prince, one who infringed the freedom which was coterminous with nobility. Irish clan chiefs evidently felt they too had legitimacy on their side to raise the 'septs' (the clans) against English domination, with its hostile state, alien religion and colonizing tendencies. But the nobility were playing a dangerous game, not least because there were anti-noble sentiments just below the surface of many popular revolts. 'Kill all the gentlemen and we will have the Six Articles up again and ceremonies as they were in King Henry's time' was the slogan of the English Prayer-Book Rebellion. During an insurrection in the southern French city of Narbonne in 1632, nobles were referred to as 'Jean-fesses' ('Jack-arses'). One peasant song from the insurrection in Austria (1626–7) began: 'Now will we sweep through the land, and our own lords must flee.'

The Swiss served as a regular example of those who had successfully thrown off their nobility. During the League of the Croquants of 1594–5, it was a commonplace that the peasants wanted to abolish noble privileges and to establish a democracy on the pattern of the Swiss. Besides, princes could use popular protest to turn the tables against their own rebellious nobility. A striking case was the 'Club War' in later sixteenth-century Finland, in which Duke Charles – the acting regent in Sweden – encouraged his peasants to rise 'if by no other means, then with stakes and clubs' against the Finnish nobles who remained loyal to the displaced Swedish king, Sigismund Vasa.

The state became the focus of unrest, especially when its own taxes were the objects of contention. With the growth of the fiscal state (see below, ch. 16) the focus of unrest became increasingly centred on its role, on the 'novelty' of its exactions and the unscrupulousness of its agents. In southwest France, it was the attempt to introduce the *gabelle* (the tax on salt) that sparked off the peasant revolt that culminated in 1548. In Saintonge and Angoumois, salt-marshes were a profitable enterprise. Communes began by imprisoning and massacring the *gabeleurs* who had been parachuted in from outside by the syndics of private tax-collectors to whom the collection of those revenues had been leased out at a profit by the state. That became a more common pattern in France in the 1630s and 40s, when local revolts became a rejection of the fiscal state, and the financiers, tax-farmers and intendants which sustained it.

It was in the nature of the little tradition of rural and urban revolt that protest was presented as supporting legitimate authority and seeking a return to a lost age of community and equity. There was a persistent belief that the king was the source of justice and that, if only the tribulations of his people (which had been masked or misrepresented by ministers and favourites) were revealed to him, he would remedy their woes. 'Down with *gabelles*' was the cry during the 'Nu-Pieds' rising in Normandy (1639). But at the same time the protesters shouted: 'Long Live the King.' In their anonymous manifesto they wanted a return to the good old days of King Louis XII. 'Death to Bad Government, and Long Live Justice' declared the rebels in Naples in 1585.

A variant of the same theme in popular protest was that of the saviour, a 'hidden king' who would miraculously return to deliver his people from their woes. It had resonances with the millenarian prophecies which could be found in the urban milieu before and during the Protestant Reformation. Old Emperor Frederick was the just ruler in whose name the grievances of the German people were expressed in 1520 at the beginning of the Lutheran troubles. It was a persistent myth in Portugal that King Sebastian had not fallen in battle in Morocco in 1578, but was still alive, the object of visionary writings in the 1630s (mostly of Jewish *converso* origins), portents in the natural world and learned disquisitions by Jesuits at Évora University. The Bolotnikov Rising in 1606–7 occurred in the wake of the dynastic struggle between Tsar Boris Godunov and the pretender to the throne, the pseudo-Dimitri, a young man who claimed to be the true heir and promised the restoration of peace and justice against Godunov. That appeal to a Pretender was so powerful that the pseudo-Dimitri was propelled to the throne after Godunov's death in 1605, thanks to a loyalist rebellion led by boyars and supported by Cossacks and Poles. Bolotnikov's supporters made it to the walls of Moscow in October 1606, although they were compelled to retreat as they alienated the very people in the capital they were trying to influence.

If protest was 'loyal' and in defence of conservative values, why was it treated as confrontational in a new way in this period, and so brutally repressed? With only a handful of exceptions, the protests were overwhelmed by force. Those cities (Ghent, 1539; Bordeaux, 1548; Naples, 1585) which rose up against their overlords paid a heavy price. Leaders of revolts were put on trial, tortured and publicly executed. The city's privileges were torn up, its walls breached and fines imposed on its citizens. In the aftermath of the uprising in Naples in 1585, over 800 people were put on trial, but 12,000 more fled the city, fearing the repression that would ensue. Peasant armies were almost invariably defeated by the greater skills and better armament of their opponents. But deliberate butchery explains the huge loss of lives that occurred in the aftermath of defeat. Over 5,000 peasants died at the battle of Frankenhausen (15 May 1525) during the Great Peasant War. The opposing *Landsknechte* (mercenary pikemen) had six casualties, two of whom were only wounded. Perhaps as many as 100,000 peasants were put to death in the two years of revolt in German lands from 1524 to 1526. Peasants died in their tens of thousands in the Hungarian insurrection prior to the battle of Mohács (1526). In the wake of the Pilgrimage of Grace, peasant bands in arms were slaughtered 'like dogs', according to Captain Cobbler, one of their ring-leaders, awaiting his fate in Lincoln jail. 'What whore-sons were we that we had not killed the gentlemen, for I thought always that they would be traitors,' he reflected. Over 5,000 peasants died in the various confrontations that brought the Prayer-Book Rebellion to an end in August 1549. At the battle of Clyst Heath alone, 900 bound and gagged prisoners had their throats slit in ten minutes. In the conflict which brought the Croat peasant uprising in 1573 to a close, Emperor Maximilian II boasted of the death of 4,000 Slovene and Croat peasants. In the wake of the 1626–7 uprising in Upper Austria, over 12,000 peasants were said to have been put to death. At the battle of Sauvetat near Périgueux in 1637, 1,000 peasant bodies were left on the battlefield. Thousands more died in insurrections than were accounted martyrs in the religious confrontations of the sixteenth and seventeenth centuries, or than were judicially executed for witchcraft.

The leaders of revolt were given brutal punishments to discourage others from following their example. The Romanian György Dózsa (or Székely), the mercenary captain turned leader of the peasant-dominated insurrections in eastern Hungary that culminated in 1526, captured after the rout at Temesvár, was condemned to sit on a smouldering iron throne with a heated iron crown on his head and a red-hot sceptre in his hand; leading fellow-rebels were condemned to bite his skin where hot pliers had been inserted, and to swallow the flesh. At Frankenburg am Hausruck in Upper Austria, Lutheran peasants revolted against Count Adam von Herberstorff's attempt to impose a Catholic priest on their community. Despite an amnesty, the count arrested the leaders of the insurrection and (following contemporary military practice) divided them into two groups, forcing them to gamble with dice for their lives.

Thirty-six men were hanged, the act triggering the Upper Austrian rebellion which followed.

The fate which awaited rebel leaders was not merely to dissuade others, but also to intimidate local notables and leaders. That was also the objective behind the obsessive concern with absolute obedience, required by God and the prince, which permeated royal ordinances, and which was the staple of the advice literature for magistrates. No effort was spared in proclaiming the dangerous consequences of rebellion, and most of the rhetoric was aimed above the heads of the people themselves. 'When every man wyll rule who shall obeye?' asked one tract in the wake of the Pilgrimage of Grace. 'No, no, take welthe by the hand, and say farewell welth, where lust is liked, and lawe refused, where uppe is sette downe, and downe sette uppe. An order, and order muste be hadde, and a waye founde that they rule that best can, they be ruled, that mooste it becommeth so to be.' Reflected in the more authoritarian tones of the literature on political obedience was the attempt to educate the larger and more disparate group of local leaders upon whom the state depended. There was a deeper concern as well. The humanist project involved linking the exercise of office to the achievement of public good. There was a persistent danger that magistrates, local officials and lesser nobles might misconstrue where their loyalties lay – to the people, or to the state. Since 'lesser magistrates' (and almost anyone in a public office could be thus described) were accorded the duty to God and the people to disobey a higher authority by influential Protestants when it failed to carry out its duties before God, rulers were more exercised by the problem of ensuring the loyalties of that growing group of lesser officials upon whom their authority depended in difficult times.

So, despite the harsh repression of popular revolts and the exhortations to absolute obedience, protest often achieved something of what had been demanded. The Great Peasant War was defeated decisively, but the succeeding Diet of Speyer (June 1526) agreed propositions to alleviate the burdens on the peasantry. In the wake of the rising in the Tyrol in 1526, the Land Ordinance conceded rights of land ownership and limitations to labour services on royal demesnes as well as changes to the laws on hunting and fishing. New fiscal impositions were cancelled or postponed and promises were made to redress wrongs in the wake of social protest, not because the people had won but because the power of local leaders had to be acknowledged. Their attempts to mitigate the effects of economic change in town and countryside – through price controls, ordinances against grain hoarding, poor relief and the purchase of food supplies for release at subsidized prices – help to explain why, despite the crumbling social cohesion in western Europe, there were not more serious uprisings.

Even so, the voices of protest were heard as being seditious, and in new ways. That was partly because they were broadcast to a wider public, and therefore more capable of being manipulated and misunderstood. There was a new nervousness about seditious talk – investigated and prosecuted with much greater determination in the aftermath of the Reformation. When the Oxfordshire carpenter Bartholomew Steere voiced his thoughts in 1596, 'that the Commons, long sithens in Spaine, did rise and kill all the gentlemen in Spaine and sithens that time have lyved merrily there', he was misinformed. But that did not prevent the English government from executing him for seditious talk. The progress of popular insurrection could be followed from the mid-sixteenth century through the newsletter service from the banking house of Fugger at Augsburg. Pamphlets issued by, or in the name of, protesters circulated their grievances and demands to wider audiences. The mimetic possibilities of popular revolt were particularly evident in the 1640s. Battista Nani, Venetian ambassador to Paris, wrote in September 1647 about the impact of the revolt of Naples which had occurred two months previously: 'The most common idea that is spreading among the people here is that Neapolitans have acted intelligently and that, in order to shake off oppressions, their example should be followed. It is understood, however, that allowing the people in the streets to shout aloud their enthusiasm for the revolt of Naples has caused great inconvenience. Therefore measures have been taken to prevent gazettes from reporting further on it.' The same forces which spread the technological changes transforming Christendom were also disseminating knowledge about protests, themselves manifestations of its diminished social cohesion.

4. Treasure and Transaction

Money lay in a potentially awkward relationship to Christendom. A monetary system placed value on precious metals, whereas Christendom's belief-community was built around worth expressed as orthodoxy, genealogy, inheritance and knowledge. That awkwardness was mostly, however, unrealized. Money was not used in a lot of exchange (i.e. the economy was only partially monetized). In addition, money had a habit of turning into wealth of all sorts – noble patrimony, ecclesiastical benefice, royal office, peasant dues – thereby aligning itself with traditional values and established power structures. Scholastic theologians offered explanations for how, within reason, money could be squared with Christian beliefs. Yet something changed in the sixteenth and first half of the seventeenth centuries. Silver became available in unprecedented quantities. The prominence of money sustained a virtual community, a republic which traded in precious metals, held together by mutual bonds of credit and trust. Europe's overseas merchant empires were created. Some people grew rich and others poor. Crucially Europe's states benefited from the power that flowed from silver, giving them resources and stimulating their competitive energies to engage in destructive conflict with one another. Money was the dissolvent of Christendom. Aligning money with Christian values began from the notion that precious metal was part of God's cornucopia, grown on earth by the influence of planets. In contemporary alchemical understanding, metals were represented by their signs (gold by the sun, silver by the moon, copper by Venus, and so on) and placed on earth by God's beneficence for mankind.

SUBTERRANEAN TREASURE

Lucas Gassel was a Flemish painter and Breughel's contemporary. In 1544 he signed a painting known as *Coppermine*, although it is probably the production of cast-iron in nearby Liège that is its subject. On the hillside is a polluted industrial landscape – mine-workings, wagon railways, adits and winding gear. In the foreground, ore is being raked and transported in wheelbarrows. A worker struggles to carry a crucible on his back, while another nearby hammers a casting out of its mould. Prominently depicted is the water-powered blast furnace that made it all possible. In the midst of the scene, a physician is pointing at a bowl of vomit from a worker suffering from exposure to toxicity. Meanwhile, a woman dressed in red carries a pitcher of wine, her demeanour suggesting that she provides more than liquid refreshment to the workers. Set against this scene, on an adjacent hillside the rural order remains intact. Gassel presents a Manichean world of ambiguous values.

Such ambivalence was common. The mining engineer Agricola (Georg Bauer) believed that mineral resources were part of God's blessings: 'in fact, one mine is often more beneficial to us than many fields'. Mining was more risky but it was more productive. You had to take greater risks and it polluted the atmosphere. But that mostly occurred in 'otherwise unproductive [mountains], and in valleys invested in gloom', doing 'slight damage to the fields or none at all'. However, abundance came with a price tag. The more there was of something, the less it was worth. That challenged notions of an inherent value in nature as well as a just price for commodities. It was a 'paradox', understood in this period as a way of expounding views that were contrary to those of the common multitude. To the unorthodox potter Bernard Palissy the industrial production of glass buttons or cheap wood-block devotional prints inevitably made it harder for skilled artisans to make a living because they flooded the market. If alchemists were successful in turning base metal into gold 'there would be such a great quantity of gold that people would scorn it to the point that no one would give bread or wine in exchange for it'.

For Palissy value came from artifice – from the hands of a skilled potter like himself – rather than nature. His contemporary Blaise de Vigenère replicated scholastic arguments against usury, saying that objects like metals were 'sterile' since they 'produce nothing' by them-selves. Moralists regarded subterranean treasure as encouraging avarice and cupidity through materiality, a quest for novelty and a worship of fashion. Agricola thought this was beside the point. Subterranean treas-ure was essential: 'if we remove metals from the service of man, all methods of protecting and sustaining health and more carefully preserv-ing the course of life are done away with. If there were no metals, men would pass a horrible and wretched existence in the midst of wild beasts; they would return to the acorns and fruits and berries of the forest . . .' The mining of alum, essential to the dyeing of cloth, substan-tiated his point. Supplies came from Phocea (inland from the gulf of Smyrna) until the Ottomans cut them off in the 1450s. In 1460, how-ever, rich deposits which could be open-cast mined were discovered at Tolfa, north of Rome. The papacy greeted the discovery as providential and declared that the proceeds should be devoted to Crusade. In reality, they swelled the papal treasury and enriched the merchant bankers (the Medici; then, after 1520, Agostino Chigi), who handled the monopoly. Chigi employed 700 workers in the mine, built a village for them (Allumiere), and purchased a port from Siena to manage the exports. He also bankrolled the elections of Popes Julius II and Leo X and lent the money for their military campaigns. Merchant capitalists needed no lessons in wealth accumulation, enterprise management or protecting their investment by political means, but their outlook was opportunistic and short-term.

Around the Meuse valley, coal mining grew fourfold between 1500 and 1650. Slag-heaps rivalled church steeples. By 1600, 'sea-coals' were shipped from Newcastle to London and to continental ports in sub-stantial quantities. Copper, tin, lead, arsenic, sulphur and mercury were mined and shipped in hitherto undreamed-of quantities. The search for raw materials was driven by the demand from more distant markets, and gold and silver were the transforming treasure of this period.

GOLD AND SILVER

It is difficult to overestimate the mystique attached to these substances. Gold thread was woven into cloth and tapestry giving them irides-cence when caught in the light. Gold and silver animated statues and paintings. Gold and silver regalia, jewellery and tableware were statements about the innate virtues of aristocracy. The search for precious metals drove Europe's overseas expansion. Jacques Cartier set out on his first expedition in 1534, as Columbus had done a generation before, with the aim of 'discovering certain islands and lands where it is said that a great quantity of gold and other rich things might be discovered'. Martin Frobisher's voyage to Newfoundland in 1576–8 was in search of precious metals. Sir Walter Raleigh understood that Philip II's Spanish empire was not based on 'the trade of sacks of Seville oranges . . . It is [with] his Indian Gold that he endangereth and disturbeth all the nations of Europe.'

In addition, gold and silver were money. Various coins were produced in local mints, franchised out to local enterprise. France had around twenty mints, Castile at least six. Almost every Italian principality and many German cities minted their own coins. Production involved striking them out manually, using a hammer and hand-held dies. The resulting coins had irregular edges, and their weight and thickness varied considerably from mint to mint. The possibilities for fraud through 'sweating' some of the metal off the coin or 'clipping' the edges were considerable. Even money-changers had difficulty in detecting variations in coinage alloy and weight. The Paris mint experimented with a rolling mill and a cutting press to add a milled edge but the invention was wasteful and expensive to install. Although its virtues as a means of preventing fraud were discussed, no European currency was milled before 1650.

Money based on more than one metal was complicated, and sixteenth-century Europe relied on three: gold, silver and billon. The value of coins was determined not just by their face value but by their weight and fineness. Billon coins were the least valuable, consisting of small amounts of silver, alloyed with less valuable metal (mainly copper) – in practice making them impossible to value intrinsically. Gold coins were the most valuable and used rarely. The majority of Europeans never spent a gold coin in their lives – one Venetian ducat purchased over 600 eggs or 240 herrings at the Antwerp market in the 1520s. They were coins that were easier to test for weight and fineness and used by bankers, courtiers and the wealthy. They were also symbols of power. In the early sixteenth century, Milan and Naples put portraits of their rulers on their coins, imitating classical precedents and turning coins into political advertisements. The French king Henry II allowed himself to be presented wearing the laurels of a conquering emperor on a *teston,* the silver coin whose name (from *testa* meaning 'head') reflected what was novel about it.

Silver coins, by contrast, were a common transaction medium. The expansion in silver coinage stimulated Europe's monetization. Silver testoons, half-crowns, angels and crowns (the English silver coins up to the coinage reform of 1551), shillings, half-crowns and crowns (thereafter), Spanish *réales* (containing 3.19 grams of fine silver) and Dutch *stuiver* (containing .94 grams of fine silver) survive plentifully in coin collections. More prestigious were the 'maxi-silver' coins of the period, the heavier *réales de a ocho* ('pieces of eight', eight times heavier than a *réale*), or the silver *Guldiner* from central Europe which became the model for the *Joachimstaler* (28.7 grams of fine silver) – and, much later, the young American republic for its silver dollars (*Talers*).

The coin-producing mints functioned at the behest of bankers, money-changers and merchants who brought the metal to them. The mints then struck the coins, deducting operating costs and seigniorage, the state tax imposed for the privilege of operating a mint. Although the authorities monitored the quality of coins, the marketplace determined the quantity struck and in what metal. Providing an adequate circulating medium, especially for smaller-scale transactions, was particularly problematic. Billon coinage was vulnerable to being melted down for its silver content, especially in times of monetary instability and inflation. The 'problem with small change' in this period was that there was never enough of it, its quality was suspect, and it was not a profitable commodity for the mints to produce. There was a mass of *blancas* (Castilian copper coins containing only 7 grams of silver) of dubious worth in the Spanish peninsula. Milanese *terline* and *sesine* (nominally worth 3 pence and 6 pence) settled everyday transactions in northern Italy. French *liards* (farthings), *deniers* (pennies) and *douzains* (12 pence) or English groats (4 pence) paid a toll, bought a loaf or were left in a poor-box. But, like inferior wine, they did not travel well. Even the finest coins were alloyed with copper to harden the malleable precious metal. English 'sterling' silver, for example, had 7.5 per cent copper content in this period, the French equivalent (*argent-le-roy*) 4.17 per cent. Impecunious princes were tempted to increase the profits from the mints by adding more of this base metal alloy and reducing the silver (known as 'debasement'). Alternatively, they could decrease the weight of the coin itself, thus minting more coins of the same 'face' value from the 'pound' (or *marc*) of fine silver or gold.

Public authorities provided a way of accounting for differing metals and coins of differing weights and fineness. They were known as 'moneys of account' and they were used for accounting purposes in all sorts of transactions. They represented a stable measure of value by which one set of coins could be compared with another. Throughout Italy, for example, all accounting was in *lire*, *soldi* and *denari*. Only the last unit corresponded to an actual coin. The others were imaginary units, of which there were 20 *soldi* or 240 *denari* to the *lira* (or notional 'pound' weight of coin). Similar moneys of account existed everywhere in Europe – the *maravedí* in Spain, the *livre tournois* in France, the Dutch *gulden* and the pound sterling in England, for example. Exchange rates existed between the physical coins and the moneys of account. Those exchange rates fluctuated in respect of the individual coins in question and in the differential value of one money of account in terms of another. The authorities set these exchange rates, which were then advertised at the mints as the purchase price for the bullion and coins presented by merchants. But the latter had the final say because if the rate was not realistic they refused to do business with the mints and traded at unofficial rates. Then, as now, there were only a small number of people who knew how the bullion and money markets worked, and an even smaller minority, clustered in Europe's emerging financial centres, who knew how to play them to their best advantage.

Europe's precious metal stocks were undergoing two transformations. First, in the 1470s, the Portuguese established their presence on the West African Guinea coast. In 1481, a fleet of eleven ships arrived and, in a matter of weeks, built the fortress at São Jorge da Mina (now Elmina, Ghana), at which they traded for 'Sudanese' gold which West Africans extracted from the Senegal, Niger and Volta river basins and carried to the coast. In 1509, the Guinea Office was founded to regulate the trade; from their account books we can determine the business's scale (roughly 0.77 tons per annum between 1500 and 1520, the height of the trade). Then, new supplies of gold opened up in the American colonies. In under a generation, the Antilles were drained of the gold that was panned out of the river silt. By 1550, 64.4 tons of gold had been unloaded at Seville from New World sources, or the equivalent of 708.5 tons of silver at the going rate of conversion.

The impact of that substantial blood transfusion for Europe's metal-starved monetary economy was less than it might seem. The imports from West Africa may have merely diverted gold that would have otherwise arrived in Europe by caravan across the Sahara to the ports of the Mediterranean. In addition, the Portuguese used some of it to underwrite their trade with India and Indonesia, for which it was an essential element. There was, however, a second, coterminous change in Europe's supplies of precious metals – a bonanza in silver- and copper-mining in central Europe – which had begun at the same time (the 1460s) and reached its peak in the 1540s. In Thuringia, Bohemia, Hungary and the Tyrol copper and silver deposits, long known to exist, became economically feasible to extract thanks to two related technological innovations, whose implementation was in response to the rising commodity value of silver.

The first was a chemical process which used lead in the ore-smelting to separate out silver from copper. The second was drainage mechanisms, harnessing water and horse power for more efficient pumps to drain deep mines. Production peaked in the 1530s at around 88.18 tons of silver per annum. Eisleben, Annaberg, Marienberg (Saxony), Joachimsthal and Kutná Hora became silver-rush towns. The boom made the fortunes of the Fugger family from Augsburg. The Lutheran Reformation was cradled where Europe's boom was most raw.

SILVER, TRADE AND WAR

Silver was complicated and expensive to mine and also heavy to transport. These obstacles explain why there were virtually no silver imports from the New World before 1530. Thereafter, however, it was a different story. After the Spanish implantation in southern Mexico in 1521, European expeditions ventured into the northern Chichimeca. On one of them in 1546 natives brought its leader (Juan de Tolosa, a Basque noble) pieces of local silver ore as a gift. That same year, a small mining settlement was founded over 8,000 feet above sea level at Zacatecas. Insensitive of local customs, the prospectors provoked a frontier war with the Zacatecos and Guachichile Indians in 1550. Prospectors found more around Guanajuato and Pachuca. Intrigued by the problem of decreasing silver yields from the ores, a Spanish merchant,

Bartolomé de Medina, brought new smelting methods from Spain (their origins probably lay in Germany) in 1554. These involved the construction of a flat patio in which the ore was finely crushed and then mixed with mercury and a salt-water solution. The resulting slimy mixture was left in the sun for several weeks until the silver had amalgamated with the mercury. Mining and extracting silver in Mexico depended on imported European materials, skills and equipment. There were iron and steel tools, lamps and oil, crushing mills and horses. The mercury was brought over in leather bags from Almadén in southern Spain, where the Fuggers held the contract for its production from 1563 to 1645.

Meanwhile, another bonanza began in the Spanish settlement of Upper Peru (now Bolivia), 400 miles inland from the Pacific Ocean. Silver ore was discovered in the Cerro Rico ('Rich Mountain', as it now became known) over 13,000 feet in the Andes above the town of Potosí, in 1546. When the surface ores became exhausted in the late 1550s, the Spaniards turned to lower-grade ores with the patio process. In 1572 the first of over twenty artificial reservoirs was constructed in the hills around, storing millions of gallons of water to power hydraulic hammers for crushing the ore. By 1600, there were around 125 ore treatment works and the town had grown to over 100,000 inhabitants. No other mountain produced such fabulous wealth. There were 15,000 mineworkers in Mexico and Peru by 1570 – and three times that number were involved in the operation as muleteers, carters, salt producers, etc. The death-toll among miners and those working with lethal mercury was grim. In the period of peak silver production in central and southern America from 1590 to 1620, official annual production was at least 7 million ounces (220 metric tons), but there was substantial under-registration – perhaps by as much as two thirds. Contemporary seventeenth-century Dutch gazettes published figures of silver imports from Spanish America that cast doubt on the official ones, so much so that the apparent decline in production after about 1620 which appears in the official figures of what was received in Seville may not, in fact, reflect a weakening of silver imports into Europe, as was once thought. In any case, by 1600 around a quarter of Potosí's output was probably traversing the Andes to the Río de la Plata and then to Brazil, Lisbon and the European market. Other large amounts were traded across the Pacific to Manila and thence to China. One of the first results of Europe's overseas expansion was that Europeans became the dominant force in the global trade in silver.

The primary European beneficiary of this speculative operation was the Spanish monarchy. It contracted for the supplies of mercury that were shipped across the Atlantic, and profited from it. It collected a tax on each bar of silver produced (10 per cent in Mexico, 20 per cent in Peru) and charged a handling fee. There were additional duties collected at the colonial ports as it was transported, including when it arrived and was accounted for at the Colonial Office in Seville, and when it was exported from there to elsewhere in Europe. The growth of royal receipts enabled Charles V to fund his military campaigns in Italy, North Africa and the Mediterranean, Germany and Flanders. Charles V's empire worked on the basis of contracts (*asientos*) with suppliers. They furnished everything from mercury, borrowing (*asientos de dineros*), down to all the supplies for military forces. The essential task of the Castilian treasury (*Hacienda*) was to match receipts to expenditures when the former were irregular and the latter immediate and impera- tive. In reality, the monarchy treated silver like a crop from a domain, one which could be harvested as and when it required. In times of dif- ficulty, it seized privately owned silver on its arrival in Seville, compelling the owners to accept interest-bearing bonds in return (*juros*). It antici- pated the receipts on its silver revenues by converting them into *juros* and, since they paid attractive rates of interest (5–7 per cent), there was no shortage of takers. When it could no longer honour its *asientos*, they too were converted into longer-term *juros*. The borrowing capacity of Castile's treasury expanded with the influx of precious metals. Spanish Habsburg treasurers could rely not merely on Spanish merchant bank- ers but on others in Charles V's empire in Europe (the Welser and Fugger from Augsburg, the Schetz from Antwerp, among others). Then, when the monarchy defaulted on its obligations and those banking houses suffered, merchant bankers from Genoa and Cremona in Spanish- influenced northern Italy took their place (among them the Spínola, Grillo, Doria, Affaitadi).

This sophisticated state borrowing became vertiginous in the second half of the sixteenth century under Philip II. The military costs of the Spanish Habsburg's dynastic empire grew larger, especially in the west- ern Mediterranean and in Flanders. The sale of government bonds was on such a scale that it threatened the liquidity of the state. Although

Philip II declared a state bankruptcy three times (1557, 1575 and 1596), he ensured that interest payments were maintained to *juro*-holders, a promise that could be honoured only on the strength of the buoyancy of silver receipts from the New World. Despite repeated financial crises and declining silver receipts in the reign of Philip IV (1621–65), the silver from the Americas remained the means by which the Spanish Habsburgs were able to retain sufficient liquidity to fight the Thirty Years War. If anything, New World silver's significance increased as revenues elsewhere faltered. Madrid authorized public celebrations when news of the fleet's arrival reached court. Five million *ducados* of additional bonds were issued between 1621 and 1640 to cover the sequestrations of Seville merchant assets when the silver convoys failed to make it.

One might imagine American silver acting like an adrenalin surge through Europe's polities, driving their appetites for war. American precious metals not only sustained the ambitions of the Habsburg dynastic empire, but they also bankrolled those of its enemies. The processes of precious metal extraction and transportation were merchant-, not state-led. The shipowners, captains and merchants of Seville became the core of a powerful American colonial trading consulate (known as the *consulado*). Seville's merchants acted as the tax-farmers for the duties on silver. They contracted to supply the convoy ships and pay the wages of their crews. They became indispensable in the handling of imported goods into Seville and out again to the Americas, estimating what could be profitably sold in the colonies. The wares were then purchased on credit from foreign merchants with factors in Seville. These debts were settled from the silver receipts once the convoy arrived from the New World. American silver flowed into Seville, but then immediately out again – to the French, English and Flemish merchants whose grain, textiles, salt and manufactured goods found their way to the markets of the New World. By the early seventeenth century, Seville merchants were acting as front-men (*prestanombres*) for their counterparts from northern Europe.

In addition, the trade and silver networks to and from the New World came to resemble the pipe-work of an old water-supply: it was full of leaks, and the greater the pressure, the higher the wastage. Dutch and English smugglers ('interlopers') established bases from which to trade directly with the Spanish New World and disrupt its convoys. Silver percolated overland from Peru to what is now Argentina, and from there onto the European market. Smuggling became almost institutionalized, a means by which the creaking Spanish monopoly was rendered tolerable to colonial America. That trend was intensified by the precious metal transfers that resulted from the Habsburg military forces in Flanders. The mercenaries from Spain, Italy, Germany and the Netherlands itself were armed, fed and clothed by means of contracts with suppliers, all of which were honoured in New World silver (or gold that had been purchased with silver). The reality was that the silver diaspora to northwest Europe hastened that region's monetization. It shifted the balance of Europe's advanced North Italian–Rhineland axis northward. It furnished the wherewithal for Spain's enemies who, by the close of the Thirty Years War, had brought it to its knees.

New World precious metals fed Europe's growing military conflicts. They also had the potential to create social change by putting power in the hands of merchants. In certain places (the emerging Dutch Republic) that occurred. But that it did not do so on a wider scale was the consequence of European states investing so much of their monetarized wealth in conflict. The investment resulted in a socio-monetary transfer. Money became invested in something else: in military valour, in noble families and office-holding élites, and in the protection of religious orthodoxy. Silver went into the pockets of Spanish Habsburg generals and military contingents, and fed the lifestyles of its imperial administrators and their families, its diplomats and informants. Spanish élite society – its nobles and patricians, its ecclesiastical and charitable foundations – invested heavily in government bonds, the bond-holders providing an important element of political loyalty to the Habsburgs at difficult times. Similar processes of socio-monetary transfer were at work among Spain's enemies too. In the state-like structure of the Dutch Republic, they resulted in the emergence of a patrician élite, 'embarrassed' by their riches in the sense that they did not want to flaunt them, devoted to another set of conservative values. In France, the emerging absolutist state became a powerful instrument for socio-monetary transfer, converting money into office-holding privilege and military service. The Bourbon monarchy legitimated the ostentatious display of wealth in buildings, apparel and aristocratic deportment of its nobilities, new and old.

TRADE AND CREDIT INFRASTRUCTURES

Some of the biggest transformations in Europe in this period were also the least publicized. Parts of western and central Europe grew financially more sophisticated. Attitudes to credit became more relaxed, and debt played a greater part in private and public life. Above all, the transactional costs of trade decreased. It became easier to shift goods, simpler to borrow money and cheaper to move it around. You could insure a ship and its cargo at major ports (1 per cent/month of the value of the ship and its cargo at Antwerp) and peacetime costs for doing so declined. Risks were reduced by information flows that were more broadly based and publicly available. By 1600, a merchant had access to published commodity prices and the exchange rates in many European trading centres. There was a 'quiet revolution' in interest rates. They fell wherever political conditions were stable enough to support the market. There were new financial instruments that enabled people to invest surplus wealth more broadly. Mercantile activity became more complex and diverse. Retailing, too, became more specialized, especially for luxury goods. In Europe's major cities, there was a widening and deepening of consumption, supported by the development of distinctive retail space. This, in turn, meant a greater emphasis on the availability and delivery of goods to market and the credit relationships to match. Unpredictability – especially war and political instability – remained, however, the principal transactional cost.

It is difficult to document changing attitudes towards the lending and borrowing of money. Almost everyone needed a loan at some stage in their lives. Even in those places where the economy was not fully monetized, there was plenty of debt to be managed. Marriage portions created rural indebtedness, as did harvest failures. Trade recessions threw artisans out of work, placing burdens on local mechanisms for managing debt. Unpredicted risks generated mercantile debts of different sorts. In Rome, for example, about 6 per cent of the population found themselves imprisoned for debt in 1582 alone. Debt litigation dominated law cases in London in the century after 1550. The small-claims court in Venice (the *Justicia Vecchia*) saw many ordinary folk come before it to settle contested debts. Almost 40 per cent sued for not having been paid for work. Just over 20 per cent of cases involved retail

debts, especially to vintners and apothecaries who allowed their customers to purchase on credit. A further 20 per cent related to debts for
services of one kind of another. 'When will you get rid of your debts?'
Pantagruel asked Panurge in Rabelais's classic *Gargantua and Pantagruel.* 'When hell freezes over, when the whole world is happy, and when
you are your own inheritor,' he replied.

The higher up you were socially, the more in debt you were likely to
be. In Elizabethan England, the duke of Norfolk, the earls of Shrews-
bury and Essex and other aristocrats regularly pledged their plate,
jewels and occasional revenues to sustain their lifestyles. In 1642, the
income of England's peers has been estimated as about £730,000 – but
their debts were double that figure. The palaces of Europe's grandees
were as much a tribute to their capacity for debt management as they
were an acknowledgement of the importance of conspicuous consumption in upholding their social status. And they were led by Europe's
princes, more indebted by far than their predecessors.

Debt and credit were present in people's lives because they had
moral connotations. Bankruptcy was widely regarded as the consequence of fraud, and the volume of legislation about it seems to reflect
its increasing incidence. Usury gave credit an even more ambivalent
moral dimension. Everyone agreed that usury was a sin, and most
people regarded it as a crime as well. They could not agree, however, on
when it occurred. In canon and secular law, usury was defined as lending for a guaranteed return over and above the sum that you had lent
out, and without risk to the lender. Humanists and theologians had
begun to question that definition on both biblical and logical grounds.
Should the Old Testament dispositions apply to Christians? If so, a sin
was committed only where the action could be equated with an intention. In the case of an annuity (a sort of mortgage) on a property, for
example, it could be argued that the money was actually buying the
rights to the fruits produced by the money that had been borrowed. The
annuity might look like a loan but it was the sale of a right, vested in
land or assets whose values were real.

Typically these issues were discussed through the prism of religion,
through which the real world was viewed, lived and judged. The debate
cut across religious divisions with Protestant theologians as divided on
the issue as their Catholic opponents. Luther tended to be conservative,
suspicious of tendentious arguments about usury – he drew swords with

the Catholic controversialist Johann Eck on it. But he accepted that there were circumstances when lending money at interest was legitimate (for example, in the case of student loans). Calvin was influenced by the clever French jurist Charles Dumoulin. The latter argued that usury should be judged by the circumstances in which money was lent, the question being the reasonableness of the amount of interest charged. There was nothing inherently wrong, he said, in lending at interest to people who would use the money productively. Calvin incorporated his views into a private letter in 1545, but asked its recipient not to let it circulate abroad.

Martin Bucer, the Protestant reformer from Strasbourg, found his views mocked in *The Market, or Fayre of Usurers*, a pamphlet published in England in 1550. It is presented as an imagined dialogue in which Pasquil and Usurer debate the issues, the latter (Bucer himself) offering to prove that usury was not necessarily a sin: 'I speake not of very great usury, as thou thinkest, but of a reasonable and decent gayne.' Pasquil's reply reflected traditional thinking on these matters in this period. There are only two sorts of lending: that which is done 'of Christian charitie', freely and for God's love, and that which is covetous. To charge interest on a loan was to commit theft. When it came to legislating on interest rates, these arguments had to be placed in the context of the world as it was. When the English Parliament did so in 1545, it allowed lending at up to 10 per cent. In the Dutch Republic, the state only controlled usury which was anti-social. But the Dutch Reformed Church decreed in 1581 that no money-lender (his servants and family included) should ever be admitted to the communion service until after they had publicly expressed their distaste for the banking profession.

The market for money was not fully in the open but it grew in complexity and sophistication. Annuities extended Europe's credit lines. You could raise money on land by instituting a 'perpetual' (i.e. hereditable) mortgage on it. More attractive still were annuities on public revenues whereby a creditor provided a municipal or state government with a lump sum in return for a 'perpetual' annual payment or a 'lifetime' yearly sum. They were popular and suited both parties. In 1520 the papacy declared annuities exempt from usury laws and licit. That was prior to taking full advantage of them itself, as did many governments. By the first decade of the seventeenth century, the papal monarchy had 10 million *scudi* of outstanding annuity-based debts in various funds (*monte*), the annual interest payments of which absorbed about half its ordinary revenues. The city-state of Genoa had the equivalent of 391.65 tons of silver in outstanding annuities by 1600, a large charge on its modest resources.

In the Netherlands, the issuing of annuities opened the door to a financial revolution by which, first the cities of Holland (Amsterdam, Dordrecht, Gouda, Haarlem and Leiden) and then the province itself stood guarantor for the debts of its Habsburg overlords. That revolution redefined the relationship between ruler and ruled in the Netherlands and opened the door to the province's financial independence which sustained it during the subsequent Dutch Revolt. By one estimate, the ordinary revenues of Castile (530 million *maravedís* in 1559) were carrying an annual 542.7 million *maravedís* in interest payments on *juros* at the time of Philip II's bankruptcy in June 1557. Each bankruptcy resulted in an increased volume of *juros* as short-term debt was converted into long-term annuities as part of the settlement with creditors. With all the annual revenues available to the crown in Castile committed to discharging the interest payments on its *juros*, the only revenues available to it were the treasure from the Indies, occasional ecclesiastical subsidies and the grants every three years from the Castilian estates.

From 1522 onwards, the French monarchy also engaged in issuing annuities through the supposedly independent agency of the municipality of Paris (*rentes sur l'hôtel de ville de Paris*), serviced by interest payments on particular revenues. In the reign of Henry II (1547–59) about 6.8 million *livres* alone were sold. By 1600, they totalled 297 million *livres*, about fifteen times the annual crown revenues. The more *rentes* the French monarchy sold, the more frequently it did so at a discount, the greater the interest charges on crown revenues and therefore the arrears (in effect, a disguised bankruptcy). After the wars of the League, Henry IV's finance minister Sully organized a selective default on interest payments. Those *rentes* which had been issued at a discount or during the Catholic League were unilaterally written off. After 1600, the issue in France was how, if at all, a sovereign king could be obliged to pay the debts he owed his subjects.

Those in cities who needed credit had a variety of professional and part-time pawn-brokers and money-lenders to whom they could turn. The growth in consumption increased the stock and range of goods to serve as deposit. In many places, goldsmiths, silversmiths and jewellers also acted as money-lenders. Outside the Italian peninsula, they became known as 'lombards' (reflected in the streets carrying that name) and, especially in Germany and eastern Europe, Jewish merchants offered a wide range of financial services. Increasingly, though, particularly in southern Europe, charitable institutions were established to keep the poor out of the hands of usurers. An outgrowth of movements for religious reform in the Italian peninsula, these pious foundations (*Monti di Pietà*) grew in scale and number as the century progressed. Most drew their capital from charitable donations, which sometimes determined that the sole function of the fund was to lend money to the poor at low rates of interest. The larger *monti* acquired impressive amounts of capital (well over half a million ducats at Rome, Verona or Turin) and offered deposit banking facilities. For reasons that are not entirely clear, poor-man's banking like this spread only patchily north of the Alps. It certainly was not for want of trying on some people's part. The English Parliament considered proposals in 1571 and the Flemish chronicler and entrepreneur Pieter van Oudegherste submitted a plan to Philip II in 1576 for banks and pawnshops throughout the Spanish empire. It never got off the ground, although there were some in Dutch towns – the most famous being the Amsterdam House of Lending (*Huis van Lening*), founded in 1614 – and rather more in the Spanish Netherlands after 1600.

Private deposit banks existed, too, run mainly by merchant bankers or their factors, their role confined to larger urban centres. Only very slowly did negotiable cheques (*polizze*) make their appearance in Italy in the 1570s, part of a limited development of giro-banks that would accept deposit transfers (*girata*). All these private banks generally worked on a fractional-reserve system of lending which ought to have guaranteed their stability. In fact, many of them failed, taking depositors' savings with them and reinforcing the view that banks were simply ways of conning money out of gullible people.

Much more significant among mercantile élites was the widespread use of the bill of exchange. The latter was already an established instrument for enabling merchants to help one another remit funds at a distance. As it gained greater legal standing and market credibility, the bill of exchange became the means by which merchants transmitted funds from one currency to another, redeemed debts abroad and carried out trade. 'One can no more trade without them,' said an Antwerp merchant, 'than sail without water.' Shrewd merchants could make profits on the operation, since to transact bills of exchange took time, during which, if the exchange rate moved, one of the parties would realize a legitimate profit. Starting in common-law England but spreading through Europe, law courts accepted that bills of exchange could be reassigned and negotiated between different parties. That opened the door to merchants generating credit for themselves on a longer-term basis by re-scripting a bill back and forth, or trading it at various discounts. By 1650, the bill of exchange had become an essential part of a sophisticated system of multilateral commercial payments.

Trade and finance flourished on news, the 'freshest advices' from other trading centres being critical in making commercial decisions. The archives of Europe's merchant élites are replete with newsletters and correspondence that mixed family gossip with commodity prices. The 16,000 newsletters for the years 1568 to 1605 in the archives of the Fugger family from Augsburg provide us with a glimpse of how one family with its finger on the pulse acquired its news. With factors based in commercial centres (Antwerp, Cologne, Venice and Rome) the manuscript newspapers provided a wide variety of news from across Europe as well as the New World, India and the Middle East. They supplied detailed accounts on matters ranging from kingly coronations to common street crimes. One issue includes the story of a debtor, playing the part of Christ in a pageant, who was arrested by his creditor, dressed up as Judas. In 1582, a sequence of newsletters was filled with descriptions of the fifty-one-day festival in Constantinople to celebrate the circumcision of the fifteen-year-old Mehmed, son of the reigning Sultan Murad. Commodity prices and exchange rates began to be regularly published, the earliest known examples being a glimpse of where Europe's principal trading centres were by 1600.

By that date, these locations mostly also had an exchange, a building where merchants could trade yearlong, furnished with additional shop facilities. In Naples, the loggia was on the Piazza del Mercato. In Venice, its equivalent was on the Campo di Rialto, the heart of the city's mercantile quarter. Hamburg's 1558 exchange was modelled on that of Antwerp, which had opened its doors in 1531. Above the London exchange, constructed in 1569, were shops (some run by women). Shops coexisted with markets and fairs as part of the growing complexity of

Europe's retailing. London's Cheapside was the city's longest and widest thoroughfare in the sixteenth century as well as the heart of its market quarter. A food market ran along one half of the street while stationers and booksellers occupied the other half. Ground-floor shops in the buildings on the street were let out for rents. Thomas Platter, a medical student from Basel, window-gazed in 1599, marvelling at the 'great treasures and vast amounts of money' that he had seen in 'The Naked Boy', 'The Frying Pan' or 'The Grasshopper' (a selection of shop-names in Cheapside). Enclosed stores offered a theatrical retail experience. In Venice, the *Fabbriche Nuove* (1550–54) was a brand-new complex in the Rialto facing the Grand Canal. Small towns in northern Italy (Imola, Pomponesco, Carpi and Gazzuolo) still bear the imprint of central streets and squares, redesigned in this period and lined with shops. Book distribution illustrates broader trends. By 1600, printer-publishers had developed wholesaling techniques to bring their products to the market, involving advertisements, catalogues distributed at the international fairs, agents and stockists. Increasingly, however, book-sellers working from shops were the people who knew their local market best.

The word 'capital' in this period meant the funded wealth of a merchant or institution, although other terms were in more common parlance, meaning the same thing. Europe's capitalism was not organized around the growth of financial structures (banks, letters of credit, etc.), industrial production and wage labour in this period. Credit, trade and transaction worked on personal agency, and Europe's merchants were more inclined to invest in land, title, office or charitable enterprise than in industrial production. Their investments were therefore not fungible (not readily transferable into liquid wealth). Personal ties, the assessment of people's credit-worthiness on an individual basis, were essential. Europe's merchant firms were reticulations of family, with often ethnic or religious connections. These family firms provided a degree of stability to Europe's commercial nexuses – although most of them were opportunistic, taking advantage of whatever trades seemed to offer the possibility of profits, and not outliving three generations.

Europe's financial system prospered under a variety of circumstances. It did not require representative institutions, though stable states helped. It could survive governments not paying their debts, though their meddling with currencies through debasement could play havoc. It was not particularly price-sensitive to credit and it supplied ample opportunity for agents, factors and intermediaries to offer specialist services. By 1650, brokers were everywhere important, and as never before. With so many financiers and their agents, and such a lot of secrecy, there was fast practice; the set-up looked more secure than it was.

RIDING THE WAVE

Monetary inflation was a fact of life in the sixteenth and early seventeenth centuries. The average price of a *setier* (a sack of grain measuring 12 bushels) of best-quality wheat on the Paris market rose from just over a *livre* in 1500 to 4.15 in 1550, 8.65 in 1600 and 18 by 1650. On a yearly basis, that was modest. Cumulatively, it was the longest period of sustained and continuous inflation to that date. The phenomenon challenged Christendom's notions of what constituted wealth and reward.

There was a lively debate in the sixteenth century about what caused the unparalleled 'dearness' of things. Sixteenth-century commentators made the connection between increasing monetary stocks and price rises, although they remained puzzled by the relationship between plenty and worth. The Polish astronomer Nicolaus Copernicus wrote extensively on the effects of the debasement of the country's coinage, noting that 'money can lose its value also through excessive abundance'. In his *General History of the Indies* (*Historia General de las Indias*, 1552), Francisco López de Gómara reckoned that the rising prices in America were 'as a result of Incan wealth passing into Spanish hands'. The celebrated Augustinian professor at the University of Salamanca, Martín de Azpilcueta (called 'Navarrus' because he came from Navarre in the western Pyrenees), generalized that insight in his treatise on usury (1556): 'Other things being equal, in countries where there is a great scarcity of money, all other saleable goods, and even the hands and labour of men, are given for far less money than where it is abundant.' The problem, as he and his fellow professors of natural law and moral theology in Salamanca saw it, was how to reconcile these market forces with the imperatives of social justice, a fair price for goods and protecting the interests of the poor.

Was inflation caused by the imports of New World silver? The connection between recorded price rises and imports is not as close as was once thought. Inflation began in the sixteenth century before the imports started, and their under-recording post-1600 destabilizes the correlation later on. This does not disprove, however, the more general proposition, supported by sound economics, that inflation had a very great deal to do with changes in the money supply, which were massive. The relevant question becomes: what prevented these changes from creating runaway, rather than gradual, inflation? We can only reflect upon the remarkable and fortuitous conjunctures that allowed a significant proportion of Europe's precious-metal windfalls to be siphoned off to stimulate trade with the Far East and with Russia. Without these safety valves, Europe's 'silver age' would have quickly come to grief.

None of this, of course, was understood by Europe's rulers. That much is evident from the coinage debasement operations carried out by various European princes, and which equally affected the money supply. The objective of a debasement was to reduce the weight of a coin or the amount of precious metal in it, and thus to increase the number of coins with a given face value that you could mint from a given amount of it. So alluring was the operation that it happened at regular intervals. The Burgundian-Habsburg administrations debased their silver coins in both fineness and weight twelve times between 1521 and 1644. The English coinage lost over 35 per cent of its silver content from *c.* 1520 to 1650, mostly in a decade of economic madness beginning late in the reign of Henry VIII and known as the 'Great Debasement' (1544–53). In France, successive debasements meant that the prevailing French silver coin in around 1650 (the *écu blanc*) contained less than half the silver of its equivalent in 1488. In German lands, mint-operators used their franchises to debase the coinage, creating a period of widespread popular hatred of the 'counterfeits' and 'cheats' (known as the *Kipper-und Wipperzeit*) that were widely believed to be behind it all, and which was believed to herald the coming of the End Time. Even the Spanish monarchy, which did not debase through the sixteenth century, resorted to a catastrophic debasement of small-value coins in 1607.

Debasement generated a contemporary debate all of its own. In England, Sir Thomas Smith, in his *De Republica Anglorum* (published in 1583, but written earlier), saw it as princely deception. Across the Channel, Jean Cherruyer (or Cherruyl), seigneur de Malestroit, a monetary specialist for the French crown, argued that, because of successive debasements, inflation was more 'imaginary' than real. It was a paradox (that is, a popular delusion) that goods had gone up in price. They had not. The same amount of silver still bought the same amount of grain, thanks to the effects of debasement. Two years later, he found his match in the up-and-coming French jurist Jean Bodin. His 'Response' to Malestroit's 'Paradox' relied on empirical evidence to show that, contrary to what Malestroit asserted, monetary inflation had occurred on a large scale. Bodin was inclined to believe (at least in the second edition) that this was the result of American silver imports. He was even more insistent that it was a sign of tyranny when princes fiddled with currencies at the expense of the public weal. It would be better to have money that contained what it said on the coin by way of its precious metal content. Bodin understood that there was a fundamental relationship between coinage and good government, although in his lifetime the values of a commonwealth were beginning to be overlaid by the harsher and more authoritarian tones of obedience to the absolute will of a prince.

By the seventeenth century, mineral wealth was seen to be something of a poisoned chalice. 'Columbus offered gold unto one of your Kings,' wrote the English political thinker James Harrington, 'through whose happy incredulity another prince hath drunk the poison, even unto the consumption of his own people.' It was God himself, agreed the illustrious Spanish diplomat Diego de Saavedra Fajardo in his *Political Maxims* (1640), who had hidden precious metals in the ground precisely so that there would be no more of them used than was strictly required for commercial purposes. Unlimited wealth, such as that from the Mexican and Peruvian mines, had been 'fool's gold'. 'Who would have believed,' he continued, echoing a famous remark by Justus Lipsius, 'that with the gold of that world this one would also be conquered?'

Underlying the debate about the worth of money, lay another, pursued by humanists on the basis of the ancients, about the proper relationship between business (*negotium*) and the quiet life (*otium*). Aristotle had taught that gathering wealth was a natural part of good housekeeping, but only so long as it was limited to the provision of necessities. In other circumstances, wealth corrupted those who accumulated it. However, some – the Dutch publicist Dirck Volckertszoon Coornhert, for example – argued that a merchant could be a good Christian by acquiring wealth in order to distribute it to good causes. In the seventeenth century, however, that debate went a stage further. French intellectuals in the 1630s and 40s ventured to argue that *amour propre* was a proper stimulus for moral behaviour, that friendship could be based on the pursuit of mutually shared but selfish interests, and that the pursuit of wealth for its own sake was not the slippery slope to corruption but in the interest of all. In the Netherlands, the Dutch jurist Hugo Grotius argued that the most fundamental law of nature was self-preservation, and that the next most natural human right was, therefore, self-interest. Pursuing self-interest (including the acquisition of personal wealth) was not, therefore, necessarily a bad thing. Not the mainstream, such ideas were nevertheless a sign of how far Europe by 1650 had come from the moral consensus which had dominated Christendom on the eve of the Reformation.

Thomas Hobbes, who had spent time in the company of French intellectuals, published his *Leviathan* in 1651. The title referred to the sea-monster, mentioned in the Bible and commonly taken as the hideous gatekeeper of Hell. In Hobbes's account, the 'Leviathan' is a morally neutral sovereign, ruling over human individuals, each governed by their selfish appetites and desires. These latter are, says Hobbes, neither good nor evil 'for these words . . . are ever used with relation to the person that useth them: there being nothing simply and absolutely so.' In a state of nature, every man has a right to everything, 'even to one another's body', which is why it was a competitive jungle in which the 'life of man was solitary, poor, nasty, brutish and short'. In Hobbes's formulation it was only the prudent pooling of self-interest which created the powers of the sovereign ruler, human beings agreeing to surrender some of their competitive instincts in order for the rule of law to frame a civil society. There was nothing, however, in Hobbes's account which made the pursuit of wealth and profit inherently good or bad, beyond what the sovereign ruler dictated it to be, and contemporaries glimpsed within the pages of his book a political universe in which social morality had become what the prince said it was.

5. Noble Pursuits

THE FORTUNES OF CHIVALRY

Nobility existed to defend Christendom by force of arms. Knighthood was the institution founded by the Church for the purpose. It centred on the rite of dubbing (or benediction), which conferred a grace upon the knight to enable him to fulfil his Christian duties. The aristocratic warrior code of chivalry, which had been promoted by the rituals and etiquette of the military orders, was gradually transformed in the later Middle Ages, partly through the influence of conduct books and a burgeoning vernacular romance literature, into a more general moral ethos. The complaint was already common by 1500 that chivalry was in decay. But early printed chivalric romances in poetry and prose in the vernacular were still hugely popular, the *Amadis de Gaule* (a French chivalric adventure, based on an earlier Spanish story) leading the way. For the young Philip II this was his favourite reading, the Arthurian romances organized at Binche in his honour in 1548 a realization of his chivalric dreams. The promotion of chivalric rituals such as dubbing and tourneys at princely courts, which declined only gradually towards the end of the sixteenth century, furnishes further evidence that chivalry became a way by which lay aristocratic élites retired from the increasing brutality of warfare into a make-believe world, peopled by perfect, gentle knights, one where troublesome clerics and protesting people did not exist.

So chivalry did not expire, but its meaning changed until, like Christendom, it became a fantasy land. Chivalry transmuted into a courtly code of aristocratic behaviour, reflecting the evolving nature of political authority and, with it, the obedience and service which were expected from its lay élites. As a military ethos it had perished amid conflicts fought not to protect Christendom from its enemies but to champion one version of Christianity against another and advance the dynastic objectives of princely houses over one another. Nobility, too, underwent considerable change in the same period. It came to signify hereditary social status, detached from military prowess. The majority of nobles in sixteenth- and seventeenth-century Europe never shattered a lance in battle even though they claimed the dignity of knighthood. To wear a sword, to claim membership of a knightly order, and to adopt the symbols and manners of chivalry became the marks of asserting noble distinction.

Giovanni Della Casa's *Galateo* (1558) turned the chivalric moral code into questions of noble distinction and comportment. Torquato Tasso restaged the First Crusade in a climate of personal and Counter-Reformation turmoil in his epic 'Jerusalem Delivered' (*Gerusalemme Liberata*, 1580). Love, heroism and self-sacrifice became the signs of true nobility in a world of moral degradation. A scene from the poem inspired the path-breaking operatic duet of Claudio Monteverdi, the 'Combat between Tancredi and Clorinda' (1624). Luís de Camões's *Os Lusíadas* (*The Lusiads*, 1572) deployed the chivalric romance to celebrate the Portuguese discovery of the ocean route to India, while Edmund Spenser's *Faerie Queene* (1590, 1596) transposed chivalry into a world of magic realism into which contemporaries could read glorified elements of the Elizabethan expeditions to Ireland and the Netherlands.

Chivalric romances were popular because they bridged the gap between noble reality and illusion. One work, above all the others, exposed that gap for what it was. Miguel de Cervantes Saavedra lived the ambiguities of the noble who sought to defend a Christendom that no longer existed, and about which he would later write in the *Ingenious Gentleman Don Quixote of La Mancha* (*El ingenioso hidalgo don Quijote de la Mancha*, 2 vols. – 1605/1615). He was from a parvenu noble family, his paternal grandfather being a merchant in Córdoba whose son became a lawyer for the treasury of the Spanish Inquisition and (thanks to aristocratic patronage) an appeal court judge. When contemporaries were asked whether the Cervantes were nobles or not, they said that they never seemed to pay taxes, that they dressed in silk, and that their 'sons were often to be seen jousting on good and powerful horses'. When the family fell on hard times, those sons sought ways of keeping up appearances while making their way in the world. But each attempt brought deception with it. Based in Seville for a time, Miguel sought passage to the Spanish New World, but was refused. Fleeing the consequences of a duel fought in the confines of the royal court at Madrid in late 1568, he entered service abroad, first in Rome to a cardinal, and then in Naples.

Like many of his contemporaries, Cervantes weighed up the advantages of being a noble of the pen rather than the sword: 'for though Letters have been the foundation of more estates than Arms, still soldiers have an indefinable superiority over men of letters and a certain splendour about them which puts them above everybody'. That led him to serve on a galleon at Lepanto along with his brother Roderigo. Miguel's left hand was smashed and his chest severely wounded in the battle. On his return to Spain in 1575 he was captured by corsairs and spent five years in an Algiers prison with a ransom of 5,000 *escudos* on his head. His family sold their possessions to help pay it, and petitioned the royal council in vain for aid towards his release. Miguel's own attempts to engineer his escape were pure adventure, it being a matter of luck that three Mercedarian friars, despatched from Valencia to secure the release of Christian slaves, were able to prise him from the clutches of a Greek renegade corsair in Algiers whose savagery was renowned. Forced to live by the pen rather than the sword, Cervantes became a munitions master in Andalusia for the Armada in 1587–8, which led to a spell in jail under suspicion of corruption, while his brother soldiered on with scant rewards in Flanders.

In prison, Miguel began writing the first chapters of what became the road novel adventures of Alonso Quijano, the retired country gentleman from a village in La Mancha, whose reading of books about chivalry so excited his imagination that he ceased to eat and sleep, such that 'his brain dried up and he went completely out of his mind'. Determined to become a knight-errant, he donned a suit of armour and renamed himself 'Don Quixote', setting off with a peasant farmer, Sancho Panza, as his squire, on a bony pony named 'Rocinante'. Don Quixote takes on all-comers in his attempt to be the knight-errant of his imagination in a world that seemed no longer Christendom. Each time he fails. In the most famous scene of all, Don Quixote spots some windmills on the horizon – part of the Extremadura landscape, they were also a symbol of Spain's Dutch rebels. 'Destiny guides our fortunes more favourably than we could have expected,' says Quixote. 'Look there, Sancho Panza, my friend, and see those thirty or so wild giants, with whom I intend to do battle ... This is noble, righteous warfare, for it is wonderfully useful to God to have such an evil race wiped from the face of the earth.' When told by the ever-practical Sancho Panza that they are not giants at all, Don Quixote replies with the optimism of the deluded: 'Obviously, you don't know much about adventures.' Sancho Panza's reply comes later in the book: 'I have heard tell that Fortune, as they call her, is a drunken and capricious woman.' The fortunes of being noble in the sixteenth and early seventeenth centuries depended more on Lady Luck than on protecting Christendom.

MARKS OF DISTINCTION

The dilemma for Europe's stratified societies was how to placate personal animus. Family feud and social envy were destructive in societies where wealth was limited, much sought after and gained at the expense of someone else. Their potential for harm was exacerbated by Reformation religious conflict. One way forward was through rituals of gesture and cultures of decorum that turned ways of behaviour into social distinction. In a society of orders, such marks of distinction were the daily manifestation of what held Christendom together.

In 1580, the Polish magnate Stanislaw Siecienski moved from Masovia to the borderland of southeast Poland around Przemyśl, a town among the noble latifundia of that region, bordering the route through the Carpathian Mountains to Hungary. There he constructed a new palace around a courtyard. Its sides represented the four quarters of the globe, and the oval towers erected at each extremity were dedicated to the pillars of the society of orders: the 'Divine', the 'Papal', the 'Royal' and the 'Noble'. The entrance was via a lake, traversed by a bridge leading to a gateway, topped by a square-shaped clock-tower. This was where the king and queen of Poland, Sigismund III and Constance of Austria, were welcomed as guests in 1608. Greetings and farewells were an essential part of the rituals of the society of orders. Nowhere were they more elaborate than in the Polish-Lithuanian 'nobleman's paradise'. To accompany the welcome there were several sorts of bowing, handshaking, kissing and knee-bending. The purpose of that tower was to enable servants to watch the road and announce approaching high-born visitors well in advance so the household could welcome them at the gate. Hats played an important part in the proceedings, doffed at the moment of the bow just deeply enough to sweep the floor. In Polish official proceedings, they were removed at every mention of the king or the pope. The physical embrace, initially regarded as a somewhat plebeian custom, became an indispensable element in noble social rituals. Peasants obligatorily kissed the hands of their lords, and minor nobility expected to do the same to their magnate superiors, who might take off their gloves, depending on the rank of the individual in question.

How you walked, dressed, spoke and rode were all signs of who you were. Books of etiquette told you how to use body language to master your emotions, and the space around you. Some gestures did not earn these books' approval, especially the male noble swagger adopted in so many paintings of this period. This posture – standing with one hand holding a baton, a whip or leather gloves, the weight on one leg and the other hand on the hip – could indicate statesmanlike restraint or peacock display. Either way it was assertive of space, moral and political. Franz Hals's *Cavalier* (1624) is not laughing with us; he is pushing his elbow in our faces.

Noble deportment was inculcated by tutors – and from around 1600 increasingly in academies specializing in the arts of riding and fencing. It was often taught through dance, that of the Polish nobility giving rise to the Polonaise, or 'walking dance', upon which travellers often commented. Transgressing social convention was increasingly difficult for those in upper ranks. King Sigismund III was ridiculed by the Polish gentry because of his fondness for playing football. Surviving family books from Polish nobles record the elaborate formulas setting down how to invite a neighbour to a hunt, to express condolences on someone's death or to congratulate them on a safe journey home. The silent revolution in Europe's thirst for communication created a greater awareness, too, of social distinction and the various ways of distancing social groups one from another. As the four towers of the Krasiczyn palace suggest, both the court and the Catholic Church had a great deal to do with the elaboration of rituals of distinction. But so, too, did the ambition to create a 'godly commonwealth' in which people knew their place and acted accordingly. This was what inspired the writings of Szymon Starowolski, himself from an impoverished Lithuanian noble family, who spent his life tutoring the sons of magnates. In the *Reform of Polish Customs* he presented an idealized world in which social gradations were each marked by different responsibilities.

Dreams of social harmony on the basis of social distinction were not new in Poland. Mikołaj Rej, a self-educated Polish noble of modest means and Protestant persuasions, made himself into a magnate owning several villages and a new town (named Rejowiec). His writings include a verse *Short Conversation between a Squire, a Bailiff and a Parson* (1543), in which the social evils of the day – ignorant clergy, grasping lawyers and the corruption of political life – were put under the spotlight. For Rej, the world was increasingly complicated. It was harder to live up to ideals of virtue and social harmony. He wanted to believe that the latter lay in the noble household where honesty was rewarded with loyalty from the servants. Yet in his verse drama 'The Merchant', he turned the conventional morality play on its head. The merchant in question is a social parasite who abandons his first wife ('Conscience') and has a son ('Profit') by his second ('Fortune'). At the Day of Judgment which ends the play (itself a parody of a Polish seigneurial court), the princes, bishop and bailiff invoke their virtues in vain and the merchant is saved, thanks to his faith in Christ's grace. In short, nothing was simple when it came to matching the ideal with the real world.

That did not stop Europe's élites from trying to make it so, through sumptuary legislation that covered a wide range of social behaviour, from dress to dining, from weeping at funerals to disorderly conduct at weddings. These laws became an increasing preoccupation of Europe's legislators, their increasing frequency perhaps evidence that they knew that they were fighting a losing battle. Yet the ordinances were not a sham; the problem was rather that legislation was an inappropriate way of preventing social distinctions being transgressed. Luxury knew no law, and rising anxieties about weakening social cohesion were reflected in reissued sumptuary laws. Legislators were on the horns of a dilemma because some luxury was to be encouraged since it demonstrated the power of a ruling élite. One of the paradoxes of the first half of the seventeenth century was that, at the same time as the more complex etiquettes of the 'society of orders' permeated its upper echelons, so the efforts to enforce them by legal means slackened. Some countries

(England in 1604) repealed their sumptuary legislation while others (the majority) silently let them pass into disuse.

The society of orders depended on social emulation. That, however, posed further dilemmas, since this was as likely to encourage the transgressing of boundaries as the reinforcement of them. To be a gentleman meant, as it had to the Cervantes family, behaving and dressing like a gentleman. Francesco Sansovino, for example, idealized the Venetian society to which he belonged as a world of social harmony where its patricians wore long black gowns in public as a sign of the ordered life of the republic. Yet he also noted the ostentatious displays of rich clothing as contemporaries engaged in conspicuous consumption. For this was a city where a humble oar-maker left among his possessions in 1633 six trunks containing forty-three shirts, where fabrics of all kinds were readily available, and where there was a market in second-hand clothing. It was not just at Carnival time that Venetians dressed up. In the painting of *The Tailor* (Giovanni Battista Moroni, *c.* 1565) the artisan in question is wearing a beautiful silk doublet and rich russet breeches while holding scissors, ready to slice into the black velvet for a patrician toga. Who, indeed, was the gentleman? Everywhere in Europe, the marks of distinction that defined gentility were becoming more elaborate. It is an understandable paradox that the ideals underpinning the society of orders became more insistently expressed even as weakening social cohesion was undermining the effort to legislate them into place.

PEDIGREE

Europe's nobility was a diverse, well-established and resilient group. Their grasp of wealth, power and status required constant and sometimes ruthless adaptation. They concentrated their resource base in landownership in some parts of Europe, diversified into other investments and activities in others. It was a survival of the fittest, since there was no more potentially violent force in European society than its nobility. The weakest members – poor nobles, rich in lineage perhaps but weak in resources – went to the wall, unable to live the life that their status dictated. They were replaced with new blood, either through artificial elevations of new families to nobility in reward for their service to monarchies and states, or through hypogamy ('marrying down') that had long protected Europe's nobility from what would otherwise have been its inevitable extinction. The ideology justifying rank and privilege was not service to Christendom but pedigree.

Genealogy had strong biblical legitimacy, through the patriarchs of the Old Testament to Christ himself. It was male-dominated since biblical begetting was largely from father and son. Pedigree was not confined to nobility or gentry, not even to human beings. It was individual and corporate, part of a chain of being that extended to the animal kingdom. Genealogy had immediate and practical significance (who inherited, who succeeded), but it was also the key to patrimony and legitimacy. In all Europe's customary laws, the concern was always the continuity of a lineage, even though it might be secured by various means. There were no better claims to legitimacy in this period than lineage. Ancestor-worship was a way of justifying the status quo and also a spur to be worthy of one's forebears. The unfortunately named Suckbitches, a modest gentry family in Devon, knew that they had made it since, as one of them said in the later sixteenth century, 'it had pleased God to continue one name [i.e. *theirs*] amongst a thousand, to enjoy a place so many ages'. That entitled them to look down on their richer noble neighbours, the Courtneys.

Recording one's ancestry was important. The early seventeenth-century Welsh antiquary George Owen Harry advised any Welsh gentleman of the 'meaner sort' to have his family pedigree written out for him. If the gentleman could not name by memory his four great-grandfathers and their wives he could only be 'out of love with himselfe'. Christoph von Zimmern spared no effort in compiling the chronicle of his Swabian noble family, complete with richly coloured blazons. Lineage mattered since evidence of ancestral right frequently figured in property disputes and claims to privilege. Ancestry could claim you a place in an aristocratic retinue, a family pew or grave, and an entry to a college or university. Humanist writers fashionably proclaimed that true nobility lay in virtue and education. It sounded plausible enough, but everyone knew that, in reality, pedigree mattered more, which was why such strenuous efforts went into proclaiming and proving it.

Lineage was paraded, painted, emblemized and documented. When the French king Francis I processed ceremonially into Lyon in 1515, the Valois dynasty was portrayed before him in a painting like the tree of

Jesse. When Archduchess Isabella entered Brussels in 1615, she did so accompanied by a wrought-iron mantle depicting her ancestors. Chancels and naves, fireplaces and charitable foundations afforded opportunities for genealogical self-fashioning. Coats of arms and heraldic devices permeated Europe's architecture and material possessions. Through funerary lozenges and monuments, stained glass and ceramics, silverware and furniture, the nobility stamped themselves on their environment, a constructive revalorization of the past, circulated to sustain the present.

What circulated was creative if not invented; new noble blood in old family bottles, spurious claims that the aggressive pre-eminence of the Russell, Howard, Cecil, Sidney or Holles families (to take only English examples) prevented contemporaries from examining too closely. Some claims relied on oral testimony. The Yorkshire-born Sir Thomas Wentworth, in high favour under King Charles I, had his family's ancient pre-eminence confirmed when his father reported that he had 'herde that our name and progenie hath for a long tyme before the Conquest bene of worship and reputation', vaguely recalling that 'thear are att this daie in the Lowe Countries records thereof in some towne'. Yet the nobility had to adapt to the increasing importance of the written record. Rulers wanted registers of who really was noble. In England, that was the task of the heralds, incorporated into a 'college of arms' in 1555. Thomas Benolt, officer of the Court of Heralds, was the first to conduct a regional inspection of all those claiming armorial bearings excluding the peerage, gentry being required to appear before him with their written evidence. The objective was not so much to limit the creation of new nobles as to regulate and profit from the privilege concerned.

Across the Channel, claims to nobility led to exemption from taxation and antipathy to noble interlopers. The response was to appoint commissioners to investigate noble titles, in which families were required to prove that their title went back three generations. The nobility of Lower Normandy was subjected to examination eight times between 1500 and 1650 and the results were not foregone conclusions. The investigation around Caen in 1634–5 found 114 out of the 994 families could not prove their titles. In other parts of Europe, such investigations were carried out more summarily. In 1626 King Gustav Adolf of Sweden unilaterally repudiated the claims of three quarters of those claiming noble status (from 400 to just 126) on the grounds that they were too poor to claim the status.

The pedigree craze led to antiquaries being commissioned to research and publish lineage. John Lambert of Kirkby Malham, grandfather to the Cromwellian major-general of the same name, counted himself an amateur genealogist and found a companion of William the Conqueror, Ranulph de Lambert, from whom he claimed to be descended, publishing forged charters that he had probably concocted himself. William Cecil, Elizabeth I's secretary of state, financed research to prove that he was descended from Welsh princes who had been companions of King Harold, his son Robert finding it tiresome ('these vain toys ... such absurdities'). By the early seventeenth century, no one would doubt the ancestry of a Cecil. By 1650, the nobility was on the way to being a more classified and defined élite, for whom lineage constituted their right to own and to rule.

Genealogies were presented in different ways, but the problem was how to represent two different realities: lineage and consanguinity. The latter was important, not least to prevent the intermarriage of close cousins. Roman jurists developed a way of charting it, but it deracinated lineage by emphasizing collateral relationships with other families. By emphasizing marriage, it suggested that lineage was not necessarily masculine, as indeed it was not. In German genealogical trees the line was sometimes presented as coming from the stomach of the woman. In England, there was a custom of presenting marriages in genealogies as handshakes from one lozenge to another, with the offspring emerging from the conjoined hands. Either way, the spotlight was placed on marriage.

How to make a good noble marriage? The experience was rather like playing contract bridge with an unreliable partner. There were so many variables to take into account: the age of a potential spouse, her likely capacity to bring heirs to the marriage, her relatives and connections, how her estates complemented one's own, what her prospects were as a potential heiress. In the circumstances, there was often not much room for affection as the basis for marriage, even if there is plenty of evidence that it could be a result of it. Celibacy was frequently the preferred option, thereby threatening the continuity of noble lineages. In parts of northern Italy (the Venetian terra firma and the duchy of Milan, for example) the custom was to restrict marriage to one male per generation in order to avoid the proliferation of collateral lines. Aristocrats could rely on princely courts as the best marriage market, and diplomats, magistrates and financial councillors as shrewd match-makers. Princes might, however, interfere. French kings regularly prevented matches or imposed others upon unwilling families. In England, the Court of Wards and Liveries, established in 1540 and abolished along with all feudal tenures at the end of the Civil War in 1646, exploited the prerogative right of the monarchy to take into its care the orphaned heirs of the aristocracy, an opportunity to exploit their estates and have a say in their marriages. Aristocrats could expect to play the marriage market well. Not so the middle and lower ranks of the nobility upon whom the fate of the class as a whole depended. The sharply rising cost of dowries – evident for all noble groups across this period – was making it harder to keep up.

LIVING NOBLY

Noble privileges lay at the heart of a society of orders. They were an essential part of 'living nobly'. Such privileges varied widely across Europe and they tended to overlap with those enjoyed by commoners. Moreover, especially in the stronger polities of western Europe, they were eroded under state pressure. They were often the subject of debates which, either implicitly or explicitly, led to anxiety and sensitivity about the nature of nobility.

The almost universal privilege was the right to carry weapons, typically a sword. Nothing charts more graphically the challenges to Christendom than the advent of the long, thin laminated steel rapier. Lightweight, carried on a belt at the waist, these weapons were designed for the courtyard rather than the battlefield. It needed skill and practice to use them against an opponent similarly armed. Manuals offered technical advice and, from the 1570s, incorporated engravings that turned interpersonal fighting into a science. Girard Thibault's *Academy of the Sword* (1626) was a sumptuous folio which included forty-six engravings of duelling duos in action. In reality, a good fencing instructor was indispensable, and there were plenty around, the best being reputedly the Italians, retained by Europe's princely aristocrats.

Duelling became an expression of noble consciousness in some parts of Europe. It had hitherto existed as part of judicial combat, a sanctioned means of settling quarrels between nobles by asking God to decide the outcome in battle. One of the last such judicial duels was the high-profile encounter between François de Vivonne, sieur de La Châtaigneraie, and Guy Chabot, count of Jarnac, in Paris on 10 July 1547. Private duelling, by contrast, reached epidemic proportions in parts of Europe, travelling northwards from Italy to France and thence to England. This was despite condemnation from on high. The Council of Trent forbade it. King Henry III declared it a capital offence in France in 1576. James VI and I outlawed it too. Writing in 1609, the Parisian diarist Pierre de L'Estoile reckoned that 7–8,000 French noblemen had lost their lives in duels in the previous twenty years. His estimate may be inflated but he was writing about a France that had lived through forty years of intermittent civil war and its accompanying encouragement to noble feud and division.

The reality was that duelling reflected how sophisticated and deep-rooted the noble honour code had become. For its aficionados, it was the public defence of honour and, as Jesuits argued in defence of duelling, since honour is as precious as property one should be entitled to defend it. Treatises on noble honour and its defence abounded, mostly unreadable and lampooned by Touchstone in Shakespeare's *As You Like It*. In fact, the majority of Italian duels were exercises not in killing someone but in the art of going through the motions of a fight while leaving the door open to an honourable reconciliation. Annibale Romei's 1585 treatise on the subject (translated into English as *The Courtiers Academie* in 1598) began from the proposition that duelling should not happen and that it had been banned. So it included sections on how to reconcile quarrels and the face-saving formulas that one could use to resolve a dispute.

Exemption from paying taxes was traditionally a key mark of nobility. In fact, it had never been an exclusive one. Large numbers of commoners enjoyed fiscal exemptions. So, for example, when the Swedish crown wanted to encourage the peasantry of Finland or the Baltic seaboard of Pomerania to serve in its cavalry in the Thirty Years War it accorded them hereditary tax exemption on their lands. Nor was tax exemption enjoyed by all nobility. Nobles in Tuscany, Venice, East Prussia and the British Isles paid taxes and their nobility was not compromised. Where tax exemptions existed, they tended to be diluted or diminished in various ways. As states had greater recourse to indirect taxes, so the nobility found themselves paying their share. In Saxony, nobles were required to pay taxes on their estates in 1529, 1541–2 and 1557, or to make voluntary 'free gifts' to the ruler's exchequer, as in 1622. Nobles were taxed for failing to turn out for cavalry service or required to pay feudal dues as tenants-in-chief. Exemptions tied to particular noble property rather than to the person were widespread. With a busy land market and the impact of generations of noble succession, a mismatch between noble status and tax exemption became prevalent.

In some places, noble fiscal exemption was a consequence of service to the prince in a military or administrative capacity, which meant that nobility was accorded to the legal and medical professions. In Spain, it was a benefit for lay members of the Inquisition. In France, the immunity was the fruit of royal office and, as the weight of the French state grew in this period, so did the number of its administrators. Office could be bought, and with it came immunity from direct tax. One of the main perquisites of French royal offices was that they fell outside the customary laws governing landed property and so were treated as 'movable goods'. So an office could serve as part of a dowry, the guarantee on a loan, the payment of a debt or to gratify a younger son who might otherwise be excluded from the inheritance. But, in addition, the exemption from direct tax could become hereditary if you could prove that your family had been noble and tax exempt for three generations. A new, articulate ruling group was emerging, sometimes referred to in the early seventeenth century as the 'nobility of the robe' from the long gowns worn by judges and officials.

Similar developments occurred elsewhere in Europe as its states confronted the changing demands upon them. From the early sixteenth century, the councils and law courts of the Spanish Habsburg empire were staffed by university-trained administrators (letrados). There, as in England, the proliferation in the ranks of its civil servants was accompanied by the added esteem which accrued to those close to power and influence. Many of Spain's senior letrados were rewarded with titles of nobility: 'If before, grandees were greater than letrados,' wrote Don Diego Ramirez de Prado to one of his brothers in 1641, 'now letrados have become the grandees.' He knew of what he spoke since another brother, Don Alonso, a member of the Council of Castile, enjoyed nobility and the spoils of office before he was arrested for peculation in 1607. The rise of administrator families challenged conventional notions of nobility. They proclaimed themselves a nobility of virtue rather than valour, one in which humanist education provided training in self-disciplined restraint, more important than the self-protection afforded by the rapier. And such education was open to those of talent and not just those of noble birth.

NOBLES BY NUMBERS

Counting Europe's nobility is not easy before 1650, and regional variations were considerable and inexplicable. In the region around Alençon in France, the nobility were relatively thick on the ground (230 per 386 square miles by 1667), five times as numerous as in neighbouring Anjou and sixteen times more plentiful than in the Limousin. France, however, was part of Christendom's heartland where, in common with Germany, Bohemia, Lower Austria, the Netherlands and the Italian peninsula, nobles were not a large proportion of the population. With some exceptions (the Basque country and Navarre, for example), they were generally not more than 5 per cent of the population, and mostly the figure was lower – sometimes close to or below 1 per cent. Europe's republics were particularly parsimonious in creating nobles. In Venice, the nobility were a high-born caste of only twenty-eight clans in the early sixteenth century, the status being preserved by admitting only a select few to appear in the Golden Book, the register of its ranks, instituted in 1577. The Swiss cantons, some city-states (for instance, Geneva) and Balkan regions (notably Serbia and Bulgaria) proclaimed that they had no indigenous nobility at all.

The need to defend Christendom against its external enemies was only one reason for its more populous noble margins. The periphery also never experienced feudal overlordship, so nobility was personal and not restricted by the legal constraints of holding a tenured barony. In some places to the east, too, group ennoblement was used as a privilege to encourage settlers into border areas and impose military obligations on them. In other regions, grants of nobility resulted from enfeebled states which had difficulty in controlling tacit ennoblement. In Castile, municipalities created nobles by accepting a head of household as a 'commoner knight' (*caballero villano*), and thus exempt from taxation on the local register, in return for a fee.

In frontier regions with smaller densities of population, the nobility managed to retain or even expand their numbers as a proportion of the population. In 1591, nobles made up over 46 per cent of the population of the provinces of Burgos and León in the north of Spain, and a majority of the population in towns such as Burgos itself. In Polish Masovia and Podlachia, the nobility composed at least 20 per cent of the population. There were places (over 1,600 in Masovia alone) where villages were composed uniquely of noble tenant farmers who rented and worked peasant holdings. The division of land holdings as a result of partible inheritance, however, reduced nobles to more or less landless status, creating the paradox of peasants with noble status.

Something similar happened to the increasingly populous nobility of Hungary. In the years following the Turkish occupation of the lower Danube in 1526, the Habsburg rulers of western Hungary took to ennobling those who would provide mounted service against the Ottomans. Serfs became nobles overnight. But the Danube basin was one of the parts of Europe where customary law protected lineage by an extreme form of partible inheritance. All the daughters as well as the sons were entitled to up to a quarter of the estate upon succession. In addition, there were strict customary restrictions on the mortgage and sale of noble estates. So, as in Poland, many Hungarian nobles became landless, serving in due course as mercenaries, traders, craftsmen and the servitors of other nobles. There were no derogation statutes (laws making the practice of 'menial' activities incompatible with noble status) and many of these nobles ended up working peasant tenures, no more capable of signing their name than their peasant neighbours. As their landed and economic capital declined, so these lesser nobles hung on to their cultural capital the more fervently. Obsessed with the militarized (Magyar, Sarmatian, Rus) mythologies of the past, living in their modest wattle houses with thatched roofs, they peered suspiciously at the outside world.

A more noticeable transformation took place among Europe's higher, titled aristocracy – its dukes and peers. Except as a special right accorded to members of royal families such titled nobility hardly existed before 1500. By the 1630s, however, titled aristocrats had mainly taken over as the means by which states admitted new families to the ranks of the highest nobility. The rise of the peerage was the result of princely efforts to control their nobility and, from the prince's point of view it had much to commend it. Letters patent for a peerage involved no investment; rather the reverse, since they could be sold or turned into a reward for services rendered. The result was an inflation of honours, the equivalent to what was happening to currencies, a progressive and corrosive devaluation in what 'honour' was worth.

Some regions acquired titled nobility for the first time (Hungary, Sweden, Denmark). Elsewhere, it was massively expanded. In England, the monarchy sold baronetcies and peerages in profusion in the early seventeenth century. King James I similarly tripled the number of English knights. In France, the expansion in the peerage included the controversial elevation of foreign families. Membership of the knightly Order of St-Michel was used as an alternative to paying those who served the king in the civil wars of the later sixteenth century. The resulting debasement in the honorific standing of the chivalric orders and the opposition from malcontent nobles to his rule led the last Valois king, Henry III, to institute the Knights of the Holy Spirit (1579), limited to a hundred at any one time. In Spain, the monarchy began to expand its titled nobility from 1520 (grandes or títulos; collateral lines – segundones or mesnaderos). The numbers of knights (caballeros) habited by the three military orders also increased. These wealthy foundations held the rights to grant admission to their order (creating caballeros de hábito) which guaranteed the essential quality of nobility (hidalguía). The status was much sought after because rigorous proof was demanded by the general chapters of the orders that those admitted were free from all trace of Jewish or Moorish blood, their pedigree equally unsullied by victims of the Inquisition. To be admitted to a military order advanced one's prospects of making a good marriage in Spanish society. With an empire to protect, however, Philip IV and his first minister, Count-Duke Olivares, put admission to the orders up for sale. The king told his council in 1625: 'Without reward and punishment no monarchy can be preserved. Now rewards may be either financial or honorific. Money we have not, so we have thought it right and necessary to remedy the fault by increasing the number of honours.' Olivares said that the privileges were given to those whose merit would have led them to be regarded as noble in any case. But the proofs for purity of blood were relaxed, and the resulting criticisms were directed at the monarchy itself as the architect of noble corruption.

In many parts of Europe, the upper fringe of titled nobility's resources came disproportionately (in comparison with the rest of the noble order) from the state. Despite their landed resources, aristocrats became dependent on their income from the emoluments of court office, provincial governorships and lieutenancies, and other lucrative revenue streams from heading up tax-farm consortia or speculating in government debt. They also sought a separate political identity. In those states where the nobility already possessed two chambers of delegates in provincial assemblies (Aragon, Hungary, Bohemia), the titled nobility wanted exclusive rights to the upper assemblies. In the Swedish national assembly the nobles were divided into a hierarchy of three groups from 1626 onwards, each voting separately. In the Scottish Parliament by the end of the sixteenth century, lairds and peers sat apart, albeit in the same assembly. Lesser nobilities were suspicious of their courtier and magnate superiors. In Poland the lesser nobility coalesced into military confederations in the course of the first half of the sixteenth century using the national and provincial assemblies (the Sejm and sejmiks) to force the crown to repossess crown lands that had been progressively sold off to magnates. From 1548 to 1563, anti-magnate sentiments were at their height, giving the lesser nobility a sense of political purpose.

The extremes of rich and poor grew greater among the nobility as in the rest of society. Poor nobles were the structural consequence of the mismatch between noble status and wealth. The political problems they posed, however, were widely recognized and becoming more pronounced. 'A numerous nobility causeth poverty,' wrote Francis Bacon in 1605, 'for it is a surcharge of expense; and besides, it being of necessity, that many of the nobility fall, in time, to be weak in fortune, it maketh a kind of disproportion, between honour and means.' Falstaff and Don Quixote were figures of fun on stage and in print, part of the evidence that mocking the nobility was fair game. In Lope de Vega's play *Fuenteovejuna* (1612–14) enraged peasants from the village of that name (now called Fuente Obejuna) murder Fernán Gómez de Guzmán, their local squire (a *comendador mayor* of the Order of Calatrava), in revenge for his oppression. The plot was more social comment than black comedy. In southwest Corsica, a handful of feudatory nobles hung on to their rights to extract tax from their peasants on behalf of the Genoese state. Exploiting their distance and isolation from the centre of power, they had extraordinary authority over their peasantry. From their fortified farmsteads the Bozzi, d'Ornano and Istria clans quarrelled, rustled sheep and squeezed all they could out of the local population. The Genoese state turned a blind eye until August 1615 when the house of the

Bozzi was set on fire and various members of the clan were butchered by their peasants. Wherever the state found itself in contention with local populations, there was generally a role among its opponents for the nobility (constrained to act or willing participants, it is often hard to judge), long in lineage, local prestige and pretension, but impoverished, disruptive, disrespectful of judicial authority and procedure, and with a sense that the world owed them something.

NOBLE FORTUNES

Rich and poor nobles had always existed, and the relationship between the two determined the evolution of noble fortunes and their relationship to the rest of society too. If there had been a Forbes ranking of the richest individuals in sixteenth- and seventeenth-century Europe (excluding its princely rulers), it would probably have indicated that the number of very rich nobles had grown substantially larger between 1500 and 1650. The opportunities for wealth acquisition and concentration became greater as aristocrats found ways of exploiting expanding state power to their advantage, tapping into Europe's capital markets (and running colossal debts as a result), and maximizing the benefits of landed power. Aristocratic wealth intersected with princely power, growing alongside it and correspondingly vulnerable when it was weak.

A snapshot album of the wealthiest nobles in later sixteenth- and early seventeenth-century Europe would certainly have to include Alonso Pérez de Guzmán el Bueno y Zúñiga, seventh duke of Medina Sidonia – holder of the oldest aristocratic title in Spain and owner of one of the most colossal fortunes of his day. It was partly based around the massive latifundia estates that the family owned in Andalusia – an estimated 90,000 vassals and a rent roll of 150,000 ducats – his landed interests covered half the province of Huelva. In 1588, he was chosen by Philip II to lead the *Felicissima Armada* after the death of Álvaro de Bazán, marquis of Santa Cruz. Historians have generally been puzzled by the appointment – by his own admission he had 'no knowledge or experience of the sea'. His fortune, however, was what counted since it enabled him to be the Armada's subcontractor. Medina Sidonia was an able manager of his estates and interests and his wealth also came from his posts at court. He already had the huge contract for building and running the Spanish galley fleet in 1574, partly because he offered not to charge interest if the treasure ships from the New World were delayed in arriving at Cádiz. When trying to decline his appointment in 1588, the duke argued that he could not possibly take it on because he was 900,000 ducats in debt; he had 'not one *real* to spend on the expedition'. Somehow, the good duke managed to raise the vast sum of 7 million *maravedís* to underwrite the underprepared and underfunded expedition at a crucial moment.

His grandson, Gaspar Alfonso, ninth duke of Medina Sidonia, found it harder to protect that fortune in the 1640s. Implicated in the Andalusian rebellion of the summer of 1641, he was stripped of his offices, exiled from his estates, forced to pay a humiliating 'gracious gift' to the crown, and could not save the head of his relative, the marquis of Ayamonte, who confessed to having supported plans for an Andalusian 'commonwealth'. His execution paralleled that of Henry II, duke of Montmorency, in France in 1632, an exemplary punishment to discourage other would-be aristocratic rebels. Despite having played leading parts in the Fronde and other uprisings in the middle of the century, Europe's aristocracy was generally treated leniently by those in charge of the state, who had discovered that keeping aristocrats at court was a more effective way of emasculating their political potential. The one exception was the English aristocracy, all of whom lost their titles after the English Civil War, saw their feudal dues abolished in 1646, and the majority of their estates and revenues confiscated as well. Since the English peerage owned about a quarter of the country (only in central Europe could comparable percentages of land in the hands of the higher aristocracy be found), it was the most spectacular and consequential capsizing of an aristocratic ruling élite anywhere in Europe before 1789.

Jan Zamoyski would also find his place among the wealthiest of Europe's aristocrats. From a family of modest gentry in Masovia, he became a leading Polish-Lithuanian magnate, first duke of Zamość, and perhaps the most underrated political figure of the period. Well educated (he studied at the universities of Paris and Padua), he put the learning to good use in a series of books (including one on *The Roman Senate*, whose principles of rule he emulated) and half a lifetime of service as Lord Grand-Chancellor of Poland from 1578 (responsible for domestic and foreign affairs) and Grand Hetman (in charge of the army) from 1581. He founded the town of Zamość, built as a model city to designs by the

Italian architect Bernardo Morando and settled with Sephardic Jews. At its centre lay the Zamoyski Palace, the focus for an aristocratic patrimony the size of a country. By his death in 1605, he was the magnate of eleven cities and 200 villages (covering about 2,500 square miles) as well as royal steward with extensive interests in a further 112 cities and 612 villages. Zamoyski shrewdly headed up the reformist-minded middle and lesser nobility of the Commonwealth who became known in some quarters as 'his people' (*zamojczycy* – a play upon his name). No one else in Europe in the sixteenth century was a king-maker like Zamoyski (he orchestrated the election of three kings of Poland). Towards the end of his life he was tempted to dethrone one of them, the Vasa king Sigismund III, whose absolutist tendencies he resisted. That was remembered a generation later when, in the time of the 'Polish Deluge' (1648–67), the Zamoyski estates were (along with those of other Polish-Lithuanian magnates) ransacked by Swedish troops.

The commander of these Swedish troops was Magnus Gabriel de la Gardie. He was then at the height of royal favour in Sweden. He had been the general of its armies at the end of the Thirty Years War (for which he received the princely reward of 22,500 *riksdalers* – more than any other Swedish general) and became Governor-General of Livonia. De la Gardie presented Queen Christina in 1650 with a silver throne for her coronation. He was just one of those aristocrats whose fortunes come from military enterprising in the period of the Thirty Years War (Johan Banér; Bernard of Saxe-Weimar; Louis, prince of Condé and others). His income equalled a fifth of that of the Swedish state, and he spent it on buildings. His largest castle (he had many) contained 248 rooms. In 1652, he inherited from his father the Makalös Palace in Stockholm, the most lavish private residence by far in the capital, transforming it into a treasure house for the precious objects that he had looted from central Europe in the war. When the backlash among Sweden's lesser nobility eventually occurred, the commission of inquiry set up in 1675 to look into the fortunes of de la Gardie and his aristocratic friends hardly knew where to begin. The commissioners eventually calculated that 4 million *riksdalers* of public assets had passed into their hands, and fined de la Gardie himself a colossal 352,159 *riksdalers*.

Cardinal Richelieu, who also began life as a nobleman of modest means, was more fortunate. He died in 1642 with his fortune intact and still in high royal favour – worth at least 20 million *livres* including 4 million in cash – a sum that would have equalled the yearly income of 4,000 of his ordinary noble countrymen. Cardinals had been among the wealthiest individuals in Europe in 1500 and, in that particular respect, the religious reformations of the sixteenth century might as well not have happened, for they were still among Europe's very rich, although in Richelieu's case his wealth came from a portfolio of state and ecclesiastical interests. Richelieu's successor as cardinal first-minister, Jules Mazarin, found it harder than Richelieu to retain the fortune which he acquired. Vulnerable to the charge of profiteering from the French state in the upheavals of the Frondes, he voluntarily withdrew from France, transferring what he could into conveniently transportable assets (especially diamonds). When he died, he left a fortune estimated at between 18 and 40 million *livres*.

Concentrating on visible magnate fortunes, and on the gap between rich and poor nobles, obscures another, more important theme in this period: the consolidation and expansion of the middle ranks of the nobility. The story here was one of group rather than individual success. The nobility kept traces of their ancient origins while being replenished with new blood and finding new ways of exploiting the human and biological resources to hand. This is the picture revealed by a study of the nobility in the area around Bayeux in Normandy for this period. The overall size of the group grew considerably between 1523 and 1666, with 477 families entering the nobility, of which half were migrants, mostly from other parts of the province. The latter replaced those families who fell extinct, or who dropped out of the noble order through poverty and not being able to 'live nobly'. But such extinction, although remorseless, was not wholesale. In the duchy of Savoy, almost 50 per cent of the noble families in 1700 could reliably claim that they had been ennobled before 1563 (the origins of just over 20 per cent were not known). The nobility of the Beauce (according to an inquiry in 1667) contained only a minority of families ennobled since 1560 – forty-two, as against eighty-seven ennobled before 1560. In the course of the sixteenth and seventeenth centuries, the English gentry doubled their share of the ownership of England's land from about a quarter to a half. The rise of the gentry was not an exclusively English affair though it remains the clearest example of the more general phenomenon.

DOMAIN TRIUMPHS

The enlargement of the middle ranks of the nobility occurred because they were able to take advantage of economic change through the management of their principal asset, land. How to expand the efficiently managed domain was the challenge for the nobility. In western Europe, it involved a combination of some direct exploitation along with farming out the rest. In eastern Europe, the expansion of domain exploitation was accomplished through serf labour. The revenues to be derived from seigneurial dues were (in common with the increasing monetization of the economy in general) increasingly paid in cash rather than in kind in western Europe. Once monetized, these resources suffered from the impact of inflation. In general, seigneurial revenues had already begun to fall as a proportion of the overall value of estates before 1500 and that process accelerated during the next century and a half. There was, however, still significant value in some of the casual revenues in a seigneurie, especially from the 'quit-rents' (*cens*) to be paid on the transfer of title from one peasant to another. Domains could be exploited further by encroaching on common land and rights of access to it (although it risked local opposition). Landlords also expanded the marginal economic advantages of their domains, especially the forests and monopoly rights. The buoyant market for wood in the sixteenth and early seventeenth centuries was one that they could tap into – especially desirable since the proceeds could be turned into ready money.

The nobility wanted to acquire more land. They did so, purchasing it for the best price they could, and were prepared to mortgage themselves to do so. One of the least noticed but most significant drivers for change in early-modern Europe was the unprecedented market in domain land. Transfers occurred on a scale that would not be seen again in Europe before the end of the eighteenth century. Princely rulers sold off to their nobilities what was left of their crown lands in order to finance the competitive expansion of their states. The Austrian Habsburg monarchy largely divested itself of its crown estates in the period between 1575 and 1625. When the French monarchy tried to sell off its royal domains it encountered the determined opposition of its own courts, but eventually face-saving legal formulas were developed to alienate it legally, as occurred in the wars of religion.

Following the Protestant Reformation in Prussia, the extensive domains of the Order of Teutonic Knights were 'secularized' in 1525: the lands of the order escheated to a new 'duke of Prussia', some of them remaining in the hands of knights who became Lutherans and converted, others being sold on. The Habsburg monarchy confiscated and sold on to its nobility perhaps half of all the property of the kingdom of Bohemia following the country's unsuccessful effort to throw off Habsburg rule in 1618–20. The Palatine princes saw their lands confiscated by the Spaniards in the aftermath of their expulsion from the Rhine Palatinate in 1621. Similar confiscations were threatened by the imperial forces as they moved northwards in the later 1620s towards the Baltic. Less than two decades afterwards, the victorious Swedish army commanders found themselves rewarded with estates in their newly acquired provinces of Swedish Pomerania. In Germany, the Low Countries and England, domain land sales accompanied the Protestant Reformation as states took over monastic properties and then sold them off. About a quarter of England's land came up for transfer in under two decades (1536–53).

In Ireland, meanwhile, the Tudor state reinforced its authority over the indigenous clans and their leaders by using an unsuccessful rebellion as a pretext for extending English law of individual property rights into a country where clan rendered them meaningless. By the principle of 'Surrender and Regrant', Irish clan chiefs were required to give up their hereditary rights in order to have them restored to them as tenants-in-chief of the English king (*ex dono regis*). This seemingly anodyne legal fiction was in reality a massive confiscation, one which laid the basis for the next century of English colonialism in Ireland. Domain title passed from the Irish lord to the English king, and what the king gave, he could take away and assign to others. The Anglo-Irish gentry living around Dublin in the area already dominated by the English (the Pale) took the lead. Aided by commercial interests in England they pushed for the unilateral confiscation of the counties of Leix and Offaly in 1557, transforming them into the Queen's County and King's County, two thirds of the land being regranted to English colonizers to form estates. This was the first 'plantation' of its kind and it actually occurred at the close of the reign of the Catholic Mary I. So religion was not essential to the English colonialism of Ireland, though it certainly increasingly served as its pretext and justification.

English aristocrats confectioned genealogies to establish their rights to possess the land of Ireland in cahoots with adventurers and administrators from the Pale. Gaelic chiefs responded with determined rebellion, only to give ground eventually before the military force of the Tudor state. The revolt of Gerald Fitzgerald, count of Desmond, which took in the province of Munster up to the Wicklow mountains in 1586, was followed (for example) by a further plantation in which almost all the region was confiscated and granted out to a small group of speculative 'undertakers', who undertook to establish their estates with English colonists and drive the Irish out. In the short term, it seemed to work. With the flight of the earls of Tyrone and Tyrconnel in 1609, a further half a million acres were confiscated and resettled by English and Scottish (mainly Presbyterian) planters in Ulster, the latter widening further the social basis of the emigration involved, since the Presbyterian dissenters from lowland Scotland were mostly not from the social élites.

The Stuart monarchy was readily persuaded that plantation was justified, and that it worked. The English attorney general, Sir John Davies, explained that earlier English colonization had failed because it had neglected to pursue determined military conquest and follow it up with the imposition of law. Both conquest and law were essential to sovereignty. Ireland must 'be first broken by a warre, before it will be capable of good Government'. Irish laws and customs seemed to Sir John Davies to prove that the Irish were 'little better than cannibals': 'all their possessions [are] uncertain' and 'every man being born to Land, as well Bastard, as Legitimate, they all held themselves to be Gentlemen'. English colonialism in Ireland was justified, not merely because it was part of God's Protestant providential dispensation and King James I's will, but because it was civilizing the Irish. Such justifications were no different from those that were used in London by the Virginia Company and its supporters to justify colonization in North America. In the later 1620s and 30s Charles I and his viceroy in Ireland, Sir Thomas Wentworth, pushed the politics of plantation to its extreme limits, confiscating Connaught, Clare and Ormonde to found new plantations of Anglican colonists in the midwest of Ireland, seeking to counter the influence of the Presbyterians in Ulster and balance the books of the Stuart monarchy. It aroused the indignation of the earlier colonial settlers in Ireland as well as the native Irish. The resulting rebellion in October 1641 led to brutality that some contemporaries compared to the massacre of

English colonists at Virginia on 22 March 1622, where land transfer was also one of the issues at stake.

Domain land transfer characterized Spanish colonization in Mexico, Peru and Chile in the foundation of latifundia domains (*encomiendas*), modelled on the ranching estates that were an essential part of the agrarian economy of the Extremadura region around Seville. Landlord rights were granted to Spanish colonists (*encomenderos*). Portuguese colonization in Brazil (especially from 1580 onwards) was characterized by sugar, and later tobacco, plantations, domain agriculture on a hitherto undreamed-of commercial scale and complexity. Back in Europe Catholic Church lands were vulnerable to transfer into lay hands, especially where the defence of the Church against the Protestant onslaught offered a convenient justification for it. In France, five successive alienations of Church wealth took place during the civil wars albeit, in many cases, with the possibility of repurchase later on being included in the sale. In Spain, the Church was divested of hundreds of thousands of villagers as its domains were sold off to pay contributions to the Habsburg monarchy's war efforts against Protestantism to the north.

Such transfers of property rights emphasized the significance of contracts, and the importance of the legal mechanisms to enforce them. Contracts of all sorts – indentures for apprenticeship, new instruments of credit and debt, trading ventures – served to abstract property rights from landed property and distance 'wealth' from 'landed wealth'. 'Contract' even became a way of envisaging political authority. The Dutch Revolt was presented and justified by contemporary theorists as occurring because of a breach of contract by Philip II, who had failed to protect the ancient liberties of the Low Countries as guaranteed by charters. Similar arguments would be applied by Protestant political theorists during the civil wars of late sixteenth-century France and, later, in the English Civil Wars. The arguments carried more weight because of the emphasis placed in some Protestant circles on the notion that God and his chosen people were bound by mutual promises and obligations, reflected in the Old Testament account of a king's relationship with the Hebrew people. Such arguments were the more convincing, however, especially in those parts of western Europe where the notion of 'contract' as a way of delineating wealth as possession had become commonplace, not least among the nobility.

Domain land transfers favoured the secular nobilities of Europe, and especially their middle ranks. Efficiently exploited landed property was the key to noble survival in the seventeenth century. Land outperformed other investments, even though (and especially in southern Europe in the 1630s and 40s) land values were faltering and even falling. But it needed management and exploitation, and that meant a new emphasis on the competence and trustworthiness of the steward, measured in the outcrop of advice books on the subject, stressing the importance of preparing and scrutinizing annual accounts and comparing them year on year to establish trends. Noble land resources tended to be legally tied up in knots by entails and substitutions to keep the estates intact, provide for mortgages and marriage portions, and help out members of the family in difficulties. So domain wealth was not easily released in an emergency. Hence the paradox, especially noticeable in the Italian and Spanish peninsulas towards 1640, of rich aristocrats with vast estates who, in conditions of chronic monetary instability and facing falling rent rolls, not to mention demands upon their resources from all quarters which they could not meet, felt themselves to be in crisis. By 1650, a section of the higher nobility had become vulnerable, victims in part of their own predatory exploitations of the state and their expanded domains. The nobility as an order was more secure, more powerful and more dominant. Without it, the diminishing social cohesion in Europe would have been more damaging and critical. It was upon the nobilities of lineage and land that the social compacts underlying Europe's *ancien régime* after 1660 would be built.

Grasping the World

6. Europe in the World

EMPIRE OF THE WORLD

Cicero once identified the Roman empire with an *imperium* over the world. He meant that nowhere else except under Roman aegis did the population belong to a coherent civil and political community. The emergence of Christendom made that 'belonging' coterminous with Christianity. Outsiders, whom Aristotle and the Greeks had taught Cicero to call 'barbarians' because they lacked 'civility', now became synonymous with 'pagans'. By the Central Middle Ages, the Holy Roman Emperor and the papacy had become joint custodians of the inherited historical and sacral claims to an *imperium* over the Christian world. The Italian writer Andrea Alciato made the bond between Christendom and the heritage of the Roman empire explicit: 'since . . . all who were in the Roman world were made Roman citizens, it follows that all Christians are today the Roman people; this principle excludes from citizenship those who in Asia, Africa and other provinces do not profess the faith of CHRIST. They are enemies of the Roman people and lose the rights of the Roman *civitas*.' Europe's first age of overseas expansion paradoxically occurred just at the moment when Christendom's universalism, along with the institutions which sustained it, was disintegrating. Overseas expansion provoked a debate about what it was to 'belong' in Europe. Humanists acknowledged that a *res publica* implied a distinction between those who were its citizens (*civitates*) and those who were not. But whether such 'civility' (and, if so, on what grounds and to what degree) extended to those peoples with whom Europeans came into closer contact after 1520 became an anthropological question, and then a judgement-call about what it was to be European.

Europe's early colonialists were unwilling to abandon Christendom's universalist ideals. Portuguese and Castilian claims to overseas dominions rested upon papal grants. The ceremonials surrounding the Hispanic possession of new lands consciously reflected a continuing sense of the *imperium* of Christendom. So the last Aztec emperor, Moctezuma II ('Montezuma'), was presented, in a carefully choreographed scene, as donating his empire on the eve of his death to Charles V, thereby reflecting biblical precedents and imperial continuities. By placing the Pillars of Hercules alongside the Habsburg arms with the tag 'Plus Ultra' ('Yet Further'), 'universal monarchy' was identified with Emperor Charles V. In the context of Christendom's overseas expansion that meant 'w*orld* monarchy'. Even after the abdication of Charles V in 1556 and the separation of the Holy Roman Empire from the *monarchia* of Philip II and his successors to the Spanish throne, the Spanish empire still retained the vestiges of larger claims for its authority around the globe.

Papal and imperial legitimation for 'world empire' became, however, increasingly irrelevant. The French monarchy contested it. Where was the clause in Adam's will, Francis I is supposed to have asked Charles V, by which the emperor had been bequeathed half the world? The English monarchy ignored it, asserting its own, independent claims to legitimacy in the name of an obligation to civilize and convert the heathen to true Christianity. 'Now the Kings and Queens of England have the name of Defenders of the Faith,' proclaimed Richard Hakluyt in *A Discourse on Western Planting* (1584), they have an obligation to 'maintain and patronize the faith of Christ' (i.e. the Protestant religion). The following year, he wrote enthusiastically of the three objectives of the 'Virginia Enterprise': 'to plant Christian religion, to traffic[,] to conquer'. All three were inextricably interlinked. As the *Mayflower* pioneer Edward Winslow put it in his *Good Newes from New England* (1624), America was the place where 'religion and profit jump together'. But each objective was separately and in relationship to each other, contested and open to rival interpretations in a way which defeated any universalist projection of Europe's expansion. And with geographical expansion came a greater awareness that the wider world was composed of different cultures and states, many of which (Ottoman, Chinese, Indian) were not only geographically larger, but as sophisticated as that of Christendom, even if their cultural values and religious systems were different. Claims to universal authority upon the old foundations of Christendom were, when looked at in this new global perspective, as Hugo Grotius bluntly said in 1625, daft (*stultum*).

A yet more fundamental issue of legitimacy was initially raised in the context of the Spanish empire in America. A Dominican theologian, Francisco de Vitoria, presented it in a lecture 'On the American Indians' (*De Indis*) at Salamanca University. 'By what right (*ius*),' he asked, 'were the barbarians subjected to Spanish rule?' Papal claims to dispose of secular dominion to whomsoever it chose could surely not extend over pagans as well as Christians. An alternative answer was that native Americans had surrendered their authority voluntarily to the empire. But that required putting a thumb over the evidence of the wilful plunder of the Conquistadors in central and southern America and native hostility towards being subjugated. A further possible answer was to say that the legitimacy of Spanish rule over the Indians lay precisely in the fact that the latter *had* been conquered, which opened the door to redeploying arguments used in the Spanish *Reconquista*. Such a response could be used, however, to equally good effect by other powers in Europe. They, too, could claim that they had conquered parts of the world and that this gave them legitimacy to rule there. The argument increased the importance of not simply 'discovering' new lands overseas, but laying claim to them.

How Europe's colonizers took hold of their overseas colonies differed, depending on where the discoverers came from and what sort of dominion they wanted to establish. A Dominican, Antonio de Montesinos, told Hispanic colonizers on the island of Hispaniola in 1511 that they would no more be saved 'than Moors or the Turks' because of their barbaric treatment of the natives. That led the Spanish crown to take legal advice on how best to establish its rule in the Americas. Thereafter it required Conquistadors to read out a document known as the 'Requirement' (*Requerimiento*; after 1573, 'Instrument of Obedience and Vassalage') before they acknowledged the subjection of (or, if they refused its terms, 'attacked') indigenous people. The proclamation bizarrely assumed that native peoples would understand the language and terminology in which it was framed, and recognize the overlordship over them to which it laid claim. In return for their recognition of that overlordship, the document promised that those acting in the name of the Spanish monarchy would 'leave your women and children free, without servitude so that with them and with yourselves you can freely do what you wish . . . and we will not compel you to turn Christian'. If, however, they refused, the representatives of the Spanish monarchy promised 'with the help of God' to 'enter forcefully against you, and . . . to make war everywhere . . . and to subject you to the yoke and obedience of the Church and His Majesty, and . . . to take your wives and children . . . to make them slaves . . . and to take your goods . . . and to do all the evil and damages that a lord may do to vassals who do not obey or receive him'. The text reflected both the practices of the *Reconquista* and the emerging realities of a Spanish empire that sought to integrate and convert (albeit by ostensibly peaceful means) indigenous peoples into Spanish colonial dominion. Struck by the absurdity of the 'free choice' offered to the Indians, Bartolomé de las Casas said that he did not know whether to 'laugh or to cry'. Spanish officials forbade the use of the term 'conquest', requiring the more innocuous 'pacification', to describe the imposition of Spanish rule.

French colonizers were particularly scrupulous to distance themselves from the forceful conquest implied in the Spanish Requirement. Instead they used Catholic benediction rituals to mark the voluntary subjection of natives to French rule. So, when François de Razilly's expeditionary force arrived at the mouth of the Amazon in July 1612 (at the island which would become São Luis de Maranhão), he sent a delegation to ask the local Tupi 'if they continued in the same wish as they had in the past to receive the French'. Only with the consent of the natives did the latter go ashore and cut a tree to make a cross which was carried in procession through various villages and then planted to serve 'as witness to each [Indian] of the desire they had to receive Christianity and a continual memorial to them and all their posterity as to the reason why we took possession of their land in the name of Jesus Christ'.

The notion of possession deployed by Portuguese mariners, by contrast, reflected the maritime and coastal nature of their claims to dominion. When a Portuguese fleet reached the coast of Brazil in 1500, Captain Nicolau Coelho put ashore to trade with the Tupi natives while its astronomer and pilot disembarked to measure the height of the midday sun and describe the position of the stars, marking a point (which could then be represented on a map) with a wooden cross, cut from local wood. This time the cross was an assertion of maritime supremacy, associated with shoreline markers. It was later contested by Elizabeth

I in 1562. When asked by the Portuguese ambassador to acknowledge Portuguese sovereignty over 'all the land discovered by the Crown of Portugal', she refused to do so on the grounds that 'in all places discovered . . . he had no superiority at all'. 'Discovery' (in the sense that Queen Elizabeth understood it, but not in the way the Portuguese did) was not 'possession'. The French navigator from Dieppe Jean Parmentier sailed two ships to Sumatra in 1529 with the aim of breaking the Portuguese spice monopoly which had resulted from its claims to the sea-routes to the East. He declared that the Portuguese manifested an 'excessive ambition' and that 'it seems that God only made the seas and land for them, and that other nations are not worthy of sailing'.

The Dutch lawyer Hugo Grotius was one of several commentators to maintain (in *On the Law of Prize and Booty*, 1604–5) that Portuguese claims to have discovered the oceans, and thereby to have established rights over the sea-routes, was to close them off to others and enforce boundaries where none existed in nature. Yet Grotius conceded that finding genuinely new land overseas came legally into the category of acquiring property which had no claimant – like finding a coin in the street. Dutch colonists were scrupulous about defining the precise latitude and contours of what they laid claim to, proving that it was genuinely 'terra incognita', or (if not) basing their legitimacy on the grounds that it had been conceded or negotiated with locals, and that it was sustained by regular trade, occupation and investment. Early English colonists in North America, by contrast, had the luxury of being able to claim that they had taken possession of unoccupied land which hitherto belonged to nobody at all and that they had conquered it from no one. They built houses and fenced off their land to delineate a 'plantation' where, as in Ireland, the justification for colonization rested on putting land to good use for God's glory in a way that the natives declined to do.

The world map bears the imprint of European claims from this period in place-names. Columbus's passion for naming the islands, promontories and rivers that he discovered was repeated by his successors in the Spanish Americas. The earliest historian of its colonial empire, Gonzalo Fernández de Oviedo, remarked that reading a Spanish navigational chart was like reading 'a calendar or catalogue of the saints that is not very well ordered'. Unlike the Portuguese (who Europeanized indigenous names), the Dutch, English and French used renaming strategies reflecting the Europe from which they came. The Dutch and the

English adopted the names of their towns, provinces, explorers and rulers. French nomenclature in North America reflected those individuals whose patronage at court would foster a new colony. Names were contested or changed along with the colonizer. The English colonist John Smith, the founder of Jamestown, asked Prince Charles for a patent giving him the authority to eliminate all the names in North America assigned by other nations in favour of English ones. For the Dutch, the fact that their names (Jakarta as 'Batavia'; the 'Mauritz' river, later the Hudson) were used by other nationalities was an additional proof of their rightful possession. Queen Elizabeth, however, was sceptical. She told the Spanish ambassador in 1580 that having 'given Names to a River or Cape . . . does not entitle them [Spaniards] to ownership'. Physical possession was what counted, and the capacity to hold on to a colony by force. By 1650, Europe's overseas empires reflected a pragmatic, possessive, competitive and unstable process of acquisition. There was no agreed framework of law or final court of appeal where *de facto* occupation, legal charters, recognitions, histories, cartographies, boundaries and ceremonies of possession could be adjudged beyond the rhetoric of claim and counter-claim, which preoccupied diplomats as much as it gave voice to the mercantilist self-interests of those who had a stake in empire, and the most to lose.

AGENTS OF EMPIRE

Authority was dispersed in Europe's fledgling empires. At their inception, a small number of people, without experience or much by way of mandate but in command of gunpowder technologies, held the initiative. In just two years from the moment of his landing in Vera Cruz in July 1519, the Conquistador Hernán Cortés and about 500 horsemen were able to defeat the Aztec empire of over 11 million inhabitants. The operation was carried out on the basis of a commission accorded him in the name of the Spanish crown by magistrates of the 'town' of Vera Cruz which he had himself established upon his arrival. In 1530, his imitator Francisco Pizarro led a syndicate which siphoned off the early spoils of the Mexican success into an expedition to Peru, initially with even fewer soldiers of fortune. Three years later, in November 1533, the fate of the Inca empire was sealed in an afternoon with the capture and sack of Cuzco. Fortune favoured these brazen few. The gold that was looted from Cuzco made Pizarro and his supporters richer than they could have imagined. In the longer term, however, their success opened an era of bitter and bloody rivalries, resolved only a generation later by a Spanish government stepping in with reluctance finally to organize the colony.

Meanwhile, in the Indian Ocean, Afonso de Albuquerque, the second 'governor' of Portuguese India, established a few fortified sites in the Indian Ocean from which to control its seaborne trade. In little over a decade, and with never more than fifteen ships and about 3,000 men under his command, he and his collaborators established the direction and strategy of a new 'state', the Portuguese State of India (*Estado Português da Índia*), through to the next century. They built military fortifications and naval bases at Cochin (1503) and Goa (1510) with which to overawe local traders. They then tried to control the strategic entries to the Indian Ocean at the Cape of Good Hope, Socotra at the entrance to the Red Sea, and Hormuz and Bahrain in the Persian Gulf. They cemented their influence by subjugating the small Muslim states of East Africa and conquering the islands of Madagascar and Mauritius. Then, in 1511, Albuquerque's forces captured Malacca, a dominant local trading state in the Far East and key to the South China Sea. It was a remarkable demonstration of the possibilities of maritime overlordship with the determined application of a small force.

Yet Portuguese success was ultimately only partial. They did not establish a lasting control of the trades in spices, silk and calicoes, not least because local shippers were still able to bring fine spices from the Moluccas through the Strait of Sunda to Atjeh in northern Sumatra, and because the Portuguese never captured Aden at the entrance to the Red Sea. The Portuguese *Estado* was based, however, on an important reality, which was that, by participating in the intra-Asian trade (mainly by extorting protection money through issuing safe-conducts to local traders), they offset the costs of maintaining their presence and diminished the need for importing bullion from Europe to pay for the Asian goods that they brought to Europe. India consumed probably twice as much of the spices produced in Southeast Asia as Europe, and China three quarters of all the pepper production of Sumatra. Capturing control of the intra-Asian trade lay at the heart of the Portuguese commercial ascendancy.

The marauding Dutch and English, who did their best to dismantle the Portuguese commercial empire after 1600, understood the lessons of monopoly maritime empires in general, and the significance of these intra-Asian trades in particular. With still more single-minded ruthlessness and greater resources than the Portuguese, the Dutch moved in to control the choke-points of pepper and spice production at the turn of the century, and to dominate the intra-Asian trade themselves. In 1596, the first heavily armed Dutch fleet arrived by sailing directly across the Indian Ocean and through the Sunda Strait to the Bay of Bantam, the most important harbour of Java, the island where pepper was grown, and the hub of maritime Southeast Asia. In 1602, the Dutch adventurers coalesced into the East India Company (known as the VOC: *Vereenigde Oost-Indische Compagnie*), a merchant consortium which financed an average of about thirteen ships a year for the East over the first decade of its existence, sufficiently successfully to become a profitable and permanent quasi-state institution. In 1612, it invited subscriptions for a terminable joint stock over a period of years. Its officers swore an oath of allegiance to the States General of the Netherlands and promised to furnish information about events in Asia while agreeing to surrender ships, capital and manpower to the Dutch authorities in emergencies. In return, they had the power to negotiate treaties, build fortifications, and enlist soldiers and crew. The company was an arm's-length auxiliary of the Dutch state.

All but one of the early fleets returned with cargoes, information and experience, cumulatively significant in establishing the Dutch presence in the East. However, not until 1610 did shareholders receive a dividend. But since shares were rarely offered to anyone beyond the initial circle of investors, their values rose. In addition, investors had a privileged position on the company's governing body, and so owning shares afforded entry to an important oligarchy. Its seventeen directors had the complicated task of planning operations in the Far East. Their three meetings a year took delicate commercial and political decisions.

The base of operations in the East Indies was first at Bantam and then, when the relationship with the inland powers on the island deteriorated, at Jakarta. The governor-general, Jan Coen, applied the lessons of Portuguese monopolistic commercial overlordship to the Dutch East Indies. Nutmeg and mace were obtained only from the Banda Islands, whose inhabitants discovered that they could sell their spices not only to the Portuguese but also to the interloping English, and at better prices than those contracted with the Dutch. Coen led an assault in 1621 using Japanese mercenaries which resulted in the massacre or flight of all but 1,000 or so of the 13–15,000 local inhabitants. They were replaced by slaves, convicts and indentured labour to run new Dutch spice plantations. It was the beginning of an ultimately successful Dutch attempt to bar Asian and European rivals from buying Moluccan spices. From there, the Dutch set about extending their influence in the East and South China Sea, where they were lured by the silver flows from Japan and Manila. Meanwhile, they and the English exploited Portuguese weakness on the eastern (Coromandel) coast of India, cleared the Bay of Bengal of Portuguese and Burmese pirates, and gained trading privileges in Bengal, thus opening up this rich region to intensive trade with both Asia and Europe. Finally, in 1616, Pieter van den Broecke, a founder-member of the company, developed 'factories' (fortified strongholds) in what the company called the 'western quarter' at the entrance to the Red Sea. Van den Broecke tasted 'something hot and black' in Mocha in 1614, one of the first Dutch merchants to sample coffee.

All sorts of people had a stake in Europe's overseas empires. The term 'merchant empire' is an appropriate one, even for the Hispanic colonial empires in America, because it was the bankers in Europe's money centres and their factors in the ports of departure that furnished the capital and determined what was bought and sold. Their agents were as essential to the trades in pepper, spices, silks and calicoes from the East as they were to the precious metals, hides, dyestuffs and sugar from the New World. Europe's naval skills and technologies were transformed by the knowledge and experience of the seamen who sailed the ships, the dockyard workers who built them, the cannon-founders who armed them and the cartographers and instrument-makers who helped them to find their passage.

The number of Europeans who went overseas before 1650 remained modest, and many of them were temporary residents. Even when there was a steady stream of settlers, as from the Hispanic ports each year for the Americas, it can rarely have been more than a few thousand individuals a year. Between Sofala (the Portuguese fort in East Africa) and Macao there were probably not more than 15,000 Portuguese in 1600. There were about the same number of Dutch 'free burgher' settlers in the East Indies by 1650, the ambitious colonization plans of Joan

Maetsuyker, governor of Ceylon (1646–50) and the longest serving Governor-General of the Dutch East Indies, being a flop. By the mid-century, however, Dutch New Amsterdam (New York) may have contained about 7,000 Europeans, while the stream of English migrants to America contributed to steady colonial growth (Connecticut, 5,500 in 1643; Massachusetts, some 16,000; Virginia, about 15,000). European settlement in the outer islands of the Caribbean, by contrast, was spectacular. Fertile land was let out to planter-settlers on easy terms, and there were ready profits to be made from tobacco, indigo and cotton cultivation. By 1640, the European population of Barbados was over 30,000 and St Kitts's about 20,000 – densities of settlement which rivalled those of the most advanced economic regions of Europe itself.

Europe's first overseas empires were held together at nodal points. On the coast of Africa and in the Far East these were factories, strategically located to run a tourniquet around points of supply and trade. In colonial America they were the ports of transhipment and embarkation and the governing capitals. By 1620, about 200 cities, built on a grid pattern to match the contemporary conception of an ideal town, had been established in central and southern America. They were its judicial and administrative hubs, nominally self-governing entities with colonial councils, but answerable to local judicial tribunals (*audiencias*) and viceroys. The latter's appearance in New Spain (Mexico) in 1535 and Peru in 1543 characterized a state that was determined to rule its colonies as directly as possible and along European lines, despite the distance.

In the majority of these nodal points, and still more outside them, Europeans were a minority. Only in the Caribbean islands, where the decimation of indigenous peoples was the prelude to their replacement by Europeans, and in the English colonies of North America, where colonization involved pushing the indigenous peoples back into the hinterland, were Europeans the majority. In the Portuguese factories of the Far East, European settlers became heads of households by intermarrying with local people of various ethnicities and religions. In Goa, for example, Portuguese lived alongside Gujarati and Muslim traders, Armenian and Jewish merchants, Indian Hindus from various castes, Nestorian Christians, as well as Malayan and Chinese traders. In the circumstances, it was remarkable that the Portuguese were not completely absorbed into local society. But that was a tribute to the power of a merchant-based diaspora, the dispersal of the Portuguese explaining why that language remained the trading lingua franca of maritime Asia after the Portuguese empire itself had declined.

In Dutch Batavia and Spanish Manila it was a similar picture. By 1650, when the walled city of Batavia that had been built in the 1620s was full to bursting point, the Dutch settled with natives because there was a shortage of European women willing to make the trip to the Far East. Their children became half-European (in Dutch *mestiezen* – 'mestizo'). The directors insisted that they could marry only on condition that their womenfolk were baptized Christians and that their children ('and their slaves as far as possible') were brought up as Christians and taught Dutch. Dutch settlers dwelt alongside ethnic Javanese and other Asians who had adopted something of a European culture (*mardikers*), as well as Chinese who could speak Portuguese but otherwise lived in accordance with their own traditions. The conquest of Spanish America, too, entailed European settlers being a minority amid the indigenous Indian population, despite the efforts to segregate one from the other. The mines and plantations required both Indian skilled and semi-skilled labour as well as imported slaves from Africa. Over time, the settler population of American-born Europeans (*criollo*, 'creole') grew to be the most significant element among the élites in Mexico and Peru and the foundation for a distinctive sense of colonial American identity.

European colonial identities were still in the making by 1650, forged by encounters with others but in a continuing dialogue with metropolitan Europe. Colonial settlers sought to distance themselves from the indigenous local population, especially when trying to answer critics back home. The sense of a 'barbarian' other was never more refined than among displaced Europeans abroad, seeking to assert their superiority. Deploying a language of improvement, López de Gómara in his *General History of the Indies* (*Historia General de las Indias*) justified the conquest of Hispaniola and New Spain on the grounds that the regions had been transformed by settlers in a way that Indians had proved themselves incapable of doing: 'We found no sugar mills when we arrived in these Indies, and all these we have built with our own hands and industry, in so short a time.' American Indians exemplified to colonists all that they were not, or should not be. They were barbarians, pagans, profligate, undependable, un-industrious and irrational, to be treated (whatever royal legislation declared) cursorily and badly, their protests (the riots which occurred, for example in Bahia in 1610, or São Paulo and Rio de Janeiro in 1640) being a sign of their untrustworthiness.

Dutch Company directors emphasized that Asian peoples should be treated fairly only because it was so often not the case. The decisions recorded in the plea-books of their officials at Batavia frequently refer to Indonesians, Chinese and Muslims with derogatory epithets (such as 'vile', 'mean'). That led the Dutch naturalist Jakob Bontius to protest against his fellow-countrymen's dismissal of Asians as 'blind heathens', 'treacherous Moors' and 'feckless barbarians'. A Dutch Reformed preacher at Amboina in 1615 compared the sobriety of local Muslims with the drunken behaviour of his fellow Europeans. The Dutch sea captain and heroic figure of the Dutch Eighty Years War against the Spanish, Piet Hein, served in both the West and the East Indies in the early seventeenth century. He witnessed at first hand native hostility towards European arrogance: 'They feel very deeply the wrong that is done them, and this is why they become even wilder and more savage than they already are. When a worm is trodden on, it turns and wriggles. Is it surprising, then, that an Indian who is wronged revenges himself upon someone or other?' He was writing in the wake of the massacre of Europeans by Indians at Virginia in 1622, one of a cluster of incidents in which ethnic and racial conflict heightened the sensibilities of being European. Rijkloff van Goens, eventually Governor-General of the Dutch East Indies, was conscious of being European when he wrote in 1655: 'we are deadly hated by all nations in Asia'.

When colonialists compared themselves with their distant mother country, they discovered themselves at once the same, and yet different from their countrymen of origin. That was a small part of the process by which Christendom decomposed into something else. Many of the early settlers in Hispanic America sought to recreate the world which they had left behind them. Others (notably the Franciscans in the missionary orders and, in a different context, the ephemeral French Protestant communities in Brazil and Florida, later the Protestant Separatists in New England and the Jesuits in Paraguay) wanted to create a European order that was better than the one from which they had separated. For Franciscan missionaries, that meant realizing the millennial dream of Christendom. Early Jesuits saw the Americas as a chance to recreate Eden. 'If there is a paradise here on earth,' wrote one Jesuit in 1560, bemused by the strange flora, exotic animals and wild terrain, 'it is, I would say, here in Brazil.'

The conversion of the Indians, in particular, was a spiritual challenge afforded by God as the prelude to the Final Judgment. But, to be valid, conversion had to be more than outward conformity. Baptism had to be preceded by instruction in the faith, preaching, catechism and education – and then accompanied by acculturation into European ways of thinking and behaving. The task proved next to impossible. Teaching, catechizing and baptizing hundreds of thousands of Indians with the small resources to hand could only be roughshod. Persuading or compelling Indians to move into towns, organized around a church and convent reserved for them so that they could be educated to European ways, came at a cost. It resulted in a hybrid Christianity, one that had some affinities with the sacral landscape of late medieval Europe, in which the cult of the Virgin was superimposed on, or conflated with, cults of corn-goddesses and earth-mothers. Pagan fertility rites were Christianized by the inclusion of a preliminary Mass and procession but they remained identifiable to local people for what they were. Such hybridity was increasingly at odds with Reformed (Catholic) Christianity in the Post-Reformation. As the Franciscans looked back on their efforts and their often critical relationship with the secular authorities in Spanish America over their treatment of the Indians, their millennial dream faded. Their deception was part of the fall of the established notion of western Christendom as a belief-community. The hopes for the coming of Christ's Kingdom were carried forward within the new confessional conflictual environment of the Protestant Reformation by New England Puritans and by the Jesuits in Paraguay, determined to complete the task of Christianizing the Indians using the resources of a global Catholic Christianity.

In the Far East, Christendom came up against different realities. The enhanced awareness of the Islamic challenge to Christendom in the sixteenth century was not simply a response to the Ottoman threat to Europe's southeastern flank. It was also because Europe came into closer proximity with Islam in the Indian Ocean and the Far East. Wherever Islam was a significant presence, the efforts of Christian missionaries proved more arduous, and local attitudes towards the Portuguese (to a lesser extent, the Dutch and English in the seventeenth century) turned hostile. This was the case in parts of the east coast of Africa, but also in the Far East. In the Banda Islands, for example, Muslim clerics outnumbered Christian missionaries and it was only in non-Islamicized parts of India, or in islands like Amboina (which

Francis Xavier visited in 1546) where Islam had yet to penetrate, that Christianity established a presence. Elsewhere in Indonesia, Islam was spreading rapidly, especially where Hinduism was in retreat. The Muslim merchant sultanates of coastal Java proved the most bitterly hostile to the Portuguese conquerors of Malacca. Similarly, the spread of Islam in southern India in the sixteenth century threatened the Portuguese presence, even in Goa (which withstood a two-year siege, beginning in 1569).

By then, Counter-Reformed Christianity was also being felt in India. There were efforts to exclude non-Christians from public office. An Inquisition was established in 1560 to investigate apostates and heretics, Nestorian Christians finding themselves treated as the latter. At a synod of the Portuguese Catholic Church at Udayamperoor (Diamper) in 1599, they were officially denounced and, for a time, disbanded as an organized community. The majority of conversions to Christianity were among Indians of low caste seeking to escape the pressures of that social system. Missionary zeal contributed to making the Portuguese hated as both pirates and persecutors among indigenous populations. If the same was not true for the Dutch in the Far East in the early seventeenth century it was because Reformed Christianity lacked missionary zeal and also because the colonialists exploited the rivalries between local Islamic powers and against the Portuguese to their own advantage.

Overseas empires depended on ships. The convoys that set sail from the river Guadalquivir (Seville and Cádiz) for the Spanish Americas and from the Tagus (Lisbon) bound for the Far East were organized and paid for by merchants. In the India Office in Lisbon, established in 1505–6 to oversee Portuguese dealings with Asia – as in its Spanish equivalent, formed a couple of years earlier – the paperwork of a merchant empire accumulated as the complexities of these colonial operations unfolded. The Asia convoy involved stamina and risk. The flotilla of up to ten ships set out between February and April from Lisbon on the outward leg of a 25,000-mile round-trip (the equivalent of circumnavigating the globe at the equator), aiming to catch the summer equatorial winds and currents off the coast of South America to take them round the Cape of Good Hope in order to work up the coast of East Africa and put in to the Portuguese factory port on the island of Mozambique, and the first opportunity for some lucrative trading. That part of the voyage was long and gruelling even when nothing untoward happened. Fresh supplies ran out, joints and gums swelled, and there was frequently dysentery aboard. It was not uncommon for up to a third of the ship's crew to die in one passage. From there, they followed the coast to the northern tip of Somalia before crossing the Indian Ocean. From Goa and Cochin, the Portuguese travelled on to Malacca, the monsoon governing the passage of the ships. The Dutch deployed a larger number of smaller vessels – up to a hundred of about 600 tons each, as opposed to the 1,000-ton Portuguese carracks.

The return journey involved setting out after Christmas the following year to catch the favourable monsoons and then, once in the Atlantic, to let the southeasterly winds take them northwest into the low-pressure equatorial doldrums, hoping to catch winds and currents which would take them back to the Azores and the European coast. At least 16 per cent of the ships never made their destination. Those which did so left Europe in ballast, carrying precious metal and copper supplemented by some trade goods and company supplies for the fortress factories. They returned low in the water, stacked with chests of spices (nutmeg, cloves, cinnamon, mace), sacks of black peppercorns, and bales of silk and cotton cloth stored between decks.

Only very high profits could justify this effort. Cloves bought in the Spice Islands and sold into the Indian market often made 100 per cent profits; the price of mace in Calicut was ten to fifteen times that in Great Banda, while nutmeg was thirty times higher. Indian textiles could sell in the Far East at double their purchase price. Much of the profit was made in the Far East. Selling spices into the European market was about the marketing of scarcity and the commoditization of mystique, so there was some elasticity of demand. But it was not inexhaustible, and the competition between the Dutch and English East India Companies led to oversupply and a weakened market price before the Dutch tightened their monopoly in the Far East and the English Civil War disrupted the activities of its East India merchants. Spices remained a risky commodity, especially when merchants had to commit themselves over a year in advance to purchase and shipment. It is not surprising, therefore, that the Portuguese sold them on to consortia of Italian, German and Flemish merchant banking houses, which then shared the risk. The involvement of merchants from northwest Europe in the financing of the spice trade was the prelude to their becoming directly involved in it through their own East India Companies.

The Spanish New World fleet operated differently. Ships did the round trip to Central America in nine months. That made servicing Spain's colonial empire a realistic proposition. The fleets were organized in convoys from the middle of the sixteenth century to avoid the depredation of French, and later English and Dutch, marauders waiting in the Bay of Cádiz. They were escorted by a navy, and there were generally two a year. One headed for New Spain and the port on the island of San Juan de Ulúa facing Vera Cruz, and the other for Cartagena de Indias on the Caribbean coast of what is now Colombia, from where it passed to Nombre de Dios or Portobelo on the north coast of the Panama isthmus to await the merchants travelling from Peru through Acapulco. In the 1520s already nearly a hundred ships per year carried merchandise across the Atlantic between Spain and its American colonies. That represented about 9,000 tons of carrying capacity. By 1600, the yearly average had grown to 150–200 ships with a total tonnage of 30,000–40,000 tons – the increased carrying capacity due to the fact that the size of vessels had doubled. On the outward voyages, they transported the provisions that colonists needed. On the return, in addition to the precious metals from the New World, came hides, indigo, cochineal and sugar. Although the volume of the cargoes varied, the change in Europe's trading scale was cumulatively massive. The products from Europe's overseas empires broadened Europe's consumables markets – and in a way which moralists regarded as threatening inherited Christian values.

THE SONS OF NOAH

Slavery was an established part of every Eurasian civilization and it had been a feature of European society in the Middle Ages. By 1500, however, most people in Christendom were free. Paradoxically, it was at just that moment that Europe's encounter with the wider world led to a rediscovery of slavery, albeit on different foundations: chattel-based and racial. Slaves were treated as the 'movable property' of their owners and European law gave unprecedented freedom to owners to do what they liked with them.

Only Africans were enslaved, their colour being a marker for social segregation. In the sixteenth century black slaves were often to be found in well-to-do European households, especially on Europe's coastal rim and in southern Europe. In Portugal, the economy came to rely on chattel slavery. It surprised the Flemish humanist Nicolas Cleynaerts, travelling in the service of Hernando Columbus (the explorer's son): 'All places are full of slaves. Captive blacks and Moors perform all tasks. Portugal is so crowded with these people that I believe that in Lisbon there are more black men and women than free Portuguese.' They were owned by the king, the nobility, churchmen and even ordinary people. They laboured in the fields, crewed Portuguese ships, cleaned the hospitals and worked around the house. They were shipped from Equatorial Africa and sold in Lisbon by the sixty to seventy slave merchants whose contracts made them wealthy. Slaves were openly for sale on the streets in manacles, neck-rings and padlocks; the purchase price was negotiated with a broker. Their only possibility of release from slavery was if they successfully ran away or were granted their manumission by their owner.

By the end of the sixteenth century, wherever Europeans settled overseas they imposed or accepted racially based slavery. The pattern was set in the colonization of the Canary Islands in the first two decades of the sixteenth century. Then, in 1518, Charles V granted licences to import thousands of blacks into the Spanish colonies through Seville (which, like Lisbon, had a large population of black slaves). From 1530, however, slaves were shipped directly from Africa to reduce mortality at sea. By 1650, African slaves predominated in the migration to the New World.

Aristotelian philosophy provided justifications for why black African slavery was part of the natural order. And the slave trade could be justified on the precedents of the crusading past. The biblical story of Noah's three sons – Shem, Ham and Japhet – became the starting-point for understanding racial difference and for justifying racialism. Whatever had gone on in the Ark to lead Noah to curse Ham was the explanation for blackness, an inherited curse and inferiority which European legal discrimination and cultural attitudes reinforced. In an account of Martin Frobisher's voyage to discover the Northwest Passage, published in 1578, his lieutenant George Best described Ham's curse as being that 'all his posteritie after him should bee so blacke and loathsome, that it might remain a spectacle of disobedience to all the worlde'. The Spanish philosopher Francisco de Vitoria thought the slave trade was entirely legitimate, so long as the slaves had been taken in a just war: 'It is enough that a man be a slave in fact or in law, and I will buy him without a qualm.' By the mid-seventeenth century, slavery was justified as an economic necessity. When the Dutch stormed the Portuguese Brazilian sugar plantations in 1634–8 to establish the colony of 'New Holland', their commander, Johan Mauritz of Nassau-Siegen, floated the idea of using free white labour in the sugar-mills at Pernambuco. But he rapidly came round to the view of the Portuguese whom they had supplanted: 'It is not possible to effect anything in Brazil without slaves ... they cannot be dispensed with upon any occasion whatsoever: if anyone feels that this is wrong, it is a futile scruple.'

The Indians were a more complicated matter. The Requirement turned them into servants of the Spanish monarchy. To make war upon, and enslave, them would be like declaring war on Seville, said Vitoria. The question was into what category of human beings did they fit? The first reaction – as with the flora and fauna of the New World – was to homologate them on the basis of superficial likeness to a known type. Oviedo, the earliest historian of the Indies, thought that Indians resembled 'Ethiopians', barbarians from North Africa. They might not be slaves by conquest but they fitted Aristotle's category of 'natural slaves', whom Vitoria had learned about while studying in Paris. Natural slaves were those whose intellects were not sufficient to control and direct their emotions. As the jurist and magistrate in the first colonial law court in the New World (at San Domingo), Juan Ortiz de Matienzo, put it, they are 'participants in reason so as to sense it, but not to possess or follow it'. The fashion for physiognomy inclined philosophers and theologians to categorize people in accordance with their bodily appearance. It was not difficult to construct a physiognomy of the Indians that confirmed that they were ruled by their passions. They made no provision for the future. Their psyche (or 'soul') was such that they could only be fully human (i.e. capable of 'virtue') through their master. That is why, so the argument went, freedom was unnatural to a natural slave.

The problem was that, as more knowledge accumulated about the Indians, the more problematic became any categorization of them as natural slaves. Francisco de Vitoria belonged to the Salamanca School, scholars whose philosophical approach involved teasing out the 'law of nature' – that is, understanding not just the principles imparted by God at Creation to the world, but what it was that enabled us to be human beings in relationship to it. In his university lectures on the issue, delivered as disquiet about the mistreatment of Indians in Peru was growing, Vitoria wanted to relate the 'affairs of the Indies' to the 'republic of the whole world'. He wanted to determine whether the Indians had been treated in accordance with 'God's law' (of which the law of nature was a reflection). He proved that they had a sense of territorial rights, a rational order to their affairs, a recognizable form of marriage, magistrates, rulers, laws, industry, commerce, politeness and civic culture. In each category, Vitoria highlighted – and thereby clarified – what would become the defining characteristics of being 'European' – how he understood that one could be truly 'human'. His thinking was a microcosm of how those who occupied the space of Europe came, through their encounters with others, to understand who they were, and in ways that took them beyond Christendom's belief-communities.

Vitoria was a university professor, weighing arguments against one another. There was, he admitted, a serious case against, as well as for, equating Indians with Europeans. Indian society had no written laws. Its magistrates were weak. It permitted polygamy, matrilineal descent and nudity in public. Above all there was evidence of cannibalism, a subject which was a European obsession because, like sodomy and bestiality, it seemed a perversion of the law of nature. Columbus had been told by the Arawaks about the 'Caribs' who 'eat men'. Bouts of human sacrifice among the Mexica were supposed to be followed by cannibalistic orgies. The Paraguayan Guaraní and the Yucatan Maya were reported to be cannibals. The Brazilian Tupinambá were said in 1554 to 'eat their victims down to their last fingernail'. Europeans believed these stories because they wanted to. It was a way of simplifying the otherwise complex and irresolvable issues of what made Indians different from Europeans. What one ate determined who one was; the better the food, the more virtuous a person resulted. So, Vitoria concluded, the Indians had a long way to go before they became fully human in the way that Europeans understood it. It was not simply a matter of their being converted to Christianity. Christianized Indians would still, in some sense, be 'barbarians' because they could not properly recognize right from wrong (food included). As the Franciscan Juan de Silva said, they were as incapable of distinguishing 'between right and wrong as between a thistle and a lettuce'. They needed 'civilizing'. That meant education, not just in the sense of schooling but in the sense of a fundamental reformation of the individual psyche, a lengthy process. In the meantime, the 'barbarian' had to be accepted as not European but 'within' the European order of things.

Bartolomé de las Casas ensured that these issues received a more public airing. He was twenty-eight years of age when he left for the New World in 1502, becoming first a planter and then a chaplain to the Conquistadors, experiencing at first hand the brutality that Spanish conquest meted out to the Indians. His first response was to found a utopian colony in which natives would be converted by persuasion, living in harmony with colonists in an ideal Christian community where Indians would have hospitals and churches and be taught how to work the land by Spanish farmers. Lacking practicality, it was a fiasco when it was attempted at Cumaná on the coast of what is now northern Venezuela. Las Casas joined the Dominicans in 1523 and lobbied on behalf of the Amerindian people. He was able to argue, along with Vitoria only with more detailed evidence, that pre-conquest Amerindian society ticked Aristotle's boxes as a civil society. Indians' conversion should therefore be by persuasion, and not by force, and their labour should be free. His greatest successes were persuading the papacy to issue a bull (*Sublimus Dei*, 29 May 1537) outlawing Amerindian slavery, and inspiring reformers at Charles V's court to enact the New Laws (1542) which regulated the labour service of Indians on colonial plantations in the New World.

Peruvian landowners, outraged by the efforts of its first viceroy, Blasco Núñez Vela, to enforce the new legislation, staged a revolt. They were led by Gonzalo Pizarro, one of three Conquistador brothers. The rebel colonists deposed and killed the viceroy, declaring Peru independent of Spanish authority. Only the arrival of Pedro de la Gasca as his replacement, promising to abrogate the New Laws, restored Spanish rule. In Mexico too, where Las Casas was appointed bishop of the newly formed diocese of Chiapas, colonial revolt became widespread. Returning to Spain in 1547 and ostensibly living a life of seclusion in the Dominican monastery of Valladolid, he waged a campaign for the moral high-ground in academia and around the emperor. The '30 Juridical Propositions', presented to the Council of the Indies in 1547, sought to exploit the differences over the succession of Charles V between the emperor and his son Prince Philip.

Juan Ginés de Sepúlveda was Philip's tutor, a humanist-trained

Aristotelian who had spent some time in Italy. He became the mouth-piece for Las Casas's opponents. Sepúlveda thought he understood the arguments for a Habsburg 'world monarchy'. He advocated a crusade against the Turks and went on to argue (in a dialogue probably composed in 1544) that America was Spanish by the laws of conquest. By those same laws, the Amerindians were their slaves. Cannibalism, incest, sacrifice, nudity – and other unnatural acts of which the Indians were apparently guilty – had to be stopped by force. Force (legal, moral, physical) could be used in their conversion on the same grounds that justified the Inquisition and the repression of Protestant heresy. The Council of the Indies referred the matter to an academic conference at San Gregorio College in Valladolid in 1550–51. Both sides gave as good as they got, and each thought they had the better of the argument. In reality, the council retained (in 1552) a watered-down version of the New Laws. If they were influenced by the debates at Valladolid, they were even more susceptible to the arguments that Indian slave labour could not produce a skilled workforce for the silver mines.

Las Casas had the last word. Sometime in 1552, an unauthorized publication appeared in Seville of a little book that he had written a decade before under the title *Brief Relation of the Destruction of the Indies* (*Brevísima relación de la destrucción de las Indias*). His motive was 'the very great and final need to make known to all Spain the true account and truthful understanding of what I have seen take place'. Recounting the conquest of the Americas, he said that the Spanish had appeared in the 'sheepfold' like 'revenging wild beasts, wolves, tigers or lions', language also used in the papal bull (*Exsurge Domine*, 15 June 1520) against Luther. The true story of Indian 'destruction' – Spanish power, greed and money – presaged the collapse of Christendom and the end of the world. Las Casas's little book was a counter-history of the Conquest. Translated into French and published in Antwerp in the late 1570s, and from there into English and Dutch in 1583, it was woven into the Protestant 'Black Legend' of the Hispanic empire, reinforcing the links between colonial conquest and maltreatment overseas and religious confrontation and massacre at home. So the debates about slavery, conversion and colonialism worked their way into mainstream controversies about the nature of power and violence.

In the New World, Las Casas's ideas lived on. For him, the Indians were co-equal descendants of Adam and Eve, perhaps even better than

Europeans because, following conversion, their Christianity would be pristine. Might they not also be the descendants of the Lost Tribes of Israel, in which case was the discovery of the New World an indisputable sign from God of the imminent coming of the millennium? That was the conviction among the first generation of Franciscan missionaries in the New World following their arrival there in 1524. Enjoying a freedom from episcopal and inquisitorial authority in the New World that was never theirs in the Old, these 'reformed' (that is, 'spiritual') Franciscans responded to the challenge of Christian mission with apostolic fervour. Franciscan millennial vision faded in the New World towards the end of the sixteenth century, but the idea that the Amerindians might be the descendants of the Lost Tribes reappeared among New England Protestants towards the mid-seventeenth century. The debates about converting American Indians would continue through the Reformation and Counter-Reformation to be a reflective encounter with what it was to be European.

THE EUROPEAN EAST

Medieval Christendom's boundaries were defined by the belief community that it embodied. The rise of the Ottoman Turks, the revival of Crusade, and the ensuing conflicts in the Mediterranean and southeastern Europe sharpened the political, cultural and religious divisions in those regions. That was not the case for Europe's Slav frontier to the east of the Polish-Lithuanian condominium and the Baltic. Geography offered no natural frontiers to demarcate those that lived in the European landmass from the rest of the Eurasian continent. As western Christendom disintegrated, the rationale for the traditional frontiers with Orthodox Christianity diminished. At the same time, the rise of Muscovy as a powerful entity, mirroring political processes which were similarly at work in western Europe, blurred the boundaries on Europe's eastern margins.

In 1480, the Muscovite princes ceased to be tributaries to the Mongol Golden Horde. The following century was a crucial period of Russian consolidation and expansion. Based on the growth of more settled agriculture around the upper Volga on the labour-scarce but land-rich estates of the boyar nobility, the Rurik dynasty of 'grand dukes' proclaimed themselves 'tsar' ('Caesar') over all Rus. Grand Duke Ivan III was offered a crown by the Holy Roman Emperor, but he rejected it. Eastern and western Christendom were separate and apart. Russian princes, he said, derived their authority from God alone. So Ivan organized his own coronation in 1503, adopting the Byzantine double eagle as his emblem and appropriating the ceremonial and ritual of Byzantium.

Muscovy grew massively in the sixteenth century. From a tiny population in 1462 of about 430,000, by 1533 2.8 million inhabitants owed allegiance to the tsar, and 5.4 million by 1584. The expansion consolidated Muscovite authority in the Polish Ukraine to the southwest, where Christendom's authority had been enfeebled by attacks from the Crimean Tatars. Muscovy equally cemented its grip on the lower Volga river basin, overwhelming the khanate of Kazan in 1552 and establishing its presence on the shores of the Caspian Sea in 1556. Many new fortress towns in stone were constructed, along with smaller forts in wood. To the east and before the end of the sixteenth century, Russians began settling in western Siberia, forts and kremlins marking its territorial expansion. By 1600, Muscovy ruled from Arkhangelsk (known in English as Archangel) on the White Sea, to Astrakhan at the mouth of the Volga on the Caspian Sea.

The power of the Muscovite state rested on the unique authority of the tsar. When the Holy Roman Emperor Maximilian I sought to comprehend what it was that Ivan III had which he did not, he received the reply: 'We Russians are devoted to our sovereigns, whether they be merciful or cruel.' That loyalty was based on the tsar's role to protect the Rus from attack by the nomadic peoples of central Asia. The tsar's authority was strengthened in the course of the sixteenth century by Muscovite military institutions, notably the professional units of harquebusiers (*streltsy*, or 'shooters'), introduced by Ivan IV in the years before 1550, and some of the trappings of a centralizing state that were common in western Europe. It also benefited from the group of loyalist retainers instituted by Ivan IV. The 6,000 secret informers (*oprichniki*) which formed that grouping swore an oath of allegiance to the tsar, undertaking to inform him of any plots or rumours against him. The *oprichnina* earned Ivan the epithet of 'the Fearsome' (or 'the Terrible') and, in the seven years from 1565 to 1572, it humbled the Russian nobility.

The consolidation of the Muscovite state made the question of the border with Europe more problematic. Russian expansion south and east, into the forests and river systems of central Asia, opened up the possibility that 'Europe' (under the aegis of a 'Europeanized' state) was engaged in a further expansion, less advertised than that which followed on from the discovery of America, but no less important. As in America, the processes were not state-led in any simple or straightforward way. The consolidation of the Muscovite state created a diaspora of those who did not choose to live in, or were forced by circumstances to flee, the land of Rus. They included peasants running away from serfdom, ruined and disgraced landholders and servitors (the victims of the *oprichnina*), common fugitives and prisoners of war. Some young Russians chose to 'go cossacking' in the service of the Don and Yaik Cossacks before returning to settle down in the Muscovite army. Some were attracted to the trade in silks, hides and saddles in the lower reaches of the Dnieper, Don and Volga rivers, and the profits to be made by those willing to take up the challenge. The southern steppe population became a mix of different ethnicities – Muscovites, Poles, Circassians, Moldavians and a smattering of Germans and Slavs – and a tinderbox for 'Pretender' rebellions against the tsar in the early seventeenth century. The repression of revolt then became the pretext for a further extension of the tsar's authority. A small but important part of the Great Muscovite Law Code (*Sobornoe Ulozhenie*) introduced by Tsar Alexis in 1649 sought to deter the mass migration of peasants that fed Russian expansion to the south and east by tying the serfs to the land.

Russian expansion into Siberia owed as much to private initiative as to state sponsorship. Enterprising Russians organized traders and trappers and funded private bands of Cossacks to break the resistance of local Siberian natives to their intrusion. They were then followed by military servitors of the tsar who collected tribute in fur for the state, which then went to fund the military emplacements that supported the expansion. Erofei Khabarov (nicknamed 'Sviatitskii') matches closest the pioneers who opened up America to European expansion. Originally a peasant, he became an enterprising farmer in western Siberia. In 1625, he undertook his first voyage from Tobol'sk, the site of the only surviving stone kremlin in western Siberia, built in 1585–6 by a contingent of hired Cossacks, on a river vessel to the settlement at Mangazeya, a new colony on the Taz river. The Taz flows into the Arctic Ocean and it offered an export route around the Arctic coast in the summer for furs to the English traders at Archangel. In 1632, he led an expedition to the Lena river, where (at the mouths of the Kuta and Kirenga tributaries) he established a farming settlement and built a salt-works. In 1649–50, he set off with a band of military servitors across the Olekma river to the Amur river watershed in eastern Asia, exploring its tributaries and provoking conflict with the Manchu, reaching Okhotsk on the Pacific coast. At the same time, before and after the severe dislocation of the wars of succession at the end of the Rurik dynasty and the beginning of the Romanovs (Russia's Time of Troubles, 1598–1613), foreign prisoners of war and criminals were forcibly relocated to Siberia. They joined the wandering peoples who crossed the Urals of their own accord to escape the Muscovite state and find a new life for themselves. Before the death of Tsar Alexis in 1676, the overlordship of the Russian tsar encompassed over 3 million square miles, larger than the Ottoman empire and dwarfing contemporary western European states.

At the same time, the consolidation of the Muscovite state made interactions between the European landmass and the Rus much more sustained. The tsars actively encouraged such contacts. They welcomed Dutch and English representatives at their court, and sought access to European gunpowder technologies. They were repeatedly hampered by their lack of direct access to the Baltic, so the opening up of the Arctic Ocean and White Sea route via Archangel changed the dynamics of the relationship. Europe's American silver lubricated trade with Muscovy, just as it did with the Far East. Prices in Russia went up in the second half of the sixteenth century. Rye, the principal grain in Muscovy, fetched 23 den'gi per *chetvert'* in around 1550, but sold for over 80 in the bad harvest years of 1586–8, and for well over 40 during the last decade of the sixteenth century. At the same time, the Holy Roman Emperor and the pope understood the significance of a strong Muscovite state as an ally against the Turks, and fostered missions to establish closer links with that objective in mind.

As in America, however, more sustained contact with Russia led to a sharpening of Europe's sense of its own identity. In Poland and Lithuania, the traditional boundary between the western and the Orthodox churches began to break down when a portion of the Orthodox Church disavowed Muscovite tutelage. A Metropolitan archbishop 'of Kiev and all Russia' was established under Polish influence in 1558 at the beginning of the Livonian War (1558–83). The Kiev Metropolitan succeeded in garnering the loyalties of the Orthodox population of Lithuania and a section of the discontented nobility of western Russia, although not that of the peasants. In 1595, the king of Poland proclaimed the union of this Orthodox Church with the papacy, a significant reinforcement of Counter-Reformed Rome's claims to a global Christianity. But the Greater Russian hinterland remained faithful to the Orthodox Metropolitan in Moscow.

With dissident varieties of western and eastern Christianity now in place, it was no longer the difference between Orthodox and western Christianity which could define Christendom. To the degree that a frontier existed, it was part of a mental map, carried by individual Europeans, and therefore ambiguous and debatable. Europe's emerging sense of its own identity in relation to America and the world at large played a part in defining its relationship to the European East. What was identified as 'savage' and 'barbarian' in the American Indian became counter-posed as 'cruel' and 'despotic' in Russian political culture and society. The English explorer Jerome Horsey, who spent seventeen years at the court of last Rurik tsars and knew the country well, was struck by its arbitrariness and brutality. Reporting on the siege of Novgorod in 1569–70 by the forces of Tsar Ivan IV, he noted that the city was ransacked by 30,000 Tatars and 10,000 harquebusiers who 'without any respect, ravished all the women and maids, ransacked, robbed and spoiled all that were within it of their jewels, plate and treasure, murdered the people, young and old, burnt all ... set all on fire ... together with the blood of 70,000 men, women and children slain and murdered'. If he is to be believed, it was a massacre that dwarfed what would occur in Paris at the massacre of St Bartholomew in 1572. He took it as defining what set Russia apart from the Europe that he knew. That was the view, too, of the Polish king, writing to Queen Elizabeth I a few years later as the Livonian War was coming to a close: 'We seemed hitherto to vanquish him [the tsar] only in this, that he was rude of arts, and ignorant of policies ... we that know best and border upon him, do admonish other Christian princes in time, that they do not betray their dignity, liberty and life of them and their subjects to a most barbarous and cruel enemy.'

One of the English merchants to visit Russia in the later sixteenth century was Giles Fletcher, a City of London official who was sent as ambassador to Moscow in June 1588 to preserve the privileges that English merchants of the Muscovy Company had gained for themselves. The company had been established in 1551 to seek out a Northeast Passage to China. Three ships left London on 10 May 1553, of which that captained by Sir Hugh Willoughby became trapped in ice off the coast of Murmansk, the poor crew freezing to death. The vessel led by Richard Chancellor found its way to the estuary of the Northern Dvina river in the White Sea where its captain was escorted ashore to make the long journey (over 600 miles) to Moscow for a meeting with Tsar Ivan IV. Chancellor returned with promises of trade privileges. By the time of Giles Fletcher's visit, the Muscovy Company had established its warehouses in Archangel, Kholmogory, Vologda and Moscow, and about twelve ships a year made the passage, a voyage that lasted as long as that to the New World.

Fletcher returned to England in 1589 and wrote about his experiences in *Of the Russe Commonwealth*. He was impressed by the scale of everything: the size and potential of the country, not to mention the rigours of its winter climate. Of the towns, it was Moscow that he recalled most clearly: over 40,000 houses protected behind three layers of curtain walls and bigger than London. The buildings were mostly made of wood and you could buy them as a kit to put up in a day. Good Puritan that he was, Fletcher noted that God's providence had ensured that timber was in such ample supply that these houses were cheap (although God had apparently neglected to consider the risk of fire). Fletcher had good contacts with the merchant élite and was overwhelmed at the scale of their emporia, reflecting the country's vast potential. Grain was plentiful and cheap. The pastoral economy created surpluses of tallow and cow-hide. Furs from northern Russia were available in profusion. Train-oil (used in cloth and soap manufacture) was produced in large quantities from the annual seal cull in St Nicolas Bay. Although Moscow's merchants dominated this economy, provincial merchants became rich too. He heard of three brothers (the Stroganovs, though he did not know their names) from Solvychegodsk ('salt on the Vychegda river'), a settlement closer to Archangel than Moscow. They were among the earliest pioneers in Siberia.

Fletcher realized that this eastern outback had huge resources. But he turned his discourse on Russia into a warning-piece to Elizabeth I.

Russia was 'a true and strange face of a *Tyrannical state*, (most unlike to your own) without true knowledge of GOD, without written Lawe, without common iustice'. Its government was 'much after the Turkish fashion . . . plaine tyrannicall'. Fletcher had in mind some anti-Puritan (and, as he saw it, absolutist) currents at the English court. His work was so outspoken that its publication was banned by order of the queen whose beneficent rule it sought to advertise. The text would, however, be published a couple of generations later during the English Civil War, playing its part in the anti-royalist propaganda of the time. Fletcher was just one of an emerging group of travellers, diplomats and merchants from Europe whose detailed knowledge of the country emerged in print in the years before 1650. Their accounts served to consolidate the picture of a Russia whose state and society might have some affinities with those of Europe, but which did not share its values.

EUROPE IN THE MIRROR OF THE WORLD

European utopian writing was defined as a genre in the wake of America's discovery. Thomas More's 'new island' of Utopia (in Greek, 'No-Place'), described in the dialogue by the sailor Raphael Hythloday, supposedly one of Amerigo Vespucci's crew, took readers outside the place with which they were familiar in order to see it, as it were, from the outside in. Utopia was all that the humanist Thomas More wanted contemporary Christendom to be. Its citizens were public-minded, law-abiding and hard-working. They abhorred waste and lived virtuously in common with one another. 'Outside Utopia, to be sure, men talk freely of public welfare, but look after their private interests only,' Hythloday reported. 'In Utopia, where nothing is private, they seriously concern themselves with public affairs.' Utopia knew no enclosure of common land for private gain. Utopian rulers did not start wars for their private dynastic objectives. There was no hereditary nobility to lord it over others and bleed the public purse for their own profit. Using a familiar Platonic allegory, More turned the newly discovered lands into a mirror for a European space in which personal acquisitiveness was undermining the law, morality and common beliefs on which Christendom rested. The lesson that More wanted his dialogue to leave with his readers was that it was better to engage in the uphill task of reforming the common weal, albeit imperfectly, than not to do so at all. Published initially in Latin in 1516, his little treatise became translated from the later 1540s (Italian, 1548; French, 1550; English, 1551; Dutch, 1553), which was when Europe's internal regional conflicts first began to mesh with confessional strife.

As Europe's religious divisions widened, so the idea of a newly discovered city on an island far away from Europe became a way of escaping from the tensions which had been created. In the Italian peninsula, the 'Happy City' ('Eutopia' was how Thomas More's island was rendered in the Italian translation) was a world imagined by the Platonic philosopher Francesco Patrizi in a work published in Venice in 1553. As the Counter-Reformation took hold, so utopian writing became a way of putting into words ideas which otherwise would have attracted censure. Ludovico Agostini included an imaginary island republic in his 'Dialogues on the Infinite' (*Dialoghi dell'Infinito*, c. 1580), while Tommaso Campanella wrote his 'City of the Sun' (*Città del Sole*) from a Naples prison in 1602. Campanella imagined what a reformed Spanish empire might be like. He pictured state-run monastic granaries, seminaries turned into workhouses, and American Indians taught craft-skills and turned into a mobile labour force, all in the service of a providential Spanish monarchy whose destiny was to rule the world. Meanwhile, his contemporary Ludovico Zuccolo used the imaginary islands of 'Belluzzi' and 'Evandria' in 1625 to present what a reformed Venice could have been, a truly 'Serene' Republic.

Thomas More's *Utopia* also appealed to Protestant Europe, especially when the politico-religious tensions of the Reformation were at their height. The belief in providence accorded Protestant utopias a millennial dimension, often heightened by their links in Protestant central Europe to reforming chemical physicians and mystic theologians. In the feverish climate in central Europe in the aftermath of the Defenestration of Prague and the appearance of the great comet in the last months of 1618, Johann Valentin Andreae published his *Christianopolis*, a model Christian society on a far-away island, whose inhabitants tell the arriving stranger that his visit was 'under the leadership of God in order that you might learn whether it is always necessary to do evil and to live according to the custom of the barbarians' (i.e. 'Europians'). Andreae's planned city had at its heart an educational and research establishment (bearing curious similarities to the observatory of Uranienborg built in the later 1570s by the Danish astronomer Tycho Brahe on the island of Hven). For Andreae, the reform of learning was essential to making human knowledge an instrument for improving the condition of humanity rather than the weapon of first resort in confessional conflict. Around the college of learning, Andreae placed the workshops, granaries and public facilities to sustain the reformed and cohesive society of which he dreamed. Francis Bacon would draw on Andreae's *Christianopolis* when he wrote the *New Atlantis*, published in 1624. Both were models on which Samuel Hartlib, a refugee in London from Elbing as a result of the Thirty Years War, would base his sketch of the island of 'Macaria', published as the second session of the Long Parliament opened in October 1641 on the eve of the English Civil War. Hartlib was not alone in seeing the links between the planting of colonies in America and the practical realization of *Christianopolis* as a reformed polity whose values unreformed Europe had rejected.

If America had just been somewhere that Europe had not known very well before, wrote the Huguenot pastor Jean de Léry, who spent two years closely observing the Tupinambá of Brazil in 1556–8, then 'Asia and Africa could also be named new worlds with regard to us'. What made America different was that it was a continent of which there was no prior textual knowledge from Antiquity. Its discovery became a full-stop answer for those who wanted to challenge the dominant Aristotelian philosophical consensus and champion the primacy of experience over received wisdom. The Jesuit historian José de Acosta found that he was cold at midday in the Tropics despite the heat of the sun. In Aristotle's meteorology, that was an existential impossibility. But Acosta trusted his own senses and 'laughed and made fun of Aristotle and his philosophy'.

The circulation of information in print about the New World was extensive. Travel and exploration narratives found a ready market. The letters of Hernán Cortés, for example, appeared in print in five languages, all before 1525. Oviedo's 'Summary' natural history of 'the Indies' (America) was first published a year later. Peter Martyr Vermigli wrote the first complete 'history' of the New World discoveries in 1530. In 1534, Francisco Jerez's *True relation of the Conquest of Peru* appeared in Spanish, German and French, while the first part of Oviedo's more comprehensive natural history was published that same year.

It was modest in comparison with the 'decades' of Antonio de Herrera's *General History of the Indies*, published in the early years of the seventeenth century (1601–15) or Juan de Torquemada's *Indian Monarchies* (*Monarquía Indiana*, 1615), a monumental history of the indigenous peoples of America. Giovanni Battista Ramusio's *Navigations and Voyages* (*Navigationi et Viaggi*, 1550) used the notion of a 'collection' of New World travelogues as a metonymy for the whole process of discovery. He dedicated the work to Girolamo Fracastoro because he 'does not, as many do, merely imitate, or go from one book to another, modifying, transcribing, and declaring other men's things'. He is a true 'discoverer' who 'travelled the world collecting many new things never before heard of'.

The encounter with other human beings outside Europe involved a judgement. The observer had to place himself in relation to that other human being, and that place was relative, complex and emotional, as well as rational. Everyone was convinced (because Aristotle and classical Antiquity in general had taught them so) that human nature was uniform. So, the closer Europeans came into contact with the peoples of the New World (and, by extension, Africans and indigenous peoples of the eastern hemisphere), the more those peoples became a mirror in which Europeans saw themselves, their differences being mapped onto and used to explain or magnify the divisions within Europe.

When Vitoria sought a comparison for the Indians in Europe, he found it in the peasantry: 'even among our own people, we can see many peasants who are little different from brute animals'. Jesuit missionaries from 1550 onwards wrote in their letters to Rome of 'these Indies' of rural Italy, places where the peasantry lived like 'savages', their beliefs seemingly little different from those of the Indians and as resistant to the 'education' that the Counter-Reformation offered them. Italians called the invading forces from beyond the Alps in the Italian Wars of the first half of the sixteenth century 'barbarians'. The French scholar Étienne Pasquier took exception to the French being called 'barbarians', but then used the same epithet for the Germans. The 'monsters' with which travellers embellished their accounts (Amazons, androgynes, anthropophagi, giants, Cyclops, troglodytes, pygmies, people with tails) became domesticated and embodied into stereotypes of other Europeans. Cornelius Gemma, professor of medicine at Louvain, published a treatise in 1575 in which the various monstrous races were enumerated. But, he noted: 'It is not necessary to go to the New World to find beings of this sort; most of them and others still more hideous can be found here and there among us, now that the rules of justice are trampled underfoot, all humanity flouted, and all religion torn to bits.' He perhaps had contemporary pamphlet literature in mind, in which (for example) the French claimed that the English, like wild men, had tails, or that Protestants were monsters in the eyes of Catholics, and vice versa.

In the second half of the sixteenth century, and especially around 1580 (when the Spanish hegemony over the Portuguese overseas empire became a reality, and when Francis Drake had returned from his 'circumnavigation'), French and Dutch writers and engravers republished the works of las Casas and others to fashion the 'good savage', the Indian who had been oppressed by the Spanish conquerors and who would become an ally against the 'Machiavellian' cruelties of their shared enemy. That year, Montaigne published his famous essay 'On Cannibals', adopting the tone of the gentleman in his study, contemplating with bemusement the world without. Montaigne referred to his meeting and trying to converse with a native Tupinambá in Rouen. He used the experience to calibrate his reactions to what was going on in contemporary France.

To do so, Montaigne drew on the freshly published account of the Protestant pastor Jean de Léry's experience of the siege of Sancerre in 1573. During the siege, Léry entered the house of one of his flock who, starving, had eaten the flesh of his three-year-old daughter. Seeing her cooked tongue on plates, Léry wondered why his visceral revulsion had not been similar when he had studied the cannibalistic practices of the Tupinambá Indians during the Villegagnon expedition to Brazil in 1556-7. As a good Calvinist, he had a clear sense of where to draw the line between 'us' and 'them', and he was in no doubt that it was not just cultural but also theological. Only God ultimately knew who were saved and who were not, and Calvin had been unambiguous: 'there is no nation so barbarous, no race so brutish, as not to be imbued with the conviction that there is a God'. Yet, in the case of the Tupinambá their superstition had become ingrained, transmitted from their forefathers, because they were the descendants of Ham and cursed. He interpreted Indian ritual shrieks as demonic possession. They were, in short, unredeemable.

Yet, back in Europe where it should have been different, it wasn't. There too, cannibalism existed, and that was Montaigne's point. 'I am not sorry that we notice the barbarous horror of such acts,' he said, 'but I am heartily sorry that, judging their faults rightly we should be so blind to our own.' When Jean de Léry recalled the ritual dances of the Indians, it was not in order to dismiss them as simply demonic: 'hearing the measured harmonies of such a multitude, and especially in the cadence and refrain of the song, when at every verse they would let their voices trail, saying *Heu, heuaure, heura, heuraure, heura, heura, oueh* – I stood there transported with delight. Whenever I remember it, my heart trembles.' The discovery of America awakened Europe to what was 'curious' and 'wonderful', but also 'barbarian'. The savages became part of what it was to be European.

7. Earth and Heavens Observed

NATURE AND DIVERSITY

The age of discovery was not merely the exploration and settlement of a new continent, the encounter with the world's oceans, and the locating of Europe within them. It was also the unearthing of a new sense of nature and the universe. Christendom's theologians believed that the natural order was subservient to God and that the created universe was a reflection of his divine will. God could use nature to stimulate us to magnify his greatness and be in awe of his creation and omnipotence. The continuing volcanic action on Mount Etna and the legendary salamander's regeneration through fire were taken by St Augustine as examples of God's intervention in nature to remind us that God could make human bodies burn for eternity. The biblical record was ample evidence that he could cause extraordinary events to occur in the natural world. Meteorites, comets, monstrous births and other strange phenomena should be taken as warning signs of God's wrath or of imminent great events. At the least, they were an acknowledgement that nature was unpredictable, shifting and irregular.

In the Central Middle Ages Christendom recovered the teachings of Greek philosophers – particularly Aristotle and Galen – which coalesced with what was already known as the Ptolemaic geocentric universe. Nature became an ordered and comprehended space, part of the universal and divinely sanctioned truth alongside theology, things that we could know for certain and which constituted 'knowledge' (*scientia*). Because divine and human truth were the same thing, natural philosophy was an integral part of Christendom's structures of belief. Given the complexity of the natural world (and the human body as a part of it), Aristotelian natural philosophy and Galenic medicine concentrated on general statements about the causes of certain phenomena. To have done otherwise would have risked compromising the certainty of knowledge, finding endless variants for which there was no explanation, and entering a world of dangerous uncertainty. So medieval philosophers created an Aristotle in their own image. They marginalized some works (the treatises on physics, meteorology, zoology, biology and natural history) in favour of others (the metaphysics). In a similar way, Galenic medicine (recovered through Latin translations of Islamic medical texts) offered explanations of human physiology and disease rather than the *practica* of therapeutic cures. Aristotelian forms, elements and the primal qualities of hot, wet, cold and dry (the basis of Galenic humoral pathology) made nature conform to 'science'.

The demands of certainty, however, meant accepting that nature was not governed by inexorable 'laws'. There needed to be room for the variants that occurred in the natural world. Nature obeyed 'rules' (*regula*) not laws. She was a divinely instituted 'Artificer', whose habits and inclinations explained the movement, gestation, generation and decay that occurred in the natural world. The Aristotelian-Galenic explanatory framework was reassuring. The large-scale picture (the macrocosm) mapped onto the smaller-scale one (the microcosm), a framework matching the local with the universal. In its homeostatic and organic universe nothing challenged God's infinity and power. Its truth was confirmed by what could be observed by everyone and by what had been experienced in the past.

Human beings saw the heavens spinning in apparently circular motion above their heads, defining time. They equally expected things to be different on earth. There, some heavy things fell to the ground whereas others did not. Solid bodies acted differently from liquids and air. Aristotelian philosophy explained this difference between terrestrial and celestial behaviour. The spheres were composed of a single element (aether) whose natural motion was circular, and which might be denser or rarer, but never substantially changed. The heavens were, like God himself, eternal and changeless. The comets which appeared from time to time were ephemera, meteorological phenomena in the upper atmosphere. Earth, by contrast, was composed of different elements (earth, air, fire, water) whose essential behaviour, motion and transformation defined their differences one from another. The complexity of terrestrial matter was considerable but not infinite. It was encased by the celestial aether and its transformation and motion were limited. Everything was, relative to everything else, local. Heavy bodies might fall, but their velocity was defined, and they would eventually find the place of rest which the universe dictated for them. Solids might liquefy and liquids might vaporize, but their new condition was one that their 'form' defined and constrained. There could be no such thing as emptiness, since space itself was defined by that which gave form to a body – length, breadth and depth. Scholastic writers even attributed to nature a *horror vacui*, a force by which nature resisted allowing a vacuum to form.

The kind of nature that came to the forefront in the course of the sixteenth and early seventeenth centuries was different. It was a cornucopia, so diverse that it could not conceptually, methodologically or institutionally be embodied in a science in the way that Aristotelians understood that term. Sixteenth-century naturalists concentrated on the discovery of the particular. That was partly what humanist philology and palaeography had been about. The Greek 'historia' meant 'learning by enquiry', and natural history was part of the rhetoric of 'discovery'. The best-known ancient natural history was Pliny the Elder's. Pliny's contemporary, the Greek physician in the service of the Roman army Dioscorides, also furnished an encyclopaedia of plants, animals and minerals with their medicinal uses. Both works attracted the attention of humanist editors. A similar focus on particularity occurred in the medical world. Physicians had always noted the symptoms which they encountered when diagnosing the ailments of their patients. But, in the newly edited texts of the ancient Greek physician Hippocrates they discovered a clinical doctor who emphasized the symptoms of a disease over diagnosing its causes.

The study of nature's particulars followed from the texts themselves. In order to establish what the words used by Pliny and Dioscorides for certain plants meant, they had to be related to examples in the real world, which required hunting them out. Similarly, Hippocrates's works stimulated physicians to write case-notes on their patients' conditions and to study particular 'cures'. The latter were often associated with thermal springs such as those at Padua. Each spa had healing properties which were specific to particular ailments. At the same time, there was a growing appreciation of botanical plants for medicinal purposes. Medical faculties sought to control the activities of apothecaries, practitioners whose commercial success attested to the success of applied knowledge of medicinal plants ('simples') and the preparation of medicines ('compounds'). That oversight entailed emulating the apothecaries, and medical faculties began appointing professors of medical botany, such posts being commonplace by the 1550s.

Medicinal cures stimulated the foundation of botanic gardens. The construction of the one for the medical faculty at Padua, opened in 1545, was directed by the Italian architect Daniele Barbaro. Its circular garden was constructed around a rampart. Drawing on military architecture, tunnels provided access to the enclosed parterres. From the rampart, students looked down on the world of nature, laid out in geometrically interlocking shapes. The design incorporated a labyrinth, and it was inspired by Vitruvius, whose works Barbaro had edited. The plan was ingenious, but it implied that medical simples were an enclosed world in which there was no more to be discovered. Later university botanical gardens were more flexible. That constructed at Leiden in 1590 – its first director being Charles de l'Escluse (Carolus Clusius) – had a capacity for over 1,000 plants and fenced-off beds to protect the rarest species. The University of Montpellier's garden used designs by Pierre Richer de Belleval to create local climates and increase the range of plants that could be grown.

Luca Ghini, professor of medical botany at the University of Pisa, was perhaps the first botanist in Europe to collect plant specimens, press them flat and dry them, and then attach them to card to form the equivalent of a botanical garden in a desiccated form, his 'herbaria'. The resulting *hortus siccus* ('dry garden') was an encyclopaedia. The herbaria of the 1530s and 1540s described about 800 vascular plants (i.e. with tissues for conducting water). In 1623, the Basel botanist Caspar Bauhin's catalogue enumerated over 5,000. Instruments for use as well as ornamentation, surviving herbaria from this period are annotated with cross-references and different vernacular identifications. Ulisse Aldrovandi, professor of fossils, plants and animals at Bologna, the moving force behind the creation of its botanical garden and the author of natural histories, described his own collections (which were opened in 1617 as Europe's first public science museum) as a 'digest of nature' (*Pandechio di natura*). Visitors regarded them as an 'eighth wonder of the world'.

These collections resulted from the exchange of information and specimens among naturalists by correspondence. Studying nature signalled one's eligibility to belong to the 'republic of letters'. The latter was a virtual community whose social composition was fluid (it included apothecaries, physicians, academics, printers, publishers, gentlemen-scholars and aficionados – with aristocratic women only at the margins). Part of the appeal of studying nature in this way was that it was immune to Europe's political and religious divisions. Its virtuosi were unlikely to be accused of atheism, given that (as they emphasized) they discovered the evidence of God in nature. Naturalists themselves were aware they were engaged in a collective enterprise, conscious that they could not master nature's diversity on their own. In the preface to his natural history of Spanish rare plants (*Rariorum aliquot stirpium per Hispanias observatarum historia*, 1576), Clusius at Leiden said that he was overwhelmed by the arrival of new specimens. His contemporary Adriaan van de Spiegel echoed his sentiments: 'no human mind, however diligent, will ever achieve a wholly perfect knowledge of plants, for their variety is infinite'.

Plant anthologies (*florilegia*), emancipated from medicinal botany, grew more detailed and richly illustrated. The woodcuts prepared by Hans Weiditz II for Otto Brunfels's *Illustrations of Living Plants* (*Herbarum vivae eicones*, 1532) could be used to identify a specimen. Leonhart Fuchs's *Natural History of Plants* (*De historia stirpium*) of 1542 provided a small-format gazetteer for plants for use on field-trips. Seventeenth-century, large-format *florilegia* concentrated on particular regions or even specific gardens. Botanical commonplace books became essential for naturalists to manage the increasing volume of information.

In Rome, the aristocrat Federico Cesi spent his fortune on patronizing the new science. In 1603, he founded the Academy of the Lynxes, named after Lyncaeus, the sharp-eyed Argonaut. Its members collected specimens, examined and recorded what they saw and communicated their discoveries to one another in special cryptographic writing. The Lincean Fabio Colonna pioneered the use of etching for plant illustration which, even more than copper engraving, conveyed their morphology and texture. Galileo Galilei was elected an academy member in 1611. He counted on their patronage to protect his astronomical discoveries and sent fellow-Linceans his *occhialino* (microscope) in 1624. By inverting telescope technology, Galileo furnished a way of discovering that nature was even more varied than one could discern with the naked eye: 'I have seen,' he wrote, 'those little animals in the grains of cheese, in truth a stupendous thing.' The academicians used the microscope to study bees. The emblem of the Barberini, a powerful Florentine family, was a trigon of bees, and Maffeo Barberini had become Pope Urban VIII in August 1623. The opportunity to demonstrate to the pontiff that the Linceans could ally papal prestige with discoveries of God's power in nature was not to be lost. The preface addressed to the new pope in the *Melissographia* (1625) explained that 'great miracles have emerged . . . and the eye has learned to have greater faith'. In accompanying publications, the Linceans included pleas for tolerating their new approach. The microscope penetrated beyond the superficially visible to discover that, in the underlying structure, nature decomposed into geometrical shapes. The reticulations of the bees' eyes mirrored the hexagonal cells of the beehive. In the Lincei portfolios, cross-sectional drawings reflect their concentration on these inward structures.

By the early seventeenth century, common-sense classifications of flora and fauna were breaking down. Naturalists' methods emphasized the importance of morphological descriptions and differences, which accentuated the diversity in nature but did not help with classification. Plant nomenclatures, initially confused by a plethora of vernacular variants, were gradually subsumed into generic classifications. Local knowledge became something more universal. But classification on the basis of what one could superficially observe (colour, texture, size) seemed no longer to work. The more naturalists saw, the less observation on its own offered a secure basis for taxonomy. As Galileo and other natural philosophers insisted, the evidence of the senses was too subjective to reveal the hidden constants in the world of nature.

What was true of botany was also true in zoology, where books on fishes (by the distinguished Montpellier physician Guillaume Rondelet) and birds (by the French ornithologist and traveller Pierre Belon) described and illustrated species on the basis of observations, relating those which they found to those discovered by the ancients and making sense as seemed best of the accretions of mythology and earlier Christian fantasy. As they confronted exotic nature from outside Europe, however, they were compelled to 'undress' the objects in nature which they had hitherto dressed up with emblematic meanings. In addition, as the animal kingdom grew larger, it posed a problem for those natural philosophers who sought to imagine what Noah's Ark had been like. The Bible stories of the Garden of Eden, the Tower of Babel, Solomon's Temple and the Flood were taken as defining the potential, but also the limitations, of human wisdom and the framing of the created order. The particularities of each story came under scrutiny, raising more questions than could be answered. To accommodate the new species in the Ark defied the laws of physics.

The conventional wisdom was that natural philosophers were 're-covering' the wisdom of the ancients. The title-page engraving of the *Universal History of Plants* (*Historia plantarum universalis*) of Johannes Bauhin, Caspar's elder brother, and his fellow-botanist from Basel Johann Heinrich Cherler, published in 1650–51, depicted a garden, surrounded by ancient worthies (Theophrastus, Dioscorides, Pliny, Galen) whose example had inspired the 'moderns'. In reality, however, the latter were discovering new knowledge, and in new ways. Natural history involved collecting 'rarities' from strange places. Finding specimens required travel, and physicians increasingly took their students on botanizing expeditions to out-of-the way places. A few naturalists travelled outside Europe (Francisco Hernández to Mexico, Leonhard Rauwolf to the Near East, Prosper Alpino to Egypt, Garcia da Orta to India), but the majority of animals and plants in the world beyond European space were known only indirectly through travellers' accounts and specimens. Even so, the result was an accretion of data about species which had no equivalent in the records from Antiquity. They included walrus with curious teeth from Russia, elks that resembled no animal a European had ever seen before, remarkable carnivorous plants from South America, and birds of paradise which reportedly had no feet because they never landed on the earth. The banyan tree (*Ficus indica*) had branches that grew upwards and downwards at the same time.

The potential for new medical cures seemed infinite. The Spanish physician Nicolás Monardes published a study of medicinal plants encountered in the New World. His book *Medical study of the products imported from our West Indian Possessions* (1565) included the first account of the therapeutic benefits of what the Spanish named 'tobacco'. Translated into English and published in 1577, the work was optimistically entitled: *Joyfull Newes out of the Newe Founde Worlde*. Only in the seventeenth century did naturalists begin to have extensive direct experience of the world beyond Europe and, with it, the capacity to separate out the untruths which their own emblematic world view, coupled with inadequate sources of information and their conception of the world outside Europe as 'strange', had perpetuated.

Nature also lay at their doorstep. Conrad Gessner went into the mountains to collect material for his botanical history. He described reaching the summit of Mount Pilatus near Lucerne as finding a new paradise. Gardens became a natural philosophers' retreat. It was not in the university lecture-room or the pages of Aristotle that truth about nature was to be found, but in gardens, kitchens, the countryside and collectors' cabinets. The study-space for nature expanded and so did its audience. The growth of urban gardens was an offshoot of the spread of urban space. Gentrified horticulture and arboriculture were a parallel development, the dominion over nature being expressed through the grafting of fruit trees or the cultivation of hybrids. Books about nature appealed beyond botanical aficionados to a wider market where the exotic and the novel in nature generated enthusiasm. In Rome, the Jesuit priest Giovanni Battista Ferrari published the first work devoted to ornamental flowers (*De Florum Cultura*, 1633). It included several illustrations of the 'Chinese rose' (*Hibiscus mutabilis*), which he cultivated for the first time in a European environment, and which changed colour in the course of a day. In the Netherlands, tulips became a commercial speculation. People were prepared to pay colossal prices for brightly coloured and rare varieties to put into gardens and window-boxes, until the bubble burst in 1637.

Princely courts fed the interest in the exotic. They were repositories for lions, tigers, Turkish hens, dwarfs, fools and automata of all kinds. Rarities, like religious relics, were treasured and became part of the pageantry of secular and ecclesiastical authority, *divertissements* from the boredom of court life. Aristocratic and courtly collectors were drawn to the power over the natural world which 'possessing' it afforded. Giuseppe Gabrieli, giving his inaugural lecture as professor of 'materia medica' at the University of Ferrara in 1543, emphasized how the subject was 'not only for humble and lowly men, but people from every social class conspicuous for political power, wealth, nobility and knowledge such as kings, emperors, princes'. He praised the d'Este princes for their patronage, and said natural history had raised 'its head from the most profound darkness' to become the 'only science of divine origins, given to men by the Gods'.

Rulers vied with one another to secure the services of naturalists. In 1544, Cosimo I de' Medici, first grand duke of Tuscany, lured Luca Ghini from Bologna to Pisa to manage his botanical garden. The papacy realized the possibilities of presenting itself as head of a global Christianity which embraced the whole of nature. In the 1560s, Michele Mercati was invited to create the papacy's botanical garden and to supervise a mineralogical museum (the *Metallotheca*). Mercati's teacher, Andrea Cesalpino, who had succeeded Luca Ghini to the chair at Pisa, left the Medici to join the papal household after Mercati's death in 1593, having already acquired a reputation for his precise classification of plants as well as a description of the circulation of the blood which prefigured William Harvey's discovery. Not to be outdone, Philip II commissioned his physician, Francisco Hernández, to go to Mexico to collect plants, animals and minerals. In 1576, he despatched sixteen large volumes back to Spain, along with thousands of specimens and illustrations, commissioned from native Aztecs. So diverse was the material that it languished in the Escorial library, though part of it found its way to Rome, where it was published by the Linceans. Meanwhile, the Valois promoted the career of their Overseer of the Royal Collection of Curiosities at Fontainebleau, André Thevet. In the following century, Johan Mauritz of Nassau-Siegen established a zoo, botanical garden and museum in 'New Holland' (Dutch Brazil). He commissioned Georg Margraf to produce a natural history (published in 1648), copies of which Johan Mauritz used as gifts. Court artists presented the natural world in beguiling ways for their audience. Jacopo Ligozzi in Florence, Teodoro Ghisi at the Mantuan court, and Giuseppe Arcimboldo in the service of the emperors Maximilian II and Rudolf II evoked the natural world as an escape from political and religious divisions while the artists of the School of Fontainebleau created cornucopian visions of nature's plenty, the richness of nature becoming a metaphor for the largesse of the French monarchy.

Collecting natural objects was a shared occupation and a means to comprehend and thereby exploit nature. Botanical gardens and anatomy theatres acquired 'cabinets of curiosities'. Physicians, apothecaries and natural philosophers were joined by Counter-Reformed clerics (the Jesuit Athanasius Kircher, founder of the Roman College Museum) and magistrates (Nicolas-Claude Fabri de Peiresc in Aix) as the fascination for collecting broadened and deepened. The largest and most varied cabinets required princely resources. The most celebrated in the later sixteenth century were in the palaces of the Gonzaga in Mantua, the Upper Castle at Ambras, owned by Archduke Ferdinand II of the Tyrol, and those of emperors Maximilian II in Vienna and Rudolf II in Prague. The latter's were so extensive that, after his death, his successor, Emperor Matthias, persuaded his brothers that the collection should be thereafter inherited by the eldest member of the family and kept in a special Treasury.

MONSTERS, MARVELS AND MAGIC

Within the medieval Aristotelian consensus, it was always possible that nature, while obeying its own 'rules', might produce accidental results – children with six fingers, comets in the upper atmosphere, and so on. Such happenings might be like the droughts, plagues of locusts, angelic manifestations and prophetic dreams in the Bible, signs from God to his chosen people. They might equally be the work of the Devil, whose ability to send 'false prophets' also had biblical attestation. Violent portents disturbed nature and so the temptation was to assign them to some demonic force. The appearance of 'monsters' (conjoined twins, for example) was transgressive, a sign that the Devil was responsible. Then again, it was possible that nature could produce 'marvels' which were simply 'prodigies', preternatural (against the natural order of things) rather than supernatural (divinely orchestrated miracles). The question was how to read the signs in the natural world.

That issue was a consequence of the emphasis on particularity and strangeness in nature, and it was not resolved before 1650. It was also a concomitant effect of the struggle to absorb new and apparently divergent phenomena from outside Europe. The New World was immense, but also marvellous and monstrous. Monstrosity signalled the breakdown of inherited, common-sense categories into which flora and fauna, as well as natural events, were classified. The emphasis on 'prodigies' in nature was another way of expressing the blurring of categories between what was 'natural' and what was not. In curiosity cabinets there were often 'monstrosities' whose deformities were the object of speculation. The Gonzaga collection in Mantua included a stuffed two-bodied puppy and a preserved human foetus with four eyes and two mouths. The objects at the Schloss Ambras included a painting of a 'wild man'.

The individual in question was from the Canary Islands, and he and his daughters suffered from a genetic ailment, resulting in a superabundance of bodily hair, which rendered them objects of speculation about monstrous barbarism. When the Linceans dissected a hermaphroditic rat or studied a deformed nestling, it was not apparent what distinguished nature's rarities from its aberrations.

The literature about monsters and prodigies irrupted before the Protestant Reformation, especially in Northern Italy and Germany. In a crescendo of rhetoric about the need for spiritual reformation and knowledge of the Bible, unnatural events were interpreted as God's anger at human sin. The survival of Christendom seemed to be at stake. Printed accounts of monsters and portents generated the impression that these were on the increase. The Protestant Reformation, coupled with the intensified Turkish threat (interpreted as God's portent about Christendom's imminent demise), transformed the culture of monsters and prodigies. The explosive events in Germany accompanying the Protestant Reformation seemed to its supporters to be God's sign that the world was living in its Last Days. 'This is now the last age, when the Gospels are resounding, and crying out against the Pope,' wrote Luther. His opponent Johannes Cochlaeus depicted Luther in 1529 as the seven-headed monster of the Beast in the Book of Revelation. Lutheran propagandists responded with the 'Seven-Headed Papal Monster', a woodcut depicting a beast with its claws trampling the Gospels underfoot and its mouth (like a lion's – a reference to Pope Leo X) threatening to swallow up countries. Reformation turmoil sensitized contemporaries to the signs in nature that what was happening was part of God's providential plan.

As the controversies of the Protestant Reformation deepened, so did the debate over monsters, prodigies and portents. Protestants saw them as warning signs from God, but Catholics interpreted them as false signs from the Devil. Religious tensions led both sides to enlarge the scope of divine intervention and to sharpen the distinction between what could be ascribed to divine forces and what might be explained by irregularities in nature itself. The natural histories of portents and prodigies, prolific from the later 1550s, contributed to a sense of apocalyptic anxiety. Their authors developed a pseudo-science of 'teratoscopy' (the study of prodigies in nature). Philipp Melanchthon's relative Caspar Peucer published a synthesis in 1553, trying to separate out 'holy prophecies' from 'natural predictions' and the 'ruses of Satan'. His objective was to demonstrate that, although the Devil had vitiated the certainties of divination, there were still signs and portents which could be ascribed to God. In Basel, Conrad Lycosthenes spent twenty years compiling a chronicle (*Prodigiorum ac ostentorum chronicon*, 1557) of prodigies and portents. He used the terms 'sign', 'prodigy', 'miracle' and 'manifestation' interchangeably to describe violent, hideous or strange events, all signs from God. And since a tenth of those which he recorded occurred in the period from 1550 to 1557, Lycosthenes saw his chronicle as proof that Christendom was under threat. The conjuncture between religious and political turmoil and a portent and prodigy literature continued into the first half of the seventeenth century, although in the salons of the virtuosi of the new science it was transposed into a culture of curiosity and *divertissement*, tinged with scepticism.

Contrasting explanations for unexplained phenomena also existed from among those who studied alternative currents in ancient philosophy. The works of the Epicureans, Stoics, Platonists and Pyrrhonists became available in printed editions, while Hebraists explored the esoteric philosophy and techniques of the Kabbalah. Amid this period of classical discovery, the life and works of Aristotle acquired a historical perspective. As the alternatives to Aristotelian philosophy came to the fore, they provided a credible basis from which to attack Aristotle himself. Neo-Platonists, in particular, thought that the 'marvellous effects' which occurred in nature could be explained by an alternative model of how the universe worked. Life-forces existed, immanent in nature, which could not be accounted for in terms of Aristotelian categories of matter and form. The world was a 'feeling animal'. The 'souls' of animate nature were instruments of these energies. The latter (often described as a *pneuma*, not exactly matter and not quite mind) linked the microcosm to the macrocosm, bodiless and embodied things in a mystic harmony. These harmonies could be detected by an adept through the power of natural magic. Through music, mathematics and spiritual and psychological magic, the magus could enter a higher world of figures and celestial influences in which the deeper truths which God had placed in nature could be accessed by human imagination.

The agenda of natural magic was ambitious. In reality, Neo-Platonists differed from one another on both the definitions and the details of how one might proceed. They had no common platform. On their own, they could not supplant the Aristotelian consensus. They were always vulnerable to the charge of being cheats and impostors, deluding people with the pretence of understanding occult celestial forces. But their impact was real enough, at least until the demands for an explanation of the universe that relied on more transparent and imposed laws of nature began to make themselves felt towards 1650. Neo-Platonist explanations seemed to be supported by a more powerful mathematics, capable of representing complex relationships in geometrical and algebraic form. The adepts of the new chemical philosophy also found in Neo-Platonic explanations a language and vision of animist complexity which provided a basis for attempts to explain chemical change. Neo-Platonists used their anti-Aristotelianism as a rhetorical platform to their advantage. More, they offered a plethora of examples of their explanations at work in nature. They emphasized at every turn that (unlike Aristotelians) their aim was to bring about something practical. They believed in and practised experiments. Above all, Neo-Platonists had all-embracing explanations for natural phenomena that did not rule out God's power in the universe. On the contrary, their picture of an animate nature reinforced the sense that God was close by, a great artificer in nature, at work in the forces of his universe. By the same token, however, Neo-Platonists had to admit that such life-forces were capable of being suborned by those who chose to be instruments of the Devil. And in the Manichean atmosphere of the Post-Reformation, the Devil was becoming a more significant enemy in what remained of Christendom.

In 1533, Heinrich Agrippa published an enlarged edition of his *Occult Philosophy* (*De occulta philosophia*) which, through its frequent reprinting and many translations, defined 'natural magic'. Agrippa was an artful vulgarizer and drew on the works of Italian Neo-Platonists (especially Giovanni Pico della Mirandola and Marsilio Ficino), Jewish Kabbalists, Hermes Trismegistus, Pythagoras and Zoroaster, which he encountered during the six years he spent in North Italy in imperial service from 1512 to 1518. 'That magic is natural,' he wrote, 'which having observed the forces of all things natural and celestial and having examined by painstaking inquiry the sympathy among those things, brings into the open powers hidden and stored away in nature.' 'Magic' was that which 'links lower things as if they were magical enticements to the gifts of higher things'. 'Astonishing wonders thereby occur,' he continued, 'not so much by art as by nature to which – as nature works these wonders – this art of magic offers herself as a handmaiden.'

Magic was not what magicians do, but what nature accomplishes with their help. By describing magic as the link between lower and higher bodies, Agrippa emphasized astrology. 'Magic is so connected and conjoined with astrology,' he said, 'that anyone who professes magic without astrology accomplishes nothing.' Agrippa did more than anyone else to give respectability to 'occult' philosophy in the sixteenth century. To illustrate the potential of natural magic he interspersed his philosophy with experiments. He used magnets, heliotropes, basilisks, dragons, electric ray fish, mandrake, opium, hellebore and dragon's wort (tarragon) to exemplify the strange powers in nature which he claimed to be able to understand and harness through natural magic.

Agrippa knew that such power in the wrong hands could become sorcery. His book was published in defiance of the Dominican inquisitors, alert to the spectre of demonology as witchcraft prosecutions became more prevalent. Agrippa was careful to include in the revised 1533 edition a recantation of magical philosophy, one which he had initially published seven years previously as part of his *On the Uncertainty and Vanity of the Sciences* (*De incertitudine et vanitate scientiarum*), another famous book which denounced human arts and sciences (especially astrology) as useless, particularly in the hands of scholastic theologians and avaricious clerics. Read in the context of the Lutheran Reformation, to which he was inclined, Agrippa wanted to say that there was no real knowledge beyond faith in Scripture. Set alongside his views in *Occult Philosophy*, the perplexity in which he left his reader made the book notorious, contributing to accusations of his supposed dealings with the Devil. Some details around the legendary Dr Faustus are attributable to Agrippa.

Occult philosophy was especially influential among the growing numbers of nonconformist thinkers in Europe whose careers as physicians, alchemists and astrologers provided them with a platform for their speculations. Girolamo Cardano, a trained physician from the universities of Pavia and Padua, established a name for himself as a mathematics teacher in Milan before setting up a successful medical practice. He already had a reputation as an algebraist who had probed the laws of probability before he published *On the Subtlety of Things* (*De subtilitate rerum*, 1550). The publisher's blurb said that the book offered its readers 'the causes, powers, and properties of more than 1500 varied, uncommon, difficult, hidden and beautiful things'. Cardano himself emphasized that reading his book was like going into a cabinet of curiosities, warning readers of its 1554 edition (by which time it had expanded to offer '2,200 very beautiful things'): 'many will read, but few, if any, will understand everything written here'.

Cardano was a serious astrologer, deploying an observational knowledge of the movements of the sun, moon and known planets to predict and explain the history of the world, and to cast horoscopes for the alive and dead. At the same time, he knew the dangers that lay in store for his reputation. His 'rivals' would cause him 'harm' if his predictions turned out to be false. Always charge a high fee for astrological consultations, he advised, and never publish anything, 'for those who do so make themselves infamous even when their predictions are true'. Cardano did not follow his own advice, however, and his first publication was a *Prognostication* (1534). The great conjunction of Saturn and Jupiter which occurred that year predicted 'that the world must soon undergo a complete renewal. Pay attention. Sacred Scripture and astrology have shown us, without doubt, that our insatiable rapacity must soon come to an end.' Four years later, he became the first astrologer to publish a collection of 'genitures' (or horoscopes) of famous people, alive and dead, based on the disposition of the planets at their birth. The result was a provocative work of literature, in which the faults and fortunes of the famous (they included Nero, Luther, Dürer and Savonarola) were exposed, but found to lie in the stars. The work invited the barrage of criticism which it duly received. But it also opened the door to invitations from princely clients (including King Edward VI of England) who were persuaded that it was better to know what the stars had in store before it happened to them.

Cardano distanced himself from Aristotelian natural philosophy. He wrote and rewrote his autobiography, examining his life as though it was a scientific subject in its own right. Occult powers had psychic as well as physical impact, and his interest in dreams as 'an admirable form of divination' was as considerable as his theories of metoposcopy (predictions of human behaviour from characteristics of the forehead) and chiromancy (predictions using palm-reading). Like Agrippa, he was aware of the dangers that could occur when magical power fell into evil hands. He emphasized that it was only when such knowledge was put to practical use to improve the condition of human life that it could be regarded as legitimate. Cardano's *On Subtlety* was the object of an attack by another natural philosopher, Julius Caesar Scaliger, in 1557. When challenged,

Cardano shrouded himself with the justification that mystic inspiration, beyond his own powers of explanation, led him on. That was not sufficient for the Inquisition in Bologna, however, which imprisoned him in 1570 because he had attempted to cast Christ's horoscope.

The Elizabethan magus-mathematician John Dee was a devoted astrologer. From his days as a student in Louvain in 1547, he kept notes of planetary positions from which to cast horoscopes. In his first published work (a set of aphorisms on mathematical astrology) he compared the universe to the harmonious resonances of a lyre. Then, following in Agrippa's footsteps, he explored the Jewish esoteric tradition of the Kabbalah. This taught that Creation descended from the perfection of God down to the imperfect material world. The letters of the Hebrew alphabet, which are also numbers, were the building blocks of Creation and the key to Holy Scripture. By making words numbers, and using Kabbalistic interpretive techniques, the underlying numerical harmonies in the universe could be detected. *Monas Hieroglyphica* (1564), his most acclaimed work during his lifetime, showed how a geometrical symbol (a hieroglyph) was one from which all other symbols could be constructed. It formed the key to a symbolic system and accompanying exegesis. In his *Mathematical Preface* (1570) to Henry Billingsley's popular translation of Euclid's *Elements*, Dee turned this Kabbalistic manipulation of symbols into a plea for the application of mathematics to the searching out of all knowledge.

That was a goal he shared with Johannes Kepler, who, abandoning his theological studies, became obsessed with applying mathematics to the discovery of heavenly harmonies. Inspired by a vision which came to him while teaching, Kepler conceived of a hieroglyph, analogous to Dee's, with which to explain why God had decided that there were only six (known) planets, and why he should have determined that they have orbits. Kepler was district mathematician in Graz until he visited Rudolf II's imperial mathematician, Tycho Brahe, in 1600 and became his assistant. Following Brahe's death a year later, he succeeded him to that post in Prague, thereby inheriting his planetary observations (the Rudolphine Tables). Kepler sought an answer to the question about the number of planets and their orbits which explained why things were the way they were in the real world. His hieroglyph was based on the five, regular 'Platonic' solids. By the principles of Euclidean geometry, they were the only possible three-dimensional objects with all faces the same. So, when God inscribed those solids into the spheres of the planets, six was the only number of planets that there could ever be, and their orbits relative to each other were inscribed and circumscribed (he followed a Copernican heliocentric picture of the universe) by the shapes of those solids. He outlined this 'geometrical Kabbalah' in *Cosmographic Mystery* (*Mysterium cosmographicum*, 1596).

Three years later, Kepler began work on his masterpiece, the *Harmony of the World*. When it was finally completed and published in 1619, Kepler expanded his Neo-Platonic conception of the universe to include the Pythagorean harmony of the spheres. His explanation began with an analysis of musical harmony. There was also a long section on astrological harmonies affecting sublunary nature, for Kepler was a convinced astrologer, albeit critical of simplistic notions as to how planetary conjunctions might dictate what happened on earth. By then, and on the strength of his and Brahe's astronomical observations, he had convinced himself that planetary orbits were not circular but elliptical, but he managed to explain that too within his Neo-Platonism.

To understand the motions of the planets around the sun, Kepler had recourse to something like magnetic force, as examined by William Gilbert, physician to Elizabeth I, in his *On the Magnet* (*De Magnete*, 1600). Scornful of Aristotelian learning, Gilbert acknowledged his debts instead to the mathematical and navigational practitioners in London – those 'who have invented and published magnetic instruments and ready methods of observing, necessary for mariners' work and those who make long voyages'. But it was Cardano who led him to his 'magnetic philosophy', in which the earth was infused with a hidden energy, a giant magnet, alive and self-moving around its own axis. To prove the case, Gilbert turned to the 'microcosm' of the world, the lodestone, and it was at this point that the practitioners provided him with the instruments to carry out 'experiments' (his preferred term) by which to tease out what navigators had already discovered for themselves, namely the existence of magnetic North, and the declination of the compass needle at different longitudes.

Astrologers, astronomers, magicians and mathematicians, like cosmographers and naturalists, became respected figures at European courts. Pope Paul III was one of several occupants of the papal throne in the sixteenth century to employ a resident astrologer. Michel de Nostredame (Nostradamus), who acquired a reputation as a medical practitioner at Salon in Provence, began producing his annual almanac in 1550. His

Prophecies (or *Centuries*) followed in 1555. Catherine de Médicis, then queen in France, had been brought up at the Florentine court, which made her particularly well-disposed to judicial astrology and the power of natural magic. She asked Nostradamus to prepare royal horoscopes for her children. When she became queen mother and regent in France, she secured his appointment as court physician and consulted him about propitious moments for her family. Queen Elizabeth's coronation was held on 15 January 1559, following the horoscope cast for her by John Dee. The queen held him at arm's length thereafter, but he busied himself as a consultant to the English Muscovy Company and the adventurers colonizing North America. Complaining of slanders against him and protesting that he was innocent of 'unchristian' practices, Dee succumbed to the enticements of a Polish aristocrat (Albrecht Łaski), who accepted him for the great magus that he claimed to be, and fell under the influence of an impostor (Edward Talbot, alias Edward Kelley) posing as a spirit medium.

Dee then turned to Emperor Rudolf II and, in August 1584, he and Kelley moved to Prague. He had an audience with the emperor, telling him that through his medium (Kelley) he enjoyed conversations with angels who told Dee that he was God's chosen prophet. He offered to make the emperor a party to these conversations. If Rudolf repented of his sins and believed in the message that Dee would convey to him, he would triumph over his enemies, defeat the Turk, and become the greatest emperor in the world. The emperor indulged his fascination for clockwork automata, his search for perpetual motion, his alchemy, and his predilection for mineralogical and botanical collecting, attracting to his court the most prominent occult philosophers and alchemists of the day. 'His Majesty is interested only in wizards, alchymists, Kabbalists and the like,' said one enemy. Dee, however, was disappointed. Rudolf wanted to maintain religious peace in the fragile political situation of the empire. Dee angled to be the emperor's magician-confessor, revealing secrets in return for action and commitment. But Rudolf's interests in magic grew out of passive resignation and spiritual pessimism. At the insistence of the papal nuncio, who was convinced Dee was a 'conjuror and a bankrupt alchemist', the emperor expelled him in 1586.

In retrospect, the last years of the sixteenth century were the high-water mark of respectability for astrologers at European courts; their courtly influence declined thereafter. The hidden homologies of the universe, on which their science depended, seemed out of place or irrelevant in the Thirty Years War, where political and military conflicts, the course of which they had failed to predict, were so immediate. Their science required substantial reworking in order to embrace a heliocentric cosmology. Mathematicians offered a more applicable and secure science, not least in relation to ballistics. Astrology and divination remained popular, but learned astrology could hardly survive the mechanistic models of the universe which followed in the wake of the widespread acceptance of Copernicanism. Then again, the Counter-Reformed Catholic Church turned decisively against leading Neo-Platonists at the turn of the century, condemning the writings of their leading philosopher (Francesco Patrizi), burning another (Giordano Bruno) and imprisoning a third (Tommaso Campanella). Even in Protestant Europe, there was a rejection of the occult formulations of its practitioners. Meditating upon Dee's *Monas Hieroglyphica*, the Protestant divine Méric Casaubon gave up in despair. 'I can extract no sense nor reason (sound nor solid) out of it,' he wrote.

By the early years of the seventeenth century, natural magic had helped to break down the Aristotelian consensus. Natural magicians had extended the intellectual space and respectability for practical knowledge and discovery and created a more positive relationship between philosophers and technical practitioners. The natural magic tradition had broadened the scope and significance of mathematics as a way of understanding the universe. Above all, natural magic had countered the tendency in the Post-Reformation period to regard everything which happened that was out of the ordinary as a supernatural event – a warning sign from God or a demonological force. Magic enlarged the space for understanding the natural.

THE ALCHEMICAL REFORMATION

Alchemical skills and practices acquired great significance. They were essential to the 'silver age'. The mercury amalgamation process advertised the possibilities of transmutation of base metals into rarer ones. Mint-operators as well as silversmiths and goldsmiths needed the techniques of assaying and cupellation. Alchemists' know-how was essential to manufacturers of guns, saltpetre, glass, printing ink, bleaches and dyes. Alchemical techniques were increasingly significant in medicine too. But there were no formal alchemical qualifications. Techniques were acquired by a combination of experience and reading the broadening range of manuals, both skills books explaining particular recipes, and compendia of authoritative (often Arabic) texts from the Middle Ages.

Alchemy also became more than an assemblage of techniques and procedures. It formed the basis of a chemical philosophy and medicine. Chemical philosophy linked itself with astrology and natural magic, offering an understanding of God as a divine chemist. The Creation was a chemical process, and the end of the world would be a chemical culmination. Chemical medicine openly challenged the pre-eminence of Galenic medicine. The response of the medical establishment was predictably hostile, exploiting the notoriety which traditionally surrounded alchemists, saying they were fraudsters. The fortunes of chemical medicine and philosophy were inextricably linked with those of the Protestant Reformation, and one person in particular.

The individual was Theophrastus Bombastus von Hohenheim, who advertised himself in an early publication, the *Predictions Pronounced upon Europe* (1529), as 'Paracelsus' – i.e. 'Surpassing Celsus', the physician of ancient Rome. In his life and career he rejected the prevailing knowledge establishment. Born at Einsiedeln, a small town near Zürich, he moved with his father, a physician, to Villach in Austria, where he worked as an apprentice in the nearby Fugger-owned silver mines before training as a physician, serving as an army surgeon, and becoming physician by appointment to the city of Basel. He drew on his experiences in publications on miners' ailments, new ways of treating wounds and the cure of syphilis. He proclaimed that true knowledge came not out of medical textbooks but from ordinary people ('I have not been ashamed to learn from tramps, butchers and barbers') and from practical experience ('I tell you, one hair on my neck knows more than all you authors, and my shoe-buckles contain more wisdom than both Galen and Avicenna').

His appointment at Basel entitled him to lecture on medicine at its university. To the scandal of the medical faculty, he refused to wear an academic gown, lectured in his German-Swiss dialect rather than Latin, ignored the textbooks and, in a gesture of public defiance redolent of Luther's five years earlier, threw one of them (Avicenna's *Canon*) on a bonfire. Not long after he was expelled, resuming an exotic life of travel which his later publications exalted as the only true way of finding things out. 'According to me, and not according to you' was his taunt to the medical establishment. He had already visited Italy, Holland, Prussia, Poland, Scandinavia and the Levant. Now he made his way through Alsace, Bavaria, Bohemia and Austria, which is where he died (in Salzburg). He did not, however, live the life of the conventional wandering scholar. There were stories: of his excessive drinking, filth and possible madness; of his turning up dressed as a beggar, or a peasant or a noble; of his preaching unorthodox doctrines to Swiss peasants (Appenzell, 1533), and raging against the authorities.

For Paracelsus, medicine was a form of protest. Prognostications, based on conjunctions, eclipses and comets, account for the majority of the works printed under his name before his death. Christ's birth had been heralded by a new star and the turmoil of religious change and (as he saw it) the likelihood of imminent social collapse would necessarily be reflected by portents in the sky, signs of the coming Day of Judgment. Such a new star (Halley's Comet) had made its appearance in 1531. Paracelsus sighted it on 21 August in the sky above St Gallen. 'All destructions of monarchies . . . are announced by portents and signs,' he wrote. Yet Christ had worked healing miracles; so a return to the true word of Christ involved a recovery of Christian healing. Medical reformation must begin with a cleansing of its temple and the exposure of the greedy and incompetent medical fraternity. In his two short tracts on syphilis, he contrasted doctors offering an ineffectual but expensive remedy (guaiacum, an American wood, whose supply was controlled by the Fuggers) with simple therapies (laudanum as a pain-killer and mercury for syphilis, mainstays of Paracelsian treatments). Vanity and avarice were Paracelsus's twin enemies of a medical reformation in which service to the common weal and care for the least privileged in the community with simple remedies lay at the core. Reacting to the contemporary taunt that he was the 'Luther of medics', he responded: 'Am I a heresiarch? I am Theophrastus . . . the monarch of physicians,' who had turned his back on the 'stone-church' of the medical establishment in favour of peasants (in support of whose cause, Paracelsus had briefly been arrested).

The majority of Paracelsus's prolific writings did not see the light of day until after his death. 'Paracelsianism' was guaranteed a long afterlife by their gradual publication and by the controversies surrounding their reception. When he fled from Basel, he left many papers in the hands of his amanuensis, who became the publisher Johannes Oporinus. Oporinus disliked Paracelsus's private life and saw no point in publishing his outpourings in Swiss-German. They languished until Adam von Bodenstein, the son of a radical Protestant and physician, became a convert to Paracelsian chemical medicine after being cured of a tertian fever by its means. Expelled from the University of Basel for his 'heretical and scandalous books', he published Paracelsian treatises. A physician in Strasbourg, Michael Schütz, became another convert to the cause, collecting and publishing Paracelsian works. Not until the early years of the seventeenth century was the Paracelsian corpus available in print, mostly written in rebarbative Swiss-German and peppered with strange jargon. A cottage industry of Paracelsian lexicons emerged to make sense of the new 'chymiatria' (iatrochemistry). Little by little, however, the key Paracelsian notions became clear – notably the three 'principles' in nature (sulphur, mercury and salt), the equivalent of the Trinity. The fundamental chemical process was separation, and it explained processes in the macrocosm (the Creation) as well as the microcosm (the digestive system). 'Chrysopoeia' and 'argyropoiea' (Paracelsian mumbo-jumbo for making gold and silver) were about progressive distillation and the removal of slag during the refining of metals.

Despite opposition from medics (among his most vocal critics was Thomas Erastus at Heidelberg), the influence of Paracelsian medicine grew in German lands in the years before the Thirty Years War. The remedies attached to his name seemed to work, and chemical physicians offered the prospect of uniting hands and minds in the discovery of the secrets of nature to the public good. Chemical physicians and alchemists enjoyed the patronage of German princely courts. Ernst von Bayern, archbishop of Cologne, was a great Paracelsian supporter. Duke Julius of Brunswick-Wolfenbüttel was a patron to Paracelsians. He regarded alchemists as key figures in his efforts to exploit the mineral resources of his dominions, rationalize the state and maximize its economic potential. Elector August of Saxony invested heavily in alchemical books for his own and his wife Anna's use. His promotion of chemistry, chemical medicine and horticulture was reflected in Dresden's court festivals. Not to be outdone, Duke Frederick of Württemberg established a mining city (Freudenstadt) and built himself a chemical research facility in the ducal gardens at Stuttgart. The chemical reformation increasingly became the preserve, however, of Protestant courts and an agent in their struggles.

Conventional physicians in Germany accommodated themselves to chemical medicine, excising the magic and religious unorthodoxy of Paracelsian ideas and their attack upon Galen, while quietly adopting the iatrochemistry. Outside Germany, the medical opponents of Paracelsianism concentrated on discrediting its proponents and debunking its credentials. In France, Henry IV's physician, Joseph Du Chesne, tried to show how Paracelsus's three principles could be found in Hippocrates. Published in 1603, his book was denounced by the Paris medical faculty. The turf-war between Du Chesne's supporters and his detractors was still being fought a generation later, Richelieu cautiously sustaining the chemical physicians against the medical establishment. Meanwhile, other opponents of Paracelsus assaulted his alchemy. In the same year that Du Chesne published his book, Nicolas Guibert printed his *Alchemy Impugned by Reason and Experience*, in which Paracelsus was described as 'the most foul and absolute prince of liars who ever was, is, or will be, excepting the Devil'.

A similar battle was underway across the Channel, where the Galenist-trained physician Thomas Muffet returned from Basel as a Paracelsian acolyte. Muffet proposed Paracelsian remedies for the London College of Physicians' licensed Pharmacopoeia. He also specialized in that part of the natural kingdom whose variety most baffled contemporaries: insects ('Little Miss Muffet' of the nursery-rhyme being his daughter). But his proposed changes were not implemented and, by the later 1620s, conservatives had the upper hand at Charles I's court as well as in the college. Charles's physician was William Harvey, and he 'did not care for chymistry', dismissing newfangled medics ('neoteriques') as 'shit-breeches'.

These quarrels masked the extent to which Galenist physicians quietly adapted to new remedies. That was particularly the case in the Low Countries, where chemical philosophy had an impact on medicine, chemical research and industrial processes. Faculties of medicine could control curricula and license physicians but they could not stifle public interest. Galenic medicine felt under threat. In Germany, debates became dominated by pure-of-heart Paracelsians in the early seventeenth century. Reflecting contemporary religious and political tensions, Johann Valentin Andreae, the Lutheran pastor from Württemberg and author of *Christianopolis*, composed a spoof pamphlet entitled the *Chemical Wedding of Christian Rosencreutz*. Published in 1616, it used alchemical allegories to represent Protestant hopes for a new golden age. By then, several publications, circulating from Kassel and perhaps also by Andreae, had introduced the public to Christian Rosencreutz, a talented alchemist and member of a secret Brotherhood of the Rosy Cross. Under the fiction of this brotherhood and its mythical adept, the chemical reformation became a dream for a more fundamental transformation of society. Repackaged, the dream would resurface on English shores in the wake of the English Civil Wars.

SEEING AND BELIEVING

One of the criticisms levelled against the mythical Rosencreutz was that he was too 'curious'. Curiosity, the cousin to libertinism and atheism, was 'the vanity of the eye'. That was the title of a book by an English cleric, George Hakewill, published in 1608 and written for someone who had gone blind. Contemporaries celebrated all that could be discovered in the world around them, just by looking. Hakewill countered by blaming sight for everything that was wrong in it: ambition, gluttony, theft, idolatry, jealousy, contempt, envy and witchcraft. He had spent time in Calvinist Heidelberg where the Protestant Reformation was acutely conscious of the dangers of idolatry, Catholic rituals being regarded, wrote Hakewill, as 'superstitious worship-in-the-eye service'.

Theologians and moralists were not sure how to respond to ocular hegemony. In Counter-Reformed France, some advocated spiritual withdrawal from the world, a way of not 'seeing' it, while the Lutheran superintendant of Hamburg, Joachim Westphal, lectured the clergy about the importance of avoiding meddlesome curiosity – in politics, religious controversy, but also in natural philosophy. For his part, Jean Calvin, who opposed Westphal on the subject of predestination, issued his warning against astrologers in 1549. Calvin did not deny that the heavens influenced what happened on earth, but he was convinced that human beings could not interpret what the signs meant, because God had not chosen to share that knowledge with us. We should adopt a 'learned ignorance', rather than presume to trespass on the Almighty's providential disposition. To imagine that we could explain portents and predictions was to step into a 'labyrinth' and open the door to the Devil's deceits.

Curiosity corroded Christendom. For all that philosophers, naturalists and alchemists celebrated the art of looking, the reality was that it was not straightforward. Everyone knew that vision could be radically impaired, and that humoral imbalances could result in delusions. Jugglers and artists could persuade the eye that it was seeing something that was not really there. What were perspective drawings, anamorphic representations, theatrical sets and prisms if not delusions? Optical effects were a common feature of magic – and telescopes and microscopes were no different from other optical magic. Francis Bacon provocatively included both 'perspective houses' (i.e. observatories) and 'houses of the deceit of the senses' (i.e. theatres) among the research facilities in Solomon's House on *New Atlantis*. The Devil was especially adept at deceiving us into thinking that what we had seen was real. How else did witches, known to be in bed, fly off to attend their sabbaths? The difficulty in interpreting what had been seen was the problem for interpreting apparitions and monsters; but it equally existed when it came to the perplexing issues of ghosts and dreams. The insecure status of how to interpret what we saw posed a danger because it confused the true from the false. Both the Protestant Reformation and the 'new learning' were about distinguishing one from the other.

Ocular hegemony was asserted in the anatomy theatre. Physicians engaged with greater enthusiasm in dissection, jostling with surgeons and demonstrators. Anatomical theatres constructed for teaching purposes in medical faculties increased after the publication by the famous Flemish anatomist Andreas Vesalius of his *On the Fabric of the Human Body* (1543). The book was based on his own anatomical lectures, attended by students, to whom he played the showman. He allowed the audience to handle the organs as he removed them from the body: 'Surely, lords, you can learn only little from a mere demonstration, if you yourselves have not handled the objects with your hands.' 'I see' is a refrain in the text, especially when Vesalius proved that Galen had passed off information taken from animal anatomies as something which occurred in the human body. Almost ninety years later, a prosperous physician and magistrate in Amsterdam, Dr Nicolaes Tulp, commissioned a portrait of himself and several surgeons engaged in an autopsy from a young artist, Rembrandt van Rijn. The resulting picture is not a simple celebration of what could be seen. The painter depicts Tulp not looking at the body himself, but rather holding the splayed-out muscles and ligaments of the corpse's hand in his own (the artist reflecting an engraving in Vesalius's anatomy), an anatomist in meditation. His companions stare intently, but at a copy of an anatomy book to one side. Rembrandt depicted a lesson in contemplation of how wonderfully God made nature and man.

Celebrating God in nature was the way by which contemporaries justified their curiosity in the world around them. By the end of the fifteenth century, 'natural theology' was used for the argument that the defence of the beliefs which underlay Christendom could be based on the evidence of God as Creator. The argument was pertinent when it came to converting Muslims, Jews or even Indians in the New World, since it represented a starting-point with which they could all agree. It was also the title of an early printed book by Raymond Sebond, made famous in the sixteenth century by Michel de Montaigne's translation of it into French in 1569. Montaigne conceded that natural theology raised a big philosophical issue, since it relied on the evidence of the human senses, which could easily be misled. So his *Apology* for Sebond's natural theology, composed in the 1570s, constituted the longest contribution to his *Essays* (1580). Christianity, Montaigne argued, depends on faith and grace, and not on reason. The human senses are fundamentally flawed and capable of being deceived, and by nature itself. Human reason was equally fallible. We can no more control our minds than our bodies. 'To judge the appearances that we receive of objects,' he wrote, 'we would need a judicatory instrument; to verify this instrument, we need a demonstration; to verify the demonstration, an instrument. We are thus in a circle. Since the senses cannot decide our dispute, being themselves full of uncertainty, it must be reason that does so. No reason can be established without another reason: there we go retreating back to infinity.' Elsewhere, and especially in his later writings, Montaigne suggested that whatever truth we might establish lay with simple people – the Brazilian Indian, for example, 'fit to bear true witness' because he was 'so simple that he has not the stuff to build up false inventions and give them plausibility'. Truth lay, as Paracelsus (and Rabelais) said it did, in the mouths of tramps, butchers and barbers.

Montaigne's circular argument was derived from a book, published in 1562, by Henri Estienne. It was a Latin translation of the *Outlines of Pyrrhonist Philosophy (Sexti philosophi Pyrrhoniarum hypotyposeon)*, the doctrines of Pyrrho as put together by a Greek philosopher and historian, Sextus Empiricus. At the heart of its various propositions was the denial that sensory experience could lead to a scientific knowledge of the external world. It was not simply that our five sensory receptors are limited and inaccurate but that (as Montaigne said) one person's are inaccurate in a different way from another's, and there was no way of reconciling them. Radical doubt along these lines became something of a preoccupation in French intellectual circles in the first half of the next century, reflected in the controversial *On Wisdom* (*De la sagesse*, 1601) of Pierre Charron and, most famously, in René Descartes's *First Meditation*, written in the 1630s. If we could no longer agree among ourselves as to the evidence of our own eyes, what chance was there for agreeing about what a citizen's role in the state was, or about what was right and wrong? Those were questions which the politico-religious conflicts of the later sixteenth and early seventeenth centuries raised. In their wake, the answers seemed to lie, not in engaging with the world and collaborating as citizens to make the commonwealth a better place, but in separating faith and reason and in detaching oneself from the political world, leaving rulers to keep the peace by force of arms and to determine what was public morality.

Scepticism was taking root, however, at a time when contemporaries 'knew' more and more. There were more facts around, and the European sense of 'fact' (as something that occurred, or was seen to be the case) made its first appearance in Italy in the later sixteenth century. For Galileo, *de facto* (*di fatto*) meant just that. 'Facts' were what, for Francis Bacon, experiments could prove. There was a recourse to factual representation of the real world too: paintings from life, true engravings and veritable histories. At the same time, there was more awareness of paradox, in the sense of something that was contrary to what was commonly seen, or regarded, as fact. The paradox at the heart of disintegrating Christendom was that, as Europeans knew more, it made less sense to them.

THE ADVANCEMENT OF LEARNING

Scientific certainties were taught at the universities, the forefront of Christendom's intellectual life. By 1500, there were seventy-eight institutions that offered a *studium generale* – a place where students from anywhere in Christendom could study under professors within a teaching programme that offered not only arts subjects (the *trivium* of grammar, rhetoric and logic, followed by the *quadrivium* of arithmetic, geometry, music and astronomy), leading to a degree as master of arts, but at least one of the higher faculties (theology, law or medicine), where students studied for a doctorate. The majority of these universities were old foundations, established by bulls from the papacy or charters from the emperor. But over thirty of them were not a century old, founded by princely patrons who understood that university education had become an important part of the formation of young men in the upper social echelons. Universities had no difficulty in attracting increasing numbers of Europe's notability in order to educate the state officials, lawyers, physicians and clergy of the future. Moreover, their students became imbued with the humanist values which gradually permeated through arts faculties. Germany stood out in the establishment of new schools of learning. The major universities were, to varying degrees, connected to the Church. In Paris, Oxford and elsewhere, theology was the pre-eminent higher faculty. That was because scholarship was about truth, the rational foundation for the belief-community at the heart of Christendom. A degree from a university was studied for in similar ways, and in accordance with a curriculum that was recognizable throughout Christendom.

University expansion continued at a brisk pace beyond 1500, driven by the same pressures that had been at work in the previous century. By 1650, the number of establishments had more than doubled. The student cohorts probably increased even more. But by 1650, a university degree was no longer universally recognized, the result of religious and political division. The Holy Roman Emperor refused to acknowledge the University of Leiden, founded by the Dutch in 1575, and so did Philip II, in whose name the university claimed a (forged) deed of foundation. Religious dissidents went abroad to study, their influx leading to the foundation of new establishments (Irish Catholics in colleges and seminaries in France, the Low Countries and Rome; Huguenots in Geneva, Sedan and Orange). Rulers used institutions of learning to validate religious change. In 1527, the Landgrave Philip of Hesse established a college without papal privilege or imperial approval in order to train the clergy for the Lutheran Reformation. Trinity College Dublin was founded in 1592 as a Puritan educational adjunct of the Protestant English ascendancy. Sweden established or re-founded colleges of higher education and universities as part of its attempts to integrate the conquered territories of northern Germany and the Baltic into its state.

In addition to universities, there were other institutions that offered tertiary education, many of which did not award degrees at all. This was especially the case in Protestant Europe. German emperors refused Calvinist high schools the right to confer degrees. For their part, Genevan pastors and magistrates staked their claim to be different from traditional universities by establishing an 'academy', delivering simply a testimonial of Protestant beliefs and behaviour at the conclusion of a period of study. By not awarding degrees, faculties became less important and the possibilities for pedagogic and curriculum innovation greater. One of the most influential models was that put in place by Johann Sturm at the Strasbourg school which he directed for over forty years from its inception in 1538. He drew on his teaching experience in the colleges of the University of Paris. Strasbourg's academy was like a secondary school and further education college rolled into one, offering a humanities school, organized into classes, with a university-style superstructure of liberal arts teaching on top, delivered by university chair-holders giving courses of instruction in different subjects on a rotating basis. The aim was to integrate sound learning and humanist values with Protestant piety and the ability to analyse material and construct persuasive arguments – a key skills-set for the administrators, teachers and preachers of the next generation in the commonwealth.

Although more universities with rights to award degrees existed in Catholic Europe, there too the range of higher educational provision broadened. The Jesuits also borrowed from the Paris collegiate model. Lagging initially somewhat behind Protestant foundations, by 1600 they overtook them, their colleges offering the most widespread and coordinated programme of further and higher education in Europe, one that universities could not match. But where the Jesuits had higher educational facilities, they were generally limited in nature, having an arts faculty with a faculty of theology tacked on. Only a small minority became degree-awarding institutions (for example, Olomouc in 1581, Bamberg in 1648). Other Catholic orders involved in higher educational provision (seminaries, for instance) chose mostly not to establish universities awarding degrees.

In both Protestant and Catholic Europe, those seeking an education for their sons readily understood the differences in objectives and attainments of these various establishments, aware that study at an academy (such as the flagship academy at Herborn in the Calvinist Wetterau counties of Rhineland Germany) might count for more than a university degree. They sought a 'general education' (*Paedagogium*) for their offspring, promoting 'learned and eloquent piety'. Only a small minority of students were expected to go on to study in the higher faculties. The objective was not the construction and transmission of an edifice of scientific certainty. They did not need the elaborate scaffolding of Aristotle's Logic (the *Organon*) to achieve their goals.

Fortunately, more elementary primers were to hand. In Lutheran Europe, Melanchthon wrote several *Dialectics*, which became very popular. In Calvinist Europe, it was the *Dialectics* of a teacher at the University of Paris, Pierre de la Ramée (Ramus), that swept the board. Ramus had taken his Master's degree there in 1536, defending as his thesis: 'Whatever is affirmed from Aristotle is contrived'. Eight years later, he published a frontal assault upon Aristotle's Logic, and then his substitute for it, the *Dialectics* (*Dialecticae Partitiones*, 1543). Ramus offered something simpler – a tenth the size of Aristotle's text. He sought to make logic into an instrument of communication ('dialectic . . . an art which teacheth to dispute well'). Rhetoric was separated off, leaving the student to concentrate on how to define the topics of a discourse and then arrange them. Students were taught the basics: to proceed from the general to the specific, from definitions to examples. Ramus's practice of dividing subjects into two main parts, and then further subdividing each of them (creating dichotomized tables) became, in the hands of Ramist-educated students, over-contrived. His proposed reform so incensed the teachers in Paris that they prosecuted him for undermining philosophy and religion. The king ordered a royal commission which, in 1544, prohibited Ramus's books and banned him from teaching. He turned to mathematics, and had a hand in another pedagogical reformist treatise, the *Rhetoric* (1548), of his former student Omer Talon.

The ban on his teaching was eventually rescinded and in 1551 he became professor of philosophy and eloquence at the prestigious institute for humanist learning, established by Francis I, the Collège de France. From that haven, Ramus launched frontal assaults on the University of Paris, where professors purchased their posts and the costs of a college degree were beyond those of modest means. Venal professors took bribes in return for dissecting dead Scholastic doctrines. His solution was to recruit professors on a competitive basis, pay them from the public purse and reform the syllabus. He created many enemies, and his Protestantism made him a target for them at the massacre of St Bartholomew, where he died in the bloodshed. The success of the Ramus/Talon textbooks was considerable. They would be the foundation-stone of the education at Herborn (and other Calvinist academies), where one of its philosophy professors, Johann Heinrich Alsted, researched an ambitious encyclopaedia of the sciences, rooted in Ramist pedagogy but drawing on other traditions too, with the aim of coordinating knowledge and reformation. There would be some 800 editions and adaptations by around 1650, and almost half that number again of textbooks by other Ramist educators, all for use in Protestant, mainly Calvinist, Europe.

The success of Ramist pedagogy was matched, in due course, by that of the Jesuits. Their model curriculum (the *Ratio Studiorum*, 1599) was widely followed by colleges – to the degree that they had competent teachers to deliver it. Because it elevated the significance of the *quadrivium* (arithmetic, geometry, astronomy and music), it needed teachers with specialist skills. Partly because of confessional competition, the range of curriculum and teaching innovation in Europe's academies and colleges was impressive. Generations of articulate and versatile Europeans were educated. But such innovation threw the spotlight back on universities, where the demands of the higher faculties for a traditional formation restricted change. There was more evidence of change than was apparent from the outside, but it did not stem the rising tide of criticism against universities for defending an 'old' learning.

That critique began from a central plank in the humanists' platform, which was that they were recovering ancient texts and learning which had been ignored by medieval Scholastics in a barbarous 'Middle Age'. The humanist history of learning was an inverted curve of ancient greatness, medieval decline and contemporary renaissance. The rejection of Scholastic learning in favour of Antiquity became a rhetorical commonplace especially to promote subjects which were not traditionally seen as scientific. In Andreas Vesalius's treatise on anatomy, as in Giorgio Vasari's *Lives of the Artists*, 'old-fashioned' Scholastic learning became a foil to advertise what was exciting in humanist rediscovery. 'Let us imagine a teacher of a university who died a century ago, and now returned among us,' declared Ramus in a public lecture, published in Paris in 1564. 'If he compared the efflorescence of humanist learning and the sciences of nature in France, Italy and England as they have developed since his death, he would be shaken and astonished' by the changes. 'It is almost as if he raised his eyes from the depth of the earth to the heavens and saw for the first time the sun, the moon and the stars.'

By 1600, the critique went a stage further. The learning of the ancients was not simply being recovered, but being surpassed. New worlds, devices, technologies and philosophies had been discovered, and they were commodified as 'novel'. A series of engravings was issued in Antwerp in the early seventeenth century to designs by Jan van der Straet under the heading 'New Discoveries' (*Nova Reperta*). The frontispiece illustrating the first series depicted the Americas, the compass, gunpowder, the clock, guaiacum, distillation and silkworm cultivation. Later sheets illustrated the manufacture of cane sugar, finding longitude by the declination of the compass and copper engraving. There was the beginnings of a debate between the 'Ancients' and the 'Moderns' (one in which George Hakewill staged an appearance on the side of the 'Moderns'). Novelty was not a curse and the advance of learning could be seriously promoted.

The Proficience and Advancement of Learning (1605) was the title of Sir Francis Bacon's first prospectus for 'discovering' new knowledge. The son of Sir Nicholas Bacon, a prominent Elizabethan courtier and Keeper of the Great Seal, Francis was trained in the law, and he expected to follow in his father's footsteps. Unfortunately, his career stalled and so, like others of his day, he occupied himself with projects which might interest the state and promote his fortunes. They included plans for a state-sponsored research library, botanical gardens, a laboratory and a museum of inventions. He was frustrated when these came to nothing. With the advent of King James I (who promoted himself as 'Solomon', a divinely inspired royal sage), he published a prudent 'mixture of the new and the old', linking the discovery of the New World to a reform of learning. 'Proficience in Nauigation, and discoveries,' he wrote, 'may plant also an expectation of the further proficience and augmentation of all Scyences, because it may seeme that they are ordained by God to ... meete in one Age.' He cited a prophetic verse from the Book of Daniel: 'Many shall run to and fro, and Knowledge will be increased.' Meanwhile, he wrote the outline of what would appear fifteen years later in Latin as the *Novum Organum* (*New Organon*, 1620). By that date, however, Bacon was a busy man, having been appointed attorney general in 1613, and Lord Chancellor in 1618. The book, dedicated to James I, was unfinished; but that was the point. The preface said that he aimed to provide the equivalent of a compass to point the way across an unknown ocean, comparing the voyage to be undertaken to that of Columbus. The book's frontispiece was of a ship in full sail, passing through the twin Pillars of Hercules (carrying the motto 'Plus Ultra') to discover new lands of knowledge.

The work was divided into two books. The first was a scathing attack on the 'vices' of traditional learning ('phantastical', 'superstitious', 'contentious'), with Aristotle the target. In the second book, he offered his alternative ('middle') way. To explain it, he drew an analogy from the bee. It 'gathers its material from the flowers of the garden and field, but then transforms and digests it by a power of its own. And the true business of philosophy is much the same.' Discovery was a collaborative process in which diligent human beings collected information about the real world in store-houses of 'natural histories', turning it through the art of experiment (learning the 'secrets of nature' by 'constraining it') and logical induction into fruitful and productive knowledge. Bacon deliberately wrote his 'logic' as a series of disjointed 'aphorisms' – each one designed to detonate thoughts in the brain. Aphorism 124 ran: 'For I am building in the human understanding a true model of the world, such as it is in fact, not such as a man's own reason would have it to be; a thing which cannot be done without a very diligent dissection and anatomy of the world ... Truth therefore and utility are here the very same things.' If Bacon hoped to engage Solomon in his enterprise, he was to be disappointed. Within a year of the publication of the *New Organon*, his enemies secured his impeachment by Parliament and he was disgraced. Appreciated on the continent of Europe for its ferocious attack upon Aristotelianism, Bacon's project became, in a popularized form, a platform for those who sought change in England at the time of the English Civil Wars.

COPERNICAN COSMOLOGY

Nicolaus Copernicus's *On the Revolutions of the Celestial Spheres* was published in 1543. Copernicus had studied in Cracow and Bologna, but retired to Frauenburg, a cathedral city on the Polish Baltic coast, in

1503. Astronomy was part of the core curriculum, taught from textbooks that explicated the Ptolemaic model of an earth-centred universe in which the planets moved around the earth on epicycles, whose centres inscribed the circles that constituted the bodies of the planetary spheres. The epicycles (and associated 'equants', formulae for planetary movement during the epicycle) accounted for variations in the speed and brightness of planets and for their periodic retrograde movement. Ptolemy's *Almagest* was available in Latin and Greek versions, but it was regarded as difficult and rarely studied directly. Humanist scholars worked to provide an introduction to it that would make it comprehensible. They also added new observations and calculations since Ptolemy's were very limited.

Copernicus's work offered a solution to two problems, one theoretical and the other practical. The theoretical one was the discrepancy between Aristotle's account of motion (which was that it must always be linear and uniform) and that of Ptolemy (which was an explanation for why planetary motion was non-uniform). Ptolemy's epicycles and equants created planets whose movement was different from everything else in the universe, like (said Copernicus) a monster whose arms and legs moved separately from each other. The practical problem embarrassed the Church. Ptolemaic astronomy could not accurately compute the calendar and the dates for Easter, and in 1514 Copernicus was invited to Rome to advise upon a solution. He declined, saying that it could not be set right until the problems of the motion of the sun and moon had been solved. Copernicus perhaps knew that part of his eventual solution had already been proposed by Arabic astronomers. But he discovered that you could not displace one part of the planetary system without 'disordering the remaining parts'. He therefore remodelled all planetary motion with the earth involved in a uniform triple motion (rotation around its axis, revolution about a point near the sun and directional rotation upon its axis) which corresponded to that of the other planets.

Copernicus did not regard this as an armchair exercise. His preface insisted that what he proposed was physically true. The celestial bodies revolved around the sun and in physical spheres, just as they carried the earth. That, however, placed his system at odds with Aristotelian physics, Holy Scriptures and daily experience. Copernicus was reluctant to see the work published and it was only after a visit from Georg Joachim Rheticus in 1539 that he released his manuscript. Rheticus was trained at Wittenberg, where Philipp Melanchthon dictated the approach to natural philosophy. Melanchthon wanted to understand God through the natural world to reveal a Creator and providential God and a model for social order too. Fallen man was surrounded by corruption, but the heavens were unaffected by the Fall. In cosmology, the observer could discover the will of God, especially since human beings, created in God's image, still had traces of capacities for knowledge with which God had endowed Adam. The publication of Copernicus's tract through the agency of a Wittenberg-trained Lutheran in Protestant Nuremberg was therefore not surprising. Even so, Copernicus's text was issued with an anonymous preface, written by a Lutheran theologian, Andreas Osiander, which readers took to be by Copernicus himself. Concerned about its consequences for Aristotelian physics, Osiander emphasized that Copernicus's astronomical system should not be taken as a representation of reality. On the contrary, it was just a mathematical way of seeing things. A reader who took it as offering a true account of the physical universe risked 'departing from this discipline more foolish than he came to it'.

Copernicus's text was a technical astronomical treatise. The specialists who read it followed Osiander's advice. Only a handful accepted the physical truth of the Copernican theory before 1600, and only four came out in print in favour of it. Even the Danish astronomer Tycho Brahe rejected the triple motion of the earth (in 1587), proposing instead a compromise in which all the planets circled the sun, while it moved around a stationary earth. In Rome, those responsible for the Gregorian Calendar (adopted in 1582), a central plank of the Counter-Reformed Catholic Church's claim to lead a global Christianity, used Copernicus's calculations, but only because it made them more accurate.

The Dominican Giordano Bruno was the most notorious of those who made no secret of their Copernicanism. In Platonic-style dialogues he explored the possibility not only that the world revolved around the sun, but that the universe was infinite and that there was a plurality of inhabited worlds. Which particular heresy provoked his arrest in Venice in May 1592 is unclear, though in the hostile environment towards Neo-Platonism in Counter-Reformation Italy it was important to watch what one said. That explains why a professor of mathematics, appointed to a temporary post at the University of Pisa in 1589, Galileo Galilei, kept his Copernicanism initially to himself. In August 1597, however, he wrote a letter out of the blue to Johannes Kepler, whose book on the *Cosmographic Mystery* he had just read. It had delighted him, he said, because he himself had long been a Copernican. 'With this hypothesis' he had 'been able to explain many natural phenomena which under the current hypothesis remain inexplicable'. He had even written a treatise in defence of Copernicanism, but could not conceive of publishing it while such views were held in derision.

Galileo's natural phenomena emerged during his experimental programme investigating motion. Working with his sponsor, Guidobaldo dal Monte, the military brother of a cardinal and a marquis, Galileo proved to his satisfaction (using inked balls thrown across an inclined plane) that the path of a projected object was a symmetrical curve, a parabola or hyperbola. It looked like a chain, suspended between two points. For him, this answered one of the objections already foreseen by Copernicus to the physical possibility of the earth's rotation: why was it that an object, dropped from a tower, fell in a straight line at its foot, and not to the west of it? The answer for Galileo was that, like his projectile or chain, it described a symmetrical curve. That was the beginning of Galileo's perception of the relativity of movement, the possibility of motion being a uniform, dynamic force, capable of being explained mathematically. By the time of the letter to Kepler, Galileo had also developed another argument in favour of the earth's movement about its axis, based on the movement of the tides. Galileo's Copernicanism was that of a convinced anti-Aristotelian, attracted to its mathematical elegance and determined upon proving its reality.

In 1609, Galileo deployed his technical skills to produce a telescope. He made one which could magnify twenty times. Four years later, he manufactured tubes that magnified thirty times; by 1615, a hundred times. With such an instrument he had the potential to attract princely patronage as well as discover evidence in support of Copernicanism. That potential was realized when Galileo published *The Starry Messenger* (*Sidereus Nuncius*, 1610) in Florence. He dedicated the work to the duke of Tuscany, Cosimo II de' Medici. That same year, Galileo moved to a well-paid post in Medici service. Galileo observed the four largest moons of Jupiter and used them as evidence of the physical reality of the heliocentric system. He christened them 'the Medicean stars' and set about persuading everyone of the reality of what he had seen. That was not so easy because the small number of high-powered telescopes which he had manufactured was already spoken for, and the instruments were not straightforward to use. But he had a two-pronged strategy for convincing those that mattered, notably in Rome. It involved convincing the experts and neutralizing the sceptics.

Initially things worked according to plan. The leading astronomer in the Jesuit College in Rome, Christopher Clavius, announced that he had seen the four moons rotating around Jupiter in November 1611. The ground was laid for Galileo's triumphal visit to the papal city. Galileo announced supplementary discoveries: the phases of Venus, sunspots and the irregular face of the moon, all, as he hoped, confirming the Copernican hypothesis. The second prong of the strategy, however, was tougher. His opponents had inherited wisdom, orthodoxy and people in high places on their side. Even in Florence, there were those who harboured doubts, probably with reason, about his religious orthodoxy. The Inquisition began its inquiries, reporting in due course to Rome. When Galileo visited that city in 1615, he had to fight his corner in a curia dominated by a conservative pope who instructed Cardinal Bellarmine to issue a warning to Galileo to abandon the physical reality of Copernicanism. Galileo was not as good a courtier as his opponents, who held more cards. It was almost impossible to prove Copernicanism from astronomical observations, especially when there was a Tychonic alternative to hand. In his efforts to neutralize the supporters of that alternative, he antagonized the Jesuits, weakening his position. Galileo returned from Rome thinking that he could continue to argue for Copernicanism, albeit without prejudice to the Ptolemaic system.

Galileo's optimism was misplaced. Initially, his prospects improved when the Florentine Maffeo Barberini was elected Pope Urban VIII in 1623. That encouraged him to carry on working on a treatise in which the arguments for and against heliocentrism were compared. The result, published in Italian in 1632 as *Dialogo sopra i due massimi sistemi del mondo* (*Dialogue concerning the Two World Systems* – the two systems in question being the Ptolemaic and the Copernican), was a masterpiece. It was imagined as an academic debate spread over four days between three colleagues. Two of them tossed arguments to and fro, but their persuasion was in only one direction: towards the reality of the heliocentric system. The third ('Simplicio') was the fall-guy, who kept feeding in old arguments which the others knocked down. Far from being 'without prejudice', Galileo's *Dialogue* ridiculed his opponents, and Urban VIII thought it made fun of him too.

That was especially dangerous in the international politics of the year 1632. Urban had spent much of his career as the pope's representative in France. He thought that country was the only guarantee against the power of Spain in Italy and Europe. But, in June 1630, Sweden, encouraged by France, entered the Thirty Years War and 1632 was the year of Swedish triumph. If France was the pope's ally, then so were the Protestants. Urban did not want to fall out with the Florentine grand dukes but the latter were, by inclination, pro-Spanish. With his loyalties divided, Urban did not need the Galileo issue as a further matter of dispute. Galileo's trial for heresy (1633) before the Roman Inquisition resulted in a suspended sentence. He was condemned to 'abjure, curse and detest' heliocentrism, sentenced to life imprisonment (commuted to house-arrest), and the *Dialogue* was placed on the Index.

Although Galileo was silenced, the *Dialogue* was translated and published in Latin north of the Alps through the offices of a French Protestant, Élie Diodati, who was a friend of Galileo's. Galileo's physics also circulated extensively and with it the vision of a universe dominated by mathematically abstracted 'axioms' which explained the real world. That was thanks to a Minim friar and mathematician in Paris, Marin Mersenne. He was an 'intelligencer' who put himself at the centre of a network of academics and antiquarians who treated natural philosophy as an alternative to the divisions in the world around. *Virtuosi* (the word came into vogue in the 1630s) had a constructive role. Stoic obedience to the powers that be might be the order of the day in politics, but in matters of natural philosophy, it was different.

Galileo's *Discourses and Mathematical Demonstrations Concerning Two New Sciences* was published in Leiden in 1638 and translated into Latin by Mersenne the following year. It offered another dialogue between three people, only this time written in a style that imitated an open-ended discussion among its protagonists, each of them struggling to match the mathematical axioms proposed to the complexity of the real world. The subjects at issue ranged from the resistance of materials (the first 'new science') to motion (the second). But this second subject was interspersed with treatises on different sorts of motion. Galileo wanted to say that these were matters on which there was certainty: that motion was uniform, acceleration being distance travelled as the square of the time, and projectile motion being a symmetric curve. Galileo's mechanics cemented his growing reputation. It was also a sign of the gathering respectability of the Copernican proposition and the emerging attractiveness of a mechanical picture of the universe.

Also in 1638, an English clergyman and virtuoso, John Wilkins, published *The Man in the Moone*, a pastiche of a work by Francis Godwin. It popularized Copernicanism while also inventing the genre of science fiction. Three years later, Wilkins plagiarized another of Godwin's works in *Mercury, or the Secret and Swift Messenger* (1641), showing 'how a man may with privacy and speed communicate his thoughts to a friend at any distance'. It was a treatise on the science of cryptography, signalling on land and sea, secret inks, mind-reading, and a prospectus for a 'real character' or scientific language. The possibilities for *virtuosi* remaining in contact with one another had never seemed greater, despite the forces of the Catholic Church. Aristotelianism was not dead, but the Aristotelian consensus was at an end. What would replace it remained opaque.

A MECHANICAL VISION

'Mechanical' in 1500 meant things that were practical and people who were manual. In the sixteenth century, however, the word acquired a different resonance: it described everything to do with machinery. That was partly because of the revival of the mechanics of Antiquity, particularly associated with Archimedes. But it was mainly because machines played a greater part in people's lives. The machinery in question – astronomical and navigational instruments, compasses, surveying equipment, pumps and hydraulics, logarithmic devices, clocks and sundials, spectacles, maps, fortifications and guns – almost always required mathematical calculation for its manufacture and use, as well as proper training for its correct operation and maintenance.

Machinery also became a world view. Clocks, for example, were not particularly reliable time-keepers, but they were automata which stood as a model for God's universe. In the new clock for Strasbourg cathedral, completed in 1574, the device stood in the south transept like a temple, 59 feet high. Fitted with a celestial globe, astrolabe and astronomical mechanisms as well as a terrestrial timepiece, it was designed to present the divisions of time from centuries to minutes. An angel turned a sand-glass at each quarter hour, the four ages of life passed in front of Death during each hour, and at the last hour of each day, Christ appeared. Clockwork planetary models graced grandees' curiosity cabinets. Juanelo Turriano spent twenty years designing a mammoth one for Charles V, to whom clocks were a passion. It was incomplete by the time of the emperor's death, and was modified to take account of the calendar reform. In 1561, Eberhard Baldewein, clockmaker to Landgrave Wilhelm IV of Hesse-Kassel, produced an astronomical timepiece based on the latest planetary tables. Jost Bürgi, christened 'a second Archimedes' by Wilhelm, manufactured another in around 1604 for Emperor Rudolf II. Calibrated for the Gregorian calendar, it displayed the most important saints' days and included two dials, one presenting a geocentric planetarium, and the other a heliocentric one. Kepler said that a later generation would rate Bürgi's work as highly as Dürer's paintings. On a clock presented to Duke Frederick III of Schleswig-Holstein in 1642, the figures of Copernicus and Tycho Brahe are engraved on the case. The legend under Tycho reads: '*Quid si sic?*' ('What if it be thus?') and that under Copernicus: '*Sic movetur mundus*' ('Thus the world is moved').

Mechanical objects were a component in Europe's relations with the rest of the world and the drive for a global Christianity. Handsome clocks were commissioned from Augsburg manufacturers by the emperor to present to the Ottoman sultan as part of the annual tribute he owed from 1548. In a letter of 1552, Francis Xavier wrote that missionaries to Japan should have good scientific knowledge because the Japanese were fascinated by astronomical and geographical information: 'They pester us with questions on the movements of the heavenly spheres, the eclipse of the sun, the waning and waxing of the moon, and the origins of water, snow, rain, hail, thunder, lightning and comets. Our explanations of these things have great influence, so that we win the souls of the people.' The Jesuit Matteo Ricci, who was given permission to spend time in Chao-ch'ing, west of Canton, in 1583, captured the attention of Chinese scholars not merely by learning their language but through the scientific objects he brought with him. In 1584, he presented the governor with a copy of a map of the world, adjusted to Chinese sensibilities, and a sundial. In subsequent years, he presented spheres, globes and sundials to mandarins, prior to his teaching cosmography, mathematics and physics in Nanking and being invited to

the imperial court at Beijing in 1605. The shape of the earth, the existence of the poles, the order and movement of the stars and planets and
the use of globes were used as knowledge capital: 'Through it,' Ricci
wrote, 'many avowed . . . today that their eyes were opened to very significant things, to which they all previously had been blind.'

The mechanical analogy was commonplace by 1600. Comparing the
confused contemporary politics at the beginning of the Thirty Years War
with the stability of the heavens, the German Lutheran pastor Johannes
Geyger wrote in *Political Horology* (1621): 'how much wiser and ingenious must this Master be who . . . indeed has created by his omniscience
the whole heavenly firmament and clockwork . . . ?' 'Surely the sky is
the great Wheele of a Clocke,' wrote the Huguenot scholar Philippe
Duplessis-Mornay. 'My goal,' declared the astronomer Johannes Kepler,
'is to show that the celestial machine is . . . like a clock.'

What began to change around the year 1600 was the degree to which
mathematically derived axioms provided generalizations about the real
world such that they could predict how it would always and everywhere
behave. The behaviour of bodies in liquids, liquids in tubes, pendulums,
levers under tension, projectiles, percussive hammers, strings, objects
dropped from high places – the possibilities grew larger. In 1618, a
young René Descartes joined the army of the prince of Orange, camped
at Breda on the border with the Spanish Netherlands, to learn the art of
war. While there, he met the local natural philosopher Isaac Beeckman.
Together they tried to solve physical problems using mathematics. Like
Galileo, whose work was as yet unpublished, they established a law for
describing the fall of moving bodies. Beeckman's 'mathematico-physics'
inspired others as well, particularly from France. By the time Descartes
returned to the Dutch Republic in 1628, he had defined his objective:
how, on the basis of applying mathematics to physical problems, to use
similar reasoning to explain everything known to the human mind?

He began writing down his notions (and dreams) in a notebook which
Beeckman had perhaps given him. Probably thinking of joining Mauritz
of Nassau's army en route for Bohemia, Descartes recorded on 10 November 1619 – but the existing copy may be defective – that he had discovered
the foundation of a 'marvellous science'. His system was rooted in a metaphysic of human knowledge that supported his mathematical physics
and his attempts to explain human behaviour. He believed that his method
ensured certainty because it grounded natural knowledge on a few

axioms whose certainty could be guaranteed by intuition, self-evidently true like proofs in geometry. Aristotelian distinctions of heaviness, lightness, hot and cold, wet and dry were banished. Nature was matter; and the essence of matter was extension, its only properties being the geometrically derived ones of shape, size, position and motion. His famous *cogito ergo sum* ('I think, therefore I am') was the dream-induced method by which Descartes hoped to establish that his intellect existed, and from which it was possible to proceed logically to prove the existence of God, the rules which he had established for the universe, the existence of matter and the solution to physical problems in the real world.

Elaborating the dream in the form of a treatise, which is what he published as the *Discourse on Method* (*Discours de la Méthode*, 1637), was easier than realizing it, for that meant studying the real world. In 1629, he told Mersenne: 'I want to begin to study anatomy.' A few months later, he wrote: 'I am now studying chemistry and anatomy simultaneously; every day I learn something that I cannot find in any book.' He undertook his own dissections, studied human and animal physiology, explored chemical medicine and geometry. Rather than being a fully fledged 'method', the *Discourse* became an introduction to three exemplifications (optics, meteorology and geometry) of a mechanist approach to the world, whose ramifications he would flesh out in publications over the next decade.

What Descartes offered was a model for a new world-system, constructed around the laws of motion and impact. His mechanical philosophy demanded a non-anthropomorphic universe and a willingness to consider God's role in nature as that of a trustworthy clockmaker, at arm's length from his creation. How the soul fitted in, and what connected it with the body, became a major critique of Descartes's system. For it required a radical disjuncture between mind and body since material objects could no longer be seen as containing 'sympathies', 'harmonies' or 'occult' qualities, implanted in them by God. Ideas were not part of the universe. They were in our heads, and to be judged critically and rejected if reality contradicted them. The universe was an automaton: 'There is a material world machine,' he wrote, 'or, to put it more forcefully, the world is composed like a machine of matter.' His frequent references to 'the machine of our body' were intentional. 'There are certainly no rules in Mechanics,' he thought, 'that do not also belong to Physics [i.e. physiology] of which it is a special case: it is no less natural for a clock composed of wheels to tell the time than for a tree grown out of a given seed to produce the corresponding fruit.' His conviction that the laws of mechanics applied to the human body was reaffirmed after a discussion of the functioning of the heart, when William Harvey's demonstration of the circulation of the blood provided him with an analogy of a pump for the human organ.

The eye was part of that machine. His dissections had revealed its physiology, his geometric skills explained its optics and his laws of physics determined the nature of light and colour. He could explain that it worked like a camera obscura. What we actually 'saw' in our brains bore no resemblance to the image that was focused onto the retina. Our brains received a decomposed signal which only our brain's cognitive processes turned into 'vision'. So Descartes's mechanical vision short-circuited debates about the mismatch between vision and reality, and rendered irrelevant scepticism about what we could know. If we saw monsters, miracles, dreams and apparitions, they were the result of our own cognitive processes. They did not exist outside our heads. What we knew for sure was the world around us: its shape, size, extension and motion.

For Descartes's contemporary Thomas Hobbes, the scientific study of optics was also a central preoccupation, and this 'mechanical vision' lay at the heart of his understanding of human society. He based his social philosophy on the primary concepts of movement and matter. Like Descartes, he drew on the discoveries of William Harvey, the circulation of the blood being a 'vital motion', the heart a 'piece of machinery in which . . . one wheel gives motion to another'. The state was no longer a commonwealth with a soul. It was an 'Artificiall Man' with a heart, explicable as a mechanical device. The motions that caused apparitions in humans moved from the senses to the brain. The cognitive perception of them was received by the heart, from whence we had the notions of pain and pleasure that constituted the motive forces of human society. The *Leviathan*'s famous frontispiece of the ruler as a composite image of all his subjects was probably inspired by an optical device that Hobbes had seen in Paris in the 1640s. Jean-François Nicéron, a member of Mersenne's circle, had designed a polygonal lens from which an image of Louis XIII was recomposed from bits of the portraits of fifteen Ottoman sultans. The state was a kaleidoscope of our own imagination. What held the political world together, like the natural world and the universe, were imposed laws. We had to make of them what we would.

8. Being in Touch

THE KNOWLEDGE HORIZON

Knowledge in Christendom had been the preserve of the few, its nature restricted by what constituted science, its circulation constricted by the privileged environments of its acquisition and transmission. The sixteenth and early seventeenth centuries witnessed an expansion in what was defined as knowledge, in the spheres where it could be gathered and transacted, in the number of those who could access it and the geographical range over which it travelled. The orbit for knowledge expanded. The research facilities in Bacon's *New Atlantis* (1624) were staffed with 'Merchants of Light', whose task was to gather 'the books, and abstracts [i.e. summaries], and patterns of experiments' from around the globe, while 'Depradators' collected them from books and 'Compilers' collated them. That dream would have been unimaginable a century previously.

Knowledge communication changed with separate but related innovations in travel, postal services and printing. The interactions between these three created the infrastructure upon which mercantile traffic depended, through which diplomatic intelligence flowed, and by which news was carried from beyond and around Europe. The republic of letters was reliant upon that infrastructure. These changes redefined what it was (in cultural terms) to be local, sharpening the division between those who had access to literacy and knew how to deploy it, and those who did not.

Such cultural tensions have been interpreted as a division between a popular and an élite culture. In the minds and debates of the learned, that cultural distance had long existed. The Devil exploited the 'superstition' of unlettered people. The imperatives for religious and moral reform that followed the Reformations (Protestant and Catholic), coupled with missions overseas, certainly increased the perception of a larger gulf between those who understood and those who had to be taught what to believe and how to behave. The demands for greater obedience to authority – expressed in ecclesiastical doctrines that were written down, sworn to, memorized and internalized, and in municipal and state edicts and ordinances that subjects were expected to be familiar with – also increased the perceived gap between the well-endowed literate and the literately deprived. The complement to the weakening social cohesion during this period was a diminishing cultural cohesion.

Knowledge was power and profit. There were limits to its circulation, imposed by stakeholders (princes, patrons, printers and stationers). Yet the cultural assumptions about secrecy were changing. Humanists advertised their role in 'exposing to the light that which had been buried in the dust of Antiquity'. Protestant theologians insisted that the Reformation brought God's truth into the open, placing the Bible in people's hands for them to read for themselves. Paracelsus said he liberated medicine from physicians. But the same Protestant theologians understood that people needed to be guided in how and what they read into biblical texts. Alchemical and Neo-Platonic texts were 'occult' not simply because they uncovered hidden forces in nature, but also because their authors thought they uncovered energies so powerful that they should be kept out of the public domain. Cornelius Agrippa was reluctant to publish the details of his magic because his readers would accuse him of being a sorcerer. 'You should communicate vulgar things to vulgar friends; but higher and arcane things only to higher and secret friends; give hay to an ox, sugar to a parrot,' was Abbot Trithemius's advice to him. Paracelsus enveloped his teachings in obscure language, partly to keep them out of the hands of empiric and quack physicians.

Although much information was susceptible to being regarded as secret, the new breed of natural philosophers and practitioners had a more open attitude to sharing their know-how with others. Sebastiano Serlio, the son of a leatherworker who trained as an artist, illustrated and published his compendium on *Architecture* (1537–51) because God had given him his talent and he should not keep it 'buried, hidden in my garden'. Daniele Barbaro justified his commentary on Vitruvius's treatise by saying that he had acquired the knowledge he had through the openness of others (such as stonemasons and mathematicians) and that he wanted to honour that debt of gratitude. The ceramics expert Bernard Palissy published his inventions in *Admirable Discourses* (1580) and criticized alchemists for their secrecy.

By the early seventeenth century, knowledge was becoming seen in some quarters as a commodity. Scholars were merchants, trading facts. The Jesuits sometimes referred to themselves as engaged in godly 'merchandise'. Samuel Hartlib, an exile in London from the Thirty Years War from the late 1620s onwards, wanted knowledge to be a public commodity at the service of the 'reformed Commonwealth'. A librarian would be a 'Factor or Trader for helps to Learning' required to 'give an account of his Trading and of his Profit in his Trade'. He proposed an 'Office of Address', following a similar venture established in Paris by Théophraste Renaudot, to act as a knowledge conduit.

Access to information was also promoted by published reference works. They became an established part of Europe's cultural life. Atlases and gazetteers, dictionaries, bibliographies and encyclopaedias proliferated. Even those for specialists grew more detailed and useful. Prior to 1500, there was just one set of planetary tables (the Alfonsine Tables) to record the movements of the planets across the heavens, a compilation based on a small number of observations from Toledo. By 1650, there were over a dozen different printed sets available. Numerous non-specialist reference works were designed to offer access to the material which Europe's notability were expected to have at their side in order to be considered well-educated. Of the over 150 dictionaries printed in Europe before 1650, some were monolingual (Latin or vernaculars). Others were multilingual, offering translations from or into one or more languages. The most widely reprinted reference book of all was Ambrogio Calepino's *Dictionarium* (1502), a work which gave the title to the genre. Beginning life as a Latin dictionary, it had 150 editions by 1600.

Bibliographies and published sale catalogues were also useful reference works, a way of keeping track of publications that were out of print, false imprints, pseudonymous works and pirated editions. Dictionaries of quotations offered miscellaneously arranged collections of useful or morally improving sayings. The first book to carry the term 'encyclopaedia' in its title was Alsted's 1630 *Encyclopaedia*. Reference works for the non-specialist became an important staple for printers and publishers. They not only sought to bring together the growing amount of information in the public domain from Europe and around the world, but also sought to collate it so that it would be accessible. The emergence of tabular diagrams to indicate content (dichotomy tables of the kind favoured by Ramist educators), indexes of people, places and topics, marginal indicators, cross-referencing, different type-faces to highlight different sorts of information at a glance, and footnotes offered ways to structure larger amounts of information.

THE POWER OF CARTOGRAPHY

Map-making exemplified the growing knowledge horizon. Printed world maps became more detailed and accurate on the basis of collated information from pilots, sailors, captains, explorers, cartographers and mathematicians. Europe's representation of the coastline of southern America, for example, took several generations of trial and error. The chartrooms of the Portuguese and Spanish monarchies became record-ing centres for details about winds, sea currents, water depths, as well as measured distances and coastal details. Despite their efforts to keep such information to themselves, it percolated into the public domain. So, Dutch knowledge of the Malay peninsula in the 1590s was relayed to Petrus Plancius by a Portuguese source, thereby orientating Dutch expeditions. The Dutch East India Company's geographical intelligence is measured in the maps distributed by its Amsterdam cartographic publisher – the Dutch published maps as proclamations of their claims to predominance in ocean sea-lanes and territorial possession. From 1617 onwards, the official cartographer for the company, Hessel Ger-ritsz, laid down a uniform protocol for the company's maps so that their grids were comparable.

Producing world maps was an art in itself. Martin Waldseemüller, an educated humanist from Freiburg, initially led the way. Working for his patron, René II, duke of Lorraine, he linked a printed world map (over 6 foot wide, the first to cover 360° of longitude and to show the African coastline) with a printed world globe and an introduction to 'cosmog-raphy'. He referred to a letter from the Florentine merchant Amerigo Vespucci, edited and published in a German translation in 1505. In it, the Florentine dressed up the New World discoveries of Columbus as his own. Waldseemüller took him at his word: 'Since another fourth part [of the world] has been discovered by Americus Vesputius, I do not see why anyone should object to its being called after Americus the discoverer, a man of natural wisdom, Land of Americus – or America, since both Europe and Asia have derived their names from women.' Six years later, he had second thoughts, preferring to call it 'Terra Incognita'. But it was too late: the accretion to the continental myth had been born, and contemporaries began similarly to understand Europe as that space represented for it on a globe.

The revised spatial representation of the continents was consolidated on world maps by the next generation of cosmographers, concentrated in Venice, the Rhineland, Flanders and Paris – places where the skills existed alongside patrons to support cartographic workshops. Their know-how was handed on through dynasties of map-makers. Gerhard Mercator collaborated on his first printed globe in 1535–6 with the engraver and globe-maker Gaspar Van der Heyden, the mathematician, surveyor and cosmographer Regnier Gemma Frisius and the imperial diplomat Maximilianus Transylvanus. Van der Heyden provided the copper plates of twelve segments ('gores') which, pasted together onto a papier mâché globe provided the image. Gemma Frisius coordinated decisions about representation. The resulting globe offered a depiction of the world from space which claimed to correspond with what was currently known. Where knowledge did not exist, the globe printed a disclaimer.

Mercator followed in 1541 with the largest printed globe yet produced. Dedicated to Nicolas Perronet de Granvelle, Charles V's minister, it offered a revised geography, putting into global context the significance of the Hispanic discoveries. It also included a spiral of rhomb lines that demonstrated the difference between Ptolemaic and magnetic North. Mercator's geography bore the imprint of the changing political and religious world. Imprisoned at Louvain as a suspect 'Lutheran' in 1543, he fled to Duisburg, abandoned his imperial patrons and became a spectator of the crisis engulfing Flanders in the 1560s. In 1566, as newly appointed cosmographer to the Protestant duke of Jülich-Cleves, he conceived how to map our knowledge of the universe. 'I had decided at the beginning,' he recalled later, 'to investigate thoroughly the two parts of the universe, the celestial ... and the terrestrial.' But he then came to see that they were united by history. The resulting cosmography therefore linked time and space, a chronology of world events from Creation to the present, supported by a world map. This was published in 1569 as a wall map, embodying for the first time in that form his cylindrical map projection. However, the explanatory panel did not elucidate how navigators should use it, still less how cartographers might reproduce it. Not until thirty years later would trigonometric tables become available from the mathematician Edward Wright to provide an explanation. For Mercator, its significance was only understood alongside his *Chronologia* (1569), published at the same time. In the latter, he synchronized world history into a chronology whose climax was an imminent apocalypse. Mercator concluded with one final, predictive date: 1576, the *Initium cycli decemnovalis*, the decade of fallow for the earth predicted by Hosea, after which the Lord would 'be as the few unto Israel'. Mercator's 'Projection' was part of a universal millennial history to which European space was related.

Wall maps grew larger with more information, but they also became impractical. The solution was to divide them into regions and compile them into books or portfolios. Mercator published one which carried the title: *Atlas, or Cosmographic Meditations* (1585). The first plates concentrated on the Low Countries, France and Germany. Other parts of Europe followed after his death, in the complete edition published in 1595. The result was pure spatial information. The sheets for Flanders benefited from the triangulation of the region in accordance with mathematical procedures established by Gemma Frisius in 1533, and made easier by its flat terrain and succession of church steeples. Those for the British Isles depicted 2,500 geographical names. Individual sheets could be replaced by new engravings as more accurate information came to hand. Cartographers increasingly emphasized the reliability of their methods of enquiry and their up-to-date representations. By 1650, printed atlases were accompanied by gazetteers of European place-names and the representation of locality in western Europe was substantially mastered.

The new geography linked space to power. Maps determined the routes of French armies invading Italy in the sixteenth century just as they plotted the fortifications around England's southern coastline, constructed by Henry VIII. William Cecil, Elizabeth I's secretary of state and Lord Treasurer, mapped noble estates, taxation assessments and local government boundaries. He probably secured the appointment of

Christopher Saxton as Surveyor of England and Wales in 1573. Similar political and commercial imperatives led the Dutch Republic and Bourbon France to sanction the publication of maps of their political space. Cartography became an instrument of empire. Diogo Ribeiro, Charles V's cartographer, developed maps for the first circumnavigation of the globe. In 1527, he updated the Royal Register or planisphere, the first map to include illustrations of navigational instruments. The astrolabe was placed on the map in the Pacific Ocean at an unmarked line of longitude, 180° east, with a tiny Portuguese flag to the west, and a much larger Spanish flag to the east. That laid claim, by means of navigation and cartography, to an anti-meridian, the equivalent the other side of the earth to that agreed in the Treaty of Tordesillas (7 June 1494) by which Spain and Portugal divided the spoils of the Atlantic between them along an arbitrary line, a hundred leagues west of the Azores.

Portugal's discovery of the Moluccan Spice Islands in 1512 furnished Ribeiro with the evidence to assert this anti-meridian, placing the Moluccas within the Spanish sphere. He was one of the Spanish negotiators at Badajoz–Elvas in 1524 that tried, and failed, to resolve the contested claims to the Moluccas by both Spain and Portugal. Cartography and navigation were equally deployed in the resolution of the conflict in 1529 with the signing of the Treaty of Saragossa. Portugal paid 350,000 ducats in return for an agreement to a line of demarcation in the eastern hemisphere that was the equivalent of 17° east of the Moluccas, which Ribeiro and his colleagues worked out as being just to the west of the furthest island of what the Spanish hoped would be their Spice Islands, and which would be colonized by Spain from 1542 as the Philippines. The sense of space which lay behind the notion of Europe was part of the assertion of a colonial dominion.

Organized space was an instrument of rule. Emperor Charles V impressed foreign dignitaries with maps emphasizing the extent of his dominions. Map murals decorated the private quarters of the Palazzo Vecchio at Florence for Duke Cosimo I. Pope Gregory XIII ordered the construction of a Gallery of Maps, almost 400 feet long, at the Vatican. A contemporary described Pope Gregory walking its length 'considering how best to administer and govern'. At the end was a portal containing an anamorphosis, a mirror displaying an image of the Eucharist reflected from a distortion in the ceiling above, thereby linking geographical and holy power.

THE SCIENCE OF TRAVEL

Despite its divisions, the European landmass was traversed, and not just by the élites. From the second half of the sixteenth century travellers had printed itineraries to guide them. In 1552, Charles Estienne published his *Guide to the Roads of France*. He was no seasoned voyager but he was a shrewd printer. His typography enabled him to fit a large amount of information legibly on to very small pages. Estienne started a trend in travel guides. By 1650, Europe's bookshops were full of *Deliciae, Itineraria* and *Descriptiones*. Rome accommodated tens of thousands of pilgrims each year. A census of 1526–7 enumerated 236 hostelries in the city, one for every 233 inhabitants. Not surprisingly, there were no fewer than 193 travel guides to Rome published before 1650.

Travel literature combined adventure, curiosities, ethnography, scientific enquiry and moral edification – all from the comfort of one's armchair. That from the New World was the equivalent of science fiction, and enterprising editors published collections of explorers' tales. Ramusio's three-volume *Navigations and Voyages* (*Navigationi et viaggi*), which popularized the travel stories of Marco Polo and Ferdinand Magellan's voyage as recounted by Antonio Pigafetta, was quickly emulated. In England, Richard Eden published travel stories organized into four sections (one for each 'corner' of the world). That was also the principle adopted by Richard Hakluyt in his *Principal Navigations, Traffiques and Discoveries* (1589).

Travel diaries came of age, desirable companions for educated Europeans on the move. Many of them found their way into print by 1650. Thomas Coryat, a clergyman's son from Odcombe in Somerset, published *Coryat's Crudities* in 1611, 'hastily gobbled up' during five months' travel to Venice. Over half the journey was on foot and he hung up his boots in the parish church on his return to prove it. His contemporary Fynes Moryson published his diary covering a decade of travel in 1617. Travelogues became a staple for fictional writing, the backbone of the picaresque novel. Diarists commented on the roads, cities, inns, beds, food and money. For Montaigne, dictating his travel diary to his secretary as he went to Italy in the early 1580s, the size, comfort and cleanliness of the inns were important. German inns were the best, with

Baden getting his five stars. Even in thinly populated rural Europe, you could generally find a bed for the night, though a traveller in Muscovy in 1602 noted with surprise that 'one can go for twenty or thirty miles without coming across a single town or village'. Moryson recommended carrying a portable bed in the coach in readiness for such eventualities.

Travellers noted curiosities in accordance with the advice contained in the advice-books on the 'science of travel' (ars apodemica). The authoritative work of the genre, probably more praised than read, was Theodor Zwinger's weighty Travel Method (Methodus apodemica, 1577). Zwinger had already made a name for himself by editing a dictionary of quotations compiled by his stepfather Conrad Lycosthenes. The travels of his youth, Zwinger explained, had been a waste of time because he had not been properly prepared. His book instructed young people on how to observe, digest and record systematically the knowledge that they gained from travel. He had been taught by Ramus in Paris so the work is a succession of unmemorable branching tables, laying out the moral and practical advantages of travel, with some useful advice on note-taking. By 1650, Europeans were travelling in and outside Europe as never before, and recording and transmitting their experiences in more systematic ways.

WRITING, READING, COUNTING

Humanists used 'emblems' to encapsulate the multiple meanings conveyed in an image. The term came from the title which Andrea Alciato gave to an encyclopaedia of illustrated epigrams which he published in Augsburg in 1531. His idea was that each emblem presented the viewer with a scene suggesting an implied or unexpected message for which it then became a mimetic device. By 1621 Alciato's work had become a 1,000-page volume with numerous imitators. 'Emblemata' found their way onto family crests, bookplates, buildings, tableware and embroidery. His first emblem for Mercury, for example, depicted the upper half of a nude male torso emerging from a pile of stones at the intersection of three roads, the god's trident pointing towards the middle of the roads. The epigram explaining the motto ended: 'We are all at the crossroads and in this path of life we err, unless the god himself shows us the way.' Other emblematists present Mercury as the winged messenger of the gods. Either way, the god became a symbol of the speed and power of reading and writing. By the 1620s, the word 'Mercurius' was synonymous with manuscript and published newsletters carrying the latest information.

The power of Mercury depended on the ability to read and write. The fissure between the literate and the non-literate constituted the biggest cultural division in European society and the greatest obstacle to its reformation. Of the two skills, writing was harder and longer to acquire. Writing-masters and school-masters realized that the printing press afforded the opportunity to publish teach-yourself manuals. The result was a raft of copybooks, directed towards teaching children to write, which stole ideas and illustrations from one another to advise the novice on how to sharpen the quill, prepare the ink and rule the paper, and when to lift the pen following which letters. Many of these copybooks taught writing and simple arithmetic as one operation. Reckoning-masters also published manuals with examples and illustrations to teach the operations of number. Arithmetic manuals were alert to the problems that those involved in commerce were likely to encounter, and mixed mental arithmetic with practical calculation. The arithmetic published by Peter Apian in 1527 was depicted in Holbein's painting *The Ambassadors*. Holbein showed it open at a page demonstrating a handy way to divide by twelve, and placed it adjacent to a globe displaying the meridian of longitude agreed at Tordesillas. It was a reminder that mathematics and literacy were important components in all walks of life.

The pressures to become literate and numerate were particularly strong in urban Europe. Trade guilds demanded the ability to write as well as read from their apprentices. In London, for example, the ironmongers' guild required a signed oath from their apprentices; 72 per cent managed it in the surviving register from 1520–50 – rising to 94 per cent in the second half of the century. The second largest group of books published in Strasbourg in the sixteenth century was technical manuals – treatises on the fabrication of dyes, pamphlets on metalworking, books on land-surveying. They were published for a literate, artisan laity who had acquired functional literacy.

This was often first-generation literacy – insatiable, unstoppable and encouraging its possessors to get the wrong end of the stick. Hans Sachs, the eponymous *Meistersinger* of Wagner's opera, was the son of a tailor who became an apprentice shoemaker. He gained his literacy at the Latin school in Nuremberg before taking off as a journeyman. When he returned in 1519 it was as a shoemaker who devoted himself in his spare time to writing. According to his own reckoning, he had, by 1567, written 4,275 master-songs, 208 dramas, and 1,558 fables, dialogues, psalms and tavern songs. There is a curious fountain in the piazza of Montereale Valcellina in northern Italy which depicts a wheel of cheese, minus one slice, with water trickling through the holes in the cheese. It commemorates Domenico Scandella, known as Menocchio, the local miller. Menocchio was another first-generation literate, more interested in finding things out from the books he read than from sermons. From reading, he told the inquisitor, he deduced that the world had evolved 'just as cheese is made out of milk – and worms appeared in it, and these were the angels – and among [them] was God'. Menocchio was tried by the Venetian Inquisition, found guilty and executed.

Many people picked up how to read informally. The evidence from the tribunals of the Spanish Inquisition suggests that significant numbers learned to read and write on their own, or from relatives. For the religious reformers of the sixteenth century, the household was an important cradle of literacy, and basic literacy was important to the functioning of catechism classes. In these and other environments, reading was not a private activity. It accommodated itself to well-established patterns of sociability. Reading was out loud; texts were recited. Taverns had printed handbills pasted to the walls for the purpose. Noël du Fail, born in rural Brittany, published a collection of old wives' tales and sayings in 1547 that he remembered as being sung and retold in the evenings by firelight. What he published was only one version of a more unstable spoken artefact. In his *Household Economy* (1529) the Lutheran reformer at Eisenach Jost Menig recommended the regular reading of Scripture around the dinner table. A Protestant linen-weaver from Cambrai explained before the judges in 1566 that he had been 'led to knowledge of the Gospel by ... my neighbour, who had a Bible printed at Lyon and who taught me the Psalms by heart'. Inside schools as well as out, peer-led oral learning, auto-didacticism and memory played an important part in acquiring functional literacy and numeracy.

What we know about elementary schools is fragmentary. Petty (*petites écoles*), back-street (*Winkelschulen*), commercial (*abbaco* – after the commercial arithmetic in which they specialized), ABC (writing), guild, private and municipal schools taught basic learning skills, and contemporaries distinguished them from the Latin schools into which they sometimes fed. City fathers regarded local educational provision as important to the welfare and standing of their locality. When asked how the town of Coburg in southern Saxony supported three vernacular schools in the 1560s, the local official replied: 'because we have so many artisans, journeymen and vine dressers here'. In urban environments, petty schools taught basic skills to large numbers of boys, but Venice is one of the few places where we can document it. In 1587, at least 26 per cent of boys between six and fifteen years of age attended schools in the city, and over half of them were in vernacular rather than Latin schools.

Historians are cautious in interpreting the evidence of how many people could write, let alone read. There is no shortage of documents which people signed. But being able to sign one's own name is not a reliable guide to one's ability to write, and still less to being able to read. A signature was not universally recognized as the best way of authenticating a document. In Hungary, for example, a seal was more important since signatures (and writing in general) were regarded with suspicion. There is also a definable difference between those who signed with ease and others who struggled to do so. The judges in the tribunals of the Spanish Inquisition were particularly interested in suspects' ability to read and write, and graded them accordingly, recognizing that there was a difference between those who had some basic ability and those who had fluency.

Two generalizations hold good. The first is that literacy was most marked in towns. By the mid-sixteenth century, up to half the population of London could probably, to some degree, read and write. European towns of over 10,000 inhabitants struggled to meet that figure before 1600 when they had high levels of immigration from rural hinterlands. In the Castilian city of Cuenca, only 25 per cent of the men born between 1511 and 1530 could sign their name, although that figure had risen to 54 per cent for the generation born between 1571 and 1590. There was a literacy vortex in early-modern towns where cultural assumptions were dominated by the lay literate who governed overall patterns of attainment and expectation. These oases of high city literacy linked the urbanized corridor running from London, through the Low Countries and down the Rhine to the cities of northern Italy.

The second is that these abilities were concentrated in the hands of men. Only 28 per cent of a sample of women who signed contracts before notaries in Lyon in the 1560s and 70s could do so with their full name. One man in three could not sign the parish register when he married at Amsterdam in 1630; two out of every three brides declined to do so. In Hungary, even aristocratic women struggled with the pen. The second wife of Count György Thurzó was illiterate when they married in 1592. Two years later, she had learned enough to write a few words in her letter to him, when he was besieging a Turkish castle in the Turkish-Hungarian wars, and he was delighted: 'You have traced some words with your own hand, my sweetheart, which is much to my liking . . . I shall bring back some fine Turkish wares as presents.' Wherever else they acquired their basic learning skills, Europe's children were not likely to learn to read at their mother's knee.

A GOOD EDUCATION

'A good education [bonae litterae] makes men,' wrote Erasmus, the best-known intellectual of his day. What he meant was that only a classical education really counted. The philosophy, theology, history and literature of Antiquity, studied through their original texts and languages, contained an integrated programme of what was needed to equip boys (mostly) with a love for the wisdom and virtues of classical Antiquity and thereby inculcate them with the civic values and Christian piety to serve the commonwealth. It is easy to overestimate the achievements of humanist pedagogues. Their advice was principally directed towards the private tutors of princes and magistrates, or the Latin schools for urban élites.

The impact of humanist educators reflected their ambitions. Out of the window went the 'barbarous' methods used by old-fashioned grammarians, obsessed with teaching dull rules of Latin grammar and syntax with the aid of a birch. Humanists exaggerated for effect. 'I have no patience with the stupidity of the average teacher of grammar who wastes precious years in hammering rules into children's heads,' wrote Erasmus in his little treatise Upon the Right Method of Instruction (De ratione studii, 1511). He sketched out instead how 'student-centred learning' could be fun. The tutor should 'lead' the student, after a short course in grammar, to the texts themselves, 'a limpid spring'. Students should read them for themselves, abstract passages from them, put them (like proverbs) around door-frames, inscribe them on rings or cups, turn them into jokes and make them part of their lives. A student would come to grasp the 'meaning and force of every fact or idea that he meets' and acquire the confidence to talk and write in the language himself. Practice was preferred over precepts, methods over specified content, and organized learning over simple memorization. The outcome was a performer: a (Latin) speaker, qualified to interpret texts, comment on them, translate, speak and write off the cuff. Eloquence (portrayed as Mercury in later editions of Alciati's emblems) was an essential skill for politics. Government in the eyes of humanist-trained princes, magistrates and notables was about persuasion.

Humanist educators did more than sketch out an educational programme; they provided teaching materials too. None was more popular than Erasmus's *Adages* and his *Colloquies*. The first showed how to abstract a passage and comment on it. Initially published in 1500 with about 800 sayings and brief explanations, it grew with each succeeding edition until it contained over 4,000 extracts by Erasmus's death. The result was a portrait of learning, organized into quotable distillations of wisdom, by turns curious and funny. Several of them survive today in vernacular phraseology (for example: 'to champ at the bit' and 'no smoke without fire'). Latin students in this period were brought up to compile their own excerpts into 'commonplace' books, portable libraries of learning that influenced how sermons were preached and books were written.

Common-placing was one way by which contemporaries handled the increasing amounts of information coming their way. Taking handwritten notes was a way of mentally absorbing the material they contained. Those who purchased books were encouraged to use tables of contents and indexes as models for how to structure their notes into topics, and to annotate the books in the margins. The naturalist Ulisse Aldrovandi found himself overwhelmed with the notes that he had taken over the years. The scholar Fabri de Peiresc was, according to his contemporary Pierre Gassendi, never to be seen reading without a pen in hand. Peiresc used the common technique of taking notes on loose leaves, and started a blank page for each new item so that he could add to it later on. Each sheet was then annotated with a heading and bound into registers so that he could retrieve the relevant note at a future date. The effort in keeping track of his notes, however, was considerable: 'he would frequently excuse himself that all in his House was nothing but a confused and indigested Masse'. Finding one's way through a morass of material was the common predicament of scholars by the early seventeenth century. Help was at hand, however, from an English school-master – Thomas Harrison, a friend of Samuel Hartlib. His 'booke-invention' of *c.* 1640 involved taking down 'epitomes' of relevant information on slips of paper and then storing them as facts in what amounted to a cabinet of curiosities: a filing cabinet.

Like the *Adages*, Erasmus's *Colloquies* also became a runaway success. It first appeared in a modest eighty-page edition without the author's permission from Basel in 1518, a manual to help boys with their conversational Latin. By March 1522 it had gone through thirty reprints. It remained a staple on bookshop shelves and student reading-lists. In this age of travel, Erasmus began with dialogues that got students practising their greetings and farewells – from the exquisitely polite ('Greetings, my incomparable patron') to the temptingly rude ('Greetings to you, bottomless pit and devourer of cakes'), with lessons in civility on the way ('To greet one who is belching or breaking wind carries politeness too far'). Erasmus played on every register of communication: written, spoken, gestured, implied, unsaid. Jokes, irony and word-play, often at the expense of his critics, reminded the alert reader that almost every word and sentence contained a surprise. The *Colloquies* were far more than an educational handbook; they were an invitation to step into a wider world of civilized learning, a 'republic of letters'.

That phrase (*res publica literaria*) was used by Erasmus to signify an imagined club of humanists. Latin was its lingua franca, and you could show that you belonged by writing in a sloping italic script instead of a vertical Roman script. Such handwriting was initially scoffed at as a novelty and then associated with heresy. But italic then appeared in print (the Venetian printer Aldus Manutius being the first to adopt it). Gerhard Mercator used it to engrave the place-names on his maps. When applied to handwriting, it saved time because more letters could be joined up. Student autographs reveal generations signing up to the club.

Membership was by correspondence. Over 3,000 letters to and from Erasmus have survived – something approaching a map of the multiple nodes linking the humanist commonwealth in the early sixteenth century: Oxford, Paris, Antwerp, Frankfurt, Basel, Venice, Vienna and Cracow. It was a self-appointed élite of the educated, the successful and the powerful, clergy as well as laity, embracing central and eastern Europe. To be a corresponding member raised suspicions in parts of Mediterranean Europe where there was an Inquisition in the wake of the Protestant Reformation. But there were ways around their hostility. Galileo did not correspond directly with Kepler but used a third-party correspondent in Prague. Marin Mersenne acted as an intermediary for other contacts in the Netherlands and England. Like Gassendi and Peiresc, Mersenne found France in the early seventeenth century ideally placed to be a communication medium between Italy and Protestant northern Europe.

Printed books were often collaborative works, their production aided by an unseen telegraphy of correspondents and manuscript circulation. Sebastian Münster's *Cosmography*, for example, would have been impossible to produce without its collaborators. Through Beatus Rhenanus, Erasmus kept abreast of what was going on in the central Rhineland. His friend and correspondent Guillaume Budé – 'the marvel of France', Erasmus called him – told him all he knew about their friends at court and the French capital. The creation of an engaged and literate public was as important to the anticipation of change in and around the Reformation as the printing press. Such a club created resentments among those who believed they did not belong, were excluded, or felt threatened by what it claimed to stand for. Besides creating political divisions, the Protestant Reformation partially decomposed this invisible republic, its gradual re-composition in the first half of the seventeenth century being one of the many signs that Europe was finding the ways and language to outgrow its religious contentions.

Within the republic of letters was an evocation of the moral and civil virtues of friendship. In his little manual on teaching, Erasmus took the example of Virgil's Second Eclogue. It was about friendship among equals, he said, where 'the stronger and the more numerous the ties of taste and interest the more durable the bond'. In parenthesis, Erasmus presented his picture of friendship among like-minded people: 'I mean the frank, open and abiding friendship which alone deserves the name.' Erasmus's correspondence exemplified the ideal – though it was a contrivance, based on Ciceronian conventions. Another Erasmian runaway success, *On Composing Letters* (*De conscribendis epistolis*, 1522), laid out how to write a good letter. It went through fifty-five editions before 1550. The exchange of letters presupposed an exchange of objects. Paintings, coins, curiosities, manuscripts – all the worldly goods valorized in the Renaissance – became objects of exchange, transformed beyond their commodity value into symbols of shared values and ideals.

There are two surviving oil paintings of Matthäus Schwarz, chief accountant at the house of Fugger in Augsburg. The earlier of the two, painted in February 1526 by Hans Maler, depicts the 29-year-old wearing a stylish hat and a costume of black ermine, and strumming a lute. In that of 1542, painted by Christoph Amberger, he is forty-five years old and has put on weight. There is a glass of red wine (a reference to his family's mercantile origins in the wine trade) and his rich clothes are set off against a Renaissance painting behind him. Schwarz has a humanist veneer but his interests seem to lie more in the practicalities of life rather than in what people were thinking or reading. Beginning in 1519, he kept a voluminous manuscript diary, entitled *The Run of the World* (*Der Welt lauf*). All that remains is its adjunct: *The Book of Clothes*, a picture book with 137 miniature pictures of Schwarz in the costumes that he wore. It runs almost literally from cradle to grave, the first image showing him in nappies and the last one as a mourner at Anton Fugger's funeral in 1560. They show him in his school uniform, leaving school (dancing on his school books) and in his outfits as a travelling merchant. That in the autumn of 1525 includes a reversible jacket, bright red on the outside, green on the inside so that, when travelling through the Tyrol accompanying silver transports for the Fuggers, he could turn green, the colour of the insurgent peasants. He is depicted tobogganing in winter, and wearing a red and yellow festive costume for the wedding of his master, Anton Fugger, in 1527. We might see this as the equivalent of a personal photograph album from the sixteenth century, evidence for a new 'individuality'. Yet, in June 1526, months before his thirtieth birthday, two miniatures of Schwarz show him in the nude. The contemporary belief was that, on Judgment Day, we appear before God naked. In reality, Schwarz's book is an account of his life in the world as others would see him – in his clothes. His self-awareness is clothed by self-fashioning. But his nakedness was not a depiction of either. Rather it was recognition that he would have to account for himself in another world, where clothes and self-awareness counted for nothing. Humanists changed European's perceptions of their place in the world. But that did not mean that they had thereby been put in touch with modern individualism.

'POST-HASTE'

Letters were at the dynamic heart of Europe in the sixteenth and early seventeenth centuries. Letters patent were the preferred instruments of state. Letters of nomination furnished you with an office in it, or a benefice in the Church. Letters of commission gave you powers to govern a province or a colony. Letters of indulgence provided promissory notes of pardon for your sins (until Protestants called foul). By 1520, resident diplomats and the regular despatches which accompanied them were becoming habitual at the courts of western Europe, drawing on the example of the northern Italian principalities (Milan, then Florence and Venice). King Francis I inherited the throne of France in 1515 with only one resident ambassador. At his death in 1547, France had ten throughout Europe in order to counter the diplomatic sophistication of its Habsburg rivals. As Europe's commercial networks expanded, so larger mercantile firms made much greater use of commission agency to operate at a distance, letters being the means by which they managed these operations. In Venice, letters of news arrived at the Rialto (the mercantile heart of the city) from across Europe, one of several nerve-centres of Europe's communications, where news was power, but not exclusively in the hands of the conventionally powerful.

The despatch of an extraordinary courier was not novel. Medieval universities had provided organized postal services of their own so that students could keep in touch with their families and be sent money and belongings. What changed was that these were supplemented by relay routes of post-horses, organized by governments but available for a fee (and at the discretion of couriers) to private individuals. The addresses on letters indicate how widely the service was used – often accompanied by messages to the carrier: 'with the speed of a bird'; 'day and night', 'post-haste', 'non celeriter sed fulminantissime' ('not just fast, but like lightning'). Franz von Taxis, the general postmaster of Philip of Burgundy, ran the postal services for the Habsburg empire (and gave us the word 'taxi'). A painting of von Taxis in around 1514 shows him with the symbols of his office: a letter-box with its silver finial, a quill-pen, a letter, a seal-ring and some gold coins. In the contract signed by Philip's son Charles on 12 November 1516 with Franz and his nephew Johann Baptiste von Taxis, they guaranteed a regular service of 'ordinary posts' from Brussels throughout the empire. The operating times stipulated in the contract were not significantly improved before the later eighteenth century.

On 14 June 1520, two weeks before his election as Holy Roman Emperor, Charles granted Johann Baptiste von Taxis the exclusive right to appoint and dismiss postmasters in his lands and call himself 'General Postmaster'. As a result, news travelled fast in the empire. The first report of the Anabaptist revolution in Münster was through the letters of its bishop, sent on to Worms and then distributed by the Taxis network. The unexpected meeting of Pope Clement VII and Charles V at Bologna in February 1530 was known in Antwerp a week later by the same route. By the early sixteenth century, the north of Italy was criss-crossed by a fast postal system. By 1568, there were five resident postmasters in Rome (those of the kings of Spain and France as well as the republics of Genoa and Venice, in addition to the pope himself), whence letters and parcels were despatched at least once a week for Venice, Milan, Genoa, Naples and Lyon (for France and the Low Countries). The Antwerp bourse displayed a timetable of carriers. From 1558, the expatriate Italian banker Prospero Provana ran a postal service for King Sigismund II Augustus of Poland which left Cracow on Sundays, reached Vienna on Wednesday and arrived in Venice the following Tuesday. By the early seventeenth century, a postal network served all the major towns in the northern Netherlands. John Taylor's *The Carriers Cosmographie* (1637) mapped the postal routes to the shire towns in England and also explained which postal carriers left from which tavern, and on what days of the week.

Postal networks served only major towns. They were expensive and things then, as now, could go wrong. But contemporaries made allowance for upsets and, when one examines how the news reports of the major events spread across Europe, it is the volume and contradictory accounts that frustrated contemporaries, not the slowness with which they reached them. Literate Europe came to depend on communication at a distance, and not just across the European landmass. With the cycles of commercial traffic to and from colonial America and the East Indies it was easy to incorporate reports and papers from overseas into domestic circulation. Jesuit missionaries were encouraged to provide information on natural history and curiosities. Their colleges beyond Europe (Lima, Goa, Macao) were, like their counterparts in Europe, nodes in knowledge circulation. San Pablo College in Lima, for example, taught missionaries, prepared and published grammars of local Indian languages, had one of the largest libraries in southern America, and its pharmacy became a renowned centre for indigenous medicinal plants. By the seventeenth century, Jesuits sent shipments of medicaments and rarities back to Europe on a regular basis, their reports then appearing as *Annual Letters* which were published from around 1550.

BOOKS SEEKING READERS

Printing was hailed as a world-changing event. Luther famously described it as 'God's highest and extremest act of grace, whereby the business of the Gospel is driven forward', a sign of the coming millennium: 'the last flame before the extinction of the world'. At face value, such remarks reinforce the impression that there was a 'printing revolution' in the sixteenth and early seventeenth centuries. In reality, however, the situation was more complicated than that. The well-established technologies of 'scribal publication' (circulation by multiple, often selective, copying of materials for limited distribution) continued to provide a convenient means for circulating ideas around Europe's republic of letters, easily adapted to its learning media, relatively unencumbered by censorship and requiring little capital investment. Yet the possibility of accurate textual reproduction in large quantities was not an anodyne change, especially when it was linked to the advent of print culture – i.e. the existence of enterprising printers, publishers, bookmarkets, distribution networks and an adapted reading public. That print culture was the achievement of this period. By 1650, it is impossible to imagine Europe without it.

Print culture was a tribute to commercial rather than technological success. By 1520, printing was out of the cradle and almost all the technical innovations that made it possible were in place. Printing presses and print-shops in 1650 looked much as they had done over a century previously. What changed was their cultural footprint. Global estimates remain impressionistic. In 1520, there were between 250 and 270 printing centres in Europe, almost all of them in cosmopolitan cities, university towns or in the shadow of a princely court. By 1650, those figures had not doubled, but there was an increasing concentration of printing presses in a limited number of lead-sites. In 1550, Paris and Lyon occupied a dominant role in France. Venice published over half the production in Italy, a preponderance matched in the Netherlands by Antwerp. Only the German market remained one in which there was no dominant centre. One should perhaps imagine 150–200 million copies being produced from these presses in the sixteenth century. The comparable figure for the eighteenth century would be of the order of 1,500 million.

Changes of that magnitude meant finding new readers and persuading them to buy printed materials in greater quantity. Alongside the triumphal trope of the providential printing press went another in the sixteenth century: that of the over-production of books. Luther deplored the 'abundance of books and writers', complaining of 'an infinite sea' and 'ocean' of books. The English martyrologist John Foxe agreed: 'since the republic of letters is indeed all but overwhelmed by an infinite multitude of books flying forth on all sides,' he wrote in his Latin martyrology, 'my labours at putting hand to pen seem superfluous . . .' There may even have been a crisis in the production of scholarly books by the early seventeenth century. We tend to think that, in the pioneer age of printing, readers were chasing after books. The reality was the reverse: books chased readers.

Europe's printers and booksellers knew how to lure them. It mattered how books looked because, for Europe's literate élites, printed books were for keeping, and not just communicating. At the top end of the market especially, they were objects of luxury and value, presented as gifts and treasured. Since books were generally sold unbound (*in albis*), booksellers offered bespoke binding services. For printers and publishers, therefore, an illustrated frontispiece was of particular significance – something to be displayed in the shopfront or pinned up at the book fair. Woodblock prints were cheaper to produce, easily integrated into the printing process and recycled from one edition to another. Copperplate intaglio printing was more expensive and copper in restricted supply. Both the engraving and printing took longer and required more skill. But the greater clarity and sophistication of the

image were advantageous when covers sold books, and engraved fron-
tispieces gradually prevailed for more expensive titles.

Title-pages tempted the reader with bold claims – true histories, pro-
digious marvels, strange wonders. They advertised new editions and
improved readability – better layouts, indexes, notes and illustrations.
Catalogues helped readers to know what was available and their layout
was improved. One sixteenth-century German printing dynasty from
Lübeck (Johann Balhorn and son) were so renowned for 'improving'
their texts from one edition to another that they became the eponym in
German for altering something until it no longer made sense (*verball-
hornen*). A mass-produced book needed features to distinguish it from
the competition and printers were sophisticated in finding ways of
doing so. German printers adopted a Teutonic rival to roman type,
known now as 'Fraktur', to give their works a distinctive appearance in
local markets. Lyonnais printers tried to popularize a *civilité* italic font
for works for the French market. Claude Garamont modelled his
Roman and Greek fonts on designs produced for the press of Aldus
Manutius in Venice, the modern Garamond typeface being based on
designs by one of his successors, Jean Jannon.

Title-pages were sometimes modified to sell into different markets, or
changed to dispose of remaining stocks. Prefaces persuaded people to
buy, men of letters badgered to provide dedications. In some regions,
printers diversified into playing-cards, greetings cards, calendars and
albums. In northern France, the founder of a publishing dynasty in
Troyes, Nicolas Oudot, began printing books of prayers, romances,
fables and almanacs very cheaply. They became known as 'the blue
library' (*bibliothèque bleue*) from their coloured covers. They were marketed regionally across northern France through pedlars (*colporteurs*)
hawking them at fairs and from town to town. Oudot's contemporaries
in Amsterdam, Paris and London sought out other markets for ephemeral publications, particularly newspapers and journals. Everywhere,
printers and publishers knew that a popular book was one that appealed
to diverse groups of readers, whose tastes and interests they had to
cultivate. By 1650, there was a striking correlation between a country's
book production and its per capita gross domestic product. The relationship was not that of cause and effect, but it reflected a new reality: that
printing had become by the middle of the seventeenth century a reliable
indicator of underlying economic prosperity.

Succeeding as a publisher required commercial acumen, business contacts and good luck. The career of Christophe Plantin, one of the most enterprising printers in sixteenth-century Europe, illustrates how it was done. Like many printers of his day, he was an émigré, arriving in Antwerp having been born in the Loire valley. In 1555, he began printing books, combining this initially with leather-work, binding and the selling of French lace. He used family and friends to raise his capital, and some of his friends were also 'family' in the sense that they belonged to the Family of Love, followers of the domestic piety advocated by Hendrik Niclaes. Plantin developed his contacts in Paris, gearing his early works to the French market, careful to balance his output between prestige publications and lower-range but steady-sale titles. By 1566, Plantin and Co. had seven presses and employed thirty-three printers, compositors and proof-readers and had moved premises from 'The Golden Compasses' (one of Plantin's regular printing devices) in the Kammenstraat to the Vrijdagmarkt. There, the *Officina Plantiniana* featured on the tourist map – as it does today.

Plantin's greatest success, however, was to use his contacts in high places to secure printing monopolies. The politics of book censorship grew in the sixteenth century out of the desire of printers themselves to protect their publications from competition. They sought 'privileges' to do so and governments realized that they could become a weapon in the battle against religious controversy. Publications therefore carried an 'imprimatur' which offered the printer-publisher economic advantages but at the same time obliged him to submit his texts for official examination. Plantin, however, landed the most tempting of monopolies. With the help of Antoine Perrenot (known as Cardinal Granvelle), he secured a royal subsidy (1568) and papal privilege (1572) to print and market throughout Catholic Europe the multilingual Polyglot Bible. In 1570, he also gained a papal privilege giving him sole rights to print and market the new breviary (the liturgy for the Roman Church) recommended by the Council of Trent. In 1571, the privilege was extended to Spain and its overseas territories. Consignments of books by the thousand were shipped from Antwerp and Plantin's publishing pre-eminence briefly assured. But no publisher was ever secure for long. In a competitive environment, rival printers in Cologne, untroubled by his privilege, produced their own breviaries. Political crises, while they generated demands for printed copy, disrupted supplies and markets. With the renewed civil war in the Netherlands in 1572, he almost went bankrupt. Even this most successful of publishers signed himself off in his letters in the later 1580s as 'from the once-flourishing' Plantin.

Libraries were the embodiment of the new print culture. The growth of private collections can be measured, in part, through surviving inventories. In Florence, Amiens and elsewhere, the evidence is of a growth in the availability of domestic printed reading-matter, and particularly in the development of medium-sized urban collections (30–200 items). Specially built libraries were also constructed for larger collections, symbolizing the link between books and power. In 1515, the Venetian Senate decided to build a library to house the books that had been left to it by Cardinal Bessarion. The Senate's resolution referred to the 'good government' that would come about through following the ancients in fostering learning. The royal library at Fontainebleau formed part of Francis I's cultural agenda, which included the founding of a royal printing house and a system of legal deposit. In Germany, princes rivalled one another in founding libraries and appointing scholar-librarians. Libraries, in short, became spaces that were either dedicated to the common weal, or (increasingly) privileged environments in which to exalt the dignity of princes.

LANGUAGES AND COMMUNITIES

Language was a barrier as well as a facilitator to communication, whether by word of mouth or in writing. How many languages were spoken in Europe in this period? The answer is not straightforward since what is classified as a European language is determined by those which have survived. A recent estimate puts the figure at somewhere between forty and seventy. The awareness of Europe's rich linguistic heritage was growing. Contemporaries often linked the quality of languages to the perceived moral character of the people who spoke them. So the philosopher and magistrate Michel de Montaigne regarded Gascon, the language spoken in southwestern France, as 'male' and 'military', while his contemporary the Parisian barrister Étienne Pasquier thought Italian was 'soft' and 'effeminate'. Both Montaigne and Pasquier subscribed to that part of the humanist agenda which made language the touchstone of education. Writers rivalled one another in promoting their own native vernacular while denigrating the claims of others. In 1542, the Italian dramatist and intellectual Sperone Speroni discussed the relative merits of Greek, Latin, Tuscan and other Italian dialects for literary composition. The poet Joachim du Bellay followed his example seven years later and condemned his compatriots for not promoting the richness of French in his *Defence and illustration of the French Language*. In Spain, humanists linked the dignity of the Castilian language to its Latin roots, although other languages in the peninsula had their defenders too. Martín de Viziana sought to prove, for example, that Valencian was the equal of Castilian in drawing its roots from the ancient languages. In 1589, Gudbrandur Thorláksson advanced the claims to purity of the Icelandic language. There was hardly a vernacular that did not have its champion.

Is this evidence for the triumph of the vernacular? The reality was not that straightforward. There was a constant tension between spoken and written languages, between the pressures of localism and the desire for uniformity. Linguistic pluralism remained a fact of life in Europe. In the Engadine valley in central Switzerland, the Salis family corresponded with one another in five different languages in the later sixteenth century. The sons away at school wrote back in Latin but the rest of the family used German, Italian, French and (the women) their native Romansch. Bilingualism was common, too, in eastern and central Europe, where speakers of Hungarian and Slovak, Czech, German, Croat or Italian lived in proximity. In Lithuania, five languages cohabited – Lithuanian, Polish, German, Ruthenian and Latvian. People readily accommodated themselves to belonging to more than one language community. Which language they chose to use, and in which context, became a social and cultural statement about who they were and where they belonged at any particular moment.

Latin was the language of Christendom. It remained the most important 'virtual language' that defined who you were, socially and intellectually. As the English schoolmaster Richard Mulcaster said, it was the language of 'the learned communitie', 'the mother tongue of the learned'. It was the last component of Christendom to crumble. In dual-language parts of Europe, Latin remained the lingua franca for justice, administration and getting about. Many municipal and court records in Poland were kept in Latin until the seventeenth century. In Vienna, *Hofkammer* officials corresponded in Latin with their counterparts in Bratislava. The records of the German and Hungarian Diets were in Latin. When English travellers wanted to make their wishes known in Hungarian inns they used Latin. A Flemish Capuchin wrote to Rome in 1633 that 'in Hungary the peasants and shepherds speak Latin more fluently than many priests do elsewhere'. Latin remained the formal language of diplomacy and of the Roman Catholic Church. The majority of books for sale at the Frankfurt fair were still in Latin by 1650. It was not the only virtual language (Jews used Hebrew and Church Slavonic was the lingua franca among the Orthodox) but Latin remained a residual trace-element and linguistic frontier delineating what had once been Christendom.

The tensions within the Protestant Reformation were reflected in its languages. Although humanists preached the utility of reformed vernacular languages, states could not impose a language. The Edict of Villers-Cotterêts (1539) referred to the 'maternal French language' as what should be used in French courts. But it did not exclude other languages from being accepted. That same year, the Polish Sejm ordered that all its laws and edicts should be published in Polish, but that did not impact on other parts of its localized administration. The Act of Union between England and Wales in 1536 required oaths to be taken 'in the English tongue', although Welsh continued to be used into the next century. The following year, the Act of the English Order limited the use of Irish in public, thereby turning English into a resented colonial language. In 1561, the Inquisition made Castilian obligatory in Catalonia, creating similar resentments, which would resurface in the 1640s. In the seventeenth century, the Swedes attempted to restrict the use of Danish and Finnish in its new empire, while the Habsburgs sought to impose German in Czech lands after the battle of the White Mountain (1620). By 1650, there were emergent dominant linguistic communities in Europe, reflecting a redefining of the local in Europe. There were also languages in clear retreat: Basque, Breton, Gaelic. For others – Catalan, Portuguese, Czech, Danish, Dutch – the prospects lay in the balance.

The linguistic choice facing intellectuals was between broadening their impact (Latin) and deepening it (a vernacular). Erasmus had no difficulty in choosing the former. Everything he wrote was in Latin, a language he spoke (with a Dutch accent). Yet, in the preface to his Greek edition of the New Testament, he advocated putting it into vernacular languages so that 'the lowliest women' (omnes mulerculae), Scots and Irish, Turks and

Saracens could read it, ploughmen sing the Scriptures at the plough and weavers keep time to them at their loom. The greatest linguistic tensions of the age of the Reformation were: what language should one use in church, and how should one address God. Latin remained the language of the Catholic liturgy. But the evidence from church visitations is that a substantial proportion of the parish clergy, at least before the impact on clerical education of Catholic reform, did not know much of it. Whether that mattered, and what language was used for sermons and homilies, is difficult to determine. Simple Latin may have been approachable to speakers of Romance languages if interlaced with the vernacular. It is not clear that their congregations would have understood a vernacular any better – unless their priest happened to be fluent in their patois.

Protestant reformers chose deepening over broadening, but with difficulty. Luther advocated retaining a Latin liturgy for educational purposes and wrote his theological works in Latin. Huldrych Zwingli, whose spoken language was a Swiss dialect, made language central to the way we understand and worship God. When he reformed the liturgy in Zürich (1525), it was in the Swiss-German of the eastern Swiss cantons that worshippers said the 'Gloria in Excelsis'. It was only in Latin that his theological works gained him a broader hearing. Jean Calvin used both Latin and vernacular French but struggled to render his works in the latter. Translating the Bible was a challenge for all the religious reformers. Martin Luther translated it into German for 'the common man' (*der gemeine Mann*). But what German? In his *Table Talk* he recognized that 'German has so many dialects that people living only thirty miles apart do not understand one another'. In his Bible translation he chose to follow the model of the Saxon court at Meissen, known as 'Meissen officialese' (*Meissner Kanzleisprache*). Vernacular Scriptures divided Protestantism over the issue at the heart of the Reformation: how one was in touch with God.

THE POWER OF IMAGES

There was significant innovation, sophistication and imagination, beyond printing, in the use of wood-block images, engravings, etchings, music- and ballad-printing, medal production and tapestry-work. Scholars, artists and engravers understood that an image conveyed layers of meaning. Mechanical reproduction assisted in the manufacture of globes, armillary spheres, sextants and astronomical rings and improved clarity and accuracy. The increased reliability of numerical tables (for geographical positions, trigonometry, logarithms and planetary ephemerides) facilitated their use. Dichotomy tables made it possible for the structure of information to be taken in at a glance. Images enabled techniques to be better conveyed and standardized. The quality of illustrations, coupled with the arrangement of image with text, contributed to the success of anatomical textbooks, botanical handbooks, mathematical treatises and atlases.

Pictures were suited to the focus on the particular. Naturalistic representations of plants closed the gap between discursive texts about nature and the direct experience of it. Vesalius supervised and paid for the eighty-three woodcut images of the human body contained in the *Fabrica* (*Seven Books on the Fabric of the Human Body*), telling the reader: 'How much pictures aid the understanding of these things and place a subject before the eyes more precisely than the most explicit language.' Scales on maps, measurements, accompanying descriptions of images and hand-coloured artefacts supplemented the sense of a denoted reality. Knowledge of the world could also be represented in diagrams and formulae which constructed ways of seeing the world and structuring knowledge. The illustrations which accompanied Descartes's optical treatise thus combined anatomical dissection with optical geometry. Engravers and artists were not merely adjuncts to the processes of knowledge representation, but active collaborators in it – sometimes figuring directly in the works which they represented.

Far from fossilizing knowledge in a static medium, pictures represented its acquisition as a dynamic process. Heinrich Vogtherr (the Elder) was the first to produce anatomical illustrations with layered flaps in order to show the body internally and externally. Hans Baldung Grien contributed ten woodcuts to Walter Hermann Ryff's 1541 anatomical atlas depicting the successive stages of a cranial dissection. Galileo's *Starry Messenger* included sequenced engravings of the irregularities which he had seen on the moon's surface and the spots on the sun as a visual narration of his astronomical theories.

Images sold books, and also ideas. Lutheran propagandists incorporated already familiar motifs (monsters and portents) into their anti-Catholic pamphlets, justifying them as 'for the simple folk'. Images could transcend the literacy gap – could become the 'bible of the poor' (*Biblia pauperum*), as the Second Nicene Council (AD 787) had called it. Zwinglian-Calvinist (Reformed) Protestantism had second thoughts, however, about pictures, especially in a devotional context. Images encouraged idolatry, and Old Testament biblical precepts proclaimed them dangerous to true faith and to be destroyed. There was no such reticence in Counter-Reformed Catholic Christianity. Images were important, as Jesuit missionaries emphasized, in the armoury of persuasion. Francis Xavier arrived in Goa in 1542 with wood-block prints, paintings and statuettes of the Virgin Mary.

The religious art of the High Renaissance and early Baroque – Michelangelo, Raphael, Zuccaro, and (later) Rubens and Carracci – travelled around the world in engravings and etchings. Luís Fróis, one of the Jesuit missionaries in Japan, reported in 1584 that over 50,000 devotional images were needed for distribution to its growing Christian community, adding that these pictures were so coveted as gifts in India and China that a priest might set out with a thousand of them, but be persuaded to part with them before he reached Japan. The solution was to found an indigenous 'school' of painters, attached to the Jesuit seminary in Japan. Begun in 1583, it was headed by the Jesuit Giovanni Niccolò. Under his direction, Japanese lay brothers copied European engravings in oil paintings on copper, wood panels, watercolours and ink drawings on a substantial scale, many of them exported to China.

Images were chosen for their appropriate effect in a particular environment. In China, for example, they were as much part of Matteo Ricci's missionary strategy as clocks, astronomy and maps. He initially replaced images of the Madonna with those of the *Salvator Mundi* because the Chinese confused the Virgin Mary with Guanyin, the Buddhist Bodhisattva of Mercy. Later, however, he and his successors took advantage of the affinity. Like his fellow-Jesuits in Japan, he also avoided the Crucifixion and scenes of the Passion because locals regarded them as humiliating. Jesuits related how pictures created great excitement among host populations. The impact of European representational art was powerful. 'This is a living Buddha,' Chinese Emperor Wan-Li said when regarding an oil painting of the *Salvator Mundi* from the Jesuit workshop in Rome, shown to him in 1601. Visitors to the Jesuit residence in Beijing in 1605 were 'amazed by the books of images' they were shown. They apparently thought 'they were sculpted and they could not believe that they were pictures'. Others were reported as saying that paintings and engravings had a supernatural quality because the eyes of the Virgin or of Christ seemed to follow them as they moved around.

Accommodation to local tastes was encouraged among those missionaries who were convinced that a softly-softly approach (*il modo soave*) was the best way of winning secure converts to Christianity. Europe's mechanically reproduced media were an important adjunct to global Catholic Christianity. An Antwerp engraving from 1550 served as the model when Nahua Indians in Mexico depicted the Virgin of Sorrows in feather-work. In 1578, the first Mexican feather-painting, based on a European engraving of Mary Magdalene, was recorded as making its way via the Philippines to China. The 153 images in Jerónimo Nadal's *Pictures from the Gospel Stories* (1593) were based on a cycle of drawings first made in Rome in the late 1550s or early 60s. Printed in Antwerp, they had a considerable impact on missions in Asia and Latin America. 'By placing an image before people's eyes,' said Ricci, 'we can explain what we could not perhaps put into words.'

Christendom Afflicted

9. Politics and Empire in the Age of Charles V

CHRISTENDOM'S FRAGILITY

Christendom had never been a political unity. The European landmass was a political kaleidoscope. Rivalries generated conflicts which the papacy and the Holy Roman Emperor could never do more than mediate. That was partly because both those institutions were themselves parties in the struggles, involvements which changed the nature of their own power and made them targets for criticism. The latter was expressed in terms of demands for reform. Reform of the Church had a long-established agenda, embodied in the clamour for an ecumenical council. Although the Conciliar Movement was in abeyance by the end of the fifteenth century, Church reform was still capable of being mobilized against the papacy by interested parties. Reform of the empire was also a well-established theme in German lands, surfacing alongside Church reform in German Diets, deployed by different people and for various purposes. Sometimes reform was used to criticize the emperor, and at other times to promote measures which strengthened the emerging political maturity of the empire itself.

The political fragmentation of Christendom was exposed in the first half of the sixteenth century. That was partly because of the emergence of the Ottomans as a significant threat. At precisely the moment when Christendom required a coordinated response to a threat from without, it was paralysed by ruptures within. Those divisions were inflamed by the composition of an unprecedented dynastic empire under Habsburg Charles V, king of Spain from 1516 until his abdication in 1556, and Holy Roman Emperor from his election in 1519 through to his death in 1558. The Habsburg patrimony occupied the strategically sensitive parts of the emerging economic heartland of the Rhineland. It straddled the Alps and the Pyrenees, and stretched down the Danube beyond Vienna. Charles V engineered his election as Holy Roman Emperor. He enjoyed the unparalleled fortunes of the New World. In various pronouncements he acknowledged that he carried the hopes of Christendom: for reform in the Church and empire, for protection from the Ottomans and for resolution of Christendom's conflicts. Some interpreted his reign in prophetic terms. He was a second Charlemagne, a *Rex Romanorum* who would renew the Church, reform the empire, repulse the Turks and – like King David – gather the sheep into one fold.

Yet it was the inevitable consequence of his patrimony that Charles V would never realize such aspirations. He was the inheritor of dynastic alliances and political agendas which had been constructed to limit Valois France. He was the heir to long-standing suspicions between the emperor and the papacy, further exacerbated by Charles's ascendancy in the Italian peninsula and by different agendas upon Church reform. The sheepfold became a battlefield. Called upon by the uniqueness of his position to articulate a new 'universal' monarchy for the protection and advancement of Christendom, his attempts to do so invited the hostile response from Valois France that Charles's claims to speak for and protect Christendom were a smokescreen for Habsburg dynastic ambitions. Although French attempts to create an anti-Habsburg alliance were not as enduring as they would have liked, they successfully constructed a narrative which detached Habsburg imperialism from the survival of Christendom as well as from the reform of the Church and empire.

The Lutheran movement in Germany was the other key element in the political fragility of Christendom in the first half of the sixteenth century. Lutheran Protestants rewrote how Christian truth was to be found and mounted a wholesale attack upon the legitimacy of papal claims to authority. How their movement called into being fresh coalitions across social boundaries, activated new political players and cemented the political maturity of the empire, independent of the emperor, is the subject of the following chapter. But it was part of the political fragmentation of Christendom, which is the subject of this one. Once more, Charles V was at the centre and again he had to play an impossible hand. He felt the inheritance of Christendom on his shoulders, which was not to be surrendered to the views of a monk who rewrote inherited traditions. Yet Charles also had to respond to the political forces in the empire which Lutheranism had summoned up, and which drew their legitimacy from the fabric of the empire itself. His attempt to gather together the different strands of the agenda for Church reform as a way of reconciling Lutherans with the Church looked, for a time, as though it might work. The papacy played along with it, especially when it seemed a way of reuniting Christendom against the Ottomans. Deep down, however, the papacy suspected imperial motives, and those who regarded Lutheranism as a theologically irreconcilable creed eventually won out.

When Charles's attempt to negotiate a resolution of the theological differences in the empire failed in the 1540s, he turned to military force. Many, especially among those who staffed the ecclesiastical institutions which guaranteed the integrity of Christendom (the Inquisition, the Dominican Order, the theological faculties of the universities), argued from the beginning that Lutheranism was a heresy whose defeat was essential to the maintenance of God's order on earth. The emperor's role was to provide the sword and buckler to defeat heresy and thereby staunch the political fragmentation which weakened Christendom. The evolution of Protestantism brought to prominence hard-line views about how Christendom should be preserved, although, in the circumstances of a fragmented Christendom, they served only to enhance its underlying fractures.

Charles's military victory over the Lutherans at the battle of Mühlberg (24 April 1547) did not defeat Protestantism. It was succeeded by the Peace of Augsburg, a settlement negotiated there by his brother Ferdinand (Emperor Ferdinand I). Signed on 25 September 1555, it was enshrined into imperial law. Charles did not want the legalizing of heresy on his conscience, and feared that it would be the cause for greater dissent in the empire. He wanted the settlement written in Ferdinand's name rather than his own, and issued instructions for the Diet to be delayed until his abdication was announced. Ferdinand did not wait, and Charles was consternated. A month later, at a ceremony in the Great Palace in Brussels on 25 October 1555, Charles V announced his wish to abdicate and to pass on to his son Philip the rights to rule in the Netherlands. Negotiations followed between Philip and Ferdinand, who overrode Charles's wishes (enshrined in a family compact of 1550) to keep the Habsburg legacy intact. Philip waived his candidacy to succeed Ferdinand as king of the Romans and future emperor. More reluctantly, he surrendered to Ferdinand his rights in northern Italy. In return, Ferdinand conceded that the Netherlands should remain under Spanish control. That deal concluded, on 16 January 1556 Charles abdicated as ruler in Spain, investing Philip with his authority over Castile, Aragon, Sicily, the islands in the western Mediterranean and the New World. The religious division of Christendom had been legalized in the empire. The Habsburg legacy was split on what would turn out to be a fatally flawed basis. And the failure of Christendom's political leadership had been confirmed.

POLITICAL CONFIGURATIONS

Europe's landmass was politically variegated. In 1520, there were some 500 more or less independent entities. Although the processes of conquest and coalescence that underlay European state formation continued, it would not be until the first half of the seventeenth century that Europe's middleweight states (which economic expansion and other developments favoured) began to gain the upper hand. Around 350 separate states would still be distinguishable around 1650. The smaller entities included republics that claimed to be maritime empires (Venice, Genoa), city-states shorn of a hinterland (Geneva, Dubrovnik, Gdańsk, Hamburg), a newly reconstituted duchy with a contested republican legacy (Florence, after 1513 the duchy of Tuscany), an emerging provincial republic (the Dutch Republic) that, by 1600, had something of a state-like structure and, by 1650, had become a colonial power. There was an old empire (the Holy Roman Empire) in the process of acquiring the trappings of a dynastic state in its Habsburg heartlands and a reinforced constitution for the rest, alongside a newer condominium that called itself a republic (*Rzeczpospolita*) but was an elective monarchy (Poland, merged with Lithuania by the Union of Lublin, 1569). Self-governing rural oligarchies (the Grey Leagues – (*Grisons, Graubünden*) – which ruled part of the Swiss Alps) coexisted alongside a loose confederation (the Swiss cantons). Numerous small principalities in the Italian peninsula, the Pyrenees, northern Germany and the Netherlands governed themselves for most purposes, though owing allegiances to bigger neighbours. Some were the volcanic craters of older 'failed' states (Burgundy, Navarre). There were elective monarchies in the east and north (Bohemia, Poland, Hungary, Denmark and Sweden) and a unique elective monarchy governing the largest state in central Italy (the Papal States).

Free space existed at the margins, in places which were at best only loosely affiliated to settled states. Bands of ethnic Poles and Muscovites known as Cossacks, some of them fleeing serfdom, made their way to the Ukraine, the 'land beyond the rapids' (Zaporizhzhia), an encampment towards the mouth of the river Dnieper. Nominally acknowledging Polish-Lithuanian overlordship, in reality they were a force unto themselves, fighting the Kazan Tatars, an ethnically mixed group of Tatars and Bulgars on the river Volga. Cossack elders, meeting in a host (*Sich Rada*), decided which commander (*hetman*) they would accept. Contemporaries referred to it as the Cossack 'republic'. There were similarities between the Cossacks and the Croatian Uzkoks (*Uskoci*, i.e. 'those who ambush'). Dispossessed Croats, fleeing Ottoman overlordship, they congregated at the fortress of Klis on the Dalmatian coast near Split. Klis withstood an Ottoman attack for over two and a half decades. When it fell in 1537, remnant Uzkoks established themselves at Senj. From there, they preyed upon shipping until, following hostilities between Venice and the Austrian Habsburgs, a peace was mediated at Madrid in 1617, which resettled the Uzkoks in the Slovenian mountains.

Barbary corsairs (Muslim pirates) on the North African coast commandeered Christian ships in the Mediterranean and conducted raids on the coasts of southern Christendom. The most notorious were Oruç Reis and his younger brother Yakupoğlu Hizir. Both became the object of legend, the former known as 'Barbarossa' or 'Redbeard'. The Barbary Ottoman states continued to be a threat to Christendom into the seventeenth century. Similar nominal authority was exercised in the name of the state by Gaelic lords, ruling beyond the English Pale, or in the Scottish Highlands; but the measure of Europe's state formation in this period was its intrusion and developing mastery over its margins.

A smaller number of states in western Europe, coalescing around a dynastic ruler, gradually became more powerful than the rest. Some of these hereditary monarchies were on old foundations, even if their dynasties were recent. The Valois had been on the French throne from 1328, although, in reality, it was a cadet branch of the family, the

Valois-Angoulême, who ruled from 1515 to 1589. The Bourbons succeeded them with the most contested dynastic claim of any monarch in this period. Meanwhile, the Tudors came to the English throne in a straightforward coup in 1485 and would, in turn, be replaced by a dynasty from a smaller, neighbouring state, the Scottish Stuarts, in 1603. The latter tried to turn their dynastic condominium into a composite monarchy.

In the Spanish peninsula, rival branches of the house of Trastámara provided the rulers to the kingdoms of Castile and Aragon until they were united in the diarchy of Ferdinand II, king of Aragon (Ferdinand the Catholic), and his wife, Isabella I, queen of Castile (Isabella the Catholic). Ferdinand justified his military conquest of the kingdom of Naples, completed in 1504, as the recovery of an inheritance which had been separated from the crown of Aragon by his uncle, Alfonso, in 1458. The result created another monarchical composite (Castile-Aragon-Naples), although it did not last long in the hands of the Trastámara since Ferdinand and Isabella only had one daughter, Joanna. Castile, Aragon and Naples became the inheritance of the successors of her Habsburg husband, Philip the Handsome. Having ruled Portugal since 1385, the house of Aviz ended with Cardinal Henry, the kingdom being incorporated into the Spanish Habsburg monarchy for two generations before the revolt of 1640 handed it to John IV, duke of Braganza.

In eastern Europe, the Jagiellon dynasty (descendants of the Livonian house of Gediminids) furnished the grand dukes of Lithuania and kings of Poland from the later fourteenth century, the two regions being linked together by virtue of being ruled by the same Jagiellon princes from 1501 to 1572. Vladislaus II, the brother of Alexander Jagiellon, king of Poland and grand duke of Lithuania after the death of his brother in 1501, was crowned king of Bohemia in 1471 and then also king of Hungary, following the death of the childless Hunyadi prince Matthias Corvinus in 1490. The result was another compound state, that of Hungary-Bohemia, which lasted through the reign of his son Louis II until he died at the battle of Mohács (1526). In the first two decades of the sixteenth century, Poland, Lithuania, Bohemia and Hungary constituted a Jagiellon dynastic sphere of influence like that of the Habsburgs. As things turned out, Louis II was the last of the direct Jagiellon line in Hungary-Bohemia, just as Sigismund II Augustus would be in Poland-Lithuania. Their heirs in Hungary-Bohemia would be the Habsburgs (albeit contested by the Jagiellon John Zápolya,

The Jagiellon Dynasty in the Sixteenth Century

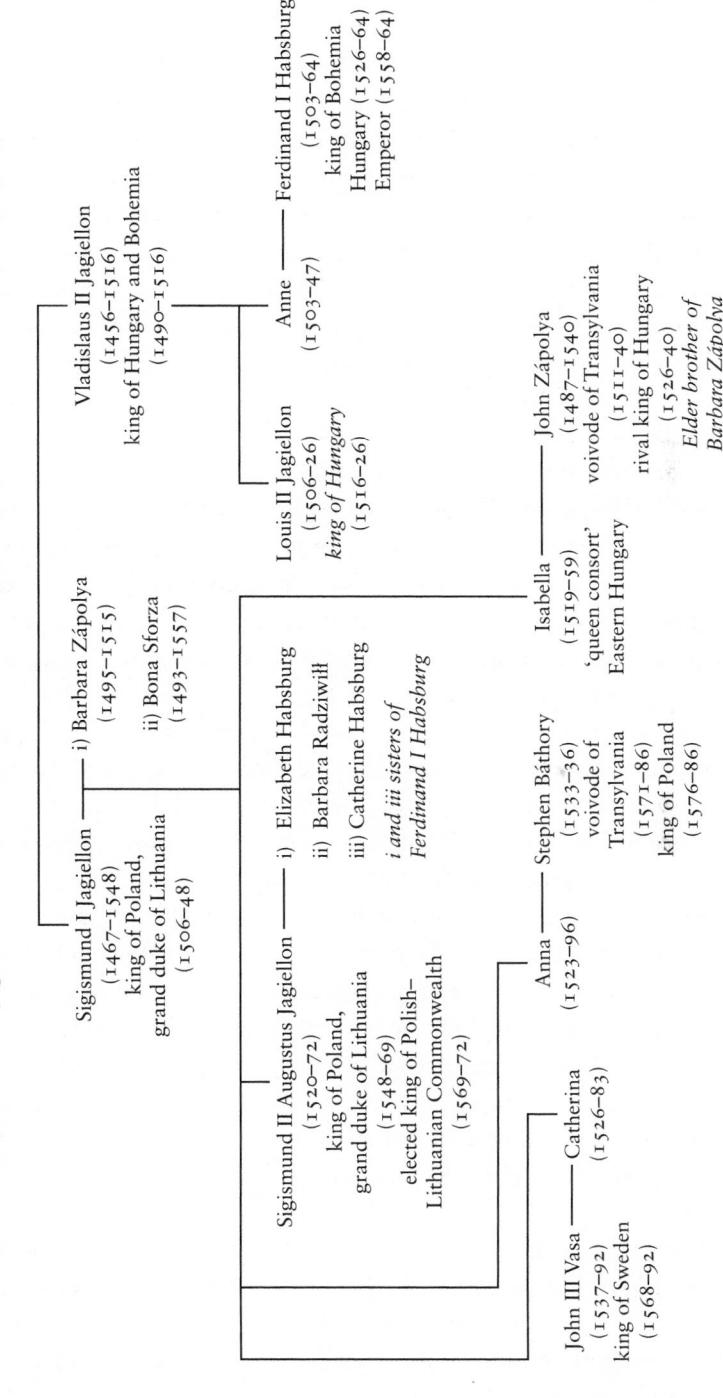

a descendant through his mother) and in Poland-Lithuania, the Swedish Vasa.

In Scandinavia, the German house of Oldenburg ruled Denmark, Norway, Iceland, Greenland, the Faroe Islands and Sweden in a dynastic union (the Kalmar Union) from 1397. In 1523, Gustav Eriksson, from the house of Vasa in the Uppland region of Sweden, led a revolt which placed him on the throne in Sweden and Finland. In 1562, Catherina Jagiellon, daughter of Sigismund I of Poland and sister of his successor, Sigismund II, married John Vasa, duke of Finland, later King John III of Sweden. The result was a Vasa dynastic sphere of influence which embraced the eastern Baltic shore towards the end of the sixteenth century, destabilizing Scandinavian politics for the next two generations.

Nowhere was there a 'nation state' in the sixteenth century. That nineteenth-century framework does not fit these dynastic enterprises, which reflected family fortune more than national identity. Compound kingdoms were the rule rather than the exception. Some of them were contiguous states (England and Wales, Piedmont and Savoy, Poland and Lithuania, Castile and Aragon). Contemporaries recognized the strategic value of contiguity but did not overestimate it. Conformity (similarities in language, customs and institutions) counted for more. In any case, the vagaries of dynastic outcome often worked against contiguity, and relatively few states were able to capitalize on its benefits.

The kingdom of France was unusual in its size and coherence. Little by little it incorporated neighbouring principalities into its domain. The seizure of English Gascony in 1453 was followed by annexations in Burgundy (1477), Provence (1481) and Brittany (1491), which retained elements of legal, institutional or cultural autonomy while absorption took place. The long, historic process of French integration resumed in the first half of the seventeenth century, but it remained work in progress. The Bourbon monarchy incorporated Béarn in 1620, annexed Lorraine in 1634 and invaded Roussillon in 1641. The kingdom of France was the object of emulation and suspicion for its integration and power.

Dynastic configurations did not seem strange until the doctrine of sovereignty, articulated in the political writings of the French philosopher and legist Jean Bodin, posed the question of where power lay. Contemporaries found that hard to answer. The Spanish jurist Juan

Solórzano Pereira summarized the experience of a lifetime in colonial administration in a compendium defending Spain's colonial project. His *Indian Politics* (*Politica Indiana*) applied Bodinian sovereignty to the Spanish empire. Spain's rule over its colonies fitted the model since they were juridically and administratively an integral part of Spain. Not so, however, its rule in Aragon, Valencia, Catalonia, the kingdoms of Sicily and Naples or the Netherlands. Solórzano called the latter 'equally important' (*aeque principaliter*), adopting a canon-law term for two dioceses which became united under one bishop. 'These kingdoms,' he wrote, 'must be ruled and governed as if the king who holds them all together were king only of each one of them.' Segmented sovereignty had advantages when it came to ruling disparate political entities. By guaranteeing the customs, laws and institutions of a particular country, composite rule became palatable to the local élites who made it work. The solution lay in the absent monarch being represented by regents or viceroys. Such ventriloquism required finesse to ensure that local notables did not feel alienated.

Composite monarchy stretched the bonds between rulers and ruled. The Scandinavian monarchy partially capsized with Swedish revolt in 1518–20. The Danish king, Christian II, led an invasion of southern Sweden which culminated in a massacre of almost a hundred leading figures of the Swedish élite in Stockholm. Among those killed was the father of Gustav Eriksson. The latter went on to lead the insurrection which defeated the Danes, before being elected King Gustav Vasa by the Swedish Estates on 6 June 1523, signalling Sweden's defection from the union.

At the same time, the composite monarchy was tested in Spain. Setting out from Flanders to claim the thrones of Castile and Aragon as regent for his mother, Joanna, whose mental illness justified his being crowned while she was still alive, Charles V (Charles I of Castile) landed at Asturias in October 1517. But the Estates (*Cortes*) of Castile and León, meeting in Valladolid in January 1518, were not convinced by the arguments that they heard for that arrangement, addressing Charles as 'Your Highness' (*Su Alteza*), while referring to Joanna as 'Majesty' (*Majestad*). The representatives of eighteen towns submitted a petition, which Charles accepted, insisting that their queen retain her household, that he marry a Castilian and learn the language and allow Spaniards into his entourage, that his brother Ferdinand remain in Spain during his absences, and that the precious metals from the New World and all the offices and commands remain in the control of Spaniards. Even the royal domain was ring-fenced from Charles V's possible exploitation. The deputies granted their new king a subsidy but were aghast to discover that their new ruler demanded yet more money in 1520.

By then, Charles had begun appointing Burgundians to positions in Spain by the simple expedient of naturalizing them. The notables of Toledo joined forces with other towns in a league (*junta*) of municipalities (*comunidades*). The clergy preached openly against the new regime and handbills were posted up in churches to rally support against the alien king. Troops sent to repossess Toledo were defeated and the *comuneros* drafted their grievances to present before Queen Joanna, recognizing her as their only legitimate ruler. They proclaimed the sacrosanct nature of agreements made between rulers and ruled and the contractual nature of monarchy. Working behind the scenes, those loyal to Charles V retained support wherever they could find it, especially in the countryside and among the Spanish gentry, who were often the leading notables (*regidores*) in towns. After a year of chaos and fighting, the *comuneros* were defeated at the battle of Villalar (23 April 1521) and the crisis passed. But, with a comparable situation in Valencia and resentments in Naples too, it was an early sign of how brittle large composite monarchies would be.

Female regents proved particularly skilful at the mediation that was required, as the succession of able regents in the Netherlands for Charles V and Philip II demonstrated. Charles's aunt Margaret of Austria (regent from 1507 to 1515 and 1519 to 1530) was succeeded by his sister Mary of Habsburg (regent from 1531 to 1555). His illegitimate daughter Margaret of Parma (regent from 1559 to 1567) was hardly given a free hand, however, and her regency ended in tears. Even when composite monarchies developed a convincing myth of rule around a notion of personal loyalty to the dynasty among the upper echelons of the nobility, it was inevitable that the competitive forces for the favour of the monarch divided the élites of one country against those of another. The instabilities of composite rule in monarchies could be covered over, but they could never be removed.

Dynasticism was the dominant legitimizing principle. Even in the elective monarchies of eastern Europe, it was deeply ingrained. The oligarchies in Venice, the most enduring republic, were as dynastic as

Europe's society of princes. House, blood and lineage ruled the upper echelons of Europe's aristocracy, legitimating power and the transfer of wealth, prestige and influence from one generation to the next. But the costs of dynasticism were high. In the later Middle Ages, it unleashed a civil war in England (the Wars of the Roses) and an international conflict (the Hundred Years War). In the sixteenth and early seventeenth centuries, those costs remained burdensome. Dynastic politics were unpredictable and unstable. Unexpected deaths created ruptures, while marriage alliances had unforeseen consequences. Above all, dynastic interests did not naturally accord with those of Europe's localities. As Europe's states became more complex governing entities, so that mismatch caused tension and division.

OLDER CONFLICTS AND THEIR LEGACIES

Exploiting dynastic alliances and inheritances and the tensions among smaller political entities to their advantage, the larger dynastic states in western Europe pursued their competitive ambitions. The resulting battlegrounds became the test-bed for new military organizations and technologies as well as different ways of doing politics. The conflict zone of the Hundred Years War in francophone Europe, concluded in 1453, left a bitter legacy that was remembered on both sides of the Channel through the first half of the sixteenth century.

In Valois France, the memory was of military devastation and dismemberment. In Tudor England, Henry VIII, crowned 'by the grace of God, king of England and France' in 1509, evoked his illustrious Lancastrian ancestor Henry V and dreamed of recovering Guyenne. By the Treaty of Westminster (November 1511), Henry VIII joined the Holy League of Pope Julius II (pope from 1503 to 1513), King Ferdinand of Aragon and Venice to drive the French out of Italy. Naval operations began the following year, but the English Guyenne expedition met with disaster. Cardinal Thomas Wolsey rose to favour in Henry VIII's eyes because he saved the day. His organizational skills were essential to the rebuilding of English naval and military forces and the success of the 1512–13 campaign east of Calais. Wolsey's diplomatic finesse ensured the conclusion of hostilities with a treaty (London, August 1514) that was presented by Henry as bringing peace to Christendom. That became the sketch for a much grander meeting, also at London, in the autumn of 1518. Wolsey's finest hour, it brought together the representatives of France, England, the empire, the papacy, Spain, Burgundy and the Netherlands to sign a mutual non-aggression pact (the Treaty of London, October 1518) by which Christendom's divisions could be laid to rest. Despite the elaborate reconciliation between Charles and Francis, organized at Guînes in June 1520 (the 'Field of the Cloth of Gold'), such hopes were disappointed. The peace marked simply a pause in Anglo-French hostilities amid the Italian Wars, which recommenced in 1521.

Renewed English intervention on the continent followed. An expeditionary force to Brittany and Picardy in 1522, after Henry VIII's treaty with the emperor at Windsor in June that year, culminated in a large English army led by Charles Brandon, duke of Suffolk (the ablest English military commander of his generation), reaching within 50 miles of Paris and wreaking havoc on the way. The gains were minimal but the costs were huge. The English Parliament refused to grant additional taxation and Wolsey devised a 'forced loan' of a third of the estimated revenues of the clergy and one sixth of those of the laity (the Amicable Grant of 1525). The levy was bitterly resented and failed to furnish what was expected of it. In its aftermath, England sat on the sidelines despite French weakness in the later 1520s, and Wolsey's downfall was assured.

In 1543, another large English expedition took place, one army led by the duke of Norfolk towards Montreuil (a failure), the other commanded by Suffolk successfully capturing Boulogne after a siege. In the subsequent peace (Ardres, June 1546), the English held Boulogne for eight years on condition that the stronghold was returned to France in 1554 upon payment of a large sum. In 1557, Mary Tudor reluctantly committed English forces in support of her husband, Philip II, and the defence of the Low Countries. In the process, Calais, England's last foothold on the continent of Europe, was lost to France in 1558. England had nothing to show for almost half a century of intervention.

The Italian Wars, to which these English expeditions were a side-show, had begun with the 'descent' of the French king, Charles VIII, at the head of an expeditionary force, through the Alps to Naples in 1494. For at least a century before then, northern and central Italy – excepting

Venice, which prided itself on its stability – had been riven by rivalries between noble clans who identified themselves loosely with Italy's pro- and anti-imperial factions. The Roman Orsini and the Este from Ferrara supported the papacy, while their bitter rivals the Roman Colonna and the Gonzaga of Mantua backed the imperial cause. The former supporters of the papal cause mostly rallied to the French, whereas the Colonna and the Gonzaga were among Charles V's more reliable allies in the peninsula. The Visconti in Milan had been imperialists too, but they had been ousted from the duchy by Francesco Sforza, a mercenary captain, who founded a new ducal dynasty on unsteady foundations. In Genoa, rival clans were also confronted by periodic upsurges of republican sentiments. In Florence, the Medici gained ascendancy over their rivals, but their power-base was also vulnerable to popular republican sentiment. There were plenty of local quarrels for the French invaders to exploit.

Charles VIII's invasion attempted to make good his dynastic claims to the kingdom of Naples, which the Angevins had ruled before the Aragonese dynasty installed itself there in 1442. The French counted on a revolt of Neapolitan nobles, which had taken place in 1486, some of whom had made their way to the French court. Charles VIII was encouraged in his endeavour by Ludovico Sforza, Francesco's successor. The French king's publicists presented the enterprise as justified by King Alfonso's 'tyranny'. The arrival of the French in Naples, they said, would put an end to burglary and robbery in a part of Christendom most vulnerable to the Turks, and install a regime of justice, the first stage in a Crusade and the recapture of Jerusalem.

In the short term, Charles VIII's campaign was a success. On 22 February 1495, the French marched into Naples unopposed, following the abdication a few days earlier of the reigning Alfonso II and the flight of his successor, Ferdinand of Aragon. They held Naples briefly, only to be ousted in due course by the regrouped forces of Ferdinand. French attentions then turned to the duchy of Milan. The childless Charles VIII was succeeded by Louis XII, who had claims to Milan by virtue of his descent from the Visconti. In 1498, Louis's army marched into the duchy and overthrew Duke Ludovico Sforza to consolidate the French power-base in northern Italy, while turning Genoa into a French dependency. In the longer term, however, the French expeditions destabilized the politics of the Italian states. They reignited latent fears in Christendom about the power of the reunited French kingdom, ones which Ferdinand of Aragon mobilized over the next two decades. In France, 'bulletins' (distant ancestors of the newspaper) were distributed in manuscript and print, presenting Italy as a 'terrestrial paradise', a rich plum ripe for the picking. That remained an alluring myth for those at the courts of Louis XII's successors, Francis I and Henry II, who were persuaded that chivalric endeavour, military adventurism, liberating Italy, personal profit and service to the king added up to an unanswerable case for further Italian adventures.

What is commonly known as the 'Italian Wars' was experienced by contemporaries as successive phases in a long-drawn-out struggle for hegemony in the Italian peninsula, which became part of a wider Habsburg–Valois conflict. This provoked an arms race in which the scale of armies grew. The War of the League of Cambrai (1511–16) was succeeded by the Four Years War (1521–6) and the War of the League of Cognac (1526–30). In the mid-1530s, a further two years of campaigns focused on Franco-imperial control of the duchies of Milan and Savoy (1536–8). The final episodes of the Italian Wars (1542–6 and 1551–9) were protracted and fragmented. French intervention marked almost every phase until 1530, after which Habsburg predominance in the peninsula was mostly assured. Chased out of Milan in 1513, French forces returned in the first year of Francis I's rule. Leading an army of 8,000 Gascons and 23,000 *Landsknechte*, he crossed the Alps in July 1515, overthrowing the Sforza dukes of Milan after two days of battle at Marignan (13–14 September 1515), where it was the timely arrival of the Venetian army to help the French that secured the victory. For a time, French dominance in northern Italy was assured by the ensuing peace at Noyon (August 1516).

Only five years later, however, Francis attacked the newly elected Emperor Charles on several fronts – in Luxembourg and Navarre. The emperor responded, having orchestrated an alliance with Pope Leo X, promising him Parma and Piacenza, by invading Milan in the name of Francesco II Sforza. The large contingent of French forces sent to recover the situation was defeated at La Bicocca on 27 April 1522. Nothing ventured, a further French army 30,000 strong encircled Milan in 1524 but could not dislodge the imperialists. In the wake of that defeat, Charles ordered his generals to push the campaign into France with an amphibious assault upon Marseille. Francis responded late in the season by leading a force across the Alps and invested Pavia. But imperialist reinforcements arrived from Germany and the French besiegers found themselves overwhelmed. Thousands of French troops were killed in the battle of Pavia (24 February 1525), or drowned in the river Ticino; 10,000 more were captured, including the French king himself.

The captive Francis was taken to Spain and kept under house-arrest, his release agreed only after he had signed a capitulation (Treaty of Madrid, January 1526), in which he formally abandoned all claims to Italy, the duchy of Burgundy and the lands of Charles's Burgundian ancestors. Francis's two sons stood surety for the treaty's fulfilment but he swore a private oath that he had acted under duress. Upon his release just over a year later, the French king took advantage of the rejection of the Madrid Treaty by the provincial estates of Burgundy to delay its ratification, while his diplomats garnered support for the Valois cause. With the backing of the Medici pope Clement VII, guaranteeing the support of both the papacy and Florence, the French put the finishing touches to the League of Cognac (May 1526), whose other parties included Venice, Ferrara and Duke Francesco Sforza, newly restored in Milan after Pavia, but suspicious of the Habsburgs. Imperial forces under the renegade French prince of the blood Charles III, duke of Bourbon, launched a pre-emptive strike in the peninsula, aiming to overrun Florence and the Papal States. Finding the road to Florence blocked by heavy snow, they made for the Romagna and then marched on Rome itself. The city's defences were so feeble that the invaders left their siege equipment behind, relying on ladders to take it. The duke of Bourbon was shot – Benvenuto Cellini claimed that he fired the bullet – as they forced their way in. In the resulting sack of Rome (6–12 May 1527) almost 10,000 of its citizens may have died and its churches and palaces were plundered.

The French seized on the impact of the slaughter in the peninsula. Another French army (up to 70,000 strong) marched across the Alps in August 1527, taking their revenge on Padua, which was captured and put to the sack, before moving southwards towards Naples. Meanwhile, the naval commander Andrea Doria seized control in Genoa, where the French established a dependency around the port of Savona. From there he assembled galleys for an assault upon Naples by sea. For a time it looked as though the collapse of Habsburg Naples was a foregone conclusion. However, victory eluded the French. Their army was decimated by plague and Andrea Doria deserted their cause, using his naval forces to relieve and retake Genoa for the Habsburgs. French forces capitulated at Savona, and a relief army, led by François de Bourbon, count of St Pol, was cut to pieces at the battle of Landriano (21 June 1529). That same month the emperor made peace with Pope Clement by the Treaty of Barcelona and set sail for Genoa, and thence to Bologna for his papal coronation (24 February 1530), in a visit which cemented imperial hegemony in the peninsula and restored battered imperial and papal reputations.

There would be further French incursions into the Italian peninsula over the following three decades, but they took place in the context of wider Habsburg–Valois confrontation. By 1530, the destabilizing effect of the Italian Wars in the peninsula had become evident. A young Florentine lawyer, Francesco Guicciardini, who would later write the most perceptive commentary upon them, already concluded in 1508 that the conflicts were 'a flame, a pestilence which has entered Italy'. They 'overturned states and their forms of government, as well as their ways of making war'. Like Guicciardini, his contemporary Niccolò Machiavelli sought to make sense of the impact of the Italian Wars. It was not merely the material consequences of warfare. The political world in the Italian states became more unstable as they sought to make alliances of convenience in league with those intervening from without and against one another.

Politics within these Italian states became more ruthless as a result. Court factions sought to remove their opponents by direct and indirect means. Political assassinations became more common. Banishment of leading opponents created further instabilities as exiles (*fuoriusciti*) tried to orchestrate their own comeback by destabilizing the regime which had expelled them. Opponents used rumour and gossip to undermine and disgrace each other. In Rome, the statue on a corner of the Piazza di Pasquino became, in the second decade of the sixteenth century, the place where political placards were posted. They were often venomous – those attacking Pope Leo X, for example, portrayed him as an untrustworthy Florentine financier who had bankrupted the papacy. By the mid-sixteenth century, when the papacy began to curb the excessive licence accorded to political posters, the 'Pasquil' had entered the political lexicon for a lampoon, and similar sites had opened up in Venice (the 'Bocca', near the Rialto) and Modena (the 'Bona', a statue on the corner of the Palazzo del Commune). Machiavelli and Guicciardini tried to understand the new princely courts. They sought to explain why Venice had survived as a republic when Florence failed to. They analysed the ways of conducting warfare. The political and military rules of engagement did not seem to abide by the norms of Christian morality. A lot depended upon good luck (*fortuna*) and naked power.

Above all, the Italian Wars undermined the credibility of the papacy and the emperor. As in the other states of the peninsula, the French invasion of 1494 proved to be a watershed for the papal dominions. Exploiting Rome's political prestige as well as its unrivalled diplomatic sources of information, the popes and their servants called on foreign military and political help to strengthen control of their dominions. Essential to the process was the kingdom of Naples, which was theoretically a papal fief. The papacy claimed the rights to confirm the ruler in Naples, a bargaining position from which it was able to extort concessions from Ferdinand of Aragon but also from French contenders to the Neapolitan throne. Giuliano della Rovere, Pope Julius II, played the new and complicated politics to perfection – 'worthy of the greatest glory if he had been a secular prince', noted Guicciardini. Having secured his election by making promises to his rival, the Spanish-backed candidate Cesare Borgia (Pope Alexander VI's nephew), he took the name of Julius. He thus recalled the memory of the fifth-century Roman pontiff who had triumphed over the Arian heresy, summoned a Church council to Rome and constructed the basilica of the Twelve Apostles. But the allusion was also to Julius Caesar, the Roman emperor who had put an end to intrigue and laid the foundations of empire.

Julius II then arrested his Borgia opponents and took over their authority in the Romagna. At the same time, he strengthened papal authority in Umbria and Ancona, while exploiting the Italian Wars to sequester Parma and Piacenza in 1512 when the French were pushed out, and Reggio and Modena as well. The pope led military forces in person to the siege and capture of Mirandola in January 1511. Not for nothing did he return to Rome through a triumphal arch that would have befitted Julius Caesar himself. Pope Julius had been the architect of the League of Cambrai (1508), which brought together the forces of the French and Emperor Maximilian I, ostensibly to conduct a Crusade against the Turks, but in reality to overrun Venice. Then, after the French crushed those assembled to defend the Venetian Republic at Agnadello

(14 May 1509), Pope Julius executed a breathtaking volte-face. He formed a Holy League, made public in October 1511, with the Spanish and Venetians against the French.

Louis XII took his revenge by organizing a campaign of satirical pamphlets and verses aimed directly against Julius, 'serf of the serfs' – a pun on the Latin title adopted in papal bulls: 'servant of the servants of God' (*servus servorum Dei*) – and 'prince of idiots'. The papacy was depicted as the source of schism in Christendom. Only temporal princes, with the French king in the lead, could heal Christendom's profound malaise. Louis XII summoned a council of the Church to meet at Pisa in November 1511, while his troops invaded the Romagna and overran Ravenna. Adjusting to the new reality, Pope Julius declared the 'little council' in Pisa 'schismatic' and summoned his own to meet in Rome at the basilica of St John Lateran. It became a talking-shop, which highlighted the improbability of achieving any progress on the agenda of Church reform by that route.

The Italian Wars made other powers realize the full extent to which the papacy itself had become infected by the new politics, and the degree to which the popes were preoccupied by the temporal affairs of the Papal States. Ultramontane princes became more openly cynical towards holders of the papal office. Louis XII described Julius publicly as the son of a peasant, who needed to be beaten into obedience. Secular rulers accommodated themselves to the new scale of papal nepotism which the Italian Wars encouraged. Above all, they invested energy and money in influencing papal elections and, since the outcomes were generally unpredictable, the result confirmed the reputations of cardinals (the majority of whom were Italians) as slippery and untrustworthy.

The Italian Wars affected the credibility of the emperor as well. Much of northern Italy had once belonged to the Holy Roman Empire and various parts still owed fealty to the emperor. Maximilian I's involvement in the early Italian Wars was proclaimed by the French as imperial aggrandizement. Charles V's inheritance of the kingdom of Naples was opposed by anti-imperial cardinals in Rome, worried that the pope would become his 'chaplain'. In Rome, Florence and Venice, and not just at the French court, the prospect of the emperor as duke of Milan was all the proof that was needed of imperial ambitions to rule Italy. Above all, the sack of Rome marred the imperial cause. Rome, the Jerusalem of Christendom, was wrecked and vandalized by predominantly

Lutheran soldiery, acting in the name of the emperor. They carved the name of Martin Luther (the graffito is still there) into the walls of the rooms in the Vatican Palace, decorated by Raphael for Julius II in 1511–12. Those who took refuge from Rome in Venice and Florence remembered the event as a tyrannical imperial assault on Italy: 'Italy, Italy ... wake up, raise your honoured head, and heed well your latest woes' went one madrigal. 'Observe how wickedly your Pharisees have deprived you of the shadow of your remaining authority ... recover your honour, exterminate the wicked faction, and its cruel tyrants.' Nothing was more calculated to undermine Charles's efforts to champion the agenda of Church reform at Rome or to increase the suspicions of those who already regarded imperial influence in the peninsula as an alien hegemony.

CHARLES V'S *IMPERIUM*: MYTH AND REALITY

'No family has ever attained such greatness and power by means of kinship and matrimonial alliances as the House of Austria,' wrote Giovanni Botero in his *Reason of State* (1589). His Spanish contemporary Juan de Mariana agreed: 'Empires grow and extend themselves through marriages. It is well known that if Spain has come to be such a vast empire, she owes it both to the valour of her arms and to the marriages of her rulers.' Marriage was, Erasmus reminded Charles V, 'the greatest of human affairs' and 'generally considered as the unbreakable chains of general peace'. Like the Jagiellons, the Habsburgs married their close relatives to consolidate the dynasty; unlike them, they married early. Early marriage ensured Habsburg fecundity; intermarriage risked their health.

A dynasty was more than a family. It was a collectivity of inherited rights and titles that transcended individuals. Ancestral traditions lay at the heart of dynastic politics. In his famous speech condemning Martin Luther at the Diet of Worms in 1521, Charles V began with an explicit allusion to 'my ancestors .... most Christian emperors, Archdukes of Austria and Dukes of Burgundy', who had all defended the faith and 'handed on these holy Catholic rites after their death by natural right of succession'. Dynastic rule was inherently conservative. A legitimate ruler did not merely claim to rule, but also to preserve the 'rights' and 'privileges' of his peoples – these being complementary and coterminous with the dynasty itself.

Dynasties functioned as clans, corporatist and hierarchical. Emperor Maximilian I, architect of the Habsburg dynastic construction, thought of himself, his daughter Margaret of Austria, and his grandson and probable inheritor Charles in the same breath, 'one and the same, corresponding to the same desire and affection'. Charles would, in due course, refer to his young brother Ferdinand as someone 'whom I love and esteem as my other self'. Their enemies, he told him, would seek to 'disunite us, divide us the more easily in order to break our common power and bring down our house'. The fear of a house being divided against itself was a dynastic commonplace since family quarrels were destructive. All Europe's ruling dynasties evolved an informal hierarchy within the clan. For the most part, the junior branches of a clan accepted the need for allegiance to the head of the dynasty and their role in advancing its common destiny in return for real protection of their personal interests.

The Habsburg dynastic construction applied these principles with finesse. Emperor Maximilian I was its principal architect. He first married Mary, the daughter of Charles the Bold, last duke of Burgundy. The death of the latter in battle in 1477 resulted in the implosion of the Burgundian state with Maximilian succeeding to its remnants. Then, following Mary's early death in 1482, Maximilian married Bianca-Maria Sforza, the niece of the reigning duke of Milan, Ludovico Sforza. He picked up the largest dowry of any prince before 1550 and rights to inherit the duchy if the dynastic cards stacked up that way. From his first marriage, he had two children, Philip and Margaret. They were key dynastic assets, and he placed them with skill, marrying them to children of the newly conjoined dynastic Hispanic union, Isabella, queen of Castile, and Ferdinand, king of Aragon. Archduke Philip (the Handsome) married the infanta Joanna in October 1496, while the infante John (Juan) married Archduchess Margaret in April the following year.

Thereafter, Habsburg success was the outcome of luck – or, looking at it through the eyes of Ferdinand of Aragon, the misfortune of the Trastámara. The infante John died in 1497 aged nineteen, while, as it were, on active dynastic service (through an excess of *copula*, i.e. sex) and left no heirs. Infanta Isabel married the king of Portugal, but died

The Habsburg Dynastic Sphere of Influence in the Era of Charles V

Ancestral Lands Austria	Burgundian Lands	Aragon, Valencia, Sicily, Naples	Castile

Ancestral Lands Austria

Frederick III
(1415–93)
emperor
(1452–93)

Maximilian I
(1459–1519) emperor
(elected king of the Romans
1486; [1493]–1519)
m Mary of Burgundy

Marguerite of Austria
m i) John of Aragon
ii) Francis I king of France

Burgundian Lands

Charles the Bold
(1433–77)
duke of Burgundy
(1447–77)

Mary of Burgundy
(1457–82)

Philip the Handsome
(1478–1506)
duke of Burgundy,
king of Castile and Aragon
(1504–06)
m Joanna

Charles
(1500–58)
king of Castile
(1516–56)
emperor (1519–56)
m Isabella
of Portugal

Eleanor
(1498–1558)
m i) Manuel I
king of Portugal
ii) Francis I
king of France

Aragon, Valencia, Sicily, Naples

John II
(1398–1479)
king of Aragon
(1458–79)

Ferdinand II
(1452–1516)
king of Aragon
(1479–1516)
m Isabella I

Joanna,
known as Joanna the Mad
(1479–1555)
queen of Castile and León
and Aragon (1516–55)

Castile

John II
(1405–54)
king of Castile and León
(1406–54)

Isabella I
(1451–1504)
queen of Castile and León
(1474–1504)

Catherine of Aragon
(1485–1536)
m Henry VIII
king of England

John
(1478–97)
m Marguerite
of Austria

Isabella II
(1501–26)
m Christian II
king of Denmark

Ferdinand I
(1503–64)
emperor (1558–64)
m Anne Jagiellon

Mary
(1505–56)
m Louis II Jagiellon
king of Hungary

Catherine
(1507–78)
m John III
king of Portugal,
prince of Asturias

in childbirth a year later. Her son, who would have inherited the thrones of all the Iberian kingdoms, followed her to the grave two years later. Infanta Catherine, Isabel's sister, was married to Prince Arthur, son of Henry VII, the first Tudor king of England, in 1501, but he too died the following year. Catherine ended up marrying Arthur's brother, Henry VIII, in 1509, in what looked like a dynastic ace of hearts. However, after twenty-five years without the male heir that the Tudor bully demanded, the ambitious hopes went unrealized.

Meanwhile, Princess Joanna, now the heiress to the thrones of Castile and Aragon, bore Philip the Handsome a string of children, each of whom offered further opportunities for Maximilian to expand the Habsburg dynastic gene pool and political influence in Europe. The daughters married crowned heads of Europe. Their brothers, the two archdukes, Charles and Ferdinand, pocketed principalities and kingdoms like coloured balls on a billiard table. Charles was only six years old when he inherited the Burgundian domains of his grandmother Mary in 1506, above all the Low Countries, with the death of his father, Philip the Handsome. Then, when his grandfather King Ferdinand of Aragon followed Philip to the grave in 1516, Charles claimed Castile, Aragon and Naples in the name of his mother, Joanna. Poor Joanna's mental health had been destabilized by the death of her husband and the birth of their daughter Catherine some months later, in 1507, but there was a degree of male ruthlessness in the way Joanna was treated. Ferdinand usurped her birthright, and had her confined to the Santa Clara convent in Tordesillas, near Valladolid, in February 1509 on the grounds of 'insanity'. That was why, when Charles landed at Asturias on the Bay of Biscay in October 1517, he first made his way to Tordesillas in order to persuade her to cede him authority to rule in her name.

Meanwhile, Charles's brother Archduke Ferdinand was not forgotten: King Ferdinand of Aragon schemed for his namesake and grandson to succeed him in Spain. Maximilian had other plans, however, which were realized in an agreement signed in Vienna in 1515 with Vladislaus II Jagiellon. The Habsburgs had already managed to extend their sphere of influence in those parts and Vladislaus concluded a pact with Maximilian that was Habsburg marital diplomacy at its finest. The two houses made their inheritances mutual in two interlinked promises of marriage. Ferdinand was espoused to Anne Jagiellon, daughter of Vladislaus, while the latter's brother Louis II Jagiellon married Mary, Ferdinand's sister.

The full significance of the deal emerged only a decade later, after Maximilian I's death on 12 January 1519.

The inheritance of the Holy Roman Empire was the one piece of the puzzle that Maximilian had not resolved before his death. It was in essence an elective monarchy, with candidates to the imperial throne being chosen by a college of seven electors. In the sixteenth century, these were the Margrave of Brandenburg, the Count Palatine, the archbishops of Cologne, Mainz and Trier and the king of Bohemia. The Electors were in a position to extract a 'capitulation' from candidates – promises they were obliged to fulfil. The broadsheets distributed from Vienna by printer Hans Weiditz played on the popularity of Charles's deceased grandfather. Under the two pillars of Hercules and the slogan 'Plus Ultra' Charles was presented as a fresh-faced Austrian archduke who spoke and wrote German. He promised to safeguard the privileges and liberties of the German nation to whom the legacy of the Roman empire had been transferred. In a draft capitulation he undertook to 'conclude no alliance or union with any foreign power in the name of the Empire' and to 'introduce no armed force from abroad' without their explicit agreement, to nominate only Germans to imperial posts and never to appropriate to himself the lands of the empire held by these same Electors. These promises would return to haunt him.

Charles's candidature faced determined opposition from several quarters, not least Francis I, the papacy, Henry VIII of England and members of his own house. Both Henry and Francis understood the significance of the impending election. The emperor was the symbolic secular head of Christendom, the guarantor of peace, justice and the integrity of the Christian West. In addition, the imperial title carried with it rights to intervene in the principalities of northern Italy, once part of the empire, and especially Milan. Henry backed out at an early stage but Francis pressed on, presenting himself as recovering the legacy of the kingdom of the Franks. His claim was supported by Pope Leo X and greeted sympathetically by Archduke Ferdinand. The Electors, however, remained unconvinced. Would not Francis I treat the empire like an annexe of the French kingdom?

Both Francis and Charles wooed the Electors for all they were worth. The Margrave of Brandenburg acted as cheerleader for the French claim, letting it be known where it mattered that he could count on the military support of Franz von Sickingen, a German mercenary knight whose most recent success had been to besiege the city of Metz to extort an outrageous ransom. Charles tried (initially without great success) to present himself as a German prince. But he had the support of the Swabian League, the 'Imperial Circle' which was in the process of organizing military forces to enforce an imperial court decision to oust Duke Ulrich of Württemberg from his territories for having annexed the imperial city of Reutlingen. In addition, Charles entered into negotiations with the Electors to neutralize their fears that he would be an over-mighty monarch. Both sides distributed colossal bribes; Charles's 851,000 florins (about two tons of gold) were borrowed from the Fugger and Welser banking houses in Augsburg, with ancillary amounts from the Fornari in Genoa and the Gualtarotti in Florence, all redeemable on his future revenues in Spain. It was the beginning of what would be the defining characteristic of Charles V's European empire – its capacity to mobilize resources from a variety of locations but to fund them increasingly from one (Castile). The Electors duly declared by a majority for Charles on 28 June 1519. Crowned king of the Romans at Aachen on 23 October 1520, he had to wait a decade before his coronation as Emperor Charles V by the papacy at Bologna on 23–4 February 1530.

There remained the problem of Charles's younger brother, Ferdinand, a prince of the blood. The emperor's advisers urged him to provide a generous patrimonial settlement, and it was put into place in two successive stages, both of which revealed Charles V's pragmatism. By the Treaty of Worms (28 April 1521), he ceded to Ferdinand the Habsburg patrimony in five Austrian duchies (Upper and Lower Austria, Styria, Carinthia and Carniola), while retaining its remaining lands in southwest Germany (including Alsace and the Breisgau), as the route to the Netherlands and too precious to surrender. By a further agreement in Brussels the following year, he devolved the government of the empire to Ferdinand, thus providing a way to circumvent the promises he had entered into at his imperial election.

Four years later the significance of that decision became evident in a way that neither Charles nor his advisers could possibly have imagined. When Louis II Jagiellon was killed in battle against the Turks at Mohács on 29 August 1526, he had no heir. What was left of Hungary outside the hands of the Ottomans had no king and no army. Charles's promise to defend Christendom acquired a desperate urgency and Ferdinand lost no time in achieving his election to the crowns of Hungary and

Croatia, Charles ceding the title of king of the Romans in 1531 to make way for Ferdinand, who had already been elected king of Bohemia. For better or worse, Ferdinand became *de facto* leader of Christendom's landward defence against Ottoman aggression. The kernel of a second Habsburg dynastic empire had been created, centred round the Danube and looking east. In these eastern elective kingdoms, however, it was the nobility which had the upper hand, and it would take the changes in the political and ecclesiastical fabric of that part of the world in the later sixteenth and early seventeenth centuries to grow the seed of the Danubian Habsburg monarchy which was planted in 1526.

How did one give shape and purpose to a dynastic empire on the scale of Charles's? The emblem 'Yet Further' had been devised by his court physician and was painted on the sails of the flagship which carried him from Flushing to Spain in 1517. What that slogan might mean was fleshed out by a clever Piedmontese lawyer, Mercurino Arborio de Gattinara. As Maximilian I's diplomat, he had worked with Julius II to put together the League of Cambrai against France in 1508 and already distinguished himself in Habsburg service. In monastic retreat, Gattinara composed a treatise on the 'new monarchical world and the triumphal future of Christendom', which was presented to Charles as he left for Spain. A year later, Gattinara was appointed Grand Chancellor of all the Realms and Kingdoms of the King, a post he held until his death in 1530. One of his first tasks was to write the emperor's speech of inauguration. It was delivered on 30 November 1519 at Molina del Rey. The Electors were told that they had been divinely inspired. Charles carried God's blessing to restore the empire and renew the *sacrum imperium* to care for Christendom – its religion and its community.

In a stream of documents, Gattinara educated the emperor to an understanding of world monarchy. 'God the Creator,' he told him, 'has given you this grace of raising you in dignity above all Christian kings and princes by constituting you the greatest emperor and king who has been since . . . Charlemagne, your predecessor.' Charles was a 'universal monarch' whose task was to reconcile Christendom in a realm of God-given justice and peace. It was a curious blend of Dante's *Monarchia* (a text which Gattinara tried to persuade Erasmus to edit) and millennial expectations.

Where did it leave the papacy? Gattinara's experience of Rome, and especially of Pope Julius, made him cynical, like many of his contemporaries. The pontiff had to be made to see the urgency of Church reform through the holding of an ecumenical council. The imperial victory at Pavia in 1525 encouraged Gattinara to urge Charles to apply pressure on Pope Clement. His advice: '[Instruct] His Holiness that if he does not want to use his office of common pastor for the tranquillity of Italy and of Christendom, then we shall be forced to use our office as Emperor.' In July 1526, he wanted Charles to summon a council himself. The pope was a ravening wolf in sheep's clothing, an instigator of conflict rather than a means to its resolution. That was before the sack of Rome gave the lie to Gattinara's high moral tone.

By the time of Gattinara's death, Charles had tired of his advice. Instinctively aware of the difficulties of imposing anything upon Rome, the emperor understood how 'universal monarchy' would be misread as Habsburg ambition. Charles had been brought up in the chivalric honour code of the Burgundians and his outlook was simpler: his priorities were decided by his 'honour' and 'reputation', Christendom being subsumed into their defence. In a speech before the papal Curia in 1536, he rejected the charge that he sought 'world monarchy'. He was simply defending his inherited lands against attack from Lutheran heretics, Turkish infidels and the perfidious French – his enemies just happened to coincide with those of Christendom.

When running his empire, Charles was not as convinced as Gattinara wanted him to be of the advantages of administrative order, legal process and reform. Charles was, by instinct, a delegator, suspicious of institutions and trusting of people. Given the size and diversity of his dominions (3–4 million inhabitants in the old Burgundian lands, 6 million in Spain, 3.5 million in Italy and 1 million more in German lands), that was probably the realistic choice. He governed with the help of an inner group of advisers, initially Burgundians, although Castilians gradually took over – a mixture of senior ecclesiastics, Castilian nobles and secretaries. The empire's financial resources were hand-to-mouth, and partly dependent on the deals that could be struck with local Estates. The kingdom of Naples and the ancestral Habsburg lands (mainly the Netherlands) offered ample ordinary revenues in comparison with the size of their populations, and especially when compared with Castile. Castile's Cortes, however, could be more easily persuaded to provide extraordinary subsidies than its Neapolitan and Dutch counterparts. Above all, Castile had other revenue streams which could be mortgaged to Charles's bankers. Without Castile, Charles's military campaigns would have been impossible. His empire was a dominion with a variable geometry, personal and tending to the ramshackle.

But this did not stop his image-makers making more of him, and what his empire represented, than he did himself. Some of them drew on mythical genealogy, insisting that Charles was descended from Aeneas of Troy, a claim that dovetailed with the belief that the dominion of the Roman empire had been conceded by God in perpetuity to the successors of Aeneas. What was the Burgundian Order of the Golden Fleece if not an evocation of Jason and the Argonauts who repatriated the Golden Fleece, destroying Troy on the way, a legend woven into the story of Aeneas as told by Virgil? Others evoked Spanish Habsburg overlordship as a 'ship of virtues' and Charles V as a new Hercules. The emperor's coronations at Aachen and Bologna emphasized his sacred imperial function. His viceroys and administrators were brought up on this make-believe.

Such myth-making was persuasive in the smaller courts of Italy, jostling for position in the Habsburg sphere of influence. Part of Gattinara's achievement was to counteract French anti-imperial propaganda. In Genoa, for example, where Andrea Doria expelled the French with Habsburg assistance in July 1528, Charles V was presented as a 'confederate' who supported Genoese liberties. Scenes from Jason's life were commissioned to decorate the southern façade of the ducal palace, and a series of tapestries from the life of Aeneas adorned it for Charles's visit in 1536. In Florence, an imperial statue was erected in 1539 as part of the festivities to celebrate Cosimo de' Medici's marriage. Not to be outshone, Federigo Gonzaga, duke of Mantua, decorated the Sala di Troia in his palace at Te for Charles's visit there, accompanying it with the Sala del Imperator, ornamented with scenes of conquering emperors. The rival court of the Este, dukes of Ferrara, commissioned Ludovico Ariosto to write *Orlando Furioso*, in which Charles V's ancestry was traced back to the gods. Such allusions did not strike the wrong note in the Renaissance, before the Reformation and its fall-out rendered their implicit paganism suspect. Yet the more Charles V's rule came to resemble an empire, the more resented it became within the peninsula and without. Three thousand imperial troops were stationed in Lombardy, Naples and Sicily from 1530 onwards, keeping the *Pax Hispanica* in Italy, but also providing a reserve force for trouble elsewhere in the Habsburg empire.

THE 'GREAT MONARCHY' OF FRANCE

The French kingdom was Christendom's largest; its population dwarfed Charles V's dynastic conglomeration. The difficulty was to persuade others that it was not a menace to them. Around 1520 Guillaume Budé wrote his treatise on *The Institute of the Prince*. Budé was a great scholar whose knowledge of Greek earned him the admiration of Erasmus. His text sought to demonstrate how the wisdom of the ancient world could form the basis of a moral philosophy for the present, and that education and learning nourished princely virtues. His work was a humanist contribution to the tradition of the 'Mirror for Princes', Erasmus having written a similar work for the young Charles of Habsburg in 1516. Budé's text has often been presented as offering an 'absolutist' vision of royal power, consonant with the traditions of French monarchy. Had he not told the young Francis: 'Kings are not subject to the laws and ordinances of their realm [...] divine law alone suffices to command them [...] [God] conducts their free will, leading them by divine inspiration'? If one puts the passage in context, Budé was not saying that princes could do as they please. He was referring only to that part of royal authority concerning the distribution of posts and favours. That was a very important part of royal authority, of crucial significance to the functioning of monarchy. But royal authority was exercised through laws and ordinances, courts and jurisdictions to which, in most matters, monarchs naturally bound themselves.

Budé's interest in royal 'distributive justice' (patronage) was because it was a 'power that must be exercised with prudence'. Prudence meant being fair towards people's merits and services and it was a princely virtue. Virtue was inculcated through the study of past examples, as Budé went on to illustrate. But he also accepted that circumstances might occur where princes lacked the necessary 'moral wisdom', either through youth, senility or debility. At such times, a prince needed counsellors whose prudence would stand as proxy for his own. Far from denying the importance of good counsel, Budé was at one with his contemporaries in emphasizing that it was only through taking advice, and knowing when it was good and when it was not, that monarchical rule really worked. The French monarchy was no threat because it was lawful, prudent and well advised.

One of the leading advisers of the young Francis I was Claude de Seyssel. In 1519, he sat down to write *The Great Monarchy of France*, completing it in a month as a gift to the king on his 'joyous entry' to Marseille. For Seyssel, the French monarchy exemplified the mystic harmony and order that accompanied monarchical rule. With an eye to North Italy and the cardinals in Rome, he wanted to demonstrate that the French monarchy was not arbitrary. On the contrary, French kings respected the laws of the land and the Church. If they did not, any prelate or man of standing had the duty to remonstrate with the king and reproach him. In addition, Seyssel argued, there were other 'bridles' to the absolute authority of the French monarch. The institutions of the kingdom, especially its judges, played a fundamental part in French governance. The power of the magistrate was 'more authorised in France than in any other country in the world of which we have cognizance'. Organized into Parlements, their task was to register royal edicts and ensure that they did not conflict with or contradict the 'police' (*politia*) of the realm, i.e. preceding laws. The Parlements also guarded the 'fundamental laws' of the kingdom, which Seyssel defined as its customary laws, the royal domain (which was 'inalienable') and the dynastic succession itself (through the Salic law).

The Lex Salica governed the Salian Franks in the early Middle Ages. Claiming a lineal descent from them, French jurists concentrated on that aspect of the Salic law which limited succession to the eldest male ('agnatic primogeniture') in order to exclude the English from the French succession during the Hundred Years War. Unique in Europe in this period, the Salic law not only barred women from the throne but also any claim that passed through a female line. By 1561 Charles Du Moulin was convinced that 'the Salic law is as ancient as the crown'.

Officially, the Salic law was the ultimate guarantee of French unity. Unofficially, however, the Valois were as prudent as the Habsburgs in arranging the pieces on the dynastic board so that, should the French crown succumb to the kind of succession crisis which had led to the kingdom's dismemberment in the Hundred Years War, it would be possible to resurrect a plausible case for a succession through the female line (see p. 288). Collateral dynastic lines were locked into the royal descent.

When a French succession crisis lay in the offing later in the sixteenth century, Catherine de Médicis followed the same moves. She married

The Succession to the French Crown in the Sixteenth Century

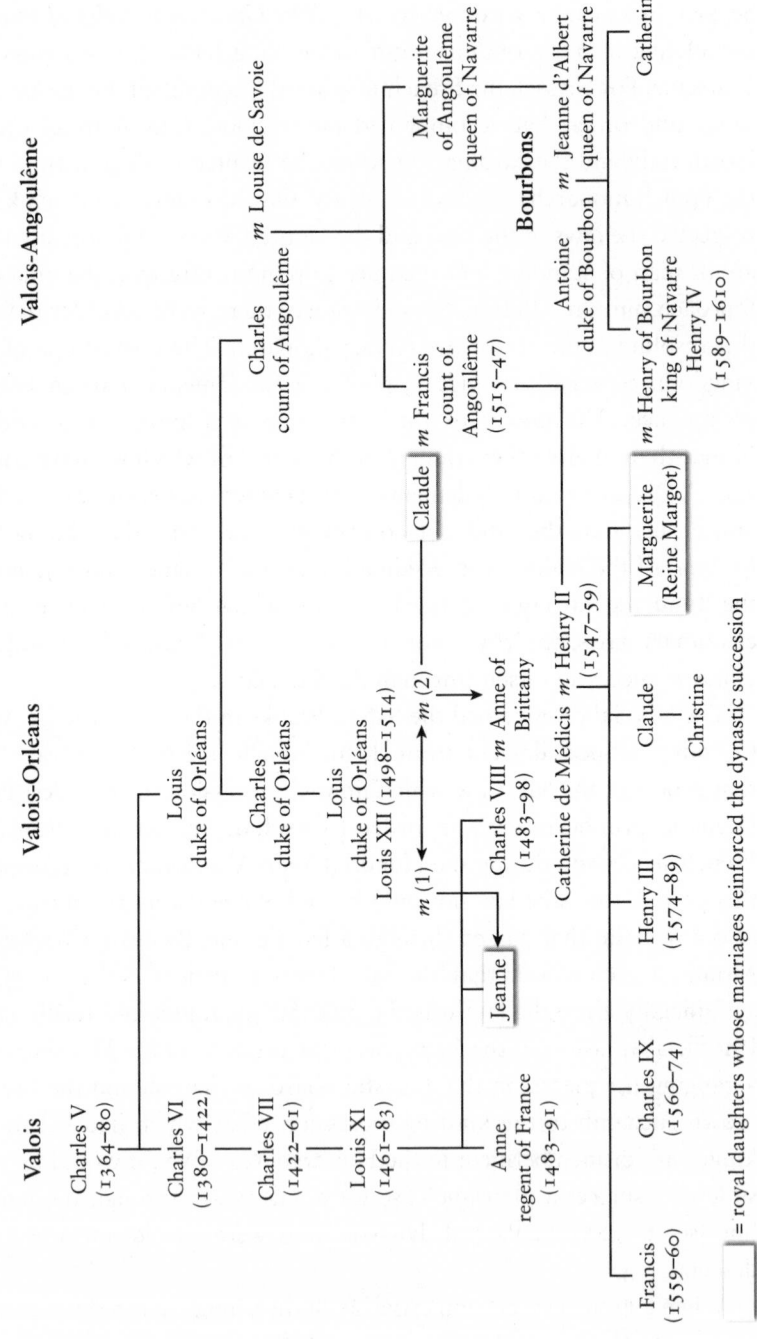

Valois

Charles V (1364–80)

Charles VI (1380–1422)

Charles VII (1422–61)

Louis XI (1461–83)

Anne regent of France (1483–91)

Francis (1559–60)

Charles IX (1560–74)

Henry III (1574–89)

Valois-Orléans

Louis duke of Orléans

Charles duke of Orléans

Louis duke of Orléans Louis XII (1498–1514)

m (1)

m (2) ⟶ Anne of Brittany

Charles VIII (1483–98)

Claude

Claude

Christine

Jeanne

Valois-Angoulême

Charles count of Angoulême *m* Louise de Savoie

Marguerite of Angoulême queen of Navarre

Claude *m* Francis count of Angoulême (1515–47)

Catherine de Médicis *m* Henry II (1547–59)

Marguerite (Reine Margot)

Bourbons

Antoine *m* Jeanne d'Albert duke of Bourbon queen of Navarre

Catherine

m Henry of Bourbon king of Navarre Henry IV (1589–1610)

▢ = royal daughters whose marriages reinforced the dynastic succession her daughter Marguerite ('la Reine Margot') to Henry of Navarre, the heir via the distant Bourbon line. Pierre de Bourdeille, *abbé* de Brantôme, recorded one of Catherine's ladies-in-waiting welcoming the possibility of la Reine Margot becoming queen of France in her own right. Catherine told her sharply to hold her tongue but, when pressed, the queen mother conceded: 'my daughter would certainly be as capable, and more so, of reigning as many men and kings that I have known'. Religion and politics contrived, however, to complicate the succession. Divided from her husband by religion and politically estranged, Margot was a broken reed when it came to securing the Valois succession. So when Catherine de Médicis met Navarre in 1586, it was with a different proposition to solve the Valois succession crisis. If he would announce his conversion to Catholicism, she would organize a divorce from Margot in order to allow him to marry her little granddaughter Christina of Lorraine. Henry would marry his estranged wife's niece to double-lock the succession to the French throne once more with a marriage. Henry's rejection of the offer reflected not so much his Protestantism as his belief that providence destined him to be the successor to the French crown, come what may. That opened France up to the most bitter succession crisis of the period.

What contemporaries most noticed about the 'great monarchy' of France was the size, organization and cultural dynamism of its court. By 1523, the royal household comprised 540 officials, and the wage-bill continued to rise in the course of the first half of the sixteenth century. This, however, takes no account of the retinues of queens, queen mothers and royal children, nor of the counsellors, notaries, royal secretaries, foreign legations and small army of hangers-on. Overall, it must have regularly exceeded 1,000 individuals – which accounts for the indiscipline accorded to it by contemporaries and implied in the ordinances which attempted to regulate it.

Organizing the court was a major operation, the responsibility of senior officials (the *Grand Maître* and *Grand Prévôt*). Transportation was important since the French court 'progressed' through the kingdom following a complex itinerary dictated by the needs of governing a large and disparate state through local élites. Italian residents at the court were exhausted and bemused by it all: 'This court is like no other,' wrote the bishop of Saluzzo to Cosimo I of Florence. 'Here we are completely cut off from business, and if by chance there is any, no hour, day or month is set aside for anyone to deal with it. Here one thinks of nothing but hunting, women, banquets, and moving house ...' The furniture, gold and silver plate, tapestries and menagerie were testimony to the sophistication of court taste, evident also in clothes, food, etiquette and an enlarged social space for women at court. Some changes reflected increased Italian influence but Burgundian court traditions also played their part alongside indigenous pressures towards a more complex civil society.

The imperative of housing an enlarged court determined the architectural activity of the later Valois as much as their desire for ostentation. Reconstructing the realm after the Hundred Years War involved the French nobility building themselves houses where defence was no longer the primary consideration. At the same time, the campaigns in Italy brought the French nobility into contact with High Renaissance classical architecture. By Francis I's reign, Italian classicism was actively encouraged by a king whom the architectural designer Jacques Androuet du Cerceau pronounced was 'marvellously addicted to buildings'. First in the Loire valley, and then after 1528 in the Île de France, the stock of royal châteaux was transformed. At Blois, an entire wing was enlarged, giving it a new façade of Italian colonnades (*loggias*) on the outer side, constructed in the style of Bramante's Vatican. Then, in the royal forests east of Blois, the new palace of Chambord was built. After 1528, Francis I set in train other transformations at the Louvre, St-Germain-en-Laye and Fontainebleau, whose decor celebrated super-abundance, evoking the greatness of the French monarchy and state.

The French high nobility were titular heads of the state's standing army of cavalry, the *gendarmerie*. The governing equivalent was its *corps* of judicial and financial officers. In the sixteenth century they began to hold their posts by inheriting or purchasing them. In 1515, there were over 4,000 of them, the backbone of the monarchy's attempts at territorial integration. Fiscal pressures increased their numbers, and the importance of venality to the monarchy's finances. Some of the surviving châteaux in the Loire valley, the playground of France's governing élites (Chenonceau, Azay-le-Rideau, Bury) testify to the wealth and aspirations of those through whose skills the French monarchy built its more unified state.

The French expeditions to Italy were France's response to Charles V's *imperium*. Charles VIII, Most Christian King (*Rex Christianissimus*), was the descendant of the crusading Saint Louis and the true inheritor of Charlemagne. If Charles was descended from Aeneas, the Trojans were French ancestors. Others argued that they were descended from Japhet, the eldest son of Noah. France was a promised land. St-Denis, the resting-place for French kings, was founded by a saint who had met Christ himself. France's rulers did not need emperors or popes to validate their *imperium*. That existed by virtue of their being anointed with a sacred phial of holy unction, held at Rheims for use in their coronation. French propaganda garnered disillusion with imperial pretentions while offering a positive alternative. French *imperium* contrasted with the notion of a *translatio imperii*, a continuity between the ancient Roman Empire and the Holy Roman Empire. It was prudent, law-giving and pious, committed to reform of the Church and peace in Christendom.

Francis I's most able diplomats – Guillaume du Bellay and his brother Martin – were skilful in articulating this French version of *imperium*. Guillaume spent his formative years in Francis's service and had been captured at Pavia. He realized it required patient diplomacy, working behind the scenes, to construct an enduring anti-imperial axis. This was what he practised in the four years he spent in Germany from 1532 to 1536. Charles V's boast that he was 'most victorious Caesar' (*Caesar invictissimus*) after his Tunis campaign was, he told German princes in 1535, a warning that the emperor wanted to subjugate them. Then, as governor in Turin and vicar-general of Piedmont, Guillaume showed that French rule had a light touch, the French king's door being open to those oppressed by the emperor.

Not immediately rewarded, the du Bellay strategy blossomed under Francis I's successor, Henry II. Over thirty royal entries to French cities (among them, Lyon, September 1548; Paris, June 1549; Boulogne, May 1550) served up anti-Habsburg propaganda. Henry was depicted with his symbol of a crescent moon – an allusion to the waxing and waning of fortune which governed human history, and also to the Church, whose decline had been evident, but which under French leadership would be reformed and once more in the ascendant. He was portrayed as a Gallic Hercules with chains issuing from his mouth to his subjects, winning loyalties by persuasion, not by force. His slogan (devised for him by an exiled Florentine, Gabriel Syméoni) was: 'Until it fills the whole universe' (*Donec Totum Impleat Orbem*), the French answer to 'Plus Ultra'. Habsburg–Valois rivalry broadened.

HABSBURG—VALOIS CONFRONTATION

That rivalry emerged in the Italian Wars to become a primary destabilizing force in Christendom in the 1540s and 50s. Genuine efforts were made in the 1530s to defuse the issues in contention but Francis's diplomatic overtures to the Protestant princes and the Ottomans were known about and resented in the imperial camp. Then, on 1 November 1535, the death without heirs of Francesco II Sforza, duke of Milan, reopened the destiny of the duchy, communications hub and strategic heart of the Habsburg empire. Francis offered a resolution around the devolution of the duchy on his second son, Henry, duke of Brittany (later Henry II). Charles countered by saying that he could accept the duchy in the hands of the king's third son, Charles II, duke of Orléans.

Meanwhile, Francis gathered a new army near Lyon and invaded neighbouring Piedmont and Savoy, while innocently proclaiming no hostile intent towards the emperor. Charles countered with an invasion of Provence (1536) which went badly, while Francis denounced Charles for his unilateral violations of the Peace of Cambrai before the Parlement of Paris and reasserted old French claims to the county of Flanders. With papal and other intermediaries, however, both sides were talked into a ten-year truce (18 June 1538) and a face-to-face encounter at Aïguesmortes (14 July 1538), where the two sovereigns agreed to a dual marriage, with Charles V's son Philip wedding one of Francis's daughters, and Charles, duke of Orléans, a daughter or niece of the emperor, with Milan as her dowry. Both monarchs agreed to combat heresy in their dominions, and Francis pledged to join in a Crusade against the Ottomans. The emperor travelled the length of France from Bayonne to St-Quentin (27 November 1539–20 January 1540) in the company of his French host, fêted as he went. Fleshing out the details of the deal on Milan proved, however, to be harder, and it was put to one side as the entente faded.

French efforts to build an anti-imperial coalition now began to show fruit. In Germany, the Schmalkaldic League of German Protestants welcomed a new recruit to their coalition in 1541: Duke William IV of Cleves, to whom the Rhineland duchy of Guelders had voted to transfer their authority in revenge for having been incorporated into the Habsburg Netherlands in 1536. King Christian III of Denmark also signed a treaty with France. The eastern flank of the Low Countries had a coordinated pro-French bloc of allies and Francis I launched his offensive in support of them in January 1542, occupying Stenay on the Moselle, the gateway to Luxembourg. Later that year, a French army 40,000 strong marched towards the Pyrenees, while French troops also mobilized in Piedmont and two other armies prepared to invade the lower Rhineland. Perpignan resisted assault and French forces could not save the duke of Cleves from having to surrender to Charles's forces, which then took up position for a coordinated invasion of northern France the following year. One by one, France's fortresses on the Marne (St-Dizier, Vitry, Châlons-sur-Marne, Épernay) fell to the emperor, who let it be known that Paris was his goal. Francis took what he could from a negotiated peace (the Treaty of Crépy, September 1544), and the terms which Charles's diplomats offered were so generous that some contemporaries wondered what the conflict had been about. The marriage proposals for Milan were resurrected and concluded. They were scuppered, however, by the unexpected death of Charles II, duke of Orléans, on 9 September 1545. Francis offered to abandon all his opposition to convening a council of the Church and promised to provide military assistance to Charles if his former allies, the Schmalkaldic League, proved unwilling to negotiate a return to the Catholic faith. The emperor had a free hand to put an end to Germany's dissensions once and for all, by force if necessary. The origins of Charles's military showdown with the German Protestant Estates in the Schmalkaldic War lay in the peace at Crépy.

Henry II picked up the French anti-imperial agenda upon his accession in 1547 and gave it his total commitment, laying the groundwork for a coordinated assault on Charles V. The French army and navy were reorganized and strengthened, an attack on Spain in the New World was explored and the finances of the state were consolidated. Boulogne was recovered from the English, Henry entering the city as a hero. French agents and commanders slipped into place in the Italian peninsula, and anti-Habsburg exiles found a place in the sun at his court. His diplomats reopened contacts with the Protestant Estates in Germany whose forces, after being crushed by the emperor at Mühlberg (April 1547), gained a second wind, rallied by Margrave Hans von Brandenburg-Küstrin. Their greatest coup was secured by Jean de Bresse, bishop of Bayonne, who entered into secret discussions with Elector Moritz of Saxony and Margrave Albrecht Alcibiades of

Brandenburg-Kulmbach in October 1551. Three months later, by the Treaty of Chambord France agreed to provide a subsidy of 240,000 *écus* immediately and 60,000 *écus* per month thereafter to the German Protestant alliance in return for their recognition of French rights to all the francophone imperial cities, 'Cambrai, Metz, Toul, Verdun, and any others that there may be'. France's diplomats had a broader plan for a new *imperium* on the legacy of Charlemagne, constructed around the ancient Merovingian lands and including the Low Countries and the Rhineland. The German princes would belong to it by free consent, the French king becoming their 'protector'. The cardinal of Lorraine even had a seal designed in which the *fleur de lys* sat amid the *cachets* of German princes.

French preparations paid off in the 1552 coordinated assault on the Habsburgs. The French invaded Italy, Germany and the Netherlands and launched naval operations in the Mediterranean and the Atlantic. The main army (35,000 strong) was led by the king himself into Lorraine. It reached the Meuse and took Toul without a fight. Metz fell on 17 April 1552 and French forces moved on to Hagenau on the Rhine. Strasbourg itself looked vulnerable. Crippled with gout and dismayed at the treachery of the Protestant Estates, Charles was forced at short notice to raise 150,000 men to defend the empire. The result was a showdown winter siege of the French by imperial forces at Metz, lasting three months from October 1552 to January 1553. In the end, the emperor was forced to retreat. French troops under the duke of Guise flaunted the imperial eagle chained to Herculean columns with the inscription: *Non ultra Metas* ('Not beyond these limits' – but also 'Not beyond Metz'). That withdrawal was the moment when Charles's brother Ferdinand realized that to forestall the disintegration of the Reich he had to come to terms with heretics.

Meanwhile, French troops invaded Corsica in 1553, opening up a civil war, while an expeditionary force struck southwards through Tuscany to bring aid to the republic of Siena. In 1552, that city had expelled the garrison which Charles V had imposed on it. In reprisal, Charles V despatched his general Gian Giacomo de' Medici to lay siege to it. The French forces led by Pietro Strozzi were defeated at the battle of Marciano (near Arezzo, 2 August 1554). After a heroic three-year siege, Siena eventually capitulated and was incorporated into the consolidated duchy of Tuscany.

In Picardy, the French were vulnerable. That was where Charles launched his counter-attack, moving the forces which had failed at Metz across to take the fortified town of Thérouanne, a French outpost in Flanders. As it was well provisioned and recently renovated, everyone around Henry II thought it could withstand anything. In reality, it fell to a surprise attack and, after a month's pounding, Hesdin followed (July 1553). Three French armies mustered in 1554 to recover the situation, devastating the southern Netherlands and taking several fortresses. With Charles V's announcement of his abdication in 1555, a brief truce and respite followed. Despite the accumulating signs of financial exhaustion, Henry II committed himself to a further Italian expedition in September 1556, led by the rising star at the French court, François, duke of Guise, a foreign prince (*prince étranger*) from the cadet line of the House of Lorraine at the French court. Just as it became bogged down in Italy in the course of the following year, France confronted a large Spanish force (over 50,000 strong), commanded in person by the young Philip II, on the borders of Picardy. Despite all their endeavours, the French could put only half that number together to defend the northern frontier. At a serious numerical disadvantage, French forces were commanded by the Constable, Anne de Montmorency. Trying to defend the frontier town of St-Quentin, his army was overwhelmed (10 August 1557). The Spanish conquered all but one of the fifty-seven French standards. Over 2,500 French soldiers were killed, many of them senior commanders. The Constable himself was captured and Paris stood open to attack. Guise was recalled from Italy, and the king and his close advisers faced unprecedented criticism.

The duke of Guise profited most from the situation. Presenting himself as the saviour of the hour, he masterminded a midwinter assault upon Calais. Remarkably, after two days of bombardment the castle walls were breached. By 8 January, the English defenders sued for peace. With Calais in his possession, Henry II had the bargaining counter he needed to secure the ransom and release of the Constable. The French dauphin, Francis (later King Francis II), was a potential instrument in any peace deal since his marriage to Philip's sister would seal the reconciliation of the two houses. As it turned out, there was an even more attractive bride for the dauphin, a match which carried the enthusiastic endorsement of the Guise. This was a marriage between Mary Stuart and Francis. Mary Stuart was not only the heiress to the Scottish throne, but was in line to the English throne as well, if (as evidently would be the case) Mary Tudor had no children and Princess Elizabeth could be kept off the English throne as a bastard. Mary Stuart was a trump card, a queen of hearts if not an ace. On 19 April 1558, the betrothal took place. The contract of marriage gave Francis the title of king of Scotland until he inherited the French throne. The two realms were joined together in their coats of arms and, in November 1558, they added England's as well. In secret clauses, however, the agreement was that, if Mary died without a child, her rights to England and Scotland would pass to the Valois dynasty and Scotland and its revenues would pass to Henry. One way or another, a Franco-British composite monarchy was in gestation.

So, too, were complex negotiations to draw a line under the long, bitter and costly Habsburg–Valois conflicts. They involved Spanish and French, and then later English plenipotentiaries, and began in earnest in October 1558. Dynastic reconciliation was cemented by a double marriage. Duke Emmanuel-Philibert of Savoy married Marguerite, sister of the French king, Henry II. That covered the French king's blushes over the surrender of Savoy-Piedmont back to the Savoy house. The other marriage was that of Henry's eldest daughter, Elisabeth, to Philip II himself – with Mary Tudor's death in November 1558, Philip II had that clause written into the treaty late on in the proceedings. The key stumbling-block proved to be what happened to Calais – after November 1558 in the hands of Protestant Queen Elizabeth I. In the end, it was agreed that France would hold it for eight years, after which it would be returned to England. France would provide a security of 500,000 *écus* as a pledge of good faith, both sides accepting that any violation of the peace would render the terms inoperative.

France kept the three francophone imperial bishoprics in Lorraine (Metz, Toul and Verdun) and, since Philip was not emperor, he merely registered a token protest at this infringement of the empire. France recovered St-Quentin and three other forts in the southern Netherlands in return for four held by France. French dynastic claims in Italy were renounced and the duke of Savoy was restored to his duchy. All that remained of the French expeditions to Italy were the duchy of Saluzzo and a few fortresses in Piedmont, including Turin. Dynastic conflict on a massive scale did not move the frontiers of Christendom much. But it created political fissures in which Protestantism flourished, and a mountain of debts which compromised the stability of those states involved.

CHRISTENDOM AND THE OTTOMAN EMPIRE

In the first half of the sixteenth century, the Ottomans' expansion was ominous. In 1521, they took Belgrade. In 1526, the central Hungarian plain opened up to their forces and Buda fell. Three years later, Sultan Suleiman I (the Magnificent) besieged Vienna itself. Eastern Hungary became ruled by the Ottomans, and Transylvania, a nominally independent vassal state, seemed likely to follow suit. The Habsburgs and Jagiellons were no longer protected by buffer states but were on Christendom's front line.

At the same time, the Ottomans enlarged their presence in the Mediterranean. The conquest of Syria and Egypt in 1517 furnished them with a long eastern Mediterranean seaboard with plenty of ports. From there, they made common cause with the Barbary states. And that was just at the moment when Christendom's intensified rivalries in the Italian peninsula, as well as the creation of the Castile–Aragon–Naples compound kingdom and then that of the Habsburg empire, made communications in the Mediterranean a central strategic issue. In 1522, the Ottomans besieged the Crusading Knights of St John of Jerusalem and expelled them from Rhodes. In the space of a short generation, Venice lost much of its maritime empire, surrendering the majority of the remaining islands in the Greek archipelago between 1537 and 1540. Only Cyprus, Crete and some bases on the Adriatic remained, and these were regularly threatened. Christendom had reason to fear the Ottomans.

Ottoman propaganda fed that anxiety. Their conquests nurtured the development and diffusion of an imperial ideology which both justified what they had acquired and proclaimed their aspirations to world dominance. Drawing on the Islamic principle of 'holy war' (ghâzâ) – especially after acquiring Mecca and other Islamic holy shrines, and absorbing the Mameluks of Egypt – the sultan inherited the title of 'servant of the two sanctuaries' and the old caliphate protection for the House of Islam (dâr-al'Islâm), with aspirations to convert the world over. From Sultan Mehmed II onwards, the Ottoman Porte nurtured the *imperium* which had been acquired with the capture of Constantinople. When the Italian portrait painter Gentile Bellini depicted Mehmed II it was as the descendant of Alexander the Great, adding at the bottom of the painting: 'emperor of the world' (*Imperator Orbis*).

Suleiman I inherited these traditions, including the title 'Distributor of the Crowns of the Great Monarchs of the World'. In 1529, he made good that claim when he installed John Zápolya on the throne of King Stephen in the Ottoman part of Hungary with the Hungarian crown, which the Ottomans seized just before it was about to be smuggled to Vienna. Suleiman ceased to sit cross-legged upon a divan to receive ambassadors and instead occupied a jewel-encrusted throne. In 1532 Venetian goldsmiths completed work on a ceremonial warrior's helmet for the sultan, commissioned by the Grand Vizier Ibrahim Pasha. Composed of four concentric crowns (one more than for the papacy), resplendent with gigantic pearls, it was deliberately designed to outshine the claims to *imperium* of the papacy and Holy Roman Emperor. The sight of it in 1532 turned Habsburg envoys into 'speechless corpses'. From Christendom's listening-posts on the Ottoman world in Vienna and Venice came troubling reports of the sultan's aspirations to conquer Rome. Ottoman geomancers and image-makers drew on the millenarian expectations that were common currency in Mediterranean lands among Jews and Christian converts to Islam, presenting Suleiman as a Muslim messiah (*mahdi*) whose reign would usher in the last days before the coming of the Islamic millennium (1591–2).

Ottoman expansion confirmed these anxieties. In 1480, Otranto in southern Italy was sacked, a reminder that the Italian peninsula was now a front line too. Each new reported sighting of the Ottoman fleet and every hostile landing by the Barbary pirates focused afresh the dangers to Christian communities around the Mediterranean. It was the fear of the Turks at the gates of Rome, as well as a response to the recent sack of the city, that led Pope Paul III to commission Antonio da Sangallo to build a huge rampart around the city. Charles V's viceroy in Naples, Pedro de Toledo, began the construction of watch-towers and defensive emplacements round the coasts. Ferrante Gonzaga supervised the building of 137 towers round the coast of Sicily.

In both the Italian peninsula and in eastern Europe the anxiety about Ottoman incursions was transmitted by printed broadsheets, ordinances for military levies, debates in councils of state, preaching, images and popular songs. In frontier societies such as Croatia, local nobles acting as the first line of defence transmitted their anxieties back through the Habsburg empire. Despite its divisions, the latter accepted its responsibility to coalesce and mobilize when faced with a threat to the East. When news reached Strasbourg of the arrival of Suleiman at the gates of Vienna in 1529, its councillors (many of them Protestant and otherwise suspicious of the emperor) did not debate whether they should come to its aid, but only how much they could levy and how quickly. The fear of the Turks was not confined to those lands nearest the danger. On the contrary, it was pervasive in the literature and consciousness of France and England and expressed eloquently by people who were never likely to set eyes upon an Ottoman.

Crusading anti-Muslim notions were reinforced by Christendom's stereotype of the 'Turk'. It traversed popular and élite discourse, was reflected in international diplomacy and political analysis, and reinforced a prevalent oppositional logic. The Turk was the enemy of Christ, as Pope Leo X said in his bull (*Constituti iuxta*, April 1517). He called on the rulers of Christendom to put aside their quarrels in order to fight 'the Turks and other Infidels' who 'ignore the true light of salvation because of the obstinacy of their minds', the 'hateful enemies of God and inveterate persecutors of the Christian religion'. When, in 1535, Charles V announced to the Cortes of Castile his intention of leading an expedition against Tunis, he justified it as an enterprise against the 'perpetual enemy of our Holy Catholic faith'.

These collective worries were often expressed in apocalyptic terms. The collapse of Christendom to the forces of Islam had often been presented as heralding the coming of the end time in the Middle Ages, but that now gained a new specificity. In the cities of northern Italy, radical preachers proclaimed the need for moral and social reform in Christendom and the emergence of a warrior prince to lead a Crusade against the Turks in a cosmic battle. The rise to prominence of the popular literature of portents and prophecies added a dimension of urgency to the pervasive anxiety about the Turkish menace. The failure of Christendom's political and spiritual leaders to defend it only intensified fears about Ottoman expansion which had nurtured apocalyptic anxieties at the outset.

That failure was evident for all to see. As the Venetian maritime empire shrank so its senators anxiously debated whether it was better to appease the Ottomans or to resist their advance. 'Every time we have made war upon the Turks,' said one of them in 1538, 'we have lost.' They despatched missives to Rome, Vienna and elsewhere seeking alliances against the 'common enemy'. Those senators had substantial investments on the Venetian terra firma. Its protection in the Italian Wars meant making alliances with some and against others rather than common cause against the external enemy. The peace treaties which brought princely conflicts to a conclusion in the first half of the sixteenth century were often justified in terms of the wishes of all parties to undertake a Crusade. So, in the Treaty of Madrid (January 1526), concluded by the captive Francis I with the emperor, both parties solemnly reaffirmed that their '*principal* intention' was to conclude their particular differences in order to concentrate on the 'universal' objective of 'enterprises against Turks and other Infidels'. Three years later, the preamble to the Peace of Cambrai (August 1529) solemnly proclaimed the necessity for all its signatories to work together to oppose the 'invasions that the Turk, the enemy of our Christian faith, has perpetrated upon Christendom during its intestinal strife'. The Peace of Crépy (September 1544) committed Francis I to furnish 600 cavalry and 10,000 infantry to fight in Hungary 'to repel the Turk and his forces'. Essential to peace-making rhetoric, these clauses advertised the frustrations of Christendom's leaders at their impotence to advance an agenda which they mostly agreed upon.

The papacy was committed to rallying secular princes behind the cause of Crusade because it confirmed its destiny as spiritual leader of Christendom and the mediator of peace among the nations. That role became more difficult to fulfil alongside that of the papal prince, whose temporal interests required it to protect and advance the Papal States and be a party to the struggles in the Italian peninsula and elsewhere. The Reformation made it harder still since the papacy could hardly call on the loyalties of Protestant princes. The more the papacy proclaimed the urgency of uniting Christendom around a Crusade, the more it advertised its own incapacity to lead Christendom. That did not stop it trying to do so. For Pope Paul III the achievement of concord among Christendom's rival princes and the beginnings of Church reform, envisaged as its complement, were the essential preliminaries to the launching of a Crusade. The Ottoman threat brought coherence to the papal envoys despatched around Europe to that effect, the cautious opening to the door of Church reform in 1536, and the papal willingness to go along with imperial efforts at achieving reconciliation with the Lutheran estates in 1539–41. For a time, the efforts looked as though they might succeed. Charles V and the Republic of Venice were willing to give reconciliation a chance. In May 1538, Paul himself became an intermediary between Charles and Francis in negotiations at Nice where both parties recognized the danger to 'poor Christendom' because of princely dissensions. Yet the moment passed. The dealings in Germany with the Lutherans reached deadlock, relations between Francis and Charles soured once more, and Church reform took on a different hue with the summoning of the Council to Trent in 1545. By Paul III's death in 1549, the papacy was no longer, whatever it would have liked, the primate of Christendom.

The Ottomans posed a direct threat to the Habsburg empire. That, however, complicated the emperor's task of rallying other princes in Christendom to the cause of Crusade. As the notion of 'Crusade' became interpreted as an anti-Ottoman offensive so it became less clear what the target of that offensive might be. Constantinople was unthinkable; Jerusalem was impracticable. More limited targets, however, were inextricably associated with the dynastic and material interests of the Habsburgs themselves. Persuading other princes to sign up to them became correspondingly harder. The defence of Vienna in 1532 offered one focus, and Charles V took advantage of the stubborn resistance of the small Hungarian fortress-town of Kőszeg to assemble a large coalition force to defend it. That army did not, in fact, draw swords with the Turks, though its achievement was presented as a crusading triumph.

Three years later, the Barbary corsair bastion of Tunis offered another target. Charles V's naval forces in the western Mediterranean had been strengthened by the defection in July 1528 of the Genoese naval *condottiere* Andrea Doria to Habsburg service. The emperor also benefited from the galleys of the Order of St John of Jerusalem, which he established at Malta in 1530 for the annual homage of one falcon. On 15 June 1535, imperial coalition forces of some 35,000 disembarked from a flotilla of a hundred warships and 300 other assorted vessels. After a month-long siege, Halq al Wadi gave way and Tunis fell (helped by a rising of its slaves). With the enemy galleys of Barbarossa lurking close at hand, the emperor held on to Tunis but withdrew to Italy. There he was fêted as a new Scipio, Carthage's conqueror. Once Charles V had proved his crusading credentials, however, his attentions were pulled elsewhere. A subsequent Holy League coalition of forces between Rome and Venice had a dismal outcome off the northwest Greek coast at Preveza on 27 September 1538, which sealed the Turkish hold on Greece. Venice made its peace with the Ottoman Porte in 1540.

Charles mounted his final military expedition against the Ottomans in the following year. It was another amphibious operation, this time directed at the North African stronghold of Algiers. Five hundred ships carrying 25,000 troops set sail late. Bad weather disrupted their landfall. The Algerians profited from the setback and launched sorties on the expeditionary force, which found itself surrounded. Those that could retreated to the vessels that had anchored at Cape Matifu, but it was almost a rout: seventeen galleys and 130 carracks were lost, along with thousands of lives.

That defeat mirrored another on land that same year at the siege of Buda. The disastrous defeat at Mohács in 1526 had ended the Jagiellon dynasty in Hungary and dispersed its aristocratic supporters. The Turks initially retired back behind the Danubian Gate after the battle, leaving Hungary as a power vacuum in which the claims to the succession of 'royal' Hungary by Archduke Ferdinand were rejected by the country's ruling noble élite in favour of one of their own: John Zápolya, who seemed most capable of restoring the Hungarian kingdom. He was duly elected King John I of Hungary at the Diet of Székesfehérvár on 10 November 1526. But within a year, Zápolya faced a serious popular uprising fomented by Archduke Ferdinand, led by Jovan Nenad, a Serbian mercenary who became known (because of a birth-mark) as 'the Black', and who proclaimed himself tsar. An army from northern Hungary, with Transylvanian help, defeated the forces of the Black at the battle of Sződfalva (25 July 1527). By then, however, Hungary's divisions had been exposed. Zápolya was crushed months later by a force of Germans, Austrians and Hungarians in the name of Archduke Ferdinand at the battle of Tokaj (27 September 1527) and he retreated into Polish exile. Gradually, Ferdinand began to build up his links to Hungarian baronial families in the west and north of the country upon which Austrian Habsburg fortunes in the future would depend, and to construct the central institutions, based at Bratislava, by which he and his successors would govern.

The major part of the Hungarian nobility turned out for Ferdinand's coronation in Székesfehérvár on 3 November 1527. But Zápolya was still around, a lightning conductor for anti-Habsburg and populist forces in Hungary and Transylvania. Promoted to the kingship of Hungary by the sultan, he consolidated his support in northern and eastern Hungary. Zápolya died in what is now Romania at Sebeş in 1540. But only the year before he had married Isabella Jagiellon, by whom he had a son – John Sigismund, born in Buda a fortnight before his father's death. His mother, acting as queen consort, oversaw her son's coronation as Hungarian king at a Diet, and ruled in his name with the support of the Ottomans and the advice of a monk known as 'Friar George'. Archduke Ferdinand chose this moment to eliminate his Hungarian rival and stake his claim as protector of Hungary. He assembled a large army (some 50,000 Germans, Austrians and others), mobilized under the command of Wilhelm von Roggendorf, his court chancellor, and besieged Buda in the summer of 1541. But the siege faltered and, worse, the Ottoman army arrived on the scene on 21 August. Ferdinand's army was defeated and the Ottomans occupied central Hungary for the next 150 years. Buda became a Muslim city. Isabella and her infant heir (with Friar George) were packed off to Transylvania. Ferdinand's call on his brother Charles for help fell on deaf ears and, for a time, how to repulse the Ottomans in southeastern Europe became a bone of contention between them. The Habsburgs failed to unite their own lands against the Turks, let alone the rest of Christendom.

Nothing indicated the changing nature of the confrontation between Christendom and the Ottomans more clearly that the 'impious' alliance between France and the Ottomans, sketched out in the wake of the consolidation of Charles V's hegemony over the Italian peninsula in 1530. Part of the Valois politics of forming countervailing alliances against what it regarded as Habsburg dynastic imperialism, the initial rapprochement was informal and through intermediaries among the Barbary pirates. Charles V knew about it at an early stage and hesitated between openly denouncing it and privately persuading Francis I to let it drop. In the wake of the Tunis campaign, and with the emperor's attack upon Provence in 1536, Francis called on the naval forces of the sultan's ally in the western Mediterranean, Barbarossa, to counteract those of Andrea Doria in Genoa. In 1537, Franco-Ottoman cooperation projected an invasion of the Italian peninsula and Pope Paul III's urgency in promoting reconciliation in these years was a direct response to the dangers the Franco-Ottoman alliance posed. Thirteen French galleys joined the Ottoman naval squadron attacking Corfu in 1537. In July 1543 Barbarossa's fleet of 110 galleys appeared off the coast of Marseille with the French ambassador to the Porte on board to take part in a Franco-Ottoman invasion of Nice (then part of the duchy of Savoy), Christians fighting alongside Ottomans against Christians. In September Barbarossa demanded that his fleet refit in a French port, and Francis placed Toulon at his disposal. All inhabitants except heads of households were ordered to leave, while the town became for eight months an Ottoman encampment.

MONSTROUS REGIMENT

There was a political paradox in Christendom's dynastic states. They were patriarchies, but women were essential to their dynastic strategies. On the one hand, power was expressed in overwhelmingly male terms. Jean Bodin (a misogynist) expressed what many contemporaries took as axiomatic: that the family, the fundamental building-block of societies and state, institutionalized male power. 'All laws and customs,' he wrote, 'make the husband the master of his wife's actions and the enjoyment of wealth which she inherits.' Such marital absolutism did not give *carte blanche* to 'wayward husbands' to do as they pleased. But Bodin was clear that the law was on the husbands' side. On the other hand, female rule was an ever-present reality in dynastic states, and to a degree that had not been so hitherto. The period from 1515 to 1621 witnessed sixteen female regencies across Europe. Put together they lasted around 140 years. In addition, five queens ruled in their own right. Queens were accorded their own apartments, retinues and status, while the Renaissance made it fashionable to extol female beauty and virtue. Christendom had to adapt itself to female rule.

Women were essential to the politics of dynastic states. Births were political events. Sex was the stuff of court politics. Wedding nights were public, notaries being among those present. Francis I and Pope Clement VII watched the fourteen-year-old Henry II and Catherine de Médicis 'joust in bed' at their nuptials. Brantôme claimed to have seen Francis II of France 'fail a number of times' in bed with Mary Stuart – the fourteen-year-old's testicles had not descended from his pelvis. Royal lyings-in were the subject of intense speculation. Rituals left no doubt as to the magnitude of the occasion. The expectant mother wore robes of historical significance to the dynasty and auspicious relics were deployed to assist the outcome – which is not surprising, given that (for example) over half the Habsburg queens in the sixteenth century died in childbed. The poor wife of John III of Portugal gave birth nine times, but only one child lived to the age of twenty. Henry VIII's first two marriages resulted in fourteen recorded conceptions, but only two daughters survived. Dynastic states were constrained by the biological fact that it was not conception, but the difficulty of bringing a pregnancy to term, that threatened dynastic continuity.

Devolving power to a regent queen reflected the dynastic clan. How much power came their way depended on circumstance. From Charles V's correspondence with his aunt Margaret of Austria and his sister Mary of Hungary it is evident that, while they deferred to his will, he accorded them a good deal of latitude. It was otherwise with Queen Isabella in Spain, made regent in 1529–32, and again in 1535–9. Charles remembered the *comuneros* revolt and she was closely watched over. Women regents were often persuaded to, or chose to, surrender their power to someone else. In the summer of 1566, Mary Queen of Scots put her trust in David Rizzio, her musician and private secretary, with tragic consequences. No political events in this period were murkier than what followed. She had married Henry Stuart, Lord Darnley, on 20 July 1565 and become pregnant. Darnley suspected that the child was Rizzio's and murdered him at Holyrood Palace in the queen's presence. The child (James Stuart VI of Scotland, later I of England) was born on 19 June 1566, and Mary entrusted her favour to James Hepburn, earl of Bothwell. Darnley sought his reconciliation with the queen and the role of 'crown matrimonial' for himself, significantly more than consort. On 10 February 1567, Darnley's body and that of his servant were found in the orchard at Kirk o' Field, Edinburgh, where they had been staying. Henry Darnley was in his nightshirt and an explosion had occurred during the night in the house. Henry and his valet had been strangled and the explosion was possibly an attempt to cover up the murders.

Mary Stuart then became the prisoner of the rampant Bothwell, on whom suspicion for the murder now fell. The Privy Council began proceedings against him on 12 April 1567, but it was for form's sake and he was acquitted that same day. Two weeks later, on 24 April, while Mary was travelling from Linlithgow Palace to Edinburgh, Bothwell ambushed her with 800 men and escorted her to his castle at Dunbar. The circumstantial evidence suggests that he then raped her. On 12 May Mary created him duke of Orkney, and three days later they married in the Great Hall of Holyrood. There followed an uprising against them in which Mary was imprisoned at Loch Leven Castle (on 15 June) and forced to abdicate in favour of her one-year-old son. After an unsuccessful attempt to regain the throne, she fled to England to seek the protection of her distant cousin, Elizabeth I. The leitmotif of these events was Mary's vulnerability in a divided realm. Women in power were the first to be blamed for things that went wrong.

In most of Christendom, queens ruled as regents but, in the British Isles, they ruled as of right. Uniquely three queens (if we count the nine-day wonder of Queen Jane, or Lady Jane Grey, in July 1553) followed in succession to the English throne: half a century of female rule. Contemporary Protestants found it easy to publish the case against women in power when it came to Mary Tudor, who put a full stop to their religious experiment. Christopher Goodman, a former professor of divinity from Oxford who had taken up exile in the Rhineland and Geneva, explained in a work he published in 1558 that female rule was 'against nature and the order established by God'. Subjects were not bound to obey queens, especially when they persecuted God's chosen ones. Also from Geneva, John Knox sounded *The First Blast of the Trumpet against the Monstrous Regiment of Women* in the summer of that same year. 'How abominable before God,' he declared, 'is the Empire or Rule of a wicked woman, yea of a traiteresse and bastard' – and no one was in any doubt that he referred to the two Marys (Tudor and Stuart). He invited their deposition forthwith, keeping his own name off the title-page for his own safety. Even the Genevan reformer Jean Calvin was in the dark about who had written it until a year later.

By then, Mary Tudor was dead and Elizabeth I had ascended the English throne. Not amused, she commissioned John Aylmer to write a riposte to Knox, a tricky assignment because Aylmer was more than half-persuaded by Knox's general case. In *An Harborowe for Faithfull and Trewe Subjects* (1559) he described its errors as the result of misplaced zeal. Elizabeth I's right to rule came from her birth, and that had been determined by the Almighty's providence. Providence had decreed that England was not a 'mere monarchy, as some for lack of consideration think, nor a mere oligarchy, nor democracy, but a rule mixed of all these'. It was a mixed state of the kind that Aristotle had favoured, a combination of 'monarchy, oligarchy and democracy'. Aylmer told people in England what they already knew: that England was a 'monarchical republic' in which they were active citizens, conscious that the safety of the state depended on them as well as their virgin queen, unmarried and heirless.

The reigns of Mary and Elizabeth posed impossible dynastic conundrums. In Mary's case, the puzzle was how to marry and secure Catholicism and the succession in a way that was acceptable to that monarchical republic, while at the same time retaining her authority as queen regnant. Her decision to marry Prince (soon to be King) Philip of Spain (25 July 1554), when she was thirty-eight years of age, solved only part of the puzzle, and then not for long. In Elizabeth's, the conundrum was the reverse: whether, and if so how, to remain single, while at the same time placating that same republic, whose concern was for the security of the public weal and the survival of the Protestant settlement. These imponderables lay at the heart of English politics for half a century, channelling its response to the Protestant Reformation.

10. Schism

THE COMING OF THE PROTESTANT REFORMATION

The Protestant Reformation was a religious schism, like that between western and Orthodox Christianity in the eleventh century only messier. It reshaped the mental landscape of Christendom. Belief took on a new meaning. Contemporaries had nothing in their experience with which to understand the transformation. Local antipathies to the jurisdictional apparatus and infrastructure of Christendom had been coterminous with its emergence but it had lived with them. Heretical movements – a way by which Christendom's infrastructure chose to characterize those antipathies – were also part of the later medieval landscape, although their adherents had been persecuted and (with the exception of the Hussites in Bohemia) crushed, reduced to localized remnants. The agenda of Church reform, expressed through the Conciliar Movement, had engaged the secular authorities in Europe in the fifteenth century, which had used the issue for their own political purposes. But its moment had come and gone, except in the German polity. Christendom was never as orthodox as in 1500.

The religious revolt of the sixteenth century did not aim to destroy Christendom. On the contrary, it's first protagonist, Martin Luther, saw himself as saving it from its enemies within. He set about the Reformation which the pope and bishops had failed to provide, thereby averting the wrath of God. By 1520, after reading (among other things) the exposure by the humanist Lorenzo Valla of the Donation of Constantine as a forgery, Luther became convinced that the Roman hierarchy was a tyranny in the service of the Antichrist. Those responsible for reform were the greatest obstacle to it. In March 1520 he wrote his *Treatise on*

Good Works. In tone, it was not an anti-papal rant but an exposition of Christian responsibilities, organized as a commentary on the Ten Commandments. When he discussed the obedience owed to 'the spiritual authorities' (i.e. the pope and bishops), however, the radical dimensions of Luther's thinking for Christendom emerged. Those authorities 'behave towards their responsibilities like mothers who forsake their children and run after their lovers'. The spiritual authorities are 'in all respects more worldly' than secular authorities themselves. They practise what they should prevent, and they command and prescribe things contrary to the first three Commandments, while Christendom decays around them. In these circumstances, 'anyone who is able to do so' should come to Christendom's aid. He called upon kings, princes and nobles 'for the benefit of Christendom and to prevent blasphemy and the disgrace of the divine name' to resist the 'scarlet whore of Babylon' (the pope). Indeed, he said, 'it is the only way left to us'.

By June 1520 when this treatise was published, the implications of Luther's critique were just beginning to be felt. By declaring that popes could be wrong, that the ecclesiastical fabric was in alien hands and that Church councils could not be depended upon, Luther reflected where he thought the foundations for authority within Christendom lay. God's Word had become flesh in Jesus Christ. Everything had changed at that moment in human history. Christ was the only source for authority in Christendom. As that moment receded, so the possibilities for corruption increased, making truth harder to recover. But God's Word had been preserved in Scripture, the agent and content of divine Revelation. Scripture needed no interpreter. Anyone with faith in God's redeeming mercy would find truth there manifest. It was Luther's radical rewriting of tradition which made the Protestant Reformation different from preceding heretical movements.

That was recognized in *The Defence of the Seven Sacraments* (1522), the treatise written by King Henry VIII in response to Luther's *Babylonian Captivity of the Church* (1520). The English king posed as the Defender of Christendom. He used biblical and patristic arguments to maintain the seven sacraments, showing that there was a concurrence of support for them which could only be a manifestation of the Holy Spirit. Luther's reply was brutal and to the point. If Christian faith depended for its veracity only upon the length of time of its credence, and the common agreement and customs of men, then it did not differ from the beliefs of Turks or Jews. Traditions and customs were no more than gossip (*Menschen Sprüche*). King Henry was like an ass who 'sticks its head in the sack'.

Luther's appeal to the Estates of Christendom – kings, princes and nobles – lay at the heart of the second reason why the Protestant Reformation was different from previous dissident religious movements. Luther's Reformation summoned up more powerful political and social forces in support of change whose alliance coalesced in German-speaking Europe. The evangelical Protestant movement drew strength from a politically fragmented Holy Roman Empire and neighbouring Swiss Confederation. New players appeared – preachers, city magistrates, printers and publicists, urban and rural mass movements – and printing and other forms of dissemination made the dynamic of the movement and its underlying political and social forces seem more powerful and integrated than in reality was the case. The tendencies to fragmentation within the early Protestant Reformation were as significant as the forces which it initially unleashed. Its survival and evolution depended on the political forces to whom Luther made his appeal in 1520.

THE HOLY ROMAN EMPIRE AND THE SWISS CONFEDERATION

These were the political map's most complex entities. Even their titles were unclear. The Reich was Roman (*Imperium Romanum*), Christian (*Imperium Christianum*) and universal (*Imperium mundi*). 'Schwitzerland' was the term used for the original allies from the region of Schwyz, around Lake Lucerne, which made up the original Swiss Confederation. Subsequently, other cantons and communities attached themselves to this core which still acknowledged the overlordship of the emperor. Then Swiss proximity to Habsburg claims and aspirations created a rift. Emperor Maximilian I attempted to annex parts adjoining Switzerland, but the inhabitants of the disputed regions formed three leagues, two of which joined the Confederation in 1497 and 1498. The more effectively organized of these was the Grey Leagues. The threat from the Habsburgs in Swiss lands, and notably from Emperor Maximilian's reforms, led to a rift. Formally, the Swiss remained within the Reich, but even the Swiss cities bordering German lands (Basel and Schaffhausen) ceased to attend the German Diets after 1530 and Swiss autonomy was an actuality – its independence recognized in the Peace of Westphalia (1648).

The border between Switzerland and the empire was only one of numerous complexities for anyone trying to work out the frontiers of either entity. The empire had three nominal imperial arch-chancellors (the archbishops of Mainz, Trier and Cologne), servicing its German, Burgundian and Italian affairs respectively, of which only the first was functional by 1500. Imperial jurisdictions in northern Italy were a thing of the past, and its Burgundian jurisdictions had become absorbed into Habsburg or Valois territorial dominions; or, in the Low Countries, were peripheral to its affairs. Even in northern and eastern Germany, where the frontiers of the empire were at their clearest, things were not straight-forward. Pomerania, Brandenburg and Silesia were territories held in fief to the emperor. The lands of the old crusading Order of Teutonic Knights were not, but when the territories of the Prussian branch of the order were secularized in 1525 they devolved into the hands of the order's Hohenzollern Grand Master. So Prussia was only part of the empire by virtue of being in the hands of the Brandenburg Hohenzollerns.

To the south of Brandenburg lay the territories of the kingdom of Bohemia (including the duchy of Silesia and the margravates of Mor-avia and Lusatia). These lands were inherited by the Habsburgs in 1526 but their status in the empire was peculiar. Bohemia was the only kingdom to exist as a subordinate entity within the empire. The Bohe-mian king was one of the imperial Electors, so his lands were exempt from imperial jurisdiction. But as a king he did not directly participate in the deliberations of the Electoral College. The Bohemians insisted that theirs was an elective monarchy. Even when Charles V's brother, Ferdinand I, inherited the kingdom in 1526, the Bohemian Estates went through the formality of 'electing' him, thereby putting down a marker for Bohemia's semi-detachedness from the empire.

The frontiers of the Swiss Confederation were defined by those of the self-governing communities which composed it, alike only in their inde-pendence from other princes and rulers. They were most subject to change in the two outer cantons of Zürich to the east and Bern to the west. Zürich was not large (about 7,000 inhabitants in 1520). By its municipal charter of 1498 it was a self-governing entity, made up of representatives from the town and its rural hinterland. It acted as the diplomatic and political instrument of the Confederation in German lands, putting out feelers to southern German cities who might be persuaded to join it, and reluctantly agreeing with Bern in negotiations (for example, in 1516 and 1521) for treaties to provide the French monarchy with mercenary forces. Bern was not much bigger than Zürich but its municipal charter was less participative. Bern's oligarchs enjoyed French monarchical protection and hoped to realize benefits from it by securing the overlordship of its neighbours around Lake Geneva. In 1536, they acquired Vaud, Thonon and Ternier, leaving Geneva as an independent city.

Neither the Swiss nor the empire had a constitution. The thirteen full members of the Swiss Confederation discussed matters of common significance at a Diet, an important forum for negotiations as, first the issue of mercenaries, and then the Reformation, threatened to tear the Confederation apart. The empire was an elective monarchy, candidates to the imperial throne being elected by the seven Electors to the empire. The emperor was expected to hold regular Diets or meetings of the German Estates, summoned by the emperor (with the Electors' permission) in accordance with a 1495 agreement known as the 'Perpetual Peace'.

Numbers fluctuated, but there were about twenty-five major secular principalities and an additional ninety archbishoprics, bishoprics and abbeys, along with around a hundred counts, who attended the second chamber. Clerical representation reflected the fact that about 16 per cent of the Reich was ruled by prince-bishops and archbishops whose dioceses extended even further than their principalities, creating disputes with neighbouring jurisdictions. The third chamber brought together the representatives of about sixty-five imperial cities, varying in size from the impressively large (Cologne) to the tiny (Dinkelsbühl – under 5,000 inhabitants). By 1500, the procedures for a Diet had become standardized. During the opening session, the imperial 'proposition' was read out, constituting the agenda for the Estates. The Estates then met separately and, if they agreed on a recommendation, it was transmitted to the emperor. When the Diet was completed, its conclusions (and the emperor's consent to them) were published as a Recess. Each Recess constituted imperial law. Among others with rights to be represented at the Diets were the imperial knights, holding fiefs through which they owed their allegiance directly to the emperor. Mainly concentrated in Swabia, Franconia and the upper and middle Rhine, they provided the emperor with a bargaining counter against larger principalities.

The juridical framework distinguished the Reich from the Swiss Confederation. A recent development, it resulted from the movement for imperial reform in the later fifteenth century, part of a broader dynamic by which the constituent elements of the empire defined their relationship with the emperor. The movement bore fruit in the Diets of Worms and Augsburg. The Diets became a more important and recognized body. An Imperial Chamber Court was established, independent of the emperor and his court. Although the emperor had the right to appoint its presiding judge, the Estates nominated ordinary judges. The court took over imperial prerogatives, its remit being to maintain peace and justice and adjudicate disputes between the emperor's vassals. It was implicitly acknowledged that the emperor could, in extraordinary circumstances, revoke laws or deprive corporations of their privileges, using plenary powers. But the prevailing assumption among the lawyers advising German territorial princes and cities was that he was bound by both natural and divine law, and that he had to aim at the common good. In ordinary circumstances, his 'public person' as supreme judge of the empire had been surrendered to the imperial court, which promoted Roman law as the basis for the empire's legal practices. In 1500, a regional structure to enforce the decisions of the imperial court and the Diets was also put in place through the institution of six Circles (regional territorial groupings).

Charles V's election in 1519 set another precedent. As a result of negotiations prior to his election, he agreed a capitulation with the Electors. His prerogatives would be exercised only with the consent of Electors and Diets. He confirmed the rights of the Electors during interregnums and imperial absences. He promised to respect the rights and dignities of all and to enforce the terms of the Perpetual Peace of the empire. Foreign treaties were to be dependent on the consent of the Electors. Charles promised to live in Germany, to appoint only Germans to serve the empire, and never to summon a Diet to meet outside the Reich. He committed himself to negotiate with Rome to reduce the ecclesiastical taxes paid by Germans, and to establish a new imperial governing council, through which to introduce further reforms into the Reich. These promises, to be monitored by Electors and Diets, became a precedent; all subsequent emperors had to subscribe to similar documents. Charles's became one more constraint (in addition to his prolonged absences from German lands), when it came to his handling of the Protestant schism.

So, unlike Switzerland, the German empire was a mature political and juridical entity. Only in the empire did Church and imperial reform intermingle. The *Reformation of Sigismund* was the most popular document to make the link. Drafted in Basel, probably in 1439, it was reprinted nine times before 1522 and imagined a priest-king named Frederick who would head up a reform in which the plain-speaking 'German' folk would vanquish their oppressors and overcome 'Latins' and their subtle ways. Since both Church and imperial reform joined the dynamic in which the empire's elements were defining their relationships with the emperor, so Luther's call for a Reformation had a particular resonance there.

Although not its instigators, the beneficiaries of reform were the princes. The empire's evolution allowed them to present themselves as its primary law-makers and keepers of the peace. At the same time, the number of German noble counts was gradually diminishing as a small group of dynasties among the higher nobility consolidated their lands and titles by inheritance and acquisition, aggregating to themselves the powers of princes. The Landgrave of Hesse is a classic example. In 1518, the fourteen-year-old Philip of Hesse claimed to rule an agglomeration of previously separate counties (Katzenelnbogen, Ziegenhain and others) along with the Hesse principalities (Upper and Lower Hesse) to constitute a haphazardly assembled principality. The process was assisted by agreements with local and regional groups of nobles, towns and ecclesiastical corporations, as well as dynastic compacts which limited the possibilities for the dynastic dispersal of their lands and titles. German princes began to introduce appeal courts into their dominions, thereby reinforcing their sense of being no longer one among many vassals of the empire but rulers of it, by virtue of, and in line with, its emerging political practices.

Even before the Protestant Reformation, princes and imperial cities attempted to strengthen their control over monasteries and dioceses within their spheres of influence. In Switzerland too, the cantonal city of Zürich chose the clergy, promoted reform in monasteries, controlled what the laity gave the Church, and used their sponsorship of sermons at Advent and Lent as a way of controlling who preached what. Princes equally challenged episcopal and papal authority in their lands. Duke George of Albertine Saxony, for example, pressured the clergy in the diocese of Meissen into submission to his influence. Margrave Albrecht

Achilles of Brandenburg enforced his rights to tax the dioceses in his domains. Landgrave Philip of Hesse sought to remove the remaining jurisdictional authority of the archbishopric of Mainz in his lands. At the Diet of 1511, German princes allied with the French king, Louis XII, to call for Church reform. For his part, the emperor, seeking to neutralize the criticism, put himself at the head of reforming endeavours in both Church and empire. At the Diet of Augsburg in 1518, Emperor Maximilian I led the opposition to the demand from Rome for an imperial levy to fund the war in Hungary against the Infidel on the grounds that it could be granted only once Church reform had been seriously undertaken. Church reform was thus an active issue in German politics before Luther came on the scene.

CHRISTENDOM'S SACRAL LANDSCAPE

Religious experience was essential to the lived reality of Christendom. Nothing is harder, however, than discovering what people really thought about religion. The religion of the laity was very different as between the learned and the unlettered. Such differences were recognized in contemporary debates (intensified by the Reformation) about what constituted superstition and magic. The concerns of the laity were influenced by and overlapped (but did not coincide) with those of the clergy. The latter were a varied order in society, some ('regulars') in monastic communities, others ('seculars') sustaining the parochial and diocesan life of the Church. The evidence for what people believed is as ambiguous as the analytical categories ('popular', 'élite', 'superstition', 'magic', 'holy', 'belief') are crude. When the Franciscans began their missionary work in the New World in the sixteenth century, the gulf between their religious experience and that of the Amerindians was immense. The same cannot be said for the distances separating the unlearned and the lettered, the laity and the clergy in Europe on the eve of the Reformation. Christian Europe had been constructed over centuries on the basis of an interaction between its élites and the rest. That interaction was intensified by the printed word. The variety and density of religious experience were considerable on the eve of the Protestant Reformation.

Lettered contemporaries were aware of it. In 1517, Antonio de Beatis, chaplain and amanuensis to an Italian cardinal, accompanied him on a visit north of the Alps. Arriving in Cologne, he admired the 'infinite number' of reliquaries in the 'large and beautiful cathedral', as well as the unique collection of skulls in the church of St Ursula, the relics of the 11,000 virgins. In the choir of the Franciscan monastery, he venerated the remains of the medieval philosopher John Duns Scotus, while in that of the neighbouring and rival order of the Dominicans he looked through the glass plate under the high altar to see the body of Scotus's antagonist Albert Magnus and was shown the chair from which he had taught. On one of the city's hills, he visited a female canonry where he discovered that, although the canonesses ate and slept in the convent, by day they walked the streets in pairs. Beatis compared what he saw with his native Italy: 'They pay such attention to divine worship and their churches, and build so many new ones, that when I think of the state of religion that obtains in Italy . . . I feel no little envy of this region and I am pained to the heart by the scant devotion of us Italians.'

Beatis found that what was 'holy' in the Rhineland was different from what was 'holy' in his native Naples. That variety appears in other evidence. Testamentary bequests recorded what people chose to will from their estates as pious bequests. An abundance of images, murals, altarpieces and carvings from the period prior to the Reformation is preserved. There is a good deal known about the popularity of religious shrines and the significance of pilgrimage. Historians can say something about the meaning of religion as framing the pattern of people's lives. Yet the variety of what was regarded as holy makes it difficult to evaluate what religion meant on the eve of the Reformation.

People bought religious literature in large quantities. The inventory of a bookseller in Amiens from 1509 furnishes some idea of what was popular. It included forty-one different titles and 1,240 volumes, of which religious works constituted the overwhelming majority. Among the most numerous were manuals to assist in domestic prayer: almost 800 copies of books of hours, including 300 alone in large print format for children. There were also Psalters (editions of the Psalms), Mass books and postils (commentaries on the Bible readings, Sunday by Sunday), books of religious instruction (the antecedents of catechisms), pamphlets expounding the Ten Commandments, the virtues or the sacraments. Finally, there were volumes devoted to the lives of the saints, the most popular being Jacques de Voragine's *The Golden Legend*. But this evidence indicates only what (literate) people were expected to read, and what was saleable. Many of the books on the shelves in Amiens were in Latin. Such literature does not tell us how readers understood what they read, nor how they integrated it into their experience.

The bedrock of the Church was the parish. Parishes covered the length and breadth of western Christianity. That was where the vast majority of the population attended Mass, made their offerings, confessed and took communion once a year. Parochial Christianity, however, was more than a religious experience. It was a set of rights to benefices which were the key to monopoly revenues (the tithe, collected in various forms) in which patrons, collators and clergymen all had interests. And behind every parish church lay wardens who cared for the fabric of the church, managed the parish chest and organized the patronal feast. In the urban world, the role of the parish in local life was perhaps not as great as it once was, but wills attest to an attachment to the church where one was baptized, and where often one's ancestors were buried. The parish represented a given, the place of religious duty, but not necessarily devotion. The incumbent vicar of a small parish outside Mainz on the eve of the Reformation explained that nine out of ten of his flock did not confess their sins and therefore did not receive Christ's body at Easter.

Diocesan visitations took place from time to time in the pre-Reformation Church and kept an eye on non-observance. They also noted clerical absenteeism (widespread, sometimes for justifiable reasons – such as undertaking diocesan duties) and, where it was brought to their attention by locals, clerical incontinence and incompetence. Both the latter, however, were less marked in surviving visitations before the Reformation than one might suppose from later Protestant critique. The reality was that, at least in rural Europe, zealous, chaste and over-educated parish clergy would probably have been regarded with suspicion. The priest's role was more that of a notable, settling family quarrels, drafting wills and providing rural credit. Locals wanted someone who would understand them.

Unlike parishes, laymen chose the confraternities – lay brotherhoods, devoted to religious and charitable service – to which they belonged. These were increasing on the eve of the Reformation and contributed to the variety of local religious experience. In Normandy, for example, confraternal 'charities' were, for some reason, far more in evidence in the dioceses of Lisieux and Évreux than in the coastal bishoprics of

Avranches, Coutances or Bayeux. They were more an urban than a rural phenomenon. Although there was no correlation between them and craft guilds, the two often blended together so that, to take just one example, at Rouen, a city with something like 40,000 inhabitants on the eve of the Reformation, there were some 131 confraternities, many of them reflecting the city's artisan trades.

The social diversity of these organizations was as varied as their role. In a few places, beggars had their own confraternity, although more typically the pattern was of social diversity in which an unofficial hierarchy of leading figures in a community acted as syndics and treasurers. Besides supporting their members in times of hardship, confraternities saw to the burial of their number and prayed for the release of their souls from Purgatory. The maintenance of confraternal side-altars, anniversary Masses and the lighting of votive candles – these were common denominators of confraternal religious experience on the eve of the Reformation. Their hymns, mystery plays, flagellant processions (the *battuti* of northern Italy) and penitential rituals were part of a flamboyance in which it is hard to imagine that an experience of religion of some sort was not present for almost all people, either regularly or episodically.

The diocesan rites, litanies and saints' days reveal the same diversity. Contemporary concerns about superstition (crudely, the manipulation of holy power for secular purposes) are readily comprehensible. Was the Christian message being lost amid the rich texture of ritual and the lush sacral landscape? What, for example, did the people of the Louron valley in the Pyrenees make of the frescoes inside and outside their churches? Painted by unknown craftsmen, they can be dated only to sometime on the eve of the Reformation. The murals offered a glimpse of the Church's answers to the questions: How are we saved? Who is saved? At the chapel of Mont, worshippers passed a fresco of the Last Judgment as they entered the church. Christ is portrayed in majesty at the end of the world like a judge, sitting in a tribunal over the world, accompanied by advocates and the scales of justice (the Devil is trying to tip them his way). The angels are blowing their bugles to awake the dead for judgment from Purgatory. The Devil, pictured as a monster, is ready to receive those sinners who are convicted to the flames of Hell. The good people of Mont, however, could take heart: Heaven is full and Hell is empty. This was, after all, an image for them on their way to and from church, and its responsibility was to save sinners. Across the valley, another chapel had the tree of Jesse painted in the chancel, a reminder of the ancestry of sacred ministry. Such images were the 'Bibles for the poor', medieval Christianity's justification for religious art. But whether, and how, these images were understood by local inhabitants is another matter.

Theologians, whose business it was, debated how salvation worked – to what degree, if any, we human beings could contribute to it ourselves. Preachers and confessors were more inclined to dramatize it, just as the Louron murals did. Image-makers, printers and preachers found death and the prospect of judgement merchandisable commodities, leaving behind the sense (probably overdrawn) that salvation was an overwhelming preoccupation of Christians. Preachers also emphasized the importance of human responsibility, our role in our own salvation. Like the Louron murals, sermons created a vivid impression of what the pains of Purgatory and Hell were like. But they also showed how suffering could be attenuated by penitence and intercession.

The Church was the primary place where such penitence was efficacious. Christ had power to forgive sins and he had passed it on to the pope for the Church to dispense. The Eucharist offered absolution for sins committed by the living and advocacy for the souls of the dead. Requiem Masses for the souls of the dead were requested plentifully. Wills show that these were becoming commodified, the more you could afford being a better guarantee of salvation. Pilgrimages to the great sanctuaries of Christendom, including the voyage to the Holy Land, were popular, but regional shrines could offer something of the same penitential status. The popularity of such shrines is attested by the elaborateness of *ex-voto* offerings from the faithful. The issuing by the papacy of rights to such pardons in the form of purchasable letters of indulgence to fund the building of hospitals, churches, even (in the Netherlands) dykes, was an extension of plenary remittance. The letters required the penitent to undertake some personal act of contrition and, in return, offered a promise of participating in the benefits of the charitable works that the sponsored institution would eventually provide to others. Such penitential processes tended to increase on the eve of the Reformation, and not merely for the self-serving and mercenary reasons ascribed by Protestants. There is no sign that the coming of the Reformation can be explained by the 'abuses' of the Church. All the evidence (construction, donations, pilgrimages, elaborate triptych altarpieces) is that it was flourishing. And the diversity of ritual and experience was held in an embrace of orthodoxy by a Church that claimed a monopoly on truth and salvation. Martin Luther's claims to a different truth and way to salvation changed that.

LUTHER'S WAY

'For the beginning was ful small, and in manner to be contemned, and one man alone sustained the malice and violence of the whole world.' This was how Johannes Philippson von Schleiden (Sleidan) pictured the early years of the Protestant Reformation in the preface to his *Commentaries* (1555), its first historian. He experienced the excitement of the new religious movement. As a Strasbourg lawyer and diplomat, he witnessed the Schmalkaldic War (1546–7), a conflict between its political protectors and the emperor, which, struggling to be impartial, he interpreted as God's providence humbling an emperor through the agency of Luther. The latter's critics saw him as an evil force, tearing Christendom apart. Sleidan read the life of Luther by one of them, Johannes Cochlaeus. In it, the author – an eye-witness to Luther's appearance at the Diet of Worms in 1521 – depicted him as in league with the Devil, driven by carnal lust and an insatiable desire to topple authority. Both sides propagated the myth that the Protestant Reformation had begun with an obscure monk in Saxony. The Protestant Reformation was not, however, a one-man show. If there had been no Martin Luther, the powerful currents for religious change would have found their catalysts – they had already begun to do so in the Rhineland and Switzerland by the time of Luther's appearance at Worms. But without Luther as the super-catalyst it would not have been the Protestant Reformation.

Luther himself was ambivalent about the dramatic events of his life. On the one hand, his contribution was modest: 'I simply taught, preached, wrote ... otherwise I did nothing ... The Word did it all.' There were no strange portents in the sky or miracles of healing, and Protestant myth-makers had to create those after his death. His birthplace was twice saved from fire in the sixteenth century, a 'great sign'. A painting of him turned out to be 'incombustible' during the Thirty Years War. Luther was, however, tempted to see himself as the particular vehicle for God's strange work. In 1531, he quoted the heretic Jan Hus, facing execution ('I might be a weak goose [in Czech, Hus = goose], but more powerful birds will come after me') and adapted the words to himself; 'they may have cooked a goose in 1415 but, a century later, it has turned into a swan'. At Luther's funeral, Johann Bugenhagen repeated the allusion, reminding Catholic opponents that Luther had died in his bed: 'You may cook a goose, but in a hundred years' time there will come a man you will not be able to roast.' His point was that God's truth could not be smothered. Looking back, drifting from memory to anecdote, Luther furnished glimpses of how he thought it had come about, but it is like looking at sepia photographs from long ago. Here is Luther in July 1505, paralysed by a near-death experience in a thunderstorm, making a vow to St Anne that he would become a monk if he survived. There is the image of Luther's 'eureka moment', a theological breakthrough while at work in his study on the third floor of a tower on the city wall, the latrine nearby – Luther's famous 'Tower Experience' (*Das Turmerlebnis*). We cannot date that one, and perhaps the photograph is not what we think it is. What Luther discovered, when, and how significant it was, is an industry of its own.

For that reason, the story is well-known and, in some respects, unremarkable. Luther was no different from many clerics of his day: a bright boy from a modest background, the kind that kept the Church going. He called himself a peasant, but that should be glossed, for his father (Hans) was a miner and married the daughter of a local notable from Eisleben. Luther graduated from Erfurt University in 1505 and made his vows to become a monk in the Order of the Hermits of St Augustine that same year, despite his father's opposition. In 1508, he began lecturing in moral philosophy at the recently founded University of Wittenberg. In 1512, he was awarded his doctorate and became professor of biblical theology, its town preacher two years later. In 1525, he was one of the last of the monks to leave his old monastery, marrying a former nun, by whom he fathered six children. Wittenberg was where the Reformation happened.

Luther becomes interesting only when he writes. His publications began in 1516 with an edition of sermons, written two centuries previously (he attributed them to the German mystic Johann Tauler), on how to be in communion with God and live a good life. It was known as the *German Theology*. Luther's preface praised the work, which would have an impact on those who wanted to take the Protestant Reformation further and faster than he did. Research papers followed in 1517: the *Disputation against Scholastic Theology* (August) and the *Ninety-Five Theses, or Disputation on the Power and Efficacy of Indulgences* (October) – the latter having a fair claim to being the shortest and most explosive academic article ever written. A century later, it was commemorated by a procession culminating at the castle church in Wittenberg. An anniversary engraving in 1617 shows Luther with a quill pen inscribing his theses on the door of the church. The nib is depicted going straight through Pope Leo X, in one ear and out of the other, and knocking off his tiara. Words, it implied, had deadly truth, the power to overturn thrones.

That, roughly speaking, was the story. In April 1518, Luther's Heidelberg Disputations, presented before the chapter of his order, won him a following in the Rhineland. His published sermons began – those on Indulgences (more popular than the *Ninety-Five Theses*), on Christ's Passion, on Death, on Work and on Marriage all appeared before 1520, the year when Luther defined what he stood for. Works poured out – something every two weeks, according to one calculation. The Reformation began as an academic and literary event.

A map of Wittenberg in 1546, the year of Luther's death, depicts a walled town with about ten streets and three gates. It was small, and almost everything on the map had been newly founded or rebuilt. At the South Gate stood the largest house in town, constructed in 1512 for the court artist and pharmacist Lucas Cranach. To the West Gate was the castle which holds the key to what made Wittenberg significant. In 1485, Saxony had been divided between two brothers – Ernst and Albrecht. 'Ernestine Saxony' retained the right as the Elector to vote at imperial Diets but lost the best bits (Leipzig, its university and castle) to Duke Albrecht. Ernst's son Frederick the Wise ruled Electoral Saxony from 1486, and made Wittenberg his capital. He demolished the old castle and built a new one, including a library. The latter was supervised by Georg Spalatin, court chaplain and tutor to the Elector's children, an intermediary between the Elector and the university.

The castle also had a new church, complete with a collection of relics. It dominated the town when it was completed in 1505. Frederick wanted to put his capital on the map. Turning it into a centre for devotion, learning and pilgrimage was a good way to do so. Part of that strategy involved establishing a new university to rival Leipzig's. It opened its doors in 1502 and Frederick's childhood friend and kinsman Johann von Staupitz was appointed dean of the theological faculty. The following year, Staupitz became vicar-general of Luther's monastic house. It was new too, for the Augustinians had arrived only in 1502. Wittenberg was neither big enough nor old enough to have much by way of vested interests. Luther would be able to appoint like-minded faculty colleagues and, with the Elector's backing, fashion its religious life as he thought best.

That new monastery was the point of departure for Luther's spiritual journey. The monastic rule that he had entered, the sermons that he heard, the theology that he read, all taught that man was a sinner who needed redemption. How that redemption worked was discussed in abstractions among theologians who were divided into various 'ways of thought' (*viae*), partly reflecting their philosophical standpoint. Sins came in all shapes and sizes, but it was generally agreed that there were seven deadly ones. These went back to Adam's disobedience. Humankind was the inheritor of that 'original' sin, and unable to 'satisfy' God's righteous anger.

Fortunately God, whose power is absolute, was willing to commit himself (as the theologians of the *Via Moderna* saw it) to a covenant to bestow grace upon human beings, and limit his power within established channels. His ultimate covenant was to send his son, Jesus Christ, into the world, who, because he was both man and the son of God, could offer the necessary satisfaction on our behalf. That grace remained available through the channel of the Church, and the sacraments, particularly baptism, the Eucharist and penance. Together, these offered the Christian congruent merit which worked alongside his own penitence, though whether attrition, a fear of the consequences of sin, was worth much in God's eyes, or whether (in time) it might lead to contrition (true penitence), and whether perfect contrition could ever exist were matters of debate. Habitual grace was, they all agreed, a supernatural gift which, when received into the soul, united the Christian with Christ, put things right with God, and taught him a new 'habit', or disposition to be a virtuous human being. Such grace was sufficient because it gave him the power to obey God, but it was not automatically efficacious since that depended on its being put into practice in his life, by doing 'what lies within his powers'. To enjoy a state of grace involved a perpetual effort, one in which penance, self-denial and self-sacrifice were the key. Detachment from the world's temptations, accompanied by monastic vows, was a good start on that long road. The Augustinian Hermits in Wittenberg took it seriously.

Luther, by his own account, was a good monk. But it did not work. In 1518, Luther described his temptations (*Anfechtungen*), dark nights of the soul 'so intense, so infernal, that no language, no pen, could possibly delineate them'. In 1533, he recalled how his mother had dealt with being pestered by a neighbouring witch. On other occasions, he describes how he was visited by the Devil in the monastery. Luther's responses were often scatological: 'But, if that is not enough for you, Devil, I have also shit and pissed; wipe your mouth on that and take a hearty bite.' In a sermon before the chapter of the Augustinian Order in May 1515, Luther's theme was that of slander and backbiting, a problem in monastic life. 'A slanderer,' he said, 'does nothing but ruminate among the shit of others ... That is why his droppings stink most, surpassed only by the Devil's.' The Devil, in other words, was in the monastery, in our mouths, everywhere. Each glimpse of Luther's earlier life seems a calculated reminder that salvation was not an academic matter, but a question of flesh and blood, life and death.

In Luther's various accounts, remembered in a way that confuses past and present, Staupitz, the Superior of his order and (it would seem) his spiritual director, pointed the way forward. In one encounter, Luther records him saying that when he was tempted to dwell too much on God's righteousness, he should instead think about the wounds of Christ, focus on the Man of Sorrows. It was Staupitz who taught Luther to think of repentance in terms of a relationship with a merciful God, rather than as a state of being judged by an omnipotent one. The point was not to discover how we are saved. We already were. The question was how, in that relationship, we trusted God.

Luther reacted selectively and comparatively to what he read. Traces of what he had been taught reappeared in unexpected guises as his thinking evolved. He became convinced that the only worthwhile theology was one that could make sense of the world and its complexity. In the process, scholastic theology was dispensed with. By 1517, Luther was an outspoken critic of its empty categories. Yet some of its influence remained with him, especially the *Via Moderna* emphasis on the dichotomy between the sovereignty of God and the sinfulness of man.

Dichotomies remained essential in Luther's thought, often expressed as word-pairs, paradoxes through which one should understand the ways in which humans relate to one another and towards God. In those relationships, always dynamic, we are contradictory bundles of potentials and desires, free and bound at the same time, sinners and forgiven of our sins, capable of the uttermost depravity but (through God's grace) able to go on loving and be loved. Luther's paradoxes perplexed his contemporaries; Erasmus said he would not go to the stake for any of them.

In the place of scholastic thinking came an intensive reading of the Bible, an investment in learning Greek and Hebrew, and the purchase of Erasmus's 1516 edition of the New Testament. Luther concentrated on the Pauline epistles in the New Testament and the Psalms in the Old Testament, using the commentary techniques that were the current method of lecturing to students to clarify his reading of the essential meaning of the text in question. In the process, something happened to his idea of what God was saying. Human speech-acts were not up to much. True, they were the basis of society (oaths, promises, pardons) and embraced the important things in life. Yet we say things and do not mean them. We promise them and do not carry them out. The Bible, however, contained God's promises and he is totally trustworthy. We do not have to hold the text this way or that, elaborate on it, turn it into a law or create a metaphysic around it. The sign is the reality, and God is simply ready and waiting for the faith which acknowledges that. With that faith, said Luther, you have something stronger than any piece of paper, any letter of pardon, any intellectually constructed paradigm. You can hold that promise up to God, no matter what happens. The 'Indulgences Affair' and what followed turned this insight into something much sharper-edged and destructive: 'Scripture alone' (*sola Scriptura*), the assertion that Scripture is the bedrock test for what constitutes God's truth.

Luther found the essence in a text from St Paul's Epistle to the Romans, ch. 1, v. 17 (itself referring back to the Old Testament): 'For therein is the justice of God revealed from faith to faith; as it is written, The just shall live by faith.' In his preface to the Latin edition of his complete works, published in 1545, Luther said that it was only when he began to lecture on the Psalms for a second round in 1519 that he construed what this passage meant; that God's righteousness was not that of a judge dispensing justice to sinners but that of a merciful father who preferred equity to justice, who wants faith alone, and wants us to live spiritually in return. 'I felt myself absolutely reborn,' he wrote, 'as though I had entered into the open gates of paradise itself.' But that was in 1519, two years into the Indulgences Affair. Had he, as many Luther scholars surmise, come to it much earlier, perhaps in 1513, when he first started lecturing, or in 1515, when he first tackled Romans?

Luther's lecture notes take us only so far in unravelling this puzzle. We can see what he chose to comment on, and who he was reading: St Bernard of Clairvaux, Jean Gerson, Gabriel Biel, Johann Tauler, Augustine of Hippo. The latter was of singular importance, the fourth-century theologian who had done most to convince the Christian Church that human beings after the Fall were not worth saving and that God's decision as to who should be redeemed was (to us humans) entirely arbitrary. He would save those whom he chose, making use of whatever slight capacity we might have to turn towards him, gradually transforming us by his grace. For some theologians, Luther's way was merely that of Augustinianism reborn – and, since Augustine had never been neglected in the Middle Ages, Luther's novelty becomes a damp squib. But in practice Luther taught something different. We are saved, he said, by Christ's righteousness. Only faith (*sola fide*), itself a gift from God, can take hold of this righteousness. That faith comes to us in an instant, not little by little. Through it, we are in a dynamic relationship with God. It is, said Luther in 1522, a 'divine work' in us.

Only perhaps quite late on, after the initial attacks on him in the Indulgences Affair, did Luther's new thinking take full shape in his mind. He called it his 'theology of the cross' and he expounded it at the meeting of the Augustinian Order in Heidelberg in April 1518, among his own brethren. One Dominican who heard him, Martin Bucer (whose subsequent contribution as a reformer in the Rhineland and England was considerable), was transfixed by what Luther said. 'A theology of glory calls evil good and good evil. A theology of the cross calls the thing what it actually is.' He went on to explain that a God of revelation tells us from on high how to behave and what to do. That is the theology of glory and it inevitably defines 'goodness' by what God says we should do and say. By contrast, a loving God is one who becomes weak and foolish to save people, present in the world, but 'hidden in suffering'. On another occasion, he expounded Exodus Ch. 33 where Moses seeks the glory of the Lord, but sees only his backside. For Luther, that is the point. No one can see God face to face and live, so God reveals himself in the most unlikely ways and places. He is hidden, but active in all the messiness of our lives. Luther re-routed theology away from the university and study and towards the hospital, the bedroom, the workplace. He said that we were all our own theologians ('the priesthood of all creation'). If that had been carried through, the Reformation would have changed Christianity out of all recognition.

BATTLES OF THE BOOKS

Luther's visit to Heidelberg was his first direct contact with the literate world of the Rhineland humanists. That world served as an echo-chamber for the 'Luther Affair'. While Luther was finding the Gospel in his way at Wittenberg, a community of Bible scholars was finding it in theirs. The centres were in Basel, Zürich and Strasbourg. Basel was the great university city where Erasmus completed work on his New Testament in 1515, the year Wolfgang Capito became cathedral preacher, professor and Erasmus's assistant. Also in 1515, Johannes Oecolampadius (the Greek for 'little lamp', his original name in German being Johannes Huszgen) arrived in Basel at the invitation of Erasmus's printer, Johann Froben. Oecolampadius helped Erasmus finish the notes and commentary to his New Testament. At around the same time, Huldrych Zwingli visited Basel to meet that 'most learned of all scholars' (Erasmus), purchasing the New Testament and settling down to learn Greek to master it. Four years later, Zwingli would mount the pulpit at the Great Minster of Zürich, capital of the large, easterly Swiss canton. Eight years on, Capito took up his post as provost of the collegiate church of St Thomas in Strasbourg, being joined there by Martin Bucer, Caspar Hedio – another Basel graduate – and Matthias Zell. These were the movers and shakers of the upper Rhineland Reformation.

Erasmus's *New Testament* became three volumes in one. He had begun with the idea of an aid to help with Bible-reading in the form of scholarly notes. He hated the old commentaries, wanting instead to have notes that took one back to what the words actually meant. As he wrote, however, he realized that the Vulgate Latin translation was not up to the mark. He needed to provide a new one to explain the notes.

But then, in order to justify his own translation, he had to give the Greek original. The eventual volume was little short of 1,000 pages in length. Three volumes needed three prefaces. The first was an 'encouragement to the devout reader'. Within the pages of this book, said Erasmus, lay Christian truth, 'the philosophy of Christ'. You did not need to be a professor or a theologian to discover it; you simply had to be a receptive, pious reader (who knew Latin and Greek . . .). How you did that was the subject of the second preface ('On Method'). It was a matter of being in the right frame of mind and aware of the communicative power of language. The third preface was an 'Apology', anticipating his critics. Finding the Vulgate wrong in over a thousand places, he expected an avalanche of criticism, so he dedicated his work to Pope Leo X to secure protection in high places.

The onslaught duly happened, not least because Erasmus had worked fast. A rival edition had been published in Spain at Alcalá for Cardinal Cisneros, archbishop of Toledo, in January 1514, and Froben hoped to steal a march on it by securing an imperial privilege for Erasmus's version. Meanwhile, another battle of the books also raged in the Rhineland. The scholar at its heart was Johann Reuchlin, known as 'Capnion' (the Greek for 'puff of smoke', or *Reuchlein*). Reuchlin had less of the wit, and none of the presentational flair, of Erasmus, but he had linguistic and philological skills. By 1515, he was northern Europe's leading Hebrew scholar.

Reuchlin was working on a great treatise on the Kabbalah (*De arte cabbalistica*) that came out in 1517. That was when he was not fending off critics. Prominent among the latter was a Jew from Nuremberg who had converted and been baptized a Christian at Cologne in 1504: Johannes Pfefferkorn. He made his name with anti-Semitic publications, beginning with *The Mirror of the Jews*. The accusations were familiar and nasty (ritual slaughter, child murder, obstinate heresy), and campaigns against Jews had begun to have an impact in Germany. Jews had been expelled from Austria in 1469 and from Nuremberg in 1498, and were menaced in Bavaria, from where they were expelled in 1519. The resulting displaced Jewish communities created racial and religious tensions which Pfefferkorn's 'mirror' reflected and magnified. In 1509, Pfefferkorn campaigned to confiscate Jewish books, and Reuchlin prepared a report the following year that dismissed both the legality and the substance of the case. He became a marked man, his work condemned by theologians at Cologne and Paris, his writings banned by the emperor and burned in public, he himself forced to appear before the Inquisition at Mainz. In 1515, his case was pending an appeal to Rome when Ulrich von Hutten's *Letters of Obscure Men* appeared. Under the guise of letters written in dog-Latin by invented nonentities to one of Pfefferkorn's supporters, Hutten (and friends – it was a group effort) made fun of Reuchlin's enemies, rubbished old-fashioned lecturers and monks, and painted a ribald picture of the papal court and its exploitation of the Germans. The literate world queued up to enjoy the controversy and to take sides. The 'Reuchlin Affair' was an opening skirmish in a larger battle of the books which turned into the beginnings of the Protestant Reformation.

THE LUTHER AFFAIR

Luther's insights might have remained just that. That they did not do so was one of the unintended consequences of what happened between 1517 and 1521. The Luther Affair has been called 'an accidental revolution' but it was an accident waiting to happen. The issue on which it began – indulgences – was not new. In this instance, the good cause in question was the rebuilding of St Peter's Basilica in Rome. It had been begun seven decades ago and was unfinished. Pope Leo X recognized the power of a symbol (and a symbol of power) and put his stamp on the project. He turned to indulgences to finance it. But the receipts came in slowly, and some rulers blocked the initiative.

In the case of the young Hohenzollern Albrecht of Brandenburg, things were different. At the age of twenty-three, he was nominated archbishop of Mainz, prince-archbishop of Magdeburg and acting bishop of Halberstadt, making him an Elector of the empire, its Arch-Chancellor and a prince in his own right. But he needed a papal dispensation for which Rome charged a fee. Here was the basis of a deal. Albrecht agreed to take charge of the sale of the indulgences in Germany for eight years, half of the proceeds going to fund the reconstruction of St Peter's and the other half to the merchants who loaned Albrecht the money for his dispensation. The operation was entrusted to a Dominican, Johann Tetzel, who had fifteen years of experience in the salvation-marketing business. Electoral Saxony, however, was one of the places where indulgence-selling was forbidden, and the Hohenzollerns were no friends of the Wettins, the house of the Saxon Elector. But Tetzel preached at Jüterborg, just over the Saxon frontier, and attracted a popular hearing.

Luther's response was to write a letter to his archbishop – Albrecht of Brandenburg – enclosing the *Ninety-Five Theses*, short and provocative, on what he saw as the abuse of indulgences. Whether the theses were ever pinned to the door of Wittenberg cathedral on 31 October 1517, as Melanchthon asserted in his funeral sermon for Luther, is a matter of doubt. Luther did not want to cause the Elector of Saxony political embarrassment, and they were not intended as a clarion call to Germany. Albrecht did what was expected of him: he sent them to the University of Mainz for examination, and forwarded them to Rome. Meanwhile, a copy was printed without Luther's authorization and translated into German. The Dominicans and others leapt to Tetzel's defence. The result was another battle of the books.

For Luther the issues were about grace and salvation. For his opponents, they were about papal authority. Books and pamphlets invited educated opinion in Germany to take sides. Opinions on Church reform ran high in advance of the 1518 Augsburg Diet. In Rome, Pope Leo X could have sat it out. But the *Letters of Obscure Men* (condemned to be burned by a papal bull in 1517), and Erasmus's withering denunciation of the warrior Pope Leo in his *Complaint of Peace*, published in Strasbourg that same year, were disturbingly personal. The *Letters* were published anonymously and Erasmus had friends in high places. They, for the present, were untouchable. Luther, on the other hand, was an obscure Augustinian monk in Saxony. Elector Frederick could surely be won over. Saxony was not that far from Prague, where the scars of Hussite heresy had still not healed. Why not make Luther into an example, a shot across the bows to others about the reality of papal authority? So the heresy process, launched against Luther by the Dominicans, was geared up, and he was summoned to Rome in August 1518.

Leo X was not entirely wrong. But he neglected two interlinked elements that proved critical. He underestimated Elector Frederick's determination to protect Luther, and he misinterpreted the gathering movement in Luther's favour. Behind Frederick's obstinacy lay a prince with a sense of his responsibility as an Elector of the German empire. In addition, in January 1519, the balance of political forces in Germany

changed with the death of Emperor Maximilian I. In the electoral campaign that followed, Frederick's vote, one of seven, was critical. Wanting
to back neither of the two front-runners (Francis I and Charles V), the
papacy initially put its weight behind an indigenous candidate: Frederick himself. The heresy process against Luther was suspended – a crucial
period for the emergence of a wider basis of support for him.

Lutheran solidarity lay initially in predictable places – Wittenberg
University and the brethren of his order, spoiling for a fight with the
Dominicans. But solidarity also emerged from less likely quarters –
among the independent knights of the empire, for example, one of
whom offered to raise an army in support of the Luther cause. It
coalesced, too, among the educated opinion that had lined up behind
Reuchlin. German resentment at the cultural arrogance and exploitation of Italians was a case which made itself, unlike one that defended
the privileges and culture of the Jews. Hutten, who was initially inclined
to dismiss the Indulgences Affair as a squabble, understood in the wake
of Luther's disputation with Eck at Leipzig in July 1519 that it furnished
an occasion to throw mud at a Church which failed to reform. At the
Diet of Augsburg (August 1518) the papal envoy, Tommaso de Vio (Cardinal Cajetan), general of the Dominican Order, struggled against the
rising tide. By the next Diet (Worms, April 1521), his successor was sub-
merged: 'All Germany is in open revolt. Nine-tenths cry out "Luther!"
And the remaining tenth ... cry "Death to the Roman Curia!"'

Luther never underestimated his opponents. Their skill was to shift
the terms of the debate away from salvation and towards authority.
First with Cajetan at Augsburg, and then with Johann Eck, Luther had
to confront issues which had not been his preoccupations up to that
date. Eck was vice-chancellor of Ingolstadt University and at the height
of his powers. In yet another controversy (Eck's *Obelisks* versus Luther's
Asterisks), and then in debate at Leipzig in July 1519, Luther found
himself fighting on a much broader terrain, rejecting the claims implicit
in canon law that the bishop of Rome was head of the Church by divine
right, asserting that councils of the Church could, and had, made mis-
takes, and accepting that many of the beliefs of Hus were 'most Christian
and evangelical'. In place of councils, canon law and church fathers, he
asserted the primacy of Scripture over all other forms of authority.

Luther's *annus mirabilis* was 1520. 'The time for silence is over and
the time for speech has come,' he wrote in his *Address to the Christian*

Nobility of the German Nation, one of three famous manifestos of that year. For the first time he addressed the broader political question of Church and imperial reform as conceived at the German Diets. Through the German nobility he appealed to the new emperor himself, that they should 'do their Christian duty and defend the Church against the Pope and see to it that a general council was summoned to reform the Church and the Christian estate'. At the same time he appealed to a 'nation' that was more than the nobility to liberate Germany from Rome's tyranny and create a true godly order. In *The Freedom of a Christian*, Luther's message was that reform and reconciliation with the Roman Church were no longer important. What mattered was how the Christian, unable to earn merit through good works, could lead a Christian life. Luther's answer was in a paradox. We were both free and unfree. We were already free from 'clerical tyranny ... the ecclesiastical prison' because we were in a direct relationship with God. Our bondage was that this freedom came with responsibilities as a Christian to carry out God's love in the world. For the present, Luther sidestepped what this might mean for our obedience to rulers and the Church.

By the time of the publication of *The Freedom of a Christian*, Luther's reconciliation with the Roman Church was a lost cause. His writings had been condemned by universities in Cologne and Louvain. The papal bull (*Exsurge Domine*) threatening him (and Hutten) with excommunication unless they recanted was issued on 15 June 1520. Luther burned it along with an assortment of books by his opponents, a reply to a parallel burning of his own books at Leipzig. The scene was set for the 'secular arm' to apply the bull at the imperial Diet of Worms, where Luther was summoned to appear. Imperial advisers sought ways of preventing the Luther Affair from dominating the discussions of Church reform. The Estates refused to contemplate the imposition of a papal ban in German lands before the individuals affected had a chance to be heard and to answer the charges. Neither side got what they wanted, although in the eventual compromise the implication was that it was for the German Diet to determine how problems affecting the Church and doctrine in Germany should be handled. Luther was given imperial protection to travel to Worms – a journey which turned into a triumphant cavalcade. Before the young Emperor Charles V in person, Luther's books were stacked up, their titles read out. Luther was invited to acknowledge them, and whether he stood by the views expressed in them. In his reply he divided them into three categories. His works on faith and morals were acknowledged even by his enemies. To renounce those would be to renounce Christendom itself. Those on the evils of the Church and the corruption of the papacy concerned how Christendom was governed. To deny them would be to deny any remedy to Christendom itself. Only in the case of the third category, polemics directed at his critics, did he concede that he might have written with more charity. Urged to give a plain answer, his response was that he would not recant unless proved wrong by Scripture, because his conscience was 'captive to the word of God'. Printed versions of his statement added the evocative words: 'Here I stand, I can do no other.'

THE PROCESSES OF REFORMATION

The Reformation began in German and Swiss lands. In the explosive decade of the 1520s it meant different things to different people, spreading through multiple media. It made new alliances across social groups and brought fresh political players into action. The exodus of monks and nuns from monasteries, the controversies raised by clerical marriages, and the polemic against 'priests' whores' (concubines) imbued the early Reformation with a sense of liberation, a sizzling sexual energy which the disturbing nudes of the Wittenberg painter Lucas Cranach, Luther's long-standing friend and supporter, reflected. That the Reformation managed to coalesce around an emerging set of churches and doctrines towards 1530 was an achievement. But it came at a cost. Coherence was achieved by defining a mainstream 'magisterial' Reformation and excluding those who failed to conform. Those tensions led, by the end of the decade, to rifts over how churches should be organized and governed, over the relationship between ecclesiastical and secular authorities, and one large, unbridgeable rift over the Eucharist.

New players emerged in part because those who might have been expected to take a lead in determining what happened did not do so. Charles V left the Reich immediately after the Diet of Worms and returned only a decade later, in 1530. From a distance, his interventions served merely to frustrate the efforts of the German Estates to resolve the differences through a national council of the Church. At the Diet of Worms, Charles nominated his brother Ferdinand as regent of the empire. But

Ferdinand had a complicated relationship with his brother. As co-heir with Charles to the dynastic inheritance of Maximilan I he expected to be granted a substantial inheritance and to be elected king in Bohemia and king of the Romans. But Charles was sensitive to the charge that the Habsburgs were trying to take over the empire by stealth. At Worms, he agreed to settle upon Ferdinand the five Austrian duchies. Then, in February 1522, he ceded to him the Tyrol, the Vorlande in Swabia and the duchy of Württemberg, recently occupied by the Swabian League and governed temporarily by the Habsburgs. The last part of this agreement was kept secret, and when it became public knowledge in 1525, it raised doubts about Habsburg intentions in the Reich. Meanwhile, Ferdinand consolidated his authority in Austria and overcame his brother's reluctance to his election to the Bohemian throne in 1526. The Wittelsbach Duke Wilhelm of Bavaria launched his rival candidature with international support. Ferdinand needed the support of the Electors and the acquiescence of the Estates to win through and he was prepared to shelve the Lutheran problem. Ferdinand inherited parts of Hungary, and thereafter his ability to lead the empire was compromised further by the Ottoman threat.

By the terms of his Capitulation, Charles agreed to set up a Governing Council. This new body was one in which the Estates had a determining part, but it had to collaborate with Ferdinand. That proved difficult. Attempts to carry forward the imperial reform programme by instigating a 'Common Penny' imperial tax to fund military expenditures failed. As the Governing Council faltered so the leadership of the empire fell back upon the Estates. But they were at sixes and sevens over how to respond to the Lutheran Reformation. Even their execution of the Edict of Worms was problematic. Elector Frederick secured an exemption from having to carry it out in his own lands. Only in Habsburg territories, Albertine Saxony, Bavaria and Brunswick was any attempt made to enforce it. The rest simply ignored it. The efforts, spearheaded by a group of imperial cities (Strasbourg, Ulm and Nuremberg), to lay the groundwork for a national council of the Church to meet at Speyer in 1524 collapsed as their own unity dissolved, one of a series of fractures in the German empire of which Lutheranism became both the cause and ultimately the beneficiary.

Among the new players on the political scene, Luther was an ambiguous figure: a non-political national hero. On his journey back from Worms he was taken out of circulation for his own safety by the Saxon

Elector and kept in prison for ten months at the Wartburg castle. The result was an outpouring of writings – on the sacraments, monastic vows, the Psalms and a translation of the New Testament into German. But Luther emerged in 1522 with no desire to put himself at the head of a popular movement or to engage with the imperial cities in their plans for a national council. He optimistically expected the dissemination of the word alone to destroy 'the swarming vermin of the Papal regime'. His main concerns were to encourage Christians to reform their own communities without being hindered by the princes. The latter he despised as 'generally the biggest fools or the worst scoundrels on earth' from whom 'one must constantly expect the worst'.

Yet, without willing it, Luther became a touchstone of Reformation. At the university in Wittenberg, among the officials of the Saxon Elect-orate, the humanists of the Rhineland and in southern German cities, he had supporters. Among the members of his own Augustinian Order, as well as more widely among the preaching clergy, his message vibrated outwards. The processes of the Protestant Reformation are laid out in the printed pamphlets (*Flugschriften*) which accompanied its first decade in German-speaking lands. Produced in handy formats and distributed on a regional basis, they sold into a competitive market. More than half of them were only eight pages long and cost a sixth of the daily wage of an artisan apprentice. Woodcuts were used to illus-trate the title-page on about three quarters of them. The variety of literary forms testified to their being derived from other means of communication – sermons, letters, poems, songs, prayers, complaints and exhortations. Although religious themes predominated, other subjects impinged too – the war against the Turks, the uprising of the commons, miraculous signs and prophecies, interest and usury. Over 10,000 pamphlet titles are known to have been published between 1500 and 1530, but the vast majority of them appeared in the decade between 1517 and 1527, and most of them were evangelical. There were possibly about 3 million pamphlet copies in circulation between 1518 and 1525. For a population of 12 million, that figure sounds mod-est; but in relation to those who could read it was impressive. Despite the impact of the Reformation elsewhere in Europe nowhere experi-enced this intensity of printed output. Only perhaps in Geneva in the 1550s and 60s would printing and the Reformation converge on the same scale.

Pamphlets were not the sole, or even the most important, means of evangelical persuasion. The early evangelical preachers were perhaps the most effective communicators of all. They dramatized the moment, speaking to audiences of this as a 'golden and joyous' time, when the 'gospel has been set free' to 'the whole world', which had previously been 'denied Christ'. God himself was now at work, and the Last Judgment and the Kingdom were close at hand. They recounted their own experience of discovering 'evangelical Christian truth', and invited an active response. The true Church, they implied, lay in the community of the faithful. The Gospel did not belong to the priests. Laymen (and laywomen) were equal to, or even superior to, priests in faith.

Luther offered no Reformation blueprint. His invitation to local Christian congregations to work it out for themselves called other actors into play and, in the evangelical movement of the 1520s, they grafted his message onto their own concerns and objectives. The Reformation in Wittenberg was an early indication of how divisive that could be. With Luther locked away in the Wartburg, the movement lay in the hands of his university colleagues. One of them, Andreas Bodenstein von Karlstadt, intoxicated by his independent reading of St Augustine and then by Luther's charisma abandoned his initial reserve. In December, students and others broke into the parish church, threw out the Mass books and pulled down the altar. They then forced their way into the city council, demanding an end to the Mass. In response Karlstadt inaugurated a 'Christian city of Wittenberg'. He encouraged the monks and nuns to leave their cloisters and, on Boxing Day 1521, announced his own engagement to a fifteen-year-old girl. The Mass should be replaced by something that involved ordinary people. The latter made their presence felt. Contingents of weavers – Luther later dismissed them as 'dreamers' (*Schwärmer*) – made their way to Wittenberg, convinced that, as he had seemed to say, God was on their side. They were unimpressed by the idea that the Eucharist was a miracle. The bread and wine were just symbols ('pictures'). To believe anything else was simply 'idolatry'. On that subject, Karlstadt had incendiary things to say. In *On the Removal of Images* (1522), he denied that images were the books of the poor. He urged his readers to destroy images before they destroyed themselves.

All this happened to Elector Frederick's anger and Luther's consternation. The latter was released from the Wartburg castle and returned to preach a week of sermons. Our world within, he began, is ours, and no one else's. None of us can die for another, and if we set ourselves up as judges over one another, Wittenberg will become another Capernaum. The message of Christian freedom was that we should make what changes were necessary but not constrain people's consciences by forcing the pace. Monks and nuns should leave their communities and marry if their consciences dictated it. The only harm images ever did anyone was in their veneration. God told Moses not to worship them. He did not say: 'tear them down'. The good people of Wittenberg had fallen under malign influence. He rebuked them for being seduced by false prophets.

Defining the issues, pace and authority to undertake change dominated the early Reformation. They were matters which Luther thought should be decided locally. When Leisnig, a town in Electoral Saxony, consulted him in 1523 on how to proceed, he told them to place the church and its parish coffer in the hands of their own community. In 1524, the Franconian village of Wendelstein drafted Church ordinances and read them aloud to their new clergyman, reminding him that he was their 'attendant and servant ... [y]ou shall not order us; it is we shall order you'. At Zwickau, Elector Frederick's 'pearl', his 'little Venice' and the largest town in the Electorate, the process was more confrontational. The town had changed with the discovery of silver on the Schneeberg, sharpening the contrasts between those who took advantage of its new wealth and those who could not. Hermann Muhlfort, the city treasurer, corruptly rode the boom, his accounts reflecting schemes for city hall improvements, street-paving, a new syphilis hospital, and the like. Also arriving in 1520, fresh from Wittenberg as another would-be Lutheran acolyte, was Thomas Müntzer. From the first, his sermons in the little church of Zwickau's wool-weaving district attracted crowds with their anti-papal rhetoric. Then Zwickau's notables grew nervous as violent incidents multiplied. Müntzer was accused of making common cause with 'ordinary louts', his 'drinking companions', who panted for 'murder and blood'. These were the so-called 'Zwickau Prophets', people like Niclas Storch, a weaver from just outside the town. Storch, like Müntzer, taught that Scripture alone did not have the power to instruct people, and that one must be enlightened by the Holy Spirit. Among the residents of 'God's Lane' (part of the weaving district), the Prophets were believed to have twelve apostles and seventy-two disciples. Gradually, by proscribing its leaders and reinforcing the authority of its church, Zwickau's notables regained the upper hand, expelling the radicals.

Karlstadt, Müntzer and Storch took the message of the Holy Spirit elsewhere. Karlstadt went to Orlamünde, south of Jena. There he removed images from the church, refused to baptize children and interpreted the Eucharist as a memorial of Christ's death. In 1524, he published his answer to Luther's Wittenberg sermons in his pamphlet *On Going Slowly*. 'If you see a small child with a sharp knife, you do not say "let him keep it, for brotherly love." You take it from him lest he wound or kill himself.' Immersing himself in the writings of late-medieval mystics, he developed a theology of spiritual regeneration in which the soul must be emptied by abandoning itself to God before being circumcised (metaphorically) and transformed into a new man and spiritual rebirth through the Holy Spirit. Baptism and the Eucharist were signs of that regeneration having taken place. Small children could not possibly experience such a rebirth, so infant baptism was not only unbiblical but impracticable. The bread and wine were symbols, since no one could be expected to believe that Christ's body was somehow everywhere. Luther retorted that Karlstadt had swallowed the Holy Spirit, feathers and all.

Similar forces were at work in the Swiss cantons of Zürich and Bern. In Zürich, Huldrych Zwingli had a determining role to play; in Bern, the official preacher Berthold Haller was an early Zwinglian enthusiast. With clarity and acumen, Zwingli projected the city and canton of Zürich into the forefront of the Reformation in the 1520s. Zwingli understood 'reformation' to mean not just a change in what went on in Church. It was the reform of the whole community embodied in that Church. The agents of reform were, therefore, those who were responsible for that community: its magistrates. That was embodied in the great public disputation in Zürich town hall on 29 January 1523. On the top table sat the newly elected town councillors, landowners, businessmen, successful craftsmen for the most part. Before them were the sixty-seven Articles, an evangelical 'planning application' as it were, submitted to the town council for discussion and approval. Zwingli was there with his supporters and his books; 600 others packed the room to hear the discussions. Zwingli's opponents were ill-represented and put their case badly. They questioned the authority of the city council to decide such matters, but Zwingli retorted that it was a 'Christian

Assembly', a 'gathering of bishops' – Zwingli's New Testament exegesis insisted that a bishop was an 'overseer'. His propositions swept on to deal with the sacramental issues and rituals. The result was a foregone conclusion. Zwingli's planning application was approved, his sermons authorized, and the clergy of the canton were obliged to conform.

The Zürich Reformation took place in stages and it was not until three years later that the Mass was abolished. But already in a sermon preached in September 1523, Zwingli's friend Leo Jud pointed out that Orthodox and western Christianity numbered the Ten Commandments differently. Orthodox Christianity had followed Judaism in making the 'graven image' commandment separate and more prominent. Western Christianity had softened it by subordinating it to the first command-ment. By the time Jud published his text, Zürich had begun to put this ban on idolatry into practice, including music as a form of aural idol-atry. Zwingli's notion of the Eucharist evolved in tandem with this detachment from all that could be 'embodied' in a sign. In the late sum-mer of 1525 he published a version of a letter originally written by Cornelis Hoen, a jurist and member of the provincial council of Hol-land, in 1521. According to Hoen, the words of institution ('This is my Body' ...) should be taken symbolically. Zwingli's adoption of that 'symbolic' view turned radical Sacramentarian opinions into a main-stream and divisive issue.

That was also the pattern of Reformation in Bern. In 1523, the patri-cians of Bern required its preacher Berthold Haller to teach only what was to be found in Scripture. In 1525, the city council abolished indul-gences, clerical dues, and the fiscal and legal privileges of the clergy. The magistrates took over the exclusive rights to appoint and dismiss the clergy in the canton. In the following year, after a rural revolt Haller found himself at the head of a popular movement in Bern whose influ-ence upon elections to the city council in 1527 tipped the balance in the local oligarchy in favour of evangelical change. Priests were allowed to marry, Masses for the souls of the dead were abandoned, and a public disputation was organized in January 1528 whose outcome determined a Reformation in Bern along the lines of that in Zürich.

The distinctiveness of Zürich's Reformation was already apparent by the time of Zwingli's death in battle at Kappel am Albis on 11 October 1531, part of Zürich's by then bitter confrontation with Cath-olic neighbouring cantons and an avatar of the conflicts between states involving religion to come. His successor, Heinrich Bullinger, declared Zwingli its prophet and first martyr. The pattern of Zürich's Reformation emerged as not only Sacramentarian, iconophobic and chromophobic, but harmonophobic as well. By then, its more radical fringe had become identifiable as those who refused infant baptism ('Catabaptists', Zwingli called them; 'Anabaptists' to us). Zwingli failed to convince them otherwise and they were arrested by the magistrates and prosecuted under an ordinance introduced in 1526, threatening them with drowning. The first to be convicted was Felix Manz, the illegitimate son of a cathedral canon in the city. Led to a boat on the river Limmat on the afternoon of 7 January 1527, he was thrown into the water, his hands and feet bound to a pole. Most of the rest fled, creating the first of succeeding Anabaptist diasporas.

Zürich's Reformation exercised an influence not only in Bern but beyond the Swiss cantons in southern Germany, across Lake Constance to the tributaries of the Danube and the Rhine. That was where most of the imperial cities lay, eighteen in the upper Rhine alone, thirty in Swabia. It was also the heartland of the Holy Roman Empire, where the majority of its Diets were held. Its leading cities were Nuremberg, Augsburg, Strasbourg and Ulm, flanked by a second rank of middling towns (Worms, Constance, Heilbronn and Nördlingen). 'Turning Swiss' was what the nobility told the emperor was happening all about them, an extension of the movement in the Grey Leagues that had once led to the Swiss secession from the empire, still a living memory. The allure of Swiss confederacy influenced the Reformation in southern German-speaking lands through the formation of Christian Federations.

But the empire's southern cities discovered that Zürich's Reformation was problematic. Their magistrates had to contend with the authority of the emperor and imperial institutions. Nuremberg, for example (the biggest city in southern Germany), hosted the Imperial Supreme Court and housed the crown jewels of the empire. Their magistrates had to balance pressure from below and within their number to carry out religious change with influence from above and within the city from conservatives. Ordinances in 1521 and 1522 invited Protestant preachers to the city and restricted alms-giving. Parts of the city became openly Lutheran. By 1524, however, the authorities were nervous – not least because their city was threatened with a papal interdict and with imperial pressure, and peasants were refusing to pay tithes. Preachers

were told to lay off their sermons, printers were restricted. When representatives from the emperor ordered them to end the city's evangelism
at the Diet of Nuremberg that year, however, it was too late. Ordinances
on baptism were announced and the Reformed Mass introduced on
1 June 1524.

In southwest Germany, the Protestant Reformation engaged other
political players and social coalitions. The military uprising of imperial
knights in 1522–3 was inspired by Luther and its leaders were evangelicals. The castle of Franz von Sickingen at Ebernburg (near Karlsruhe)
became a centre for evangelical printing and the third place (after
Wittenberg and Nuremberg) to host an evangelical Reformation.
Sickingen also enjoyed the adherence of Hutten, whom he had met
during the Swabian League's military engagement against Duke Ulrich
of Württemberg in 1519. Hutten supported Sickingen as the national
movement's leader which Luther refused to be. Between them they hoped
to turn the disaffections of imperial knights and lesser nobles into a
military force that would 'create an opening for the Gospel' in the middle
Rhine. Noble feuds had encouraged the growth of noble leagues in
Swabia and the Wetterau counties. In August 1522, about 600 Rhineland knights met at Landau and swore to a 'fraternal' association under
Sickingen's leadership. He then launched a feud against the
Elector-archbishop of Trier. But the general uprising Sickingen hoped for
failed to materialize. He did not capture Trier; instead, he was killed in
May 1523 when his own fortress at Burg Nanstein in the Landstuhl was
besieged. Hutten fled to an island in the Zürichsee, where he died of
syphilis in August 1523. The Estates prevented the failure of the Knights'
Revolt from threatening their own destiny as an order within the empire.

The Great Peasant War of 1524–6 was a more complex phenomenon, and on a larger scale. It brought to a climax the pressure-cooker
atmosphere of the early German Reformation. A climactic happening
had been predicted by astrologers. In February 1524, the planetary conjunction in the sign of Pisces was the presage for a world-changing
event, perhaps a new Flood. About fifty printed works have survived
from the year 1523, predicting a disaster, some depicting it as a popular
uprising. Some of the Alsace rebels claimed that they had merely been
the agent of God's will as written in the stars.

For heuristic purposes, the Peasant War is often parcelled up as the
'rural Reformation', the counterpart of the 'urban Reformation',

although in reality the divide is an artificial one. Luther's message had an impact beyond urban landscapes. The nobility acted as a conduit for evangelical ideas. Parts of Luther's message went down well in the countryside, where there were clerical lands, rights and monastic presence. The idea that Church wealth had been acquired by false pretences took root. Zwingli's influence was still clearer. By teaching that the Gospels were the touchstone of Reformation, he opened the door to questioning tithes, for where was their biblical justification? In 1523, the refusal to pay tithes began in the Rhineland and Franconia and spread southwards. In Zürich, tithe resistance became the signature of those impatient with slow change, starting around Witikon and Zollikon, villages just up from the lake and supported by Wilhelm Reublin, later one of the most articulate Anabaptists.

To call it a Peasant War hardly captures the flavour of this exceptionally widespread movement of rural commoners and townspeople, seeking redress for grievances that were not new from an empire which in their eyes manipulated a contrived (Roman) law against their customary rights and privileges. The means at their disposal were numerous: mass political assemblies, petitions and 'articles' setting out their grievances, boycotts of tithes and other dues, ransacking of monastic and noble properties. Only in the later stages did peasant bands congregate into 'armies'. The evolution of this variegated outbreak of people-power is hard to describe because it differed from region to region and its outcomes were dependent on local circumstances. In the Black Forest, the wealthy abbey of St Blasien and the counties of Lupfen and Stühlingen became the focus of tithe-strikes in the summer of 1524. Joining the upswing was Waldshut, a small town on the Rhine above Basel with a radical pastor, Balthasar Hubmaier.

As the movement spread into Upper Swabia, it became more overtly evangelical. Large bands of peasants assembled in a carnival atmosphere on the eve of Lent in February 1525. Their leaders made common cause with the newly appointed preacher in the small imperial city of Memmingen, Christoph Schappeler. Memmingen had just emerged from a conflict with the bishop of Augsburg over its rights to appoint its own preacher. The magistrates supported Schappeler both because of their own growing evangelical convictions and in response to guild pressure. One of Schappeler's adherents was a furrier, Sebastian Lotzer, an outspoken pamphleteer who preached the coming of the end of the world, interpreting his own awakening to the gospel as a sign of his prophetic power. The leaders of the peasants in the villages around Memmingen entered the city and either Schappeler or, more probably, Lotzer helped turn their grievances into the famous Twelve Articles of Memmingen, published in March 1525. Within a couple of months, these had been reprinted at least twenty-five times, a blueprint of complaints and a rallying cry.

Those articles offer an insight into how religious language and objectives were mixed with other grievances into a 'gospel of social unrest'. One thread running through them was the sense of a common man (rather than peasant), independent of imposed authority and reliant upon a local community. Behind that community lay a notion of 'divine law', inscribed in traditional and communal justice. Trying to define the religion in this peasant resistance is rather like breaking down a compound into its chemical elements. It misses the point. Religion was the bond which gave impetus, dynamism and danger to the movement. The peasants certainly had political aspirations. In its most radical manifestations, the Peasants' War articulated the right of the commons to depose ungodly rulers. A pamphlet entitled 'To the Assembly of the Common Peasantry', published in Nuremberg, imagined tyrant rulers being replaced by free communities of peasants living alongside urban communes and nobles and under the distant authority of a beneficent emperor. 'Turning Swiss' remained part of the dream of the Peasants' War.

The radicalism of the Peasants' War emerged in a different way in the last months of Thomas Müntzer's life. After he was expelled from Zwickau in 1521, his nomadic existence took him to Prague and eventually to the small Saxon fortified enclave of Allstedt, where he led a radical Reformation and bitterly attacked Luther as the mandarin of Wittenberg. On 13 July 1524, he preached an incendiary sermon before Duke John, co-regent in Thuringian Saxony and heir apparent of his brother Frederick. Taking a text from the second chapter of Daniel, he interpreted Daniel's dreams as a call to arms against lords who oppressed the gospel. Briefly establishing a league of about 500 citizens, he fled over the walls on the night of 7–8 August 1524, moving on to Mühlhausen in Thuringia, a small imperial city. There he fomented unrest, promoting an Eternal League of God, with whose support he deposed the city fathers (16 March 1525) and elected a new Eternal Council in their place. It was from there that he wrote apocalyptic letters to supporters, inviting them to rise up and smite their enemies.

On 10 May he set off with his contingent to support a peasant band assembled at Frankenhausen and, imagining himself a latter-day Gideon, led his followers to annihilation by princely troops just outside the city on 15 May. He himself was captured and was decapitated outside the walls twelve days later. It was not the end of the Peasants' War but it was a defining month, not least because Luther published his tract *Against the Robbing and Murdering Hordes of Peasants*. Partly in response to Müntzer's call to arms, Luther condemned the peasants for 'terrible sins'. The springtime of evangelism was over, and a divorce had occurred. For what we know today as the 'radical Reformation' was, in its origins, not a thing in itself but rather one half of a fraught relationship which now ended.

The dynamics of the early Reformation emphasized two realities. The first was that religious change was capable of creating an alternative vision of the political and social future. The second was that the Reformation set in train broad coalitions for that change. In the rural world, the coalitions were shortlived; in the urban world the trends were more varied. Where coalitions with a head of steam from artisans and householders were led by agitators prepared to outface the authorities, the movement for religious reform succeeded in displacing the existing regime. Where well organized coalitions met a less implacable regime, the result tended to be a negotiated settlement and a more gradual transition towards a reformed Church order in which the old guard embraced the new coalition and defused it. Where coalitions were weak and poorly led, and faced determined opposition, they failed. As the cycles of social and political urban ferment worked their way through, the outcome was a series of political and religious compromises.

By the later 1520s, the results were beginning to emerge. The magistrates in scores of imperial cities in Franconia, central Germany, the Rhineland and the Swiss margins legislated to accept the Protestant Reformation. The cantons of Zürich and Bern did so too. In southern Germany, where the influence of evangelical Protestantism had been considerable, the number of imperial cities which introduced reforming Church ordinances by 1530 could be counted on the fingers of one hand. In northern Germany and on the Baltic coast the evangelical movement was also only just beginning to get under way, though it would eventually be as significant there as well. In larger German territories, the early princely adopters of Lutheranism – Electoral Saxony (led by John the Constant, who succeeded Frederick the Wise in 1525) and Philip of Hesse – were few. The most energetic princes in northern Germany still opposed Lutheranism, convinced that the Estates would find a way to conjoin imperial and Church reform. More numerous were those who sat on the fence, remaining loyal to the old Church, but not standing in the way of the spread of evangelical preaching in their territories so long as their own authority was not threatened.

The secularization of the Prussian territory of the Teutonic Order in 1525 served as a case apart – not only because it was not properly part of the empire but also because its acceptance of the Reformation rode on the back of a collapse of the order in the face of double threats from peasant disorders within and Polish takeover from without. The prevailing hesitancy seemed in line with the Recess of the Diet of Speyer in 1526 which decided that each Estate should conduct their affairs in religion 'as [they] hope and trust to answer to God and his Imperial Majesty' until the meeting of a general council of the Church or a national assembly.

That gave the princes and cities of the Estates what would become known as the 'right of Reformation' (*ius reformandi*) – the right to determine the religion of their subjects. On that basis Philip of Hesse and John the Constant of Saxony set about framing the establishment of territorial churches in their dominions, with Melanchthon and Luther offering the justification for why a ruler, divinely ordained, had the Christian duty to promote the Gospels in the lands under his authority. The Speyer Recess was, however, provisional and it could be reversed. In the later 1520s, the territorial stakeholders of the empire began to form confessional allegiances. At the succeeding Diet of 1529, also summoned to Speyer, the imperial and Catholic camp was stronger. Archduke Ferdinand rebuilt Habsburg alliances in southern Germany. Duke George of Ducal Saxony, the most articulate of Catholic North German princes, made no secret of where princely duties lay. God sought revenge on the 'Martinians' who had introduced heresy into Christendom. He would not thank those who had failed to act in its defence. The Diet of 1529 revoked the previous Recess and enforced the Edict of Worms wherever possible. The majority of the Estates agreed, and proceeded to ban any further religious innovations. Zwinglianism was also abolished in the empire, and anyone convicted of adult baptism was condemned to death.

A few of the Estates reacted to this Recess by publishing on 19 July 1529 a minority decision, or 'Protest' (hence the name 'Protestantism'), signed by a number of princes and the representatives of fourteen imperial cities. Using the argument that a majority decision could not annul a unanimous decision of a previous Diet, and that a decision of conscience about religion was between an individual and God, that Protest became the foundation for the Lutheran Reformation. Charles V himself was present at the Diet of Augsburg, whose proceedings dominated the following year (April–September 1530). The Arch-Chancellor invited written statements on the religious question. Lutheran Protestants responded with the Articles of Torgau, which dealt mainly with questions of ecclesiastical organization. Philipp Melanchthon, who attended the Diet, also included a statement of doctrine, presented under the signature of eleven princes and two imperial cities to the Estates on 25 June 1530, which became known as the Confession of Augsburg. The 'evangelical' Estates of the Rhineland and southwest German cities, where Zwinglianism had gained its adherents, submitted their own confession, known as the Tetrapolitana (after the four cities in whose name it was presented: Strasbourg, Constance, Memmingen and Lindau). The Lutheran Reformation was now a distinct entity.

THE POLITICS OF THE LUTHERAN REFORMATION

The Protestant minority in the Estates faced an uphill task. Although the emperor was absent from German lands through the 1530s, his authority in the north and west was reinforced through the Low Countries. In the west, it was strengthened by the Catholicism of the dukes of Lorraine and the Habsburg county of Burgundy. Even the oppositional rivalry of the Wittelsbachs in Bavaria was eased when Duke Ulrich was restored to his duchy of Württemberg in 1534. German territorial rulers remained wedded to the concept of the empire and loyal to the emperor as the guarantor of political stability and order in the Reich. Only gradually did the spread of Protestantism among the nobility change the balance of forces.

The Schmalkaldic League, formed in 1531 of the protesting minority of territorial entities, was a novelty in imperial politics – a transregional confessional alignment with its own treasury, troops, meetings and, by the end of the 1530s, foreign policy. Most wise heads continued to imagine that the empire's divisions were temporary, and that they would be resolved around a moderately reformed German Church. The latter seemed the most credible option to those who regarded the recovery of political unity as the prerequisite for progress on other fronts. That was why theologians, legists and diplomats met for discussions in or around the Diets at Augsburg (1530), and Regensburg (1541) and at various colloquies in between. Each time they failed, to mutual recriminations. Only gradually was it clear that German princes and cities had to decide for or against the Reformation.

Emperor Charles V, spurred to action by the international scene as well as by a Catholic league of German princes, sought to reverse the creeping advance of Lutheranism by military force. Exactly when that decision was made is not clear, but the ground was laid by the succession of Duke Maurice to Ducal Saxony in 1541. His forthright approach galvanized Catholics in the empire and intensified the anxieties of the Schmalkaldic League, which by then had become weakened. Philip of Hesse's bigamy enfeebled its claims to stand for the Christian duty of princes. A joint attack on Brunswick-Wolfenbüttel by Hesse and Electoral Saxony depleted their joint treasury. The pope's call for a general council of the Church to meet at Trent in 1545 ended efforts to seek a regional solution to the empire's divisions by a council. Above all, the Peace of Crépy (September 1544) gave Charles the assurances he needed that France would not intervene on behalf of the Schmalkaldic League.

The military campaign launched by the emperor against the Protestants was carefully planned and brilliantly executed. He secured the support of Ducal Saxony and Bavaria by promising both of them Electorships. In addition, he offered a marriage between the son of Duke Wilhelm of Bavaria and one of Ferdinand's daughters, and (to Duke Maurice) the administration of the lucrative dioceses of Magdeburg and Halberstadt. Then, on the eve of the Diet of Regensburg in July 1546, he announced to the Protestant Estates that he was obliged to act against 'disobedient princes', outlawing the Landgrave of Hesse and Elector of Saxony for an alleged breach of the imperial peace. That cleverly turned the issue at the Estates towards the preservation of imperial law and jurisdiction. Realizing that they were facing a military showdown, the southern members of the Schmalkaldic League mustered over 50,000 men, while key Electors of the empire (Mainz, Cologne, Trier, Brandenburg) announced their neutrality. The emperor's troops took time to arrive but the League was held at bay. Ferdinand's mobilization, too, was hampered by the rebellion in Bohemia, and Duke Maurice's troops initially refused to fight alongside Spaniards. Eventually, however, a combined Saxon and Bohemian army invaded Electoral Saxony, defeating the Elector's forces at Mühlberg (24 April 1547) and capturing the Elector himself. On 19 May, just over a year after Luther's death, imperial troops entered Wittenberg without a fight. In his *Commentary on the German War* (1549), the Castilian historian Luis de Ávila y Zúñiga wrote that the imperial army crossing the Elbe reminded him of Caesar crossing the Rubicon. In 1548, Titian painted the emperor on horseback drawing on Dürer's image of the horsemen of the Apocalypse.

Determined to exploit the victory, Charles V summoned the Diet to Augsburg. With his troops standing by, he issued the Interim of 1548, making some concessions to Protestant sensibilities, but essentially re-imposing Catholicism and threatening the privileges of those who held out against his authority. The Protestant states mostly gave way, with the exception of Magdeburg, an early adopter of the Reformation (1524) and a long-standing member of the Schmalkaldic League. In the aftermath of the Interim, refugees swelled the numbers within the walls as the city prepared to defend itself against the forces of Duke Maurice of Ducal Saxony. In a siege lasting over a year, the duke's troops burned the suburbs and fought off attempts to relieve it, losing 4,000 men before Magdeburg negotiated a capitulation in November 1551. Within the besieged city, a remarkable transformation took place, masterminded by theologians and publicists who were mostly not its native inhabitants. Hartmann Beyer, Matthias Flacius Illyricus and Nikolaus von Amsdorf authored pamphlets which proclaimed themselves as the true spiritual inheritors of Luther's message and Magdeburg as 'Our Lord God's Chancery'. Nikolaus Gallus was the author of the 1550 *Confession, Instruction and Warning*, which argued for the responsibility of the magistrates of the city (as 'lesser magistrates' in the empire) to resist the unconstitutional and unjust actions of the emperor.

The siege of Magdeburg was a manifestation of the politics of conviction, where religious identity would be coterminous with political loyalty, both couched in historically rooted salvation myths. Its resistance demonstrated that armed opposition on religious grounds could succeed. Once the siege was raised, Duke Maurice, gamekeeper turned poacher, led a new revolt of princes against the emperor in 1552 which adopted the argument of the 'lesser magistrate' to its own cause. Charles V was forced to concede in law precisely that *ius reformandi* which he had tried to eliminate militarily. The Peace of Augsburg (1555) furnished the framework for the later Reformation in German lands, legalizing Lutheranism in the hands of established authority.

PROTESTANT DIVISIONS

The Reformation placed the spotlight on controlling the relationship between what people believed and how they behaved. The significance of the written 'Confession' was that it sought to do just that. It is no coincidence that the first of these, the *Schleitheim Confession* (1527), was Anabaptist. In the wake of the defeat of the Peasants' War, scattered remnants endeavoured, under the pressure of those who denied everything they stood for, to put in place their vision of the Church, such as it had existed in the days of the Apostles. They were mostly country people. The *Schleitheim Confession* was a declaration in time and space – many later Anabaptists would express their own beliefs differently. Anabaptists' theology was often of secondary importance to the way that they lived their lives. To live in, but not of, the world created hard choices. These included whether, and in what circumstances, they should acknowledge the rule of princes who, they thought, were not Christian at all. A Christian community of goods was another common ideal, albeit differently realized among Anabaptists. In Swiss and southern German Anabaptism, it was compatible with family households as the primary focus for living and believing. In Moravia, however, a further Anabaptist diaspora led to Anabaptist missions to smaller towns (Nikolsburg, Brünn and Znaim) and then (after internal divisions) to settlements on noble estates. Proclaiming themselves the true adherents of Jacob Hutter, a charismatic Anabaptist from the Puster valley, they lived in communities of about 500 people in which elders organized communal houses, crèches, schools and craft-production, keeping themselves to themselves in a world that, by and large, let them be. In Germany, Austria and

Switzerland, the Anabaptists contended with persecution – Protestant as well as Catholic. In time they learned to adapt to it, avoiding military service or other duties against their consciences, outwardly conforming to the religion of the prince, ensuring that their children married only Anabaptists, and keeping the faith. Territorialized, confessional religion encouraged such outward conformity, allowing Anabaptism to remain a minority presence across central Europe. Where local conditions favoured it, as in southeast Moravia or in the chaos of the emerging Dutch northern provinces, it may have been the religion of about 10 per cent of the population by around 1600. Princely persecution and urban magisterial surveillance did not eradicate it. Anabaptism stood for issues which the Reformation had raised but not resolved.

The growing superstructure of Protestant theologians drafted Lutheran and Zwinglian confessions and cemented the 'magisterial Reformation'. In fact, the process had already begun with treatises defining Reformation beliefs. What Luther regarded as canonical beliefs emerged in his 'Large Catechism', published in April 1529 for study by the growing cohorts of students in theology from Wittenberg. That generated the 'Small Catechism', which Luther intended for use in domestic environments and schools. The Reformation changed what religious belief was about. Confessional Christianity became a credal religion in which secular and religious authority had a joint stake in administering tests of belief and monitoring behaviour.

Protestant princes seized the initiative to define beliefs. After the Recess of Speyer, Philip of Hesse summoned his clergy to Homburg in October 1526 and, with the assistance of a former Franciscan from Avignon, François Lambert, proclaimed a Reformation for his principality which included changes to its schools, hospitals and poor relief. Luther took exception to it, and collaborated instead with Elector John the Constant in the elaboration of a Wittenberg model, one that was adopted in the Electorate and widely copied elsewhere in Lutheran lands. Church services were standardized around Luther's German Mass, monasteries and church fabric were administered by secular authorities, evangelical pastors were appointed by them, and a regular process of parochial visitations instigated, taking princely control of the Reformation into the parishes. Not surprisingly, the centralization of principalities in Germany often coincided with the period when Protestant princes consolidated their rule through religious change.

The princely Reformation turned out, not only in Germany but elsewhere in northern Europe, to be a conservative affair. The Swedish Reformation is a case in point. Building on the newly accomplished revolt from Danish rule, Gustav Vasa dispossessed the Church of its lands, threw out the Danish senior clergy and appointed his own, and instituted a Reformation in which the Swedish Mass retained altars, crucifixes, candles, vestments, the Virgin Mary and saints' days. All that changed was the use of the vernacular instead of Latin, the communion in both kinds, and the suppression of incense and holy water. Cautious Reformation proved enduring, but its solidity came at a price. It relied on top–down religious structures in which secular forces played a dominant role. Where that occurred, the fear of the 'outsider' (initially Catholics but then also non-Lutherans) was one facet of an obsession with 'order', manifested in legislation governing people's social and moral behaviour.

By contrast, the Reformation's explosive dynamics lasted longer in the urban landscape. There, and especially in the Rhineland, Zürich offered an alternative model, less conservative and with different relationships of power and communication. These latter focused on the relationship between words and things, between the spiritual world and the world as it is. Luther had one intransigent view on that matter, Zwingli another. Landgrave Philip of Hesse tried reconciliation at the Colloquy of Marburg in early October 1529, attended by Zwingli, Luther and associated cohorts of theologians. The dispute turned on the Eucharistic 'words of institution'. Luther theatrically wrote them in chalk on the table at the beginning: 'This is my Body' (*Hoc est corpus meum*). Fierce argument ensued about how these should be interpreted, in a literal or metaphorical sense, and there was no meeting of minds. Luther felt the political pressures to come to a compromise, but he was 'shackled, I cannot escape, the Word is too strong'. Zwingli's dream of a 'Union' was shattered and a fundamental rift, leading to two different lineaments of the Reformation, occurred. Schism was not just in Christendom, but within the movement which (without intending to) was tearing it asunder.

11. Reaction, Repression, Reform

Christendom rested on cultural, social and political foundations reflecting the institutions and habits of thought which sustained its fabric and vitality. So, in the heartland of Latin Christendom lay the patchwork of Italian bishoprics (as many as the rest of western Christendom put together) and religious foundations which, along with the existence of the Papal States as a regional power, conditioned the reception of Protestantism in the Italian peninsula. A frontier legacy dictated the Iberian peninsula's reactions. The existence of Jewish and Muslim minorities and of Judeo-Christian and Morisco converts under the impact of the Christian *Reconquista* determined responses to Protestant ideas in that part of the continent. North of the Alps and Pyrenees, different conditions had an impact on the direction of religious change.

Resisting whatever threatened society and its values had been a sustaining force in Christendom. In the sixteenth century, that resistance was complicated. Two uncertainties were intertwined. One was the nature of Church reform – a cause to which many individuals and groups were committed, but which had been pursued in different ways by various individuals and groups without establishing common cause. The second was the emerging Protestant version of Church reform, which was difficult to evaluate. Was it, as Martin Luther claimed, the only option for reform? Or was this a fundamental challenge to Christendom? Protestants did not speak with one voice so it was difficult to answer these questions. Sometimes Protestants echoed what many already thought. Even the distinction between 'justification by faith' (or rather God's saving grace to man, a continuing and respectable Augustinian theological theme) and 'justification by faith alone' (excluding 'good works') was one whose significance only gradually became clearer. In northern Italy, for example, the Benedictine monks in Padua, part of a reformed group centred on the monastery at Monte Cassino (known as the 'Cassinese congregation'), studied the writings of the early Greek fathers to prove that this was a false dichotomy, and that human works and divine grace were both necessary to restore human nature to the way God intended it to be. So much was wrapped up in the language and tone by which Protestantism was conveyed.

From 1521, Lutheranism was a heresy, condemned by the papacy, Louvain, the Sorbonne and Cologne. But political circumstances, combined with its own dynamic, turned Luther's Reformation into something that could not be immediately eliminated. That made the institutional response complex. Secular and ecclesiastical authorities did not see eye to eye. In addition, Protestantism was not the only threat to Christendom. In Mediterranean Europe, the Ottomans were closer, Protestants a second-order issue. Many hoped someone else would deal with the Protestant problem or that prayer and reform would bring about Protestants' reconciliation to the Church. There was a divide between those who sought to turn back the spread of Protestantism and those who wanted to adapt to it, turn its own weapons against it. Where that internal debate was intense, the response to the Reformation vacillated.

TARES AMONG THE WHEAT

St Augustine not only inspired the Protestant Reformation, but was also the preferred theologian when it came to justifying religious intolerance. Responding to the threat from the North African sect of Donatists, the bishop of Hippo argued that coercion could legitimately be employed to induce the recalcitrant to see the error of their ways. Using the parable of Christ at the banquet (Luke 14:23), Augustine said that 'compel them to come in' (*compelle intrare*) was the biblical legitimation for using force against heretics, an astringent medicine, inducing repentance in the erring individual. But what if repentance was not forthcoming? Later Patristic writers were clear that obstinate heretics had to be exterminated, limbs amputated to preserve the rest of the body in good health. The Spanish Franciscan Alfonso de Castro constructed *compelle intrare* into a biblical justification for colonialism. Becoming counsellor to Emperor Charles V, he then published an encyclopaedia of heresy in 1534. A later work, *On the Just Punishment of Heretics* (1547), earned Castro his reputation as the heretics' 'scourge'. He wrote it on return to his native city of Zamora from the Council of Trent, surprised to hear people openly criticizing the emperor's wars against German Protestants.

Castro set about proving them wrong. The death penalty was a legitimate punishment for obstinate heretics. If Luther had been executed, the German mess would not have occurred. Going easy on heresy merely stacked up problems for the future – and anyone who thought its punishment should be left to God alone must be crazy. That was in the context of the parable of the tares (Matthew 13), often a starting-point for those who took a strong line against Protestantism. Castro later put *compelle intrare* into practice. He spent the last years of his life preaching in Antwerp, the largest city of the Netherlands and a viper's nest of heretics. In the responses to the Reformation, those from the Spanish peninsula were unusual. Protestant heresy was successfully repulsed and by means of the state. The heartland of Christendom's largest dynastic empire had a unique experience of Reformation.

Spain's exceptionalism rested on its history as a frontier state. Muslims had dominated parts of the Spanish peninsula for centuries. With them Jews had settled in both Christian and Muslim realms, all three religions cohabiting in a complicated coexistence (*convivencia*). But the Christian kingdoms of the peninsula were dedicated to its reconquest, something which they achieved with the fall of Granada in 1492. *Convivencia* became a thing of the past. The Jews were given an ultimatum to convert to Christianity or leave the country, similar moves against Muslims following shortly thereafter. The result was emigration, but mass Christian baptism too. The latter created 'New Christians', former Jews (*conversos*) and Muslims (*moriscos*). In both cases, their religious traditions included arguments for outward conformity, while practising privately and believing otherwise. But dissimulation became a problem when the state aligned itself with faith. Dissimulation towards the one implied dissension as to the other. Ferdinand and Isabella established the Spanish Inquisition in 1478 as an ecclesiastical court under their direct authority to deal with that problem. King John III of Portugal followed suit in 1536. Very different from the medieval Inquisition, the Holy Office was a state bureaucracy, staffed by officials trained in canon law, operating under a papal charter but usually independent of Rome's authority. Its initial role was to supervise new converts and it was given the resources to do so – local informers, officials to guard ports and frontiers, overseers to control what was printed, prisons and archives. Inefficient by modern standards and frequently overstretched, sometimes criticized by the Cortes in the peninsula and ecclesiastics, it made its presence felt, establishing an orthodoxy of behaviour and belief.

The result can be judged in terms of what people read and how they came by it. Printing arrived late in the Spanish peninsula, an imported technology. In Seville, for example, three generations of the Cromberger family (originally from Germany) undertook New World printing, a profitable contract and one that they took care not to compromise by printing anything heterodox themselves. Printing was limited to major cities and university towns, which made the control of indigenous production easier. Building on the system of licensing printers, the Inquisition proved effective at overseeing who printed what, as well as what was being imported. The Spanish Index of Prohibited Books, first published by the royal council in 1551, was comprehensive.

The Spanish market for Bibles and devotional literature was buoyant. Erasmus, among others, met the demand. His success, however, was ephemeral. From 1525 onwards, his works fell under suspicion of having fostered the devotions of those whom the Inquisitor General proclaimed as 'Illuminists' (*Alumbrados*). In urban centres of New Castile, in university circles at Salamanca, and in the households of the upper aristocracy, private prayer groups discreetly practised the attainment of inner penitence as a route towards total abandonment to the love of God. To the Inquisition, this challenged the conjuncture between conformity of belief and behaviour. Although there is no evidence that the Illuminists read Protestant books, they were tarred with the Lutheran brush.

The Illuminists were treated leniently. Under the surface and despite the Inquisition, their influence survived. The Spanish humanist who became Charles V's chancellor, Alfonso de Valdés, saw no problem in corresponding privately with Luther and Melanchthon, or in expressing his contempt for the papacy in his defence of the sack of Rome in 1527. But the Inquisition kept an eye on him and might well have taken things further had he not died in 1532. By then his brother, Juan de Valdés, had left for Rome to write the first of a series of works whose circulation in Spain and Italy served as a litmus test of heterodoxy.

By 1550, only one individual had been executed by the Inquisition for Protestantism, and under forty people had been investigated. But in 1557, a consignment of letters and Genevan anti-papal books fell into the wrong hands. Suspects in Seville were rounded up and arrested. Charles V was informed and almost his last letter to his son Philip II demanded exemplary punishment for those caught. The fraught international situation provided the context for a series of *autos-da-fé* (from the Latin *actus fidei* or Act of Faith) which began in Valladolid on 21 May 1559 with the new king, Philip II, in attendance. The most remarkable arrest was that of the primate of Spain himself, Bartolomé Carranza de Miranda, archbishop of Toledo. Politically motivated, the Carranza investigation on a charge of heresy generated paper and suspects. What the Inquisitors uncovered was bigger and more coordinated than they had hitherto imagined. Students attending foreign universities were recalled. Vigilance was imposed on border-crossings. Foreign print-workers fell under suspicion – mostly heresy by hearsay for, although they worked with books, it was not from their pages that they derived the nonconformity of which they were suspected. These were watershed years for Protestantism in the Spanish peninsula. In the end, only about a hundred Protestants were executed in Spain from 1559 to 1566 – under half the number put to death in a similar period under Mary Tudor, a quarter of those killed under Henry II in France, and only a tenth of those executed in the Low Countries in those same years. After around 1560, the tiny minority of Spanish Protestants took up exile north of the Alps, their writings blackening the reputation of Philip II and the Inquisition.

LIVING JUSTIFIED

In 1543, an anonymous book appeared in Venice entitled the *Most Useful Treatise of the Benefit of Jesus Christ Crucified* (*Il Beneficio di Cristo*). Enigmatic, it set out how it felt to be justified, and what it meant for ordinary people to be able to say that Christ was their brother. The work was the bestseller of an Italian Reformation that never was. So ruthlessly was it pursued by the Inquisition that no copy appeared to survive until, 300 years later, one turned up in a Cambridge college library. Its story reflects the problematic history of the Italian response to the Protestant Reformation.

That the work was printed in Venice is no surprise. The city's presses were renowned. Not dominated by the Habsburgs, the Venetian Republic also kept its distance from Rome. Unlike Spain's, Italy's borders were porous and Protestant ideas circulated widely. Students came across the Alps to study in Venetian universities. Merchants transacted business north of the Alps as a matter of course. All the signs are that, at least until the *Benefit of Christ* was published, the works of the Protestant reformers were known and available in northern Italy.

Who wrote the *Benefit of Christ*, and why? In August 1566, Pietro Carnesecchi revealed in a trial before the Inquisition in Rome that the author was 'Don Benedetto', it being later revised by Marcantonio Flaminio. Carnesecchi was a papal secretary whose address-book gave the Inquisition the identities of the *spirituali* (those who wanted to reform the Church from within). The name of Flaminio points to other influences among Italian evangelism, a now contested term for those who sought a route to ecclesiastical reform that avoided Protestantism. A poet and philosopher from Venice, Flaminio became a member of the household of the reforming bishop Gian Matteo Giberti in 1528. That was the year when Giberti withdrew to his diocese in Verona, one of the wealthy towns on the Venetian terra firma. Giberti already moved in the spiritual circles of the Roman Oratory of Divine Love and the Theatines. Now he set out to create a model diocese. His initiative was among many that counted as the Catholic Reformation – meaning those attempts to reform the Church from within. There was also talk of Flaminio encouraging lay study of the Bible, preaching and frequent communion. Retiring to Naples on health grounds in 1539, Flaminio joined a circle of reform-minded men and women around Juan de Valdés, especially Bernardino Ochino and Giulia Gonzaga, and drank the pure wine of Valdesianism (a complex theological blend of Erasmianism, Illuminism and Lutheranism). It was in Naples that Flaminio met 'Don Benedetto', whom detective work by Italian historians revealed as a monk from the Cassinese congregation. Its influence is detectable in the *Benefit of Christ*, whose initial version was probably written in 1539.

With the death of Valdés in 1541, Flaminio and others from Naples moved north to join the household of Reginald Pole. Pole was an English aristocrat and cardinal who had first arrived in Italy in 1521 to study at Padua, but who returned in 1532 as an exile in protest at the Henrician divorce. His social eminence made him a soulmate to Gasparo Contarini, a Venetian patrician and ambassador who had been made a cardinal by Pope Paul III in 1535. Between them, Pole and Contarini encapsulated the false hopes of reform in Italy in the 1530s and 40s. They both sat (with Giberti) on the commission (the Council for the Reform of the Church) established by Pope Paul in 1536 in expectation of a general council. Its report was a dead letter. Even more hopes were raised when Contarini was appointed papal delegate to the Colloquy at Regensburg in 1541, where he entered into direct negotiations with German Protestant theologians, securing with them an agreed statement on justification by faith. After the talks broke down, Contarini was portrayed as a dangerous compromiser.

Contarini died under a cloud, some said poisoned by his enemies, in 1542. Among the most prominent of Italy's 'philo-Protestants', Bernardino Ochino and Peter Martyr Vermigli fled in fear of the newly founded Papal Inquisition, deciding that their future lay north of the Alps, the beginnings of a brain- and spirit-drain of would-be reformers. By then, a revised version of the *Benefit of Christ* had been published, and it was accused of being a compendium of Lutheranism. Few Italians who read it were probably aware of how much of it came from Protestant sources. Its popularity in the 1540s corresponded to the decade when crypto-Protestant beliefs threatened to create a mass movement. In Modena, Bergamo, Siena, Lucca and elsewhere in Tuscany, dearth and social tension combined with religious dissent. In Venice, Padua and Ferrara, crypto-Protestant conventicles became more public. Meanwhile, in Rome, the opponents of Contarini (called 'zealots' by his diminishing band of supporters) now had the upper hand, led by the Neapolitan Gian Pietro Carafa, future Pope Paul IV. They sought to prove that the *spirituali* were naive compromisers, and that the Roman Inquisition had arrived (1542) just in time. By the end of the 1540s, the impact of repression began to be felt. The majority of those under suspicion drew a line under their previous beliefs. The minority who could do so, or felt moved to, joined the émigrés across the Alps, increasingly in Geneva. In the mountain valleys of Savoy and Piedmont (and in Calabria, around Montalto to the south of Naples), Waldensians (survivors of a late-medieval heresy) linked up with Genevan Protestants. Moulding their beliefs to the latter, they provided an underground Protestant network that survived beyond 1560.

A handful of émigré intellectuals were attracted to freedom north of the Alps, but could not stomach the confessional straitjacket of Geneva. These included Lelio Sozzini, whose father was a professor of law at Padua and who studied there himself. Moving across the Venetian border into the Swiss Alps in 1547, he wrote treatises which existed only in manuscript in his lifetime, in which he envisaged the resurrection being just for the righteous, the souls of the rest dying along with their bodies. Such speculation worried reformers in Zürich and Geneva, and Sozzini's views on the Trinity were suspect too. After his death in 1562, his nephew Fausto Sozzini continued where his uncle had left off and, remarkably, did so while working quietly as a secretary in the service of the Medici in Tuscany. He published his uncle's writings only after leaving Italy in 1574, his later peregrinations in Transylvania and Poland spreading what became known as anti-Trinitarian Socinianism by the end of the sixteenth century.

Italy did not have a Protestant Reformation, and historians ask why that was. Was it because it was too timid, polite and aristocratic? Was there a failure of leadership or of ideology? But this is to judge things in the peninsula by what happened in Germany. The story of the *Benefit of Christ* introduces other issues: the difficulties in undertaking reform from the inside without causing religious division, at a time when the peninsula was the focus of intermittent international conflict; and how to spread Protestantism and keep the candle of Church reform alight, even as the forces of repression were massing.

BEFORE THE PLACARDS ... AND AFTER

There are parallels between the reception of the Protestant Reformation in Italy and France. If Italy's was the Reformation that never was, France's was the Reformation that might have been. As in Italy, Luther's ideas circulated quickly in France after 1519, thanks to books, students and preachers. In August 1524, Guillaume Farel published the *Lord's Prayer and Creed* in French, a disguised translation of Luther's *Little Book of Prayers* (1522). Published under the nose of the Sorbonne it was the most daring Protestant book to appear in France before 1534. Fewer than eighty Lutheran editions across the whole of France in the 1520s was a drop in the ocean when set alongside the 2,500 other works known to have been published in Paris alone during that decade. In a letter of 1524, Guillaume Farel wrote: 'Good God how I rejoice when I see how the knowledge of the pure grace of God has spread abroad the greater part of Europe! I hope that Christ will eventually visit France with his benediction . . .' That hope was expressed, however, while hostile reactions to Luther gathered, orchestrated by Noël Béda, a professor of theology, director of one of the colleges in Paris and rector of the Sorbonne. In what became a leitmotif of the French Reformation, the anxieties about religious change were accompanied by fears of a cataclysmic event – in this case, the fears of a second Flood in 1524. One magistrate in Toulouse was so convinced that he built himself an ark against the eventuality.

In the diocese of Meaux reforming aspirations confronted the forces of reaction. Its bishop was Guillaume Briçonnet, whose ideas for his diocese mirrored those of Matteo Giberti at Verona. Visitations and synods were followed by something more unusual. Determined to reorganize its rural preaching, he established mission stations, manned by a group (the Meaux Circle) holding known reforming convictions. Foremost among them was Jacques Lefèvre d'Étaples, a biblical scholar and friend of Erasmus. The others were mostly his friends and disciples. Briçonnet was confessor to the king's sister Marguerite of Navarre and he counted on her protection. It was not enough. After Francis I's capture at Pavia, the Queen Mother Louise de Savoie became regent in the king's absence (1525–6). Meaux, a cloth town suffering hard times, began to take the Reformation into its own hands. Catholic posters were torn down and anticlerical chants echoed in the marketplace. Lefèvre fled to Strasbourg, while Briçonnet's diocese was investigated for heresy by a commission of judges from Paris. In the aftermath of the 'Affair' of Meaux, the network of Marguerite of Navarre was all that protected Briçonnet and like-minded humanist reformers.

Although there were patronesses of reform in Italy their influence was nowhere that of Marguerite's. She was a royal princess, had a huge patrimony, and used this to create niches of safety for those who were reformers who refused to be stereotyped as 'Lutheran' or 'Protestant'. Her first book was the *Miroir de l'âme pêcheresse* (translated eleven years later as 'Mirror of a Sinful Soul' by another princess, Elizabeth Tudor). The mirror in question reflected much else besides Marguerite's soul – criticisms of ecclesiastical abuses and doubtful doctrines, but also a path by which a Christian could find his own way towards God. More revealing, though only through a glass darkly, was her later work, published in 1547 as *Marguerites de la Marguerite des Princesses* (1547), a collection of *chansons*, poems and play-texts, no doubt composed at an earlier date. A vehicle for protecting and furthering the careers of those of advanced religious opinions in France, Marguerite also invoked her right as a princess to avoid committing herself confessionally. In the early 1530s, prudent behaviour allowed the 'evangelicals' to congregate. It was Reformation by stealth.

The 'Affair of the Placards' stopped it in its tracks. On the night of 17–18 October 1534, an anonymous printed billboard (*placard*) entitled *True Articles on the Horrible, Great and Insupportable Abuses of the Papal Mass* was posted up in Paris, other cities and even (it was reported not long after) on the door of the king's bedchamber in the château at Amboise. Two copies still survive, written (as is now known) by Antoine Marcourt, a pastor at Neuchâtel, the first French-speaking city in Europe to become Protestant. It attacked 'papists' who 'pretended' that the Mass was a 'sacrifice', covering up in a 'big word' (transubstantiation) the 'invention' that Christ was corporally present in the consecrated bread and wine. Parisian Catholics were outraged. Expiatory processions were organized and 200–300 people arrested. In December a special judicial tribunal was formed to find and judge those responsible. There was a procession, led by the king himself. Six victims were burned in public and a public crackdown began. The 'Affair of the Placards' played into the hands of the enemies of reform. Marguerite kept her distance, staying at Angoulême and Nérac. In her entourage was the son of a minor ecclesiastical official with a humanist training in law, Jean Calvin. At the end of 1534 or early the following year, he made his way to Basel.

JEAN CALVIN AND GENEVA

Calvin was in voluntary exile. Basel offered safety but not security. Fortunately for him, his cousin Pierre-Robert Olivétan lived there. Evangelically inclined like Calvin, he was completing his French translation of the Bible, to which Calvin provided prefaces. That addressed to 'Those who love Jesus Christ and his Gospel' was an evocation of all that God had created. Published in Neuchâtel, Olivé-tan's Bible (paid for by the Waldensians) was a remarkable achievement. Calvin later altered it, but he did not change the way in which Olivétan chose, wherever possible, to render the Hebrew in terms that had no trace of the old religion. 'Bishop' became 'surveillant'; 'priest', 'pasteur'; 'chalice', 'cup'; 'church', 'temple', etc. The glossary of French Protestant-ism was under construction.

Some of Basel's printers were committed to the evangelical cause. In March 1536, two of them published the first Latin edition of a book that (in a very different form) would become indissociable from the name of Calvin. It was initially entitled *Of the Christian Religion, the Institution*. Calvin had perhaps travelled with a draft of the text on paper or in his head. In form, it was a manual of Protestant orthodoxy. But it was also intended as an apology for the French 'evangelicals' facing post-Placard repression. In a preface addressed to Francis I, Cal-vin countered the suggestion that they were the sixteenth-century equivalent of terrorists. The *Institution* of the title implied 'manual', but it also meant 'foundation'. Protestants, Calvin told the king, supported the pillars of the Christian faith. They were not the cause of trouble; that was the fault of others. He quoted 1 Kings 18: 'it is not we who spread errors abroad or incite tumults; it is they who contend against God's power'.

The work opened with a sentence whose formula came from Cicero: 'Almost all sacred doctrine consists of two parts: knowledge of God, and of ourselves.' That combined knowledge was 'nothing else than a firm conviction of mind whereby we determine with ourselves that God's truth is so certain, that it is incapable of not accomplishing what it has pledged to do by his holy Word'. Calvin was paraphrasing a pas-sage from Paul's Epistle to the Romans (10:11), which would be the work on which he published his first Bible commentary four years later in March 1540. By then, he had thoroughly revised the *Institution*. Pub-lishing this second edition (renamed the *Institution of the Christian Religion*) in 1539, he now envisaged it as complementing his biblical commentaries. The work was intended 'to prepare and instruct candi-dates in sacred theology in the reading of the divine Word', and to contain the 'sum of religion in all its parts' so that, when it came to expositions of the Scriptures, he would be able to 'condense them' since he had already laid out the underlying fabric. Thereafter, through to the final Latin edition of the *Institutes* (as they are known) in Calvin's life-time (1559), its text grew, taking into account the weight of his learning and the need to complement his Bible commentaries as they appeared. In subsequent editions, that crucial first sentence was also changed, subtly but significantly. Under a heading which emphasized that 'the knowledge of God and that of ourselves are connected', Calvin now began the sentence 'Nearly all the wisdom we possess . . .' – i.e. the knowledge that we fallen creatures can manage about God. Theology for Calvin was not God's truth but our imperfect attempts to grapple with the truth which God had chosen to give us. In the Scriptures, God 'prattles at us, like nurses with babies', to 'accommodate the knowledge of him to our slender capacity'.

For Calvin, the role of a commentator was to understand the author. In Romans, he entered into the mind of Paul of Tarsus. We cannot know God in his essence. We can know him only by his creation and by the fact that he embodies righteousness and goodness. We human beings crave the latter, but we are incapable of achieving it. We live in an 'abyss' of sin, a 'labyrinth' of our own making, and the righteousness in God condemns us. For Calvin, the 'justification' that is the essence of the Pauline Epistle was how the Creator restores us, the unrighteous. God finds the way to do that, just as he had for Abraham. He allows Christ to 'indwell' in us such that we are 'engrafted in Christ' or 'coalesce with Christ'. The sacraments are 'instruments' to nourish our faith, 'seals' which imprint the promises of God on our hearts and confirm the certainty of grace. That happens at God's good pleasure and not to everyone. The twin sons of Isaac belonged to the tribe of Israel, with whom God had made a covenant. But God chose Jacob and rejected Esau. That, too, belongs to God's righteousness though we cannot comprehend it. We can be sure, though, since this is the message of the Scriptures, that God chooses his faithful, that there is no salvation without election, that human merit has nothing to do with being elected, and that he never abandons those who are called.

This was Calvin's radicalism: a double predestination, some being saved and others damned. It took the dichotomy in Christendom between the believing core and the periphery of infidelity and turned it into a division within Christendom's core. That said, predestination was not as emphatic in Calvin's thought as it would be for some of his adherents. Predestination spoke to them about the more divided Europe in which they lived. For Calvin, predestination was not an invitation to anxiety about God's justice but a full stop to speculation on the matter. To the question: 'Am I saved?' he replied that belonging to the Church and knowing Christ in one's heart were signs of election. That was liberation from angst. There was no need to build an ark. The rest was about living with Christ in the world, a conflictual maze of human passions. But God's creation was not without order, and in human affairs we had a 'duty of love' towards our neighbours, citizens, rulers, even though they may not be Christians themselves. It was the scattered communities to whom Paul sent his epistles that became Calvin's models for the tribulations of the godly in the world.

Geneva, where Calvin arrived by chance in 1536 and stayed to give Bible lectures, was no such model. It was a medium-sized city of about 12,000 inhabitants, mostly French-speaking, crowded within newly rebuilt defensive walls, and located on a hill overlooking the western end of Lake Geneva. It had been ruled by a prince-bishop who owed overlordship to the dukes of Savoy. In 1526, however, the Genevans rejected their bishop and the magistrates confiscated Church wealth. But there were divisions over how the Reformation was to proceed. Guillaume Farel, a former member of the Circle of Meaux who had left because it was not radical enough, came to the city for the first time in 1532. True to form, he was confrontational and was lucky to escape with his life. But then, on 21 May 1536, the Genevans suspended Roman Catholic worship, destroyed images and adopted the Reformation. Either Calvin or, more likely, Farel drafted the 'Ecclesiastical Ordinances' and 'Confession' which the magistrates decreed should be sworn by all inhabitants of the city. That oath, and strong-arm tactics in getting people to adopt the new measures, produced a reaction. When the city authorities ordered their new 'pastors' to conform to the Eucharistic practices of its Swiss neighbour and erstwhile 'protector', the canton of Bern, Farel and Calvin refused to celebrate Easter communion and were banished. Calvin only returned reluctantly three years later, in 1541, and on his own terms. The intervening period spent in Strasbourg under the tutelage of Martin Bucer was a training course in how to establish a Church so that it nurtured the best in everyone without compromising its core values, how to survive in the confessional crossfire between Zürich and Wittenberg, and how to become respected in the unstable politics of the upper Rhine and western Swiss margins.

That stood Calvin in good stead in the 1540s as he sought accommodation in the religious differences among Protestant communities. The first sessions of the Council of Trent indicated that there was nothing more to be expected from reconciliation with Catholicism. Calvin already regarded Charles V as a latter-day Nebuchadnezzar, sent by God to punish the Protestants for their disunity. The Lutheran defeat at Mühlberg in April 1547 seemed to prove him right. Securing unity among Protestants, however, looked next to impossible, given the differing views of the Lord's Supper between Wittenberg and Zürich. Calvin set out his convictions on the sacraments in a *Short Treatise*, written in Strasbourg but published only once he returned to Geneva. They were the ways that God met our feeble capacity for understanding, outward signs which had no power in themselves. By how we come to regard them, however, and through the effect of faith, they embody everything that faith is and does in us. By that embodiment the Lord's Supper becomes more than a sign. 'Let us,' he said in the 1543 version of the *Institutes*, 'learn not to take away the thing signified from the sign', for 'the truth must never be separated from the signs'. That made it harder for Calvin to persuade the 'patriarch' ('Antistes') of Zürich, Heinrich Bullinger, to make common cause with Geneva. After a visit, Calvin wrote to him that 'although I am conscious in myself of a more inward union with Christ in the sacrament than you express in your words, yet this ought not to prevent our having the same Christ; or our being one in Him. It is only perhaps through this inward *consensus* that we can unite with each other.' That is what Calvin achieved in 1549 when he signed up to the Zürich Consensus (*Consensus Tigurinus*). Its twenty-six articles were a theological compromise. Its opponents accused it of being 'syncretist' – a term first deployed by Erasmus to mean a convenient agreement between two parties to make a common front against others. They were mostly right. But it was the beginning of something else: a bicephalous (Calvin *and* Bullinger) 'Reformed' Protestant tradition which offered a defensible theological inheritance at the time when Lutheranism was hardening its confessional stance.

Calvin set about establishing a constitution for the Genevan Church. On 20 November 1541 the city's magistrates agreed to his draft with some amendments to protect their authority. The Ecclesiastical Ordinances created a self-regulating, visible community of believers, whose pastors led the congregation but were appointed and watched over by laymen. It was an ecclesiastical polity in which there was a process of mutual 'edification'. Other posts – teachers ('doctors'), poor-relief administrators ('deacons') and Church councillors ('elders') – had the same procedures of appointment and surveillance. The arrangements reflected Calvin's study of the early Pauline Church and his legal background. They reveal his preference for collegiate governance. The pastors were required to meet together once a week for Bible discussions – the origins of the 'Congregation of Pastors', in time a formidable institution, respected both in the city and abroad. At the heart of the Church lay the 'consistory', a self-regulating council of laity and clergy to oversee the morals and wellbeing of the community. The Protestant cities of Zürich, Basel and Bern had established 'marriage courts' to resolve matters previously handled by ecclesiastical courts. Calvin's consistory was different since it oversaw the morality of the congregation at large. In practice, the pastors became the paid servants of the Genevan state to whom they owed allegiance, and the appointments of elders were ratified by the city council. Only the power of excommunication remained solely in the hands of the consistory.

Calvin sought new pastors for the Church. There were many vacancies but a shortage of candidates meeting his exacting standards. An early casualty was Sebastian Châtillon (Castellio). Calvin had invited him to teach in the college at Geneva and become a pastor. It looked like a good appointment. Their relationship soured, however, over theological differences which reveal Calvin's insecurity. It took the arrival of other exiles to turn the Genevan pastorate into a loyal, stable preaching ministry. With that Calvin was better equipped to deal with the opposition which tried to discredit and remove him. In 1546, the influx of refugees became the initial focus for his opponents, some of them well-placed Genevan citizens. In the gathering storm, the affair of Servetus (Miguel Servet) was one of several in which it was difficult for Calvin to strike the right note. Servetus was a physician from the Basque country who had fled the Inquisition, and whom Calvin already knew for his unorthodox opinions on the 'sleep' of the soul after death. Servetus published a translation of the Bible in 1542 which drew on Jewish, Gnostic, pantheistic and Neo-Platonic traditions of biblical exegesis. Shortly thereafter he wrote his main work of systematic theology, the *Restitution of Christianity*. Servetus hoped that his anti-Trinitarian theology would serve as a way of reuniting the Jews to Christianity. Copies circulated before it was published – Sozzini was among those who knew of it. Calvin's reaction, when he was sent some passages in 1547 for comment was hostile. When the book was published in 1553, it carried Calvin's comments in a preface. He was incensed at having his name linked to a work that he regarded as blasphemous, sought to have it banned at the Frankfurt book fair, and alerted the ecclesiastical authorities in France (where Servetus was living) through an intermediary to have its author arrested. Servetus escaped to Geneva, where he was arrested and imprisoned in August 1553.

There had to be a trial. Calvin was represented at it by his secretary, Nicolas de la Fontaine. Written and oral testimony was presented, and Servetus defended himself with ability. The Genevan ministers concentrated on passages from Servetus's earlier works to prove that his interpretation of the Trinity was blasphemous, and thereby punishable by death. Blasphemy, however, was difficult to demonstrate, especially when the individual in question had hardly set foot in Geneva and was not an inhabitant. Calvin brought in the big guns of other Reformed churches to lean on the magistrates, who pronounced the guilty verdict on 27 October 1553, and Servetus was burned to death that same day. The affair haunted Calvin for the rest of his life. He published a treatise that sought to out those (especially in the Italian exile community) who might be tempted to think as Servetus had done. Then he tackled head on the right of magistrates to punish heretics. Trying not to sound like Alfonso de Castro, he distinguished between coercing people's beliefs and defending true doctrine. When it came to the latter, Calvin claimed biblical authority for the obligation of princes to use the sword to maintain right religion in the community.

Early the following year came a frontal assault on Calvin in a book by Castellio entitled *Concerning Heretics and Whether They Should Be Persecuted*, published under an assumed name and with a false imprint. The main body of the work was a miscellany of texts, mostly from the writings of the Protestant reformers (including Calvin), in which they opposed the use of the death penalty for heretics. The dedication (to Duke Christoph of Württemberg) began with an imaginary scene. Suppose the duke announced a visit to his subjects and ordered them to put on a white garment in his honour. Imagine his reaction when he found them quarrelling among themselves, stabbing and killing one another in his name, and not a white shirt in sight. Would he not find this reprehensible? Yet, if Christ (who had himself been executed for heresy) returned to earth, that is what he would encounter. Christians should look into their own souls and not condemn others. The role of magistrates was to maintain civil society, not judge theology. The work quickly gained a hearing in France. Had not Calvin sold a pass, justifying anything that the French king might do to Protestants in the name of maintaining right religion in his own kingdom?

In Geneva, opposition focused on the question of whether exile newcomers should be allowed to purchase the rights and status of bourgeois in the city. To allow them to do so would provide a windfall to the city treasury, but at the same time it would change the city's political composition and consolidate Calvin's grip since they were his adherents. Genevans opposed to Calvin attempted an insurrection on the night of 18 May 1555 but it failed. Its leaders were put on trial and executed; others fled into exile. The magistrates admitted an influx of refugees into the bourgeoisie and the political complexion of the city was transformed in Calvin's favour. For the last decade of his life (he died in 1564), Calvin's Reformation in Geneva was politically secure.

Calvin preached (stenographers copying down what he said) week in, week out. He ranged over the issues of the day, brought them to the doorsteps of Genevans and raised the expectations and commitments of what Reformation entailed. The magistrates enforced the efforts of the Church with legal enactments that changed public life. They outlawed dancing, controlled theatrical performances, limited the names allowed at baptism, and increased the penalties for promiscuity, blasphemy and drunkenness. It was not all repressive, though. When it came to matrimonial legislation, which Calvin helped to draft, the resulting ordinances were practical-minded and liberal. They lowered the age of majority, acknowledged the place of women in the choice of spouse and allowed for divorce in certain circumstances. The consistory court turned Calvin's Reformation into a social transformation. It met weekly, with the numbers of cases brought before the elders growing year on year, almost until Calvin's death. That increase explains why Genevans felt that the Church was becoming more intrusive in their lives. Geneva's reputation as a godly 'New Jerusalem' spread widely, as admired by its advocates as it was ridiculed by its detractors. Florimond de Raemond,

Montaigne's contemporary as a magistrate in Bordeaux, sneered at the French Protestant exiles flocking to the place they called 'Hieropolis' (Holy City).

FAILED REPRESSION, RETARDED REFORMATION

After 1539, the French Reformation presented contemporaries with a paradox. The most powerful state in Europe committed itself to repression and failed. With the Edict of Fontainebleau (June 1540) heresy became a state crime, the legislation being strengthened through to the comprehensive Edict of Châteaubriant (1551). France did not need an Inquisition because its magistrates and local governors served the turn. The brutal extermination of the Vaudois (Waldensians) in April 1545 at Mérindol (in Provence) and Cabrières (in the enclave of the Comtat Venaissin) furnished the proof. Yet, even this exceptional case exemplified the difficulties of repression since those responsible were in turn investigated by a special judicial tribunal for abuse of power. This was just one sign of the incoherence of French repression. Those fearing judicial investigation could always (temporarily) make it across the border to the communities of exiles in the Rhineland and western Swiss margins in the late 1540s and 50s. From 1549, Geneva kept a register of the refugees who applied to become resident (*habitant*) in the city. It included over 5,000 names up to 1560 – mostly heads of households. The total number of exiles must have been more than twice that – doubling the indigenous population of the city.

Legislation was too little, too late. That was particularly evident in the control of Protestant printed literature. Up to the early 1540s, the French authorities had it more or less under control. Then a group of mainly Paris printers put their expertise to good use in Genevan exile, remodelling the market and favouring the large-scale diffusion of Calvin's works as well as the Genevan Bibles and Psalters. Not only did the French authorities fail to stop barrel-loads of merchandise making their way across the border, or pedlars taking them to fairs and markets, but they could not unwind the lines of credit that Geneva offered to its retailers, let alone the networks of correspondents by which manuscripts entered the kingdom. After 1555 indigenous Protestant presses established a foothold in Lyon and Rouen, ready to satisfy the demand in the 'wonder years' of French Protestantism of 1560–62. By the 1550s, the French judiciary was investigating fewer suspects and condemning even fewer of them. Even the transfers of prisoners from one jurisdiction to another became imperilled by the ability of Protestant vigilante groups to ambush and release them.

Heresy legislation at home was failing but France's political leaders seemed not to notice. Their sights were set on what was happening abroad, and the royal commitment to the pursuit of heresy had always been subject to the countervailing pressures of international diplomacy. French foreign policy east of the Rhine depended on the support of German, mainly Protestant, princes. Even after the death of Marguerite of Navarre in 1551, Henry II continued to be indulgent towards those in his entourage with dissident opinions. There was a naive sense of optimism among France's governing groups about their ability to foreclose, if necessary, upon heresy. For their part, French magistrates were anxious not to create martyrs. The judges understood that the exemplary value of extreme punishment was easily negated by a culture of martyrdom. The Christian martyr was a familiar figure, perpetuated by hagiographical traditions. But the judicial repression of heresy created a theatre of martyrs. And there were Protestants willing to play that role. On 23 August 1554, the Genevan printer Jean Crespin presented a compilation of their trials to the magistrates in Geneva, asking for permission to publish it. Anxious about its rhetorical impact, they recommended that the words 'saints' and 'martyrs' be replaced with less loaded terms. Calvin weighed in against them and Crespin's book was published without changes. In his preface, Crespin insisted on the pedagogic value of martyr narratives. Better than an old-fashioned saint's reliquary, a martyrology recounted the experiences of contemporaries – ordinary people, flesh and blood, placed in extraordinary circumstances, defending and explaining themselves as best they could, witnessing to faith while knocking a nail in the coffin of the authority that judged them. The *Book of Martyrs* was a compulsive read. Regularly expanded and reprinted to 1609, it contributed to the common patrimony of Protestant martyrologies.

Protestantism in France became indistinguishable from the spread of Calvinism after the end of the 1540s. Calvinism provided a language of opposition: critical, caricatural and convinced. In Agen, for example, the school headmaster taught his students that the lighting of candles in churches was a relic of paganism. One of those pupils later mocked a priest in the street, saying: 'Go to work, priests, you should tend your vines!' Another young man from the same town met ladies on their way from Mass and told them that they had 'just received a paste God'. On All Saints' Day 1552, a group of men gathered at the door of the cathedral in Rouen to gatecrash the sermon, crying out 'What a Fool!' while their companions in the pews mewed like cats. In 1559, at Provins, Catholics were openly mocked in the streets as 'lepers' (cagots). In cemeteries, at roadside shrines and on the exterior decor of churches, Christian imagery was desecrated in acts of anonymous iconoclasm. In Noyon, Calvin's birthplace, a statue of Christ in the local churchyard was torn down and dragged by its feet one night in August 1547 and suspended from the gibbet in the central square of the town. Acts like this were a defiance of authority, an advertisement that those in charge could no longer control heresy. How were Catholics to respond? The priest and prolific pamphleteer of the 1550s Artus Désiré pointed the way. Turning print against the Protestants, he constructed a stereotype of these 'storm-troopers' (francs-taupins) of 'deformation', priapic prophets of Antichrist who would be eliminated in the coming cosmic battle that heralded the End Time.

Calvin's reaction to these developments was a paradox. Rather than encouraging his fellow-countrymen to man the barricades, he held back. He wanted Calvinist communities to come together in mutual charity, but he counselled caution. Many would 'taste God's truth' who would eventually 'be lost to perdition'. They should not rush into forming churches, and they should on no account confront royal authority directly. Geneva's missionary effort, despatching trained pastors to these congregations, began very late. As a result, the Reformation in France was not 'made in Geneva', and the case has even been put that Calvin botched things, his prudence leading to the growth of a movement that he could neither direct nor manage. Geneva did not impose its church order, discipline and confession on the emerging French churches. Rather, it found itself willy-nilly turned into a source of authority for the divided, scattered and leaderless churches in France which needed the doctrinal and disciplinary security Geneva provided. Little by little the French churches emerged from the shadows after 1555 in a way that neither royal authority nor Geneva could effectively control. Their leadership passed in due course to the French nobility, with consequences that were very different from anything Calvin had intended.

THE RHINELAND AND THE NETHERLANDS: MAGISTRATES, REFUGEES, REVOLUTION

The Rhineland from Basel northwards offered a Reformation haven. It is not a matter of understanding its success – for instance in Strasbourg (1529) and Frankfurt (1533) – but of explaining why it failed elsewhere. In this fragmented space, a Reformation in one place created reaction and opposition in another, with human movement, coerced or voluntary exiles, acting as convecting currents for and against the Reformation. In one instance, it got out of hand. The Rhineland was the communication corridor for the Habsburg dynastic empire, its messengers and military forces. Some areas were its hereditary lands; others served as its recruiting grounds. Where they could, these regions stood against religious change, assisted by local vested interests.

For the magistrates of Rhineland cities where the Reformation was implanted, the issue was managing change. That was not easy, especially in a place like Strasbourg, which was a breeding-ground for religious opinions of all sorts. If there was no major social unrest there, it was because the city fathers appreciated the limits of their own authority. Within its walls you might encounter, besides the majority adherents to the magisterial Reformation, steered forward by Martin Bucer until he was forced to leave in 1547, Lutherans, Sacramentarian Zwinglians, adult baptizers, spiritualists, epicureans (i.e. liberal-minded humanists), French evangelicals, émigrés from England and the Netherlands, critics of tithes, usury and monasticism, and Chiliastic millenarians.

Strasbourg was where an opinionated furrier from Schwäbisch Hall, Melchior Hofmann, encountered Anabaptism for the first time in 1529. In a commentary on the Book of Daniel, published in 1526, he announced that the Last Judgment would occur in seven years' time. He was convinced by Ursula and Lienhard Jost and Barbara Rebstock (the 'great prophetess of the Kalbsgasse'), all three known for their trances, that not only were the last days upon them but that he was himself the new Elijah. Hofmann proclaimed Strasbourg as the spiritual Jerusalem where Christ would set up his kingdom on earth. Imprisoned by the magistrates, Hofmann managed several times to escape to the lower Rhineland and the Netherlands to spread his messianic views. In 1533, back in Strasbourg, he courted arrest. The city's magistrates obliged. He was just one of a stream of individuals committed to radical religious change that they had to keep an eye on.

Refugees from France, the Netherlands, England and Scotland in the Rhineland could join a 'stranger' church, a community set apart from the ambient Lutheranism. Fourteen such churches had a tenuous existence in the period from 1538 to 1564, the leading ones being in Strasbourg, Basel, Frankfurt and Wesel. They were self-governing congregations, open to being seduced by those in their midst who sought moral and doctrinal purity. They looked to Calvin to resolve their quarrels and became the first Calvinist churches outside Geneva. This 'refugee Reformation' spread outside towns. Tucked in the Vosges mountains and on the margins of the duchy of Lorraine lay the mining communities around Sainte-Marie-aux-Mines in the Lièpvre valley, where mining flourished in the sixteenth century. Anabaptists from Zürich settled there in the 1530s, making a living by farming the upper valley. They were joined by German-speaking Lutheran miners and then, later on, by French-speaking Calvinist refugees. Somehow this valley of religious pluralism in the later sixteenth century survived amid the outcrops of territorialized confessional religious uniformity and confrontation all around, an exception protected from persecution by its overlord and by its own obscurity.

In the Netherlands, the challenges facing the magistrates were similar to those in Strasbourg, but with striking differences. Their overlord was Habsburg, and their wealth underwrote the emperor's military campaigns. Ghent was the biggest city in Flanders. Antwerp, the jewel of Brabant, was not far behind it. Amsterdam, the largest town in Holland, by contrast, was a small place of not more than 2,500 houses. To a degree unique in Europe, these places' prosperity depended on traded goods. Just as bales of Flemish cloth sold at Wittenberg market, so Luther's works found their way to the Netherlands. Over thirty editions of his writings were translated into Dutch by 1530 – and there would be many others from Protestant reformers in both Dutch and French to cater for Walloon and Dutch markets.

The cultural attitudes of the élite percolated through to the wider cross-section of the population. People here were expected to be able to read, think and act for themselves. The surviving evidence from heresy investigations suggests the down-to-earth ways in which ordinary people understood religion. Wendelmoet Claesdochter from Monnickendam, revered by Dutch Protestants, dismissed holy unction to anoint the sick as 'good only for salads or for greasing boots'. Eloy Pruystinck, a slater from Antwerp who visited Wittenberg in 1525 and disputed with Melanchthon, thought that everyone possessed a holy spirit, and that faith was desiring for one's neighbour what one wanted for oneself. Plain folk echoed what they heard on the streets or in taverns – that the clergy were worthless, that fasting brought on headaches and that to say that bread and wine were turned into Christ's body and blood was mumbo-jumbo.

How were the patrician families at Antwerp, Ghent and Amsterdam to manage such dissent? Dutch magistrates were integral to urban literate and corporate culture, epitomized by the Chambers of Rhetoric that convened artists, artisans and merchants under municipal patronage. By the middle of the sixteenth century, virtually every city in the Low Countries had one such society – Antwerp had several – and Ghent ran an annual competition for the best play-text on a chosen theme. The surviving texts reveal this civic culture. There were familiar satirical targets (worthless priests and fat monks) and moralizing tones. In the Ghent competition of 1539, the Gillyflower Chamber from Antwerp offered a play around the proposed theme: 'What is a dying man's supreme hope?' Their answer was unambiguously Protestant.

Within weeks of the play's performance, Ghent rose in revolt. Some patricians were outraged by the emperor's attack on their privileges, symbolized by a charter that he had forced them to accept at the time of his 'Joyous Entry' into the city in 1515. Others belonged to evangelical circles, or were fired up by the mounting costs of 'voluntary loans' that Charles V had exacted. A group of guildsmen arrested patricians who were rumoured to have made secret deals with the emperor for the further infringement of the city's privileges. To the shouts of day-labourers (the 'Screamers'), the odious charter was cut into pieces in front of the City Hall, while a new committee of aldermen instituted changes, beginning with the compulsory sale of grain at reasonable prices. Ghent's revolt fizzled out before the end of the year. Charles V visited the city at the beginning of Lent in 1540, rewrote its privileges and banned its

Chambers of Rhetoric. Ghent epitomized the early Reformation in the Netherlands: a low-grade war of words, an outbreak of street violence and civic opposition.

Charles V was determined to stamp out heresy in the Netherlands. He succeeded, albeit at a price. As the later experience in Italy was to prove, exceptional circumstances were required for the Inquisition to be accepted. In Milan, the citizens rioted when Philip II tried to introduce it. In Naples, they threatened a revolt in 1547 leading to the temporary withdrawal of the proposal. In the Netherlands, there was similar opposition. Yet that did not prevent a troika of civil, ecclesiastical and pontifical tribunals being deployed to carry out edicts (*Placarten*) against Protestantism. The legislation created a hybrid definition of heresy as a form of treason, more heinous than counterfeiting coins. Once someone was convicted, there was no latitude. Penitence changed only the method of execution. Treason meant the expropriation of the property of the condemned to the state.

This was alien to the patricians, some of whom were caught in the legislation themselves. Antwerp refused to publish the anti-heresy edict of April 1550 because it demanded that no one could take up residence without a certificate for Catholicity. That compromised trade with Protestant England and the Baltic. Groningen (only incorporated into the Netherlands in 1536) also bridled at interference from Brussels. Dissidents escaped there to lie low. After 1530, heresy edicts denounced the negligence of the police or the leniency of local magistrates. It was uphill work for the special commissioners and local inquisitors appointed to investigate heresy. Given local opposition, it is the more remarkable that so many went to the scaffold – perhaps 1,300 women and men between 1523 and 1566. There was a high rate of conviction (in Flanders 60 per cent of those investigated) and remissions were rare (less than 1 per cent were released on letters of pardon). Repression removed potential Protestant leaders and brought patricians into a reluctant conformity. Where France failed, the Netherlands appeared to succeed.

That success was at the price of alienation. It did not happen openly, given the spectre of revolt and the lack of any aristocratic leadership to which the alienated could turn for support before 1560. The numbers of exiled Protestants from the Low Countries in Bremen, Basel, Emden (in time, a northern Protestant 'Geneva') and London grew, beginning in the 1540s. The resulting 'stranger' communities abroad sustained an underground network of Protestant contacts and congregations which the authorities had greater difficulty in quashing. The success of Charles V's persecution deprived the fledgling Protestant movement of those who would naturally have been its conservative leaders. In so doing, it opened the door to an Anabaptist movement that was less dependent on élites. Precisely because the Anabaptist movement in the Netherlands lacked a civic leadership which would have kept it in check, it developed a radical potential that was to be found nowhere else.

So Melchior Hofmann's apocalyptic message had an impact among Dutch artisans. Hofmann visited East Friesland, rebaptizing adults in Emden and elsewhere in 1530. He called on them to 'separate themselves from the world' through the 'true sign of the covenant' (rebaptism) in order to be among those saved in the coming Apocalypse. One of his disciples, Jan Volkertszoon, a clog-maker from Hoorn, returned to Amsterdam. Under the noses of the authorities, he rebaptized those whom he persuaded to 'forsake the world and the flesh, to cleave to God and to love their neighbour'. He was eventually executed at The Hague in December 1531 along with others. Shocked, Melchior Hofmann ordered rebaptism to cease until, as he expected, the Apocalypse occurred in 1533.

Jan Matthys, a baker from Haarlem who had been rebaptized by Hofmann, did not follow that lead. Convincing himself and his fellow Melchiorites in Amsterdam that he was the true Enoch, the Prophet foretold in Revelation, he rebaptized those who came to him on All Saints' Day 1533 and left his first ('shrewish') wife for another. He then despatched his followers, two by two, to proclaim the coming of the Apocalypse. Two of these apostles, Gerrit Boeckbinder and Jan van Leyden, sailed across the Zuider Zee to Münster, the episcopal city to the east of the Netherlands which had recently turned Protestant. Arriving there in January 1534, they announced themselves as Enoch and Elijah and proclaimed it as the New Jerusalem, Matthys joining them a month later along with other Dutch Anabaptists. A 'Great Exodus' followed. Between 14,000 and 16,000 believers from Holland gathered for the flight from 'Egypt'. Twenty-seven ships with about 3,000 aboard left Monnickendam and arrived at the Zwarte Water river near Genemuiden (Overijssel), where many were promptly captured and disarmed. No one resisted, because they expected Jeremiah to take them into the land of Canaan. In Münster, Matthys rebaptized the majority of the population with the encouragement of Berndt Knipperdollinck, a cloth merchant and one of the two new burgomasters elected to the Anabaptist city council on 22 February 1534.

There then began a Reformation like none other. Monasteries and churches were looted and images were smashed. Under the pressure of a siege from forces organized by the bishop and Westphalian princes, Lutherans and Catholics who refused to be rebaptized were expelled. Their property was placed in central warehouses, silver melted down to make coins inscribed with: 'The Word of God made Flesh Lives in Us'. Inhabitants were enjoined to call one another 'brother' and 'sister' and to live in a community bound by love. Communal ownership of commodities was established along with publicly directed labour services. A blacksmith who challenged the legality of proceedings was stabbed and then shot by Jan Matthys in a town council meeting.

After Easter 1534, Jan Bockelson ran naked through the town and fell into a silent ecstasy. When his speech returned three days later, he called for a new Sanhedrin government of the city by twelve apostolic elders. In the legal code which followed in August, Bockelson proposed polygamous marriage on the biblical precept of 'increase and multiply'. The proposal was not immediately accepted by the elders and it was only after an uprising that it was made law. In September, Bockelson was proclaimed 'Prophet-King of Zion'. The streets and gates of the town were renamed in celebration of the New Jerusalem. Sundays and feast-days were abolished and the days of the week reconfigured alphabetically. Divara, Bockelson's chief wife, was proclaimed queen and she held court with him in the marketplace, which was where the throne of New Jerusalem was erected. Pamphlets in support of the Anabaptist kingdom were smuggled out to encourage risings elsewhere. In Amsterdam eleven naked streakers (*Naaktloopers*) ran round the streets to proclaim the 'naked truth' of what was happening in Münster. The siege lasted seventeen months before the city capitulated on 24 June 1535. The Anabaptists were promised safe quarter but their leaders were put to death. Knipperdollinck and others were publicly tortured with red-hot irons, their bodies suspended from the tower of St Lambert's church in cages, which remain there still. Jan Bockelson was found in a cellar. For several months thereafter he was paraded in shackles around Germany as an object of curiosity before he too was tortured to death.

The Melchiorites are the unloved foster-children of the Reformation. Catholics used Münster as a sign that the Reformation was the instrument of the Devil. Magisterial Protestantism disowned it at every opportunity. Within Anabaptist historiography the Melchiorites have been sidelined as an illegitimate and unrepresentative brand. In reality, Melchiorite Anabaptism was not entirely defeated at Münster. It lived on for a time among the sect which acknowledged Jan van Batenburg, the bastard son of a minor nobleman from Gelderland, as the new David. The Batenburgers believed that the kingdom of God would be established by military power and thought polygamy was legitimate. Melchior Hofmann went on smuggling pamphlets out of his Strasbourg cell, singing 'woe on you godless scribes of Strasbourg'. Among those caught up in the events at Münster was Menno Simons, a priest at Witmarsum. Convinced that there was no biblical justification for infant baptism, Simons preached against those 'false teachers' who 'traffic in strange doctrine' and usurp the role of Christ the King. It was under his influence that Dutch Anabaptism was led towards 'spiritual resurrection', about which he wrote eloquently, a new birth which comes when one is reborn into God's family. The emphasis that he placed on the family and upon spiritual struggle had its impact on others in Dutch separatist congregations, notably David Joris and Hendrik Niclaes, whose 'Family of Love' percolated into unlikely places in the sixteenth century, including small English towns and Elizabeth I's court. The Münster rising was a reminder of what the Protestant Reformation had stirred up but not settled: the sources and guarantees of theological, social and political order and God's plan for the world.

REFORMATION IMPORTS

In eastern-central Europe, the Protestant Reformation was an import, dependent on propitious circumstances for its success, particularly on its adaptation to the linguistic and cultural milieu, on local support and on the fortuitous outcome of the conflicts that it raised. The guardians of tradition and legitimacy proved critical to the success or otherwise of the proselytizers of the new faith. Knowing what was to happen later (a Catholic revival and the Thirty Years War), it is easy to ignore the fact that there were significant regions (northern Bohemia, Moravia, Silesia,

Lusatia, the Baltic littoral, parts of Greater Poland, northern and eastern Hungary) where the Catholic Church was reduced to an ineffectual minority. The largest Protestant church building in the sixteenth century was St Mary's in Gdańsk – a huge brick barn beside which the Polish monarchy was constrained to erect a small Catholic chapel so that it had somewhere to worship when it visited the port.

Protestantism challenged not only the Catholic Church but also royal authority. The elective monarchies of eastern Europe mainly clung on to the old religion – associating it with the traditions and mythologies that surrounded their rule. Only the voivodes (i.e. palatine rulers) of Transylvania, a new dominium that emerged after the battle of Mohács, adopted the Protestant religion. The Polish crown, however, was twice occupied by those who had accepted Protestantism before they were elected to it: in 1575 by István Báthory, Zápolya's successor in Transylvania, and then in 1587 by Sigismund III Vasa, king of Poland.

The elective monarchies depended for their authority on the local Estates. In Bohemia and its associated crown lands (Moravia, Silesia and Lusatia), in Poland, Hungary and in the Austrian archduchies, power lay with the nobility. The result was a partially emasculated Church and a tendency to concede religious determination to a local level and accept the reality of the pluralism that resulted in the name of guaranteeing noble privilege. In Poland, King Sigismund II Augustus surrendered whatever may have been his personal inclinations to the necessity of the entente with the Polish Diet. A decree of 1555 and further decisions of 1562–3 weakened Church courts. By 1569, when Protestants almost equalled Catholics in the Polish Senate, some deal had to be struck. In January 1573, the Confederation of Warsaw (signed by Catholic, Protestant and Orthodox representatives) agreed a mutual peace between the various religions. Its terms were confirmed by Henry of Valois at his election to the Polish throne in 1573, and then by his three successors, thereby almost turning it into a fundamental law.

In Bohemia, royal military and financial authority was also dependent on agreement with the Bohemian Diet. Laws were enacted only with the approval of these Estates and both the Supreme Court and the provincial government were composed of representatives of the nobility. The latter acquired much of the wealth of the clergy and the authority to nominate to local benefices. If they nominated Protestant ministers, nobody could stop them. In Moravia, the Diet, the sovereign judicial court and local officialdom were all in the hands of local nobility. The latter had no difficulty in resisting King Ferdinand I's attempts to reimpose Catholicism. It was the governor of Moravia, Wenceslaus Ludanic, who, at the Diet of Brünn in 1550, defended evangelical teaching and reminded the king of his coronation oath. Facing a majority vote against him, Ferdinand accepted a negotiated religious pluralism which made Moravia the avatar for the Peace of Augsburg in the Holy Roman Empire.

Protestantism prospered in eastern-central Europe, where it won over the local nobility. It was on their lands and under their influence that it thrived – spectacularly so on the estates and with the patronage of Prince Nicholas Radziwiłł, Voivode of Livonia, Grand Hetman of Lithuania and a gatekeeper for Calvinism in Poland. It flourished more modestly under the influence of magnates like Count Stefán Schlik and members of his family, who had founded the silver mine at Joachimsthal and had estates in the region around Loket in western Bohemia. The Schliks established Protestant grammar schools and employed Lutheran ministers. Here, as elsewhere, Protestantism accompanied imported German know-how in glass manufacture, linen and textiles.

The importation can be measured through the efforts to produce vernacular Bibles. Fundamental to the success of the Protestant endeavour, it was compromised by the linguistic diversity of these regions and by the fact that many of the languages in question had unstable written forms and, in Slav, a variety of alphabets. The commercialization of book production (which secured its success in western Europe) was compromised in the east by the small markets for individual translations, and the underdeveloped printing and distribution infrastructures. Production was all the more dependent, therefore, on aristocratic patronage, the collaboration of clerics and the availability of vernacular translations. In some places, that had not happened at all by 1650. There was no Bible translation into Macedonian or Bulgarian before the nineteenth century, no Estonian Bible before 1739, and the first Latvian translation appeared in 1689. The first Finnish New Testament came in 1553, but the complete Bible followed only in 1642. Remarkable, by contrast, was the achievement of Primož Trubar, the Protestant reformer from Carniola. Working in exile, he produced the first two printed books in Slovene, a Protestant catechism and a learn-to-read manual, before going on to complete a translation of the New Testament.

It lies alongside that of Antonius Dalmata (Anton Dalmatin), who, with Stipan Consul, achieved the first translation and printing (in glagolitic characters) of the Croatian New Testament, at Tübingen in 1562. Only in Bohemia was this effort anything other than uphill. Uniquely in eastern-central Europe, Bohemia had a pre-Reformation vernacular Hussite Bible and a church organization to resource new translations. Two partial ones preceded the comprehensive New Testament in Czech of Jan Blahoslav, which began to appear in 1564 and in due course became part of the Kralice Bible (1579), funded and coordinated by the Czech Unity of Brethren.

In eastern-central Europe Protestantism spread through Germanic culture. Communities of German merchants dominated the Hanseatic towns of the Baltic littoral. German miners worked in Bohemia and Hungary, and Saxon nobles had estates and interests in northwestern Bohemia. Through their efforts Protestant gymnasia were established, the pride of towns such as Elbing and Joachimsthal. But Protestantism also infiltrated indirectly, by means of mercantile contact and through students from eastern Europe studying at Wittenberg (there were eighty-eight from Bohemia there in 1530) and, increasingly after 1550, in the Calvinist academies in Germany. There were also communities of German extraction in eastern-central Europe whose affinities to that culture drew them to Lutheranism. Kežmarok, a town settled by Saxons in the thirteenth century, stands in the shadow of the Carpathian Mountains in northern Hungary. Its priest, Thomas Preisner, read out Luther's *Ninety-Five Theses* from the pulpit in 1521. The events of the Reformation were followed closely in the German-influenced mining towns of what is now central Slovakia (Banská Štiavnica, Kremnica, Banská Bystrica). That influence mostly did not extend to an elaborate Church organization beyond the local level, although ordinances, a common order of services and a confession emerged in the early 1530s in the Hanseatic towns of the Baltic, and later in Bohemia, Hungary and Poland as confessional differences made their mark.

People aligned themselves religiously in accordance with their attitude towards German culture, which limited the spread of Protestantism. Magyars, Slavs, Croats, Slovenes and Poles did not identify with it. Jews looked to Judaism for their identity, Ruthenians to Orthodox Christianity, Tatars to Islam. Where the Reformation aligned itself with indigenous identities, it was in its dissident forms, both because Protestant dissidents tended to be driven out towards the extremities, and because they too identified with Protestantism that was not German Lutheran. So in Hungary there would be a significant Anabaptist presence as well as a vigorous Calvinism. Transylvania would become a Calvinist state in the later sixteenth century.

In Poland, too, Calvinism was the form of Protestantism that made the greatest impact, partly thanks to the efforts of Jan Łaski (John à Lasco). The only Polish Protestant theologian with an international reputation, he had spent time in Basel and Emden among the 'stranger' churches before becoming superintendent to the 'stranger' congregation in London from 1550 to 1553, where his ingenuity was put to good use in settling quarrels and framing constitutions and confessions that met its needs. Leaving at the accession of Mary Tudor with a shipload of refugees, he settled in Brandenburg before returning to his native Poland in 1556. There, he put his talents to good use, lobbying in high places (he became a secretary to King Sigismund II Augustus), winning over Polish gentry to Calvinism, and bringing together the Lutherans, Calvinists and exiled Bohemian Brethren into a common agreement at Sandomierz in 1570. That was an accord framed against the anti-Trinitarians (i.e. Unitarians), a force to be reckoned with. In Poland, they had split off from the fledgling Calvinist Church in 1556 and established themselves as the 'Ecclesia Minor' or 'Polish Brethren', while, in Transylvania, Voivode John Sigismund Zápolya made no secret of his Unitarian leanings. Fausto Sozzini, Łaski's equal as a theologian, spent the winter of 1578–9 as the personal guest of George Biandrata, the physician to the Transylvanian court at Cluj-Napoca, before moving on to Poland, where he became a spokesman for the Polish Brethren, feared by his critics and a thorn in the side of confessionalized Protestantism.

The Reformation in eastern-central Europe moulded itself to established ethnic, political and social contours. It was anaemic, created no martyrs and lacked a divisive edge. Bohemia was the exception. Its indigenous Reformation had occurred in the previous century. It already had a new religious doctrine (that of Jan Hus), 'Utraquist' (*in utroque specie*, in both kinds, bread and wine) churches independent of the papacy, and the potential for radical change among Taborite sects with their social theology. By 1520, however, Taborite radicalism was a spent force, channelled into the Unity of Brethren, which rejected violence and concentrated instead on the spiritual struggle within. Although they had bishops and elders, the Brethren were, as their name suggests, an affiliation of congregations in which the laity had the upper hand. The Utraquist Church became a Czech clerical establishment, cautious to the point of myopia when it came to embracing Lutheranism. Only a minority within the Utraquist Church was open to Protestantism. Among the Unity of Brethren, however, a rapprochement with Lutheran Protestantism occurred. In 1535, their confession of faith reflected the Augsburg Confession and they drew strength from their affinities with the Lutherans in Germany.

The noble leaders in the Bohemian Estates tried to turn those affinities into a political movement in 1547. King Ferdinand used the opportunity of a fire in the archives to rewrite the terms on which he had been elected to imply a hereditary principle. In response (rashly, since they had no support from Moravia, Hungary or elsewhere), they declared their backing for John Frederick, Elector of Saxony, and the Schmalkaldic League, denied the request from Ferdinand for men and arms to aid the imperial cause and rose in revolt. The League's defeat at Mühlberg in April 1547 signalled their own. The Brethren, the towns and prominent German Lutherans paid the price of the rebellion. The Brethren were exiled (some of them seeking refuge in Moravia, others in southern Poland), while the towns lost their self-government and Lutheran counts were dispossessed of their property. The nobility in general was pardoned and the 'liberties and privileges' of the Estates openly maintained, but with a significant caveat. In their 'Recess' (resolution) upon the land ordinance of 1549, the nobility of the Bohemian Estates accepted that 'the privilege of the Bohemian lands embodies this principle, that the eldest son of each king shall become king of Bohemia after the death of his father'. Eastern-central Europe would be largely spared the political instability that occurred in western Europe in the second half of the sixteenth century. But this clause implying the end of the elective monarchy in Bohemia returned to haunt the nobility seventy years later at the beginning of the Thirty Years War.

The Reformation in the British Isles was also largely an importation from abroad. Unlike eastern Europe, the area was dominated by strong monarchies – the Tudors south of the border and the newly strengthened Stuarts to the north. That masks the degree to which it was influenced from outside, not least because the Reformation began with an 'Act of State', the 'Great Matter' of King Henry VIII's divorce from

Catherine of Aragon. By the law of consequences much followed thereafter. Henry VIII's divorce came at the wrong moment for both the papacy and Emperor Charles V (who was Catherine's nephew) and they mishandled it. Papal authority in England was dismantled by legal means, steered through the English Parliament by the king's minister, Thomas Cromwell. The Act in Restraint of Appeals (abolishing legal appeals to Rome, 1533) declared that 'by divers sundry old authentic histories and chronicles it is manifestly ... expressed that this realm of England is an empire' – an assertion of the English monarch as the equal of the emperor, with an imperial (closed) crown to prove it. In addition, it envisaged that empire as a 'body politic ... divided in terms and by names of spirituality and temporality' which owed the king a 'natural and humble obedience'. The Act of Supremacy (1534) declared the king 'by authority of this present Parliament ... the only supreme head in earth of the Church of England'.

Cromwell made the most of this supremacy and dissolved the monastic fabric of England in a little under five years in the face of popular resistance. None of this, however, amounted to a proper Protestant Reformation. Henry VIII's regime was never short on advertising itself, both to its subjects and abroad. A copy of Stephen Gardiner's *On True Obedience* (1535) and the Henrician *Protestation* found their way into every ambassadorial briefcase. The pope had earlier rewarded King Henry with the title 'Defender of the Faith' after his *Defence of the Seven Sacraments*. So Henry sought to preserve the common faith of Christendom, albeit within a monarchical-led Church, shorn of those elements that had aroused the wrath of its critics. Lutheranism did not enter into the Supreme Head. Those around him more open to evangelical opinions (such as Archbishop Thomas Cranmer) quietly tore their hair out or became victims of the cut and thrust of Henrician politics (Anne Boleyn, Cromwell). Among the minority of early English enthusiasts for the Reformation was an Oxford-trained academic, William Tyndale, whose Protestant evangelism took him abroad, almost certainly to Wittenberg as well as to the Rhineland. There, he translated the Bible into memorably plain English (with a trace of his Gloucester roots). Henry VIII hated it, and so did Sir Thomas More. The latter was in the Tower of London by the time of Tyndale's arrest. If More did not pay the person who ultimately betrayed Tyndale, then the king himself was the instrument of his execution by inquisitors in the Low Countries.

Henry VIII could not, however, will what happened beyond his grave. His son and heir, Edward VI, was a minor, nine years old in 1547. The 'godly imp' was given the best education money could buy. His tutors included the classical scholar John Cheke, who came out of the closet to declare for Protestantism in 1547. Edward's uncle, Edward Seymour (brother of Jane Seymour, King Edward's mother and Henry VIII's third wife), became Protector and the king's council was a roll-call of those whose Protestantism had, like Cheke's, been well hidden. The Reformation experiment that occurred in the six years from 1547 to 1553 was a borrowed one, 'act two of a continental drama played out earlier and on a different stage', as a recent historian put it. But it was eclectic, the result eccentric and resisted locally.

Archbishop Thomas Cranmer recruited theological talent abroad. In the aftermath of the imperial victory at Mühlberg it was a good time to be looking. Bernardino Ochino was smuggled out of Augsburg, given a new suit of clothes and the books he asked for, provided with a non-resident post at Canterbury and attached to the 'stranger' church in London. His writings, suitably translated, had a big impact. His fellow-countryman Peter Martyr Vermigli was recruited to a post in Oxford. The bishops were his friends – Latimer, Ridley, Ponet and Hooper. It was his theology of the Eucharist that was mediated through Cranmer into the 1552 Book of Common Prayer. Other foreigners included Martin Bucer (a chair in Cambridge), the Hebraist Immanuel Tremellius (Tremellio – one of Vermigli's colleagues from Lucca) and Jan Łaski – all part of Cranmer's idea (which emerged in March 1552) for a general council of the Church that would trump the Council of Trent. The project never got off the ground and England's Protestant experiment was caught short with Edward VI's sudden death in 1553. Among the unfinished business was the 'Reformation of the Laws', the project to replace canon law on which Vermigli, William Cecil and others spent a great deal of energy. In that sense, as in others, England was not more than half-Reformed by the time of the king's death.

His successor, Mary Tudor, came to power in a coup against a Prot- estant minority, determined to try to hang on through advancing the claims of Lady Jane Grey, who was rapidly caught and executed by forces loyal to Mary. That minority knew the vulnerability of the English Protestant experiment. Thomas Cranmer advised Vermigli and others to leave the country in September 1553. As they packed their bags, the archbishops of Canterbury and York, with the bishops of London and Worcester, were marched off to prison, round one of the operation to undo the Protestant Reformation. Everything depended on targeting the organizational fabric of Protestantism, using the supremacy of the English state over its Church against it, and winning the battle to secure a particular view of 'true obedience'. It was achieved with the re-imported talent of Cardinal Reginald Pole, who arrived back as cardinal legate in November 1554. No one knew better, given his Italian experience, how to articulate that obedience in such a way that the key debate under Mary was not about winning hearts and minds, but about securing conformity. We shall never know how successful the campaign to re-Catholicize England would have been; it was truncated by the death of Mary in November 1558. Over 300 people were burned at the stake – mainly in the south of the country. Others left the country to join the 'refugee Reformation' in the Rhineland and in Switzerland, one of them being John Foxe, the English martyrologist. His efforts to document the Marian persecution and set it in the context of the wider pattern of God's intervention in history became part of Protestant England's birthright.

What Foxe does not tell us is that, by 1558, the authorities had despatched most of the Protestant leadership that had stayed behind, and were mopping up the remnants – the 'sustainers' of the movement – harder to find, but by then quiescent. Had Mary lived longer, it is difficult to imagine a circumstance in which English Protestantism would have easily revived. It would have had no help from France or the Low Countries. In Scotland, the regency of Mary of Lorraine (1543–61) was just culminating with the marriage of her daughter (Mary Stuart) to the Valois dauphin, Francis II, in 1558. With the establishment of common Franco-Scottish nationality in 1557, Scotland seemed destined to be part of a French dynastic empire. The accession of Elizabeth I to the English throne in November 1558 turned everything on its head. A period of unparalleled instability in the politics of western Europe was beginning. With it emerged transnational, politico-religious affiliations that sought to create Christian commonwealths in Europe that were very different from the Christendom of the past.

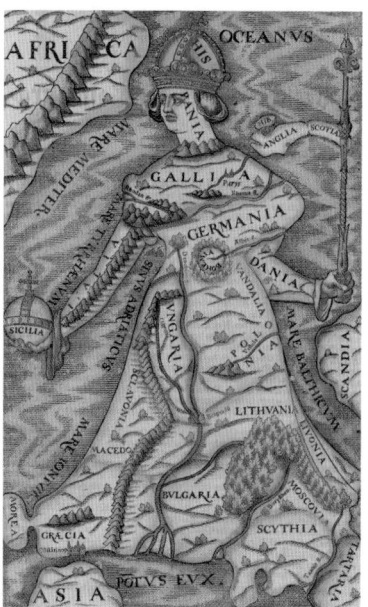

1. Luther's Wittenberg collaborator was Lucas Cranach the Elder. His erotic version of female beauty worked its way into the Wittenberg Reformation. Depicting Hesiod's close of the silver age (from around 1530), he evokes the dawn of a dangerous epoch.

2. The humanist Johannes Bucius Aenicola first conceived this cartographic depiction of Europe as a queen, published in 1537. The image was popularized through an engraving in later editions of Sebastian Münster's *Cosmographia*.

3. Thomas Cockson's engraving *The Revells of Christendom* offered a satire on international politics in the wake of the Twelve Years Truce (1609).

4. Annibale Carracci popularized the painting of everyday subjects. In *The Bean-Eater* (early 1580s) an Italian scoffs his beans with a wooden spoon. His meal includes bread, vegetables, onions and a glass of wine.

5. Isaac van Swanenburgh depicted various stages of cloth production in a cycle of paintings from the sixteenth century. They later decorated the Leiden clothiers' guildhall, where cloth production was inspected and regulated.

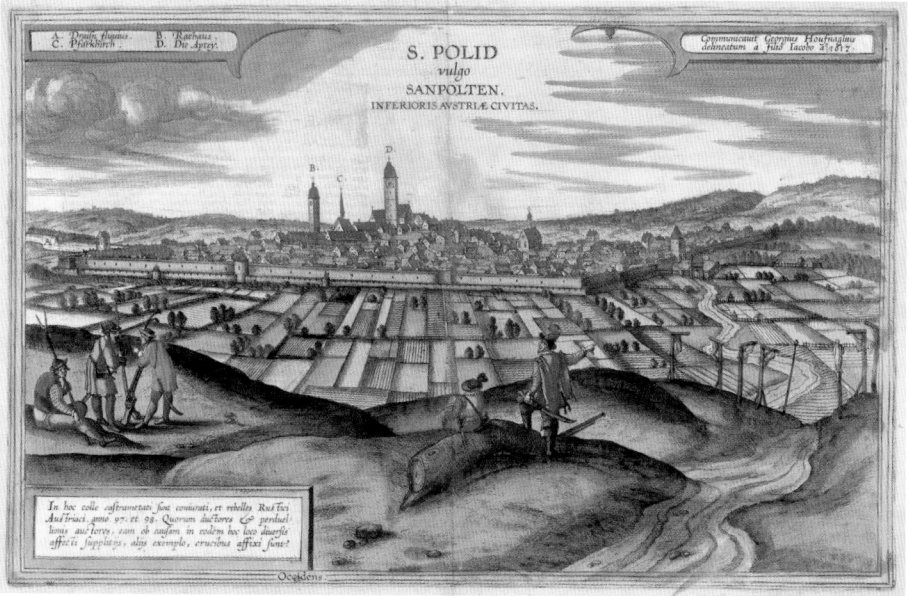

6. Sankt Pölten, a town in Lower Austria, featured among the cityscapes in the final volume of the *Civitates Orbis Terrarum* (1617). Georg Hoefnagel had engraved the scene in the wake of the brutal suppression of a peasant insurrection in 1597. Some of its sixty executed leaders are depicted on gallows outside the city walls.

7. The *Rathaus* (municipal court) in Lübeck around 1625, meeting in an arcade facing the market square. The painting depicts a woman pleading her suit before the municipal judges.

8. The silver from the mine at Potosí (Peru) was carried by llamas to the coast, the first stage of its journey to Europe and the Far East. This engraving appeared in the geographer Théodore de Bry's description of the Americas (*Americae*, 1602).

9. Théodore de Bry's description of the Americas included the Tupinamba people, depicted as living sociably. Their cannibalism struck Europeans as disconcerting since it evoked the massacres within Europe in the wake of the Protestant Reformation.

10. The arrival of European traders, as seen from outside Europe. This detail, taken from a Japanese folding screen (*byōbu*) in around 1600, shows *namban* ('southern barbarian') Portuguese disembarking in Japan with their goods.

11. Franciscan ethnographer Bernardino de Sahagún employed Aztec artists, trained in European representational techniques, to illustrate his *General History of New Spain*. Here the artist depicts domestic pagan rituals involving the summoning of the Devil.

12. Bonaventura Peeters the Elder paints a thriving harbour (probably Archangel in Northern Russia) in 1644. Hunters arrive with their goods, while the large ship being loaded in the harbour flies the Danish flag.

13. Two of the remarkable illustrations from the sixteenth-century Augsburg bourgeois Matthäus Schwarz's manuscript account of his life through the clothes he wore.

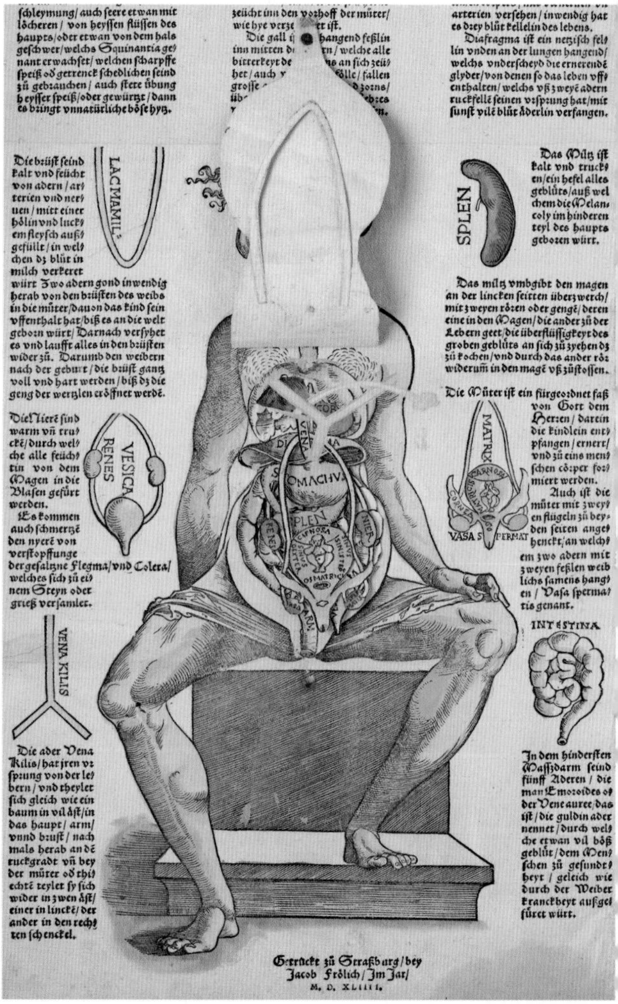

14. Among the many innovative uses of print technology were broadsheets for medical students (this one published in Strasbourg in 1544). The illustrations incorporated paper flaps which, when lifted, offered a printed equivalent to an anatomical dissection.

Getruckt zu Straßburg/bey Jacob Frölich/Jm Jar/ M. D. XLIIII.

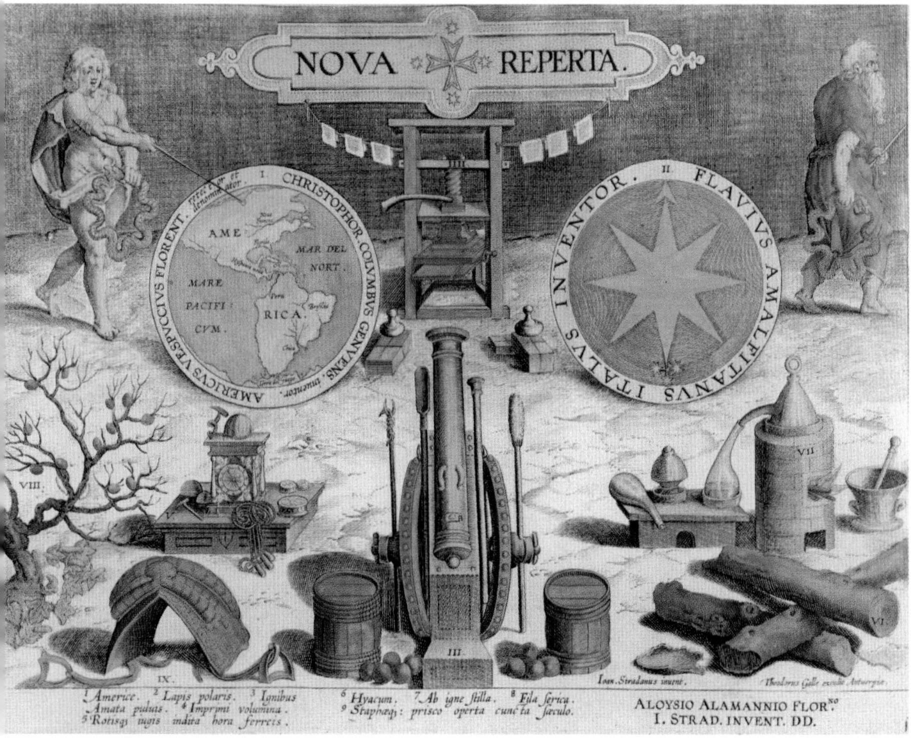

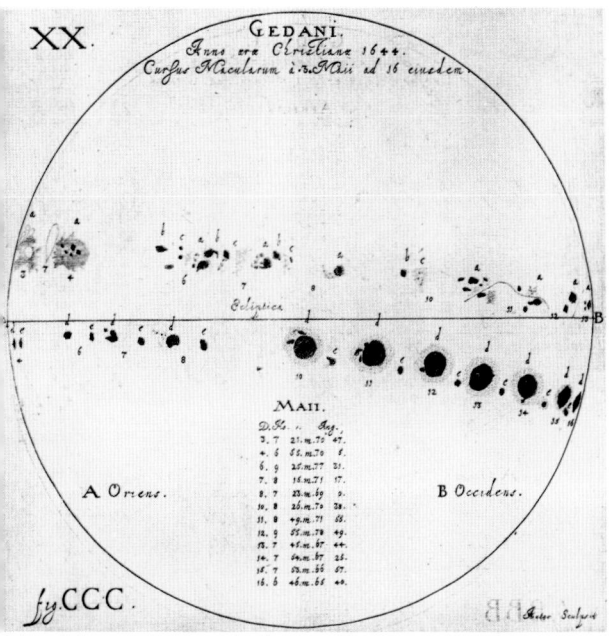

NOVA ✠ REPERTA.

15. The frontispiece engraving to the successful 'New Discoveries' (*Nova Reperta*) compilation by the Flemish publicist Jan van der Straet (Stradanus). The discovery of the New World takes pride of place, accompanied by other wonders of the modern world. Aristotle discreetly exits stage right.

16. Telescopes enabled observers to track sunspots accurately. The Gdansk astronomer Johannes Hevelius published the sunspots he had observed in composite illustrations in *Selenographia* (1644; illustrated here in the 1647 edition), confirming that sunspot activity had become rare by the mid-seventeenth century.

17. Nature's prodigies and abnormalities stimulated the curiosity of Europe's courts, philosophers and naturalists. Antonietta Gonzales inherited her rare genetic abnormality from her father. Painted here by Lavinia Fontana in 1583, she became notorious, featuring in Ulisse Aldrovandi's collection of monsters.

18. Adriaen van Stalbemt's painting of an aristocratic cabinet of curiosities in the early seventeenth century is an imaginative depiction of how nature, science and the arts are capable of enticing and beguiling the human senses.

Christian Commonwealths
in Contention

12. Conflicts in the Name of God

CHRISTENDOM'S NEW FRONTIERS

In the wake of the Reformation, Christendom was compromised. Its universal ideal had become tarnished, its infrastructure weakened. The Roman Church initially was left without a coherent response to the Protestant assault upon it. The emperor, seeking to defend Christendom, had become an instrument in its divisions. Incapable of rallying forces against the Ottomans, he had also failed to prevent the spread of Protestantism in the empire. The splits in Christendom seemed unbridgeable. Even the notion of 'religion' reflected the divisions which lay at its core. Before 1500, the 'religious' were the monks, those who were in regular orders, and whose vocation was to pray for Christendom. Following the texts of Roman Antiquity, Christian humanists used the term 'religion' to describe beliefs in a god who was not necessarily Christian. Protestant reformers adopted the term to sharpen the distinction between the 'true' religion of Christians and the 'false' religion of their critics. 'New religion' and 'Reformed religion' became common parlance. Catholics, by contrast, continued to see one faith, the rest being 'heretical' and 'schismatic', judging, as the English Jesuit Robert Persons put it, 'all other religions besides their own, false, and damnable'.

There was, of course, a polemic concerning which Church the inheritance of Christendom rightfully belonged to. The Royal Injunctions, drafted by William Cecil and issued by Queen Elizabeth I in 1559, demanded of English congregations: 'You shall pray for Christ's holy Catholic Church; that is, for the whole congregation of Christian people, dispersed throughout the whole world, and specially for the Church of England and Ireland.' Everyone subscribed to the belief that there was only one, true, Catholic Church, but whether the latter rested on the Roman claims to Apostolic Succession or on the grace of God, dispersed through individual congregations, was the point at issue. When an English recusant Catholic was interrogated on his religion, he was asked: 'Art thou a Papist, a Protestant, a Puritan or what Religion art thou?' At a loss to know how to respond, he answered that he was 'but a poore Catholique', that reply being taken as a sign of his popish tendencies. Precisely because 'religion' had become a confused category, 'confessional' statements alongside disciplinary injunctions to define outward conformity became significant. Religion became what a creed said it was.

A new religious frontier emerged; or rather, since the Reformation was a movement in Christianity's tectonic plates, it was more like the jagged fault-lines created by a violent tremor. Borders in the post-Reformation religious world were, like its politics, unstable and complicated. Rulership consisted of concatenations of rights which did not add up to a contiguous landmass. Diocesan boundaries rarely matched political frontiers. Patronage rights to appoint clerics ended up having been sold or transferred into the hands of aristocrats and others who might not follow the religious convictions of the ruler in whose land those benefices belonged. Anyway, people no longer necessarily adopted the beliefs of their overlords.

As time went on, the frontiers which mattered most were those in people's minds, the result of conflicting religious identities constructed into boundaries by an oppositional process. These boundaries were erected through education and indoctrination – the preaching, catechizing, Ten Commandments, churchgoing and religiously impregnated conformities that dominated public life. In divided communities, they took shape as negotiated agreements and legal enactments, arrived at in the shadow of contestations which had made them necessary in the first place. For those growing up with the politico-religious contentions of the later sixteenth century, there was nothing irreversible about the political and religious choices that they made, especially in the earthquake zone between an emerging Protestant northern Europe and Catholic southern Europe. From Scotland in the west (which was where the tremors of a Calvinist Reformation first shook a monarchical state to its foundations in 1560) to Hungary and Transylvania in the east, religious loyalties lay in doubt, and the affiliation of communities and states in question was fought over. These contestations afflicted Christian commonwealths in France, Scotland, Savoy and the Netherlands in the 1560s, but they were annealed to broader and internationalized conflicts in the last decade of the sixteenth century, ones which also reflected the end of the silver age, emerging economic dislocations and weakening social cohesion. The seismograph of military activity registers a spike of unusual intensity in the 1590s, a prelude to the peak of even greater intensity in the mid-seventeenth century.

CHRISTIAN COMMONWEALTHS IN STATE AND CHURCH

The Christendom which survived the Reformation earthquake was attenuated. Its universalist claims were maintained within the orbit of the Counter-Reformed Catholic Church, although they would be effectively reworked into a global Christianity. Christendom still existed in common parlance, especially when vocalizing the anxiety raised by the Ottomans. It also continued within the weaker notion of a collectivity of Christian commonwealths, each exemplifying different versions of what it meant to live in a belief-community. The 'Christian prince' and 'Christian commonwealth' were dominant political ideals, expressed in works claiming to be mirrors for princes and instructions for magistrates. 'Magistrate' was the contemporary term for whoever had the 'power of the sword' (*ius gladii*) in a commonwealth, the right to punish and chastise.

Advice literature for rulers emphasized that it was not intended exclusively for them. Every reader – citizen – could hold such a text in their hand, as one would hold a mirror to one's face, and learn from its pages. Such literature offered an ideal of rulership in order to show how reality was distanced from it. Machiavelli's *The Prince* was regarded as ever more scandalous as the century wore on precisely because it subverted the genre, approximating the virtues of rulership to the reality. Seneca's 'The love of the people constitutes the prince's most impregnable fortress' was a favourite dictum. Machiavelli justified the opposite proposition: 'It is better for a prince to be feared than loved.' Erasmus's *Institution of a Christian Prince* (1516) turned the 'people' into more than a rhetorical trope. Their interests determined whether a ruler was to be judged a tyrant or not. The ruler is 'born for the common good'. In times gone by, he was 'appointed by popular agreement' – the 'power to punish' being assigned to magistrates by the commonwealth. As humanist antiquarians in the sixteenth century discovered more about the early history of the 'Gauls', 'Saxons', 'Scots' and 'Sarmatians' (the myth adopted by the Polish *szlachta* about their origins), they broadened the evidence for the origins of power lying with the people.

By contrast, a tyrant assumed power by usurpation or conquest, ignored the good of the people and followed his own fancy in pursuit of private gain. Appearing on almost every page of Erasmus's treatise, the people are like the chorus in a Greek tragedy, echoing the mutual obligations between ruler and ruled. In a Christian commonwealth, he said, 'there is a mutual interchange between the prince and the people'. The public good legitimated power in a Christian commonwealth, rendering it virtuous and moral. The people (as a public construct) were the fact of life upon which government rested.

German historians prefer to call this a period of 'confessionalization'. The confessions were not simply Catholic and Protestant. Set against the Lutheran Augsburg Confession were the Reformed (Calvinist) Confessions. By the early 1560s the latter included those for Basel (1534) and Geneva (1536), the *Consensus Tigurinus* (1549), the Hungarian (1557), Gallican (1559) and Belgic (1561–2), and the English 'Thirty-nine Articles of Religion' (1563). The animosity between Lutheran and Reformed Protestant Christianity was, in polemical terms, at least as venomous as that between Protestants and Catholics. The Tridentine Profession of Faith (issued by Pope Pius IV's bull *Iniunctum Nobis* of November 1565) offered a united Catholic response. Alongside the desire to unify beliefs came a desire to impose the same religious observances: to sing the same psalms, recite the same prayers, celebrate the same feast-days. These were defined through Church disciplines, synods and councils. The question for Christian commonwealths was: to what extent were they going to become confessionally Christian? Not to do so threatened the existence of the notion of 'right religion'. To do so risked being pulled apart by religious divisions and destroying the commonwealth's values of concord, peace and harmony. There was no answer to that conundrum.

What made the puzzle more perplexing was that the commonwealths were evolving. State and Church became more closely aligned in the wake of the Reformation. The enlargement of state control over Church affairs was a growing reality in Protestant Christendom. Not only did states assume a greater role in the appointment and supervision of clerics, they also took on responsibilities for poor relief, education and (with police regulations governing marriage, family life and moral behaviour in public) the daily lives of their subjects. In some places this amounted to a conscious process of state-building – bureaucratic, top–down conformity working better in a smaller state like Württemberg than in a larger entity such as Elizabethan England. Confessionalization became a way of projecting a sharper sense of religiously conceived identity – whether in the hands of aristocrats who sought to rally support for their cause, or in those of godly rulers, presenting themselves as leading an elect nation.

Yet sharpened religious identities did not always lead to political unity. There was no more powerful political myth in the later sixteenth century than English anti-Catholicism. It had coalesced quickly around the dynastic succession of Elizabeth I, in doubt throughout her reign. Its resurgence owed a great deal to her excommunication by Pope Pius V (*Regnans in Excelsis*, 25 February 1570). English Protestants projected an image of Catholicism which displayed, as though in a mirror, their own unease. Far from reflecting national unity, they felt disunited in comparison with the perceived enemy. The various conspiracies to unseat Elizabeth, inspired among English Catholic exiles abroad in the late 1570s and 80s – some with papal encouragement – gave weight to their fears. The Spanish Armada amply confirmed every one of them. But those in Elizabeth's councils of state tended to exaggerate the unity of their enemies and misread their intentions. Sir Francis Walsingham, her principal secretary of state, placed a heavy reliance on networks of spies, code-breakers and agents provocateurs, whose intelligence served to reinforce prevailing anxieties. The latter risked permanently alienating the significant minority of the English population, which had remained loyal to the old faith but was prepared to stay loyal to the new regime. English anti-Catholicism led to a psychosis of fear about dissembling Jesuits, that 'mischievous broode of caterpillars' whose powers of persuasion were almost magical. Each victory over a perceived threat from this insidious enemy – the defeat of the Spanish Armada (1588) and the Gunpowder Plot (1605) – became the occasion not to rejoice in the name of Protestant England, but to fret about the narrow escape which had just been avoided. Each success was turned into an instrument of perpetual memory to the disaster which might have been. English Protestants did not find their religion led to national unity. Instead it was the expression of their doubts and anxieties.

Was there also a commonwealth in the Church? The notion of a Christian commonwealth was a battleground in post-Reformation ecclesiology as well, a central focus to the conflicts of the later sixteenth century. The Roman Catholic Church championed sacerdotal power, making it a central plank of the decisions at the Council of Trent. Calvinists, by contrast, developed a model of the Church as a commonwealth, in which the Church was responsible for, and overseen by, its *presbyterium* (Calvin's term for the office of bishop). There was only one true Catholic Church but it was divided into congregations, each chosen by God's grace, with Christ as their head. A true Church was one where, according to Calvin, the Word of God was purely announced and the sacraments properly administered. His successor in Geneva, Théodore de Bèze (Beza), added a third category, Church discipline, emphasizing their ecclesiological distinctiveness. A true Church was also one where there was a godly order. That was embodied by the officers of the Church – pastors and elders, making up the 'consistory' (translation of the Latin for 'Church senate') – carrying the charge of the *presbyterium*. Elders, in particular, had the power to make and enforce the laws of the congregation and to elect the pastors in a 'free and legitimate [i.e. public] election', seeking the consent of the congregation for the choice they made. They also had the authority to depute to Church assemblies (synods) in the model Gallican Discipline (1559). Consistorial-synodical Church government posed a threat to divine-right episcopacy and traditionally conceived sacerdotal power (to which other forms of power were related), which is why Calvinism was at the core of the contentions in Christendom in the later sixteenth century.

WARS OF RELIGION

This period is commonly called the time of Europe's 'wars of religion'. In reality, these were political contentions in which religion was the way by which conflicts in the commonwealths of state and Church were manifested. The divisions over religious beliefs and practices were polymorphic and unpredictable, a cause and a consequence of religion becoming a central dynamic in public and private affairs. Dissension manifested itself at different levels, pulling apart the mutual obligations between the ruler and the ruled. Virulent doctrinal and dogmatic conflicts took on new forms, often concentrating on where the 'true Church' was to be found. Armed conflicts descended into civil wars, iconoclastic uprisings, local civil disorders, noble-led rebellions and peasant revolts. 'Symbolic' confrontations (burning in effigy, the organized destruction of books and so on), verbal and visual aggression, judicial repression, extreme physical violence (massacre) all contributed to what destroyed Christian commonwealths and tested Christian churches. Martyrologies narrated and commemorated suffering in the face of extreme violence. Antagonism over religious buildings, rights of worship, contested social space, prayers, processions and ceremonies were the outward manifestations of conflicts which challenged the authority of magistrates, pastors and priests within the commonwealth, and led people to question whether Christendom still represented any common values.

Managing the potential for divisions on the grounds of religion was complicated. 'Toleration' was not what was expected of a Christian magistrate, still less of a minister of the Word. Luther introduced the term into the German vocabulary, only to dismiss what it implied. 'Faith suffers nothing, and the Word tolerates nothing' was one of Luther's paradoxes, meaning that God's Word allowed no compromises. A magistrate was no more expected to tolerate the existence of another religion than to permit the existence of demonic forces and witchcraft. To tolerate something was to allow an evil to be perpetuated because one did not have the conviction or authority to stamp it out. None of the religious confessions was fundamentally tolerant of the existence of other religions. Magistrates were repeatedly exhorted to use the power of the sword to maintain the authority and status of the Church and its confession in their dominions to the exclusion of others. Rulers needed little persuasion of the righteousness as well as the right-mindedness of uniting their lands and peoples under one uncontested faith. The widespread conviction was, as the French lawyer Étienne Pasquier put it, that the 'general foundation [of a state] is principally dependent on the establishment of religion, because the fear and reverence of religion keeps all subjects within bounds more effectively than even the presence

of the prince. Therefore the magistrate must above all other things prevent the mutation of religion or the existence of diverse religions in the
same state.' Heterodoxy was an invitation to God's wrath.

Calling the later sixteenth century the era of the wars of religion
underestimates the polymorphy of religious dissent and the degree to
which religion became the prism through which questions of power and
identity were viewed. It excludes the equally significant experience of
religious pluralism. Religious dissent did not necessarily lead to conflict.
Contemporaries appreciated that religion was a superficial rallying cry
for people's loyalties, a smokescreen behind which people could pursue
their individual interests. If anything, the conflicts made them hypersen-
sitive to the squalid hypocrisy of their opponents. Everyone could agree
that the bitter and divisive conflicts of the period were part of the dis-
array of Christendom, but, for many, religious pluralism was an even
more insidious sign of its decay and imminent demise.

RELIGION AND POLEMIC

In 1566, a satire appeared from the Genevan presses. It offered a
wall-map and description of the 'Papal World' identifying the various
cities and provinces (the 'Kingdom of Good Works', the 'Clerical Provinces', and so on). The papal prison is depicted as 'Purgatory' and the
Castel Sant'Angelo in Rome as the seat of the Antichrist. This was an
infernal cosmography in which the world is divided between good and
evil. All around are the tentacles of an octopus with a gaping mouth,
holding in its clutches the vulnerable Protestant kingdoms, led by
twenty-four 'Reformers' (an allusion to the Elders of the Apocalypse),
protecting truth with their fists. The engraving set out to shock, exaggerating the power of its opponents to create a syndrome of anxiety. By
presenting Rome as an international menace its authors looked to
eschatology. In the struggle against the forces of darkness, the righteous
armies of Protestant truth were justified in taking up arms, for were
they not God's agents in a global conflict?

The authors of the work hid behind a pseudonym: 'Frangidelphe
Escorche-Messes' ('Freedom-Loving Scorch-Mass' or, with Rabelaisian
transposition, 'Scorch-Bum'). In reality, it was written by Jean-Baptiste

Trento, whose career was a paradigm for Protestant controversialists of the later sixteenth century, a refugee from Vicenza who smuggled Protestant books into Italy disguised as a fur-merchant, before ending up in the London house of the English spy-master Francis Walsingham, the executor of his will. Its engraver was Pierre Eskrich, German by origin and an immigrant to Lyon, who took up refuge in Geneva as a Protestant. Responsible for the maps in Genevan Bibles, he knew how to draw an octopus because he had done so for Guillaume Rondelet's natural history of fishes. Trento and Eskrich belonged to a small world of well-educated and talented migrants whose religious convictions contributed to Reformation polemic. Suspicious of those in authority, they directed their anger at what they saw as abuses of power and untruth.

By the end of the century, the Latin-derived word 'controversy' had acquired a new resonance, and the Greek-derived word 'polemic' appeared to describe the war of words over dogma and ceremonies. Contemporaries listed words calculated to give offence. The Catholic Willem van der Lindt published a catalogue of them (over a hundred) in Cologne (1579). Beside the familiar 'Lutheran', 'Zwinglian', 'Papist' and 'Anabaptist', it included 'innovator', 'libertine' and 'middle of the roader' (*moyenneur*). Blasphemy, too, was seen through the lens of heresy or dissimulation, for the power of words to hurt was itself rewritten. Images and music charged words in new ways. Liturgical chants and canticles were parodied. Protestant martyrologists report their victims defying the authorities by singing psalms or spirituals. The French Protestant Psalter, translated into verse by Clément Marot, was the runaway bestseller from the 'wonder years' of the French Reformation (1560–62). In Antwerp, those who forced open the gates of the city in August 1566 did so with Psalters in their hands. In 1561, Mary Queen of Scots was escorted back from France to Holyroodhouse through the streets of Edinburgh with Catholic litanies from the assembled crowds. Later on, during the League in Paris, a Catholic song-book was published so that those engaged in mass processions could follow the words. The civil wars in France and the revolt in the Low Countries acquired their character through pamphlets. On the streets, in military skirmishes, in the print-shops, conflict was about words as well as actions.

THE 'YEAR OF WONDER' IN THE NETHERLANDS AND A TIME OF TROUBLES

An Antwerp contemporary christened 1566 the 'year of wonder' (*jaer van wonder*), that 'atrocious disturbance' of the Christian religion and the 'great mutiny' of the nobility. It began in southern Flanders when a hat-maker (Sebastiaan Matte) led an outdoor Protestant prayer-meeting at Steenvoorde, outside the monastery of St Lawrence on 10 August, the saint's feast-day. When Matte finished, the crowd went into the convent and smashed any religious image they could find. The 'Iconoclastic Fury' (*Beeldenstorm*) had begun.

From West Flanders, the movement spread. Richard Clough, an English observer in Antwerp on 20–21 August, wrote that it was like 'hell, where were above 10,000 torches burning, and such a noise as if heaven and earth had got together'. Next day in Ghent there was a riot on market-day and image-breakers set to work. Children set up saints' statues in the street and ordered them to say: '"Long live the Beggars" or we'll cut your head off' – before executing them. Cloth-working towns and villages around Lille followed suit before the movement spread northwards into Holland and Gelderland. The local authorities were left on their own to deal with a crisis the scale and nature of which had no precedent. Ill and 'sick at heart', the regent, Margaret of Parma, agreed to a Declaration on 23 August in which she temporized with the nobles. Lamoral, count of Egmont, Stadholder of Flanders and Artois, reported rumours of armed uprisings, open-air meetings and demands for a full 'religious peace' (*Religionsvrede*) like the Augsburg settlement in Germany. Philip de Montmorency, count of Horn, Stadholder of Gelderland and Admiral of Flanders, received reports of image-breaking and insurrection, as did William, prince of Orange. In a further revolutionary move, from Valenciennes and Tournai came plans to raise 3 million florins with which these towns hoped simply to buy their freedom from Philip II. In December 1566, Protestant synods at Antwerp and elsewhere mobilized for a general insurrection, while towns loyal to the regent looked to their own security. In the showdown that followed, the rebels were routed outside Antwerp, while the movement collapsed further north. Valenciennes held out for a time, hoping for aid from French Protestants, but it never came.

With hindsight, the uprising is more predictable than it was at the time. In the cloth-working villages and towns of Flanders, what you sold in half-finished cloth determined the food you could buy for the week ahead. In the winter of 1565–6, the markets for cloth and grain were disrupted by trouble in the Baltic. But these were not just food-riots that went wrong. Frustrations, long-standing anticlerical sentiments and more immediate anxieties were channelled into the movement. Thousands of people congregated behind hedges or in fields to hear preachers. Pieter Brueghel the Elder's painting entitled *The Preaching of John the Baptist* captured these moments. Men, women and children, dressed in their best, crowd around the preacher. The miracle was that these self-proclaimed preachers spearheaded such an organized movement.

High politics fomented the upheaval. Horn, Egmont and Orange set themselves in opposition to Antoine Perrenot, Cardinal Granvelle, the minister whom Philip II put in charge to instigate the Inquisition and apply heresy laws strictly. Sensing themselves marginalized, the aristocrats sought to involve the States General in opposing fiscal innovations that were heading their way from Spain, putting together an informal league. Within a year, anti-Granvelle handbills appeared from nowhere. Dunce's caps (in imitation of the cardinal's biretta) and buttons with the insignia of six arrows tied about the middle ('strength through unity') followed. Their campaign worked and Granvelle was removed in 1564. Building on this success, the aristocrats deputed Egmont to go to Spain in January 1565 to negotiate further concessions. He returned with oral promises, believing that Philip II was so preoccupied with the Ottoman siege of Malta that he would acquiesce to the concessions they asked for. In reality, Egmont was duped. With Malta secured and a laden silver fleet from the Indies, Philip signed the 'Segovia Letters' (17 and 20 October 1565, from his palace of El Bosque de Segovia) signalling no compromise.

The grandees reacted to their sense of the public mood. Within days pamphlets and handbills appeared and the aristocrats mustered support for a national petition (known as the 'Compromise'). Signatories turned up in person, and onlookers cheered the nobles who went to the palace to present it. Three days later, Brederode appropriated a description of the 'Compromisers' as 'beggars' (*gueux*), declaring himself the founder-member of a new Order of Beggar Knights. *Gueux* souvenirs went on sale. One might call this a political party if expectations had not run ahead of organization or objectives. The noble adventure into mass politics contributed to the volatility of the situation, which, in turn, demonstrated that the nobles did not control events.

The rebellion collapsed of its own accord in early 1567. In Spain it was decided that the 'heretic rebellion' had to pay a heavy price. Fernando Álvarez de Toledo, duke of Alba, led the repression. With half a lifetime of service in the Hispanic empire to his name, he entered Brussels on 22 August 1567 at the head of regiments of *tercios* (infantry units in Spain's army). The Netherlands had entertained Charles V's military forces in the past, but never as an army of occupation. Alba then masterminded the arrest of Egmont and Horn at the council table in Brussels. They were tried and publicly beheaded in the main square of Brussels on 5 June 1568. He instigated a commission (known to contemporaries as the 'Council of Troubles') in September 1567 to mete out punishment to those implicated in the rebellion. The arrests began on Ash Wednesday, 3 March 1568, pictured in Pieter Brueghel the Elder's *Massacre of the Innocents*. The executions continued as William of Orange and his brother, Louis of Nassau, launched unsuccessful military offensives from Germany in 1568 and 1569. The documents of the Council of Troubles record a total of 12,302 tried – an underestimate since many of those investigated locally did not make it into their files. Of these, over 1,000 were executed and 9,000 had their property confiscated. Alba later claimed that repression had earned 500,000 ducats for the Spanish treasury. A diocesan reform was carried through, the first stage to re-Catholicization. Communities were made to repair damaged churches and to pay for the occupation through new taxes, of which the most controversial was the 'Tenth Penny', an excise tax of 10 per cent. The Estates played for time, voting a temporary levy in 1569. When that expired in July 1571, Alba raised it on his own authority, billeting troops on those who refused to pay.

The memories of revolt and repression were nurtured among fugitives in Germany and England. They joined those who had already left before 1566 to set up Calvinist churches in exile. A general assembly (*Konvent*) convened at Wesel in October 1568, attended by sixty-three Calvinists from the exiled groups. Three years later, twenty-nine leaders congregated in a synod at Emden in October 1571, where they agreed fifty-three articles which defined the discipline, theology and framework of the Dutch Reformed Church. Officially, they did not support Orange's military invasion to topple Alba. Unofficially, they became the guardians of a memory of what had happened and an impetus to what followed.

MASSACRES IN FRANCE AND AN UNREALIZABLE PEACE

In 1559–60, dynastic crisis, financial meltdown and religious dissension shook the French monarchy. France became beset by conflict that turned to civil war, beginning in 1562 and continuing thereafter in a cycle that was partly driven by its own inner dynamic. Destructive and divisive, hard fought on both sides, the first phase of the civil wars lasted only thirteen months. The Peace of Amboise (March 1563), which brought it to a close, was brokered by a monarchy that sought to recover the initiative that peace represented. But fighting broke out anew in 1567. The pacifications at Longjumeau (March 1568) and Saint-Germain (August 1570) followed, both of them shortlived. War irrupted again in 1573 and the pacifications which succeeded them – the Peace of Beaulieu of May 1576 (soon called the 'Peace of Monsieur' after the king's brother, who had mostly secured it), the Peace of Bergerac (September 1577) and the Pacification of Nantes (April 1598) – drew lessons from their predecessors.

King Henry II was accidentally killed in a tournament in Paris on 30 June 1559, held to celebrate the marriages which sealed the Peace of Cateau-Cambrésis. The kingdom passed to his fifteen-year-old son, Francis, but Francis II lived only another eighteen months before succumbing to an ear infection. In December 1560 his ten-year-old younger brother succeeded him as Charles IX. A decade of minority rule/tutelage was in prospect. French Protestants interpreted these events as God's judgement upon the Valois, a question mark over their rule.

That question mark was accentuated by unassigned royal debt and the repression of Protestant heresy which failed to deliver the unity that it promised. In another Valois showcase wedding in April 1558, Francis had married Mary Stuart, the daughter of James V of Scotland and Mary of Guise. Breaking with the past, Francis II looked to his ultra-Catholic in-laws to chart the way forward. These were his uncles by marriage, Charles of Guise, cardinal of Lorraine, and his brother, François, duke of Guise. Their rise to power signalled the eclipse of Anne de Montmorency, who had dominated the court for most of three decades. Montmorency's family and circle of influence embraced all those who would emerge as the military leaders of the French Protestant movement over the next decade. They included Louis de Bourbon, prince of Condé and a cadet prince of the blood, Jeanne d'Albret, queen of Navarre and the wife of Condé's elder brother, Antoine de Bourbon, and Gaspard de Coligny, sieur de Châtillon. Anonymous libels, verses and handbills made their first appearance in 1560, alluding to the Guise 'ivy' that sucked the lifeblood from the Valois monarchy, and the Lorraine 'pyramid' that would supplant it.

These aristocrats made common cause with the emerging Protestant movement. Calvin courted them in 1558. Jeanne d'Albret had become a closet Protestant, perhaps as early as 1555. Louis, prince of Condé, visited Geneva in August 1558. Coligny and his brother François used their captivity after the battle of St-Quentin to read Calvin's works, and to reflect. But many remained undecided, including Antoine de Bourbon, who, although he arrived at court in March 1558 accompanied by a Protestant chaplain, even attending a Protestant rally, kept his options open. He, more than others, seems to have been alert to the difficulties opening up for France.

Those dangers manifested themselves in March 1560 in a plot to 'free' the king from his 'imprisonment' by the Guises. The plotters' leader was a squire from the Périgord (Jean du Barry, seigneur de La Renaudie) whose Protestantism went not much deeper than his disgruntlement at a failed lawsuit and a visceral hatred of the Guises. He rallied together discontents and contacted Protestant preachers in Paris. The prince of Condé and Calvin gave him no overt encouragement. To gain access, Renaudie's plot used the excuse of presenting a Protestant petition to the king at Amboise. Foiled at the last minute, the leaders were hanged from the castle gate. The resulting repression fostered resentments and a myth of Guise tyranny. In late May 1559, French Calvinists held their first synod, where delegates from sixty-two churches approved the Confession and Discipline for a presbyterian and synodical Church government. By the time of their second synod at Poitiers in March 1561, there were hundreds of congregations. They focused on towns but achieved a critical mass in Lower Normandy and an arc from

La Rochelle south and east towards Geneva. Their movement's growth seemed unstoppable, and so, too, did the sectarian tensions that accompanied it. 'Huguenot', a term of abuse, came to prominence in 1560, probably deriving from a neighbourhood in Tours, around whose gate (la Porte Hugon) Protestants congregated.

Catherine de Médicis, who assumed power as regent in the name of her son Charles IX in December 1560, tried to build a consensus to tackle rising sectarian tensions and the government's debts. She did so through summoning the Estates General, the kingdom's Parliament, to Orléans in December 1560. Chancellor Michel de l'Hôpital dressed up the ancient wisdom of *amicitia* and *caritas* in a famous opening speech to the Estates General in December 1560. 'Gentleness,' he said, 'will serve better than rigour. Let us shun these diabolic words, the names of parties, factions and seditions: "Lutherans", "Huguenots", "Papists", keeping only the name of "Christian".' Failing to agree about anything, delegates were recalled to Pontoise in the summer of 1561. Under pressure, the clergy (one of the estates in the Estates General) reluctantly offered to repay debts. But that offer came at the price of refusing a formula for religious concord.

Catherine's 'gentleness' had to be undertaken without the support of the Estates General. Religious repression was dismantled, culminating in the edict of January 1562, which offered Protestants the rights to meet and worship. Each move became a stimulus to the Protestants to ask for more and an invitation to local confrontation. Image-breaking, which already exposed the anarchist and sacrilegious tendencies of the French Reformation, became more organized, in some places with an anti-monarchical gloss. At Orléans, the heart of the recently deceased Francis II was disinterred and fried before being thrown to the dogs. At Bourges, the tomb of Jeanne de France, the daughter of Louis XI and a proto-saint, was dismembered and burned.

Catholics reacted violently. The first massacre of Protestants took place at Sens, which was where a Dominican ('Jacobin') friar inflamed the local population. On 12 April 1562, over a hundred Protestants were tied to poles and drowned. At Toulouse, thousands perished after the city was retaken in May 1562 following a brief Protestant ascendancy, their assailants degrading their victims. Some believed that they were acting on God's behalf, thinking the Last Days to be at hand. Many more perished in the ensuing war. Protestant forces, some raised and funded by local churches, fought against royal troops. At the siege of Rouen (September–October 1562) Antoine de Bourbon was a victim. At the battle close by Dreux (19 December 1562) thousands perished and Condé and Montmorency were captured. At the siege of Orléans, military headquarters of Condé, the duke of Guise was shot dead by Jean Poltrot de Méré, a Protestant who had infiltrated the royal army. Under torture, he said that he was acting for Gaspard de Coligny. True or not, a feud between Coligny and the Guise family resulted – one of many vendettas in the civil wars.

The early edicts of pacification underestimated the task in hand. That of 1563 consisted of fifteen articles; that promulgated at Nantes thirty-five years later had ninety-five articles and a further fifty-six particular clauses to regulate issues of detail. In 1563, the 'privileges' accorded the Protestants were limited, and mainly directed to satisfying the Protestant nobility. Detailed application was left to royal commissioners who relied, where they could, on governors and lieutenants to assist them. They referred many matters to the council of state, which found itself overwhelmed. Royal legislation ventured into controversial terrain – controlling, for example, what preachers said in the pulpit, or how many (of which religion) should sit in municipal councils. Places of worship and burial became contentious issues. Many Protestants suspected that they were the victims of the peace. Only gradually did local communities learn how to live with their differences. In some places local councillors were elected from both confessions. In others, especially where there was a real or imagined threat to a local community from without, its leaders agreed to 'live in union and friendship' with one another. France was not irretrievably ruptured into two opposing groups.

Catherine de Médicis drew these positive elements together in a royal progress round the kingdom with Charles IX. The court left Paris in January 1564 and did not return there until the spring of 1566, the comprehensive Ordinance of Moulins (February 1566) aiming to rebuild the monarchy on the basis of 'piety' and 'justice' whose twin pillars served as the motto of the young king. At Moulins the royal council reconciled Henri de Guise and Coligny, the latter swearing that he 'had never, or caused, nor yet approved of, Guise's assassination'. The evidence was, however, that the pacification had not taken deep roots. In September 1567, the Protestant leadership mounted a further plot (the

Conspiracy of Meaux) to 'liberate' the young king. Condé, Coligny and his brothers were unsettled by Alba's repression in the Netherlands, and discomfited by their own failure to come to the aid of their co-religionists. They were additionally nervous at rumours of a plan to eliminate them, one they deduced must have been the subject of the discussions between the French and Spanish courts at Bayonne. Pope Pius V's condemnation in June 1567 of the Huguenots was assumed to be its opening salvo. But the Huguenots were always good at imagining conspiracies against themselves, and never much good at carrying out their own. The Conspiracy of Meaux was foiled at the last moment, and it left Charles IX and Catherine de Médicis with a sense that the Huguenots' real aim was to kill the king in the pursuit of their ambitions.

Following the death of the Constable Anne de Montmorency at the battle of St-Denis (10 November 1567), the command of the royal army was given to the king's younger brother, Henri de Valois, duke of Anjou, later Henry III. Barely sixteen years of age, he attracted the service of young Catholic activists. Leading a campaign to southwestern France, Anjou's forces defeated the Huguenot army at Jarnac on 13 March 1569. Wounded, Condé prepared to surrender, but one of Anjou's officers stabbed him in cold blood. Those serving Anjou felt let down by the Peace of Saint-Germain (August 1570). By its terms, Protestants were accorded four stronghold fortresses in the kingdom as guarantees of their security. Pope Pius V, who made no secret of his desire to exterminate Protestant heresy by force, told Catherine the following month: 'The day will come when Your Majesty will repent of having agreed to such a dangerous peace.' Protestants, too, their leadership now in the hands of Coligny and Jeanne d'Albret, sneered at the 'limping, badly-seated peace' (it had been negotiated by the gammy-legged Marshal Biron and the sieur de Malassise). Hard-line Catholics looked for the moment when it could be undermined.

Paris offered them the opportunity to do so. It had provided loans to the king and paid for its own fortifications. The demands upon its citizens to mobilize for their defence and protection moved authority in the capital away towards those who organized its local militia. Its parishes sustained independent-minded Catholic clergy, who identified their cause with that of their city. In 1569, three Parisians were condemned to death for having held illegal Protestant assemblies privately. After their execution, their house was dismantled and a commemorative pyramid erected in its place. Following the pacification of 1570, the king reluctantly agreed to the pyramid's relocation. On 2 December 1571, the masons set to work but a crowd prevented them. It was finally moved at night on 19–20 December under armed guard, which sparked off a riot the following day. Paris was combustible.

That does not explain the massacre that began before morning light on 24 August 1572, the feast-day of St Bartholomew. The dynamic of events went beyond anyone's ability to control. Catherine de Médicis negotiated a marriage between her daughter Marguerite ('la Reine Margot') and the Protestant son of Queen Jeanne d'Albret, Henry of Navarre. It was a high-profile, confessionally mixed marriage to cement the pacification. Henry entered Paris on 8 July and the marriage itself was solemnized on 18 August at Notre-Dame. Music, poetry and pageantry created a marriage-fantasy in which a 'Paradise of Love' (the tournament of 20 August) brought together Protestant and Catholic nobility in a charade.

Then, on 22 August Admiral Gaspard de Coligny was shot and wounded as he walked towards his lodging after attending the king's council. Coligny wanted to recover French anti-Habsburg momentum abroad. He and Condé signed an agreement of mutual cooperation in August 1568 with William of Nassau and his brother Louis. They aided the French Protestants in 1569 and served in their high command. This was an obligation to be reciprocated when, on 24 May 1572, French forces launched an expedition into Flanders in support of the Sea Beggars, who had taken Brill the previous month. Philippe Duplessis-Mornay drew up a memorandum justifying intervention in the Netherlands as the way to unite France in an expedition abroad. The royal council considered Coligny's proposition just as the French forces became bogged down, and rejected it. As Coligny pursued the idea, international tensions placed him in the spotlight.

His would-be assassin was Charles de Louviers, sieur de Maurevert, who shot him from a house belonging to the duke of Guise's tutor. Maurevert was a killer with past form and no one knows whether he was acting on his own account or (as the Huguenots surmised) for the Guises. Sensing their vulnerability, the Huguenot nobility threatened reprisals. Those around the council table of Charles IX took the threats seriously and, at a meeting or meetings held sometime on 23 August, opted for a selective elimination of the Huguenot leadership – a collective decision, taken to protect the king and his state. Catherine de Médicis certainly participated, but (equally certainly) she was not alone. Contemporaries pointed the finger at the king's younger brother, Henry, duke of Anjou, and the Italians in royal service. The execution was hasty and improvised. The Provost of Paris was told to close the gates of the city, chain all the boats in the Seine to the right bank, guard the bridges and summon the militia. During the night, the young duke of Guise and others set out from the Louvre for Coligny's lodgings with an armed contingent. A captain from Bohemia assassinated Coligny, then the body was thrown into the street, emasculated and beheaded, and taken towards the river. Other senior Protestant figures met similar fates. For three days, the city gates remained closed while the massacre continued, the Seine turning red with the blood of the victims. A partial enumeration of the bodies picked out from the Seine downstream gives no real way of estimating the number of victims – there may well have been up to 3,000 Parisians killed. Surviving Protestants later reluctantly described their harrowing experiences.

The king acknowledged his part in the events, declaring before the Parlement on 26 August that 'what has happened has been by his express command, and in no way because of Religion, and not in contravention of his edicts of pacification [. . .] but to forestall and prevent the carrying out of a wicked and detestable conspiracy by the Admiral [. . .] against the person of the king and against his State'. For Protestants this was a tyrannical act, and its victims were martyrs. The massacre became an international controversy and fatally undermined the monarchy's efforts at pacification in the next reign.

The Paris carnage inspired massacres in a score of other towns and cities, where at a minimum estimate a further 3,000 Protestants met their death (and the figure may well have been double that number). In Bordeaux, the Jesuit Edmond Auger, author of a manual on religious warfare, preached from the cathedral pulpit on Michaelmas Day 1572: 'Who has carried out the judgment of God in Paris? The angel of God. Who has done so in Orléans? The angel of God [. . .] Who will do so in the town of Bordeaux? It will be the angel of God.' Over thirty years later, the Catholic League pamphleteer Louis Dorléans referred to the St Bartholomew massacre as a 'propitious holocaust'. Many Protestants in northern France returned to the Catholic faith. But Protestantism's dynamic was sustained in southern France. It could still count on prominent noble families. Above all, the movement had urban strongholds south of the Loire. La Rochelle, a maritime port of some 20,000 inhabitants, refused to obey royal authority and organized its defences. Surrounded by the sea and marshland, it was vulnerable only to the north. Royal forces concentrated their attack at that point in a siege that lasted six months (February–July 1573) before it was abandoned.

The Huguenots already had the rudiments of a military and political wing. In December 1573, they went a stage further, calling delegates to Millau. Ninety-seven deputies attended, mostly from the Midi, a mixture of gentry, pastors, officers and urban notables. Criticizing princes and charging magistrates with the responsibility of limiting the excesses of those in power, they agreed a corporate structure for their 'party'. Using the model of the Estates General as well as their own synodical government, they vested authority in a general assembly consisting of deputies chosen by provincial assemblies and which would convene every six months. Its role was to legislate, decide war and peace, fix levels of taxation, agree loans in their name, and appoint delegates to a council which would oversee the activities of their elected political leader. For a time, local activists were in command. When the assembly met again at Millau in July 1574, they elected Henri de Bourbon-Condé (the son of Louis) as their 'chief, governor-general and protector'. Within months, they made common cause for tactical reasons with the 'malcontent' governor of Languedoc, Henri de Montmorency-Damville, and, a year later, with another leading Catholic prince of the blood, the king's brother, François d'Alençon. There was little that anyone could teach those Protestant activists about how to use their know-how of local terrain and resources. Even so, they were among the 'lesser' of the 'lesser magistrates', people from small towns and communities without wider experience and confidence in public affairs. They knew that the pattern of the civil wars in France was one of short-term conflict followed by rapprochement, and they were not interested in forming a new state on their own.

So the civil wars in France intensified for a while post-1572. Yet the malcontent and Protestant aristocratic leadership kept the door open to reconciliation and, in due course, the French monarchy responded. The Peace of Beaulieu of May 1576 came unstuck within months. That of Bergerac (the 'King's Peace') of September 1577 was compromised by the faltering authority of the king in question (Henry III) and his mis-understood efforts at reform. An entire generation was overshadowed by the fears generated in the civil wars, relived in new conflicts in the later 1580s. Only in retrospect was it a dry-run for the processes of remembering and forgetting, reconciliation and reconstruction that would begin in earnest in France with the signing of the Peace of Nantes in 1598.

HUGUENOTS AND BEGGARS AT SEA

The most militarized contentions over religion in later sixteenth-century Europe occurred where the state was most developed. That was because the authority of the state was so often contracted out to individual par-ties in complex ways – through office-holding, tax-farming, the hiring of mercenary soldiers or the privateering of naval warfare. Religious parties opposed to the state battened onto that privatized power, inter-nationalizing it and turning it to their own purposes. Nothing illustrates that process better than what happened in Atlantic waters. It was already common practice for riverine states to encourage merchants to build ships that were leased to the state in time of war through 'letters of reprisal' or allowed to prey upon foreign vessels in return for a por-tion of the prize being returned to the state. That opened the door to private endeavour after the establishment of the overseas empires and their rulers' unsuccessful attempts to limit direct trade with their colonies to themselves. Privateers and their backers regarded that colo-nization as based on an arbitrary division of the world, decided by Pope Alexander VI in 1494 'as if God had made the sea and land only for the Spaniards and Portuguese'. Those were the sentiments of Henri Lancelot de Voisin, sieur de La Popelinière, a Protestant historian and would-be buccaneer. In a book that fostered the popular notion of a 'terra australis' or 'southern world' that lay yet undiscovered, he totally refuted the idea that Spain and Portugal could treat the rest of the world as a private fief. He supported the activities of his fellow-countrymen from the 1550s onwards who undertook expeditions to establish other colonies and profit from seized Hispanic ships.

Privateering became part of the developing conflicts in France and the Netherlands. English-based buccaneers became very active in the

1560s, Elizabeth I and her ministers being economical with the truth when they denied their involvement. French Protestants used privateering to defray their war costs. They were joined by Dutch contingents after the failure of the first revolt. Count Louis of Nassau needed ships to support his planned invasion of Friesland in 1568. But its failure deprived the privateers ('Sea Beggars' or *Watergeuzen*, as William of Orange called them) of their base on the Ems estuary and they joined the French and English in the Channel. By 1570, there were about thirty Dutch privateers in operation, working out of English ports and responsible to William of Orange as and when they felt like it. In 1571, Elizabeth I came under pressure to expel them from English ports and, on 1 March 1572, she obliged. The Beggars had to find a new base of operations. La Rochelle was closed off, and on 1 April 1572 they landed in the small fishing port of Brill on the island of Voorne in the Maas estuary. The town was taken, its church ransacked. It was not a popular uprising, but it triggered an insurrection against the hated Spanish tax known as the 'Tenth Penny'.

The resentment against the Tenth Penny and Alba's regime was concentrated in Holland, north of the river Ij, and in Amsterdam. The Spanish withdrew their forces to defeat the Huguenot-led expedition to the south. Then, from his ancestral lands at Dillenburg in the Rhineland, William of Orange began another invasion on 7 July. Still more towns, this time in Brabant and Flanders, declared for the revolt. The tide turned back in Alba's favour as military reinforcements arrived and Orange's men failed to relieve the siege on Mons while Alba's sacked Mechelen. Alba justified the latter as a legal reprisal. On 11 December 1572 Spanish forces began their siege of Haarlem, the gateway by land to Holland's 'Northern Quarter', which was where Orange retreated with his remaining troops, having 'decided to make that province my tomb'.

IN HELL'S DESPAIR

Contemporaries followed these events with bewilderment. What should they call the deputies of the provincial States of Holland, summoned to The Hague by Alba but who had chosen to meet at Dordrecht instead? To Philip II and the government in Madrid, they were rebels. Elizabeth

I regarded their representatives with condescension. Philip van Marnix appeared before them on Orange's behalf with the simple objective: 'to see the day when these Low Countries may recover their former bloom, prosperity and ancient liberty'. He outlined a provisional government for which Orange would be the Stadholder and in which Protestants and Catholics would live together. But it was just a sketch. The financial arrangements were inadequate, and events proved how difficult a confessionally unaligned commonwealth would be. Convinced that Alba was a 'tyrant', they sent envoys to Gouda 'to obtain access to the charters of Holland' and make copies of their privileges. In 1575, the States of Holland created their own university (Leiden) and signed an act of union between themselves and Zeeland. Dutch pamphleteers accused Philip II of wanting to rule the Low Countries 'freely and absolutely'. In his published *Apology* of 1581, William of Orange defended himself against Philip II's condemnation, in turn branding the Spanish king a tyrant. 'Let him be a King in Castile, in Aragon, at Naples, amongst the Indians, and in every place where he commands at his pleasure: yea let him be a king if he will in Jerusalem, and a peaceable governor in Asia and Africa, yet for all that I will not acknowledge him in this country ... whose power is limited according to our privileges, which he swore to observe.'

In July 1581, the States General issued the Act of Abjuration (*Plakkaat van Verlatinghe*), declaring the rulership of the Netherlands vacant because Philip had 'deserted' the Dutch. It prohibited the use of his name on legal documents, released magistrates from their allegiance and proclaimed a new oath to the States General. The act's preamble, drawn from Duplessis-Mornay's *Vindication against Tyrants* (1579), offered a legal basis for their decision, reinforced by arguments from the Frisian humanist Aggaeus van Albada and Gouda's leading politician, François Vranck. Albada's starting-point (drawn from Spanish sources) was that 'all forms of government, kingdoms, empires and legitimate authorities are founded for the common utility of the citizens, and not of the rulers'. The community had been oppressed by its prince and, since it had no other overlord from whom to seek redress, it 'is entitled to take up arms'. Vranck argued the case for the delegated powers of the States General, a body reflecting 'the whole state and entire body of the inhabitants'.

The Dutch Revolt turned into a nasty civil war whose memories became historicized in the foundation myth for an emerging Dutch Republic. In St Bavo church at Haarlem, behind the Calvinist communion table, stands a painting where the altar once was. Texts, painted on a black background, describe Christ's Last Supper, a reminder to Calvinists of the bread and wine they were about to receive. On the back of the painting, facing the ambulatory where non-confessing townspeople walked, was another reminder, headed 'If only hunger had offered no struggle/Spanish violence would have fled from Haarlem'. Sixty-seven lines of poetry testified to the hardships endured in an eight-month siege (December 1572–July 1573). When the city capitulated, sixty burghers and most of its garrison were hanged, the siege becoming integral to Haarlem's identity, evoked in a new civic motto ('Virtue conquers Strength') and linked to the crusading tradition of Haarlemeers who had relieved the siege at the port of Damietta in the thirteenth century. Through memorials like this, the defence of Calvinism and civic liberties became the dominant narrative of the revolt.

Religious high-mindedness and political principle took second place to the sieges, ransacking, flooding, treason, exile and endurance that were the truth of it. Wouter Jacobszoon, an Augustinian prior from Stein, near Gouda, fled to Amsterdam when the Beggars took over in June 1572. He kept a detailed record of what he saw and heard. 'Marvel,' he said, 'at this troubled, tormented and wild, desolate time in which we have lived', convinced that God was visiting a terrible judgement upon the Netherlands. 'As long as people have been assured about their external freedom and their own welfare,' he commented on 4 September 1572 on the Beggar atrocities, 'they care not whether God's temples are despoiled, the holy statues broken, whether God's servants, the priests . . . are mocked . . . God has abandoned us.' In Amsterdam, he reported Beggar bravado on the streets, recorded the satirical coins they minted, the songs they sang, the plots they dreamed up, even the games that children played. On 3 June 1574, Father Wouter's diary records the fires he saw burning in the 'waterland' to the north of Amsterdam, from where a traveller reported finding thirty bodies naked in a ditch, killed by the Beggars in an ambush. He thought it was worse than living under the Turks.

How would it end? For Philip II, the answer was with the defeat of the rebels. He recognized, however, that this was a matter of politics as well as military force. Alba had understood the latter but not the former, and he was replaced by the governor of Spanish Lombardy, Don Luis de Requesens, who arrived in November 1573 with an army of 60,000, and was convinced he could win quickly in the Northern Quarter so long as he could open the dykes and flood it. But Philip II rejected the idea on the grounds of the 'reputation for cruelty that it would earn us'. Requesens was instead engulfed by a tide of army mutinies for lack of pay. Mutiny was a problem on both sides, but because of the size of the Flanders Army and because it was garrisoned in towns, this had greater impact. Mutinies started with veterans advertising their grievances in meetings, and then holding inhabitants to ransom. Requesens died on 5 March 1576, knowing that it was only a matter of time before, following Philip II's decision to suspend interest payments on his debts in November 1575, catastrophe struck.

On 25 July 1576, Spanish mutineers sacked the town of Aalst and made common cause with other contingents. On Sunday 4 November, Requesens's replacement Don John of Austria arrived in Luxembourg with powers from Philip II to send home the army and concede whatever was necessary to make peace. That same day, Spanish troops invaded the rebel-held town of Antwerp. In several days of burning and looting, over 1,000 houses were destroyed and 7,000 people lost their lives. As with the massacre of St Bartholomew, engravings and newsletters broadcast the event, making the 'Spanish Fury' part of the anti-Spanish 'Black Legend'. Four days later (8 November) the States General (including representatives from Holland and Zeeland) agreed to the Pacification of Ghent and to expel the occupying army. That might have settled the Dutch Revolt had the decision not been taken to postpone discussion of differences over religion, for it was over those that it came unstuck less than three years later.

A religious peace had been a feature of the accords signed between Orange and the towns of Holland and Zeeland who joined the Beggar cause. Although Catholic worship in public was forbidden by the States of Holland in February 1573, Catholics, Lutherans, Anabaptists and others were in practice left alone to worship as they wished in private. The 'authorized Church' in the new order, however, was Calvinist. Reformed churches emerged with speed, taking over ecclesiastical fabric and putting it into the hands of pastors, deacons and elders. But it appeared more solid on paper than *in situ*. The letters from consistories to London tell another story: a shortage of ministers, the impossibility of meeting because of the war, and the tiny numbers in the congregations. Holland and Zeeland were Calvinist only in the sense that parts of western Europe today are Christian. The Ecclesiastical Ordinances of the States of Holland (1576) made it clear, too, that the magistrates had the final say in who should be pastor, what preaching went on and the upkeep of church fabric. Baptism was open to all, not just confessing members of the Calvinist community, so churches and cemeteries became, in some sense, civic space.

That 'civic Calvinism' was not the kind that motivated pro-Orange forces that emerged in 1577 in the urban southern Netherlands. Orange's popularity there focused the widespread disenchantment with everything that had made a mess of people's lives over the previous decade. In Ghent, two Calvinist magistrates arrested the duke of Aerschot and his servants on 28 October 1577 and staged a municipal revolution, putting in their place a special committee ('The Eighteen') of artisans. In February 1578, the Calvinists of Ghent exported their revolution, marching on Oudenaarde and engineering little revolutions at Kortrijk, Bruges and Ieper. Wherever they were successful, magistrates were removed from office and replaced with Calvinists, Catholics were summarily expelled and images smashed. Most significantly of all, on 26 May 1578, the Calvinists of Amsterdam staged a coup, arresting Catholic magistrates and clergy, and expelling them from the city. Philip II's concessions to the States General now, a year later, looked like a mistake. His worst fears about the nature of 'heretic rule' were coming to pass in a Calvinist revolution in Flanders. With peace in the Mediterranean and a treasure fleet of fifty-five ships conveying over 2 million ducats of silver from the New World in August 1577, he had the resources to intervene once more. In addition, after the death of Don John in September 1578, Philip could appoint someone in his place who was both a brilliant general and an able political strategist: Alexander Farnese, Prince (in 1586, Duke) of Parma and Piacenza.

Farnese was Philip's cousin, and had been educated at the Spanish court with Don John. Serving as the latter's attaché from 1577 he understood the problems at first hand. His strategy was to allow time and the logic of events to work in his favour. So they did, beginning with the decision of the provincial Estates of Hainaut, Artois and Walloon Flanders (6 January 1579) to secede from the Estates General, blaming the 'heretics' who had shown 'such fury'. Nine months later, the Estates signed a treaty at Arras with Farnese, reaffirming their obedience to Philip II and their Catholicity in return for the removal of Spanish troops. Farnese obliged, knowing that they would eventually need him. From his fortress base at Namur, he responded to calls for aid from towns, and after each successful intervention he made an accord with the citizens in question. There were no reprisals. In return, each town agreed to re-Catholicize and grant a right of exile (*ius emigrandi*) to Protestants. Meanwhile, he lured the nobility back with promises of pardons and pensions, Philip II's 'golden bullets' as one frustrated Dutch commander called them. Farnese's strategy, involving a reconquest of the towns along the Scheldt (Mechelen, Antwerp, Ghent) to create a line of defence for the provinces of Flanders and Brabant, began to emerge.

Most daring was Parma's siege of Antwerp. The sack of 1576 created lasting resentments and the city would not be won back with concessions. The siege lasted for over a year (July 1584–August 1585) and involved the construction of a pontoon bridge across the Scheldt (2,400 feet long) with defensive earthworks at both ends. Despite Dutch efforts to ram the bridge with fire-ships and a battleship (the *Finis Belli*), they did not succeed. Spanish troops behaved themselves when they entered the city, and Protestants were given two years to emigrate. Tens of thousands left Antwerp alone and, although estimates differ, well over 100,000 migrated from the southern Netherlands northwards overall. Leiden and Amsterdam swelled with thousands of Walloons, Brabanters and Flemings. Farnese determined the contours of the new split Netherlands with the establishment of a re-Catholicized south. Clerical authority was re-established and that of the magistrates re-affirmed. They in turn proclaimed loyalty to the Habsburgs. It was not quite business as usual, however, because the Dutch blockaded the Scheldt and post-war reconstruction took years. Farnese's troops remained in place despite his promises to remove them. A new wave of mutinies in the 1590s caused major unrest. As elsewhere in Europe, they were a decade of food shortages in the southern Netherlands. For contemporary diarists, dearth was headline news, not the military campaigns tending to a stalemate with the north.

The future of the northern Netherlands remained undetermined for longer. The provisional government of Holland and Zeeland, established back in 1572, was the model for the document which the provinces of Holland, Zeeland and Gelderland signed on 23 January

1579 at Utrecht, agreeing to act in perpetuity 'as if they were a single province' on matters of peace and war. The Union of Utrecht necessitated the appointment of a council, a treasurer and other officers, but in other respects, the right of each province to govern itself as it saw fit was expressly safeguarded. Whether other provinces would join the union would depend on what happened. Acting together through what remained of the authority of the States General, they abjured the sovereignty of Philip II on 26 July 1581. That was supposed to smooth the way for a transfer of power to the king of France's youngest brother, François d'Alençon, now duke of Anjou, who arrived on cue with a small army in August 1581.

But Holland and Zeeland refused to sign up to Anjou's 'sovereignty' (Jean Bodin, the expert on that issue was one of his advisers) and the States General could not deliver the authority that he would need to govern. He seized Dunkirk, Diksmuide and Ostend from the Spanish on 17 January 1583 but failed at Bruges and Antwerp. The principal casualties of the 'French Fury' in the latter were not the citizens but the French troops – perhaps 2,000 of whom were slaughtered. Anjou's intervention in the Netherlands merely enlarged Farnese's reconquest options. Anjou's death on 10 June 1584 was followed a month later by the murder of William of Orange, assassinated in the Prinsenhof, the palace (formerly a convent) that the city of Delft gave him as the centre for his provisional government. The hired Spanish assassin shot three bullets, two of which missed. Who would direct, with what resources and on what basis, the war against Farnese remained to be determined.

Those issues were clarified in the two decades after 1585 in decisions made in the context of the broadening conflict with Spain, encompassing England, Ireland and France. The seven provinces of the United Provinces of the Netherlands were not united by religion. The religious peace that had been proposed by Orange in July 1578, and which was tacitly acknowledged in the Union of Utrecht, was not a rallying cry. Indeed, towns and provinces in the north often found local reasons to expel Catholics as risks to security. Their southward exodus (less numerous than migrants the other way) consolidated Catholic Flanders. The Netherlands was not the haven of religious liberty that it imagined itself to be later in the seventeenth century. Yet, on the basis of a political culture and the memory of recent strife, and drawing strength from the military victories orchestrated by Mauritz of Nassau, William of

Orange's son, as well as his cousin William Louis, the United Provinces of the Netherlands learned to be a state-like structure with which the rest of Europe had to deal.

THE SPANISH MONARCHY AND ITS DOMINIONS

Philip II came to the Spanish throne in 1556, inheriting dominions in Europe and overseas. He had grown up knowing nothing else and adapted himself to its service and ideals. He relished the opportunities that empire afforded. Regent in Spain since 1543, he had a good working knowledge of affairs as duke of Milan (from 1540) and king in Sicily and Naples (from 1554). He spent several months in England as king consort to Mary Tudor in 1554. From there, he crossed the Channel to attend the ceremony in Brussels on 25 October 1555 when his father surrendered power. Less than two years later, Philip's army routed the French at St-Quentin on 10 August 1557. With the Peace of Cateau-Cambrésis (April 1559), he set off south to Castile by way of his Italian possessions.

His advisers had some difficulty giving conceptual shape to Philip II's rule. To call it an empire would have further strained the delicate relationships with Philip's uncle Ferdinand, whose election to the emperorship of the Holy Roman Empire had finally been accepted by the Diet in 1558. Yet they believed in Christendom, and thought Philip II was pre-eminent over other powers in it, and that on the basis of undeniable fact. Fernando Vázquez witnessed Spanish legates in the closing sessions of the Council of Trent in 1563 claiming precedence over the French on just those grounds. A year later he wrote a treatise explaining that Spanish 'power, dominion and extended territories' justified its preferential status (*praelatio*) among Christian commonwealths. Not only that, the Spanish monarchy's precedence was warranted by the extent of the service that Philip II could render to Christendom, and by his ability to represent the voice (*vox populi*) of its Catholic people. Not only France but the Holy Roman Empire should acknowledge Spain's pre-eminence.

Philip's decision to locate his monarchy in Castile cemented the resource logistics of his father's empire, but it begged more questions than it answered, given that so many of his inherited dominions lay out-side the Spanish peninsula. Castilian humanists absorbed the notions of mutual obligation in a Christian commonwealth but it was not clear how that could work on such a scale. Castilian jurists emphasized instead the importance of kingship as the source of law. That provided the basis for Philip II's use of edicts (*pragmáticas*) issued under the king's 'absolute royal power'. The capacity of Philip II to provide a single law that ran throughout his various kingdoms gave the Spanish mon-archy its conceptual framework and legitimacy. Royal image-makers fleshed out the details in tapestries, engravings, statues, ceremonial entries, architecture and music.

Their themes included dynastic continuity and inheritance, wrapped up in the traditions of the Catholic kings of Spain, with a dose of Habs-burg mythology. Monarchical traditions in Spain did not include rituals of enthronement, anointment and the royal touch. So the monarchical image was fabricated from the events themselves, reaching its apogee in the annexation of Portugal. The royal entry into Lisbon (1581) included a triumphal arch with Janus surrendering the keys of his temple 'as if to the lord of the world', while another carried the message: 'The world, which was divided [. . .] is now linked into one, since you are lord of everything East and West.' Alonso de Ercilla, who had served at St-Quentin and then gone to Peru, composed his epic narrative poem on the Araucanian war as an epitome to Philip II's monarchy. A medal was struck in 1583, showing the king in portrait on the face and, on the reverse, a terrestrial globe with the inscription NON SUFFICIT ORBIS ('The World is not Enough') around it.

This globalizing myth – a universal monarchy which did not dare to call itself an empire – was encapsulated in the Escorial, the heart of Philip's monarchy. Constructed over twenty-one years from 1563 onwards, it was a monastery, a palace and a mausoleum, with architec-tural allusions to Solomon's Temple. Its liturgical, ceremonial and physical space was organized in such a way that the king was the inter-mediary between God and the world, the guardian of the martyr Church and the descendant of Hispanic kings and saints. It emphasized the unquestioned power of rulers as the reflection of God's will. Philip II declined to go on progress round his kingdom on the grounds that it demeaned his majesty, and increasingly withdrew from the world. A late portrait of him by Pantojà de la Cruz hung in the Escorial library. It depicts a pale figure in black and grey within an ethereal space: abstract power, devoid of context. The Escorial embodied an idea of power that conjoined secular and sacred, hierarchical and hieratic. Small wonder that the image of empire of which it was the microcosm should be the focus of Protestant fears – or that its notion of power should have become an imprisonment.

The paradox was that, although the imperial idea Philip II came to embody was particularly Spanish, the empire was not. It was a conjoint enterprise because Spain (the Castilian and Aragonese dominions until 1580, the whole Hispanic peninsula afterwards) lacked the human and natural resources upon which to build it. These lay in abundance in its other dynastic inheritances, in its overseas dominions and in the territories of its satellites. Only 12 per cent of the army that fought at St-Quentin were Spanish; the majority were Germans (53 per cent), Netherlanders (23 per cent) and English (12 per cent). Of the 67,000 troops in the Army of Flanders that Alba mobilized in 1572, about 18,000 were Germans, a further 29,000 were Netherlanders; only 10,000 were Spanish. Such diverse recruitment was normal for the armies of the period. The difference was that the Spanish had served and trained elsewhere in the empire beforehand. That was particularly the case for the Spanish *tercios*, 'the sinews of the army', who were accorded the privileges that went with empire.

Specialist skills and services for the empire often came from Italy – the accountants, map-makers, geographers, armament manufacturers, shipbuilders, pilots and engineers. The pontoon bridge over the Scheldt at the siege of Antwerp in 1585 would have been impossible without the technical expertise of two Italian engineers (Gianbattista Piatti and Properzio Boracci) who were able to realize what Farnese wanted. In 1581, the king was told by one of his officials that all the royal engineers in Spain were foreigners. It was a German who supervised the making of bronze cannon in the Spanish peninsula in the 1590s, Portuguese, Basques and Germans who provided the pilots for the Atlantic voyages and French pilots that steered the Armada up the Channel. The majority of the ships that fought the Ottomans at Lepanto had been built in the Italian peninsula. The financial sinews of empire were in non-Spanish (mainly Genoese) hands.

Distance and resources dictated the habits of empire. The superiority of Philip's intelligence services was recognized. On 15 October 1569, he told the French ambassador at his court 'with a smile on his face' of the victory at Jarnac, the news from his own government arriving a week later. Spanish diplomats trafficked for information at the highest level in Europe's courts. Thanks to information from the English ambassador in Paris, Sir Edward Stafford (on the secret Spanish payroll from January 1587), Philip II had precise details of English naval preparations. His forces would have forestalled Drake's raid on Cádiz harbour on 29 April 1587 had the information arrived sooner.

Distance remained the enemy of the Spanish empire because of its geographical extent and diversity. The challenges it faced were simply beyond anyone's capacities. The more the commitments and engagements in its name needed management, the stronger the idea of empire became. The more frequently its soldiers, diplomats, clerics and administrators travelled the dominions, the more that idea was invested in their hands. The Spanish empire in the Americas was run as an administrative state, which meant decisions had to be taken thousands of miles away. The more information came in the more difficult it was to sift, analyse and decide. The solution was to procrastinate. The pressures are revealed in Philip II's annotations on the stream of despatches which passed through his study. He expressed his hesitations and reflected on the burdens of office which his instincts of duty amplified into micro-management on an imperial scale.

Opportunities existed for those with a vivid imagination to elaborate plots against the Spanish which then became part of the imperial rumour-mill. They gained credibility in the circumstances of heightening international tensions, exacerbated by the suspicions caused by religious differences. Usual diplomatic channels were often disrupted by the withdrawal or summary dismissal of ambassadors. Others wanted to expand the frontiers of empire to their own advantage, pressures which were difficult to control. Juan de Oñate, son of a Conquistador, who married the granddaughter of Hernán Cortés, presented the viceroy of New Spain, Luis de Velasco, with a proposition to move the northern limits of Mexico 1,000 miles northwards into the Rio Grande. He promised to provide resources for the expedition. The viceroy, in consultation with Madrid, offered priests and artillery and awarded him the title of governor (*adelantado*) of the new land. Setting out in January 1598, he laid claim to 'New Mexico', accepting the 'obedience' of the Pueblo Indians to Spain and suppressing resistance with brutality.

What logic justified this expansion of the empire? Even the viceroy in New Spain thought it was 'worthless land'. New Spain's existence in the empire depended on the meekness (and sickness) of the Pueblo in the face of their new rulers.

Meekness was not the response in Chile to the south of the Biobío river. Pedro de Valdivia and followers built a fort and founded Concepción on the northern banks of the river in 1550. From there, they moved south, inflicting defeats on the local population and dividing them into overlordships. Prospectors and miners from Santiago followed in search of gold deposits. The Indians of Tucapel were less impressed, and contrived a trap for Valdivia, who was killed and eaten, leading to an uprising which initially lasted four years, and almost drove the Spaniards out of Chile. In 1598, the governor of Chile was in turn ambushed by the Indians of Arauco, captured and eaten, the prelude to a spontaneous rebellion of subjugated Indians in southern Chile in which Spanish towns were wiped out. By 1600 perhaps half the Spanish population in Chile had been killed. That was the year when a Spanish captain, Alonso González de Nájera, set out for Chile to report on the Araucanian conflict. His solution: a line of forts, a permanent army, the extermination of the local Indians and their replacement by more quiescent Africans. The war with the Araucanians went on, and his report was buried in the archives of a global empire, one of hundreds of problems on which Madrid wanted to have the last word, but over which it was obliged – by distance, logistics and exhaustion – to prevaricate.

The burden of sustaining the universal monarchy required an appeal to common endeavour. In reality, and for most of the time, the empire rested on the resources of Castile and its overseas dominions. The resulting game of robbing Peter to pay Paul passed for 'grand strategy'. The initial tensions stemmed from demands to protect the empire against the Ottomans in the Mediterranean. In the summer of 1560, the Ottoman fleet ambushed a Habsburg force sent by the viceroy of Sicily to the island of Djerba in North Africa. Spanish intelligence indicated that Ottoman power posed a threat to its communications in the western Mediterranean. The resulting galley construction was colossal, rising from fifty-five in 1562 to 155 in 1574. The costs of the galley fleet in the early 1570s matched those of the entire Flanders Army, a war on two fronts which was unsustainable; Philip II's suspension of payments (bankruptcy) of September 1575 was the result.

The 'resource envelope' of the Spanish empire expanded with the acquisition of the Portuguese dominions in 1580. In 1578, King Sebastian of Portugal died at the battle of Alcácer-Quibir in Morocco. Sebastian had no direct heirs (he was rumoured to have been so afraid of being impotent that he refused to have sex) and that spelt the end of the reigning House of Aviz. Sebastian was succeeded by his great-uncle, Cardinal Henry, who was sixty-six years of age and childless (see opposite).

The pretenders were numerous. António, known as the 'Prior of Crato', was the only direct male heir, but he was the illegitimate son of an elder uncle. When Henry died, the dynastic strength of António's case was recognized by the deputies of the Third Estate in the Portuguese Cortes of June 1580 but it was not matched by political forces on the ground, and he spent the rest of his life as a pretender in exile. Catherine de Médicis, whose lawyers thought she had a claim too, assembled a naval force in 1582 in defence of the Prior only for it to be shipwrecked off the coast of the Azores. An English expedition sent for the same purpose suffered the same fate in 1589. The only other native Portuguese claimant was Catherine, duchess of Braganza. They were all outmatched by Philip II of Spain, whose father (Charles V) had married Isabella of Portugal, Cardinal Henry's sister. Philip besieged Lisbon by sea and invaded by land, forcing António to flee in August 1580. He was installed as King Philip I of Portugal at Tomar in April 1581. There would be 'false Sebastians' thereafter, pretenders who legitimated popular revolts against Spanish overlordship. But Philip II respected Portuguese institutions. Portuguese aristocrats (already intermarried with the Spanish) were nurtured and the country's merchant colonial élites protected. Even Portuguese dynastic traditions were blended into those of the Spanish Habsburgs.

The demands to maintain the Hispanic empire grew in the wake of the Portuguese acquisition. Although mainland Portugal was a peaceful transition, the Azores archipelago acknowledged Dom António, Prior of Crato, Sebastian's illegitimate cousin. With French and English support the Azores held out until a Spanish expeditionary force of sixty ships destroyed Dom António's larger fleet in a battle off the island of São Miguel. In 1583, an even larger armada (ninety-eight ships and over 15,000 men) took the last remaining island of Terceira.

French and English engagement there mirrored their increasing

Pretenders to the Portuguese Crown in 1580

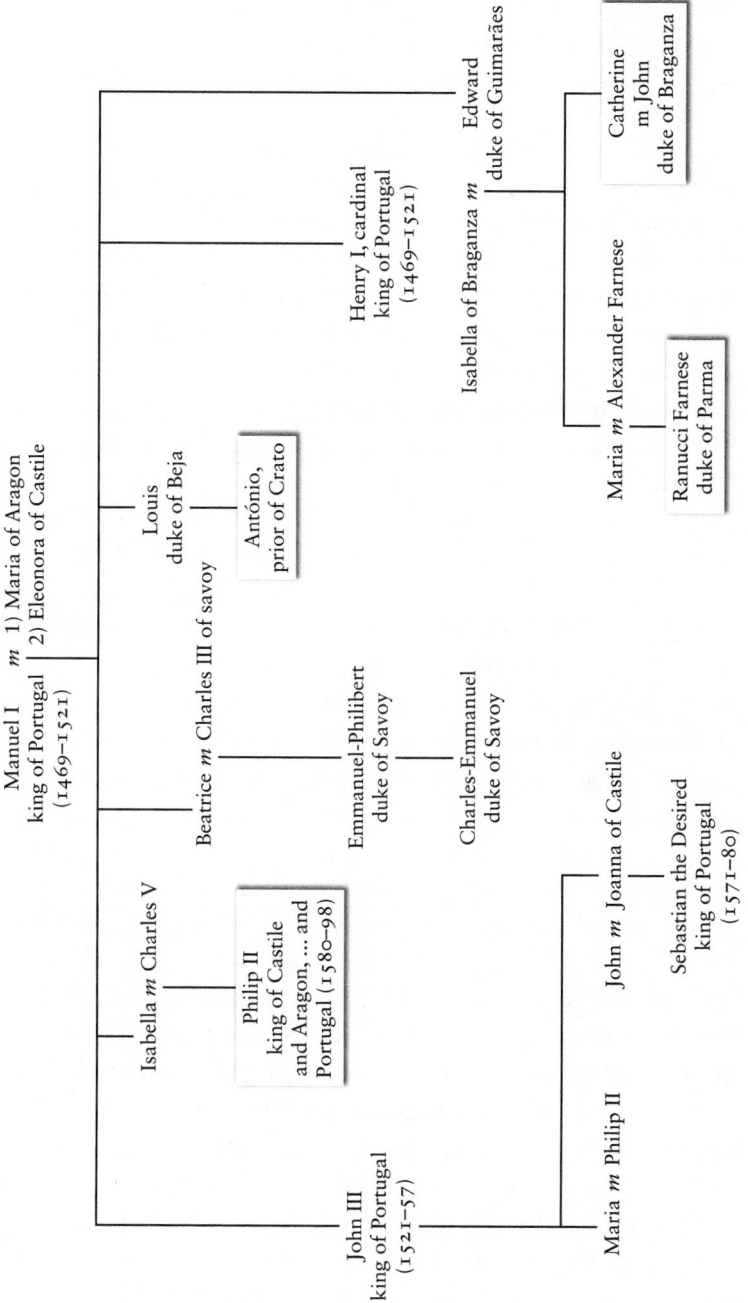

involvement in the Flanders war to the north. After Anjou's enterprise in the Netherlands failed and he died, Elizabeth I signed a treaty with the Dutch (20 August 1585). She agreed to supply 6,000 troops, and pay a quarter of their defence needs, and installed a commander to run the war-effort in the wake of William of Orange's assassination. Spain's approach to England and France had similar characteristics. It began with dissident groups, who offered Spain their advice and support while painting an optimistic picture of the prospects for Spain's intervention. In the English case, disenchanted Catholic émigrés served as the conduit. At the closing sessions of Trent in 1563, there were discussions about unseating Elizabeth and replacing her with Mary Queen of Scots; Philip II grew weary of unrealistic propositions from Rome on how to do so. But after 1580 he became persuaded that such an intervention was an integral part of, as he put it, 'the war in the Netherlands, which is as holy as a war can be'. In France, Catholics across the Pyrenees and on the northeastern borders (Picardy, Champagne) sought men and money from Spain to turn the civil wars in their direction. Here too, Philip II became persuaded that a pre-emptive intervention to block the heretic Henry of Navarre from the French throne (he became the direct heir after Anjou's death in 1584) was not only necessary but in accordance with God's will.

In each case, there was a preliminary 'cold war', typified by diplomatic tension and plots. In 1570, a Florentine financier, Roberto Ridolfi, who was involved in the abortive 'Rising of the Northern Earls' in England the previous year, tried to interest Alba and Philip II in an invasion of England and the unseating of Elizabeth. The plot was uncovered and Ridolfi's messenger was arrested and tortured. On the evidence which he revealed, the duke of Norfolk was arrested and executed in 1572. In November 1583, Francis Throckmorton, a cousin of the queen's first lady-in-waiting, was convicted of plotting to assassinate the queen and put Mary Queen of Scots on the throne, this time with the support of Mary's in-law, Henri, duke of Guise, and the Spanish. In September 1584, at the initiative of the Guises, Henri and his brothers Louis, cardinal of Lorraine, and Charles, duke of Mayenne, met at Nancy to conclude the Catholic League, composed of ultra-Catholic malcontent nobles and a fringe movement of Parisians, convinced that it was their duty to prevent the heretic Henry of Navarre acceding to the French throne. In December 1584 (or, more probably in January of the following year) Henri de Guise signed a secret treaty with Spain at the Guise family seat of Joinville in Champagne. Spain promised to pay an annual pension of 200,000 *écus* against Guise's undertaking that, come the death of the reigning king, Henry III, he would work to install a Catholic prince of the blood (Charles, cardinal de Bourbon) on the throne. In October 1585, as another plot to assassinate Queen Elizabeth materialized (the Babington Plot, after Antony Babington, an English Catholic whose revelations led to Mary Queen of Scots' execution at Fotheringay on 8 February 1587), Philip II committed himself to 'the Enterprise of England' (the *Impresa da Inglaterra*).

Spanish schemes for an English invasion dated back to the summer of 1559 when Philip sailed down the Channel from the Netherlands en route for Spain. Then, as later, he rejected the proposition as risky and impolitic. He had played a role in instigating the rebuilding of the English navy in 1557–8, and knew its potential. A moderate Protestant regime under Elizabeth I could be lived with, so long as it did not adversely impact on the security of Philip's dominions. That assessment, however, began to change in the early 1580s, following Drake's circumnavigation voyage of 1577–80, the growth of English piracy in the Atlantic and Caribbean, its intervention in the Azores on behalf of Portuguese rebels, culminating in its expeditionary force to the Netherlands in 1585. Without any formal declaration of war, Spain's preparations for the Armada began early in 1586. It took over two years to assemble, almost from scratch, the projected naval force. The huge engagement tied down the efforts and resources of the Spanish state, delaying the fleet's departure in 1588 until late in the season. Even as the 122 ships arrived off Land's End towards the end of July, the strategic difficulties of the operation had not been resolved. The duke of Parma had consistently warned that it could not be undertaken until he had recaptured a large enough port on the Dutch coast, and that it would divert resources from the campaign in the Netherlands. Obliged to keep his forces close by the coast through the early summer of 1588, he eventually gave up hope, standing down the crews on his own ships just as the Armada made its way up the Channel.

Storms in the Bay of Biscay scuppered two English efforts to engage with the vessels in Spanish waters in June and July. Sceptical as to whether the Armada would embark so late in the season, the English fleet of sixty-six vessels was caught resupplying in Plymouth Sound. It succeeded, however, in giving chase to the huge crescent of Spanish ships making their way up the Channel. The Spanish force held its line despite numerous English attempts to engage and the expending of a good deal of its ammunition. It lost only two ships (and both of these to accidents) as it moved towards the Dutch coast. Then, however, the Spanish admiral, the duke of Medina Sidonia, elected to anchor off Calais on 6 August. That furnished the opportunity for the English to organize a fire-ship attack, accompanying strong winds blowing the Spanish fleet into the North Sea. Four Spanish ships were lost but the rest made their getaway northwards. The vast majority of Spanish losses came as the fleet made its way round the British Isles back home.

The defeat raised doubts about Spanish invincibility, not least among its Dutch rebels and among the opponents of the Catholic League in France. In 1590, and again in 1592, the Spanish army was diverted to aid the Catholic League in France. Spain's strategic theatre expanded as its military engagements multiplied – in Brittany, Picardy, Normandy, Languedoc and (via the duke of Savoy) in Dauphiné and Provence. Meanwhile, the Dutch Stadholder, Mauritz of Nassau, launched offensives to push the Spaniards out of the northeastern Netherlands and secure the river strongholds.

THE CATHOLIC LEAGUE IN FRANCE

The death of the last direct heir to the French throne (François, duke of Anjou) on 10 June 1584 opened up a struggle for succession which, aligned with religious fault-lines, struck at the bedrock of dynastic politics. No one had written the script for a unitary dynastic state with a sacral kingship where the succession lay in the hands of a Protestant prince, the Bourbon Henry, king of Navarre. Henry had a huge landed patrimony, the majority of which came from the Albret-Foix-Armagnac inheritance of his mother, Jeanne d'Albret. The Pyrenean kingdom of Navarre had mostly been dismembered by Spain, but a title still remained, attached to the independent principality of Béarn. There, women could inherit, queens could rule as of right, and its rulers could be deposed for not upholding its customs. Under the influence of Queen Jeanne, the principality became a Calvinist stronghold. The Protestantism which Henry had inherited from his mother was intertwined with the destiny of Béarn. From his father (Antoine de Bourbon) he inherited, however, his distant claim to the French throne, and a tradition of rejecting any confessional straitjacket. Mortally wounded at the siege of Rouen in 1562, Antoine had been taken by barge up the Seine to Les Andelys, where he received the Mass and the last rites from a Catholic priest, expressed his wish to live and die according to the Augsburg Confession, and had the Scriptures read to him by a Calvinist physician.

After Henry of Navarre married the Catholic Marguerite de Valois in 1572 (against the wishes of his mother), he abjured his Protestantism in the wake of the massacre of St Bartholomew only to recover it once more as he quit the French court four years later. By the mid-1580s he had surrounded himself with Protestants and Catholics loyal to the cause of the Bourbon succession to the French throne, which he presented at home and abroad as a matter of princely predestination. He rejected religious conversion to accommodate the needs of the moment, and used his refusal as a way to assert his authority over others.

The others in question were the Guises – Henri, son of François, and other members of the Guise family, notably his two brothers, Charles and Louis. The Guises were nowhere near as wealthy as Navarre – but they looked to their relatives the dukes of Lorraine for support, and beyond them to Spain. The Guises were marginalized by Henry III, and their discontent nurtured their support for the Catholic cause. They projected the defeat of Protestant heresy onto a broad canvas. In a letter dated 2 April 1587 to the Spanish ambassador in France, Don Bernardino de Mendoza, Guise gave his word that he would 'not dismount from his horse' until the Catholic religion was re-established in France and his opponents ruined. That was two months after the execution of his cousin Mary Stuart in England. Reported in Paris on 1 March 1587, that event advertised the 'cruelties' to which English Catholics were subjected (and, by extension, what they could expect from Navarre's accession to the throne). It demonstrated that a twice-crowned head could be excised to truncate a religiously inconvenient succession (which is why Mary Stuart was executed). Libels circulating in Paris blamed Henry III for not having saved his sister-in-law. They were the work of the 'Sixteen' (la Seize, from the policing arrangements which divided the city into sixteen sectors). Bourbon royalist historians dismissed that group as fanatics but, in reality, they enjoyed support from well-established citizens. Thanks to an informant, Henry III escaped two coups in February and March 1587. Another, on 2 September 1587, came close to realization. The Catholic League was a media event, Parisian printers taking the lead, followed in due course by other print centres in France.

The Guises had an ambivalent relationship with the Sixteen, an organization which they had not willed into being and could not readily control. Henri de Guise had no plan beyond that of mobilizing Catholic loyalties. He would probably have preferred to devote his energies to the battlefield. As it was, he became engaged in publicity to emphasize his esteem and impose his will on the king. That was a dangerous game, especially when the king in question knew that the Guises were on the Spanish payroll and suspected (with good reason) that the libels circulating about his homosexual relations with the *mignons* were part of the ongoing game of cat-and-mouse. On 9 May 1588, the duke of Guise's entry into Paris turned into a victory parade. When the king ordered Swiss mercenaries into the capital before sunrise on 12 May they were met by the insurrection they were supposed to prevent. Barricades of chains, reinforced by paving stones, barrels and staves, stretched across the streets. That afternoon, the duke of Guise stepped onto the streets, not as a battle commander but in white satin breeches, greeted as the saviour of Paris. The following day, Henry III fled the capital through the Tuileries garden, his humiliation overwhelming.

The game of cat-and-mouse went on for the rest of the year. Weakened by the collapse of his authority, Henry III summoned deputies to an Estates General at Blois on 16 October 1588, where he hoped to recover the initiative. But, turning the pro-League sentiments of the deputies to his advantage, Guise used the occasion to impose himself once more upon the king. On the morning of 23 December, Henri de Guise was called to the king's apartment, where Henry's bodyguard assassinated him, the cardinal of Guise being put to death similarly the following morning. The king called it a *coup de majesté*, Étienne Pasquier a *coup d'état*. Pope Sixtus V called it a tyrannical act, and excommunicated him (24 May 1589).

As news of the Guises' death spread, there was a spontaneous uprising by Catholics against the king. On 1 January, a wall-painting of the assassination was put up in the church of Sainte-Geneviève-des-Ardents in the capital. On the following day, the tombs of some *mignons* were ransacked and royal coats of arms torn down from city buildings. The first of many processions took place twenty-four hours later. On 7

January Sorbonne theologians approved a 'withdrawal of obedience' from Henry III, now known as 'Henri de Valois' or, in the anagram ascribed to the Paris preacher Jean Guincestre, 'Vilain Hérodes'. Recognized royalists fled the city as the Parlement was purged on 13 January and its first president, Achille de Harlay, imprisoned. A new League municipal government was put in place with a Council of the Union to coordinate its activities with other League-declared municipalities elsewhere. Almost without asking for it, Mayenne, the one Guise brother who had not been at Blois and who had escaped the king's vengeance, had a cause to fight for, a provisional government to work with and an enemy to defeat.

That enemy was the legitimate king, which made the League and Mayenne sound more anti-monarchical than they really were. With not many options left, Henry III made common cause with Henry of Navarre and together they assembled an army of 40,000 men to besiege Paris in the summer of 1589. At his military headquarters in St-Cloud on the morning of 1 August, a monk, Jacques Clément, drew out a knife and stabbed the king, who died a day later. Clément was himself killed by the king's bodyguard. To League Catholics, he was a martyr, inspired by God, and the floodgates of vituperation against the last Valois king opened. In retrospect, that marked high-water for the League, whose problem of how to conjugate Catholicity and kingship was just beginning.

Their candidate to the throne was the octogenarian uncle of Henry of Navarre, Charles de Bourbon ('Charles X'). He was kept prisoner by Navarre in the fortress at Maillezais, allowed no contact with the outside world, had no direct heirs and died there on 9 May 1590. In his name and under the fiction of his authority, Mayenne and the League conducted a provisional government. That stretched the legal fiction of the separation between state and king, for it was not clear to what extent Mayenne could exercise the royal powers of nominating magistrates, deciding on disputed municipal elections and appointing bishops in the king's name. These issues concerned the League in Paris, where the Sixteen became a municipal power bloc, running the city. But with no military success to his name and increasing criticism of his rule, Mayenne purged the General Council in Paris in March 1590.

Mayenne's greatest hope for defeating Navarre lay early on in August 1589. The royalist nobility did not rally to Navarre and, with no more than 12,000 in his army, the Protestant king retreated to Dieppe to await English reinforcements. With a force over twice as large, Mayenne failed to dislodge him from trenches around the castle at Arques (21 September 1589). On 30 October, Navarre's men appeared before the walls of Paris. On 14 March 1590, the armies of Mayenne and Navarre engaged once more, this time at Ivry. Again, Navarre's forces were smaller than those of his opponents, but it took him only an hour to dismiss Mayenne from the field. Over 6,000 League supporters lost their lives and a myth was born. Henry IV told his troops on the eve of battle to follow the distinctive white plume of feathers in his helmet if their standards were captured. Henry IV's image-builders used that as divine approbation for his right to the throne.

The victory at Ivry heralded a quasi-siege of Paris. It was eventually broken by relief convoys from Parma in early September 1590, although by then 30,000 Parisians had died of starvation. Mutual recriminations grew amid rumours that Navarre had spies in the city, or that he might convert to Catholicism. Royalist sympathizers (known as *politiques* to their opponents) became targets of suspicion. In the autumn of 1591, a new Council of Ten, formed of activists from the Sixteen, was instituted to tighten Paris security. They drew up a 'red list' (*papier rouge*) on which the fate of suspects was indicated ('P', 'D' or 'C': Hanged, Stabbed or Thrown Out [*Pendu, Dagué* or *Chassé*]). On 15 November 1591 the leading magistrate of the Parlement of Paris was arrested on the orders of the council, along with two other judges, all three being summarily executed in prison. Mayenne's return to the capital on 28 November 1591 signalled the end of the Sixteen as he replaced the governor of the Bastille, disbanded the Council of Ten and hanged three of the Sixteen's leaders. The rest fled or lay low.

Mayenne's reason for liquidating the Sixteen lay not simply with events in Paris. On 2 September 1591, the Council of Ten wrote to Philip II to invite him to assume the French crown. That opened up the issue to which Mayenne had no solution: the royal succession. After the death of Charles X, Catholic supporters could only imagine that they were in an interregnum, it being up to an Estates General to elect a new ruler. In January 1593, Mayenne eventually convened it (or rather, a rump of a constitutive assembly) in Paris. The duke of Feria arrived in February 1593 as Philip II's personal envoy to promote the election of the Spanish infanta Isabella Clara Eugenia to the throne. The proposal had some dynastic logic to it – she was the granddaughter of Henry II and Catherine de Médicis. But it was too open an interference in French affairs. Indeed, Feria had already made Mayenne various promises if he would support the proposal. On 14 May, the candidature of the infanta was officially launched before the Estates.

Three days later, on 17 May, Henry of Navarre announced his intention to convert back to Catholicism. His decision was timed to consolidate the gathering voices of opinion in the League Estates and elsewhere towards a Navarrist solution. On 20 June, the League Estates declared that they could not accept a foreign prince as their sovereign and, a week later, on 27 June, the Parlement of Paris agreed a text which demanded that Mayenne respect the Salic law as the 'fundamental law' of the kingdom. While Parisian preachers denounced Navarre as an untrustworthy heretic turncoat, a lampoon of the League Estates began to circulate entitled the 'Satyre Menippée', facetiously presenting its deputies as high on a Spanish drug called 'catholicon' (a little pill shaped like a Spanish doubloon). Navarre's conversion finally took place on 25 July 1593 at St-Denis, the sepulchre of the kings of France. The king never said 'Paris is worth a Mass', though the phrase is suggestive of the new political logic of 'reason of state' that was emerging as an answer to politico-religious conflicts. He did call it a 'somersault', indicating the risks that he knew he was running. The abjuration opened the door to a slow reconciliation in France, beginning with a general truce (six days after the abjuration) and a declaration on 27 October that all those who rallied to the king would be automatically pardoned. Henry IV entered Paris with his forces at daybreak on 22 March 1594 with hardly a shot being fired. While the king made his way to Notre-Dame, the remaining Spanish garrison discreetly left by another gate.

RELIGION AND POLITICS

The use of violence to maintain a community of belief by force became a contentious issue in the divided politics of Christendom in the later sixteenth century. Its political culture had developed, in theory and practice, ways of controlling violence and accentuating the legitimacy of rulership and authority in the name of the commonwealth. A chivalric honour code determined what was, and was not, acceptable violence and encouraged notions of what constituted legitimate behaviour in warfare. The instruments of law, the Church and urban authority increasingly controlled the private pursuit of vengeance, feud and other forms of interpersonal violence. In the sixteenth century, however, the state played a greater part in people's lives, especially in western Europe. The Reformation furnished the circumstances and arguments for saying that there were limits to the powers claimed by those states. It is no coincidence that the violence that erupted in political life was fiercest where the powers of states were strongest and where the influence of religious change was most fiercely contested. Nor is it surprising that the arguments about violence – about limiting the power of the state to commit it, and giving others the responsibility to control it – were first heard among exiles and migrant communities, where the politics of conviction were at their strongest. Ideas about 'rights of resistance' and 'rights of revolt' had a cross-national – and ultimately cross-confessional – dynamic that reflected the conflicts to which they were related.

Jean Calvin, the theologian to whom the early Protestant communities in exile turned for advice, understood the anxieties that religious change provoked. God alone had the power, he said in the first edition of his *Institutes*, to deal with tyrannical princes. Individuals who refused to obey legitimate authority should expect to pay the price for doing so. They were best advised to live somewhere out of a tyrant's reach. Yet, under the influence of the theologian Pierre Viret, Calvin introduced nuances. In the closing passage to the final, 1559 edition of the *Institutes* he acknowledged that there might be intermediary authorities, like the Ephors of ancient Sparta, whose responsibility was to 'restrain the will of kings'. That was how Lutheran theologians in Hesse and Saxony justified princely resistance to the emperor in the 1540s, and it had resurfaced in the siege of Magdeburg in 1551. Calvin refused to go further and accord any legitimacy to a private individual in revolt against authority.

But that was not the case for English exiles in the Rhineland. John Ponet argued (in *A Shorte Treatise of Politike Power*, 1557), just as John Knox (in *The First Blast of the Trumpet*, 1558) and Christopher Goodman (*How Superior Powers Ought to be Obeyed*, 1558), that resistance against established authority could be justified, though they differed in detail over the justifications which they offered. Knox, writing in prophetic mode, regarded the rule of queens (Mary of Guise, Mary Stuart and

Mary Tudor) as against God's will, communicated to all men through nature. They were tyrants by their own acts and (though in his Scottish writings he was less clear-cut) this justified the taking up of arms by the godly. Ponet was more attentive to law and precedents. Admitting that the English people had deposed tyrants in the past, he nevertheless advised that: 'Christen men ought well to consider and weighe mennes commaundementes, before they be hastie to doo them, to see if they be contrarie or repugnaunt to goodes commaundementes and justice: which, if they be, they are cruell and evill, and ought not to be obeyed.'

Such were the roots of the arguments for a 'right of resistance' expressed by those whom the Catholic writer William Barclay called 'monarchomachs' – those who wanted to 'overthrow monarchy' (*monarchiam demoliri*). The most notorious works, conceived in part before but published after the massacre of St Bartholomew, included François Hotman's *Francogallia* (1573), Beza's *The Right of Magistrates* (1574) and a work published under a pseudonym recalling Junius Brutus, Rome's republican founder, entitled *Vindiciae contra Tyrannos* ('Defences' – but also 'Revenges' and 'Legal Recriminations' – 'against Tyrants', 1579), a work in which Philippe Duplessis-Mornay had a hand. These were more than pamphlets for the moment. They treated the issue of the limits of political obedience at a general level. Beza revived the notion of a legal 'contract' and linked it to the theological conception of a 'covenant'. He thought that there existed not simply a pact between people and ruler but also between God, ruler and people. The people could invoke God's sanctions against a ruler who broke his engagements (to people or to God). Hotman deployed his knowledge of the early history of the Franks to prove, as he supposed, that they had deposed through a 'public assembly' kings who exceeded their powers. That authority could be resurrected. The author of the *Vindiciae* argued further that the people not only should disobey and resist a prince whose authority was tyrannical and ruining the true Church, but should also call on foreign princes professing 'true religion' to come to their aid.

Although not acknowledged explicitly, such arguments had an impact on Catholics who, in similar circumstances, looked for reasons to limit or reject constituted political authority. In Spain, their ideas found an echo in the writings of the Jesuits – Emmanuel Sá, Tomás Sánchez de Córdoba and Juan de Mariana. The last of these had been an academic in Rome, Paris and the Low Countries before he returned to Spain in

1574 to become a senior figure in the Toledo Inquisition. In his *On kingship and its institution* (1599) he argued that, although sovereigns held their authority ultimately from God, it was mediated to them by communities. Kings had to put themselves at the service of the people, who could deliver judgement in the name of God upon what kings did. Disaffection was a judgement which princes should heed or face the consequences in terms of Godly-inspired sanction (which might be removal from office by one means or another). Mariana explicitly approved of Jacques Clément's regicidal act, referring to it as 'the eternal glory of France'. In the face of the rising incidence of assassination attempts on the rulers of Christian commonwealths, the 'mutual obligation' between ruler and ruled – that which guaranteed the love of the people for its prince – had never seemed so remote from reality. It is hardly surprising that the contentions over religion in the second half of the sixteenth century should lead in some places to a more absolute conception of power, and in others to a distancing of the state from confessional politics.

PATRIA AND RELIGION

'Nationhood' existed in this period and was often evoked, becoming part of the contentions over religion. But people meant different things by it and deployed it in contradictory ways. Soldiers fighting for Charles V at the battle of Mühlberg (1547) cried 'Santiago, Spagna' though many of them were not Spanish or from Habsburg dominions. Those serving in the Dutch armies in 1576 wrote to mutineers from the other side: 'We are from the same nation as you, all Spaniards.' Chronicles of the Spanish peninsula equated the Spanish with Castile and its language, but that was at odds with the senses of belonging in the other kingdoms of the peninsula. Philip II invited a national response to the capture of the Spanish fleet and sack of Cádiz by the earl of Essex in 1596, but the Castilian Cortes of the year before were already sceptical about such appeals, replying that the only commonwealth which now existed was 'a common misery for every one'.

The Reformation, however, added meaning to nationhood. Luther appealed to Germans against slippery and corrupt Rome. French Protestants reworked the myths of free Gaul, whose liberties were enshrined in assemblies which elected and deposed rulers. In German Protestant principalities the references to *patria* became more insistent. William of Orange presented himself as the saviour of the 'fatherland' and a 'patriot'. But he was of German birth, spoke French for preference, and had publicly to repudiate the accusation that he was a stranger in the Netherlands.

To most people, *patria* meant their native town or province, 'everybody's country, fatherland, the town, village, hamlet or any other place where one is born', as a Dutch dictionary put it in 1562. In Dutch, the word *Vaderland* also denoted 'heaven' in the translations of Luther's Bible, giving a religious particularity to patriotic evocation in the Dutch Revolt. But the revolt's supporters were more united by their Hispanophobia than by their patriotism. Within their churches distinctions still existed between Hollanders, Brabanters and Walloons. The growing exiledom in the Reformation nurtured a patriotism that romanticized the past into a land that never was and fostered xenophobia which distorted the present and warped the future.

National consciousness was a way by which those who believed in the Christian commonwealth spun out myths about a collective past in which the people collectively had a positive role. Scholars and antiquarians gave their histories a new veracity by printing the accompanying evidence from early charters. The results were noticeable, especially in Protestant Europe, where the upheavals of the Reformation created new states or made people see old ones in new ways. By the end of the sixteenth century, there were four new published histories of Scotland, one each for Denmark and Sweden, no fewer than fourteen for Poland and five each for Bohemia and Hungary. English Protestant writers evoked the past variously ('England', 'Britain' and 'Albion'), but when they projected it onto the institutionalized present it acquired a more defined ethnocentricity. That was as true of Holinshed's chronicle of English kings as of Foxe's martyrology. France's scholar-jurists delineated how their national myth was embodied in living organisms that were part of its commonwealth, especially its sovereign law courts and (Gallican) Church. When English common-lawyer antiquarians evoked the ancient constitution, they imagined a commonwealth in which they belonged and to which they contributed. That commonwealth was, however, what the civic and religious turmoil of the Post-Reformation was all about, and what it placed in doubt.

13. Living with Religious Divisions

CONVICTION AND CONFORMITY

'Either the Reformed religion is good or it is bad; there is no middle . . . there is as little in common between the Reformed teaching and Roman fantasies as there is between white and black.' That view of a Dutch Calvinist, published in 1579, is replicated from different sides of the emerging religious frontier in western Christianity. The English Jesuit John Radford thought that Protestantism and Catholicism were 'as farre as heaven and hell asunder'. These divisions were often presented as part of the cosmic struggle between Christ and Antichrist, God and the Devil. Only a half-hearted hesitant, said the London cleric William Gouge, could fail to 'shew a holy zeale in our anger'. These were clerical opinions and, in the second half of the sixteenth century, churchmen took the lead in fashioning religious convictions into an instrument for reinforcing ecclesiastical authority and imposing confessional uniformity. But their views found an echo among the laity. In 1615, the Calvinist minister of the Dutch village of Wassenaar was called before the synod by his own flock, who complained that he preached 'without rebuking the Papacy or other sects'. Officials in the diocese of Ulm noted that villagers knew the issues at stake in polemic controversy but they could not recite the Ten Commandments or the Lord's Prayer. The growing body of Catholic and Protestant martyrologies and the burgeoning narratives of personal conversion stories were deployed for polemical purposes, but they emerged from the experience of people confronted with uncomfortable religious choices in the Post-Reformation.

Religious identities were manifested in ritual and liturgy. These acted as markers for disputed doctrines, the finer points of which many lay people may not have understood. But it required no great learning to comprehend that devotions to the Virgin Mary and to saints were about some people being holy and having power to intercede with God. Equally, the laity's taking of communion in both kinds, the wine with the wafer or bread, was readily perceived as a symbol of the priesthood of all believers. But whether the communion came in the form of a wafer or a piece of bread, whether one received it standing up or sitting down, where the communion table was placed, whether children were exorcised and, if so, how many times they were sprinkled with water, and whether the priest wore vestments or not – these distinctions became contentious, acquiring an importance that is impossible to understand without taking into account the significance of religious conformity.

The possibility had opened up from the earliest days of the Protestant Reformation in Wittenberg that there were ceremonies and rituals which might not be specifically forbidden or commanded by God. These might remain 'things indifferent' (*adiaphora*). Accepting that there were religious matters over which one could agree to disagree was at the heart of a bitter debate. In the wake of the Interim of Augsburg (the imperial decree of 1548 and first step towards the legalization of Lutheranism in the empire) in Germany, the argument split strict (Gnesio-) Lutherans from 'Philippists' (the supporters of Philipp Melanchthon), the latter seeking accommodation with the emperor to arrive at a civil peace. The dispute emerged again in the Puritan controversies with Elizabethan bishops in England in the later sixteenth century. The problem was that to admit that there were 'things indifferent' opened the door to individual choice. Religious conformity became more important as the risks of dissent grew greater. Identical beliefs and practices, practised everywhere in the same way and at the same time, constituted an aspiration to a unity which had never existed hitherto in Christendom. As the religious frontiers grew more menacing, so it mattered more to belong within a community whose uniformity matched an enhanced sense of spiritual unity.

Conformity was hard-wired into post-Reformation society. It ensured, for example, that, although we must suppose there were as many homosexual men and women as in any age, their voices are rarely heard, so universal was the ambient social and moral pressure and so repressive the legislation against those found guilty of homosexual acts. Religious conformity generally meant sharing the views of those in the congregational pew next to you. But there were many for whom it signified something larger. The English Puritan William Bradshaw, for example, felt more at home with Calvinists abroad than he did with the conforming members of the Church Established who were his neighbours. With globalizing Catholic Christianity in mind, a Spanish ambassador to Switzerland told co-religionists there in the early years of the Thirty Years War that 'they should feel a closer kinship to a Catholic Indian or African than to a heretical . . . countryman'.

For most people conformity meant doing what everyone else did in their immediate neighbourhood, which was to attend the local church, whose bells represented the dominant lived experience of religion: a call to attend church, or to signal a burial, a marriage or a public anniversary. The local church intersected with local civic life. It organized elementary schooling and distributed poor relief. Orders of local manorial courts were read out at the pulpit, and official bulletins were pinned up in the porch. Not to attend church raised a question mark over whether one belonged in the community. To be excluded from receiving communion through excommunication was a mark of shame. To tolerate excommunicates – and, by extension, nonconformists – was to invite God's wrath. Correspondingly, when catastrophe hit local society, the most readily available explanation was that the community had collectively sinned and must assuage God's anger. When fire destroyed the English city of Dorchester in 1613 it became act one of its spiritual conversion into a Puritan stronghold in pre-Civil War England. The pressures for conformity were generated within localities, and they probably grew greater as social cohesion became more threatened, demographic resilience weakened and weather patterns turned more unstable.

Yet the reality of religious division in the later sixteenth century was that the emerging frontiers ran down the main street of communities, and not simply between states and political entities. Managing the resulting tensions depended on the size and organizational ability of the religious minority concerned, the diplomatic skills of local community leaders and their ability to reach an accord with one another, and the existence or not of outside pressures, including from individuals with interests in stirring things up. In retrospect, we can see where and when flashpoints occurred. Processions, feast-days and funerals were moments when public space was occupied exclusively by one religion, and when people were in physical proximity. Venerated objects – the images of saints, relics, Eucharistic wafers – went on public display. Those who did not take part were targeted. The French libertine poet Théophile de Viau recalled an occasion when he and a fellow-Protestant found themselves in the Catholic town of Agen in 1618. A priest, wearing his vestments and carrying the Viaticum, passed them on his way to a dying parishioner to perform the last rites, preceded by an acolyte ringing a bell. Passers-by fell to their knees, hats doffed, while de Viau and his friend just stood back. Their irreverence attracted the fury of the crowd, and it was only the intervention of the magistrate which saved their lives.

What happened in Agen was part of living with religious division in what was left of Christendom. Such incidents remained localized and sporadic in most cases because people's commitment to their religious beliefs was trumped by their other commitments: not to transgress the law, to behave charitably towards their neighbours and to accept the judgement of their betters. People who were divided by religion retained much of what they shared in common. The Polish Jesuit Piotr Skarga acknowledged as much when he wrote of Polish Protestants: 'heresy is bad, but they are good neighbours and brethren, to whom we are linked by bonds of love in the common fatherland'. A community at odds with itself was as evil as a civil war in a Christian commonwealth. In the wake of the first French civil war, when Protestants captured the city of Lyon and damaged its ecclesiastical fabric, the magistrates insisted that the well-bred children of the town parade, two by two and hand-in-hand, Protestants with Catholics, to attend King Charles IX at his visit in 1564. Dressed identically, the members of both faiths offered the king the town's loyalty. Only the small jewelled crosses pinned to the caps of the Catholics distinguished them from the Protestants. That was part of the communal mechanisms of repair when localities were torn apart by violence in the name of religion. The Christian commonwealths of the later sixteenth century depended on them.

LIVING TOGETHER APART IN SWISS AND GERMAN LANDS

The earliest experiments in living with religious diversity occurred in Switzerland and Germany. Two major alternatives existed, and there were attempts at both. The first consisted in negotiating shared space, including (in some places) church buildings and resources – known in the sixteenth century as a *simultaneum* (from *simul*, at the same time). The second involved a segmentation of the communities in question, such that they each had their own space, which typically corresponded to the religion of the ruler. The latter pattern was incarnated for German lands by the Peace of Augsburg (1555), in which the dominant principle was that the religious configuration of geographical space followed the religious inclination of its rulers – known by the Latin phrase, first coined in 1586, as *cuius regio, eius religio*.

Most of Switzerland implicitly divided up along the lines of the second option. Different cantons decided their confessional affiliations, leaving those who were in the minority confession to choose whether to stay and conform, or to leave and live elsewhere. But, in the area which had briefly witnessed the first 'religious wars' in sixteenth-century Christendom, the first and second Kappel wars (1529–31), there was an experiment in sharing space. In the disputed lands of the Thurgau on the borders of the Zürich canton, the 1531 treaty which ended the conflict created arrangements in which Catholic and Reformed congregations shared churches. Catholic priests baptized and married Reformed members of the congregation indiscriminately. Abbots carried out visitations of Reformed clergymen. The bishop's chancery in Constance appointed Reformed Protestants to serve as pastors. Local people were given the right to choose collectively and individually the faith to which they wished to adhere.

The Thurgau breaks the notion of the sixteenth century as an age of religious wars; yet, through to the early seventeenth century the arrangements worked. By the terms (*Landfrieden*) of the 1531 treaty, each party was guaranteed privileges – interpreted by the Catholics as the continuing existence of parish priests, boundaries and the spiritual jurisdiction of the bishop of Constance. Protestants had the right to continue worshipping in their faith. Both sides accepted that local communities determined what happened on the basis of majority votes. Articles of the treaty guaranteed that individuals who remained Catholic could practise their ceremonies in private or in public, 'without attack or hatred' – the clause which formed the basis for the sharing of churches for religious worship. Finally arrangements were put in place for the division of church property in proportion to the numbers in each faith. That it worked was the result of a stalemate in the balance of religious forces. But people also adapted it to their perceptions of what was right and proper.

In German lands, the experiment in religious pluralism was on a grander scale, set in place by the Peace of Augsburg. The jurists who determined its details found it hard to accommodate religious pluralism within the territorial diversity of the Holy Roman Empire. Although the agreement was 'perpetual' and its terms took precedence over other laws and privileges, it applied only to Catholics and Lutherans who subscribed to the Augsburg Confession. Zwinglians, Calvinists and Anabaptists were excluded. Princes and imperial knights were given the right to determine the religion in their territories, while those subjects who did not wish to comply were accorded the right to emigrate (*ius emigrandi*). Ecclesiastical jurisdictions over the domains of those rulers who chose to become Protestant were suspended. Imperial cities with both confessions present within their territories at the time of the Peace of Passau in 1552 were to be bi-confessional. The most delicate issue was what should happen in the ecclesiastical territories. In the face of concerted Protestant opposition, the 'ecclesiastical reservation' clause (*reservatum ecclesiasticum*) declared that, when a princely prelate became Lutheran, he should forfeit his bishopric. To appease Protestant princely sensibilities, King Ferdinand issued a declaration (*Declaratio Ferdinandea*) which guaranteed freedom of conscience for Protestant nobles and cities within such ecclesiastical territories. That declaration was never part of the Peace of Augsburg, although Protestants later regarded it as such. Above all, the guarantors of the peace were those who had the greatest stake in the construction of a viable framework for preserving the integrity of the Reich: the Estates of the empire, its officials and jurists, and the emperor.

The history of the empire in the later sixteenth century is the working out of the Peace of Augsburg as part of the consolidation of its polity. It is a success story in the face of continuing Lutheran expansion, a gathering Catholic counter-offensive, and the problem of those excluded from its terms. Despite the pressures for religious conformity, German princes and their officials understood that the empire could work only with a measure of religious pluralism, and that religious restraint and flexibility were necessary in the name of preserving the common peace. That attitude came easily to Ferdinand, proclaimed Emperor Ferdinand I in

1558. He had brokered the agreement and, deprived of Habsburg ancestral lands with the exception of the Erblande (the Österreichische Erblande, or hereditary lands in Austria), Bohemia and Hungary, he was the ruler of a composite monarchy whose core dominions were insufficient to resource it. He was dependent on the German Estates to defend a 530-mile-long vulnerable eastern frontier, open to attack from the Turks. In a militarized zone over 40 miles deep, it required over 20,000 soldiers to garrison the fortifications that kept border incursions to a minimum. By his death in 1564, Ferdinand's debts topped 10 million florins, the equivalent of five years of annual revenues. The cost of servicing this debt consumed three quarters of the latter, while the garrisons on the eastern frontier needed 1 million florins a year, which was about what he owed his soldiers when he died.

The situation was more delicate for his successor, Maximilian II. Brought up with an enduring bitterness towards Charles V, who had tried to exclude him from the German succession in 1551, he made common cause with German, especially Lutheran, princes whenever the opportunity arose. He was elected to the Bohemian crown in 1562 and the Hungarian one a year later, and his court became a magnet for those who were unwilling to be shoehorned into a confessional way of thinking. His court preacher, Johann Sebastian Pfauser, was a crypto-Protestant. His librarian, Kaspar von Niedbruck, was in regular touch with Lutheran reformers and collaborated with the rigorist Lutheran Matthias Flacius in the history of the Christian Church published from 1559 onwards and known as the *Magdeburg Centuries*. The *Centuries* assembled the materials for a history of Christendom as that of a godly minority who supported God's truth against the forces of Antichrist and iniquity. Jacob Acontius was also in Maximilian's early entourage before he left for Swizerland and England. In a *Dialogue* composed for his Habsburg patron, Acontius urged him to be a new King David, seeking his own way to Christian truth. Clerical efforts to straitjacket truth into confessional certainty were merely part of 'Satan's stratagems'. Rome and Madrid highlighted the dangers of a potentially Protestant emperor in waiting, and Maximilian II trimmed his sails to secure the succession after the death of Ferdinand in 1564.

Once emperor, however, Maximilian was as committed to the Peace of Augsburg as his father. Protestant princes in the empire appreciated his anti-papal rhetoric and drew comfort from his signs of

The Austrian Habsburg Dynastic Inheritance, 1550–1648

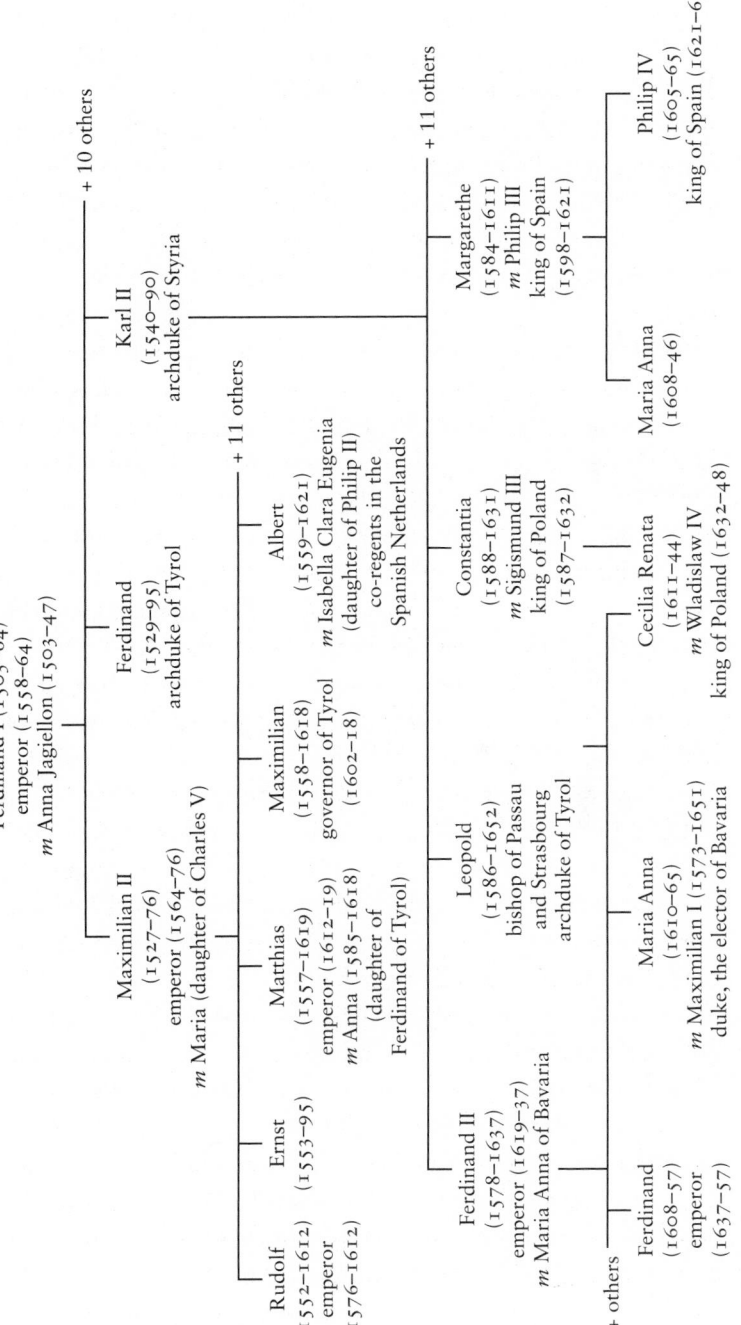

sympathy towards the Lutheran cause. Catholics accepted at face value his protestations of loyalty to the old faith, aware that dynastic pressures were working at the court of the Austrian Habsburgs in their direction. Emperor Ferdinand's will divided the inheritance three ways among Maximilian and his brothers. Maximilian retained Bohemia, Hungary, and Upper and Lower Austria. His younger brother Ferdinand inherited the Vorlande (Vorarlberg – the westernmost part of Austria – and the Habsburg dependencies to the Rhine and beyond) and the Tyrol. Karl, younger still, was given Inner Austria (Styria, Carinthia and Carniola).

Although Maximilian's share of the Austrian lands was shorn of its most populous parts, he retained control of Linz and Vienna, and could draw on the revenues of Bohemia. Hungary, which lay outside the empire, continued to be a burden rather than a blessing. However, the courts at Innsbruck (Archduke Ferdinand II) and Graz (Archduke Karl II) became nurseries of Catholic resurgence – sponsors of reversionary movements against Maximilian. Vienna now seemed a long way away from the empire and more vulnerable to Turkish incursions. Innsbruck stood in the way of the established Habsburg routes from Vienna to the Rhine; Graz blocked the links south of the Alps to Italy. The logical alternative as an imperial capital was Prague, which is where Maximilian's successor, Rudolf (elected king of Hungary in 1572, and of Bohemia in 1575) set up court in the first year of his reign in 1576.

Rudolf II was more difficult for contemporaries to pin down. Spending his formative years between 1563 and 1571 at the Spanish court, he was more warmly disposed towards both his Spanish Habsburgs and Catholicism than his father. But his convictions allowed him to oppose the papacy when necessary (which proved to be frequently). He became progressively less interested in what went on in church, attending services less often and not taking the sacrament at all after around 1600. He kept company with a curious mixture of humanists, most of them Italians in exile and under suspicion for their religious views, and Protestant refugees. Rudolf ostentatiously eschewed the Counter-Reformed activism of his uncles. In his own lands of Upper and Lower Austria, it was under the governorship of his brother Ernst that the energetic reestablishment of Catholicism was carried forward. But although Rudolf continued to sustain the Augsburg settlement in the empire, building bridges with moderate Protestant princes and recruiting their offspring to serve him, the suspicions about where he stood began to undermine those on whose loyalties he depended. What had been praised as prudence in his predecessors became criticized as indecision in Rudolf. Constructive ambivalence in the name of the common good came to be seen as dissimulation. The Augsburg settlement began slowly to unwind.

The politics of that settlement in the empire depended on the willingness of the Estates to make it work. That the Diets of the Reichstag in the second half of the sixteenth century managed to be constructive, despite the often bitter debates over imperial reform, taxes to defend Hungary against the Ottomans, and the difficulties of putting the Augsburg terms into practice, was a tribute to the numerous leagues and associations among the princes, cities and imperial knights. Organized regionally, and reflecting in part the consolidation of the regional Circles for peace-keeping and implementing imperial decisions, they transcended religious boundaries and offered the means by which compromises could be arrived at. Since the Augsburg Peace was inscribed into the fundamental legislation of the empire, its implementation was directly dependent on the imperial court, whose legitimacy was reinforced by the resulting increase in its case-load. About 9,000 cases were heard by the court in the period between its inception in 1495 and 1555. In the following period from 1555 to 1594, 20,000 lawsuits were instigated from all parts of the empire. The number of judges increased, but the pace in hearing cases diminished. Delays did not initially matter too much, because many instances were settled out of court. In addition, the imperial Aulic Council offered a second port of call, albeit one more under immediate imperial control and staffed with Catholic judges. But it, too, saw an increase in its case-load, even during the period after 1580 when it was more frequently accused of decisions biased against Protestant plaintiffs. Law proved a useful instrument to diffuse the issues raised by the Augsburg settlement.

The initial difficulties centred round the ecclesiastical territories and bi-confessional cities. Protestants ignored Catholic calls for the restitution of ecclesiastical property and continued apace with the secularization of bishoprics, while the Estates fudged the issues of restitution and migration. But a consensus was maintained because of the ongoing Ottoman threat, and because the call to rebellion from an imperial knight, Wilhelm von Grumbach, who tried in vain to raise another knights' war, rallied moderates on both sides. Even in the early 1580s, when there were disputes over the interpretation of the Augsburg Peace in the imperial city of Aachen (1580–84), the archbishopric of Magdeburg (1582) and the Electorate of Cologne (1582–3), compromises were patched together. Meanwhile, in bi-confessional cities such as Augsburg, Dinkelsbühl and elsewhere, the different confessions found ways of living together, albeit side by side, in different quarters. When it came to the Gregorian reform of the calendar in 1582, the symbol of the emerging aspirations for a global Catholic Christianity, there was no meeting of minds. It was introduced unilaterally into the empire by Emperor Rudolf, but German Protestants regarded it as a papal ploy and refused to accept it. For a time, there were two calendars in use, Lutheran merchants in Augsburg dating their letters and bills of exchange ten days behind those of their Catholic counterparts.

By the mid-1580s, however, the willingness to reach compromises ebbed away. A new generation came to power which (knowing nothing else) overestimated the solidity of the Augsburg accord. The balance of religious forces gradually began to change as the dynamic of Protestant growth faltered. In Bavaria, where a domestic crisis in the 1560s had resulted in the crushing of internal noble opposition to the ruling house, Duke Albrecht V expelled all those in his duchy who did not subscribe to the Tridentine confession. Thereafter, Albrecht V and his son Ernst imitated Protestant strategies of securing ecclesiastical offices for their family's relatives, extending Bavarian influence under the guise of furthering the cause of Catholic renewal. The lessons of the Bavarian strategy were not lost on other aspiring German princes, unsuccessfully in the case of the Prince-Abbot Balthasar von Dernbach (elected controversially to the Benedictine abbey of Fulda in 1570, he overplayed his hand), more deftly by the Elector-archbishop of Mainz when he reasserted Catholicism in his territory at Eichsfeld in 1574.

Meanwhile, the civil wars and troubles in France and the Netherlands spilled over into German lands. Troop movements disturbed the Rhineland and northwest Germany. Both the Spanish and the Dutch rebels appealed for military help and political support from the empire. Johann VI of Nassau, William of Orange's younger brother, was a Wetterau count, had close links with the Rhine Palatinate and sought to mobilize the Estates of the empire in favour of his brother's cause. Meanwhile, the turmoil in France was followed with a keen interest in Germany, the presses in Strasbourg and Cologne publishing newsletters of its military encounters and engravings of its massacres and battles. The hostility towards the Spanish, already an element in German politics, came to the fore in evocations of the 'Black Legend' of Philip II that were already a staple of Protestant propaganda in England and the Netherlands. The repeated appeals from French Protestant leaders for military support from beyond the Rhine met with a favourable response. Mortgaging resources which they mostly did not have, the Huguenot high command signed capitulations with Wolfgang of Bavaria, duke of Zweibrücken, one of the empire's mercenary opportunists (for French invasions in 1562–3 and 1569–70); and then Johann-Casimir, Calvinist co-religionist and son of Frederick III of the Palatinate (for invasions in 1575–6 and 1587).

These interventions placed the spotlight on one of the fundamental weaknesses of the Augsburg settlement, the exclusion of the Calvinists from the terms of the accord. The adoption of Calvinism as the official religion in a minority of territories and cities of the Reich, beginning most notably with the Palatinate's official adoption of Calvinism in 1563 under Frederick III, created an alternative and dissident voice in the Estates. Calvinists gradually undermined the efforts at cross-confessional agreements and compromise. Palatine lawyers took a hard line on issues of migration, arguing that the Augsburg Peace had, at least implicitly, granted rights to stay, as well as rights to depart, to religious dissidents. Palatine councillors seized the opportunity to argue the case that the Augsburg accord was being twisted against the Protestants by Catholic forces, engaged in a conspiracy and set upon suborning imperial authority. The price paid for standing outside the terms of the Augsburg settlement was the quasi-exclusion of the Palatine Electors from the Electoral College.

The death of Duke August I of Saxony in 1586 removed the last significant figure from the generation of the Augsburg Peace. His successor, Duke Christian I, led by his chancellor Nikolaus Krell, supported Johann-Casimir, the interim ruler of the Palatinate in the later 1580s and veteran of intervention in France to help the Huguenots. Following at a distance, but equally influenced by their advisers in the same direction, the dukes of Brandenburg gradually orientated themselves towards Calvinism as well – although it was only in 1613 that Elector John Sigismund formally announced his conversion. By the 1590s, with the Habsburgs contemplating a major Ottoman war in Hungary and requiring the unequivocal financial support of the Estates, the fractures in the empire were becoming less bridgeable. The Diets split along religious lines over the issue of majority voting, while delegates accused the emperor of asking for more resources than he needed. Both the Estates and the imperial legal system became increasingly paralysed. Rudolf II's brother, Archduke Matthias, declared in frustration in 1603 that 'Germany is a divided polity and no longer a united corps.' It would have required remarkably skilful negotiation by a prescient emperor to unscramble what was gradually becoming an instrument for generating suspicions. As it was, Emperor Rudolf faced a conflict with his brothers, creating the circumstances for a central European storm.

RELIGION AND THE *RES PUBLICA*: POLAND-LITHUANIA

The vast Polish-Lithuanian Republic (*Rzeczpospolita Obojga Narodów*) was no stranger to religious diversity. Since 1386, the kingdom of Poland had lived in a condominium with the duchy of Lithuania, to which Royal Prussia was added after it was wrested from the Teutonic Knights in 1454. As Poland expanded into southern Ruthenia (what is now the Ukraine) in the later Middle Ages, it went beyond Christendom, since the majority of the Ruthenians adhered to Eastern Orthodox Christianity. The grand dukes of Lithuania, hitherto pagan, accepted Christendom only when they concluded their dynastic alliance with Poland in 1385, and Lithuania remained a frontier region for Christendom in the sixteenth century. Its parishes were few, the remnants of paganism still to be seen, and the majority of the Ruthenian population, especially in White Russia (Belarus) were Orthodox. They employed the Cyrillic alphabet and remained loyal to the patriarch in Moscow. Polish monarchs saw little harm in encouraging peoples of other faiths to take up residence in this empty countryside, offering communities status and recognition in return for settlement, and welcoming individuals who could offer specialist tax-farming, administrative and management skills. They were easily integrated into cities and on the estates of Polish magnates, the latter accommodating individuals who would serve in their households as secretaries, tutors and librarians and administer their domains efficiently, especially on the latifundia which Polish magnates were in the process of establishing in the Ukraine and Belarus. Since the majority of nominations to ecclesiastical posts were in the hands of lay magnates, whose scions served as senior clerics, the authority of the Church was diminished. When bishops tried to act against priests who married, or against the nobles who protected them, the latter were known to turn up at the ecclesiastical tribunal with armed retinues to face down the judge. Even if sentence was passed against them, it was overturned at the meeting of the Sejm (the Polish Diet) or its local equivalents.

Nothing illustrated the emerging peripatetic cosmopolitanism of this period better than the migration of Ashkenazim (Yiddish-speaking Jews) from Germany, Bohemia and Moravia, driven eastwards in the late fifteenth and early sixteenth centuries as Christendom's panic about its integrity turned into spasmodic pogroms against them. Poland and Lithuania became home to what was easily the largest Jewish population (towards a quarter of a million) in Europe. Settling first in the towns of western Poland (Cracow, Poznań and Lvov), they moved eastwards to Lithuania and the Ukraine, where, joined by Karaite Levantine Jews, they served as agents and middlemen for Polish colonizers. The communities practised the liturgy and rituals which they inherited, and their rabbinical leadership was initially strengthened by the Polish monarchy being involved in their most senior appointments. Only gradually, partly as a result of the declining influence of the Polish monarchy, did Jewish communities assert their rights to appoint their 'great ones, the cedars of Lebanon, the sages of secrets' (the rabbis) and regulate their own conduct through the Jewish equivalent of the Sejm, the 'Council of the Three Lands' (Poland, Lithuania and Royal Prussia).

The Jews were joined by other religious groups, extruded to the margins of Christendom by its own internal fissures. Pińczów, home of the powerful Oleśnicki family, welcomed the exiled Bohemian Brethren in the later 1540s. Nicholas Oleśnicki allowed them to settle on his estates at Oleśnicki, and then set about turning Pińczów into a reformed Jerusalem, a model of how to find the political and social solutions to the problems of Reformation. At its heart lay the Pauline monastery, founded by his family, and which he turned into a Protestant academy, the 'Sarmatian Athens', where the Protestant translation of the Bible (the 'Brest Bible') was undertaken.

Pińczów was just one of a scattering of community experiments which were spawned by independent-minded thinkers, the majority in self-imposed exile from the Italian Reformation which never was. Stanislas Lubieniecki, the seventeenth-century historian of those who later called themselves the 'Polish Brethren' (in opposition to the Calvinists and Lutherans), recorded their learned idealism, but also their often fierce debates. Francesco Stancaro, whose writings inspired the Pińczów experiment, initiated discussions about the divinity and humanity of Christ. Fausto Sozzini (Socinus), invited to take up residence at Pawlikowice by the magnate Krzysztof Morsztyn in 1583, championed anti-Trinitarianism. Martin Czechowic, who became the principal teacher in the Calvinist school at Vilnius established by the great Lithuanian magnate Prince Mikołaj 'Czarny' ('the Black') Radziwiłł, adopted Anabaptist beliefs ('I consider the baptism of infants as the beginning of Papist ignorance') and extreme non-violence. Meanwhile, Jacob Palaeologus spent a few years in Cracow in the late 1560s, arguing for inter-faith dialogue between Christians, Jews and Muslims, before withdrawing to Transylvania. When Luigi Lippomano was sent to Poland as nuncio in 1555, he started a list of the 'heresies' he encountered, but then he gave up, and added: 'and all other pests'. When he arrived in the Lithuanian capital Vilnius, where the magnate colonizers had their principal residences, he was appalled: 'This city is a Babylon harbouring all nations that exist on earth ... but very few good Christians.'

Protestantism flowed in through those channels of religious heterodoxy as well as mediated through cultural contacts and exchange. The German-speaking urban communities of Royal Prussia were mostly Lutheran by the 1550s, purchasing their freedom of religion from the Polish crown and integrating it into their separate identity within the condominium. Many Polish magnates identified with what they saw as a cultivated, cosmopolitan and urbane Calvinism. The Calvinist churches established under their patronage, especially in the region around Cracow to the south, served their own households and retainers, but most magnates saw little point in responding to synodical pressure to compel their peasants to attend, allowing them instead to follow Catholic or Orthodox services as they wished. Even within aristocratic families, there were often religious divisions between spouses. Polish Protestantism did not have deep social roots, and it was vulnerable to internal schisms.

19. In 1525, the Augustinian monk Martin Luther married Katharina van Bora, a former nun. Aware of the polemical significance of the event, Luther encouraged a picture campaign to proclaim the event. Pairs of portraits like this (from Lucas Cranach's workshop) were widely distributed.

20. By 1520 Luther had convinced himself that the papacy was the Antichrist. Protestant anti-papal propaganda thereafter developed this into a well-worn theme. In this satirical portrait of the Aldobrandini Pope Clement VIII around the jubilee of 1600, the pope is the Devil in disguise.

21. The destruction of Christendom's sacral landscape accompanied the Protestant Reformation from an early stage. The removal of this crucifix from outside the city gates of Zürich in 1524 was organized by Claus Hottinger, a supporter of Huldrych Zwingli, with help from a weaver and a carpenter. They wanted to sell the wood to aid the poor.

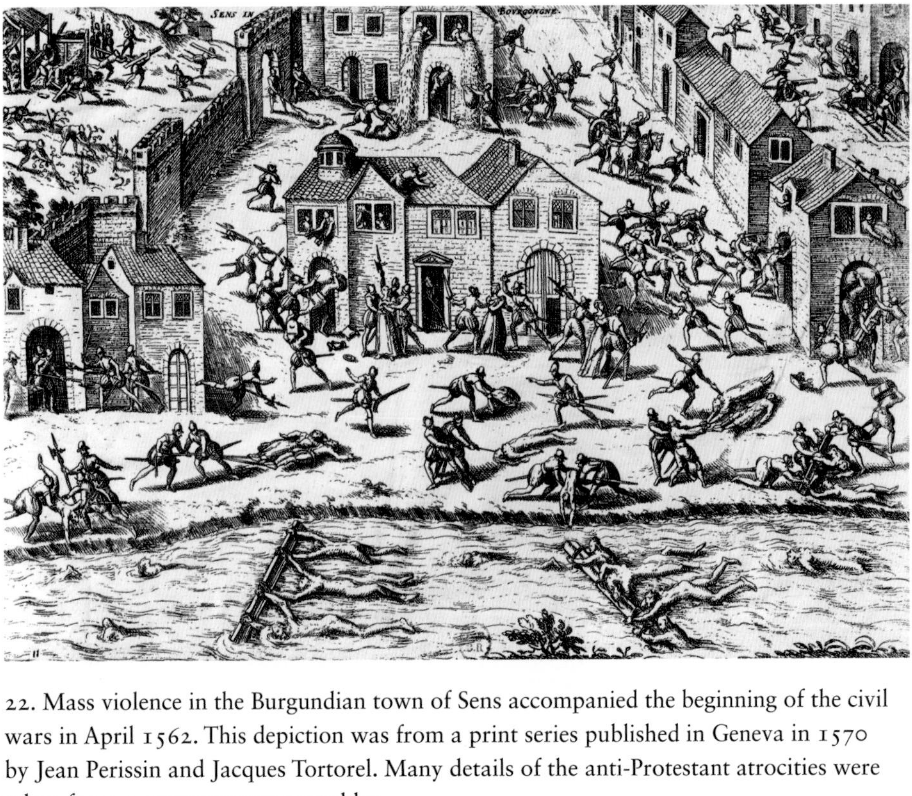

22. Mass violence in the Burgundian town of Sens accompanied the beginning of the civil wars in April 1562. This depiction was from a print series published in Geneva in 1570 by Jean Perissin and Jacques Tortorel. Many details of the anti-Protestant atrocities were taken from a contemporary pamphlet.

23. Turcophobia was prominent in the pamphlet literature of the sixteenth and early seventeenth centuries. War against the Ottomans in Hungary became linked in Germany to domestic religious and political conflicts, and reflected apocalyptic anxieties.

24. Pierre Dan was a French Trinitarian, the order founded to liberate Christian captives from corsairs and Ottoman lands. The narratives and engravings in his *History of Barbary and its Corsairs* (1637) stimulated readers to support his efforts to secure the release of Christians.

25. The victory of the Holy League fleet against the Ottomans in the Gulf of Lepanto (7 October 1571) resulted in an outpouring of propaganda. This painting, based on a Venetian broadsheet from 1572, imaginatively re-creates the battle and identifies its prominent participants.

26. Charles V was the last emperor of the Holy Roman Empire to be crowned by a pope. His coronation – depicted here in a Venetian painting from the later sixteenth century – took place on 24 February 1530 at Bologna.

27. The reform of the Julian calendar dropped ten days to bring it back into line with the seasons. Recommended by the Council of Trent, it was introduced by Pope Gregory XIII in 1582 following the advice of a committee of experts. Thereafter, Protestant and Catholic Europe lived according to divergent calendars and celebrated Easter at different dates.

28. Pompeo Leoni worked as a sculptor at the Spanish court. He cast this head of Philip II in silver in around 1580. The statue was acquired by the Austrian Habsburg Rudolf II, who admired his Spanish cousin and imitated his artistic collections.

29. Hercules personified male, noble virtue and promoted the heroic leadership of monarchs. A sustained propaganda campaign portrayed Henry IV as the 'Gallic Hercules'. In this painting by Toussaint Dubreuil from around 1600, the Herculean king slays the Lernaean hydra, symbolizing the vanquished Catholic League.

30. The Catholic League mobilized support in French cities against Henry IV by processions. Attributed to François Bunel the Younger, the scene depicted is probably the last procession in Paris (4 February 1593) before the king's entry into the city a month later.

31. Gustav Adolf's arrival in Germany in 1630 was carefully timed to coincide with the centenary of the Protestant Augsburg Confession. His propagandists also played upon his reputation as a military leader. This broadsheet, issued in the king's name, emphasized that he was an instrument in God's divine plan.

32. Lennart Torstensson, field marshal of Sweden's forces after 1641, typified the commanders who dominated the later Thirty Years War. By the time of this painting (1648) he had become governor of the western provinces of Sweden.

33. Pictures of military plunder occupied a significant place in artwork, as they did in people's experience and imagination. The slaughter by marauders is depicted in this painting by the Antwerp artist Sebastiaen Vrancx, who lived through the depredations in the Netherlands and Germany.

34. The German miniaturist Leonard Kern specialized in small alabaster sculptures for the cabinets of curiosities of aristocrats. This example depicts an atrocity from the Thirty Years War.

35. Catherine de Montholon was one of a new breed of devout French Catholic women. From a distinguished Paris family, she joined the Ursulines in Dijon after her husband's death in 1611, offering a generous dowry if they accepted the austerity required of female nuns by the Council of Trent.

36. The court of Marie de Médicis served as a model for other queens. Anton van Dyck painted her in Antwerp following her exile from France in 1631, capturing her regal but defiant resignation in the face of adversity.

37. The painter Domenico Gargiulo depicted the popular uprising in his native Naples in 1647 against alien Spanish rule, its wartime exactions and the complicit local nobility. Don Giuseppe Carafa, one of the latter, was a principal target of the mob.

38. 'The World is Ruled & Governed by Opinion' was a broadsheet published in 1641 on the eve of the British civil wars. It depicts 'Opinion' as a parody of 'Justice', sitting in a tree whose dangerous fruit is pamphlets – of which the broadsheet itself is paradoxically an example.

The Polish-Lithuanian Commonwealth acted as a kind of pressure vessel, containing the potentially dangerous religious fission between these various communities. When the Ruthenian political writer Stanislaw Orzechowski – his mother was Orthodox and his father was Catholic, a common mixture in sixteenth-century Ruthenia – looked for a contemporary parallel to the Polish polity, he found it among the 'wise Venetians', a stable balance of king, aristocracy and commonality in which the king was the head, the senators the teeth, the nobility (*szlachta*) the body (with their free vote in the Sejm as its heart), and commoners the legs and feet. As in Venice, humanist scholars developed the notion of the Polish-Lithuanian Commonwealth into an emotional as well as a rational principle of political order, one which was reflected in private papers and historical accounts and also illustrated in the frescoes of magnate houses and town halls. The prevalent foundation-myth was that the Polish nobility were descended from Sarmatians, warrior heroes who successfully resisted Roman attempts to conquer them. By the late sixteenth century, when Poland was faced with the beginnings of Swedish expansionism, the Sarmatian legend became an important counter to the equivalent myth of Swedish origins among pre-Christian Goths and Vandals. Noble students were taught how to play their part in the Commonwealth through law, rhetoric and patriotic behaviour.

Those values inspired the 'Polish Interim', agreed by the last Jagiellon king, Sigismund II, in May 1555, and borrowed from German precedents. The king was declared a 'common father' in matters of religion. Every Polish lord was permitted to introduce into his estates and house any scriptural mode of worship he desired until such time as, with the king's consent, a national council was summoned to discuss reforms in the Polish Church. Sigismund's secretary, Andrzej Frycz Modrzewski, recommended the king should tolerate all religious views since that would encourage different groups to fight out their differences in private, rather than in public. In his commentary on *Reforming the Republic* (1550) he returned to a view, often echoed among scholars and statements in the later sixteenth century, that 'violence, prison, the stake, and the flame touch only the body; only the Word of God can touch the soul'. Then, following Sigismund's death in 1572, the Warsaw Confederation of 1573 met in the shadow of the massacre of St Bartholomew to consider the election of Henry, duke of Anjou. The latter was rumoured to have instigated that massacre, and the Confederation enshrined the Interim within a framework of law alongside far-reaching declarations of the elective nature of the Polish monarchy (the *Pacta Conventa*). The Confederation solemnly agreed that 'we who differ over religion [*dissidentes de religione*] will keep the peace with one another, and will not for a different faith, or a change of churches, shed blood nor punish one another by confiscation of property, infamy, imprisonment or banishment, and will not in any way assist any magistrate or officer in such an act'. Henry of Anjou was obliged to swear that 'I will defend the peace between those differing over religion' before he was elected to the Polish throne.

What made the Polish Act of 1573 remarkable was that it legalized a religious pluralism which did not emerge as a consequence of civil war. It was agreed among nobles, but imposed from above, and against the inclinations of the majority of the Polish population. The result was a kind of religious condominium with fragile roots. Polish Catholic bishops refused to sign up to it. Its enforcement – mainly through the local meetings of nobles before and after the Sejm – was irregular and incapable of preventing spasms of religious violence. A year after the agreement, Catholic crowds (mainly students) set fire to the Bróg, Cracow's Protestant church, on Ascension Day. It went up in flames in another attack in 1591. In 1605, the Lutheran pastor in Vilnius was beaten to death by a Catholic mob on All Saints' Day. The prominent anti-Trinitarian Fausto Sozzini was attacked on the street and his life threatened in Cracow in 1594, while, on Ascension Day 1598, a group of students forced their way into his house in Vilnius, burned his books and papers, and dragged him to the marketplace, threatening him with death unless he recanted. Especially in Ruthenia, Jewish communities were vulnerable to a hostility that was aimed as much towards their role as instruments of colonization as towards their religion.

The Commonwealth eventually could not contain the various *dissidentes de religione*, and especially in Ruthenia. The instruments of Catholic renewal – especially the Dominicans and Jesuits – gradually compromised the monarchy and the Polish magnates, and destabilized fragile Orthodox–Latin Christian relations. Faced with a new, confessionally articulated Roman Catholic Christianity, that part of the Orthodox Church which was most exposed to western Christianity sought to reform itself along similar lines. Under the patronage of a leading Lithuanian magnate, Constantine Ostrogski, an academy (*Academia Ostrogska*) was founded on his estates. Its alumni served as professors in the brotherhood schools of Orthodox notables in Vilnius and elsewhere while its professors produced and published the Orthodox Bible ('Ostrog Bible').

In 1589, Jeremias II, re-elected ecumenical patriarch in Constantinople for a third time two years earlier after a stormy career, visited the Polish Commonwealth on his return from Moscow, where he had been enthroned an Orthodox patriarch. Seeking to reform the Orthodox episcopate, he deposed the Metropolitan bishop of Kiev and summoned a synod of the Ruthenian Church of Rus to Brest to discuss episcopal reform. Meeting in 1595, delegates doubted the motives and independence of the patriarchs in Constantinople and Moscow, and sought to free themselves from the intrusive patronage of Polish kings. They agreed thirty-three articles (the 'Union of Brest', 1596) in which they affirmed the Orthodox liturgy but accepted the authority of Rome. How odd, indeed, it was that the Uniates were accepted enthusiastically by Pope Clement VIII into the Roman Catholic Church while denying all the ritual tenets which were causing so much bloodshed elsewhere in western Europe. But the agreement was a triumph for globalizing Catholic Christianity – the pope even wanted them to accept the Gregorian calendar, but they demurred on the ground that it would cause uprisings. At Ostrogski's instigation a counter-synod met to oppose the Union and champion Orthodoxy.

The destruction of Christendom began to affect Orthodox Christianity as well, with long-term consequences for Poland. Uniate bishops discovered that, despite the support from Rome, they were not welcome within the councils of the Commonwealth. Under the proselytizing influence of Dominicans and Jesuits, many Orthodox Christians simply converted to Roman Catholicism. In Ruthenia (the Ukraine and Belarus), although much of the Orthodox hierarchy became Uniate, the parish clergy and people did not. The Cossacks held on to their Orthodox faith and turned it into a manifestation of their exclusion from Polish Commonwealth. There were many Poles who felt that the Cossack rebellion of 1648 was a religious war, waged against them and the Commonwealth itself.

WITH, AND WITHOUT, A STATE CHURCH: THE DUTCH REPUBLIC AND THE BRITISH ISLES

The variable geometry of the relations between Church and state over-lay the dilemmas of religious diversity in Protestant Europe. Those relations reflected the processes which had resulted in a Protestant ascendancy as well as the nature of the particular polities in each case. The religious settlements were essentially unstable, and so was the position of their religious minorities. In general, where there were hierocratic Churches and strong monarchies, the position of religious minorities was weak. Where Churches were weaker, had more complex relation-ships with the state, and where political power was more distributed, the possibilities for local and national agreements generating religious pluralism were correspondingly greater.

In the emerging Dutch Republic, the circumstances of the revolt led to a complex situation in which there was no state religion. Instead, there was a 'public Church' – the 'Reformed Church of Dutch expres-sion' (to distinguish it from its partner, the 'Reformed Church of French expression' for those French-speaking exiles from the southern Nether-lands). The Reformed Church was acknowledged by secular authorities in individual provinces and states as the only Church. No other *public* religious services were allowed in the republic. The Dutch Reformed Church was endowed with the privileges of a public body, and it inher-ited formerly Catholic churches and property. Its prayers were those which opened and closed public meetings. Its days of public prayer dominated the civic calendar. Since it was the public Church, however, its own divisions – evident during the Arminian controversy of the early seventeenth century (see below, ch. 17) – amplified political discussion and social divisions, mirroring the provincial and particularist struc-tures of its government.

The existence of a public Church still left the door open to private services of those who did not belong to it. The latter occurred in places of worship whose existence was publicly acknowledged (Jewish syna-gogues, Arminian churches) or in people's houses, the homes of so-called 'clandestine' churches. That constructed for Catholics in Amsterdam by the stocking merchant Jan Hartman included a chapel that could seat

150 congregants in the attic of his house. So the public Church had no exclusive authority in the republic. Although its numbers steadily grew, only between 12 and 28 per cent of the adult population of those regions in Holland and Friesland for which reliable estimates can be formed accepted the confession and discipline of the Dutch Reformed Church in around 1600. Catholics, Anabaptists or those who simply wanted to avoid committing themselves to the Reformed Church could be married in town halls in front of aldermen. They could be baptized and buried as they wished. In many villages, newborn babies of all confessions were baptized by a Reformed minister in the Reformed Church building without that being taken as a sign of adhesion to the Church itself. Since the church building was often also where the school was, the local archives were stored or public meetings were held, it became more of a civic space. Devotees (*Liebhebbers*) might attend the sermon on Sundays but then leave before the communion. The nature of the public Church, and its confessionally ambiguous standing within local society, encouraged people to develop the language and way of behaving towards one another over religious matters such that religion became less a question of confessional purity and more a matter of enforcing a commonly understood public morality, with rules of etiquette specifying where and when it was appropriate to talk about it. Still a matter of surprise and comment in the early seventeenth century, the negotiation of religious diversity became less so towards the middle of the seventeenth century. By then, it was possible to argue – both in the Netherlands and further afield – that the stability of the Dutch Republic owed something to its handling of religious diversity, and that its commercial success had benefited too.

The Scottish Reformation was a political and religious revolution which everyone who was involved in it tried to explain away as something else. Protestant militancy, orchestrated by John Willcock and the indefatigable John Knox, rode the crest of a brief and unexpectedly successful insurgency against the regency of Queen Mary of Lorraine, widow of King James V. The secular leaders of that insurrection, the Lords of the Congregation – discontented magnates – seized the moment of Mary's inopportune death in June 1560 and summoned a Parliament, which abolished the Mass, eliminated all previous laws 'not agreeing with Goddis holie worde', adopted a new confession of faith, and considered a blueprint for a new Church, later known as the First Book of

Discipline (1560). This contained proposals for how the revenues of the Church were to be redistributed to the Kirk, and it was left to an assembly of the latter to endorse it separately that same year. Mary's successor, her daughter Mary Queen of Scots, did not return to Scotland from France until May 1561. Although she refused to ratify the decisions which had been taken, she did not try to turn the clock back.

That was partly because the Kirk, the new consistorial-synodical Church order, remained for many years a work in progress. In particular, its relationships with political authority had yet to be decided. The material basis of the Scottish Church had been eroded by the laity's acquisition of ecclesiastical lands in the years before the Reformation. That could not be undone. Nor did the new order destroy the structure of the old. Monasteries were not dissolved, but left to a lingering decline. Priests were kept in place and, when half of them refused to conform to the Kirk, they were allowed to retain their revenues as a pension. Notionally a third of the revenues from Scottish livings (*teinds*, or tithes) were assigned to pay the stipends of the Kirk, but that arrangement depended on the willingness of local magnates to fund a minister. Although the Scottish crown nominally sequestered the rights to appoint to ecclesiastical benefices, in reality lay patrons continued to treat Church livings as their property rights.

Who ran the Scottish Church? The question was a matter of ongoing debate. The First Book of Discipline proposed ten superintendants whose duties roughly corresponded to those of bishops. Five were nominated by the assembly before, at Leith in January 1572, it accepted the notion of 'godly bishops' nominated by the crown and confirmed by the king (or regent). Just as superintendants and bishops coalesced, Genevan-inspired churchmen attacked 'pseudo-bishops' as unscriptural and unlawful: 'it aggreit not with the woorde, that Bishoppis sould be pasturis of pasturis' declared the assembly of 1577. The first consistories ('presbyteries') began to emerge in their place. After 1586, jurisdiction over presentations to benefices and the discipline of the Church were transferred from bishops and superintendants to presbyteries. Yet bishops did not entirely disappear. Although they were deprived of their temporalities by the Act of Annexation (1587) – their lands were absorbed into those of the nobility in all but two dioceses – they continued to have a civil existence in the Scottish Parliament.

The result was an underfunded Kirk, suspicious that the monarchy was not according it the support it needed, whose ministers (irregularly spread around the country) it did not properly control. Its economic weakness, however, did not diminish its aspirations to establish a godly society in Scotland. It was helped by the lack of a challenge from the Catholic minority there until it was too late to make a difference. Catholics enjoyed support among the nobility (one English report claimed that a third of the Scottish lairds were Catholics in 1600). Yet they were localized, and help from abroad came too late for any political opposition to unseat the emerging Protestant ascendancy. And the Kirk made strenuous efforts to convert lairds and clan chiefs, publicizing its successes as a tribute to its efforts to impose a godly Reformation. Meanwhile, it pursued its implantation of consistory courts (Kirk Sessions) in scottish parishes and the establishment of colloquies for ministers (presbyteries), both instruments of ecclesiastical discipline sitting aslant to the remnants of Scottish episcopacy.

The Kirk hoped to achieve its godly Reformation with the backing of the lay authority but, if not, without and against it. Although the Scottish Parliament was willing to sanction the Kirk's demands for a hard-line public morality, its support in other respects was lukewarm, as was the nobility's. In return, the ministers in the Kirk interpreted the mutual obligations of the Christian commonwealth and the responsibilities of their free assembly as a licence to criticize the monarchy and nobility publicly, and at will. That was problematic since the Scottish monarchy was poor (the revenues of the crown estimated at around £40,000 Scottish as compared to ten times that amount for the Church). Its power-base (the result of a triangulation of forces with the Scottish nobility) was destabilized for a generation. Mary Queen of Scots brought to the monarchy the revenues of a dowager French queen, but they came with strings attached, which made her a puppet in the hands of her Lorraine family. The latter was unable to comprehend and still less to help her in the wake of her two disastrous marriages. In the resulting civil war, she was forced to abdicate in favour of her one-year-old son and flee to England in 1568. That son, James VI of Scotland, did not come of age until 1578, and he only began to govern his kingdom under his own authority after 1584. The intervening rule by regency and council was a time when the mutual obligation of the Christian commonwealth between ruler and ruled generated faction, feud and calculated disobedience. In the meantime, the Kirk groped towards a working relationship with the monarch, playing the factions among the Scottish nobility to its own advantage, its self-confidence enabling it to act as a beacon in an unsteady world.

James VI in due course discovered the means at his disposal to curb the independence of the Kirk. His tutor, George Buchanan, had taught him about the history of Scotland, and especially how 'the nobilitie of Scotland hes power to correct their kingis'. But when he came to publish his own *Trewe Law of Free Monarchies* (1598), it was partly to answer the leading intellectual of the Kirk, Andrew Melville. To Melville's claim that 'Thair is Christ Jesus the King, and his kingdome the Kirk, whase subject King James the Saxt is, and of whase kingdome nocht a king, nor a lord, nor a heid, bot a member,' James's reply was unequivocal: 'Kings are called Gods by the propheticall King David, because they sit upon God his Throne in the earth.' To the Kirk's claim that presbyteries were the model of a Christian commonwealth, validated by Scripture, he replied that they were 'the mother of confusion and enemie to Unity . . . quhilke can not agree with a monarchie'.

The supporters of Andrew Melville overreached themselves and gave James the opportunity to respond. In March 1596, the general assembly openly attacked the king's 'banning and swearing' and the queen's 'night-walking, balling, etc.' and discussed plans to train a militia in every parish. In September, Melville lectured 'God's silly vassal' James on his subordination to those 'whom Chyrst hes callit and commandit to watch over his Kirk'. In the autumn, David Black, minister in St Andrews, was called before the Privy Council to answer for a sermon in which he had pronounced that 'all kings are devil's children'. Then, on 17 December, a riot in Edinburgh became the occasion for James to summon the Kirk assembly to Perth (February 1597) and Dundee (May 1597), encouraging attendance from the Highlands by ministers hostile to Lowland Presbyterians. Together they chose those who went on to become superintendants, later bishops, in the Scottish Parliament.

James's ambition to reinstall episcopacy in Scotland went beyond the notion that bishops were part of the Scottish kingdom's traditional three estates. Once he was king in both England and Scotland (1603), it became a central component to uniting the churches of 'Britain'. A Presbyterian Kirk might suit a republic like Geneva, but not 'the great frame of sovereign empire' that was the Stuart monarchy. At the Glasgow Kirk assembly of 1610, bishops were given the power to preside over presbyteries and synods, assigned the right to confirm excommunications, granted authority to conduct diocesan visitations and directed to appoint ministers. The Kirk's attempt to rescue some of the mutual obligation of the Presbyterian commonwealth was rejected by the Scottish Parliament when it ratified the agreement in 1612. At the general assembly in Perth (1618), institutional uniformity between the Scottish and English Churches was extended to ceremonies and worship. The Kirk was threatened with 'the anger of a King' into accepting Five Articles (kneeling for communion, private baptism, episcopal confirmation, and the observance of Christmas and Easter as holy days), ratified by the Scottish Parliament in 1621. The result was a rising tide of Presbyterian concern that the 'libertie' given to the Kirk, the 'chief bulwarke of our discipline', had been undermined. Refusing to kneel at communion and celebrate holy days were easy ways in which both pastors and their congregations could manifest their dissent. Despite Privy Council crackdown and the dismissal of ministers who refused to conform, and James's placatory offer in the 1621 Parliament not 'in his days [to] press any more change or alteration in matters of that kind without their own consents', an opposition movement had been born, the fruits of which would emerge in the 1630s.

The Elizabethan Settlement, passed by the first Parliament of Elizabeth's reign in 1559, was a restoration of how things had been in the reign of Edward VI, with some concessions to keep as many serving clerics on board as possible. Whether it was what the young queen wanted is impossible to determine since she disguised her own preferences. The problem was that the settlement was, to many people's eyes, a double contradiction in terms. Firstly, it was a Church and religion based on a Parliamentary act; and recent history had proved that what Parliament set up, it could pull down. To Catholic polemicists, this was its key weakness. As the English Catholic Thomas Stapleton said: 'the faith of England is no faith all builded upon the authority of God and his ministers ... but is an obedience only of a temporal law, and an opinion changeable and alterable according to the laws of the realm'. Elizabeth's first archbishop of Canterbury, Matthew Parker, assembled a team of antiquarians to prove the contrary: that the English Church rested on ancient foundations with apostolic claims to which Parliament, by law, had restored it.

Secondly, the Elizabethan Settlement legitimated a fundamentally

Catholic ecclesiastical structure, with bishops, Church courts, canon law, and the liturgy and rituals to match. But it was run by Protestants who saw, both in Scotland and on the continent, what a truly Reformed Church looked like. They hoped in due course to bring it up to date in order to keep popery at bay. Any change to the settlement was, however, what Elizabeth solidly and successfully opposed, sometimes confrontationally – in a succession of English Parliaments, MPs sought to instigate changes by legislation, which were rejected – and more often by the back door, through the existing clerical hierarchy and structures. That, however, placed Elizabeth's bishops in a quandary, since many of them recognized the need for further change but knew that their voice was falling on deaf royal ears. The bishops did not warm to the task of bringing zealous Protestants to book. Yet they understood well enough that the issues concerned their own authority. The controversy over the wearing of surplices and full clerical dress in public (the 'Vestiarian Controversy') which ignited in the wake of the Convocation of Clergy in 1562–3 was destined to have a long run. Debates within the Church and at large over what its clergy chose to wear, say and do in their own parishes symbolized whether, or not, there would be a separate and ordained priesthood within the Christian commonwealth.

The English senior clergy understood, too, that there were good reasons for retaining clerical vestments, outward and visible signs of their claims to antique authority, if it served to keep that large section of conservative, Catholic-inclined English laity from causing trouble. Keeping Catholics on-side, however, grew less important in the balancing equation after the late 1560s. English court politics became split over two marriages: that of Elizabeth herself, and that of Mary Queen of Scots, following her exile to England in 1568. The fall-out from these quarrels forced Thomas Howard, fourth duke of Norfolk, vacillating champion of Catholic sympathizers, to flee the court. His arrest was followed by an abortive rebellion in the north of England in 1569–70, the most significant in Elizabeth's reign. Led by the Catholic earls of Westmorland and Northumberland, it was suppressed, and Norfolk was executed in 1572. English Catholics had played their political cards and lost. Zealous English Protestants, laymen and clergy alike, looked forward once more to pushing the case for a further Reformation in the Church.

The Puritans (the name which 'hotter Protestants' acquired from their opponents) faced, however, repeated frustrations and disappointments.

Their hope was that the clerical hierarchy would somehow bring about changes itself. The best chance of that happening came and went with the appointment of Edmund Grindal as archbishop of Canterbury in 1575. Two years later, though, he was placed under house-arrest by the queen for refusing to suppress 'prophesyings' in the Church, that is, gatherings of the clergy (with lay people present) to hone their understanding of Scripture. Where Grindal saw a much needed way of reforming the Church, Queen Elizabeth perceived an open door to clerical independence and lay nonconformity.

Grindal's disgrace opened the door to a new generation of bishops led by John Whitgift, made archbishop of Canterbury in 1583, whose emphasis was upon conformity. Under their authority, and in the shadow of more serious Catholic dissent, organized with help from abroad, Puritan-minded clergy were brought to book. The Puritan laity who sought to put in place a shadow Presbyterian-style Church organization in localities in East Anglia was stopped in its tracks. Only a small minority chose the path of 'separatism' – self-imposed exile. By 1603, the triumph of the English clerical hierarchy over its Puritan dissidents looked complete. In reality, however, Puritanism remained, if not a blueprint for further Church reformation, a widespread aspiration for a further, moral reformation of society. Many of those who cherished that aspiration were also among those who believed that England was a Christian commonwealth, a bicephalous monarchical republic. They felt they had a stake in deciding its future, alongside a monarchy whose legitimacy to rule they did not wish to place in doubt. As in Scotland, post-Reformation politics in England – the handling of its religious divisions – furnished the unresolved tensions that would return to haunt them all in the seventeenth century.

COHABITATION OF THE FAITHFUL AND UNFAITHFUL

English Puritans lived the dilemmas of a religious minority. Their instinctive reaction was to look back to the true martyrs for the Protestant faith, exemplified in Foxe's Book of Martyrs, for inspiration as to how to behave. The pattern of martyrdom that Christendom had cherished and which the early years of the Reformation had nurtured was to refuse to renounce dissident beliefs and resist secular or ecclesiastical laws. Catholic priests and lay folk drew on similar traditions for their opposition. So, when the Catholic priest William Hart was executed at York in March 1583, he went to the stake without flinching, urging his mother (in a letter written shortly before his death) to rejoice that he was soon to become 'a most glorious and bright star in heaven'. Sir Thomas Tresham, a Catholic gentleman from Northamptonshire, wrote of the extortionate Recusancy fines that he was obliged to pay as a kind of martyrdom, comforting himself with the conviction that, when it came to religion, 'no manne canne make himself a cushine to leane upon to ease his elboes'. A woman who was 'sett upon two laddars lyke a cuckyingstole' for heckling the bishop of London during the Vestiarian Controversy rejoiced in her punishment, praising the Lord 'for that He had made hir worthy to soffer persecution for ryghtwysnes, and for the truths sake'. There was no great dividing line between standing out against the forces of an ungodly Church or un-Christian common-wealth, and taking militant action against them.

Yet, at the same time, the boundaries between resistance and compli-ance, conformity and nonconformity, were negotiable. When English Catholics became the target of intolerance, they more often responded by connivance rather than resistance, appearing in church just enough to convince local magistrates of their loyalty to the regime, while paying no attention to what went on and ostentatiously clacking their rosary beads or, like John Vicars, a Hereford brewer, walking up and down the aisles in order to avoid hearing the sermon. The preoccupation with confessional religious conformity encouraged precisely the dissimula-tion which it was designed to prevent. The Familists – disciples of Hendrik Niclaes – attended Church of England rituals while adhering to their family-orientated and mystical creed. Dissenting Puritan clergy found ways of adapting lawful conformity to their consciences. Jesuits became renowned for offering faithful Catholics casuistical responses to leading questions about their faith, even though churchmen on all sides regarded 'Nicodemites' (after Nicodemus, who came to Jesus 'by night') as dangerous. 'Cohabitation' could always be justified as preserving relations with one's neighbours and participating in the Christian com-monwealth whose existence was at stake in the conflicts of the later sixteenth century.

14. Churches and the World

CHURCHES AND STATES

The Protestant Reformation fractured the Christian Church into believing congregations, each claiming to be the inheritor of the 'true Church'. That was a recipe for ongoing debates which were sharpened by the belief that salvation depended on belonging to the true Church. The alternatives were elaborated for ordinary people in the emerging confessional apparatus of liturgies, catechisms, confessions, biblical translations, ecclesiastical disciplines and programmes of religious education. They all emphasized to ordinary people the emerging divisions in Europe.

Protestantism had, in addition, a double logic which affected the role of the Church. The first was its impact on the latter's material fabric. Wherever it took root, the Protestant Reformation broke established patterns of landed wealth, tithe income and spiritual dues. Secular authorities were no longer anxious about being charged with sacrilege in attacking Church wealth. Protestant reformers had provided them with the pretext to appropriate it under the guise of attacking abuses. In 1525, Luther assured the Elector of Saxony that the revenues of the Church belonged to the state and that, after paying the clergy and establishing schools and charities, the surplus was the Elector's. In 1534, Duke Ulrich of Württemberg confiscated monastic properties for his own purposes. His example was followed by a string of others. King Henry VIII dissolved the English monasteries, yielding the crown a profit of about £1.3 million between 1536 and his death in 1547. That was accompanied by the transfer of advowsons (i.e. rights to nominate to benefices) to the crown. These rights were – along with the chantry foundations (1547) and church plate (1549–53) – sold on to laymen. In Denmark, the monarchy began to alienate Church property to its nobility in the 1520s, even before its official Reformation. By the end of the 1530s, episcopal property had been appropriated by the monarchy and the monasteries secularized. In 1527, the Swedish king Gustav Vasa held 3,724 domain estates and the Church 14,340. By 1549, the Church had none. Although Zwingli and Bucer maintained that Church property should be vested in the community, secular rulers being merely its administrators, magistrates discharged their responsibilities stingily. The Protestant Reformation marked a large transfer of wealth and the partial dismantling of the clerical estate.

The material and social change in the role of the Church in Protestant lands was the more marked because it did not happen to the same extent in Catholic Europe. Some Catholic princes used the Protestant threat to extract resources from their clerical estates. In France, the papacy agreed to the partial alienation of Church wealth (with the possibility of its being repurchased) in order to fund royal campaigns in the civil wars. The dukes of Bavaria threatened to give concessions to their Protestant minority in order to extract more revenue from the clergy. Olivares included the Spanish Church in taxation in the 1630s, the opposition from Rome and from within its own ranks being met with reprisals. Yet in Mediterranean Europe the Catholic Church maintained its material wellbeing. Catholic reinvigoration had its foundation in clerical wealth and privilege, the unsolved dilemma being how to release them to support the Church's endeavours where they were most needed.

The second logic of the Protestant Reformation reformulated the relationships between Church and state. Its critique of the theological foundations of sacerdotal authority meant adding a sleeve of spiritual dignity to the 'secular arm'. Among the emerging Protestant political entities, the affairs of churches – from the appointment of pastors to parochial life – came to be managed (in Lutheran Europe) through a branch of the princely council and its representatives, nominated Church officials ('superintendants'). Luther's insight on such matters was that all Christians are, at the same time the subjects of two divinely established realms (*zwei Reiche*). One was the spiritual kingdom of faith, ruled by Christ and his Word, over which secular rulers had no jurisdiction. The other was the kingdoms of this world, ruled by princes who owed their authority to God and who were responsible for the peace and wellbeing of the subjects entrusted to their charge, but not for their consciences. In practice, however, the demands of the Reformation and the inclinations of its princely adherents eroded Luther's idiosyncratic interpretation. Other Protestant reformers were more inclined to accept the humanist notion of a commonwealth as a moral space in which the godly ruler had the 'office' to promote faith, piety and right behaviour among his subjects. More important, then, was to provide rulers with examples to encourage them to discharge their obligations. Pious Old Testament rulers and early Christian emperors became models of how the godly ruler should root out impiety and establish true worship in accordance with God's law.

That was all very well so long as the ruler was godly and understood where the limits of this public obligation lay. The difficulty was that the Protestant Deborahs and Hezekiahs of the age often failed to live up to the mark, seeming to behave more like the Old Testament's dissemblers and tyrants. In addition, the separate jurisdiction of ecclesiastical courts was mainly abolished in Protestant Europe. Church courts had dealt with, among other things, blasphemy, witchcraft and conjuring, and marriage. New laws and tribunals had to be established by magistrates and enforced in courts that were more civil than ecclesiastical. When Calvin (following the lead of Johannes Oecolampadius in Basel and Martin Bucer in Strasbourg) tried to define more precisely the authority of the Church through establishing a consistory court in Geneva and vesting in it the power of excommunication, he was criticized by other Protestants, more favourable to secular authority, as wanting to create a 'new popery'. Thomas Lüber (Erastus), a physician in Heidelberg, gave his name to the notion that civil magistrates, or rulers, exercised sovereignty in their states, and that Churches possessed no coercive power. That in fact became the norm in Protestant Europe.

The godly ruler was not the preserve of Protestant Europe. Catholic princes also successfully asserted their control over the Church, despite their need to acknowledge the authority of Rome and to respect the jurisdictions of bishops. In France, the Concordat of Bologna (1516) gave the French monarchy the right to appoint the incumbents of the 106 episcopal sees and 800 abbeys of the kingdom, a right exercised with scant regard to the religious or reforming credentials of candidates. In Spain, Savoy, the hereditary lands of the Austrian Habsburgs and elsewhere, monarchs treated the rights to nominate to senior benefices in the Church as an extension of royal patronage, and faced down the papacy in controversial appointments. Only in the Italian peninsula did the pope still nominate directly to episcopal sees.

Throughout Catholic lands there were ecclesiastical autonomies – autochthonous traditions deriving their strength from their foundation myths and saint cults. These proved delicate to harmonize within the claims to universality of a reinvigorated Roman Catholic Church and also resistant to state control. Only in France did they coalesce into something approaching a movement ('Gallicanism') with roots in the Church, academy (the Sorbonne) and judiciary (the Parlement of Paris). Gallicanism drew on Conciliarism, and had an agenda to protect the liberties of the French Church from royal and papal intrusion. It served as a focus for those in Catholic Europe who feared a resurgent caesaro-papalism in Rome.

The relationship between Church and state was one part of the relationship of the Church to the world. Protestant and Catholic clerical establishments had to respond to the challenge from the wider world, to the new confessional politics, to the uncomfortable reality of more powerful states and to new ways of understanding the physical environment. Both had to inculcate a sense of what religious belief and observance should be.

MISSIONS ABROAD

Europe's expansion globalized Christianity. As many as 10 million people may have been baptized as Catholic Christians in the Americas by 1550. Perhaps 2 million Filipinos had been baptized by 1620 and over 200,000 in Japan. This endeavour was independent of movements for Catholic renewal in Christendom. It relied on the patronage of the Hispanic monarchies and the competitive efforts of Franciscan, Dominican and Augustinian friars. Only gradually, especially after 1550, did the new religious orders like the Jesuits make their mark. The figures for conversions are not to be taken at face value. Enthusiastic missionaries overestimated their success, evaluating their achievement in accordance with a preconceived view as to who was capable of being converted, and to what degree. Most converts had little understanding of the religion they were adopting, and the arguments used to encourage conversion were elementary. In Mexico, and later in the Philippines, locals were often encouraged not to attend the Mass because they might not understand it. In Japan, the Jesuit Francisco Cabral was reluctant to go into theological details with his Japanese neophytes lest they became experts and created heresies.

Europeans were struck by the contrasts between Catholic Christianity and the indigenous societies with which they came into contact. In Peru, for example, the custom was that no man would marry a woman without a trial sexual engagement first. It was hard for missionaries to persuade the Peruvians to abandon premarital sex in favour of a Catholic marriage pattern that outlawed it. Taking those difficulties seriously meant accepting that conversion was a long, slow process. The Jesuit José de Acosta (in *On Procuring the Salvation of the Indians*, 1588) distinguished three levels of non-Christians. The first were those whose level of civility he equated with Europeans (the Chinese and the Japanese). They could understand and commit themselves rationally to Christianity. Second were those peoples, such as Aztecs and Incas, who had no literacy but had a civil society, and whose religious rituals were intermingled with grotesque departures from natural law (for example, human sacrifice). They needed both persuasion and a firm hand. Finally, there were the nomadic and semi-nomadic peoples of southern and northern America, and imported African slaves, who were scarcely human and had to be treated as children, weaned from their nomadic ways, 'reduced' into villages before they could be evangelized. Christian civilization – its language, civility and morality – limited Acosta's ethnography. He saw missionaries' duty as 'to advance a step at a time, educating Indians in Christian customs and discipline, and silently removing superstitious and sacrilegious rites and habits of rude savagery'.

Mission involved understanding native cultures and traditions. That resulted in an appreciation of difference. The pioneering Franciscan ethnographer Bernardino de Sahagún spent fifty years conducting fieldwork among the Aztecs. He recorded his findings in the *General History of the Things of New Spain*. It included over 2,000 illustrations by native artists trained in European representational techniques. Philip II, aware of the dangers that such study of native culture and history might cause, confiscated the manuscript and ordered its return to Spain. The limits to ethnographic understanding were set by the assumption that

Christianity was the only true religion. Missionaries were therefore inclined to regard other religions as the products of ignorance, or worse. Francis Xavier's first reactions to Japan in 1549 were: 'this land is full of idolatries and enemies of Christ'. The Portuguese Jesuit Diogo Gonçalves, who arrived in Goa in 1590 and worked in Malabar from 1597 until his death, wrote a comprehensive guide to mission which he despatched to Rome in 1615. When he described Hindu religious traditions he repeatedly referred to their deities as 'demons' and their beliefs as 'diabolic superstitions'. Yet such an attitude created a dilemma. The more native beliefs were regarded as pagan, the more urgent was the task to eradicate them, and the larger became the task of Christianization.

The number of missionaries was tiny in comparison with the task. The latter's enormity was emphasized by opposition from local peoples, more likely when missionary campaigns sought to obliterate the traces of pre-Christian civilization. In the violent Mixtón rebellion of 1541 in New Galicia (Mexico), monasteries and churches were targeted, friars mutilated and converts had their heads washed to 'de-baptize' them. Christianity became the religion of the conqueror. Two decades later, highland Peruvian Christianity was rejected in a rebellion known as the 'Dance Sickness' (in Quechua: *Taqui Unqoy*), adherents wanting to restorate ancient spirits (*huacas*) and end Spanish rule. The revolt was suppressed with terror, culminating in the execution of Tupac Amaru, the last claimant to the Inca throne. Violence did not win Christian converts but it was never far below the surface in the European colonial world.

The earliest missionaries overseas were the friars in Central America who concentrated on the settled areas of the Mexican plateau. Mass conversions were the norm, with Franciscans and Dominicans encouraging encampments for Christianized Indians that integrated Indian and Spanish ways of living. Natives provided a percentage of their labour and tribute, through which churches were constructed, often on the site of pre-conquest temples. By 1650, the Catholic Church was an established presence in Spanish colonial society. The five archbishoprics and twenty-five bishoprics of Spanish America became rich landlords, more so than the archbishopric and two bishoprics of Portuguese Brazil by that same date. The basilicas that graced American vice-regal capitals suggest a comfortable transplantation of Catholic clerical society to the colonial New World.

Underneath the surface, however, the story was of compromise between local religious systems and Christian doctrine. Mexicans fused Christian and pre-Christian beliefs and practices, especially in their households and attitudes to the surrounding natural environment. It proved difficult to eradicate the sacred topography, ritual calendar and older Andean deities. By placing churches in pre-conquest temple locations, and adopting open chapels looking onto a platform crowned with a cross at the centre of an enclosed patio, they resembled former sacrifice sites. Confraternities, public feasts and saint cults coalesced with pre-conquest traditions of feasts of the dead, dressed in Christian clothing. Saint cults invited appropriation as part of a continuing ancestral memory. For their part, African slaves in Brazil identified Christian saints with their own spirits (*orishas*) and protectors, adapting Christian rituals to their own calendar. It was European notions of 'idolatry' and 'witchcraft' which paradoxically provided the evidence for the survival of pre-Christian ancestors and deities. Hernando de Santillán explained in his *Relation of the Origin, Descent, Politics and Government of the Incas* (1563) that it was 'the Devil who speaks through them [spirits]' and recounted how over 400 temples had recently been found within reach of Cusco at which offerings were still being made. The implication was clear: the Americas needed an Inquisition. Two generations later, and almost fifty years after the establishment of the Mexican Inquisition, Hernando Ruiz de Alarcón (*Treatise on the Heathen Superstitions that today live among the natives of New Spain*, 1629) documented continuing beliefs in the *nahualli* (mountain spirits). Like the officers of the Inquisition, however, he could not distinguish between those to be ascribed to native credulity and those attributable to the Devil.

Where there was no sedentary native population and no basis for ranch labour or parishes, missions adapted the monastic tradition to minister to Amerindians. The latter were 'reduced' to live in a compound, a defensive space for a community, protected from settlers on the look-out for native labour. Missions began in New Mexico and then spread to Brazil, Paraguay and among the Canadian Hurons. The history of the reductions in the middle and upper Paraná, Uruguay and Tape rivers in the first half of the seventeenth century was recounted by the Jesuit Antonio Ruiz de Montoya in *The Spiritual Conquest of Paraguay* (1639). He described how a handful of Jesuits corralled over 100,000 natives into almost forty mission compounds. Indians were encouraged to cultivate tea (*yerba mate*), cotton and wool, and their products were sold at Santa Fé or Bogotá. In these compounds, the New World became the Church (and vice versa) as Jesuits forged a mission-led reformed commonwealth. Contemporaries who read Montoya's work thought it was a fantasy.

Published mission narratives fed the European market for travel literature, geography and natural history. Francis Xavier's first *Letter from India* (1545) began reports on flora, fauna, climate and native customs by missions. By the time of José de Acosta's *Natural and Moral History of the Indies* (1590), Jesuit natural history and geography had grown considerably. Ignatius Loyola, the Society of Jesus's founder, insisted from the beginning that a means of advancing the Jesuits' work was through 'having much inter-communication'. By the time of his death, the circulating of newsletters had become normal practice, the purpose being that 'each region can learn from the others whatever promotes mutual consolation and edification in our Lord'.

Europe's communicative energies are exemplified by its missions. Their linguistic achievements were phenomenal. Over 120 languages, all spoken rather than written, were in existence in Mexico on the eve of the conquest. Within two generations, the Franciscans produced phonetic alphabets using Latin characters, which made possible grammars and dictionaries in twenty-two of them. In Mexico, as in other parts of America and in India, the strategy was to promote the use of one language as the vehicle for missionary literature. The first catechism in Nahuatl was published in 1539, in Tamil in 1554, in Chinese characters in 1584, in an African language in 1624. These books were then deployed in church and school environments, reprinted with colonial presses. The Flemish Franciscan Pieter van der Moere founded the first European school in the Americas in 1523 at Texcoco, and went on to direct the San Francisco school in Mexico City, which in its heyday had almost 1,000 students. He also developed a hieroglyphic-based catechism for use with Indians, first published about 1548.

Humanist educational methods depended on acculturating the pupil to the processes of learning. Missionaries had similarly to adapt Christianity to present it in a form that could be assimilated. In the Philippines, for example, the Ten Commandments, the Creed and Christian prayers were turned into verses which could be chanted. Missionaries equally chose to adopt local clothing, or observe local etiquette. Matteo Ricci, the Jesuit who worked in China from 1583 until his death in 1610, accepted the dress and social rituals of a Confucian scholar and acquired a knowledge of Mandarin. He adapted the Christian liturgy to the Chinese calendar, omitting parts which might lead to offence, while (with Chinese assistance) translating Confucian classics into Latin. For Ricci, Catholic Christianity was not alien to Confucian values. In his Mandarin explanation of *The True Meaning of the Lord of Heaven* (1603), he combined Aristotelian logic, Christian doctrine and Confucian concepts to provide a basis for assimilating the two. Meanwhile, in India, Robert de Nobili adapted Christianity to local customs. He dressed like a local high-caste Hindu scholar and shaved his head, keeping only a tiny tuft. He studied Sanskrit and Tamil, and composed Christian catechisms and apologia in Tamil, adapting its vocabulary to Christian concepts. As with Ricci, however, he caused controversy both among fellow Jesuits and with missionaries from other orders and the archbishop of Goa. The disputes were resolved only by a ruling from Rome in his favour in 1622. The debate over 'accommodation' did not greatly impact on Europe's mission abroad; but it revealed the tensions within a globalizing Catholic Christianity back home.

MINISTRY AT HOME

For Catholic apologists the success of mission abroad was a sign of divine favour. What could Protestants point to by way of comparison? The lack of Protestant mission was a charge that those in the Dutch Republic and England (both with colonies) answered with difficulty. Adrian Saravia, a Dutch refugee deacon at Westminster, argued that Protestants had a duty to respond to Christ's injunction to preach the Gospel to every creature. Dutch preachers took up the cause, and a seminary was founded for would-be missionaries at Leiden in 1622. But it did not last long. Protestant missionary endeavour was the result of private initiative rather than public commitment. Protestantism saw itself as engaged in a fight for truth and survival back home. Localized and fragmented, Protestant Churches lacked the organization for mission abroad, which, in any case, was redolent of popish hegemony. If natives did not respond to the Word, it must be because God did not want them to hear it.

So Protestant Europe focused its energies on 'ministry', which was what replaced sacrificial priesthood. Ministry was a public office, connected to a specific congregation – the parish – which the magisterial reformers accepted as the base unit. That office required a special vocation but not celibacy. That was how Melanchthon, Bullinger, Bucer and Calvin sidestepped the implications of Luther's initial pronouncements that we were all our own priests. How was one called to that vocation? It was, said the magisterial reformers, a reflection of the order in God's divine will. Luther's preference was for a succession of ministers through ordination, which he understood as the apostolic succession in the Church, albeit not a conferring of grace but a confirmation of its already being present. In Zürich, by contrast, Zwingli divided the vocation of ministers into an 'internal' (spiritual) one and an 'external' (magisterial) one, thus allowing the state or its representatives a legitimate say in who should be appointed to the ministry. Protestant Churches generally accepted their obedience to the powers that be as the price of order and decorum. Calvin followed Martin Bucer in Strasbourg in expanding the offices of the Church into a variety of vocations.

In the English Protestant Church, the changes were more ambiguous. The clergy could marry, though many (including Queen Elizabeth I) found it unseemly. An ambivalent theology denied the sacrificial nature of the Eucharist, but Anglican ministers remained priests. Within European Protestantism's variable ecclesiastical geometry, there was a greater insistence that the validity of this new ministry was determined by what the individual in question did and, even more importantly, said. The minister's educational attainments and learning, family life and local standing, preaching abilities and 'good conversation' – these became the outward and visible signs of his vocation. But these were ideals, and inclined to inflate. And since ministry was in a relationship to those being ministered to there were always doubts. Protestant anxiety about uprightness and vocation began early on.

Finding ministers to fit these demands was not easy. In German and Swiss lands, old priests were mostly declared new ministers, but incumbents had little idea of what to preach and how to hold the new services. A whole generation had to be educated for a different ministry. In the first generation, there were not enough adequately trained Reformed ministers, and salaries were inadequate. Even in Elizabethan England, the supply of well-trained clergy was problematic. Very gradually, however, the Protestant investment in higher education paid dividends. By 1600, only about 25 per cent of Lutheran clergy entering the ministry in the empire did not have a university degree.

Educational attainment was not a passport to effective ministry. The relationship between ministers and their congregations was ambivalent, and educated pastors in the rural world created suspicions. In rural Electoral Saxony and Brandenburg, as in English shires, the proportions of those with a degree among the rural clergy were lower than in urban environments. Not only was there a hierarchy of posts, with urban ones attracting the more highly qualified candidates, but rural patrons looked for other qualities in their local pastors than their academic attainments. The more the Protestant clerical ministry stabilized, the higher the levels of ministerial career and family endogamy, such that the sons of ministers in their turn married into the clergy and became clergymen themselves. That increased the focus on the parsonage as the place where Christian good conduct was exemplified. Such an exemplification was more important, given the focus on the family in Protestant life and culture. But repeatedly the unrealistic expectations of ministers put them at odds with their congregations. Communities not only expected their ministers to be learned, sober, upright and modest, but they also wanted them to preserve local traditions.

The clergy therefore were under contradictory pressures. Visitors and superintendants in German Protestant lands wanted them to catechize everyone, but not be too harsh with those who could not learn the catechism by heart. They wanted the minister to maintain harmony with his congregation, and yet abstain from revelry and threaten unrepentant parishioners with exclusion. They wanted him to preach, but then found church wardens complaining when sermons were too long. The problem was that the stabilization of a Protestant ministry made it the focus for precisely the same anticlerical suspicions which had fuelled the Reformation in the first place. The lesson from a century of attempting to put in place a new ministry was that it could be done properly only with the assistance of secular authorities. But in many places Protestantism was not the religion of state; and in those where it was rulers did not offer the support required.

As Protestant Churches embedded themselves in society, so 'discipline' (the shaping of public behaviour and morality) became part of an underlying anxiety about order. Protestants abolished confession and penance, but they had yet to identify the ways by which the Reformation could become more than an aspiration. Luther and his collaborators began with the hope that it would happen on its own as part of God's providence. Their subsequent disillusionment was the reverse side of the coin to the naive enthusiasm that elementary education would change people's convictions. Second-generation Lutheran pastors lamented that the heroic age was over and that the Reformation's opportunities had been squandered. Calvin, a second-generation reformer, sought to root discipline in the Protestant polity. The disciplining of the laity was driven by the unease that religious change had made little impact on the population at large.

In Lutheran Germany, ecclesiastical discipline became based around marriage courts, consistories and parish visitations. By the second half of the sixteenth century, the last of these were regular affairs. The visiting committee subjected pastors, sextons, schoolmasters and local officials to a detailed questionnaire, focusing on church attendance, catechism and ungodly living. Visitations in urban environments were often greeted with sullen uncooperativeness. In rural parishes, however, the visitors found what they were looking for, and it was an unedifying spectacle. Nobles often set the tone by 'holding the servants of God's word in contempt'. Attendance on Sundays was poor, and even worse at catechism classes. 'You will find more of them out fishing than at service,' said one protocol. Parents held their children back, claiming that they could not afford the school fees, or shirts and clogs. There were endless reports of those for whom gambling was a profession, of 'epicureans who do not believe in the resurrection of the dead', of Anabaptists and gypsies, and of those who swore, quarrelled, fought and drank too much. Threats, said the pastors, were useless. We warn them, reported one protocol, but the reply comes: 'Why pray? The Turks and the Pope are not after us.' The only remedy was to use the instruments which had already proved inadequate, and which would turn up more information of what seemed like failure. Protestant confessional Christianity was a complex message. To understand it required literate skills and an investment of time and energy.

In Reformed (Calvinist) Protestant environments, discipline became the mark of the true Church. In Geneva, it took the form of the consistory, composed of lay elders, a syndic and the ministers of the city, meeting each Thursday. Thousands of pages of registers record its intrusions into private lives. In the years after Calvin's death, one in fifteen of the population of the city appeared before it; 681 individuals were 'suspended' from being members of the congregation, the most common sanction it applied. Excommunication was rarer, reserved for those who had treated suspension with contempt or had been found guilty of serious breaches of public morality. To the degree that suspension incurred social penalties, it worked. But Geneva was a small place, one where the magistrates took their role seriously, supporting the consistory.

At first sight, the Genevan consistory is evidence for the increasing importance of moral regulation in the Protestant Reformation, proof that social discipline was part of confessionalization. Yet the consistory was as much interested in religious uniformity as in moral uplift. The persistence of Catholic rituals, and the ease with which the city's ordinances were evaded, led Calvin to propose in January 1546 the institution of an annual visitation of Geneva's rural parishes, followed by domestic visitations by members of the consistory in 1551. In Geneva, and elsewhere, the Protestant Reformation heightened the significance of religious conformity, which in turn increased anxieties about the degree to which God would visit his anger on a city for its immorality. The anxiety about social discipline arose from a concern for religious purity.

The consistory court often tried to reconcile the parties in cases of marital breakdown, the elders being concerned to uphold the dignity of marriage and the sanctity of a promise before God. Almost a quarter of the cases involving sexual misdemeanour that came before the Geneva consistory in the years 1568–82 involved couples who, having made promises of marriage, had sex before being actually married. The consistory insisted that betrothals be honoured but it had little interest in making men and women marry who had shared physical intimacy, even if the result had been an illegitimate child. Elders knew the complexities of interpersonal disputes and the vulnerability of individuals, especially women. They appreciated that people lied in their testimonies, that their stories were one-sided, and that the consistory was fed tittle-tattle as evidence. They understood that there might be little to be gained from an exclusion or excommunication of an individual, and nothing at all from passing some cases on to the civil magistrates. Where the consistory was disposed to take a judgemental view, it weighed up carefully the need to minister to individuals (particularly women) in difficulties, against that of preventing scandal. Even in Geneva, the consistory was not part of a top–down supervision of moral reform. Genevans found ways to cover up their sexual transgressions from the consistory. Their womenfolk knew how to exploit the court as a weapon in defence of their own honour. There were always limits to the 'godly reformation'.

CATHOLIC REINVIGORATION

Protestant pessimism was inspired partly by the revival of Catholicism as a religious and political force in Europe. In eastern and central Europe, the balance of confessional forces tilted back towards the Roman Catholic Church in the first half of the seventeenth century. To Protestants, this was inexplicable. How was it that a Church whose incapacity to reform itself had been evident for centuries, and which they believed to have been deserted by God, could find the energy and will to declare that it had been right all along? The concept of a 'Counter-Reformation' (*Gegenreformation*) was first articulated by nineteenth-century German Protestant historians who needed a name for whatever it was that had begun as a reaction to Luther and continued through to the Peace of Westphalia (1648), which was when they thought it came to an end. For other Catholic historians, the idea of a Counter-Reformation accorded too much weight to the forces of reaction to Protestantism, to its politico-ecclesiastical manifestations, and to its overall coherent orchestration. What happened was not simply reactive, but animated by movements in the Church that predated Luther, and which had local roots and lacked coordination, but which inspired a revived spirituality that survived beyond the Peace of Westphalia into the eighteenth century. For that, the term 'Catholic Reformation' has often been preferred.

That revival went beyond 'Tridentine Catholicism', which suggests an ecclesiastical programme of reform, put in place by the Council of Trent (1545–63) and then implemented across the Catholic world in accordance with some central directive. The Catholic Church was a complex organism which responded in contradictory ways to the changes around it. To speak of 'Catholic revival' suggests an emphasis on the 'missionary church' which, despite the importance of the overseas engagements as well as those in eastern Europe and the Levant, does not do justice to the way the Roman Catholic Church came to stand for a certain sort of stability and relationship to the past, a particular kind of spiritual authority, and a way of communicating truth to its believers. Catholic reinvigoration proceeded on the basis of that appeal.

New and reformed religious orders were essential to that reinvigoration as it affected ordinary men and women. As missioners, preachers, educators, confessors, catechists, hospital-workers and ministers to the dispossessed, the vagrant and abandoned, they reconfigured the Catholic pastoral landscape. The success of Catholic confessionalization cannot be understood without them. As with overseas mission, the older orders remained significant. The Dominicans probably doubled their numbers between 1500 and 1650. The Franciscans in their various branches grew at approaching the same rate. Although there was official reluctance to create new orders, the pressure to do so came from below, from the charismatic figures and groups that responded to the changing world around them.

Among the plethora of new congregations and orders, the most significant and numerous were the Capuchins, the Jesuits and (of the many new congregations for women) the Ursulines. From the tiny initial group around the young Italian Observant friar Matteo Serafini, the Capuchins grew to a company approaching 30,000 by 1650, a major influence in the Italian peninsula as preachers and workers in times of plague. In 1574, the congregation had crossed the Alps to France, Spain and Germany, active wherever re-Catholicization was underway and with a reputation for accompanying people in times of uncertainty. The Basque nobleman and ex-soldier Ignatius Loyola had only nine companions when the bull establishing the Society of Jesus was issued in 1540. By his death, the Jesuits numbered about 1,000, divided into twelve provinces, and they had established thirty-three colleges. A decade later, there were 3,500, and 13,000 by 1615. Their churches, houses, colleges and universities were scattered unevenly across southern and western Europe but they were especially present in urban centres. In smaller towns, their buildings often stood out as the most imposing and distinctive.

The Ursulines began as a community of single women and widows around Angela Merici from near Brescia. They devoted themselves to helping in hospitals for incurables, looking after orphans, and instructing girls in the elements of Christianity and literacy. Protected by Archbishop Carlo Borromeo of Milan, they became a common sight in

North Italy, many residing at home and taking only private vows to their congregation, but increasingly conventualized. The papal territory of Avignon provided the bridgehead into France, where, from the early years of the seventeenth century, there were communities of Ursulines in most cities, serving the sick, working with prostitutes, and teaching the catechism and rudiments of reading and writing to young girls.

The charismatic founding figures of these new orders had little in common. The orders which they founded were very different from one another in their constitution, their relationship to the rest of the Church and their internationalism. Their own contribution to their foundations was disparate. In one key respect, however, they are alike. Ecclesiastical reform was not part of their vocabulary; 'Spirit', 'God', 'the world' and 'works of mercy' were. Matteo Serafini was from a modest background in the duchy of Urbino and became a Franciscan at the age of seventeen. Like Angela Merici, he drew on late-medieval Franciscan spirituality and in 1525 left his monastery to become a drop-out, finding refuge in Ancona and Calabria, begging for daily bread and turning up in towns to preach repentance. When he and his companions arrived, they were greeted as 'hermits' (*scapuccini*) and the name stuck. The Capuchins would not have existed, however, without support in high places. Their patrons included Catarina Cibo (duchess of Camerino and niece of Pope Clement VII) and Vittoria Colonna (widow of Ferrante Colonna and friend of Michelangelo), through whose influence the Capuchins obtained papal recognition in 1528. Matteo was elected its first vicar-general in 1529, but his relationship with the order he had founded was ephemeral. He resigned his office to return to his alternative lifestyle. In Venice, where he died in 1552, he entered a law court with his cowl over his head and a pole with a lantern on it. When asked what he was looking for, he replied: 'I am looking for Justice.' The reinvigoration of Catholic spirituality drew on the uneasy consciences of those in the urban world.

Ignatius Loyola dictated his life story in around 1553–5 to his Portuguese confidant in Rome, Luis Gonçalves da Câmara. It began in 1521 with a great turning-point, when he was wounded at the battle of Pamplona, and ended, equally abruptly, with his arrival in Rome in November 1538, before the founding of the order. He furnishes us with an aseptic account of his own spiritual journey that began with slow recuperation in the family castle at Azpeitia, reading the lives of the saints, and took him to the Benedictine monastery of Montserrat in Catalonia, where after a night in vigil he laid down his sword and dagger and took up a pilgrim's staff and beggar's clothing. At nearby Manresa in 1523 he discovered the *Imitation of Christ*, a work of late-medieval spirituality. He surrendered himself to prayer, fasting and self-flagellation, abandoning conventions and letting his hair and fingernails grow. Little by little he tempered these austerities as his soul-searching, accompanied by strong visions, produced a renewed sense of serenity.

His notes on these experiences formed elements of the *Spiritual Exercises*, published in Rome with papal approval in 1548. The *Exercises* offered a 'way of proceeding' in a series of 'weeks' for those facing an important crossroads in their lives. They centred around a particular approach to meditative prayer with Gospel texts in which individuals enter into dialogue with Christ, Mary and God the Father, feel acutely their sins, acknowledge the disorder in their lives, accept all that is wrong with the world, and put themselves in a new relationship towards it. As an exercise in spiritual communication, it was unique. Its impact on the Jesuit Order and beyond was profound.

Dressed as a pilgrim, Ignatius lived for the next fifteen years from begging, much of it on the streets. Occasionally he fell foul of the Inquisition for his unconventionality. He became a student in Paris and made friends with like-minded souls. They decided to go to Jerusalem or, if that did not work out, to Rome to offer themselves to the pope for whatever he judged 'for the greater glory of God and the good of souls'. They met up in Venice in January 1537 where, waiting for a ship to Palestine, they worked in hospitals. By now informally referring to themselves as the 'Company of Jesus', they appeared in Rome in November 1538 where, as with the Capuchins, it was through a contact in high places (the Venetian Gasparo Contarini) that they secured assent for the 'Formula of the Institute', the background document for the papal bull of September 1540, developed into the 'Constitutions' by Loyola and his secretary, Juan Alfonso de Polanco. Unlike the founder of the Capuchins, Matteo da Bascia, Ignatius continued to play a decisive role in the Jesuits until his death in 1556.

The Jesuits were the 'Church Militant'. The Formula opened by describing a member of the society as 'a soldier of God beneath the banner of the Cross'. The 'Christian soldier', however, was a familiar metaphor and had no specifically military connotations. When the Constitutions referred to the 'Superior General' of the order (of which Ignatius was the first), it was not in the sense of a military general. Only some years after Ignatius's death did Jesuits (notably Jerónimo Nadal) begin to compare him directly with Luther, a new David against Goliath, called to God the same year that Luther hitched himself to the Devil. The Jesuits dedicated themselves to absolute obedience to the pope because their rule forbade them from becoming involved in the diocesan life of the Church. Unlike other regular orders, they were not bound to celebrate the canonical hours in common, so they could be free for preaching, teaching or tending the sick and dying. They could go 'anywhere in the world where there was hope of God's greater glory and the good of souls'. Their ministry was, for several decades in the sixteenth century, unique, offering a new relationship between the regular orders and the world at large, recruiting and operating on an international scale. Loyola and his successors as generals of the order reflect the talent which the Jesuits recruited.

The Formula envisaged their role as itinerant preachers to include teaching outside as well as inside churches. They exported Spanish traditions of setting religious texts to simple tunes, sung by the children in the streets. Printed colloquial catechisms in the Protestant fashion were adopted by the Jesuits too. Jesuit preaching was part of teaching, both being blood-brethren to the sacraments of penance and the Eucharist, the well-springs of activity in the world. That activity included assistance to those suffering from disasters, accompanying convicted prisoners to the scaffold, establishing orphanages and rehabilitation centres for prostitutes, and mediating in local quarrels. Although divided over the persecution of Jews in Europe, the Jesuits continued to accept New Christians (*conversos*) into their ranks (Ignatius was never more radical than when he said that he would have liked to be of Jewish blood in order to be of the same race as Christ) and ministered in the ghettoes of Venice, Rome and Avignon. They instituted lay confraternities, the student society established at the Roman College in 1564 under the auspices of the Virgin Mary being the model for the Marian congregations that became fashioners of lay piety and a 'Third Order' adjunct of the Jesuits. Their engagements with the world posed moral dilemmas. From the beginning, the Jesuits treated casuistry (non-pejoratively 'the study of cases of conscience') as an essential subject of study – as vital as its complement, rhetoric, to the ministry of the Word. Taking the best of the confessors' manuals as their texts, they entered the minefield of older theological battles about how human inadequacies ('sins') were to be handled by the Church and the extent to which human beings, if at all, could participate in their own salvation.

Nothing was more challenging to both Catholic and Protestant Churches than the humanist notion that education could create pious and responsible citizens and change the world. By 1560, the Jesuits' commitment to education began to dwarf their other responsibilities. Polanco, writing in the name of the second general, Diego Laínez, declared: 'every Jesuit must bear his part of the burden of the schools'. A burden it was, one that the Jesuits took on without foreseeing its consequences when they opened their first school, in Messina, Sicily. It was a great success. By the 1550s, Jesuit schools opened at the rate of almost five a year; and the rhythm continued throughout the rest of the century. The Protestant Latin schools could not match that achievement. The Jesuits did not charge tuition fees but relied on endowments and foundations from aristocratic patrons and city councils, the latter relieved to hand over educational provision to a professionally competent body. Students were divided into classes, moving after examination from one class to a higher one, and skills graded accordingly. Pupils were offered a progressive curriculum that emphasized relevance to the contemporary world. Active learning was encouraged through homework, composing and delivering speeches, memorizing and reciting poetry, playing musical instruments and acting in theatrical dramas. With a good range of teachers, Jesuit schools could aim to provide a broad education. They defined what a Catholic upbringing for boys should be. Jesuit colleges were not seminaries but the training grounds for the more diverse social élites of Catholic Europe. They became the principal driving force for re-Catholicization.

Educational endeavour cost the Jesuits dearly. 'The Society is being ruined by taking on so many schools,' wrote Gioseffo Cortesono, the rector of the German College in the late 1560s, the most expensive of all the Jesuits' educational establishments, founded to spearhead re-Catholicism in Germany. By that date there were too few Jesuits for the number of its colleges, not to mention other commitments. Not all those who joined the order had done so to become college teachers. The more the Jesuits concentrated on that objective, the more problems they discovered. Some schools were only marginally viable and had to close, with debts and rancour on all sides. As the society came to grips with these difficulties, it became more worldly-wise. That widened the door to critics who argued that the Jesuits were too popular and accommodating for their own good. There was common ground between those who, in the early seventeenth century, criticized Jesuit moral theology for its 'probabilism' (the belief that, in difficult matters of conscience, one could safely follow a doctrine which was 'probably' true – attacked by critics as an open door to laxity), attacked prominent Jesuits for arguing that there were occasions when it might be legitimate to resist a prince, and intimated that it was an ambitious society, promoting its own wealth and interests at the expense of everything else.

The impact of Catholic reinvigoration owed a great deal to women. Here, however, the contradictions between the challenges of the world and the ecclesiastical response became more marked. Of the thirty or so new religious orders and congregations, the majority had female branches, and nine were devoted exclusively to women. All of these new foundations, with the exception of the Discalced ('bare-foot') Carmelites, founded by Teresa of Ávila and the only one founded by a woman that included men, stressed active ministry in the world. But how was active ministry by women to work in practice? There was no shortage of women entering convents. Some defied their own families to do so, drawn to the alternative lifestyle that it afforded, the opportunity for independent female space, the chance to follow pursuits that would not have been theirs, and a spiritual domain towards which they felt drawn. Contemplative nuns were, although theoretically brides of Christ and dead to the world, in discreet and regular touch with it, through their families, their correspondence and their prayer. Teresa of Ávila was the most remarkable contemplative nun of her generation, but she would have denied that her form of meditation and prayer did not engage with the world. As she travelled around Spain promoting her Carmelite order, she repeatedly complained about the tension in her life. 'On the one hand, God was calling me,' she reflected. 'On the other, I was following the world.'

The ecclesiastical response to the female religious was increasingly restrictive. At the final session of the Council of Trent, the reform of monasteries and the religious life was debated. Celibate and monastic life had been a Protestant target and the subject could not be ignored. The council reaffirmed female enclosure, reinforced in 1566 when Pius

V decreed that all female religious communities not practising enclosure must be suppressed. The primary motive was to control sexuality, both women's and men's. Chastity was the definition of the female religious life, and the only way to protect nuns' virginity was through strict enclosure.

As things turned out, however, the Tridentine decree was not completely enforced. The Ursulines exploited their connections with Archbishop Borromeo, gradually accepting enclosure but maintaining devout activity. Jeanne de Chantal and François de Sales's Order of the Visitation ('Visitandines') briefly flourished in Savoy and France in the early seventeenth century as a community of female widows, whose family commitments or fragile health prevented them from entering religious orders but who wanted their dedication to God to be reflected in social mission. Mary Ward emigrated to the Catholic Low Countries in 1606 and was inspired by the Jesuits to establish her own order (the Institute of Mary) in 1609. The growing presence of Mary Ward's sisters, coupled with their association with the Jesuits and their refusal to accept enclosure and use a regular habit, earned Sister Mary many enemies. Her ladies were dismissed as 'noxious weeds' and 'galloping girls' and she was condemned as a heretic in 1631, her order being suppressed the following year. But, as Louis XIV was later to discover with the nuns of Port Royal, putting women behind bars did not isolate them. Religion empowered women in various ways. François de Sales became a father-confessor by letters to godly widows whom he encouraged to follow their consciences and devote themselves to God. His correspondence was published in his *Introduction to the Devout Life* (1609), a book which showed how men and women could participate in religious life. Only the most misogynist of religious reformers could ignore the role of women, especially when they so often showed themselves more pious than their male counterparts.

THE COUNCIL OF TRENT AND THE PAPAL PRINCE

On 4 December 1563, Cardinal Giovanni Morone asked the conclave of 268 prelates at the Council of Trent if they accepted its closure. Cardinal Charles of Lorraine then pronounced the acclamations, beginning 'to the blessed Pope Pius, our Lord, pontiff of the Holy, Universal Church' and ending with: 'Anathema to all Heretics!' The Auditor of the Sacra Rota (the papal Supreme Court), Gabriele Paleotti, reported that many wept for joy, while those who had opposed one another in its deliberations now congratulated one another. They celebrated the end of the longest-running Church council for a millennium.

The council began its work eighteen years before in December 1545. Its convocation had been delayed by the papacy's reluctance to commit itself to a body whose authority might become a challenge to the papal monarchy. It was further hampered by politicking between the Valois and the Habsburgs, the emperor seeking a council that would keep the door open to Protestant mediation. Once it was in session, its proceedings were delayed by issues of protocol, who presided (papal legates), who could speak and vote (the legates conceded freedom of speech but gained a victory on limited proxy voting) and differences over the agenda. The emperor wanted disciplinary reforms to be treated first and doctrine later. The papacy wanted clarity on doctrine and no further compromises. The upshot was a compromise in which both issues were treated hand-in-hand. That formula guaranteed that the council was not about achieving a reconciliation of Christendom but a refutation of Protestant schism.

The politicking continued after the first session (from December 1545 to March 1547), delaying the second until May 1551, by which time the council moved to Bologna in the Papal States in order to satisfy the papacy's anxiety about imperial influence at Trent. That session in turn was brought to a halt for almost a decade, during which time Gian Pietro Carafa was elected to the papal throne as Pope Paul IV in May 1555. Paul IV drew his inspiration from the caesaro-papalism of medieval popes. He mistrusted councils, especially one so far from his control, and hated the Habsburgs, berating them for signing the Peace of Augsburg (1555) and briefly involving the papacy in a disastrous war with Philip II in 1556. Ascetic and autocratic, Paul lavished his attentions on the Roman Inquisition. Former papal legates at the Council of Trent (Morone and Pole) were among its suspects. Not the least of the battles fought out at Trent was the endgame of the influence of *spirituali* among Italian churchmen and theologians.

Paul IV died in 1559 and his successor, Giovanni Angelo Medici (Pope Pius IV), signalled a change of direction from his predecessor, whose two cardinal-nephews were eliminated, one strangled and the other hanged. Pius IV's acknowledgement of the need for the council to finish its work was that of a realist who recognized that the world was changing. Catherine de Médicis, the regent in France, as well as Emperor Ferdinand I, wanted a fresh start. Philip II preferred it to resume where it had left off, and that was the view which prevailed under Pius IV. When the council reconvened in Trent for its final session in January 1563, its greatest crisis was yet to come. The most contentious debate of all concerned the residential requirement of bishops in their sees. Spanish bishops championed the position that the right of residence was demanded by divine right and God's law. If that was the case, it ruled out papal dispensations and threatened the role of the cardinals in Rome as well as papal authority. Eustache du Bellay, bishop of Paris, joined the Spanish in protesting that the real novelty was papal supremacy, which created a 'temporal tyranny' in the Church. The Jesuit Laínez supported the Roman Curia, saying that the pope was the successor of the Apostles and that anyone who claimed authority otherwise was a heretic. The view won the order few friends, especially among the French.

The deadlock hastened the death of two papal legates in rapid succession in May 1563. Only the recall to Trent of the papal diplomat Cardinal Morone saved the day. He secured the support of Cardinal Charles of Lorraine and the voting power of the French and imperial delegations for his compromise proposal by which the residence of bishops was required because they were representatives of God's vicar on earth (the pope), who, by implication, could also issue dispensations as and when he needed to. This was just one part of the wide-ranging decisions, agreed on 11 November 1563, which constituted the kernel of the institutional changes proposed at Trent. They included new norms for the appointment of bishops and an injunction about preaching. Bishops were required to hold diocesan synods annually and provincial councils every three years, and to visit every parish in their diocese once a year, and they were accorded increased authority over ecclesiastical corporations and orders, especially cathedral chapters.

What had the fathers at Trent achieved? In the case of doctrine, they had a clear target in Protestant theology. Protestants never doubted that its canons were aimed against them. In reality, however, the delegates at Trent knew next to nothing about Zwingli and Calvin. Luther was the enemy, viewed through the eyes of his Catholic theological critics. Yet the confrontational presentation of Trent's theological decisions masked the reality that its decrees were, in many respects, statements of an agreed middle ground, avoiding areas where there would be disagreement. So Trent's decrees broadened the sources of Revealed Truth beyond the Bible to include apostolic traditions, but then refused to state precisely what those traditions were. In the long decree on Original Sin (sixteen chapters and thirty-three canons), the fathers skirted round the difficulty of defining the nature of grace and its efficacy, as well as free will. This laid a long fuse that would in the next century detonate acrimonious division. It began at Louvain in the 1560s with the teachings of Michel de Bay and exploded with those of his pupil and successor Corneille Janssens (Jansenius). The council had nothing to say on Marian worship. It discussed the issue of vernacular translations of the Bible, but made no recommendations. Although various decrees called for 'superstitious' uses of religious ritual to be abolished, they did not specify where the lines were to be drawn. There was no overall Tridentine theological system though there were some themes, of which the most notable was that the clergy should act as a conduit of theological truth. Somewhere at Trent, the humanist dream of a direct experience of the Word of God gave way to ecclesiastical mediation and the reinvigoration of a clerical order, separate and special in the world.

The fathers at Trent worked within the limits of their experience. Their decrees reflected their sense of what was possible. No bishop of the New World was present and the Americas were never discussed. Delegates saw no alternative to the benefice system. There were canons about clerical decency and ecclesiastical order but no Tridentine aesthetic, musical or artistic. The churchmen recognized the importance of education, especially seminaries for the clergy, but failed to provide the necessary resources. Trent offered conservative renewal. Above all, its impact depended on its implementation and, as with the Protestant Reformation, this pushed the burden downwards, towards the locality. Tridentine reform became episcopal reform, and specifically Borromean reform.

That was because of the dominant presence of Carlo Borromeo, the model episcopal reformer, even in his own lifetime. He was promoted to the archdiocese of Milan in 1560, one of the largest and richest in Christendom. The loyal adjunct of his uncle Pius IV, he appeared at Trent in its last sessions among the Curialists. When the council ended, and following the death of his brother Federico and the election of Pope Pius V, he returned to Milan in 1566 and dedicated himself to his pastoral duties. Already in 1564 and with the aid of Nicolas Ormaneto (a disciple of Cardinals Ghiberti and Pole), his vicar-general, he had organized a meeting of 1,200 parish priests at a synod to promote Trent. He went on to conduct eleven diocesan synods and six provincial councils, and a campaign of parochial visitations that was not quite yearly (the Tridentine decrees were unrealistic) but enough to see a new level of clerical oversight of the laity. Confessors were instructed not to give absolution until penitence was really in evidence. New confraternities ('of Christian Doctrine') channelled the energies of the devout laity in ways that complemented the Borromean reinvigoration of religious life.

Borromeo's obsessive campaigning was partly derived from his Milanese locale. Although he was accorded latitude by the papacy, Rome was wary of his tendency to be his province's pontiff. The Spanish authorities were exasperated by his confrontational attitudes. The cathedral canons hated him and there was at least one attempt on his life. He accepted the new regular orders only on his own terms and his relationships with the Jesuits were bad. In reality, Borromeo was neither the first, nor the only, reforming bishop of his age. Nor was his authoritarianism the only style for Tridentine episcopal reformers. However, Borromeo's flair for publicity and his close relations with Popes Pius IV and V ensured that his version of clerical authority prevailed towards 1600.

By then, the holding of diocesan councils and synods was reaching its apogee across the Catholic world. Even so, only a minority of bishops could be seen as zealous reformers. In France, for example, of the 108 bishops in office in 1614, a quarter had not been ordained, thirteen were under-age by Tridentine definitions, a sizeable minority had other posts that regularly took them away from their dioceses, and only thirty-eight ever held a diocesan synod. Although Rome played a greater part in validating episcopal nominations (especially through the nuncios), it could hardly gainsay local princely and aristocratic influence. In Germany, for example, many prince-bishops were political as well as ecclesiastical appointments. So Prince-Bishop Ernst of Bavaria had a glittering career in the Tridentine Church, becoming a bishop at twelve years of age in 1566, and going on to enjoy being prince-bishop of

Liège, Hildesheim and Münster with no acknowledgement that Trent had happened. Bishops readily identified Catholic reform as the enforcement of their own authority and traditional ecclesiastical structures. Since the benefice system was so entrenched, and secular courts could (as in France) intervene to protect parish priests, bishops had an uphill task to establish effective control over their diocesan clergy. Even so, the education of the parish clergy did gradually improve. Diocesan visitations reflected a Sisyphean effort to embed religious change, especially in rural areas. As the clerical order confronted different local conditions and problems, ecclesiastical reform became more variegated.

Tridentine reform acquired Rome's imprimatur thanks to a succession of energetic pontificates: Pope Pius V, Gregory XIII and Sixtus V. It was complemented by the evolution of the papacy towards something that resembled a monarchy. That implied a different relationship towards the Papal States, the 'Lands of St Peter' that constituted the principalities of the bishop of Rome in the middle of Italy. Because of its elective nature, the evolution was uneven. Nonetheless, under the Medici popes (Leo X and Clement VII) and the influence of the wars in the Italian peninsula in the first half of the century, the papacy's concern became to increase its political authority in the peninsula. At the same time, it consolidated its hold within its own dominions, reducing the privileges conceded to communes and nobility, and acquiring new territories in the rough and tumble of the Italian Wars. Papal households grew in scale, matching its pretensions.

Essential to the emergence of the papal prince was the changing role of the College of Cardinals. The latter had been the senate of the Latin Christian Church, theoretically an inseparable and indistinguishable component of papal authority. During the 'Luther Affair', the college still met in consistory several times a week, considering all matters relating to the Church throughout the world. With the growth in power of the papal prince, that of the College of Cardinals waned. It met twice a month to rubber-stamp decisions. The number of cardinals grew as pontiffs shored up their position within the college by making new appointments to secure a loyal majority. Cardinals became mainly chosen from a small number of powerful Roman and northern Italian families, who lost their autonomy while retaining their authority as power-brokers. Their palaces were as large as their retinues, their furnishings and cuisines equipped for the social events that occasioned their soaring expenditures. Rome was still a world of gossip and intrigue in which the material issues of the Church such as property, income and pensions continued to weigh heavily.

On hand to nurture the friendships of cardinals, play upon their enmities and lubricate their lifestyles were the papal nephews. Under the pontificates of Pius IV, Pius V and Gregory XV the cardinal-nephew became a 'favourite'. As with favourites to secular princes, however, the cardinal-nephew's position was a delicate one. Sooner or later, the uncle would die. To assure his own future, the nephew had to keep on good terms with as many cardinals as possible, even while he sought to maintain the interests of his uncle. And secular rulers, especially the Spanish Habsburgs, had a large purse and tempting ecclesiastical offerings in Spanish Italy to offer cardinals who were prepared to play their tune. That was important because the cardinals elected the next pope. At the Conclave, the factions which emerged were complicated, the politics labyrinthine and the outcomes difficult to predict. The Spanish Habsburgs took to influencing matters by declaring openly who would be unacceptable (the *exclusiva*), a veto that reinforced their presence until the revival of French influence in the seventeenth century and the reform of the Conclave procedure by Gregory XV in 1621.

Little by little, cardinals became handmaids of papal power. The process began with the establishment of the Congregation of the Holy Office, the committee of cardinals which supervised the Roman Inquisition. Further placed under papal direction by Paul IV and reorganized by Pius V, the Inquisition became a weapon in the armoury of papal hegemony. Other congregations were added until, when regularized by Sixtus V in January 1588, they totalled fifteen. Through these committees the cardinals were closely involved in papal executive decision-making, both in the Papal States and in the wider Church.

The Council of Trent became essential to the emerging double sovereignty of the papal monarchy – of the Papal States on the one hand, and of the Church Universal on the other. With the ending of the Italian Wars, the risk had been that the papal monarchy would become a client of the Spanish Habsburgs. Trent offered the papacy a larger religious and ideological justification, the instrument for Catholic reinvigoration in the world at large. Pius IV and his successors seized the opportunity, realizing that, in so doing, they subsumed the reform of the Curia (their own backyard) into something wider. In issuing the bull confirming the council's decrees, Pius IV used for the first time the title 'Bishop of the Universal Church' which had been accorded him in its last session.

The implication was immense. All ecclesiastical jurisdictions henceforth derived from the papacy and all bishops were simply his vicars. The new Index of Prohibited Books of 1564 reworked that of Paul IV. A new Profession of Faith was declared in November of that year, incorporating an oath of obedience to the pope, to which everyone entering office in the Church was required to subscribe. The Roman catechism of 1566 was issued on the basis of Tridentine decrees. It was followed by the Breviary (1568), Missal (1570) and Sixto-Clementine Bible (1590–1604) – just a few examples of Rome's capacity to use the printing press to sustain its enlarged claims. These were encapsulated by the reform of the calendar by Gregory XIII in 1582. By harnessing cosmography and mathematics to its Universalist claims, Rome changed the calendar by ten days and, with it, the liturgical year. It invited the rest of the world (the Persians, the Chinese) to adopt it. In Protestant Europe, however, it was rejected. Christendom became divided by chronology as well as by confession.

The papacy's image changed. Essential to the consecration of a new pope was the ceremonial procession from Saint Peter's to St John Lateran, his episcopal seat, a triumphal coronation parade in which the new incumbent was carried with the symbols of his power (throne, crown and canopy) on a litter across the city along the *Via Sacralis*. The ceremony highlighted the pope's sovereignty in his own state and in the world at large. In the triumphal procession of Sixtus V in 1585, the canopy was carried by Japanese envoys who understood the message: that the Catholic Church put Christendom in a global context. St Peter's, extended with a nave in the form of a Latin cross to accommodate the crowds, was consecrated by Clement VIII in 1594. It was the biggest church in Christendom and, by the mid-seventeenth century, it was complemented by the colonnaded piazza in front of it. Pope Urban VIII commissioned Gian Lorenzo Bernini to construct the baldachin over the high altar. Above its twisted bronze columns and canopy sat a cross on top of a golden globe.

The archaeological explorations of the Roman catacombs at the end of the sixteenth century provided further evidence for the historic continuity of Catholicism against Protestant innovation. The bodies and relics of saints supplied new objects of devotion for churches in Rome and for export elsewhere. From the Jubilee of 1600 onwards, papal programmes catered for the growing numbers of pilgrims, including an improved road system, public fountains and obelisks. Rome's literary salons began to refer to the new papal governing style as 'absolutism' under the pontificate of Clement VIII. For aficionados, the *History of the Council of Trent*, published pseudonymously in London in 1619, was required reading. It did not take long for them to divine that it was written by the Venetian Paolo Sarpi, a natural philosopher, Galileo's friend and a considerable theologian. The subtitle to the work hinted at its anti-papal objective: '. . . and particularly the practices of the court of Rome to hinder the reformation of their errors & to maintaine their greatness'. Using original documents, Sarpi developed the theme that had already won him the hostility of Rome during the Venetian Interdict (the censure of the city by the Vatican in the years 1606–10). Rome's absolutism had ruined the efforts of 'godly men' to 'reconcile' the Reformation through a council, and turned it into an instrument that made Christendom's divisions 'irreconcilable'. Worse, papal absolutism subverted the efforts of bishops to regain their authority and arrogated to Rome 'an unlimited excesse' of power. Sarpi's clever work cemented a hostile image of papal absolutism.

The sovereign popes of the later sixteenth and early seventeenth centuries set about reforming the Curia, Christendom's most elaborate bureaucracy. That they did not succeed is not surprising, but it was not for want of trying. It was a revenue stream in its own right with the sale of offices and 'reversions' (transfers to another incumbent). While spiritual revenues (the income from the Church at large) grew sluggishly, the temporal revenues (the income from Papal States' taxes) rose, contributing three quarters of papal revenues by 1600 and making the Papal States one of the most heavily taxed parts of Europe. Contemporaries recognized, however, that the papal monarchy was not a strong military power; it was a medium-sized player sheltering under Spanish Habsburg overlordship. The papacy remained a clerical state which benefited the few. The Borghese pope, Paul V, the Barberini pope, Urban VIII, and the Pamfili pope, Innocent X, would consolidate their family's fortunes as in a dynastic monarchy, but that did not sit comfortably with the Tridentine spirit which Rome had appropriated.

THE CHURCHES AND THE
SUPERNATURAL

Belief in the supernatural was a social reality. It explained what happened by way of good and evil in the world. It was especially a way of understanding misfortune. It linked the present with the past and the future in ways that gave coherence to time and space, and accorded God a central place in the direction of affairs. Within an overwhelmingly Aristotelian metaphysic, the learned had been taught to expect that there were spirits in the cosmos. In a world view dominated by ultimate stasis, that was how the permanent motion of the sun and planets was explained. Equally, human beings had souls as well as bodies. Explaining how the two were linked was the essence of moral theology.

Beyond the central premise of the supernatural and its accompanying social reality lay a series of debates that had preoccupied intellectuals before the Protestant Reformation, and also coloured the way in which they understood the beliefs of the unlearned. The debates crossed disciplinary divides. Physicians questioned the experiential evidence relating to the cures that cunning men and wise women supposedly worked. Lawyers cross-examined suspected impostors and fraudsters. Theologians established the distinction between beneficent and malevolent uses of the supernatural. They tried to define the limits within which Church liturgical apparatus (holy water, incantatory prayers, exorcism, crucifixes and so on) could be used to access the power of the supernatural, and by whom. The Church claimed that such power existed and that it was there to wield it.

Two related developments made these debates more central and controversial in the sixteenth century. The first was the impact of Europe's communication dynamics upon the knowledge and spread of information about the supernatural. It made the supernatural more present, more active in people's lives, and more menacing. Miracle stories, accounts of monstrous births, unexplained shapes and colours in the sky, cases of witchcraft and demonic possession fitted neatly into the confines of small printed pamphlets, rapidly diffused and feeding a market in sensational stories in which the veracity of the account seemed verified by circumstantial details. Stories of werewolves, apparitions and ghosts were part of a literature of diversion which fed into novellas, stage-plays, ballads and songs. Antiquarians documenting the natural history of their locality uncovered an 'enchanted' world, even in Protestant Christendom, where it was supposed to have been abolished. The works of learned demonologists not only commented on one another, furnishing compendia of carefully dissected and critically discussed phenomena, but also incorporated their own experiences of witchcraft prosecutions. Protestant theologians and moralists similarly developed compendia of godly interventions in the lives of individuals and communities, using them as examples of how God's inscrutable providence worked in the ways of the world. They encouraged individuals to keep diaries of the particular providences which occurred in their daily lives. Parish visitations and inquisitorial investigations turned up more evidence of the pervasive nature of popular access to magical, supernaturally derived powers. 'Enchantment' was more diffused and less controllable.

The second change was the result of the Protestant Reformation. By focusing on the immediacy and presence of God in the world, Protestants magnified the reality and menace of the Devil. Among Catholics too, the sense of living in a world in which God's ongoing and proximate battle with the Devil was also made more immediate by the emphasis on heresy as a form of *maleficium*. Crucially, however, the debates that had preceded the Reformation about when and how it was legitimate to deploy supernatural power, and by whom, became polemicized as between Protestants and Catholics. By radically shifting the grammar (the understanding) and the semiotics (what things stood for) of salvation, Protestant theologians created a platform from which to criticize the Catholic Church as 'superstitious'. Catholic theologians responded in kind, purging traditions of elements for which there seemed no adequate theological grounds or experiential evidence on the one hand, but defending the power of Catholic rites against their critics on the other. The controversies became ones that were not between 'learned' understandings of the power and danger of the supernatural, and how these differed from unlettered or 'popular' ones, but between and across the learned, each side demonizing the other. These broad-ranging controversies made it more difficult to fabricate hard and fast rules to regulate the supernatural and establish acceptable behaviour. The toughest confessional battles of this period were over the theology, reality, efficacy and appropriateness of prodigies, providences, possession, exorcism, apparitions, prophecies, dreams, magic and witchcraft. Only towards the middle of the seventeenth century did those skirmishes retreat into less confessionalized debate.

Such arguments fed through into theologically led campaigns or magisterially mediated prosecutions of those seen to be falsely claiming access to supernatural power, or doing so with the intention of making money for themselves or doing other people harm. In parts of Europe such campaigns turned into missionary terrain for the reordering of popular culture, aiming (in the case of Catholic reinvigoration) to suppress pilgrimages and healing shrines, and eliminate magical and protective rites. Such zeal was evident in the case of witches. There may have been more witchcraft victims than there were victims of religious persecution in this period. Estimates vary, but there were perhaps between 32,000 and 38,000 witches executed in the period from 1450 to 1715, the majority of them before 1650. It was not principally a misogynist campaign, linked to changing attitudes to women. Most of the victims were accused by their neighbours, and many of their accusers were themselves women, while about a quarter of those convicted were men. Whether a witch was convicted depended on all sorts of local elements, which included the existence or otherwise of forms of local reconciliation, the determination of local élites to prosecute such cases, and the nature of the juridical framework in which such prosecutions took place. Witches were prosecuted only when states, magistrates, local notables and clerics took such matters seriously. That they did so reflected the fact that witchcraft became a state offence, prosecutable before secular courts, as well as an ecclesiastical offence. That change occurred partly as a result of the Reformation, but also because of the heightened anxieties raised by those confessionalized debates.

Local patterns varied enormously. They depended in part on how those tensions were focused by political and social divisions. But witch-hunts were also set in motion by those in authority who projected their anxieties in this particular direction. In Scotland and elsewhere, the new judicial presence of the state in localities provided an avenue for prosecutions that had not existed previously. On the other hand, the Italian and Spanish Inquisitions were sceptical towards witchcraft and made few accusations. In the fervour of Tridentine visitation and the attempt to win converts to Catholicism, Cardinal Borromeo proved an energetic witch-hunter, despairing at the leniency of the Inquisition. His precedent was followed by some Catholic prince-bishops in Germany in the Thirty Years War, under whom some of the worst witch crazes occurred. Already before 1650, the debates among the élites in western Europe about the nature and reality of supernatural power were beginning to have an impact on the willingness of those in authority to entertain such prosecutions. Magistrates began to be more cautious in the face of the criticism they might incur for pursuing them. Christendom needed to be protected from the malevolence of the Devil. Europe was not so sure.

15. The Waning of Crusade

Christendom had defined itself for centuries in opposition to the belief-communities to its east and south. Both Byzantium and the West could claim to be the heirs of Christendom and its protectors against Islam. But after the schism between eastern and western Christianity in the eleventh century there followed centuries of estrangement and antagonism between Byzantium and the West. Western Christendom's crusading project served to weaken rather than strengthen the Byzantine empire, which was further undermined in the fifteenth century by the emergence of independent Slavic kingdoms, which looked to the West, as well as Ottoman settlements and pressure from the East. The fall of Constantinople to the Ottomans in 1453 marked the end of Byzantium, an empire whose durability had served as a bulwark in the Mediterranean and the Balkans against the rise of Islam.

With Byzantium's collapse, the West became the sole protector of Christendom against Islam. The Christian reconquest of the Spanish peninsula was complete by the end of the fifteenth century, leading Spain and Portugal to confront Islam directly in North Africa. They erected fortified bastions along the North African coast, while avoiding trying to conquer the mountainous and Islamized Maghreb. In the East, Christendom now faced the powerful Muslim Ottoman empire, rising from the ashes of Byzantium in the eastern Mediterranean and the Balkans. That reawakened Christendom's crusading instincts. Yet the objective of the Crusades – the recovery of the Holy Land – had been clearly defined, whereas resisting the Ottoman empire was not. And as Christendom's divisions deepened in the wake of the Protestant Reformation, so its response to the Ottoman threat became more incoherent. The Ottomans proved adept at exploiting those divisions. As the distance between crusading fantasies and pragmatic political, strategic and commercial realities grew wider, so the notion of Crusade itself fragmented and waned, and with it the idea of Christendom which had given it coherence in the first place.

CHRISTIANITY AND ISLAM IN AN AGE OF RELIGIOUS CONTENTION

By 1550, the threat to Christendom from the Ottomans was real, their advance into European lands inexorable. With energy and creativity they cemented their hold on the Hungarian plain around military and governing centres (*sanjaklar*), which they established to control the Danube and its associated watercourses. The capture of Belgrade in 1521 was followed by the collapse of Hungary in 1526. Buda was pillaged by the Turks in 1526, besieged in 1529 and then finally occupied permanently in 1541. Esztergom was besieged six times before it finally fell to the Ottomans in 1543, to become the front-line fortress and frontier *sanjak*. Meanwhile, Temesvár was conquered in 1552, thereby broadening and consolidating the Ottoman footprint north of the Balkans. The Turks adapted to local customs as the price for cementing their hegemony. The post-conquest cadastral surveys in central Hungary allocated local resources to support material infrastructure locally in order to make good their claims that they were not a predatory regime. There were tax exemptions and compensation for civilian populations most affected by Ottoman garrisons, paid for from central funds or transfers from the Egyptian treasury.

Moldavia, Wallachia and Transylvania were unstable, porous, multi-cultural and religiously diverse overlordships where the success of those in authority depended on how they brokered their acceptance with the various local groups, and played off their neighbours against one another. The Ottomans understood how to exploit local grievances and disputes to keep local rulers loyal to them. They embraced Wallachia as a quasi-independent protectorate. It was occupied by garrisons but never subjected to a cadastral survey, nor was its land granted out as prebends (*timar*) to reward Ottoman cavalry (*sipahis*) or serving officers in the imperial army (janissaries). That served as the pattern for Moldavia as well, where a failed attempt by local nobles to recover their independence from Ottoman rule in 1538 signalled its more permanent absorption into Ottoman overlordship.

Transylvania was more complex. It was the densely wooded region to the east of Hungary, whose scattered population was divided into Hungarian (Magyar) nobles and peasants to the west, Turkish peasants and Slavs to the east, Lutheran German immigrants in small towns, and self-governing communities of Szekler forest folk. The princes (voivodes) of Transylvania could not hope to defend their lands against an outright attack by any of their larger neighbours (Poles, Habsburgs, Turks). Their countrymen could raise cavalry on a voluntary basis, but only for the summer months. They needed a protector. But opinions were divided in Transylvania as to where that protection should come from. Around 1550, some (especially in western Transylvania) looked to the Habsburg archduke, and later emperor, Ferdinand I. Others supported John Sigismund Zápolya, a remnant of the Jagiellon dynasty through his mother. He was twice elected king of Hungary (1540–51 and 1556–71), mainly thanks to the protection of the Ottomans.

Rivalry between John Sigismund and Ferdinand was also fomented by religious differences. Transylvania had become a haven for Reformed Protestant proselytizing and, in due course, for Unitarians. The beliefs of the latter seemed to offer the possibilities of syncretism between Christianity and Islam. That appealed to many groups in eastern Transylvania, especially the Szeklers, for whom Islam was a close and not-so-feared neighbour. The Ottomans played on those differences to establish their hegemony while allowing the local Diet to elect its own princes and exacting no hostages or tribute. In Transylvania, a neo-Calvinist prince ruled with Ottoman blessing. Under Turkish aegis, Latin-rite Christians, Calvinists, Lutherans and Unitarians had a recognized place in Transylvanian life, while Orthodox Christians were tolerated. As with the frontiers between Protestant and Catholic Christianity, so those between Christianity and Islam were nowhere as neat as the proponents of Crusade and Holy War on either side would have liked them to be.

The Ottoman empire was (somewhat like the pre-Christian Roman empire) an amalgam of cultures and traditions which its expansion fostered. Islam provided its foundational legitimacy. The sultans conceived of themselves and their social order as Muslim and their state as an Islamic one. Yet, by 1550 the empire spread over three continents and embraced 15 million people. The Ottomans learned how to match the protection of the House of Islam with the practicalities of ruling diverse peoples. Ottoman religious and military élites maintained the primacy of Islamic law but were flexible about how they did so. The interpreters of Islamic law (*müftis*) presided over mosques and religious schools (*medresses*). They were independent of the regime and could be the focus of opposition to it. But they were trained in the Sunni Hanafi school of Islamic law, which offered justifications for religious syncretism in terms of the eventual conversion of those who were not originally of the faith. By contrast, those who administered the Islamic law locally (*kadis*) were appointed by the state, priest-magistrates who drew upon Sultanic law as well as local customs and traditions, while seeking to interpret them within the framework of their understanding of Islamic law (the Shariah). At the same time, Armenian, Greek Orthodox and Jewish communities all had their own courts within the empire, and judged people in accordance with their own laws. Genoese, Venetian (and then, later, French, English and Dutch) residents were also allowed their own courts in the trading centres of the empire. Even within the House of Islam, the Ottomans accorded space and legitimacy to the dervish orders. Christians, Jews and Armenians of talent found their way into Ottoman military and administrative élites.

While religious dissent had initially encouraged Christendom to define itself as a belief-community through the exclusion of those who did not subscribe to its beliefs, the Ottoman empire was able to expand in the same period on a basis of qualified inclusion. So although European lands had few Muslims in their midst the Ottoman empire embraced a mixture of Christians of different traditions. The majority of its Balkan subjects were (with the exception of some parts of Albania and Bosnia) Christians. There were minority Christian populations in Anatolia and concentrations of Christians in Middle Eastern mountain regions which had traditionally served as refuges (Mount Lebanon, Sasun and the Tur Abdin). Many Christians in the Ottoman empire acknowledged their allegiance to either the Greek Orthodox patriarch, or the Apostolic Armenian patriarch, both located in the Ottoman capital. Both Church hierarchies were recognized by the Ottoman bureaucracy. But there were many Christians in the Asian and African provinces of the Ottoman empire who were neither Orthodox nor Armenian – Copts, Jacobites, Maronites and Nestorians.

From the later sixteenth century onwards, the globalizing Christian ambitions of Catholic Christianity sponsored attempts by European missionaries from the later sixteenth century onwards to make common cause with these Asian and African Christians and to wean the Orthodox and Armenian faithful to the Latin cause. Their objective was to form a 'Uniate' Church (that is, one in communion in Rome) as had occurred in the Polish-Ukrainian borderlands among the Orthodox faithful after 1595. In the Ottoman empire, however, such efforts backfired – not least because Ottoman officials, reluctant to intervene in what they regarded as Christian quarrels of no concern to them, endorsed the rival authorities of the two patriarchies. By the middle of the seventeenth century, the contentions over religion in Constantinople were focused around protecting Catholic missionaries (attempts led by the French monarchy) from hostility originating, in most part, not from Muslims but from the Orthodox and Apostolic Armenian patriarchs.

Western Christendom's ideologues talked up the need to respond to the Ottoman threat with a Crusade against the Infidel, ignoring the reality that the Ottoman empire was a pluralist entity in which Christianity had an acknowledged place. In a parallel fashion, Islamic religious leaders periodically proclaimed the need for a Holy War (ghâzá), while Ottoman rulers simultaneously sought to retain the multi-ethnic and multi-confessional basis of the empire. Like Christian princes in the West, however, the sultans had to respond to the popular expectations for spiritual renewal in their midst as well as pressures for a greater degree of religious orthodoxy and state-sponsored confessional identity. In both Christian Europe and Ottoman Islam there were mutual and contradictory pressures – some for confrontation and others for co-existence. The resulting ambivalence explains the ebb and flow in the relationships between Europe and the Porte: mutual tensions, followed by renewed and contingent accommodation.

Ottoman expansion in the Mediterranean constituted a particular focus for Christendom's fears. That was where it was most readily understood within an eschatological context. The prophecies of Joachim of Fiore from the years of Christendom's crusading fervour taught that the Turks were a manifestation of the Antichrist whose final overthrow would signal the End Time. They were joined by other prophetic proclamations with their origins in the last years of Byzantium. In Venice, Florence and elsewhere in Italy, such writings were more widely diffused in print, and given credence in the years of heightened tension from the Turkish menace. As the Ottoman siege of Cyprus unfolded in 1570 so the Brescian alchemist Giovanni Battista Nazari published one of several works to appear from Venetian presses that year predicting that the Venetian Lion, the Imperial Eagle and the Papal Lamb would together slaughter the Turkish Dragon. Equivalent prophecies circulated in the Muslim Mediterranean world as it approached its own millennium (1591–2 in the Christian calendar). One of the most widely distributed predictions within Christendom (appearing in twenty-three printed editions in the years from 1552 to 1600) was that the Ottomans would capture 'the red apple', interpreted in the West as the city of Rome.

The Mediterranean was the heart of an economic world straddling continents and civilizations. Its urban centres and hinterlands were linked by patterns of exchange which were both collaborative and competitive. What went on at one end of the Mediterranean was rapidly known, talked about and emulated at the other. Intermediary groups (Armenians, Jews, Moriscos, Christians who had converted to Islam either voluntarily or by coercion and others) served as conduits of information across religious and cultural divides. Venice, Europe's great entrepôt with the East, had a guild of official translators (dragomen) who acted as intermediaries with the Ottoman empire. These intermediaries relayed Christian and Muslim prophetic voices in the Mediterranean echo-chamber, each urging on the anxieties of the other. One sign of the waning of Crusade was the decreasing economic and cultural influence of the intermediary Mediterranean trading diasporas in the seventeenth century, and the shift in the centre of gravity of Europe's eschatological and millennial speculation. By the 1620s it had moved away from the Mediterranean and the fear of the Turk, to be relocated in the hands of Protestant interpreters in the upheavals of central Europe.

The Ottoman military conquest of Syria and Mamluk Egypt in 1517 was followed by the acknowledgement of Ottoman suzerainty by the Arab advocates of Holy War in the Maghreb and the corsair states along the North African coast. The latter's licensed depredations on Christian shipping were the way whereby the Ottomans sustained their overlordship along the shoreline of the southern Mediterranean at little cost to local populations. They also acquired a naval competence with which to challenge successfully the combined maritime strength of Venice and the Habsburgs in the second Ottoman-Venetian War (1537–9). As a result, the Ottomans established their pre-eminence in the Aegean and over the majority of the eastern Adriatic coast. Just as the Ottomans exploited local frustrations against the incompetent Mamluks, so they were adept at fomenting Greek Orthodox resentments of their Latin Catholic overlords in the Aegean islands to establish their hegemony. By 1550, Ottoman naval forces were never more than a day or so away from a port and supplies for their galleys in the eastern Mediterranean. That gave them a considerable advantage over the navies of Christendom when the latter ventured on long-range expeditions east of Malta.

The Ottomans were well informed about the religion and politics of Christendom, thanks to the Jews, converted Moriscos and Christians in their service. The Muslim empire's westward expansion depended on exploiting Christian divisions and rivalries. By 1550, however, it was reaching the strategic limits dictated by the geography of its land supply-lines. Ottoman military maps tell the story of how important these were, as do their ambitious projects to link the Don and Volga rivers (first conceived in 1563), to build a Suez canal (1568) and another linking the Black Sea with the Sea of Marmara through the Sakarya river (begun in 1591). No amount of local outsourcing to supply the strategically placed outpost garrisons could replace the need to march men and equipment to the campaign front line. Equally, the materials and crews to man their Mediterranean fleets were not summoned out of thin air. They required logistic planning and forethought. Even more important in limiting Ottoman expansion to the west was the reality that the further they penetrated into the core of European land-space the more they encountered peoples who were acculturated not to accept Muslim rule and prepared to resist it.

Nor was the Islamic world itself immune to religious division. Developments here, as in other aspects of the Middle East, bear comparison with those in the West. In 1501, the Grand Master of the Safaviyeh Order, a Sufi group of mystics from what is now northwest Iran, proclaimed himself Shah ('king') Ismail in Azerbaijan and Iran and established his capital in Tabriz. Claiming to be the direct male descendant of the cousin of the Prophet Muhammad, he succeeded in imposing Shi'ism as the religion of what coalesced under his authority and that of his successors as the Persian Safavid empire. Thousands of Shi'a adherents (fundamentally divergent from Sunni Islam) were massacred by the

Ottomans in Asia Minor in an effort to repress the heresy in the first half of the sixteenth century, while the supporters of Ismail desecrated Sunni graves and sought to advance Shi'ism by military means, regarding the shah as both a religious leader and a military chieftain.

The periodic wars that broke out between the Ottomans and Safavid Persia in the sixteenth and first half of the seventeenth centuries took resources and focus away from Ottoman expansion to the west, which in turn further opened the door to a coexistence with Europe. With the Portuguese (and later the Dutch) holding sway in the Indian Ocean and hovering at the entrance to the Red Sea, the possibility that Europe would make common cause with the Safavid rulers of Persia was a constant preoccupation in Constantinople. Further Islamic dissent also appeared in the sixteenth century from the Saadi, an Arab dynasty located in southern Morocco, whose members claimed to be (like the Safavid) directly descended from the Prophet's family. At the Ottoman Porte, as in the capitals of Europe, the relationships between East and West came to be seen in terms of global strategic imperatives rather than a Crusade.

PEACE IN CHRISTENDOM: WAR AGAINST THE TURKS

The antagonism in Christendom towards the Ottomans was fundamental, the evidence for it pervasive. Yet beyond the calls to mobilize resources and efforts to defend a common faith lay debates in and around the councils of Christian princes about the best strategies and military techniques to deploy, and fundamental disagreements about whether what was needed was the defence of what remained in Christian hands (and in which regions to concentrate) or the recovery of what had been lost. Those divergences were occluded in the rhetoric of the double goal to bring peace to Christendom in order to confront the Muslim foe. The moral authority of the papacy and (to a lesser extent) the emperor were both implicated in the quest for that mostly illusory twin objective. Partly as a result of papal insistence, the diplomatic correspondence and international negotiations echoed to the importance of achieving a peace in Christendom in order to unite against the 'common enemy'. Sent by Pope Julius III to negotiate an accord between the

French king, Henry II, and Emperor Charles in 1554, Cardinal Pole wrote a discourse that was a classic statement about how true peace between Christian princes was a gift from God. That gift was the more to be sought after, said Pole, because 'truly nothing but your dissensions and wars' was to blame for the Ottoman capture of Belgrade or the fall of Rhodes. The papal dream of a united Christendom as the necessary precondition for a war against the Turk remained on the agenda throughout the sixteenth century since it was one to which Protestant and Catholic Christian princes jointly subscribed, even though little else united them.

That papal dream was still active at the end of the sixteenth century as the 'Long War' against the Ottomans in Hungary showed no signs of reaching a successful conclusion for the emperor's forces. That conflict underlined Pope Clement VIII's efforts to reconcile the French king, Henry IV, with Philip II, culminating at the Peace of Vervins (1598). The Cardinal-Nephew Pietro Aldobrandini wrote in October 1596: 'These peace talks are of infinite importance to His Holiness because he sees in them a service to God and Christendom, and the true means of exterminating heresies and subjugating the Turk.' That was the last moment in Europe's major diplomatic encounters when the rhetoric of peace in Christendom in order to unite against the Ottomans played a significant role. Protestant powers in northern Europe ceased to take it seriously. The international diplomatic role of the papacy retreated. In the initial stages of the Westphalian negotiations in 1645–6, the papal nuncio Fabio Chigi corralled the delegates from the Catholic powers in Münster to arrive at a common peace in order to resist the Ottoman offensive in the Aegean, begun with the siege of Crete in 1645. His Venetian counterpart, the experienced diplomat Alvise Contarini, tried to do the same among Protestant delegates at Osnabrück, even exaggerating the dangers for the sake of the audience. Like Contarini, however, Chigi was dismayed by the results, confiding to the nuncio in Venice that evoking the Turkish threat worked 'the opposite of what he had expected'. Delegates, he said, 'hear the Turk spoken of as though it was merely a name, a creation of the mind, an unarmed phantasmagoria'. By the time the negotiations neared completion, the papacy had to make a choice between not sacrificing Catholic gains in Germany during the Counter-Reformation, and supporting peace in order to pursue the Turkish threat. It chose the former.

There was one occasion when the papal dream came close to being realized. In May 1571, negotiations for a Holy League were concluded in Rome on the initiative of Pope Pius V. The agreement was signed by a majority of the Catholic maritime states in the Mediterranean (the Papal States, Spain, Venice, Genoa, Tuscany, Savoy, Parma, Urbino and Malta). Their maritime assets combined to make up the League forces placed under the overall command of Don John of Austria. Twenty-six years old, the illegitimate son of Emperor Charles V, and brought up almost as a brother to Philip II, he completed the repression of the Morisco rebellion in southern Spain before joining the fleet at Genoa in August. His flotilla then made for Messina, where other League ships assembled in September. On the 17th, Don John stepped ashore and made his way through a ceremonial parade of Spanish troops, arranged the length of the harbour, to attend Mass in the cathedral. In the bay were 208 galleys, six galleasses and a further sixty-six frigates. From one of the ships, Pope Pius V blessed the armada and presented it with the League's crusading banner. The expeditionary force was crewed by 44,000 sailors and oarsmen. Its ships were armed with 1,800 guns and carried 28,000 soldiers. It was the largest naval force mounted by Christendom, and the largest ever deployed against Islam.

The Ottoman fleet had already left port in June 1571. It was composed of over 250 ships, crewed by 50,000 sailors and oarsmen, and carried 31,000 soldiers. Its first objective was an assault on the strategically important and rich Venetian colony on the island of Crete. Always vulnerable because of underlying Greek dislike of Venetian rule, it was additionally weakened by the Ottoman capture of Cyprus the year before. Although the island's principal fortress held out, the island was ransacked before the Ottomans besieged Kotor on the coast of Montenegro, the fortress capital of the Venetian colony of Albania. The Ottomans were alert to the rumours of Orthodox Christian unrest in their Dalmatian *sanjaks* of Delvine, Avlonya, Ohrid and Elbasan. Open revolt had just broken out in the southern Peloponnese (the Morea), and Ottoman intelligence knew that its leaders had sent emissaries to Philip II and the Venetian Senate. The Ottoman amphibious force moved to suppress the rebellion in August before mounting an assault on Corfu, the Greek island at the entrance to the Adriatic.

Seeking the Ottoman navy, Don John's fleet engaged with it in the Gulf of Lepanto, which was where the Ottoman fleet had their arsenal, on 7 October. The Turkish commander, Müezzinzade Ali Pasha, a senior figure in Ottoman councils and favourite of Sultan Selim II, promised liberty to his Christian galley-slaves if he won the day. John of Austria simply told the crew of his flagship: 'There is no paradise for cowards.' The battle was bloody and decisive. By four o'clock in the afternoon it was over; 7,000 or more League sailors and soldiers had perished, along with at least seventeen ships. Ottoman losses were overwhelming: 20,000 dead, wounded or captured, fifty ships sunk and a further 137 captured along with the mainly Christian slave crews. Ali Pasha himself was captured and decapitated, his head displayed on a pike above the mast of Don John's flagship. Janissaries continued fighting, even after the battle had been lost. When ammunition ran out they threw oranges and lemons at the enemy.

The significance of the Holy League and of the battle of Lepanto did not lie in the destruction of the Ottoman navy or a decisive shift of strategic power. The ships were quickly replaced. When Grand Vizier Sokollu Mehmed Pasha, the brilliant Bosnian janissary-trained administrator, was asked the following year about the losses at Lepanto, he replied: 'The Ottoman state is so powerful that, if an order was issued to cast anchors from silver, to make rigging from silk and to cut sails from satin, it could be carried out for the entire fleet.' Replacing the trained crews turned out, in fact, to be the harder task. The League failed to follow up their naval victory, never contemplating the recapture of the island of Chios (which the Ottomans had captured from the Genoese in 1566) or Cyprus (taken by the Ottomans after the long siege of Famagusta in 1571).

The League was disbanded in 1573. The Venetians made independent overtures to the Porte to safeguard their commercial Levantine interests, leaving Spain (now embroiled in a major war in the Netherlands) to summon alone what resources it could to defend its position on the North African coast. In touch with the Dutch rebels, the Ottomans mounted a successful attack on Tunis in 1574 with a naval force larger than either of those which fought at Lepanto. That gave them a secure base from which to invade Morocco in 1576 and unseat its dissident sultan, Abu Abdallah Muhammad II Saadi, and replace him with his compliant uncle and rival, Abu Marwan Abd al-Malik I Saadi. The Ottomans thus reminded Christendom that they could still bring war close to Europe's heartlands. Abu Abdallah fled to Portugal and sought

to engage King Sebastian in his restoration. Although he failed to interest Philip II in the project, Sebastian launched an expedition to Morocco
which had all the hallmarks of a Crusade. His expeditionary force of
17,000 troops joined the 6,000 Moorish soldiers of Abu Abdallah, but
they were overwhelmed at the battle of Alcácer-Quibir ('Battle of the
Three Kings') on 4 August 1578. Sebastian was last spotted, Don
Quixote-like, leading the Portuguese nobility into Ottoman lines of fire.

Alcácer-Quibir was a humiliation to be forgotten. Lepanto, by contrast, was turned into a fairy-story, complete with a handsome prince
(Don John), wicked ogres (the Turks), a prize to be rescued (Christendom) and a fortuitously successful outcome. The naval battle's significance
was that it was commemorated in a surfeit of celebration. Don John
became a crusading icon. Rome treated the commander of its galleys,
Marc'Antonio Colonna, to a hero's welcome. Sculpted bronze medals
were distributed from the papal mint in memory of the victory, while
Giorgio Vasari was commissioned by the papacy to undertake a fresco
cycle for the Sala Regia (where it accompanied a painting to celebrate
the massacre of St Bartholomew). In Venice, the captain-general of the
Venetian galleys, Sebastiano Venier, was apotheosized in a painting by
Tintoretto in which he was depicted standing on the deck of his flagship
while the battle raged, assisted by a heavenly host. His renown secured
him the election as the Republic's Doge at the age of eighty.

The legend of Lepanto reassured those in Christendom who had
come to believe that their internal divisions were so great that the Turk
could never be defeated. Yet the reality was more sobering. Even after
the League had been signed, there were anxieties that Venice was negotiating a separate agreement with the Porte to safeguard its maritime
empire. Persistent disagreements over the command of the forces as well
as their eventual objective had delayed the departure of the fleet. Key
players in Christendom had stood aside from the League. Europe's Protestants ostentatiously ignored it. King Charles IX of France preferred to
hang on to the Capitulations of 1569, privileges offered to the French
on the eve of the Ottoman Cyprus campaign in order to foster disunity
among Europe's princes. Emperor Maximilian, too, rejected the League
in favour of an Ottoman-imperial accord which had been negotiated in
1568. Portugal pleaded its commitments in Morocco and the Red Sea.

By the end of the sixteenth century, the balance of forces in the
Mediterranean reached an unstable equilibrium. In Hungary and the

Balkans, a similar unsteady balance rested on the border defences in the Danubian marches and the relationships between the Ottomans and their Balkan and European protectorates. The Ottomans inherited fortresses hitherto in Hungarian Christian hands – those along the Danube and across to Lake Balaton in Transdanubia as well as those in the Novigrad Mountains and all the major castles along the river Tisza and its tributaries: some 130 installations which they garrisoned by 18,000 soldiers and 7,000 cavalry. The Austrian Habsburgs, confronted with their own weakness and the vulnerability of that part of Hungary remaining in their hands, chose appeasement as the only option, accepting in 1568 a truce which included annual payments of tribute to Constantinople. Gradually thereafter, the Habsburgs assembled their own defensive crescent along the 600-mile frontier from the Adriatic to northern Hungary, guarding it with over 20,000 soldiers. In 1590, they negotiated, albeit on disadvantageous terms, an eight-year extension of the truce. But conflict along this armed border escalated into a war that began in 1591 (as the Habsburgs saw it) and 1593 (as the Ottomans thought) and dragged through into the next decade, being concluded only by the Treaty of Zsitvatorok in 1606. Contemporary observers in Christian Europe were convinced that the Ottomans took advantage of the lull in the conflict with Persia in order to challenge the new Habsburg strategic fortifications.

Pope Clement VIII, following in the footsteps of Pius V, tried to turn the Hungarian conflict into an opportunity to unite Christendom under papal initiative. This time, however, Protestants were not even solicited to join in, so deep-rooted had become Europe's religious fracture. Instead the 'Long War' became the moment when the revived forces of a globalizing Catholic Christianity were brought into play. Venice, Savoy, Ferrara, Mantua, Parma and Urbino, Genoa and Lucca were all approached to support what the emperor declared to be a Crusade. Princes and their spouses found themselves the object of solicitous letters from the Holy See. To the east, the pope sought a commitment from the king of Poland and, beyond Europe, he dreamed of a grand alliance with the Cossacks, the grand duke of Muscovy and Shah Abbas I of Persia. An embassy from the latter was received in Rome with suitable ceremony in 1601. International subsidies were raised, and money transhipped through financiers and intermediaries largely outside Habsburg direct control. Yet the results in material terms were disappointing.

The papacy despatched three forces under Francesco Aldobrandini and additional subsidies, but Spain proved a reluctant backer, at least until after 1598. The fleets of Naples and Sicily, on which Pope Clement had relied to launch diversionary sorties in the Mediterranean, limited themselves to cautious sallies, save for one ambitious raid on Patras in 1595. Henry IV of France was as generous in his support for the principle of intervention as he was hard-headed and reluctant to deliver anything material. The Habsburgs managed to finance their war-effort only thanks to a generous reading of an agreement at the 1570 Diet of Speyer to the effect that imperial territories were obliged to provide quarter and subsistence for an army engaged in the common defence of the empire.

In the end, the outcome of the 'Long War' turned not on the lack of unity in Christendom but on the behaviour of the Ottoman client-states. The military hostilities in central Hungary destabilized the loyalties which the Turks had developed among the competing dynasties in Moldavia, Wallachia and Transylvania. These regions were as seriously affected by the climatic irregularities of the 1590s as the rest of the European landmass. In addition, the greater demands for raw materials, foodstuffs and subsidies to support the Ottoman forces in Hungary sharpened resentments towards their overlords. An important contingent of the armies fighting for the Ottomans in Hungary came from the Crimean Tatars (they furnished over 50,000 troops in 1595 and succeeding years). Each year, the sultan despatched 'boot money' to the Crimea in order to enlist their support. Once it was received, the Tatar host set forth along one of several routes, one of which took them across Transylvania, and another through Moldavia and Wallachia, and then up the right bank of the Danube. The Tatar reputation for laying waste the lands through which they passed, stealing animals and capturing peasants to sell as slaves was amply deserved.

With Ottoman attempts to limit depredations bearing little fruit, local opportunists offered to protect local people from Tatar predators and seized the moment to lead revolts against their Ottoman overlords. Leaders, looking for support from the Habsburgs, the Ottomans and Poland came and went in rapid succession. Aaron Emanoil ('Aaron the Tyrant') in Moldavia was twice prince before he was captured in Transylvania and imprisoned by Sigismund Báthory. Michael Viteazul ('Michael the Brave') became prince in Wallachia with Ottoman support in 1593 but, even as the Long War began in Hungary in earnest, Pope Clement VIII tempted him into an alliance with neighbouring upstart princes. He was variously prince of Wallachia, Transylvania and Moldavia (and, for a brief period, of all three at once) until he was assassinated on the orders of the Habsburg imperial commander, Giorgio Basta, in 1601. Sigismund Báthory held on in Transylvania, partly because of his dynastic connections with Poland, but also thanks to a 40,000-strong army, led by a Hungarian Calvinist nobleman, István Bocskai. But, with Ottoman military pressure too great for him, Sigismund eventually resigned in October 1598 in favour of one of his Polish cousins, leaving the region in turmoil.

Giorgio Basta attempted to reimpose Catholicism by force in Transylvania after 1599, following the initiative set by Archduke Ferdinand in Styria. His effort was thwarted, however, by an uprising, organized by Bocskai with covert Ottoman support. Bocskai's army went on to defeat the Habsburg forces in two crucial battles (Álmosd and Bihardiószeg). In 1605, Bocskai was elected prince of Hungary and Transylvania at the Diet of Szerencs. The Long Turkish War drew to a negotiated conclusion in 1606 with the Ottomans having little but modest fortress gains on the Hungarian plain to show for their efforts, but with much more to be hoped for from the Transylvanian insurrection against the Habsburgs. Sultan Ahmed I despatched a crown to Bocskai, offering him the kingship of Transylvania in return for nominal vassalage to the Turkish Porte. Bocskai prudently refused the offer in favour of a deal with the Habsburg Archduke Matthias, who was compelled to recognize the authority of a Calvinist prince in Ottoman Hungary and Transylvania.

French diplomats and royal publicists were the first to find the arguments which would become widely accepted to justify alliances with the Infidel. When the Dutch jurist Hugo Grotius came to publish his *Law of War and Peace* (1625), he asked 'whether it was permitted to make treatises and alliances with those who are not of the true religion'. The issue was as relevant to princes making alliances across the European confessional divide as to powers making common cause with those outside Europe. Grotius's answer was straightforward: 'that caused no difficulty because, by the law of nature, the right to make alliances was common to all mankind generally, such that a difference of religion created no exception'. Even so, Grotius was obliged to refute the biblical arguments against the proposition, and to counsel caution. Prudence dictated, he advised, that one should not enter into such an alliance if 'it put Pagans and Infidels in a position of overwhelming power'. Europe's rulers should see themselves as belonging to a Christian family with a shared duty to 'serve Jesus Christ' and help one another when 'an enemy of [their] religion smites the states of Christianity'. It was the customs of international diplomacy among the European 'society of princes', with their permanent embassies and diplomatic immunities, and shared (albeit often contested) conventions of precedence which the Ottoman state refused to acknowledge and participate in. In this respect Europe had created a sense of its political identity by 1650 which necessarily consigned the Ottomans (their political system now increasingly regarded as 'despotic') to the margins.

CRUSADING ECHOES

The rhetoric of anti-Turkish mobilization eventually wore thin through overuse as well as through an increasing mismatch between the idealistic commitments that it evoked and the political and strategic realities on the ground. The word 'Crusade' entered the English and French vocabularies in the later sixteenth century, just as the reality was vanishing over the horizon. But there would still be those in whom the call to war against the Infidel found an echo. Thomas Howard, duke of Norfolk, wanted to respond in 1529. Philippe-Emmanuel de Lorraine, duke of Mercoeur, was inspired to put the military experience he gained in the French Catholic League to good use in the Long Turkish War. Leaving France in 1599, he led the imperial forces which recaptured Székesfehérvár, home of the mausoleum of the kings of Hungary, from the Ottomans.

The dream of a Crusade in defence of Christendom infected the imaginations of more modest individuals too, both Protestant and Catholic. The Elizabethan adventurer Edward Woodshawe was arrested in 1575 for attempting to levy men in his English locality for a 'journey against the Turk'. John Smith, whose expedition to Chesapeake Bay and survey of the lower Potomac led to the publication of the map of Virginia in 1612, earned his title of 'captain' by fighting the Ottomans in Hungary and Transylvania. In 1616, the Capuchin François Le Clerc du Tremblay was given a mission to Rome by Louis XIII's new secretary of state, Cardinal Richelieu. He presented a project for a European Christian militia, open to both Catholics and Protestants, whose mission would be to protect Christendom against its Muslim aggressors. The scheme was the brainchild of Charles de Gonzague, duke of Nevers. The idea was to divert the destructive energies of religious discord into the common cause of a renewed *Respublica christiana*, albeit organized no longer under the banner of the Church but of those of its crowned heads. Meanwhile, the duke of Nevers sought the backing of the emperor and even equipped five galleons to transport the Crusaders to Greece in 1621. This was, perhaps, Christendom's last truly crusading act. No sooner conceived, it was consigned to oblivion by the onset of war in Europe. The Thirty Years War demonstrated the destructive power of Europe. In doing so, it put paid to Christendom.

For nobles, the call of Crusade offered an opportunity to perfect their military training and to acquire chivalric glory. But the overwhelming majority of those who found themselves engaged in military or naval operations against the Ottomans were mercenaries for whom it was simply a campaign, the deprivations and brutality of which eroded any sense of idealistic engagement they might have had. Even the Knights of Malta (and their equivalent, the Italian Order of San Stefano) found their fervour fell on increasingly deaf ears towards the close of the sixteenth century. Christian corsairs disturbed ordinary commercial relationships, said Venetian senators, who succeeded in persuading the authorities to confiscate the property of the Knights of Malta. Their views were echoed by French consular representatives in the Levant in the early seventeenth century, Henry IV forbidding French subjects from undertaking privateering in the eastern Mediterranean. The papal Curia, anxious to protect the lives of Christians in Ottoman custody, not to mention its investment in the port of Ancona, multiplied its representations to the Grand Master of Malta against Christian corsairs.

COMMERCE, CORSAIRS AND CAPTIVES

For centuries, the papacy had forbidden commerce with the Infidel. In the sixteenth and early seventeenth centuries, the prohibition was incorporated into the traditional annual Maundy Thursday bull (*In*

Coena Domini) of excommunications and anathemas against all those who threatened Christendom. By the second half of the sixteenth century, the bull included injunctions against those who traded in weapons, horses and war supplies, and grouped together Protestant heretics with Saracens and Turks. Publishing and enforcing such measures, however, became an uphill task in the face of commercial pressures and princely resistance.

Even in the Italian and Spanish peninsulas, the prohibition encountered problems. Rulers in Venice, Naples and elsewhere turned a blind eye to contraband trading. Outside the Mediterranean, the bull was only patchily observed in the empire, ignored by France and mocked in Protestant Europe. One of the important bargaining counters used by the English and Dutch to secure a privileged position for their merchants in the Levant was their offer to furnish the high-grade armaments which the Ottomans needed. As Christendom waned, so did the capacity to hold any commercial front against the 'common enemy'. That was even more notably the case in respect of trade in alum, the key chemical for finishing cloth. The Papal States had a monopoly on its production (from the alum deposits mined at Tolfa) so long as imported alum from the Levant was prohibited. Christendom was crystallized in a mineral salt, the profits from which went, said the papacy, towards Crusade. But the monopoly became a low-grade dispute between the papacy and the cloth-producing centres of Catholic Europe, while it was ostentatiously ignored in Protestant lands for which the cloth-trade with the Levant was a commercial opportunity.

The Ottoman state had long been accustomed to granting privileged access to its markets to selected merchant communities from the West. Genoese merchants had enjoyed a privileged status from 1352. The Venetians, Florentines and Neapolitans followed in the fifteenth century. The privileges were granted through 'capitulations' (a 'charter' with individual 'chapters'), legal documents issued by the Turkish Porte and not strictly speaking diplomatic treaties. The purpose of these permissions from the Ottoman point of view was to regulate the status of those granted safe-conduct (*aman*: 'amnesty') to reside temporarily in the House of Islam although they were not Muslims. Capitulations granted merchants *aman* status in Ottoman lands without being treated as *zimmi* (non-Muslims, living under Islamic rule): subjects of the Ottoman state, and having to pay taxes and tribute accordingly. The capitulations were more concerned with merchant legal status than with granting advantageous conditions for the trade in particular goods to specific nations.

What changed in the course of the later sixteenth century was the granting of such privileges to mercantile communities beyond the Italian peninsula and (with it) the Ottoman state's willingness to utilize capitulations as a political instrument. In 1569, the Sublime Porte granted capitulations to the French monarchy's representative Claude du Bourg, part of the Ottoman attempt to divide its European neighbours on the eve of its assault upon Cyprus. The position of French merchants from Marseille in the Levant was strengthened just at the moment when the war between Venice and the Turks (1570–73) created a commercial opportunity for interlopers. That moment was not lost, however, upon English merchants, whose ships had started to sail to the eastern Mediterranean. Two English merchants in the Levant trade organized a safe-conduct for their factor William Harborne to travel to Constantinople, where he arrived in 1578. English policy-makers appreciated the significance of making common cause with the Turks against Spain. Queen Elizabeth's letters addressed Sultan Murad III as 'the most august and benign Caesar'. The sultan granted a capitulation to English merchants in 1580, and in his letters to Elizabeth I he lavished praise on the 'pride of women who follow Jesus, the most excellent of the ladies honored among the Messiah's people, the arbitress of the affairs of the Christian community'.

The English initiative opened up a race for competitive advantage. Not to be outdone, the French ambassador negotiated the cancellation of the English privileges and the granting of more exclusive terms to the French, including the requirement that other nations sail to Turkish ports under the flag of France. In 1583, Harborne returned to Constantinople as Elizabeth I's ambassador to the Porte, the first of a regular ambassadorial presence that became, by the early seventeenth century, one of the most important diplomatic postings for the English state. The English Levant Company, formed in 1581 (united with the Venice Company in 1592), focused the efforts of English merchants trading in the Mediterranean. Taking advantage of France's civil wars in the late 1580s and 90s, English merchants consolidated their presence in Turkish markets, dealing especially in importing currants from Patras, Zante and Cephalonia and exporting English cloth. In 1601, the English negotiated a reduction in customs dues on their traded goods to only 3 per cent, along with other commercial advantages which their rivals were unable to match before 1650.

In the first half of the seventeenth century, those rivals included the Dutch. Merchants from the rebellious provinces in the northern Netherlands began direct commercial contacts with the Ottoman empire in the 1570s. Ottoman strategists appreciated the significance of encouraging the enemies of Spain in northern Europe. So, when Cornelius Haga led a delegation from the Dutch Republic to Constantinople in 1612, generous capitulations to the Dutch followed. Haga became a permanent Dutch ambassador in Constantinople and, by the time he returned to the Netherlands in 1639, the Dutch had consular posts throughout the trading centres of the Ottoman empire from Patras to Tunis and Algiers and minimal customs duties, better than the French or Venetians. Europe's trade with the Levant blossomed in the first half of the seventeenth century. Pepper and silk from the Far East were transacted through Ottoman ports, but the more important trades were in local products, including cotton from Anatolia, silk from Aleppo and mohair from around Ankara ('angora' being the English corruption of that place-name, dating to this period), dyes and Arabian coffee. By 1620, over 200 tons of raw silk was imported each year from Aleppo, with the French competing with the English for predominance in the trade.

The flourishing commerce between Europe and the Levant offered a tempting target for pirates. From the last decades of the sixteenth century onwards, the seizure of ships and their cargoes and the capture of their crews became a major source of concern for those engaged in the Levant trades, but also a stimulus to increased contact and cross-cultural trade between Europe and Islam. Privateering was a fact of life in both Atlantic and Mediterranean waters. Many thousands of Ottomans and Moroccans (including Jews and Orthodox Christians as well) were captured and sold as galley slaves on Maltese, Spanish, Italian and French ships. North African corsairs worked both Atlantic and Mediterranean waters, lingering off the Gulf of Gascony in summer months, and even plaguing the coasts of Ireland and Iceland, where one community of 400 people was seized in a single raid.

The public focus of concern in Europe was increasingly on the Barbary corsairs operating out of North African ports (Salé, Oran, Algiers,

Bougie, Tunis, Djerba and Tripoli), who preyed on commercial shipping and ravaged Mediterranean coasts from Andalusia to the Abruzzi. The privateering exploits of the corsair states of North Africa were organized by Berbers, Arabs, Levantine and Sephardic Jews, Moriscos from Spain and Christians who had settled there and converted to Islam. Known as renegades, this latter group made up at least half of the Barbary corsairs in the early seventeenth century. They included sailors who had been captured at sea and enslaved, and who then converted as a way of recovering their freedom. Others were privateers who found it a path to riches and status. Jan Janszoon van Haarlem, commonly known as Murat Reis the Younger, for example, learned the tools of privateering in northwest Atlantic waters under a Dutch flag before making his way with the ship under his command to Salé on the Moroccan Atlantic coast. From there, he attacked Spanish vessels (his ship flying the Dutch flag) and others (flying the red half-moon Ottoman flag). He in turn was captured by Barbary corsairs in the Canary Islands in 1618 and taken as a slave to Algiers, which is where he converted to Islam. From there, he joined the privateering ventures of Sulayman Reis (Ivan Dirkie de Veenboer, also originally from the Netherlands) in the Mediterranean. Then, when Algiers concluded treaties with European powers, it was no longer a port where privateering cargo could be offloaded. So van Haarlem moved back to Salé and, calling himself 'Grand Admiral', led the 'Salé Rovers' in privateering operations over many years.

The conditions for enslaved Christians in North Africa were hideous. Relieved of their clothing, valuables and dignity and held in chains, once ashore they were treated as booty. Beautiful women or young boys were picked out for the harem and entourage of the local ruler (the 'bey', 'dey' or 'pasha'). Skilled individuals were siphoned off to join the shipyards or local medical services. The rest were put up for sale in the local bazaar. Once they had been auctioned to their new master, their price was stamped on their heads or shoulders. They then worked as agricultural and domestic workers or on board ships, poorly fed and often brutalized. In Algiers, Tunis and Tripoli they were lodged at night for a fee, paid for by their owners, in special jails (*bagnes* or *matemores*), some originally designed as underground granaries. In fetid conditions they were chained to the walls each night and kept under close surveillance. Yet, through commercial intermediaries (for whom ransoming captives was part of the trading and money flows of the

Mediterranean) and the activities of Catholic orders (whose mission was to highlight the plight of these slaves and achieve their release), they were often in touch with their friends, families and communities back home. Families realized assets to secure the release of captured relatives, aided by municipal and ecclesiastical institutions. Protestant traders in La Rochelle signed contracts to negotiate ransoms, and Catholic orders on occasion accepted alms from Protestants to release 'heretics' from enslavement, welcoming the occasion for proselytizing which it afforded.

Most releases occurred after negotiations which were part of wider commercial transactions. Arriving back home, ransomed slaves became the spotlight of publicity campaigns by the Catholic order which had organized their release. So, in an event that was far from unusual, over a hundred slaves redeemed from Salé arrived at Brouage on the western French coast in 1630. Their release had been negotiated by the Mercedarian Order, whose founder, Pierre Nolasque, had been canonized two years previously. From Brouage the redeemed captives were led in procession to Paris. As they passed through towns, they reenacted their freedom to cries of 'Vive le Roi'. Published slave narratives and engravings depicting slavery and redemption became part of the publicity of the Mercedarian and Trinitarian orders, competing with each other to attract the patronage of those in authority.

The impact of this publicity was ambivalent. On the one hand, it revitalized an old story of crusading Christendom. The Mercedarian Pierre Dan's *History of Barbary and its Corsairs* (1637) included gruesome engravings of slave tortures, compulsory circumcision and incarceration which evoked images of religious bloodshed from Christendom's recent past, while coupling them with other images of ransomed slaves celebrating their redemption. Yet it was increasingly evident to contemporaries that ransoming Christian slaves was not a priority for Christian rulers. On the contrary, they were more concerned not to alienate Ottoman rulers or compromise their bilateral agreements with the chiefs of Barbary corsair strongholds in order to safeguard their own commercial interests. So, when ten corsair ships arrived in Dutch ports in the 1620s to sell their booty and repair the vessels, there was embarrassment among the Dutch authorities who were bound by their capitulations to treat them with respect, even though some of them were captured Christian ships with Christian slaves on board. King Louis XIII turned a blind eye to Capuchin reports of the suffering of hundreds of French slaves in Morocco and the plight of French subjects in Algiers until, with Huguenot resistance enfeebled, the French government offered limited support to local initiatives for ransom and repatriation. European states were aware that there was generally more to be gained from negotiation with local powers on the North African coast than from clumsy and counter-productive military interventions.

EUROPE IN THE OTTOMAN MIRROR

European powers increasingly regarded their trading links with North Africa and the Levant as advantageous. That led to a gap between popular perceptions of the Turks and the emerging, more complex reality. The stereotype of the Turks had deep roots in the past. The pervasive media of the period (pamphlets, ballads, stage-plays, sermons and even children's games) reinforced it. But the image fragmented as different elements were superimposed upon one another, the process reflecting Europe's changing perception of itself.

The perception of the Turk Infidel, the sworn enemy of Christendom, continued to carry weight. In his bull of 19 September 1645, Pope Innocent X authorized the levy of a subsidy of 400,000 crowns on the clergy to assist Venice in the war it had just declared against the Ottomans 'since it is a well-known fact that the impious tyranny of the Turks seeks nothing other than avidly to launch itself against Christian people, exterminating the Christian religion and entrenching its abomination in its place'. The stereotype perpetuated notions of the Turk as cruel, barbarous and (increasingly after 1600) despotic. The narratives of naval encounters, battles and sieges with Ottoman forces rarely failed to evoke in gruesome detail the sufferings meted out by the Ottomans upon their Christian victims. Equally, the burgeoning accounts of those who had been captured by Barbary pirates or who had served as slaves in Ottoman service and then been repurchased almost always emphasized the arbitrary and despotic brutality of their captors. The 'barbaric' cruelty of the Turks was seen as a fundamental part of the Ottoman psyche, manifest in the arbitrariness of Ottoman politics and confirmed in the supposed Ottoman contempt for Europe's cultural heritage. Polygamy and sodomy were treated as adjuncts of a barbarism that was as hard-wired into the

Turkish psyche as savagery was into the American Indians'. Europe's sense of its values and superiority was fashioned much more in the shadow of the Turkish Crescent than in the mirror of America.

The stereotype of the Turk endured despite an increasing fascination with Ottoman language, culture, institutions and religious beliefs. Humanists opened the door to comparing Christian and Islamic civilizations. But their comparisons also sharpened senses of difference, reinforcing existing preconceptions as well as enhancing senses of innate superiority. Francesco Guicciardini respected the achievements of recent Ottoman sultans in his *History of Italy*. But he also regarded Turkish society as aggressive, cruel and intolerant. The Flemish writer Ogier Ghislain de Busbecq and the French philosopher Guillaume Postel made the case for Ottoman justice, moral virtues and military excellence. But their admiration had another side to it. Postel's influential work *On the Republic of the Turks* (1560) had as its stated goal to 'provide, through a well-founded knowledge of the enemy, the means of resisting him'. Busbecq used his treatise on the Turks of 1581 to outline a plan for how Christendom could defeat the Ottomans. His famous *Turkish Letters*, published in the 1580s, praised Ottoman soldiery, the Turkish sense of social equality, and their hospitality to travellers and care for the poor. But he also emphasized the ruin of Christendom's Greek heritage and the selfish reluctance of Christian princes to support a common cause to help Orthodox Christians.

The French geographer Nicolas de Nicolai had been part of an early French delegation to the Porte in 1551. His detailed *Four Books of Navigations* (1568) was a classic of the humanist science of travel and observation. Its detailed plates turned the work into a costume-book of Ottoman life. Those costumes were reproduced in London stage-plays, where Muslims figured with greater frequency, just as they appeared in the street scenes of Amsterdam when painted by Dutch artists in the seventeenth century. In real life, more citizens of London and Amsterdam would have encountered a Muslim abroad by 1650 than a Native American.

Ottomans and Europeans gradually found that they had interests in common. The humanist Paolo Giovio was one of the earliest to be fascinated by the Ottomans. His *History of the Turks* (1531) was at the beginning of what became in the course of the later sixteenth and early seventeenth centuries a flood of 'turcica' – poetry, songs, lyrics, dramas, novels, broadsides and travelogues. He had eleven portraits of Ottoman sultans in his 'gallery of the illustrious' at Borgovico on Lake Como, copies of those presented by Barbarossa to Francis I at Marseille in 1543. Portraits of 'The Great Turk' (Suleiman the Magnificent) found their way onto the walls of English gentry. His presence in English parlours was complemented by Turkish carpets, silks, cushions and spices. Currants from Zante were a delicacy that fetched high prices in London. Meanwhile, in the Netherlands tulips became objects of fashion and obsession just as they were at the Ottoman court. The tulip was described in detail in Busbecq's letters and, perhaps thanks to his influence, tulip bulbs made their appearance in Europe in the early 1560s. By 1630, 'tulipmania' had overtaken the Netherlands in what turned out to be one of the earliest speculative bubbles, imploding with an Amsterdam stock-market crash in 1636. The 'Dr Tulp' in the famous painting of the lesson in surgical anatomy by Rembrandt was so-called because he had changed his name to match the flower of his dreams.

The more thinking Europeans saw and heard about Ottoman society, the more intrigued and impressed they became. The French naturalist Pierre Belon, whose detailed account of his voyage to the Levant was published in 1553, had much to say in their favour. They were everything that Europeans ought to be, but so often were not. Their houses and streets were clean (babies were even put in nappies so as not to spoil the carpets). They ate healthily (garlic and onions) and did not drink. Their goods were well crafted and their clothing beautiful. Jean Bodin (who read the travel accounts of Belon) saw much to admire in Ottoman society and government. He compared the sultans to French kings, neither of them tyrants, both applying good laws with humanity. But the French monarchy lacked the military discipline of the janissaries. Equally, no European state could seemingly match the financial resources and efficiency of the Ottoman empire. Its forced recruitment of young Christian boys by talent scouts to be trained up in a competitive environment to provide the best administrators, scholars, military commanders and naval officers (*devshirme*) was universally condemned as a barbarous slavery, but there was a sneaking admiration for a system in which (Christian) merit trumped family, patrimony and inheritance. 'The Turkes are the only modern people, great in action, and whose Empire hath suddenly invaded the world,' wrote the English traveller Henry Blount in 1636. He reflected a European orientalism of respect tempered by anxiety.

Christian States in Disarray

16. The Business of States

TRUST AND OBEDIENCE

War among and within Christian states was more intense in the three decades before 1650 than at any time after 1500. In the first half of the sixteenth century, the disputes among the constellation of states in the Italian peninsula had drawn others in like a gravitational force, assisted by the pull of Habsburg overlordship and its dynastic confrontation with the Valois. The size of military establishments increased dramatically, abetted by technical changes in fortifications and firearms transforming warfare on land and at sea. Military escalation was encouraged by the Ottoman threat as well as the windfall inheritance of the Habsburgs and the hostile reactions to it of other powers. The costs of war, and the fiscal and organizational demands which it made upon Europe's rulers, exponentially increased. Then, beginning with the winter siege of Metz by imperial forces from October 1552 to January 1553, the calendar of military operations was enlarged. The months of campaigning became virtually year-round. In addition, a strategy of mutual attrition took hold and military expeditions in more than one theatre against an enemy became common. Continuous attritional warfare increased its fiscal and administrative burdens and its impact.

Post 1559, the focus of warfare moved to the Low Countries and the 'Spanish Road' (as the French termed it) that linked Flanders via Franche-Comté and the Alpine corridors to the Mediterranean and the Hispanic peninsula. The Army of Flanders, sent to repress the Dutch rebellion in 1567, became the largest continuous army of occupation that Europe had yet seen. Like the Italian peninsula earlier in the century, the Low Countries became a vortex which internationalized

Christendom's divisions, this time along confessional lines. The frontier antagonisms with the Ottoman empire and more localized conflicts in the Baltic added to these fissures – notably the Baltic Seven Years War (1563–70) and the Long Turkish War (1593–1606). Above all, the civil and religious tensions provoked by the Protestant Reformation created a confessionalized view of international politics in the minds of publicists, diplomats and strategists, and punctually also in the emergence of Protestant and Catholic power-blocs.

Christendom's deepening tensions in the second half of the sixteenth century remained unresolved. They served as an *alla prima* background upon which were superimposed the swirling struggles of the period from 1618 to 1648. Three interrelated conflicts with their epicentre in central Europe have become known as the Thirty Years War. In reality only the war in Germany lasted that long. Attached to it was a renewed struggle between the Spanish Habsburgs and the Dutch Republic (1621–48), as well as an open struggle for hegemony between France and Spain (1635–59). At the same time, there were separate, though related, wars in the British Isles (the Scottish and Irish Rebellions; the English Civil Wars, 1638–51), in Poland ('The Deluge', 1648–67), as well as a renewed contest in the Mediterranean between Venice and the Ottoman empire (the Cretan or Candian War, 1645–69). They were longer-lasting than earlier wars, more interrelated and unpredictable, and harder to resolve. Those with a confessionalized attitude to international politics were angered and bewildered by alliances and engagements made across religious boundaries and justified in the interests of the state. Wars were fought with exceptional bloodshed and consumed the lives and resources of those drawn into them from wider regions and at greater levels of engagement. The events in central Europe from 1618 onwards occupied combatants from across the European landmass. They compromised the stability of Europe's states when they were under mounting pressures from within.

Internal state tensions were delineated by two periods of political crisis, the first (in the last decade of the sixteenth century) being the prelude to the paroxysm in the mid-seventeenth century. At their heart lay the decay in political certainties and a corresponding search for new ones. The arbiters of Christendom's conflicts – the papacy and empire – had abandoned that role. Christian rulers stepped into their place, drawing their legitimacy and power from notions of dynastic continuity and sacral authority, derived directly from God through lineage and consecration. In addition, humanists had validated the notion of a 'Christian commonwealth', one which depended on an understanding about the objectives, means and exercise of authority between rulers and ruled. The problem was that the religious confrontations of the second half of the sixteenth century weakened that perception, raised question marks about the actions of those in power, and divided rulers from those whom they ruled. The relationship between Christianity and kingship changed.

At the same time, the powers and responsibilities of the state increased. There were more government agencies and greater activity, regulation and intervention in people's lives and an emphasis on codification – of laws, but also of religious practices and social behaviour. The business of states grew, which required organization and cost money. Peacetime expenditures mounted exponentially, especially through cost-inflation in the housing, feeding, entertaining and management of princely courts – increasingly the heart of state-centred initiatives. The expenses of diplomatic and military establishments (such as garrisons) and of campaigns spiralled vertiginously. Those required to pay were bound to ask questions, especially as economic dislocation afflicted parts of Europe after 1580. Those questions fed into criticism of rulers and demands for fundamental political and institutional reform.

The broadening scope of state activity also increased the number of those upon whom rulers relied. Rulers became more dependent on mediated power, beholden to those to whom they had delegated their authority. The greater the reach of the state, the more important it was to secure the compliance of these intermediaries. They were no longer simply the viceroys or power-brokers who had traditionally acted as the eyes and ears of rulers. They included the entrepreneurs who ran the mints, the contractors who supplied the food for the princely household, the judges who had often purchased their offices (which then became an adjunct of their private wealth), the consortia of financiers who farmed customs duties and taxes, and the mercenary military officers and naval privateers who, by the early seventeenth century, had become semi-permanent heads of financial-military enterprises, operating in the name of states.

Such mediated authority was essential to the power of the state. But the contracting operations on which they were based raised questions about who was paying for what, to whom and for how much. The representative assemblies which had traditionally acted as channels of petitions and mouthpieces and defenders of local interests were sidelined, powerless to criticize subcontracted power, or compromised by the reality that some of these agents were in their own midst. Moreover, since the arrangements for mediated authority were the reflection of the power and influence of those who headed up the deals, there were good reasons for those who were unsuccessful in their bids, or who found themselves insufficiently rewarded for their services, to vent their dissatisfaction under the guise of charges of corruption, embezzlement or favouritism in order to disgrace their opponents. The result fed into a more profound and generalized disenchantment as the relationship between government and governed grew more distant and tense.

Those strains were more evident in regal unions, those where dynastic happenstance put states with different customs into an alliance under one prince. The religious confrontations of the second half of the sixteenth century posed challenges to composite monarchies, especially where religion was not a common bond. Even where it was, 'core states' shouldered a disproportionate share of the burden, justified by the development of more exclusive myths of rule. In Castile (for the Spanish Habsburg empire), Inner Austria (for the Austrian monarchy) and Protestant England (for the Stuarts) it took the form of a sense of an exclusive place in God's providence. In each case, the privilege of executing the Almighty's destiny carried responsibilities for which rulers demanded loyalty and a unique role for themselves.

Yet there were limits to the ability of dynastic rulers to broaden their appeal. Patriotism was potentially as divisive as claims to religious truth. The lesson Europe's dynasts drew from the politico-religious turmoil of the later sixteenth century was that religion politicized their subjects, legitimizing the latter's willingness to hold those in power to account for their actions. Religion encouraged clerics to think that they were independent from, if not superior to, lay powers. Rather than broadening the political spectrum, princes and advisers developed more exclusive claims to govern, emphasizing dynastic rights and patrimonial and patriarchal authority, justified on biblical and natural-law grounds. Wherever post-bellum politics sought stability in an authoritarian figure, one-man rule ('absolutism') offered a focus for loyalty which

masked the failure of dynastic rulers to embrace wider political sentiments. There was a renewed emphasis on the sacrality of hierarchies
and princely divine right to rule. Sacred monarchy had existed in the
sixteenth century as a heterogeneous assemblage of rituals and ceremonies. In response to royal weakness, and a spate of princely
assassination attempts, statesmen, judges and clerics constructed a more
coherent picture of monarchical sacrality. In rites of consecration and
interment, court ceremonies and choreographed royal appearances,
there was a stronger emphasis on deification and on the majesty which
distinguished a prince from ordinary mortals.

What happened when the majesty in question was that of the
papal monarch? How did Europe's states and princes negotiate their
new sense of prerogative power with the Counter-Reformed papal
monarchy? Papal secular authority had been fought over in Christendom's most divisive debate before the Protestant Reformation (the
eleventh-century 'Investiture Controversy'). In the period from 1590 to
1630 the issue resurfaced, only this time the result was to foster mistrust
of the papacy among Europe's princes and reinforce the divinity that
hedged kings. The Italian Jesuit Robert Bellarmine furnished persuasive
arguments for the pope's indirect secular power (indirect in the sense
that it was derived from the pope's spiritual authority). His writings
became a focus for critics of papal claims to secular authority in a
succession of high-profile international debates.

The latter began with the papal excommunications of monarchs in
the late sixteenth century, the starting-point for discussions of papal
secular power and the target of Protestant polemic. They continued
through the storm raised by Jesuit writings, justifying tyrannicide under
certain circumstances. Those views were exploited by Gallicans in the
wake of an attempted assassination of the French king, Henry IV, in
1594 (and then the real thing in 1610). The arguments about papal secular power had unexpected outcomes. The counter-case for mistrusting
the ultramontane objectives of the papacy was strengthened. So too was
that for regarding tyrannicide as an act of parricide and desecration.
Bellarmine's apologies for papal indirect power became centrepieces in
controversies over the papal interdict of Venice (1606–10) and the Oath
of Allegiance (1606) required of English subjects in the wake of the
Gunpowder Plot. The resulting polemic brought the English king, James
I, into confrontation with Bellarmine. Another Italian Jesuit, Antonio

Santarelli, took up the cudgels when Bellarmine died. But his treatise on *Heresies, Schismatics ... and the Power of the Roman Pontiff* (1625) was banned and burned in Paris while the Jesuits disavowed its contents. Only in retrospect was it evident that these quarrels had reinforced the divinity of kings and fostered mistrust of papal claims to intervene in secular affairs. Criticism of papal authority, hitherto the preserve of Protestants, now came from prominent Catholics as well.

Humanist conceptions of the Christian commonwealth implied duties and responsibilities for lesser magistrates. The latter also had the power of the sword. They might include the delegates and representatives in Estates and Parliaments or law officers, militia companies, guild-masters and aldermen. But as the intermediaries of the state grew, so did the numbers of those with a stake in the commonwealth. The turmoil of post-Reformation politics had its impact on the way in which such intermediaries envisaged their part in rulership. The comparable experience to the civil wars of the later sixteenth century in Antiquity lay in the Roman empire of the first century AD after Caesar Augustus and in the Peloponnesian War between Athens and Sparta in the fifth century BC. Their historians – Tacitus and Thucydides – taught that, in a world where one could be wrong-footed by events, prudence was the order of the day. Notables (such as Cicero and Quintilian) who had been educated in rhetoric to become tribunes of the people were now urged to see the other side of the coin. Eloquence could inflame people's passions. Speech was the vehicle of demagogy. Rhetoric was appropriate only in republics. Polemic and controversy were the instruments of religious conflict. The role of the notable was to mind his own business, think his own thoughts, distance himself from the populace and demonstrate his obedience to the state.

The model for such behaviour was to be found in the writings of the Stoics, especially Seneca. In the wake of the politico-religious contentions of the later sixteenth century and against the backdrop of the gathering maelstrom in Europe, the Stoics offered an honourable retreat (*otium cum dignitate* being the subject, in fact, of one of Cicero's orations) from the rough and tumble of public affairs into a more private world (a salon, a garden, a *stoa*). There, statesmen, princes and notables would be free to reflect on, express and discuss the Stoic philosophy of mastering the passions (the root of misguided actions by misled common people) through fortitude and solace. These ideas appealed especially to lay notables, and were particularly congenial to those in Calvinist Europe who had been brought up to think of their role as bringing the world of passions into conformity with God's law. Constancy, prudence, taciturnity in the face of criticism, acceptance of the part which one had been asked to play in public life, even if it might demand behaviour which defied traditional morality – these were the values around which the politics of the first half of the seventeenth century turned. They drove some to idealize a retreat from public life even as they inspired others to lead opposition to, and revolt from, authority.

International and domestic politics in the first half of the seventeenth century placed exceptional demands upon rulers' sagacity, requiring them to communicate and negotiate with one another and with their people, while at the same time denying them the experience, opportunities and expectations to do so. It is hardly surprising that, with notable exceptions (Henry IV, Gustav Adolf), they failed the challenge. In addition, there were dynastic hitches caused by royal minorities and the accession of those who were mentally or emotionally challenged by the role which they were expected to play. Europe's mid-seventeenth century paroxysm was the outcome of a deficit of trust and accountability.

THE CRAFT OF STATES

By the early seventeenth century, the term 'state' was beginning to eclipse some lexicons ('commonwealth') or add meaning to others ('realm', 'dominion'). By 1650, 'commonwealth' was more exclusively associated with republics – and (in 'The English Commonwealth', proclaimed after the execution of Charles I) radical change. The French philosopher Jean Bodin belonged to the last French generation before 1789 to use the term 'commonwealth' (*république*) without being embarrassed by its associations with writers who emphasized the accountability of rulers. His was the first generation to suppose that (taking as his target the writings of the Protestant 'monarchomachs') a ruler who was elected or in other ways accountable could not, by definition, be sovereign.

Bodin's *Six Books of the Commonwealth* (1576) began thus: 'A commonwealth is a lawful government of many households and that which is theirs in common, with sovereign power.' He defined sovereignty as 'the absolute and perpetual power of a commonwealth, which the Latins call *majestatem* ... the greatest power to command'. Sovereignty, embodied in the power to make law, was unqualified and indivisible. Although Bodin conceded that the people might be collectively sovereign, that was an impermanent form of rule. His definition of sovereignty pointed inescapably towards singular, monarchical (in Bodin's case, masculine) authority. 'Since after God,' he said, 'there is on earth nothing greater than sovereign princes ... it is necessary to take care of their quality in order that their majesty may be respected and revered in all obedience.' Bodin went further. A sovereign prince is one who is exempt from obedience to the laws of his predecessors and even from his own. Of course, there were limits to that sovereignty. Practically speaking, a sovereign could not confiscate the property of his subjects or break agreements with other sovereigns without committing political suicide. More importantly for this lawyer-philosopher who sought his ultimate truths in the big picture, a sovereign could not set aside the natural law. That was what sanctioned private property and the family. Natural laws were created by divine authority which also legitimated sovereign power. If a sovereign contravened natural law, he would illegitimate his power and become a tyrant.

Bodin encountered critics from the start and answered them in the modified Latin version of his work, published a decade later. For many, however, his notion of sovereignty begged more questions than it answered. Had not Bodin supererogated papal claims to pre-eminence and placed them in the hands of princes? Where did sovereignty leave the privileges and jurisdictions of the Church? Where was Christendom in Bodin's republic? Jesuits Robert Bellarmine and Antonio Possevino attacked his writings as belonging to an emerging category of *politiques*, those who undermined religion from within. Most of his works were placed on the Index of Prohibited Books in 1596. Meanwhile legists in the Holy Roman Empire adapted Bodin's ideas, dressing them up within a framework of public law and Christian traditions. But it was totally implausible for them to understand the empire in terms of a theoretically indivisible sovereignty any more than could their counterparts in the southern Netherlands or in Spain.

In Bodin's native France, however, sovereignty was integrated into the French jurist Charles Loyseau's conception of social hierarchy in his *Treatise on Orders* (1610). In due course, sovereignty sharpened the prerogative rights of the French monarchy. Richelieu's counsellor Cardin Le Bret used it as a legal chisel to chip out the domain rights of the French monarchy in Lorraine. That was where Le Bret served as a royal intendant from 1624 to 1632 (the year his treatise *On the Sovereignty of the King* was first published). In its third recension of 1642, he incorporated into his text the experience he gained as a commissioner in tribunals summoned to convict prominent crown servants of treason. To those on the receiving end of this sharp-edged sword of sovereignty (Henri II, duke of Montmorency, and Louis de Marillac, a French *maréchal*, both executed in 1632 for rebellion; Henri Coiffier de Ruzé, marquis of Cinq-Mars, the king's favourite, ditto in 1642, among others) the state had become a force that the greatest in the land had to reckon with.

Politics was emerging as an academic discipline in its own right, and with a literature to match. Regarded as a branch of moral philosophy through most of the sixteenth century, it began to be taught separately in Protestant Europe in the first half of the seventeenth century and was accorded its own professors. The growth of the 'scientific' literature on politics initially owed a great deal to exponents in the Italian peninsula who, under the guise of studying and commenting on Tacitus, found a way of discussing Machiavelli's ideas without mentioning his name. As one Italian commentator wrote in 1588: 'These political studies have become lately very respectable, and no man thinks that he would be able to gain honour in the world unless he understands the reasons of state ...' The following year, the Piedmontese Jesuit Giovanni Botero published his book *On Reason of State* (*Della Ragion di Stato*), remarking that he was 'greatly astonished [during his travels] to find Reason of State a constant subject of discussion and to hear the opinions of Niccolò Machiavelli and Cornelius Tacitus frequently quoted ...' He drew on his experiences as secretary to Cardinal Carlo Borromeo before entering the service of Charles Emmanuel, duke of Savoy, whose entourage served as a think-tank for the craft of state. Botero defined reason of state as 'knowledge of means capable of founding, keeping and increasing a dominion'. His experience led him to concentrate on princes, and how they hung on to power. Everything depended on the obedience of subjects, which was assured by princely virtue. That virtue was achieved through the science of statecraft, which involved moral and political philosophy, geometry and architecture, and above all history, which taught the rules of prudence.

Taking the Spanish empire and the global Catholic Church as his cue, Botero used comparative economic geography to measure the power of a state. In his *The Causes of Greatness of Cities* (1590) he asked a question which the emerging divergent patterns of growth in Europe made especially relevant: why did human population not grow proportionately to landmass? His answer was that places like northern Italy, France and the Netherlands were 'great' (that is, 'rich'), not because of their natural resources or their political systems but because of the commerce and industry which sustained their populations. Trade was God's gift to humanity, and the oceans were a providential path to universal commerce.

In his *Universal Relations* (completed in 1596) Botero offered a comparative analysis of the power of states, using the model of Venetian ambassadorial reports. He linked the increasing functions of government with the need for regular, extraordinary revenues, but indicated that the latter had to be related to the greatness of the country in question or proportionate to its economic resources. Princely virtue was to be expressed not merely in military prowess but in civil projects which increased a country's riches. His examples included the public works programmes of Italian princes (for example, at Rome under Pope Sixtus V), fostering the local skills' base through state sponsorship, and using tariffs to promote domestic industry. 'Mercantilism' (or, rather, the political economy underlying reason of state) came to be a defining political virtue among armchair state-builders in the age of the Thirty Years War. Botero's works were required reading for the Spanish *arbitristas* and French mercantilists.

Botero's writings had critics as well as followers. Did reason of state not furnish the arguments for the state being above the law? Did it not provide a licence for princes, in the name of the state, to violate religion, honesty and decency? Was it not a passport to princely opportunism, a vehicle for closet Machiavellianism? In 1621, the Venetian Ludovico Zuccolo noted that 'barbers ... and other artisans of the modest sort comment and discuss in their shops and meeting-places on reason of state'. Antoine de Laval, writing in France in 1612, was dismayed to discover that the term was 'frequently on everyone's mouth'. Revealing the hidden and real reasons behind actions undertaken for motives that were presented in other ways became a means to criticize the duplicity of those in power. For Henri, duke of Rohan, writing in self-imposed exile in Venice after his failed leadership of the French Huguenots, all politics boiled down to 'interest': 'princes rule people, and interest rules princes'. 'Interest' (in the sense of 'that which makes a difference to oneself') emerged alongside reason of state as part of the language of politics.

For the Jesuit advisers of Maximilian I, duke of Bavaria, and the publicists of Bethlen Gábor, who justified his allegiance to the Ottomans, his overlords, as a necessary 'opportunity' to consolidate his rule in Hungary, reason of state was a handy vehicle to justify otherwise controversial decisions. Such decisions were taken in accordance with a morality that had to be squared with political necessity, but their logic would remain opaque to those not party to how power worked. In his panegyric of Louis XIII, Guez de Balzac explained in *The Prince* (1631) that when 'saving the[ir] country' from 'slavery' to Protestants or Spanish Habsburgs, necessity 'excuses and justifies everything'. Gabriel Naudé's *Political Considerations on Coups d'état* was published in 1639, though it had been written earlier. Only a few copies were distributed to 'strong minds' (*esprits forts*) who understood that statecraft involved 'a violation of public law for the benefit of the public good'. Duplicity was essential to power and not necessarily immoral. Statecraft meant making alliances with those who were not of the same religion. It was not infidel Turks but Christian princes who used religion as a cover for political ambitions (he cited Henry VIII's revolt from Rome and the massacre of St Bartholomew). 'Reason of state' writings had a double effect. On the one hand, they reinforced popular perceptions that their rulers were not to be trusted. On the other, they epitomized changing political values.

MEN OF BUSINESS, MEN OF STATE

In farewell to the University of Padua after his studies, the Polish nobleman Wawrzyniec Goślicki published a treatise on the Polish Senate, dedicated to King Sigismund II. Shakespeare seems to have fashioned Polonius, the wind-bag senator in *Hamlet*, around its author. Pondering what constituted successful government, Goślicki focused on the interaction between monarch and citizens. 'Some suppose,' he mused, that the welfare of the state 'proceedeth of good laws: others have thought that civill education doth enforme it; others imagined that the temperature of the heavens doth make men apt for civill life; some also do thinke it proceedeth from the endeavour of good Kings'. The Polish king should remember, said Goślicki, that his state rests on the 'publique consent of all the *Polonian* Nation', on men like himself. Goślicki's analysis was not misplaced since the Polish Commonwealth accorded the nobles a major role. They were educated for, and expected to have, the opportunity to be of public service.

The problem was that the assemblies in which notables like Goślicki played that part were being sidelined. Senates, Diets, Estates and Parliaments in all but a few commonwealths found their role diminished or their activities discontinued. In an environment in which sacral kingship, the mystique of monarchy, sovereignty and prerogative rights played an increased part, the place accorded to assemblies whose activities reminded people of the commonwealth ideals was diminished. Instead, princely courts offered an alternative forum and a different ethos for notables. Manuals of etiquette taught notables the rules of civilized decorum at court. Civil life became not about public consent to rule but obedience through attendance, courtesy and the masking of one's true feelings behind flattery or silence.

That said, the opportunities for those who wanted to participate in affairs increased as states became more multifaceted. That was exemplified in both councils and courts – the formal and informal power structures working together coextensively at the power-centres of states. Government by council was an established reality even in monarchies with the most absolutist of pretensions. In the elective monarchies of northern and eastern Europe, the royal council enshrined the aristocracy's participation in power. In the United Provinces of the Netherlands, the twelve members of its Council of State, descending from its Burgundian namesake, became the executive committee of the States General. The burgeoning number of councils led to smaller inner privy councils, specializing in the great affairs of state for which confidentiality was essential. Membership was often predetermined by rank and status. In France, the princes of the blood regarded themselves as council members by right. In Poland, the chancellor, treasurer, commander of the army and the bishops were councillors *ex officio*. To exclude such individuals was to risk the charge of being autocratic, the prisoner of favourites and prey to one voice in counsel to the exclusion of others.

The problem was that of increasing and overwhelming affairs. One way of dealing with it was to allow everyday administration to be handled by 'professionals'. Justice at its highest level was delegated to separate sections of the royal council. In France, its judicial (*conseil d'état privé*) and financial (*conseil d'état et des finances*) branches gradually emerged as separate entities in the second half of the sixteenth century. In the Spanish empire, there were already separate councils for the Inquisition, the military orders and the *Cruzada* (especially levied with papal consent) by the accession of Charles V, who soon added others for war, and then finance. In the German empire and most of its princely territories, the court council (*Hofrat*) spawned judicial courts (*Hofgerichte*), modelled on the imperial Chamber Court. The raising of revenue, handling of indirect taxes, management of debts, payment of servants, nomination of clergy and even diplomacy all became more complex.

Princely councils adapted their membership to include those with professional competence, albeit to different degrees. In the sixteenth century, almost all the members of the Council of Castile were university graduates. In France legally trained Masters of Requests prepared dossiers for the council but its membership was still dominated by nobles. In England and Scotland, experience, capacity, family ties and loyalty continued to be more important than a university education. The tendency was towards collective decision-making. In Spain, permanent councils were supplemented by temporary commissions (*juntas*) on particular issues. Pope Sixtus V followed the Spanish example, formalizing the existence of fifteen councils ('congregations') in January 1588, thereby transforming the cardinals into pontifical administrators.

The growing complexity of government business and council proliferation made coordination necessary, especially when princes were disinclined or unable to fulfil that function themselves. Coordinators functioned at an uneasy interstice between the informal and formal power structures, particularly clearly demonstrated in Rome by the cardinal-nephew, the papal superintendant and viceroy for state and foreign affairs. Scipione Borghese was an archetypical cardinal-nephew, running the papal state for Pope Paul V. From his personal apartments, Borghese chaired administrative congregations, handled patronage, received letters of state and selected which should be read out to the pope. Yet he did not exercise this authority independently, and informal and formal power structures complemented one another. The secretaries staffing the congregations, responsible for drafting letters and memorials on which decisions were made, also saw themselves as members of the Borghese family, loyal to both Pope Paul V and the cardinal-nephew. Scipione Borghese signed the paperwork and ran the apparatus, but he was not singly responsible for its decisions.

In other instances, the coordinating role of favourites grew out of traditional military and judicial offices. In France, the first favourite at the Valois court was Constable Anne de Montmorency. At the court of the Austrian Habsburgs, the equivalent figure was the high steward or court marshal. Elsewhere it was often the chancellor (or the Keeper of the Great Seal), titular head of the judiciary but often responsible for government and administration too. Where favourites owed their influence to proven ability, martial reputation or the rich patrimony of an established noble family they tended to become entrenched in power (Count Oxenstierna in Sweden, Cardinal Richelieu in France, Count-Duke Olivares in Spain). Competent favourites had their own favourites, their personal entourages being a means to secure their position. Their servants included secretaries of state and members of the aristocracy. Richelieu's critics called the secretaries of the French state his *créatures*; the young aristocrats whom Count-Duke Olivares groomed for service were known as *hechuras*, his clients as *olivaristas*.

There was a logic to the increasing prevalence of favourites in European states from the end of the sixteenth century. As Francis Bacon (a favourite himself) observed, the more kings distanced themselves from their subjects, the more they craved friends: 'For princes, in regard of the distance of their fortune from that of their subjects and servants, cannot gather this fruit, except ... they raise some persons to be, as it were companions and almost equals to themselves.' The English playwright Ben Jonson portrayed the rise of the favourite as the inevitable result of undermining the commonwealth in favour of absolute rule. Tacitus was the source for his play *Sejanus His Fall* (1603), in which Tiberius's favourite utilizes the underhand guile of reason of state in order to become the emperor's heir before hostile public opinion and a spy engineer his gruesome end. To Jonson's near-contemporary Christopher Marlowe, homosexual infatuation explained the rise of Piers Gaveston, the 'night-grown mushrump' in *The Troublesome Raigne and lamentable death of Edward II* (1594). This was a glance at the French court of Henry III, whose emotional dependence on a succession of *mignons* was crudely portrayed by Catholic League critics as sexual deviance. Jonson's target was the court of James I, where the king's grooming of attractive young men was evident. Contemporaries could hardly ignore it and the correspondence between the king and his own *mignons* (Robert Carr, earl of Somerset – to 1615; then George Villiers, duke of Buckingham) suggests more than dalliance.

Favourites needed to maintain the monarch's confidence. Ambassadorial correspondence describes the familiarities (smiles, bows, courtesies, lavish gifts, shared passions …) whose flow secured their ascendancy and put paid to their critics. These were never far away – especially since the targets of their disapproval were responsible for the execution of controversial policies and made themselves wealthy through the outsourcing of state power to private contractors. Rivals engineered the fall of favourites through whispering campaigns, focusing the increasing mistrust of those in power upon a particular individual. A royal frown raised questions; not being invited to a notable public event or to attend council was proof that disgrace had occurred, whether or not a favourite occupied an office of state. James I's favourite Robert Carr was imprisoned in 1615 after a scandal involving the murder of his friend Sir Thomas Overbury. George Villiers, duke of Buckingham, escaped impeachment by Parliament but courted unpopularity for his incompetent foreign expeditions and corruption, and was assassinated. Thomas Wentworth, earl of Strafford, ran the gauntlet of the many enemies he had made in his administration of Ireland in the 1630s, his impeachment on a charge of treason being the first scalp claimed by the Long Parliament in the Bill of Attainder (April 1641). Strafford was assured of Charles's support: 'upon the word of a king, you shall not suffer in life, honour or fortune'. A month later, the king assented to his execution under the threat of popular insurrection. Yet Strafford was initially accorded the luxury of an impeachment. Not so Louis XIII's Italian favourite Concino Concini, assassinated on the king's orders outside the Louvre in April 1617. His body was exhumed the following day by the Parisian crowd, ritually hanged from the gibbet at the Pont Neuf before hands, hair, beard and genitals were cut off, what remained of his body being dragged round the streets before being fed to dogs. Naudé thought such excess prevented this from being a perfect *coup d'état*.

The significance of secretaries of state underlined another dynamic within European states. Decisions were increasingly registered and conveyed in written and printed forms. Great matters of state continued to be registered under a Great Seal. The change came through papers issued under the ruler's privy (or personal) seal. Letters of commission, contracts, nominations to offices, permissions, verifications and passports – such documents lay at the heart of the relationship between Europe's political élites and its governing entities. The paperwork represented a dramatic rise of power at a distance. Almost 6,000 letters of Catherine de Médicis have survived – a fragment of an estimated 30,000 original missives. When she complained to Henry of Navarre about the burden, he retorted bluntly: 'you thrive on this work'. Philip II, too, laboured at his documents into the night, reading despatches and writing or dictating his replies, complaining of exhaustion, eye troubles and headaches. In May 1579, for example, he received 1,200 petitions. His secretary Mateo Vázquez de Leca reported the complaint of the king that he had to sign 400 letters a day. Couriers and postal services were as important as military garrisons in the governing structures of Europe. The threat of being swamped by paper dictated the need for a favourite and pointed the way towards subcontracting as much state business as possible.

The archives of Europe's states were transformed from repositories of charters to arsenals of state authority. The change was not the result of foresight. More often than not over-ambitious projects led to disorderly, half-abandoned solutions. In the case of the papal archives, Pope Pius V wanted the chaotic paperwork in the Castel Sant'Angelo organized, recopied and installed in the apostolic palace – an archive for the monarch of global Catholicism. That was akin to instructions issued by Philip II in 1561 to his newly appointed archivist to create a central repository for his empire, or to Elizabeth I's establishment in 1578 of the Public Record Office. By the early seventeenth century, most states could boast an archive. That paperwork, which is what has tended to survive, reinforces an impression of the institutional weight of the state, even though it was the less documented princely court which remained of central significance to the dynamics of politics and rule.

MAKING THE JUSTICE-STATE WORK

A good prince delivered justice. The reality was not as simple as that. A plethora of local jurisdictions lay in private (seigneurial, ecclesiastical, communal) hands. In general, justice was local, cheap and unprofessional (open to favour and worse); or it was distant, expensive and professional. There was no shortage of demands for justice. The mounting case-loads and burgeoning complaints about delays and legal chicanery were, in part, the result of the pressure from below and towards the state to settle the disputes which a less face-to-face society, regulated in new ways and at a distance by paper, created. The problem was that people's aspirations were mutually incompatible: a local system of justice that was both professional and cheap.

States could multiply the number of royal tribunals to bring professional justice within the reach of localities and expand the kinds of cases they handled. By 1650, there were more magistrates, offering justice in the prince's name, than there had been in 1520. The judicial sector grew; but the more it grew, the less 'public' it was. In the duchy of Bavaria, for example, the modest 162 individuals on the duchy's payroll in Munich in 1508 grew to 866 by 1571. In France about 7–8,000 office-holders in justice and finance worked for the king in 1515. By 1665, this had grown to a corps of about 80,000. In most of Protestant Europe, Church courts were abolished and secular magistrates became the law-givers in ecclesiastical matters. But the majority of these officials, especially in France, had purchased their posts and, by the early seventeenth century, the reversion of their offices (the right to sell them on to a person of their choice). Judicial and financial offices were equally sold to wealthy competitors in Rome and in some of the smaller states. Office-holders came to regard their salaries as interest on the capital they had paid into the state's coffers.

Another way to expand the reach of princely justice was to codify customary laws. Customary law developed widely in medieval Europe, especially in areas where Roman law was not taken as the basis for the justice offered in local jurisdictions. States encouraged magistrates to harmonize and publish customs. The increasing importance accorded to princely edicts was a response to the demand for reform in societies where greater mobility, and living within broader spheres of influence, created demands for social regulation in new ways. Aspirations for reform touched on major aspects of public living – from the price of foodstuffs to the regulation of clothing and the control of prostitution. There was an obsessive concern with managing everything that moved: goods, prices, diseases, heretics and vagrants. That meant creating local inspectors, controllers and certifiers – but their offices, too, were typically sold off or farmed out to a contractor. That 'police' ordinances were often reissued was less a sign of their failure than of the educative power of legislation. This was the golden age of the 'justice-state', intrusive in people's lives.

Most ambitiously of all, Europe's rulers received petitions from their subjects and offered redress on the basis of equity. Jean Bodin made equity a cornerstone of sovereignty, whose majesty was reflected in the power to answer petitions from subjects with prudence and mercy, reflecting the divine law of which the prince was the embodiment. French monarchs expanded the competence and utilization of Masters of Requests, magistrates who received petitions on the king's behalf and reported on the equity of the case to the royal council. In Florence, the first duke of Tuscany, Cosimo I, encouraged subjects to write to him directly if they experienced problems with the law. He saw it as limiting corruption and presenting himself as the champion of the people. A sculpture, commissioned from Vicenzio Danti in 1564 and placed in the duchy's newly constructed state offices (the Uffizi), depicted Cosimo with, to one side, a male figure representing law ('Rigour'), and to the other, a female statue holding a measuring rule ('Equity'). The requests came from ordinary people, phrased as appeals to the prince's clemency in such a way that equity became a school in which the duke's subjects learned the language of obedience and deference to the state. Making a speech in 1616 before the English Star Chamber, King James I praised the equity court of Chancery as an extension of his God-given rule, 'the dispenser of the Kings Conscience, following always the intention of Law and Iustice . . . in this it exceeds other courts, mixing Mercie with Iustice'. For the early Stuarts, as for other princes in the early seventeenth century, justice was equated with exercising a prerogative and prudential power, exclusively that of the sovereign.

NERVES OF STATE

This was also the first age of the 'finance-state'. Fiscal extraction expanded to hitherto undreamed-of levels and long-term borrowing became an established reality. The establishment of tax-states was a slow process. Aristocrats lived off their domains. At the beginning of the sixteenth century princes were expected to do likewise. In places, some rulers still did so. In the Danish Oldenburg state, the Landgravate of

Hesse, Sweden – wherever the money economy was thin – the country-side was divided up into areas around a castle which acted as the focal point for collecting revenues in kind and cash. Part of the cash surplus went forward to the royal treasury. In northern Europe domain-extraction even increased for a while by the impact of the Reformation and the absorption of former ecclesiastical domains into royal hands. What dribbled into the central treasury, however, was limited. Domain-based revenues meant bullying officials into presenting better accounts, and organizing warehouses to store and sell the surplus. The other option was to alienate (or 'privatize') the domain into private hands in return for a one-off payment or a regular return.

Taxation was an opportunity for states to tap into the economic growth of the sixteenth century. In Denmark this involved the revenues from the Sound Tolls at the entrance to the Baltic (which gave the Danish monarchy a unique tax security) along with excise taxes on the sale of beer (*Cise*). In Hesse, the limits of domain-extraction were reached in the 1550s when the Landgrave's debt reached a million florins or ten times its annual income. The result was the creation of a repartition tax on a personal basis, nobles as well as non-nobles, and the introduction of excise taxes, which (as in Denmark) proved a money-spinner. Where we can measure it, taxes rose and (even taking inflation into account) sometimes spectacularly so.

Castile, the fiscal heartland of the Spanish Habsburg dynastic empire, saw its overall revenues (including those from New World silver) increase from around 1 million ducats in 1522 to about 10 million ducats in 1598 (around 500 tons of silver). In France, the receipts to the treasury increased from about 3.46 million *livres* in 1523 to 17.6 million *livres* in 1599 (more than 200 tons of silver, over 70 per cent of the value of the silver imports from the New World). In Austrian Habsburg lands the establishment of the tax-state occurred late in the sixteenth century when the Long Turkish War pushed taxes up sixfold. The levies in Austria and the Tyrol alone totalled the equivalent of 6.6 tons of silver per annum by the early seventeenth century. Even privileged cities such as Augsburg or Nuremberg experienced a rise in fiscality – the taxation in the latter reached the equivalent of 8.1 tons per annum in some years. In the kingdom of Naples, revenues rose from not far short of 440,000 Neapolitan gold ducats in the early sixteenth century to around 2.5 million ducats in 1595 (the equivalent of 42 tons of silver). The English monarchy, where most taxation was a matter of negotiation with the Parliament, also experienced a modest real increase in revenue in the sixteenth century. Nor were such increases limited to princely territories. The revenues of republican Venice rose from about 1.5 million Venetian gold ducats in 1500 to 2.45 in 1600 (the equivalent of 66 tons per annum of silver). The Papal States, too, became a significant fiscal-state. The growth in public credit in the sixteenth century would have been impossible without such rises. The interest payments on that credit meant that princes were not better off but their states became bigger enterprises.

The tax-state was consolidated in the first half of the seventeenth century, especially among the belligerents in the Thirty Years War. Castile's revenues climbed from 10 million ducats in 1598 to 18 million in 1654. France was the most precocious fiscal-state of all. According to the accounts presented at its council of state and finance, income grew to an astronomical level at the beginning of its direct military intervention in the Thirty Years War in 1635 – over 2,200 tons of silver and a notional 20 per cent of the country's grain production. In the Dutch Republic, taxation reached a peak in the 1630s and 40s. In Denmark, the tax-state became a significant feature in people's lives for the first time. In 1629–43, the annual amount raised in taxes was twice as great as in the period of 1600–1614, of which nearly two thirds was spent on the permanent army, and much of the rest on the navy.

There were only a few exceptions to the general consolidation of the tax-state in the first half of the seventeenth century. In the case of Poland-Lithuania, the union cemented at Lublin kept revenues and expenditures separate. In Lithuania, the domain was state property rather than the king's. Supposed to support the costs of the state, it failed to do so. Instead, it was pledged against loans and leased out to nobles in return for low rents. When, in the wake of the Swedish invasion of Estonia and Livonia (in whose survival the Lithuanians had the greatest interest), the leaseholders were persuaded to pay more (the *kwarta* – introduced in 1633) to a new state treasury, the Lithuanians ensured that there was no inspection of domains and the proceeds remained minimal. In the face of the crisis of the Cossack insurgency of 1648, the Lithuanians, who did not usually fund the costs of campaigns in the south, did reluctantly accept an emergency hearth tax and higher excise dues, but this was hugely resented.

The state's major revenue streams came from Poland. But chronic monetary instability in the early seventeenth century (the intrinsic value of the Polish silver coin dropped by 41 per cent in the years from 1604 to 1623), exacerbated by the collapse of the international grain market following the outbreak of warfare in the Baltic and Germany, undermined its receipts. As in Lithuania, the majority of the royal domain was leased out at low rents to the nobility, from which the Polish Sejm reluctantly granted the *kwarta* in 1633. But its leaseholders paid only token amounts and only a small proportion (about 15 per cent) of the domain (the so-called 'table' estates, treated as prerogative revenues) turned in a significant return. So the Polish monarchy increasingly depended on extraordinary taxes granted by the Sejm, the most significant of which was a land tax, based on a land survey carried out in 1563. Although Polish kings attempted to use the military crises of the Swedish and Muscovite wars to instigate reforms, they were controversial, created distrust of the monarch, and were never carried out because Lithuanian and Ruthenian magnates and nobles knew that, if a new land survey were conducted, it would expose the extent to which they were not contributing. The only alternatives were revenue expedients (among them, a hearth tax and a 'winter-bread' (*hiberna*) levy) but their financial returns were outweighed by their political costs to the stability of the Commonwealth. The introduction of an excise on beer, vodka and wine in 1629 as a wartime measure was the most promising expedient but the divisions it created were so great that its introduction was only possible as a local levy from which the crown saw none of the proceeds. The 1648 Cossack rebellion exposed the fatal political and fiscal fragilities of the Commonwealth.

In England, too, the tax-state languished in the early seventeenth century. In 1603, James I inherited an English treasury that was solvent. The crown lands offered considerable potential for additional sources of revenue and the customs, the largest source of royal revenue, did not yield their full potential. Like the Polish-Lithuanian Commonwealth, the British monarchy kept the revenues and expeditures of its three kingdoms separate. Although Ireland never paid for itself, Scotland just about managed to, and the major burdens of state were expected to be carried by England. But, as in Poland, that created political problems. The larger court which the regal union demanded, not to mention the place in Europe which its scale now invited, expanded expenditures and created debts which were criticized by English Parliaments when they met. The determined efforts to manage royal finances and cut costs by Lord Treasurer Lionel Cranfield in 1617–24 only reduced the annual deficit to £160,000 at the end of James I's reign. In the meantime, because of the way that the English monarchy paid its servants (offering them the opportunity to enjoy fees, pensions and annuities) such zeal to control expenditure merely increased the impressions of corruption.

The accumulating debts of the British monarchy were managed through the farm of the customs to various courtiers who headed up merchant syndicates, and through hiving off prerogative functions and revenues to contractors. The attempts at radical change failed, most notably in the 'Great Contract' of 1610, when king and Commons nearly reached an agreement to abolish some prerogative revenues in return for a guaranteed annual financial sum from Parliament. The negotiations failed because the political will was lacking on both sides, but the principles were revived in 1621, 1626 and again in 1641. The Stuarts were reluctant to sacrifice prerogatives which embodied a high conception of monarchy. Parliament-men were not sure how to levy an annual tax, knew that they would face criticism from the constituencies for doing so, and were more than half-persuaded by the ambient criticisms of a corrupt court.

In the 1620s, the Stuarts sought, as was usual, to fund their modest and ill-judged military interventions in the Thirty Years War by calling on Parliaments for assistance. MPs were shocked at the amounts they were being asked to pay, but military costs had risen much faster than the limited English experience of the changed realities of continental war had prepared them for. In addition, although the Parliaments of 1621, 1624, 1625 and 1628 were generous by their own lights (that of 1628 granted five subsidies, more than Elizabeth I had dared ask of her Parliaments in the 1590s), the results were of increasingly less value to the Stuarts. The 1628 subsidies were worth £275,000, in return for which the Parliament demanded that the king raise no revenues except the ones he was legally entitled to. But that sum was nowhere near the million pounds that the king needed. A subsidy was, like the Polish land tax, notionally a tax on the annual value of a person's land. As with the Polish Sejm, English Parliaments did not control the assessment of the subsidies they voted, and the fall in yield – from £130,000 in the middle of Elizabeth's reign to £55,000 – reflected inflation, increased population mobility and the reality that, in a system of local self-government, prominent individuals could not be challenged to pay their share. As the financial returns from holding a Parliament diminished in the 1620s, so their political costs grew, since their debates increasingly focused not on how to raise revenue but on fundamental laws in Church and state, culminating in the Petition of Right (7 June 1628). Agreed by both Lords and Commons and ratified by a reluctant king, it attempted to restrict non-Parliamentary taxation, forced billeting of soldiers, imprisonment without cause and the use of martial law.

Disengaging from the Thirty Years War, Charles I raised money in the 1630s as best he could. Like his Polish counterparts, he resorted to revenue expedients based on his prerogative rights. This enabled him to raise forced loans and grant patents for monopolies on producing or selling goods, a slippery slope (very, in the case of the soap monopoly) towards an excise. In 1630, he dusted down his entitlement to fine people who had not been knighted at the coronation – a successful wheeze, raising the equivalent of two and a half subsidies. Similarly, he exploited his rights to enforce the laws designed to protect the forests. But, as the Venetian ambassador observed in 1635, these were 'false mines for obtaining money, because they are good for once only, and states are not maintained by such devices'.

Charles's other expedient was 'Ship Money', a prerogative levy to expand the navy that was apportioned out to county sheriffs, whose responsibility was to negotiate its payment by local parties as seemed equitable. That resulted in rating disputes, for (as a contemporary remarked) 'in every place there are some malevolent spirits that labour to poison and censure . . . blasting this for an imposition, an innovation against the liberty of the subject'. The imposition was initially successful, apparently giving the lie to a sense of deepening resentments towards the Stuarts in England during Charles's Personal Rule – the eleven years between 1629 and 1640 when he ruled without recourse to Parliament. Yet there were warning signs of organized resistance. A Puritan network, based in East Anglia but embracing the Buckinghamshire gentleman John Hampden and the earl of Bedford, existed through meetings of the Providence Island Company. They sought leave to challenge the legality of the writ and, in 1637, Charles I allowed Hampden's case to be heard in the Exchequer. Hampden's counsel included Oliver St John, legal adviser to the earls of Warwick and Bedford. St John argued that if, as the writ claimed, there was an emergency then (given the time-frame since its issuance) the king should have summoned a Parliament to deal with it. Hampden's other lawyer challenged prerogative right more generally. On the latter the king won the case. Chief Justice Finch declared that 'no acts of Parliament make any difference' to the king's prerogative power to raise money for the defence of the realm.

The case, far from stiffening the sinews of resistance, did not disrupt the continuing collection of the levy. Only in the context of the Bishops' War in Scotland (1639), with its competing demands upon localities to levy and equip troops for the army, did the grievances of the 1628 Petition of Right resurface and the Privy Council's grip on the levy of Ship Money falter. By then, however, Charles's failure to achieve solvency through prerogative revenue-raising was completely exposed. In 1639, £328,000 of future receipts had been anticipated, bills went unpaid and (with the death or bankruptcy of his leading lenders) his financial backers were reduced to the customs farmers and his own servants (Laud and Strafford).

Indirect taxes on foodstuffs, wine, beer and salt were favoured innovations around council tables for new revenue streams since they could be seen as prerogative rights and it was said that they were paid for by outsiders or hidden in the sale price of a product. The Swedish chancellor, Axel Oxenstierna, declared that such taxes were 'pleasing to God, hurtful to no man, and not provocative of rebellion'. People were not easily fooled. Single-product excise duties were effective where a prerogative right could be claimed and where there were commodities of high value and resilient demand in buoyant economies. But when they were on commodities of lower value in cash-poor environments, and introduced with more dubious legality, they caused revolt. Taxes on salt were a tried and tested part of the finance-states of Genoa and Venice among others. But in the central regions of France salt taxes worked by demanding people make compulsory purchases of the product. The result was widespread fraud and periodic revolt against the hated *gabelles*. In the Spanish peninsula, too, the introduction of excise duties in the 1630s provoked provincial rebellion. The Dutch Republic was the first to move towards an excise – it may have invented the word – on a range of goods. In its urbanized environment, it formed a fiscal basis to the new regime. When France followed its example with a *pancarte* (so-called from the tariffs that were posted at the entry to main towns), it provoked a revolt and was withdrawn in 1602, and only cautiously reintroduced as a wartime measure later on in 1640. In England, too, Charles I's efforts to expand state revenues on the basis of the prerogative rights in the 1630s resulted in a groundswell of resentment.

Fiscal innovations relied on stronger administrative structures for tax-raising, even though much of the collection still happened in local communities. They required new officials, treasurers and accountants. In France, a new officer (the *trésorier de l'épargne*) was established in 1523, flanked by treasurers of finance, and (from 1542) by sixteen regional treasury offices (*généralités*). In Habsburg Spain, the central financial council (*Consejo de Hacienda*) had powers over Castilian revenues, separate councils being responsible for overseeing the revenue-raising in other kingdoms and principalities. Thanks to the skills of the *Hacienda* its budgets were remarkably accurate. Spanish treasurers held together complex financial operations over large distances, dealing with colossal sums of money. Despite not having a centralized treasury, they kept track of income and expenditure, knew the consolidated and floating debts of the empire and recognized when things were getting out of hand.

Despite this strengthening of state officialdom, the consolidation of the fiscal-state was mainly achieved by the contracting out of revenue-raising and expenditure. Salt taxes, customs duties and excises – but also the provisioning of princely courts and armies – were leased out to consortia of tax-farmers and providers on a contractual basis. Tax-farming guaranteed revenues in ready money. In some states, it gave courtiers or others around the prince an opportunity for manipulation and bribery when arranging the lease. Above all, the resources could be anticipated as a loan while the burden of collecting tax was passed on to those (consortia typically included wealthy merchants and officials) who had the access to the money and the experience to handle the complicated operations of tax-collection in liaison with local agents. The downside was that tax-farming left the state at a degree removed from what was being levied in its name, not able to calculate (let alone diminish) the profits made by the tax-farmers in question while suffering from the unpopularity among the public at large which its perceived rapacity created.

By the first half of the seventeenth century, contracting out was a fact of life. Along with the consolidation of the finance-state went the broadening of the numbers of people engaged in contracting operations. By

1650, the 60,000 or more office-holders of the French state were complemented by the hundreds of contractors (*partisans* – those who had signed
a *parti*, or contract) and thousands of agents (*commis*) operating for
them. Contracts furnished the state with money, credit and expertise, but
they were arrived at in a complex, secretive and surreal world. Although
tax-farming contracts were officially auctioned to the highest bidder, the
contractor-financiers operated under assumed names, and ensured that
there was either only one tender or none at all. The French government
was engaged in a perpetual cat-and-mouse game in time of war, forced to
ensure a flow of funds by making deals with tax-farmers who became, at
the same time, its lenders. The legal mechanism for investigating their
peculation was known as a 'justice tribunal' (*chambre de justice*) but it
could not be instigated during an emergency lest those whom it was
established to prosecute ceased to lend money to the state. Although the
financiers' transactions were secret, they flaunted their wealth in lavish
Parisian town-houses and lifestyles. The more contractor-financiers were
a law unto themselves the more significant the boundaries between the
public and the private became to their critics and the more the gap
between the French capital and its provinces opened up. Their opponents
called them 'snakes' and 'blood-suckers'. Their critics grew more numerous and vocal as the precariousness of the contractor-financier pyramid
of debts and obligations became more evident.

Spanish subcontracting of its fiscal operations to financiers through
asientos was already well established. So, too, was its periodic inability
to meet its contractual obligations, resolved by suspensions of payments
on its contracts (bankruptcies). As the Spanish monarchy's debts coagu-
lated under the fiscal pressures of the Thirty Years War, so its efforts to
find ways of keeping the empire financially afloat grew more desperate.
A further bankruptcy in 1627 was accompanied by a debasement of the
currency in order to devalue government debts. In addition, Olivares
brought into the Spanish contractual system some new players –
Portuguese-Jewish business families, resident in Seville and Madrid, who
had cash reserves from their Far East, Brazilian and northern European
operations. Olivares tempted them in by issuing pardons for relapses
into Judaism before 1626, guaranteeing them immunity from the confiscation of their investments by the Inquisition, and giving them offices
within the *Hacienda*. He then played them off against the Genoese
financiers with whom they came to share the burden of financing the

Spanish monarchy in the 1630s. By the early 1640s, the collapse of Spanish fiscality was imminent as all rents and taxes were committed twice over for at least five years in the future. Repayment of capital debt ceased and those on interest payments were threatened. The real value of revenues in Castile and elsewhere diminished as the impact of harvest failures and demographic decline affected southern Europe. From the mid-1640s, silver imports from the New World also shrank in volume and value. New taxes were politically impossible in an empire where provincial revolt became endemic in the 1640s. The solvency of the New Christian Portuguese bankers was undermined by Spanish military and naval disasters in the Atlantic. In 1645, as a *conversos* firm in Madrid failed, others refused to lend more money to the government. The Peace of Westphalia was accompanied by a double Spanish bankruptcy (1647, 1652) in which Portuguese and Genoese bankers faced ruin.

The French fiscal-state was the most precocious in the first half of the seventeenth century and its evolution offers the starkest example of these broader processes at work. Offices and annuities formed the core of the constituted debt of the French monarchy. The sale of royal posts was already very extensive and institutionalized in the French kingdom by 1600, but reached new intensities in the period of the cardinal-ministers (Richelieu, 1624–42; Mazarin, 1642–61). New categories of office were invented, some were 'semesterized' so that two or three people could share the same job and senior judicial posts were put up for sale. Critics of these measures drew on the ideals of the Christian commonwealth to declare that justice was being sold and the state corrupted. In 1604, the right to inherit offices was also turned into a tax (and known as the 'Paulette' after the first person to whom the tax-farm was contracted). The sale of annuities through the Paris municipality underwent a transformation as its administrators' offices were put up for sale. That paradoxically removed any pretence that the *rentes* were being issued by a body that was independent of the state. By the 1640s, tax-farming embraced all the revenues of the French state including the *tailles*. In 1637, tax-farmers were given discretion over which assignations on particular receipts should be honoured, and which should not – thereby giving them power to determine what happened to revenue inflows. The payments of interest on *rentes*, like officers' salaries, fell further into arrears – those for the last quarter of 1635, the year that France entered the Thirty Years War, were eventually paid as it signed the Peace of the Pyrenees in 1659. In the looking-glass world of French finances in the 1630s and 40s, taxes had never been so high, but the state coffers had never been so empty.

As the demands for war finance became more desperate, so the recourse to short-term loans at high interest rates increased. The interest on loans was paid through mechanisms (*comptants*) which bypassed scrutiny through the accounting processes of the French monarchy. The loans came from fortunes which had been made at the expense of the state to which they would then be re-lent. Even Richelieu and Mazarin themselves participated in lending money to the state, for which they too were handsomely rewarded. Richelieu's *créatures* included key figures in the extraordinary financial machine, individuals upon whom he could rely for their loyalty and discretion. State sovereignty became a legal coach-and-horses legitimation, justifying forced loans and allowing intendants sweeping powers in justice and finance to suppress provincial and popular revolts.

In various regions of France, peasants went into open revolt against tax-farmers. In places like Rouen, Bordeaux and Provence, the regime's opponents included magistrates whose investments in royal offices and *rentes* had been compromised and local nobles who were alienated from the Paris-led financial merry-go-round. The French thinker Blaise Pascal spent the early 1640s in the Auvergne in 'honourable retreat' because his father had been a party to the revolt of Parisian *rentiers* of March 1638, and been forced into refuge to avoid reprisals. The budgets presented to the French council of state and finances were imaginary figments, reflecting financing contracting and the manipulation of power which sustained it. Parisian magistrates attempted to resist these innovations in a movement of legal opposition short of rebellion which then turned into the revolt of the Fronde, and their actions coincided with an undeclared bankruptcy in the French state.

The Dutch fiscal experience was different from that of France. Although the United Provinces was a tiny state it was subjected to similar demands to raise unprecedented taxation for war. The Dutch participated in almost every anti-Habsburg coalition in the Thirty Years War. They supported the Bohemian rebels in 1618. The Elector Palatine, Frederick V, took his court into exile at The Hague. When the Spanish launched their offensive in 1625, the Dutch led the anti-Habsburg alliance involving Denmark. In 1624, their coalition included the French and, from 1630, Sweden. Dutch armies, navies and garrisons were more sustained and significant in comparison to its population than those of France. But there was no bankruptcy, and outsourcing and subcontracting were kept in check. The deputies in the States General distributed the burdens of taxation agreed at a federal level around the provinces by means of quotas. Excises were farmed on yearly contracts but the accounting procedures were not bypassed. When the customs were briefly farmed out in 1625, opponents in the Estates of Holland successfully challenged the experiment with complaints about the profits of the consortium concerned and its illegal actions.

Provincial Estates introduced a great variety of taxes and at high rates. In Holland, the tax burden per head increased by 21 per cent between 1621 and 1650. In Leiden, 60 per cent of the price of beer, 25 per cent of the price of bread and 14 per cent of the price of meat went in tax. But the number of open protests was limited to a major disturbance following the new impost on butter in 1624 and some unrest in Frisia in 1637. Above all, the long-term debt was written out as permanent and transferable rents and life-time annuities. Much of it was borne by the 'generality', i.e. by the States as a whole, which meant that the low rates of interest in the core of the republic (Holland, Utrecht and Zeeland) were shared by them all. Because it was shared out on a quota basis, the public debt of Holland, the largest state, increased the most. By 1648, estimates of its total amount ranged between 125 million and 147 million guilders – more than thirty times its size in 1618. Yet there was no bankruptcy.

The first Receivers-General of the Union came from the Doubleth family – émigré merchants from Mechelen. Their house at Voorhout in The Hague, near the Binnenhof, where the States General met, served as the state's unofficial treasury. They too made a fortune from putting their business acumen and willingness to take risks to the benefit of the state. They were accused of corruption by deputies at the Estates. Their books from the year 1618 had still not been accepted for audit a decade later. The provincial Estates and the States General kept a realistic eye on what was happening in the state's finances. In the end, it was the dispersed nature of the political and financial institutions of the United Provinces which inspired investors with confidence. That, coupled with the economic good fortune of the Netherlands, ensured that interest rates remained low. Subscribers were ready to lend money to the state. High taxation as a result of war was not necessarily the agent of crisis in mid-seventeenth-century European politics.

Rulers in the early seventeenth century liked to boast about their financial and military power. In reality, both depended heavily upon infra-state financial apparatuses associated with political will. The English ambassador reported how Henry IV led him along the embankment in Paris between the Louvre and the Arsenal 'vaunting' that he had the military hardware at one end and the treasure at the other to fight 'even to the end of a very long war'. Duke Charles Emmanuel of Savoy told Henry on his visit to Paris in 1601 that the distinction between Savoy and Piedmont was that 'I get out of Savoy what I can, and from Piedmont what I want.' Bavarian Duke Maximilian I was baffled that he managed to extract so much from his territories in 1632, reflecting that it would have been impossible for his predecessors to have achieved it. The business of states was that of money, what Cicero had described as the 'nerves of the state' (*pecunia nervus rerum*). The hard-edged reality of the Leviathan states was the recognition that, as Duke Maximilian had put it in 1611: 'a prince who is not wealthy at times of adversity has neither authority nor reputation. If he loses these, the management of public affairs will collapse.'

THE BUSINESS OF WAR

Military change profoundly affected Europe's states. It is sometimes called a 'military revolution', although that does not adequately delineate the chain-reactions, occurring over a long time-frame, which transformed the way that states defended themselves. What began in Italy in the fifteenth century was still being felt in the early eighteenth century. An arms race, unleashed in part by the way in which firearms and artillery affected the conduct of war, changed what soldiers wore, the equipment they carried, and the training and preparation that they needed. It transformed the role of the cavalry and its tactics. It altered the wounds they inflicted on one another and their chances of being killed. Firearms produced a step-change in the capital investment upon war. Weapons had to be purchased and stockpiled. Stronger fortifications required more investment in fixed-capital structures, which entailed maintenance and year-round garrisoning. Stronger fortifications meant longer sieges, stretching normal campaigning beyond the summer season and the equipment required. There was an equivalent arms race at sea, resulting from mounting guns on ships and a consequential shift in tactics to a style of combat based on firepower, similar to that used by artillery in sieges.

The visible result of military change was fortifications whose traces still mark the European landscape – distinctive arrow-headed bastions of earth, the lowest parts reinforced in stone or brick to prevent the ramparts from being degraded, with outer-works known as ravelins (triangular), horns (twin-pointed) and crowns designed to deliver a curtain of fire upon would-be besiegers. Engineers were in demand, lured by projects and rewards from one prince to another as states increased their protection with the latest designs of fortified strongholds. Military manuals in the early seventeenth century were replete with ballistic details. Growing international tensions in Europe in the early seventeenth century are reflected in the thousands of miles of newly constructed or modernized fortresses. They included those built by engineers for Henry IV's head of fortifications (the duke of Sully) from Savoy to Picardy on the French frontiers. Engineers for the Dutch Republic and the Spanish Habsburgs built defensive lines along the rivers in the Netherlands and in the lower Rhineland. The Austrian Habsburgs countered those built by the Ottomans across the Hungarian plain.

The importance of these fortresses in contributing to a military revolution can be exaggerated. Sieges were long and complicated affairs, expensive in materials and lives. Artillery was cumbersome and only fired mortar rounds slowly. As in naval warfare, the mobilization for siege warfare was a hostage to fortune. French commanders in the Thirty Years War found themselves committed by strategists in Paris to sieges which absorbed massive resources, the limited strategic gains being offset by a failure to hold a stronghold somewhere else. Shrewd military commanders in the Thirty Years War and English Civil War avoided sieges. What mattered was operational effectiveness, and for that the military equivalent of subcontracting was an important way for states to provide well-trained and reliable troops, feed and pay them, and motivate them to undertake the arduous route-marches and campaigns which the attritional warfare of the Thirty Years War demanded. Military 'devolution' (outsourcing) was as important as military 'revolution'.

The resort to mercenaries to supplement the resources of a prince was well established, especially on the frontiers of Christendom, where the empty political spaces were occupied by militarized groups (such as Cossacks, Uzkoks and others) which had a tradition of combining raiding and piracy. Privateering was an established way of contracting for naval forces. *Condottieri* from leading families in the Italian peninsula (the Sforza, the Gonzaga) furnished forces to the Habsburg and Valois combatants in the Italian Wars, their contracts sometimes including a retainer (*condotta in aspetto*) to ensure that their men were held in readiness for another campaign. The best-trained forces of sixteenth-century Europe were its mercenaries. The Swiss infantry forged the technique of organizing a defensive square of soldiers with halberds, protected by a fringe of pikemen. That, in turn, was adopted by the Spanish *tercio* and German *Landsknechte*. The latter were mercenary soldiers, raised through the Holy Roman Empire by smaller German territorial princes and nobles whose units were then contracted out to princes. The effectiveness of the Swiss infantry squares depended on skills that were spread through the companies, coupled with leadership.

Those qualities were acquired by experience. Swiss soldiers were recruited from close-knit peasant communities, comrades staying together in their contingents. Their commanders came from families where military service was regarded as an honourable career. The double-pay pikemen at the flanks of the companies were especially crucial to their solidity under fire. The *Landsknechte* had a more diverse basis for recruitment (including, after the Reformation, religious diversity) but many of them saw it as a professional calling. Each company had its elected officers who were responsible for troop movements, lodging and supplies, and who represented the interests of the soldiers to the captain. As in the Swiss companies, the men were divided into small groups who trained together. German contracting colonels came from among the smaller territorial princes or imperial nobility, but officers were 'acclaimed' by the soldiers at large, assembled in a circle, the body which also collectively enforced military discipline. The notorious flamboyance of mercenaries' clothing – multi-coloured jackets, slashed breeches and outrageous cod-pieces – reflected the cultural and social assumptions of men who flaunted their sexuality and killing prowess.

Cavalry companies (*Reiter*) were much in demand, another part of the German soldier-business. Military changes made the traditional 'man-at-arms' – a man on a horse, protected with plate armour – a specialized and expensive military weapon. Units of heavy cavalry still survived in France, Venice or Milan into the seventeenth century, satisfying noble pretensions, but mostly they were replaced by bands of mounted cross-bowmen and handgun-men, deployed with some armour protection. German *Reiter* specialized in the pistolier tactics known as *caracol* – from the Spanish for 'snail' – which created or exploited a collapse in the infantry squares of an opposing army. Such techniques were primarily responsible for the Protestants' Mühlberg defeat (1547). It required considerable experience to undertake such manoeuvres in battlefield conditions.

Elongated campaign seasons, larger armies and attritional warfare expanded the opportunities for contracted-out military forces. At the same time, the insolvency of princes increased the attractiveness of sharing the costs of raising, equipping, paying and supplying armies with a military contractor. The military 'enterpriser' acted as both contractor and creditor. Enterprisers existed throughout the military hierarchy, from colonels and privateering captains through munitioneers and purveyors, up to generals and admirals. Their relationships with states varied, depending on what they offered (and were asked) to undertake. The willingness of enterprisers to expand their range of activities, to advance princes and governments credit, and to take on operational responsibilities, may of itself have intensified military engagements.

Operational-financial contractors existed in naval as well as military spheres. The Mediterranean galley squadrons of the Habsburgs were built, outfitted and maintained by private contractors. Genoese galley fleets were contracted to the Habsburgs. Three of the ships in the 1588 Spanish Armada were built by private contractors, and 45,000 of the 60,000 tons of the fleet that year came from hired merchantmen. Captains (Francis Drake and Walter Raleigh being notable examples) used their ships as business ventures. They raised their capital in consortia, running privateering operations or hiring their vessels to the state, as opportunities dictated. 'Get a good ship and judiciously manage her' was the advice to indigent younger sons of English gentry, brought up to believe the exaggerated stories of the profits accruing to Elizabethan adventurers.

The biggest profits from military contracting were to be made in munitions and armaments supplies. Genoa, Hamburg and Amsterdam acted as the centres, but they relied on secondary providers. The Genoese merchant houses of Stefano and Balbi provided the armour and arms to Spanish forces. The Marselis brothers were among the Hamburg munitioneers who serviced the needs of the armies of northern Europe. The Amsterdam armaments manufacturer Elias Trip built armed vessels for the Dutch East India Company, but hired them out to the Portuguese and Venetians during the Twelve Years Truce (1609–21), and then contracted them to the Dutch and the French. Louis de Geer, whose industrial concerns included the development of the Swedish copper and iron works in the 1620s, was approached by the Swedish general Lennart Torstensson in 1644 to provide a fleet of thirty-two crewed and armed Dutch ships against Denmark and Norway (Torstensson War, 1643–5). De Geer was happy to oblige – at a price (466,550 *talers*).

French and Dutch Protestant forces in the later sixteenth and early seventeenth centuries recruited German infantry and cavalry. They were signed up for the duration of hostilities rather than for a campaign. The capitulations which laid out the terms of the contract were signed in the Rhineland cities where their commanders organized their financial backing. Although the core of the Army of Flanders was provided by Spanish veterans, the majority of the troops which served were raised by similar means. Then, in 1603 the government of the archdukes in the southern Netherlands handed over its operational management to the Genoese enterpriser Ambrogio Spínola, whose credit was better than that of the Spanish government itself. In the Long Turkish War the regiments in the Austrian Habsburg armies came from Italy, Spain and France as well as Germany, their cosmopolitan forces including many Protestant and Catholic enterprisers who followed where opportunities beckoned.

The importance of training increased with the spread of partially mass-produced portable firearms. These included the heavy-duty musket (supported by a rest on the ground when fired) and the lighter arquebus. These weapons were initially fired by a matchlock, a primitive mechanism that dropped slow-burning match-cord into a flash-pan to ignite the powder with the operation of a hand-lever. But dog-locks, wheel-locks and flint-locks – devices to produce a spark to ignite the charge – became more widely available. The introduction of the flint-lock is often credited to Marin le Bourgeois, a French gunsmith (and lute-maker) patronized by the French kings Henry IV and Louis XIII. But there was a trade-off between weapon weight and performance. Only larger-bore muskets could pierce armour at over 200 paces and, until the Thirty Years War (when the rifling of gun-bores that had begun to make hunting firearms more accurate was applied to military weapons), they were inaccurate. Portable firearms therefore depended on being used en masse and at close range with pikemen still essential to protect infantry in battle. Such developments placed even greater emphasis on drill and experience.

Gradually in the earlier seventeenth century the preference emerged for a more linear deployment over the more traditional large square blocks of troops. In his *Art of War* (1521) Machiavelli was among the first to stress the benefits of that formation. Contemporaries were aware of the disadvantages too. Linear formation lost the cohesion of the square. If challenged upon a flank, the long line had to pivot – a laborious manoeuvre, needing practice and officer oversight. Similar trade-offs were in play in the experiments with lightly armed, mobile cavalry organized into smaller units and shallow lines, offering great battlefield manoeuvrability but at the cost of the cumulative weight of a deep column of cavalry pouring into enemy positions. The Spaniards retained their company squares and it does not seem to have been a disadvantage to them. The French were slow to adopt newer cavalry formations but it did not compromise their victory at Rocroi (19 May 1643). Battlefield tactics did not spearhead a military revolution.

There was a profusion of printed books, covering every aspect of war. In words and diagrams, with lead soldiers, wooden models and mechanical toys, it was a subject of intense discussion. 'Evrie day,' noted the Elizabethan soldier Roger Williams, there were 'newe inventions, strategems of warres, changes of weapons, munitions, and all sorts of engines newlie invented.' For all that one learned in books, however, there was nothing like the experience of the real thing. The warfare of the late sixteenth century had created the pools of expertise which influenced soldiers of the next generation. The school of Alessandro Farnese, Spanish commander in Flanders in the 1580s and 90s, was highly prized. So too were those of Henry IV and Mauritz of Nassau and his cousin William Louis. The results were watched and to some extent copied in Protestant Europe in the next generation. In a letter to Mauritz in December 1594, William Louis mooted the idea of five rotating ranks of musketeers (based on the Ancient Greek military writer Aelian) to replicate the hail of fire which the Romans reputedly achieved with javelins and sling-shooters. It turned out that it took ten ranks to achieve that result. Intensive drilling was essential, as explained in Jacob de Gheyn's *Arms drill with arquebus, musket and pike* (1607), the most successful military manual of its day.

Humanists championed the virtues of conscripted militia and criticized the unreliability, venality and lack of zeal in mercenary soldiers. Their case supported the vision of a Christian commonwealth in which citizens defended the *patria* in support of their prince. The reality was, however, that wherever conscripted citizen armies were attempted (for example, Machiavelli's Florentine experiment in 1512 and the French 'legions' of the 1540s), they were a failure. Cheaper, they were poorly trained and tended to desert. Justus Lipsius (who knew little about armies but a lot about Tacitus) influenced the next generation with his critique of flamboyantly dressed mercenaries who were a law unto themselves, and his arguments in favour of disciplined, conscripted troops. 'I likewise require modestie of apparell' runs the English translation of Book V of his *Politics*, where he presented his blueprint for 'a severe conforming of the souldier to valour and virtue'. Military enterprisers in the Thirty Years War and English New Model Army generals disciplined their troops not because they read Lipsius but because they had a stake in the units they commanded.

The regiments which campaigned in the period from 1620 to 1650 were raised and maintained in a variety of ways. There were forces that were financed, administered and directed by the state (parts of the French and Spanish armies, the core of the Swedish army, the New Model Army) at one extreme of the spectrum. General contractors (such as Albrecht von Wallenstein, Ernst von Mansfeld and Bernard of Saxe-Weimar) who ran armies almost as private states in their own right lay at the other. In between there were entrepreneurs offering packages of military and naval force but under the overall control of statesmen, partially state-controlled operations, where some elements (munitions, supplies and so forth) were contracted out, and specialized providers of munitions and other services. Particular circumstances dictated the degree to which military forces were contracted out. What they all had in common was a willingness to fight longer and harder, with higher proportions of casualties. Some of the battles of the Thirty

Years War (Rheinfelden, 1638; Freiburg, 1644, for example) lasted over twenty-four hours. At the second battle of Breitenfeld (1642) half of the imperial forces lay dead or wounded or had been taken prisoner; 30 per cent of the opposing Swedish troops were dead or injured. At the battle of Jankau (1645) Lennart Torstensson's Swedish army of German mercenaries was pitched against the imperial forces led by Melchior von Hatzfeld. Four to five thousand of the 16,000 soldiers on the imperial side were killed or missing by the end of the battle, and a similar number were captured by the Swedes. Regimental soldiers were tough, resourceful and adaptable – prepared to undertake forced marches of hundreds of miles and then pitch into battle without delay.

Such commitment was not generated by loyalty to an individual ruler, except when he was also a battlefield commander as in the cases of Gustav Adolf and Oliver Cromwell. It owed little to religious or patriotic zeal. The armies were composed of different nationalities: Gustav Adolf's army in northern Germany in 1631 comprised 43,000 Swedes and 36,000 Germans, Scots, Livonians and Latvians. The Army of Flanders was Spanish in name but cosmopolitan in composition. An Italian colonel in imperial service might recruit German or Hungarian soldiers, supplemented by men from Italy or elsewhere. Colonels and commanders did not generally impose confessional adherence on their forces. Religious pluralism was the consequence of recruiting and retaining soldiers for their experience rather than their zeal. Many of those fighting in the English New Model Army (1645–60) did so for religious reasons, and Cromwell became notorious for appointing those of humble means but strongly held Protestant beliefs ('I had rather have a plain russet-coated captain that knows what he fights for and loves what he knows, than that which you call a gentleman and is nothing else,' he wrote to the earl of Manchester). But when their junior officers and ranks became politicized over back-pay in the years from 1647 to 1649 they supported the Independents, who rejected a state-imposed religious confession. Scottish Calvinists who, like Robert Munro, joined Gustav's army 'for the cause of religion', fought for a Lutheran of decidedly broad-minded views, at odds with the ecclesiastical establishment of his own country, subsidized by Catholic France. Maximilian of Bavaria's determination to insist on Catholic officers in his army inherited a broader tradition, encapsulated by the Jesuit Antonio Possevino's 1569 manual, *A Christian Soldier* (copies of which were distributed to troops before Lepanto), which drew on crusading traditions. By 1650, those were traditions in clear retreat.

Military commitment was generated within fighting forces them-selves. Battlefield commander-enterprisers had a personal financial stake in the survival and success of their units. Their own reputations as well as the fortunes of their backers rested on the operational decisions they made. Survival depended on developing and retaining experienced sol-diers. Whatever short-term gains there might have been in recruiting dregs, in the longer term it was 'able' seamen and 'old soldiers' whose experience counted for most. Securing their services meant recruiting from as broad a background as possible, offering competitive pay, equipping them well, increasing the numbers of double-pay men in the ranks and enhancing prospects of advancement. Year-on-year cam-paigning, with the reality of different states competing for what military enterprisers offered, strengthened the contemporary perception in the Thirty Years War that soldiery was a career. Among the 15,000 troops of the Bavarian army which disbanded in 1649, six regiments had served continuously since 1620, and a further six had been in action for over two decades. A majority of regiments in German forces had perhaps seen a minimum of six years of continuous campaigning. Most important of all, battlefield commanders were responsible for feeding and paying their men. Their own credit lines and logistic support were essential to their military success.

'. . . SENT TO LIE ABROAD'

Christendom's established political hierarchies fractured as its unity col-lapsed. That was reflected in the exclusive titles which princes accorded themselves and the resulting squabbles in Europe's chanceries. The pride of place traditionally accorded the emperor was contested by Valois monarchs, who claimed to be the 'eldest son of the Church' (following the salutation offered to Charles VIII by Pope Alexander VI at Christmas 1494), a title contested in both Madrid and Vienna. At the concluding session of the Council of Trent, Philip II asserted his own pre-eminence over other European princes, despite alarm in Rome. Standing on cere-mony was at the heart of the diplomacy of this period. The English ambassador to the court of Louis XIII, Lord Herbert of Cherbury, recalled in the 1630s an anecdote of Philip II reproaching an ambassador for aborting a negotiation over a quarrel about ceremonial. The ambassador was said to have replied: 'How so . . . Your Majesty is nothing but ceremony!'

Conventions determined how princes conducted their relationships. They habitually wrote to one another as 'my brother', 'my sister' or 'my cousin' – and such appellations were often the dynastic reality. By serving as godparents to one another's offspring they took one another's names, echoing a princely affinity that was expressed in their choices of spouses and marital strategies for their children. Most peace negotiations of this period revolved around a princely marriage and, even if they did not result in uniting hearts and minds, their political significance remained considerable. Eleanor of Austria, wife of Francis I by the Treaty of Cambrai (1529), widow of Manuel I of Portugal, served as intermediary between her husband and brother, Emperor Charles V. Elisabeth de Valois, Philip II's wife following the Treaty of Cateau-Cambrésis (1559), served as a conduit between the French court and Madrid from 1565 until her death in 1568.

Catherine de Médicis was not alone in the second half of the sixteenth century in making marital strategy a plank of international policy. By then, however, confessional divisions complicated diplomatic marriages. For the majority of Europe's ruling houses it became hard to conceive of a successful marriage crossing confessional boundaries. When Queen Elizabeth opened negotiations in 1579 with the French king's younger brother, François d'Alençon, duke of Anjou, they foundered on a vociferous English dislike for the French (Catholic) match. The fear that a cross-confessional marriage was the first step to a dynastic change of confessional allegiance was not illusory. Protestant John Vasa of Finland eloped with the Polish Catholic Catherine Jagiellon in 1562. When John became king of Sweden in 1569, Catherine's influence led to a Catholic-inclined church order and the reintroduction of Latin in Swedish church services. John and Catherine's son Sigismund was brought up a Catholic in Poland at the instigation of his mother and inherited the Polish throne. But he was eventually deposed from the Swedish throne in 1599 by his uncle Charles (Charles IX of Sweden) because of fears about Sigismund's Polish background and Catholicism. The Peace of Westphalia was distinctive precisely because it was cemented with no dynastic marriages. It was also the first major international peace treaty in Europe not to be endorsed by the papacy.

Spectacular summits encapsulating the society of princes in the sixteenth century (for instance, the Field of the Cloth of Gold, June 1520) went out of fashion as absolute rule distanced monarchs not merely from their subjects but also from one another. By contrast, diplomatic agency grew in importance. Permanent diplomatic representation was a well-established custom among the principalities of northern Italy in the fifteenth century. In the sixteenth century, the need to have 'an honest gentleman sent to lie abroad for the good of his country' – as England's Venetian diplomat Sir Henry Wotton remarked – became overwhelming. The dukes of Ferrara, Mantua and Parma and the state of Venice regularly had agents in Paris, Madrid and Prague in the sixteenth century. The papacy established a network of nuncios in the pontificates of Leo X and Clement VII, just as the forces of the Protestant Reformation emphasized the importance of winning friends and finding out what was happening.

By 1600, most of Europe's states north of the Alps had regular diplomatic representation that would become the hallmark of the European state system. There were debates and hiccups along the way. One issue was whether diplomatic representation was appropriate when princes were not in alliance with one another. Another was to what extent it was appropriate, and in what circumstances, to have an ambassador accorded to a prince of another faith. Other concerns were voiced about ambassadorial conduct and privileges. By the early years of the seventeenth century, the permanent ambassador had come to stay. The ambassadorial presence consolidated the society of princes and emphasized the exclusiveness that was at the heart of absolute claims to rule.

Why individuals agreed to serve as ambassadors is a complex question. They were not well rewarded. On the other hand, diplomatic service was a ladder to higher things since ambassadors had the ear of the prince. Diplomats were also at the heart of Europe's information inflation. Diplomatic despatches became longer and more frequent. Ambassadors were part of power-networks and corresponded with more people. Don Francés de Álava, the ambassador of Philip II at the French court of Charles IX in the 1560s, assured a correspondent: 'night and day in this household we do nothing but write to all parts of Europe'. The Spanish ambassador in Venice in 1587–8 received 1,000 letters from fellow

Spanish diplomats. The mental distances among Europe's power élites shrank as they accessed this information. Securitizing it became more important. Ciphers grew more common; breaking them more pressing. Mauritz of Nassau's servants cracked the ciphers used by Bernardino de Mendoza, the Spanish ambassador in Paris. Henry IV's mathematician François Viète broke the Spanish codes in the 1590s, revealing Spain's plans at a crucial moment in the Catholic League. But information inflation did not always mean greater knowledge. On the contrary, it heightened suspicions about the intentions of others.

17. States in Confrontation

The early seventeenth century reassured those battered by Christendom's religious contentions, political divisions and international conflict. Henry IV's statecraft measured up to the reality of religious division in France, his negotiators offering just enough concessions to the armed Protestant minority in the Edict of Nantes of April 1598 to win them over without losing the support of moderate Catholic royalists. Where previous edicts had come unstuck, this one survived. Then, following a papal initiative, peace was signed between Philip II and Henry IV at Vervins in May of the same year, bringing to an end three years of war and a decade of Spanish intervention in France. The ambitions of the independent-minded and expansionist Duke Charles Emmanuel of Savoy were cut down to size by a French military intervention, peace in the French Alps being secured at Lyon in January 1601. The Peace of London ended maritime warfare between Spain and England in August 1604. A settlement at Zsitvatorok closed the wearisome Austrian Habsburg war with the Ottomans in October 1606. Conflict in the Netherlands was brought to a standstill by the Twelve Years Truce, signed in Antwerp in April 1609. In the empire, there was an ongoing political impasse, but the peace had held since 1555 and no one openly challenged it. Austrian Habsburg lands were being pulled in different directions, their tensions focused in a succession crisis. Even there, however, in the decade before 1618 it appeared as though the problems could be solved by doing deals behind closed doors.

Jacques-Auguste de Thou, president of the Parlement of Paris and Henry IV's librarian, read these events as offering a basis for the reunion of Christendom. It would not emerge from the papacy, the emperor, a Church council or theologians. It would be achieved by Christian states, intellectuals and diplomats. Off-stage, not courting public endorsement, they would work quietly, step by step, putting into practice the lesson of prudence taught by the study of history. Just as the negotiators of those treaties had done, they would build reconciliation around the points of Christian doctrine upon which everyone agreed. In December 1603, the Catholic de Thou wrote to congratulate the Protestant King James VI of Scotland on his ascent to the English throne. He presented the monarch with a copy of the first volume of his history of the French civil wars (the *Historia sui temporis*). Its preface (dedicated to Henry IV and a classic *politique* justification for state-engineered religious pluralism) offered the Edict of Nantes as a model for how statecraft ended civil wars. 'Moderate conversation and ... pacific conferences' achieved more than 'flames, exile and proscription'. James endorsed the sentiments in reply. He had never personally been 'of a sectarian spirit nor resistant to the well-being of Christendom'. There was no 'work so worthy and important' as 'the solace and universal peace of Christendom'.

De Thou's library hosted a think-tank, uniting scholars convinced that confessional division, exacerbated by appeals to religious fanaticism, could be resolved by finer spirits. James devoted his time to reaching across denominational and national divisions. In 1603 the 'blessed Union, or rather Reuniting of these two mightie, famous and ancient Kingdomes of England and Scotland, under one Imperial Crown' served as one model. The Hampton Court Conference a year later, which tried but failed to persuade the English bishops to take seriously Puritan demands for reform, provided another. Both had their critics but the king pressed on. Internationally, his hopes were buoyed up by the controversy provoked by the papal Interdict of Venice (1606–10) and the criticism of Jesuit-led justifications for the pope's indirect secular powers. Convinced Catholic Gallicans as well as moderate French and Dutch Protestants looked to the Church of England as a possible way forward: an inclusive state Church and episcopal government without oppressive authority. James elicited support in unlikely quarters. In Rakow, Jerome Moscorovius dedicated his translation of the Unitarian catechism to the English king, explaining that Unitarians had always seen Christian controversies as against the word of Scripture. Senior figures in the Greek Orthodox Patriarchate made contact with the English king, seeing in him an ally against Catholic missionaries and papal envoys in the Ottoman empire. The imperial astronomer

Johannes Kepler dedicated his *Harmony of the World* (1619) to James, recalling 'what attention the prince of Christendom gives to divine studies'. Scholars queued up to offer methods by which the Christian religion could be reduced to scripturally validated tenets to which both Protestants and Catholics might adhere.

Christendom had become a pipedream for irenicists – those who sought to reconcile Europe's religious differences. It was a chimera because the basis for its aspirations lay in acts of state and diplomacy which shelved rather than solved the politico-religious tensions of the day. One by one these accords either came to bits or proved irrelevant. Jacobean diplomats were on hand to bring the parties to a contested succession in Jülich-Cleves to a negotiated peace (Xanten, 1614), but they did not eliminate the sources of the conflict. Denmark and Sweden, rivals for hegemony in the Baltic, were brought round the table by James's diplomats to sign a peace accord at Knäred in 1613, but their enmities were not dissipated. The English envoy Sir Thomas Edmondes brokered reconciliation between the prince of Condé, Huguenot grandees and the Queen Mother, Marie de Médicis, in 1616 after tension and sporadic war in France threatened the Peace of Nantes. In 1617, she and Louis XIII began the re-Catholicizing of the principality of Béarn. The king's triumphant entry there in October 1620 became the occasion for renewed hostilities with the Protestants which ended inconclusively at the Treaty of Montpellier (1622).

Meanwhile, the Peace of Zsitvatorok between the Ottomans and the Austrian Habsburgs was open to different interpretations from the moment it was signed, both sides accusing the other of bad faith and non-compliance. James's ambassador to the empire in 1612–13, Sir Stephen Sieur, found his efforts to reconcile the different parties in the Reich blocked at every turn. In 1618, a panegyric to peace was published in London entitled *The Peace-Maker* and dedicated to King James. Throughout the British Isles (even Ireland, 'that rebellious outlaw') the king had brought an olive branch. Other disputes on the continent had been happily resolved. *The Peace-Maker* did not mention that Protestant and Catholic power-blocs had begun to dominate the international stage once more. That was evident in the repression of a Catholic rebellion that year in the Valtelline, the all-important route-way for the Spanish Habsburgs through the Alps, linking Lake Como and the Inn. Nor did the author of *The Peace-Maker* foresee the outcome of the Bohemian rebellion that same year which, with the non-renewal of the Twelve Years Truce following in 1621, was the undoing of James's agenda.

Not only were the reconciliations of the early seventeenth century chimerical, they also fostered the illusion that a resolution to the problems posed by the outbreak of conflict on a large scale in central Europe (when it occurred in 1618) would be just around the corner; that the diplomatic and political measures which had worked once, would do so again; and that Christendom could be reconstructed by a dedicated peace-maker and the backing of a Christian state. What happened in the 1620s proved that nothing worked out as it was predicted. No one foresaw in 1618 that a king would be driven out of his kingdom (Bohemia) by military force and dispossessed of his lands (the Palatinate), his supporters executed and exiled. No one imagined that French Protestants would be militarily emasculated (the Peace of Alais, 1629), the terms of the Edict of Nantes confirmed but serving as the only legal safeguard the Huguenots had to their increasingly vulnerable privileges. No one predicted that Spain's army in the southern Netherlands would gain the upper hand against the Dutch in the 1620s; or that the balances of forces in the Reich between the emperor and the princes would be totally reversed by military means; or that the Austrian Habsburg emperor would have the opportunity to behave like a sovereign prince in the empire (the Edict of Restitution, 1629) as well as in his ancestral lands. The most serious oppositional movements of the first half of the seventeenth century were different from the contentions of the later sixteenth century because they were reactions to what had taken people unawares, rearguard campaigns conducted by desperate people hanging on to the values of vanishing Christian commonwealths and defending themselves from what they regarded as assaults upon their religious integrity.

POLITICAL VIRTUES IN
A DANGEROUS WORLD

The rationale for the Christian commonwealth was trumped by sovereignty and reason of state. Where did that leave those who believed that their birth, education, social role and religious experience entitled them to a *vita civilis*, a role in the state? They too had experienced the turmoil of post-Reformation politics. They had learned how difficult it was to square one's private beliefs and conscience with what was required when one held office. They had been attacked in public for what they had said and done. They had supported political causes only to be disillusioned, let down by their leaders or by events turning out differently from the way they expected. They needed a new way of looking at the world.

Justus Lipsius offered just that. He was the most widely read and influential thinker of these decades. For a time he was a dominant figure and rector at the new Dutch university of Leiden, where he published his *Two Books on Constancy* (1584). That text took the form of a dialogue in a garden, a familiar *locus* for dignified retreat. In emphasizing constancy, Lipsius drew on Seneca to show his contemporaries how they could free themselves from the slings and arrows of outrageous fortune (*publica mala*) by being dispassionate (Stoic *apatheia*) towards them. Wars and disasters were sent by God as instruments of punishment and reward, to be accepted with Stoic realism. The man of virtue (*vir virtutis*) had the 'immovable strength of a mind that is neither elated nor downcast by outward or fortuitous circumstances'. Obedient to the powers that be, he cultivated an inward life of reflection by which he remained true to himself.

Lipsius's *Six Books of Politics or Civil Doctrine* (1589) demonstrated how to reflect on political life. It was a labyrinth of Tacitus quotations ('this learned and laborious fabric', said Montaigne). Its audience (he refused to publish it in anything other than Latin, his advice being aimed at élites) was invited to treat it as a commonplace repository, one whose organization left them with the task of excerpting those passages which spoke to them, thus developing their own 'constancy', or reflective distance from the powers that be. Attentive readers discovered that his advice was reason of state with a moral top-dressing. It was better to 'bear up' (*ferre*) with rather than 'throw off' (*auferre*) rulers. 'Civil war is worse and more miserable than tyranny,' he declared. It was not imprudent for a prince to be deceitful so long as it was done 'moderately and for a good purpose'. In diplomacy, Lipsius advised: 'The Prince may . . . sometimes have to deale with a foxe, play the foxe, especially if the good and publike profit . . . require it.' Dissimulation was presented within a framework of political morality in which the end (stability and order) justified the means and the citizen was a bystander. Did prudence and virtue extend to a prince 'tolerating' a religion different from his own in his state? Experience indicated that religious dissent had torn Christendom to pieces. In a phrase he was later to regret, he wrote: 'here is no place for clemencie; burne, sawe asunder, for it is better that one member be cast away, than that the whole body runne to ruyne'. At the same time he recognized that there came a point when political virtue dictated the opposite. Once dissidence threatened to overwhelm the state it was better to give it latitude so long as it did not disrupt its stability.

Lipsius's ideas entered the mainstream, creating a political approach. His French emulators (they included members of de Thou's circle) distanced themselves from the populism of the wars of religion and created a salon-world in which politics became a talking-shop for the initiated. 'We are here among loyal friends; I think that what we say here will not pass beyond the threshold of the door,' wrote Guillaume du Vair in his dialogue *On Constancy* (1594), a pastiche of Lipsius's. Nicolas Faret's *The Honest Man* (1630) manufactured the stereotype of how to be a citizen in an absolute monarchy. Subtitled 'The Art of Pleasing at Court', it showed how, following Lipsian precepts, one could navigate a world of false friendship and flattery while still remaining true to oneself. London play-goers were treated to Shakespeare's *Tragedy of Hamlet* (1601), whose hero tests the Stoic outlook which he, along with his student friend Horatio, had imbibed in Wittenberg when they return to the corrupt Danish court. Notebook in hand, Prince Hamlet contrasts his own constancy with its absence in his mother. As the plot unfolds, Hamlet asks questions about the nobility of suicide, dissembles his own grief and uses dissimulation to uncover others' guilt.

Behind this new politics was a discourse about secrecy. When Henry IV converted to Catholicism, his Catholic League critic Louis Dorléans complained that the king was like an oyster which 'only opens up when and to whom it pleases him to do so'. Knowing when to speak and when to hold one's tongue was one of the emerging political accomplishments. In 1612, Alessandro Anguissola, counsellor to Charles Emmanuel, duke of Savoy, presented his prince with a chapter from his book *On princely good government*. Entitled 'On Dissimulation' it justified why the essence of good government was for a prince to distance himself from those around him, how his conversation should expressly *not* reveal what he was thinking. The Spanish Jesuit Baltasar Gracián y

Morales warned that our ears are the back door of truth and the front door of deceit: 'Truth is more often seen than heard. Seldom does it reach us unalloyed, even less so when it comes from afar.' Dissimulation was like the ink a cuttlefish uses to defend itself, a way of self-preservation.

Systemic dissimulation made it harder for Europe's diplomats to process the contradictory signals which they received. Those in authority were suspected of having mixed motives and therefore hidden agendas. They were no longer perceived as saying what they meant, or meaning what they said. That was how Thomas Middleton chose to present diplomacy in his play *A Game at Chess* (1624). The chess match turned out to be a game of bluff and counter-bluff representing contemporary diplomatic relations between London and Madrid. The characters included a traitorous king's pawn, a turncoat bishop, and a black knight in the shape of the Spanish ambassador at the Court of St James, Diego Sarmiento de Acuña, Count Gondomar. In Middleton's satire, the heart of the issue was what constituted political virtue.

PAX HISPANICA

In *c.* 1616 the Dutch artist Adriaen Van De Venne painted a scene in which a large party including the Archduke Albert of the Netherlands and his former enemy Prince Mauritz of Nassau enjoyed a picnic, their hats off and musical instruments to hand. The fields were tilled since the military forces in the background were on standby. The picture is an allegory of the Twelve Years Truce, which was the apotheosis of twenty-three years from 1598 to 1621, known as the *Pax Hispanica* (*las Pazes* or the 'Spanish Peace'), in which Spain sought a rapprochement with its enemies. The diplomacy which lay behind the various peace agreements of that period was tortuous, however, because, in each instance, they were acknowledgements of defeat. The *Pax Hispanica* was a lukewarm peace, a shallow intermission with continuing low-key hostilities.

The Spanish empire's military corridor (the 'Spanish Road') to northern Europe became more indispensable as the Atlantic sea-lanes were still vulnerable to privateering. The Spanish control of the Balearics and Elba provided cover for the western Mediterranean sea-lane. Spanish troops occupied the coastal enclave of the Marquisate of Finale in 1570, purchasing it outright in 1602. Genoa was a pro-Spanish republic. The duchy of Milan was the administrative and military hub of the Spanish Road. Pedro Henriquez d'Azevedo y Alvarez de Toledo, Count Fuentes, tightened Spain's military grip on the duchy and the lands around it (Mantua, Parma, Monferrato). From Milan, Fuentes threatened the duchy of Parma with military occupation, placed a garrison at Piacenza and concluded an alliance in 1600 with the Grisons (the Grey Leagues), the easterly canton of Switzerland whose name was derived from the local alliances which governed it. This allowed Spanish troops to traverse the Alps via the Valtelline. The significance of the latter as an imperial asset increased after the duchy of Savoy signed over to France the territories which enabled it to close at will the westerly Alpine corridors across the Little St Bernard or Mont Cenis to Annecy or Chambéry and then across the Rhône at the Pont de Grésin into Franche-Comté.

Spanish intentions were difficult to read because of their own hesitations about the wisdom of a strategy of peace. Philip II's will dictated that his son Philip III (who succeeded him in 1598) continue the war in the Netherlands. Philip III had been initiated into government from the age of fifteen. Earnest, pious and no inspirer of others, he devolved routine business to a *valido* ('most worthy'), someone who was privy (hence *privado*) to the king's will – in the event, Francisco Gómez de Sandoval y Rojas, count (duke in 1599) of Lerma. The king did not attend councils of state and did not see all the diplomatic traffic. How long Lerma's influence at court would last became a further uncertainty as doubts about the wisdom of the *Pax Hispanica* spread. Some argued that it might be prudent to accept peace on reasonable terms. On the other hand, said others, if it compromised the protection of Catholicism and failed to secure the integrity of Spain's empire, then attack was the best form of defence. Many of those brought up in the service of Philip II believed that peace undermined Spain's reputation. They noted the degrading of Spanish colonial and economic assets as the Dutch, English and French competed to secure a hostile presence on the coast of Brazil, while the Dutch and English undermined the Portuguese empire in the Far East.

Some thought that the solution to Spain's dilemmas lay in a 'project' (*arbitrio*) – which they sometimes declared so important that it could be disclosed only in a private audience or circulated in manuscript. Proclaiming the virtues of their chosen remedy in print was part of the projectors' strategy for winning themselves an audience. They capitalized on a sense of moral decline in the wake of Spain's recent plagues. National 'reformation' accompanied international 'reputation' – and both conjoined to undermine Lerma's peace. Don Baltasar de Zúñiga in Prague returned to sit on the Council of State in Madrid in July 1617, the leader of those who felt that the *Pax Hispanica* had given away too much. He steered Spain towards intervention in Bohemia and central Europe, and then towards renewing the war with the Dutch in the spring of 1621. That year, Philip III died, to be succeeded by his sixteen-year-old son, Philip IV. Zúñiga befriended the heir and ingratiated his nephew, Don Gaspar de Guzmán (Olivares) into his service. Philip IV instructed his secretaries that all papers requiring royal signature were to be passed to Olivares. The latter turned reputation and reformation into a programme to preserve Spanish Habsburg hegemony.

Adding to uncertainty, policy was made not only in Madrid. Four days after the Peace of Vervins, Philip II had bestowed his title to the Netherlands on his eldest daughter, Isabel Clara Eugenia, and her betrothed, his nephew, the (ex-cardinal) Archduke Albert of Austria. By a secret clause, they accepted the maintenance of a Spanish army in Flanders under a Spanish general, and their marriage contract enjoined them to recover the lost provinces of the Netherlands. They could have a court and influence, but Madrid held on to strategic and military matters. Yet things did not work out like that. The archduke was on the ground and took matters into his own hands. He masterminded the siege of Ostend (July 1601–September 1604: a 'long carnival of death', 35,000 men dying in its siege trenches) and opened direct talks with England and the Dutch. Delaying putting his signature to the truce until the last possible moment, Philip III was reported to remark: 'deep down in my conscience remains the idea that once this truce is ended it will be suitable to make war'.

There were conflicting assessments of the Spanish empire's financial strength and its will to mobilize resources. The English diplomat George Carew called it 'an unsteady giant'. The evidence was ambiguous, even to those within the Spanish administration. Despite bankruptcy, Philip II mounted two further armadas against England in 1596 and 1597; 136 ships, 13,000 men and 300 horses were despatched in the latter – almost as large as that of 1588. Philip III launched a final, equally unsuccessful one in 1601. The Flanders military establishment cost in excess of 60 million florins in the four years from 1596 to 1600, yet because of the borrowing costs and the expenses of the new court in Brussels, only a proportion of the money ever made it to the forces on the ground. Unpaid, the troops mutinied. Contemporaries monitored the arrival of silver shipments from the New World – in 1600, the third silver fleet of the year landed with 8 million ducats, bringing the crown receipts that year to about 4 million ducats, enough (as one of the king's advisers said) 'to take care of things suitably'. Yet, at the same time, devastating plague decimated the population in parts of Castile. In June 1602, the Spanish government issued a new coinage for low-denomination transactions in copper (*vellón*) whose face value was in excess of its weight in metal. The French and Dutch minted counterfeit coins and smuggled them into the peninsula, exchanging them for silver at a profit. The results damaged still further the tax-raising capacity of Castile. By 1607, Spanish revenues were anticipated up to 1611 and another default occurred. Only an agreement with a syndicate of Genoese bankers in May 1608 kept the Flanders Army in the field. Contemporaries recognized that peace was because of exhaustion, but no one knew how long it would take for Spain to recover.

Uncertainties led to procrastination, a logical response to a confusing world. It was not merely Philip III whose habitual delays were interpreted as laziness. James I also exasperated those in his service for endlessly putting things off. Delays, however, created opportunities for others to manipulate uncertainty to their advantage. The Spanish Netherlands became a magnet for displaced Catholics from France, the northern Netherlands and the British Isles. The last of these reported over-optimistically on the possibilities for overthrowing James I, while confessors and Tridentine-inspired clerics and administrators in the ecclesiastical lands of the empire and the duchy of Bavaria inspired projects for German re-Catholicization.

In England, in the United Provinces and in the smaller German Calvinist courts, peace opened up different debates. International politics in western Europe in the second half of the sixteenth century moulded the outlook of policy-makers as well as military officers into a perception of two conflicting religious power-blocs. They saw the Spanish Habsburgs as a threat to the integrity of Protestantism, one which required unending vigilance and, in propitious circumstances, a pre-emptive strike. The 'Protestant Cause' grew out of educational, religious, military, diplomatic and family experience, reinforced by correspondence and reading. In England, Francis Walsingham, the earl of Leicester, Philip Sidney and the earl of Essex all found themselves of one mind with Philippe Duplessis-Mornay at the court of Henry of Navarre. Their brand of constancy was different from that advocated by Lipsius. It was tinged with the belief that the forces of 'iniquity' (as Duplessis-Mornay termed the Antichrist) stalked the world in Habsburg colours, and that only by armed intervention would they protect the 'fortress of God's sanctuary'. They expected to be in a minority around the council tables of Protestant princes. Calvinists especially cultivated the belief that they were among the righteous minority of those who would be proved correct. When they lost the argument (as manifestly they had with the coming of peace), they sought reinforcement among those who felt themselves excluded from influence in the state.

In England, the peace with Spain opened the door to foreign affairs being a subject for debate and controversy in the Parliaments of James I. In the 1620s it was both the objectives and conduct of Stuart foreign affairs which served as a way for a minority of politicized Puritan voices to mobilize and to pressurize the king. English Puritan-minded congregations held fast-days along with their Calvinist co-religionists in France and the Netherlands at moments of international tension. They collected money for the relief of places and persons. In the universities and the London Inns of Court, like-minded students sought new heroes (King James's children – Prince Henry; then, after his death in November 1612, Princess Elizabeth, the bride of Frederick V of the Palatinate in the following year) on which to pin their hopes.

The decentralized government of the young Dutch Republic afforded scope for those who opposed the Twelve Years Truce. Its political classes (the 'Regents', or members of the oligarchies in towns providing delegates to the provincial Estates and the Estates General) had differing views. It required time and patience to come to a common mind. Johan van Oldenbarnevelt deployed his skills in negotiation, first as stipendiary town clerk ('pensionary') to the city of Rotterdam and then as Advocate of the Provincial States of Holland, which paid the lion's share of the Dutch military budget. He was, as the States of Holland declared when he was executed on 13 May 1619, 'a man of great business, activity, memory and wisdom'. Oldenbarnevelt used those skills to negotiate the 1609 truce to safeguard Holland's commercial interests, arguing that it did not compromise the republic's integrity. Mauritz of Nassau, later prince of Orange, was unconvinced. Spain would refortify. The landward provinces (where he was Stadholder) would be vulnerable. A generation's military experience would be lost when regiments (where his support partly lay) were disbanded.

As it happened, the argument over the truce was fought out on other grounds. Oldenbarnevelt and a majority of Regents from Holland and Zeeland made no secret of their sympathy, cautiously expressed in the theological language of the day, for the views of the Amsterdam pastor Jacob Hermanszoon (Arminius). The issues went to the heart of what the Dutch Calvinist Church stood for during the revolt: Calvinist predestination, and behind that the godly nation, as well as the right of the Church to excommunicate those who did not uphold doctrinal purity. Arminius died the year the truce was signed. The year after, his supporters presented a petition in five articles (the Remonstrance) to the States of Holland and Friesland. They upheld Arminius's right to cast doubts on the strict Calvinist interpretation of predestination in a polity where the Church of the state was not a state Church. In sermons, debates, placards, handbills and around Sunday lunch-tables, the views of Remonstrants (the supporters of Arminius) and Anti-Remonstrants grafted themselves into literate, well-informed, but insecure Dutch society. Churches were ransacked, ministers heckled and Oldenbarnevelt (a Remonstrant) eventually arrested by order of the States General on 23 August 1618, along with several of his supporters (including the jurist Hugo Grotius). Eight months later, Oldenbarnevelt was beheaded after a commission of the States General declared him guilty of crimes against the 'generality', that being their interpretation of what they now saw as the dangers of the truce which he had negotiated in 1609. These events were followed intently in London, Paris and Madrid. Olivares took the lesson from them that there could not be a better moment to renew the war against a divided republic than when the truce expired in 1621.

Others in Protestant Europe – beyond the politicians, courtiers and soldiers – also believed that Spain was not to be trusted, and that its empire should be attacked while it was weak. They offered their services in espionage and know-how, resulting in security alerts and plots. Some of the latter were real and dangerous, others the phantoms of overexcited imaginations. The Gunpowder Plot (5 November 1605) was a terrorist attempt to decapitate the English government with the intention of replacing King James by his daughter Elizabeth, who would be then married into the Spanish royal family and converted to Catholicism. Guy Fawkes had spent a decade in the Army of Flanders and knew what gunpowder could achieve. More speculative was the conspiracy that implicated Philippe Duplessis-Mornay, Henry Wotton and others in the wake of the Venetian Interdict controversy. The plan was to use émigrés and discontents in Venice to engineer a revolution. In January 1617, Thomas Edmondes was among those who plotted with Walter Raleigh to attack Genoa under cover of an expedition to seek for gold in Guiana. That plot was no hoax, and it came centre-stage in Raleigh's trial and execution in 1618 when he incriminated his co-conspirators. Who knows, however, what was behind the report, accorded credibility by Brussels in 1621, of a plot afoot to fill a ship in Holland with barrels of gunpowder and bring the cargo to 's-Hertogenbosch and blow up the main gates of the city? In October 1623, an accident occurred in Blackfriars, London, when a gallery serving as a chapel adjoining the French ambassador's lodging collapsed, killing Catholics assembled below to hear a Jesuit preach. Prince Charles had just returned to London from Madrid empty-handed after his quixotic quest to win the hand of the Spanish infanta Maria. The coroner declared it a tragic accident but London pamphlets and ballads told another story. It was a providential act of God: 'No Plot, No Powder' ran one headline. Real or false, accidents or contrivances, such reports exaggerated the sense of a world on the brink.

GALLIC HERCULES

Spanish diplomats understood that suspicions could be turned into a hatred of Habsburg hegemony. They responded with offices, promises of pensions, tempting possibilities of marriage, lucrative benefices. In the case of James I, they played on his conviction that the confessional divide could be bridged through the wisdom and majesty of a Solomon prince (himself). Their efforts created pro-Spanish cliques in the courts and politics of their rivals – whose adherents became accused in turn by their opponents of being proxies for the Catholic designs of a foreign power. Such resentments were held in check so long as there was no realistic alternative to Spanish ascendancy. The revival of French authority under Henry IV changed that, as registered in the Italian peninsula. Venice was the first Catholic state officially to recognize Bourbon rule. The papacy (under Pope Clement VIII) distanced itself from Spanish dependency and recognized Henry's absolution, then accepted the annulment of his first marriage (to Marguerite de Valois), thus opening the door to a second – to the daughter of the grand duke of Tuscany and an archduchess of Austria, Marie de Médicis, in October 1600. That year, rumours circulated in Rome and Venice that the French king wanted to be elected king of the Romans. In October that same year, Henry led a military campaign into the duchy of Savoy. Months later, 'Fire-head' (*testa d'feu*) Duke Charles Emmanuel was brought to the negotiating table in Lyon. The treaty allowed the duke of Savoy to retain the fortress of Saluzzo, while France acquired Bresse and Bugey, its most significant strategic gains since the siege of Calais in 1558. With these gains France threatened the westerly route of the Spanish Road.

About that time Toussaint Dubreuil completed his painting of Henry as Hercules slaying the many-headed Hydra, probably for the newly renovated Fontainebleau. The 'Gallic Hercules' became a commonplace among the king's image-makers – armed with a club and belabouring the Cerberus of the Catholic League (1592), triumphing over a falling centaur (1600 – the duke of Savoy), cleansing the Augean stables (*c.* 1604 – the reform of the kingdom) and carrying the world on his shoulders (a reflection of his European conception of his authority). The French 'royal Hercules' had usually been depicted with chains coming out of his mouth – a representation of how the French monarchy persuaded people into virtue and obedience by eloquence. That was characteristically abandoned by Henry IV, for whom the emphasis was on action, not words. He reminded notables, magistrates and clergy that it was words (sermons, speeches, rabble-rousing) which had caused France's civil wars. His role was to cut the Gordian Knot of dissension. Argument was futile since the king's actions were unquestionable. It was authoritarianism with kid-gloves.

France's reconstruction was coaxed into reality by Henry IV's charisma, a recovery of monarchical authority on old foundations. The pacification at Nantes in 1598 was an ambitious and successful attempt to use law to define and implement religious pluralism. The expansionist dynamic of French Protestantism had evaporated during the civil wars. By 1600, Protestants were perhaps no more than 5–6 per cent of the kingdom, the majority of their 700 or so worshipping communities concentrated especially in the south. But its political organization matured. The general assembly of the Huguenot party met in six different places in five years from 1593 to 1598, and in almost continuous session from April 1596 to June 1598 while the negotiations leading up to Nantes were in progress. The party's military strength was underwritten in the Nantes agreements with royal undertakings to pay for fifty garrisoned strongholds (*places de sûreté*). But the French Protestants were divided among themselves and lacked a 'protector' whom they could trust. In addition the terms of the edict stipulated that, in future, their general assemblies could be held only with royal permission. The peace defined where and how they could worship and offered the prospect that they would not be excluded from the state. Royal commissioners took on the burden of settling local issues that a general edict could not resolve, and legal tribunals (*chambres de l'édit*) with bi-confessional membership settled lawsuits between Protestants and Catholics. If religious pluralism became a fact of life in some parts of France it was on the basis of local agreements to live and let live, meaning that the frontiers between the faiths were not legally determined and rigid but fluid and evolving.

Henry IV also unilaterally wrote off some of the crown's debts while the Protestant superintendant of finance, Maximilien de Béthune, duke (in 1606) of Sully, patched the leaky pipe of royal income and became unpopular by controlling royal expenditure. Partly under Sully's impetus, Henrician reconstruction had its showcase mercantilist projects. In Paris, these resulted in the completion of the Pont Neuf over the Seine and an associated new square (the place Dauphine), an esplanade along the river between the (reconstructed) Louvre and the Arsenal, as well as the place Royale (now the place des Vosges), an Italianate piazza in an up-and-coming part of town (the Marais).

The smack of firm rule from the first Bourbon was most keenly felt by France's grandees. Their role in the civil wars had been considerable. They were between and among Europe's sovereign princes, intermarrying with them and participating in their competitive dynasticism. Some of them were persuaded to see the world through the confessionalized lens of international power-blocs. France's aristocracy was open to outsiders because cadets from foreign lineages were made dukes and peers. Their aspirations, mingling with those of the Bourbon princes of the blood, constituted an important dynamic and instability in the first generation of Bourbon rule. The nobility 'complain more about the peace than about their pensions', wrote François d'Aerssen, the Dutch envoy, in 1602, 'and willingly lend an ear to all novelty and stirring'. At that moment, Charles de Gontaut, duke of Biron, a marshal of France who fought alongside Henry IV in the League, went on trial before the Parlement of Paris for high treason – for accepting a Spanish pension, concluding a treaty, perhaps conspiring to kill the king. Henry IV released incriminating evidence and Biron's execution at the Bastille (31 July 1602) was a reminder that kings were not just aristocrats with crowns. They were demi-gods – Hercules – and they could cut off the heads of the greatest in the land.

The Gallic Hercules's view of his place in the world did not accord with that perceived in Madrid. Their differences emerged most starkly at the end of Henry's reign. Less than a month before the signing of the truce in Antwerp, on 25 March 1609, John William, duke of Cleves, Jülich and Berg, died without direct heirs. His duchies sat astride the Rhine, controlling the approaches to the Netherlands. The area was confessionally mixed, and exiles from the Spanish Netherlands had established Calvinist churches in the lower Rhine duchies, a confession not included in the Peace of Augsburg but gaining ground. They enveloped the Archbishopric-Electorate of Cologne, the most important ecclesiastical principality of the lower Rhineland. Its Catholicism was guaranteed by the imperial mandate ('Ecclesiastical Reservation') which Protestant princes understood differently from Catholics. But during the Cologne War (1582–3) the Archbishop-Elector converted to Protestantism and attempted to impose a Protestant Reformation upon his Electorate with ramifications that Counter-Reformed Catholics were anxious to undo. Both Madrid and Brussels wanted to strengthen their military position in the lower Rhineland for any future offensive at the end of the truce. Jülich was the most heavily fortified town on the left bank of the lower Rhine. If it fell into Protestant hands, it would compromise the Habsburg frontier in that region.

The principal pretenders to the duchies were both Protestants. The emperor tried to parachute in an interim imperial administrator (Archduke Leopold) to keep the peace. Leopold arrived with a token military force, no support in the mainly Protestant towns and a majority of the nobles against him. His appearance on the scene was a threat to the Dutch, who responded with military preparations in the spring of 1610. Henry IV sensed that the moment had come for a show of force. As in Savoy a decade previously, he envisaged a short, sharp intervention to assert French influence in a crucial theatre. His diplomats interpreted the Brussels archdukes' refusal to surrender the young bride (Charlotte de Montmorency) of Henry's cousin (Henri de Bourbon-Condé) to the king as a sign of bad faith. Both Condé and his fiancée had fled to Brussels late in 1609 following Henry IV's infatuation with her and his cousin's refusal to play the part of cuckold. In the early summer of 1610, an army of 32,000 infantry, 5,000 cavalry and artillery assembled in Champagne. The king commissioned a painting of himself as Hercules fleeing Venus (love) in favour of the goddesses of hope and virtue. In contemporary aristocratic culture, Hercules was often represented as an all-too-mortal god, caught between his base desires and his more noble virtues. Lipsius would have approved of the message of a painting that encouraged the king to sublimate the former for the latter. Henry IV was on his way by coach from the Louvre to the Arsenal to discuss final military plans when he was assassinated on 14 May 1610.

The truth behind the assassination will never be known, though the events can be reconstructed and the assassin, Jean-François Ravaillac, was cross-questioned in detail. Ravaillac was a downwardly mobile younger son from a broken marriage. He was poor, suffered from nightmares, heard voices, wrote delirious verses and insisted that it was 'the judgment of God' which led him on. He was interrogated and tortured, but his story remained the same: he had acted on his own. If he had been influenced by Jesuit-inspired writings about tyrannicide, it was by osmosis. Other evidence for the involvement of disgruntled grandees in the assassination comes from tainted sources. And yet the timing of the event was so consummate that it is difficult to exclude the possibility of a plot from abroad. Diplomats had credible advance warning of an assassination attempt emanating from Brussels. The receiver-general of Archduke Albert dispensed a large sum that year for undisclosed activities by agents in France. There was perhaps more than one murder plot in May 1610, Ravaillac being the assassin who got there first. Whatever the truth of the matter, France was plunged into a minority government with Marie de Médicis at its head. Only a token force was despatched to Jülich, a compromise was reached and Spain expanded its garrisons in the area. In Paris, prudence dictated cooperation with Spain, cemented by a double marriage between the two ruling houses. If France retreated from a wider role in Europe for a while, it was not altogether abandoned.

THE AUSTRIAN HABSBURGS DISCONCERTED

In July 1609, Henry IV told Archduke Albert's ambassador that Emperor Rudolf was no longer master in his own realms, and not even in Prague. That assessment of the emperor's failure to direct affairs in the lands which made up the Austrian Habsburg ancestral patrimony was commonplace. Two years later, Rudolf was forced to abdicate from the Bohemian crown by his own brother, Archduke Matthias. Eight months later, Rudolf himself died with nothing more than the title of emperor to his name. Matthias had succeeded to the Bohemian and then the imperial throne in a dynastic crisis which reflected the broader tensions within the Habsburg ancestral domains. Matthias's ambition to succeed his childless brother led him to make promises which, in the circumstances of the succession, he was then unable to fulfil. As he was childless himself, the succession problem was merely postponed, while Emperor Matthias had to contend with the suspicions which he had raised among his opponents. Everyone expected that the Habsburgs would negotiate their way through their various difficulties, but the Bohemian Revolt of 1618 detonated a crisis in the Habsburg lands which was resolved by force, spilling out into the German empire.

The origins of the dynastic crisis lay in Emperor Ferdinand I's partition of the ancestral lands between his sons in 1564. The division created a separate archduchy for Ferdinand's second son (also Ferdinand) in the Tyrol and Further Austria and another for Karl in Inner Austria (Styria, Carinthia and Carniola). The archduchies responded differently to the common and mounting fiscal and administrative pressures upon the Habsburg patrimony around the turn of the century from the Long Turkish War. Emperor Rudolf failed to make common cause with those committed to keeping the empire working. Meanwhile, deepening divisions in the Reich precluded its members from contributing more to the military campaigns in Hungary. The emperor was thrown back on what he could negotiate from his ancestral lands through their Diets, dominated by local nobles and notables, where Protestantism had gained a firm foothold. Each meeting of the Diets in the various lands advertised their bewilderment with the emperor's erratic behaviour and emphasized his enfeeblement. Meanwhile, the archdukes handled local governing groups in ways that seemed to them best.

One group of lands in the 1564 partition lay in the Tyrol. There, Archduke Ferdinand had the fewest difficulties. Lutheranism had not made much headway and local secular and ecclesiastical élites were easily rallied behind a Counter-Reformation drawing on neighbouring Bavaria, which served as a shop-window for how to consolidate authority around revived Catholicism led from the top.

Archduke Karl faced different problems in Inner Austria, a second parcel of ancestral domains. Here Lutheranism had a secure footing among the local élites. In his negotiations with the Estates he was obliged to concede a general religious freedom, confirmed in the Pacification of Bruck (1578). In 1595, however, Archduke Ferdinand II ('Ferdinand of Styria'), Karl's eldest son, took over the reins in Graz, capital of Inner Austria. Following his father's wishes as well as the injunctions of his Bavarian mother, Archduchess Maria, and the Jesuits, Ferdinand turned the Counter-Reformation into a political programme of confessional absolutism. Its hallmarks were a twin allergy towards Protestantism and notions of mutual obligation between ruler and ruled. Its objective was to demonstrate how, with determined leadership, a prince could galvanize conforming élites into imposing the Counter-Reformation decisively and quickly.

Protestant nobles initially hoped to get Ferdinand's written agreement to continue the concessions made at Bruck as a quid pro quo for the Diet formally recognizing him as their ruler. When he refused, contending that he was a *princeps absolutus* and not a *princeps modificatus*, they accepted him anyway. He later claimed that the Diet had no right of appeal over his head to the emperor, that the privileges which the Protestants claimed had no basis in the 'consent of all the people' (*consensus totius populi*), and that his father had not bound his successors. His decisions were based, he told a delegation from the Diet, on an 'inspiration from God the Holy Spirit'.

In September 1598, he decreed the expulsion of all Protestant preachers from Styria. A year later an ecclesiastical commission began work. Led by a bishop and accompanied by state officials and militia, it worked its way round towns and villages. Books were publicly burned and Protestant graveyards desecrated. Commissioners expelled the Protestant preacher if one still remained, and then called the local community together. In exhortations which mingled the evils of Lutheranism with the benefits of conversion, the Ottoman threat and obedience to the prince, they then installed a Catholic priest, commissioned repairs to the church, and ordered Sunday and Catholic feast-day observance. Remaining Protestants were given notice to leave. Around 11,000 townspeople and 1,000 nobles chose exile but the popular revolt which some of Ferdinand's counsellors had predicted did not erupt. The achievement of Ferdinand's programme took place in the peculiar circumstances of the Turkish War, the growing political paralysis of the empire and the coming to maturity of a first generation of Jesuit-trained members of the local élite. Styria's success became the blueprint for confessional absolutism elsewhere in the Austrian Habsburg domains, and then in the Reich. The origins of the Thirty Years War are not to be sought in the Hradschin Palace in Prague (which is where the 1618 rebellion began) but on the Stadtkrone in Graz. That was where Ferdinand turned the Hofburg into his governing headquarters, next door to the Jesuit church and college (endowed with new buildings by Ferdinand in 1609), and where, appropriately, his imperial mausoleum would later be built.

A final group of ancestral lands, inherited by Ferdinand I's son and heir, Maximilian, came in three different parts: Upper and Lower Austria, Bohemia and Hungary. In Austria, the local nobility had a secure position in the Diets. In Bohemia and Hungary, the elective powers of the Diets made them stronger, the balance of powers and obligations as between prince and Diet being open to contesting interpretations by both sides, starting with the electoral principle itself in Bohemia. Although Ferdinand I had affirmed the principle of primogeniture after the 1547 rebellion, the Diet did not regard itself as bound by that decision.

In all these lands, Protestantism was an established presence, with rights of worship guaranteed through the Diets, and especially to the nobility. In 1568, Maximilian granted freedom of worship to nobles in Upper and Lower Austria. By the end of his rule, they were overwhelmingly Protestant and, through their influence, so were over half the parishes. In Bohemia, Lutherans collaborated with Utraquists and the Bohemian Brethren and, in 1575, the Diet presented the *Confessio Bohemica* (based on the Augsburg Confession) for Maximilian's assent (he gave it only orally). In neighbouring Moravia, a Calvinist minority was vociferous, while in Silesia all the nobility and most of the towns had been Lutheran for a generation. Although the major offices of state remained nominees of the emperor and in Catholic hands, the Protestants in the Diet developed parallel institutions to safeguard their privileges. Finally, in that enclave of northern and western Hungary which the Habsburgs counted their own, Protestantism was also in a majority. With the Turkish threat on their doorstep, neither Maximilian nor Rudolf could afford to ignore the political reality in Hungary, which was that its Diet was in contact with the other Diets in Habsburg lands and elsewhere, and that any opposition to Habsburg rule was guaranteed sustenance from Transylvania (or/and) the Ottomans.

The Austrian Habsburg succession was further complicated when Emperor Maximilian II left that last set of domains, his share of the inheritance, uniquely to his son Rudolf II. That broke with the precedent set by Ferdinand and, in 1582, Rudolf's four surviving brothers demanded compensation for their exclusion. They were offered posts within the Habsburg portfolio, but Matthias, Rudolf's third brother, refused to sign away his inheritance. Three years in the Netherlands as Stadholder (1578–81) did not cover him in glory. He spent the 1580s sulking in Linz. In 1593, he was put in charge of the Habsburg forces in the war against the Turks, and two years later became next in line to his brother Rudolf after the death of Archduke Ernst. By then, however, his frustration with the emperor's failure to support the war against the Turks was coupled with a desire (fostered by family rivalry) to emulate Archduke Ferdinand's Styrian experiment in Upper and Lower Austria. In 1599, Matthias appointed Bishop Melchior Khlesl as his chancellor there. It was on Khlesl's initiative that the archdukes met to draft an ultimatum to place before Rudolf, that he should appoint a successor.

Rudolf was jolted into actions that made an already delicate situation worse. He refused to discuss the succession. Instead, buoyed up by military successes in the Turkish War, he tried to show that he could emulate the Styrian programme and keep the archdukes in their place. The Hungarian Diet was told in 1604 that issues of religion were no longer up for discussion, while the royal towns of Silesia were informed that their Protestant institutions and worship had no legal basis. At the end of 1604, already discontented Hungarian Protestants made plans to join the Transylvanian István Bocskai in rebellion, while the Bohemian Diet looked on anxiously at what was happening in Silesia.

Exploiting the emperor's increasing weakness and isolation, Matthias manoeuvred himself into becoming the imperial governor in Hungary. There, faced with the reality of revolt, he made peace with the Hungarian rebels (June 1606), István Bocskai and the Ottomans. At the meeting of the Hungarian Diet in Bratislava in February 1608, Matthias struck a deal with the Hungarians and the Upper and Lower Austrian Diets, to which the Moravian Diet became a party at a later stage. István Illésházy, Protestant leader in the Hungarian Diet, was made a Palatine baron. Under his influence, and that of Georg Erasmus von Tschernembl, the Calvinist leader of the Lower Austrian Diet, the Estates offered homage to Archduke Matthias (thereby implicitly renouncing the emperor), so long as they were guaranteed their religious and political privileges, including the right to have only indigenous people appointed to the offices of state in their localities. In April 1608, Archduke Matthias had an army to hand and his cheer-leaders (Illésházy and Tschernembl) on side, ready to march on Prague and force the emperor's hand.

Spanish diplomats and the papal representative brokered a way out of the impasse. The emperor reluctantly accepted the treaty with the Turks. He ceded to Matthias all his rights over Hungary, Austria and Moravia, and promised him the succession in Bohemia. Sensing their time had come, the Bohemian, Silesian and Lusatian Diets, which had stood aside from the 1608 agreement at Bratislava, entered into a solemn alliance in June 1609, vowing in biblical terms to defend their religious freedoms 'to the last drop of blood'. They acknowledged their loyalty to the king of Bohemia but not to the Catholic officials in Prague who claimed to act in his name. Faced with a group of Protestant delegates who had forced their way into his apartments in the Hradschin Palace in Prague, Rudolf responded by offering in a personal guarantee (Letter of Majesty, 9 July 1609) what they wanted by way of religious and political privileges. Bohemian nobles, knights and towns with imperial charters could follow whatever religion those chose, and each group could elect ten 'Defensores' from the Estates, in reality an alternative government.

Rudolf's desperate efforts thereafter to recover his hopelessly weak position made things catastrophic. He asked his nephew Archduke Leopold to return with troops which had been deployed in the Jülich-Cleves dispute and liberate him from both Archduke Matthias and the Bohemian Estates. On their way down the Danube, some of them mutinied, while others looted parts of Austria and Bohemia. When they arrived in Prague in February 1611, the Diet simply removed all authority from imperial officers and put the Defensores in their place. In April, they summarily deposed Rudolf from his Bohemian crown and then used the Letter of Majesty as the basis for a confirmation of all their rights and privileges before electing Matthias in his place in May 1611. The contours of the crisis in Habsburg lands which broke out seven years later were already largely sketched out.

A CENTRAL EUROPEAN STORM

Matthias's election as emperor in 1612 did not diminish the Austrian Habsburg crisis either in the empire or in the ancestral lands. He presented himself to the imperial electors as a conciliator. Only intermittently involved in the affairs of the wider empire himself, he let Bishop (after 1615, Cardinal) Khlesl take the initiative. But the latter was mistrusted by the Reich's senior figures as a scheming newcomer. The fact that he was prepared to negotiate with Protestants seemed, at least to Archdukes Maximilian and Ferdinand, to prove them right, so they orchestrated his downfall in 1618. Khlesl's earliest initiative was to summon a Diet to Regensburg in August 1613. But he was held in suspicion by Protestant delegates when he proposed reforms to the imperial court to break the deadlock in its proceedings. Equally, his proposals for the empire to assist Matthias with his inherited debt of over 5 million guilders and the ongoing costs of maintaining the Hungarian frontier fortresses met with few supporters. Prorogued to the following year, and then abandoned, this was the last Diet to be held in the Reich for forty years, its paralysis the cause of its dissolution.

Khlesl's way forward in the empire then consisted of independently brokered bilateral compromises by which he could create a coalition of imperial loyalists which would gradually subsume Catholic and Protestant separatism. That separatism had become entrenched in the formation of confessional defensive leagues in the empire. The Protestants, led by Christian of Anhalt (Palatine in the Upper Palatinate, who had come to see politics in terms of opposing confessional blocs) and Philipp Ludwig of Pfalz-Neuburg, buried their Calvinist-Lutheran divisions and signed up to a confessionally delineated defensive Protestant Union at Auhausen (May 1608). Duke Maximilian of Bavaria responded with an association of German Catholic states (July 1609). Khlesl's efforts to weaken these leagues were helped by events. Although Christian of Anhalt's diplomatic initiatives included treaties with England (1612) and the Dutch (1613), the Protestant Union lost the backing which it had from France and Brandenburg, and never enjoyed any from Saxony. With an enfeebled membership and divisions, the Protestant Union was hardly a going concern in 1618, and collapsed in 1621. Maximilian's Catholic League fell apart even sooner, undermined by rivalries which the Habsburgs fomented. The more the confessionally based leagues weakened, the more Matthias was held in mistrust within the empire.

Meanwhile, in the ancestral lands Archduke Matthias's election as emperor did nothing to reduce the potential for confrontation. In Hungary, the threat to Habsburg survival was real and imminent. In Styria, Archduke Ferdinand demonstrated what a determined Catholic solution to all these problems would be. In Bohemia, a group of Protestant nobles won concessions in writing which acknowledged the Defensores as their independent guarantors, out of imperial hands. Matthias even agreed that the next Bohemian Diet would consider proposals to extend their powers, making them responsible for Bohemian military defence and foreign policy and allowing them to form a common front with other Diets in the ancestral lands.

Matthias's transfer of the imperial court to Vienna made him closer at hand for Hungarian problems. But it put him correspondingly further away from Prague and the influence which the imperial court could bring to bear there. At two general Diets of the Austrian, Bohemian and Hungarian lands in 1614 and 1615 Matthias played for time, exploiting the disunity among the opposition and counting on compliant Moravian and Bohemian nobles with whom he could work. The latter included the Bohemian chancellor and one of the Defensores, Zdenek von Lobkowitz, and, in Moravia, Karl Žerotín. The failure of the Diets disillusioned some and radicalized others, but seemed to strengthen Emperor Matthias's position.

With the emperor childless, there was a further succession issue looming. Faced with the crisis in their midst, however, the Habsburg brothers renounced their claims in favour of Ferdinand of Styria, the only archduke with offspring. Philip III, as a grandson of Maximilian II, technically had precedence, but the Spanish ambassador in Vienna, Íñigo Vélez de Guevara, count of Oñate, concluded a secret treaty with Matthias and Ferdinand in March 1617 whereby the latter would cede Habsburg possessions in Alsace and on the right bank of the Rhine to Spain in return for its support for his unopposed election to the Bohemian and imperial thrones. With that deal in the pocket, Matthias summoned the Bohemian Diet, which reluctantly elected Ferdinand king of Bohemia on 5 June 1617, crowning him three weeks later. Only two nobles openly opposed the election. Ferdinand then engineered his election by the Hungarian Diet to the crown of St Stephen, the coronation taking place in Bratislava on 1 July 1618. It was there that he received the news that his representatives in Prague (the Regents) had been summarily despatched from a window.

The Defenestration of Prague (23 May 1618) was an orchestrated act of rebellion from a minority of desperate nobles. The archbishop of Prague, Johann Lohelius, had already begun to anticipate the prospect of Ferdinand's accession by replacing Protestant pastors with Catholic priests on crown lands whose administration Matthias had entrusted to him. Protestants insisted that the Letter of Majesty extended freedom of worship to crown lands, but the emperor claimed that these were now in the hands of the Church and that its stipulations did not apply. When they petitioned Emperor Matthias in March against this sleight of hand, they were threatened with arrest. Aware that the support for rebellion was not wholehearted, a minority of Protestant notables met once more on 22 May in Prague, where one of their number (Heinrich Matthias, Count Thurn – a recently sacked imperial privy councillor) declared that it was time to throw the emperor's representatives 'out of the window, as is customary', a reference to the defenestration which had begun the Hussite revolt. The following day, singing hymns to keep up their spirits, they marched up the stairs to the room in the Hradschin where the Regents held court and despatched three (two Regents and a secretary) through a window.

On the 24th, the Protestants formed a provisional government (the 'Directors') and raised an army. The stakes were extremely high. The rebel leaders had no international backing and risked execution and reprisals, while for the Habsburgs the imperial crown lay in the balance. The comparison with the first act of the Dutch Revolt just over fifty years previously came to people's minds. But there was a difference in the desperation of the rebels and the determination of their opponents. The Directors cast around for allies elsewhere in the ancestral lands but the response was noncommittal. The Moravians refused to join in. Christian of Anhalt and the remnant of the Protestant (Evangelical) Union of princes in the empire were unwilling to support a rebellion against the emperor. But, holding out the prospect of being elected to the Bohemian crown, Christian persuaded the maverick duke of Savoy to finance a contract army under Count Ernst von Mansfeld, whose military experience had been won in the Turkish War but who had never been paid for his services. Playing for time and relying on the secret treaty with Spain, the imperialists began mustering their forces. Emperor Matthias died on 20 March 1619 and events moved to their climax.

Bohemian forces under Count Thurn invaded Moravia to force its Diet to join the rebellion, and then turned towards Vienna, arriving in its suburbs and hoping for a rebellion from within which never materialized. The Silesians, Lusatians and Lower and Upper Austrian Estates concluded a confederation with the Bohemians, its articles offering a vague blueprint for a mixed monarchy in which Protestantism had a defined place and where power lay in the hands of the nobles. But Mansfeld's forces were trapped by a contingent of Habsburg cavalry and decimated. On 19 August, the Bohemians deposed Ferdinand on the grounds of manifest tyranny. A week later, they elected Elector Frederick V of the Palatinate as their new king. Frederick's acceptance of the offer reflected the world view which prevailed around his council table in Heidelberg. Ludwig Camerarius, his leading privy councillor, was a Calvinist with a correspondence network which put him in touch with most of those in northern Europe who had been brought up as activists in the Protestant cause, and who argued for a pre-emptive strike against the imperialists.

In reality, Frederick was recognized as king in Bohemia only by Denmark, Sweden, Venice and the Dutch Republic, and only the last offered any resources to keep him on his throne. Frederick V could hardly let his co-religionists down and was influenced by his inheritance and connections. Through his bride, Elizabeth Stuart, King James I was his father-in-law, and she led him to believe that there would be support from that quarter. There had been a Palatine prince on the imperial throne two centuries previously (Ruprecht III), so why not another? When Elizabeth arrived in Prague she gave birth to their fourth child and he was named Ruprecht ('Rupert of the Rhine'). Frederick thought he could count, too, on collaboration from Bethlen Gábor's forces from Transylvania for a joint assault on Vienna before the end of the year.

Ferdinand consolidated his position as well. He was unanimously elected emperor at Frankfurt on 28 August 1619 and mustered his forces. The military defeat of the Bohemians, when it came, was swift and total. Saxony and Brandenburg supported the emperor, and so did Maximilian, duke of Bavaria, in the name of the Catholic League (Treaty of Munich, October 1619). The League had an army under a seasoned general, Johann Tserclaes, Count Tilly. At the battle of the White Mountain (8 November 1620), a chalk escarpment near Prague, 30,000 Bohemians were routed in about an hour by the conjoined imperial and Bavarian army. The Confederates might have regrouped to hold on to Prague but Tilly's cavalry so scattered the remnants that they put up no resistance. Frederick, now the derided 'Winter King', fled east to Silesia and then back to the Palatinate. It was how Emperor Ferdinand chose to exploit that victory which turned the Austrian Habsburg crisis into the Thirty Years War.

CONVERGING CATHOLIC
INTERESTS OF STATE

Ferdinand's success made confessional absolutism conceivable more broadly within the Habsburg ancestral lands, starting in Bohemia. On 21 June 1621, twenty-seven Bohemian rebel leaders were executed in the town hall square in Prague. The victims' speeches were drowned out by drums in case they proclaimed their martyrdom to a cause. Jan Jessenius, the brains behind the rebellion, was secured to a chair before his tongue was cut out prior to his being decapitated. The heads of the victims were displayed on spikes on top of the Charles Bridge – the six facing east towards the castle were those of the nobles who had revolted against their prince, and the six facing west towards the Old Town were those of burghers. Over 1,500 nobles were tried before a court and more than 600 of them were deprived of their estates (along with a further 250 Moravian nobles). Some received partial monetary compensation but it was in a currency that was deliberately debased and the Bohemian economy was by this point shattered. Ferdinand used the expropriations to reward those who had been loyal to the imperial cause, to strengthen the power of the Habsburg state and to re-Catholicize the region. Calvinist and Lutheran ministers were expelled along with all Anabaptists, and religious freedom was abolished. Urban privileges were curtailed. Then in 1627 the nobility was confronted with the choice between converting to Catholicism and taking up exile. That same year a 'Renewed Constitution' (*Verneuerte Landesordnung*) was proclaimed in both Bohemia and Moravia which declared the Bohemian crown hereditarily Habsburg and Catholicism the sole religion. The country ceased to be a constituent element in the Habsburg kingdom and instead became an imperial crown land, its Diet a consultative body in which the upper clergy was restored to its place. Over 150,000 Bohemians chose exile.

Aware of the ramifications of confessional absolutism, Emperor Ferdinand tailored it to local environments to minimize the backlash. In Silesia, the repression was less harsh. In Lower Austria, the opposition was divided between a minority of nobles who swore an oath of allegiance to Ferdinand in 1620 – and were then guaranteed personal religious freedom – and the rest, who were not. Then, once those who had openly resisted his rule had been dealt with, he modified the 1620 undertakings to a simple guarantee of freedom of conscience, prohibiting remaining Protestant nobles from having churches and schools in their castles, on the pretext that they caused sedition. Upper Austria, by contrast, was treated to a similar fate to that of Bohemia. In 1624, Protestant preachers and schoolmasters were given a month to leave the country. All other Protestants except nobles were told to convert or leave by Easter 1626. A resulting uprising was suppressed with the help of Bavaria and, by 1630, 100,000 Austrians had joined the exiled Bohemians. In Hungary, Ferdinand's rule still hung in the balance. Bethlen Gábor periodically assaulted it from Transylvania until his death in 1629. Thereafter his successor, György I Rákóczi, continued the struggle, making ineffectual common cause with Sweden and France until

Emperor Ferdinand III made a peace with him in 1647 (the Treaty of Linz), opening the door to Hungary's confessional absolutism later in the century.

The emperor's jurists argued (with reason on their side) that they were merely putting into practice *cuius regio eius religio* in Habsburg lands, granting a right of exile (*ius emigrandi*) in each case as required by the Peace of Augsburg. What happened in the empire after the Bohemian defeat called into question, however, the basic fabric of the Reich. Frederick's defeat in Prague foreshadowed his deposition from the Palatinate. Rejecting an offer of leniency if he acknowledged the emperor's authority, he was unilaterally outlawed by the emperor in 1621 (imperial lawyers advising that no trial was needed because his crime was 'notorious'). His survival depended on mercenary forces under Count Mansfeld, the Lutheran Margrave of Baden-Durlach, Duke Christian of Brunswick-Lüneburg and a token force of 2,000 from James I. Spanish troops advanced on the left bank of the Rhine into the Lower Palatinate under General Ambrogio Spínola, while Count Tilly's League forces occupied the right bank, taking Heidelberg on 19 September. Frederick fled into exile in the Netherlands. There then followed a confiscation of the Elector's assets. Adding the left-bank lands of the Lower Palatinate to what it had been promised under the 1617 treaty, Spain increased its stake in the Rhineland.

Emperor Ferdinand had built up big debts to Duke Maximilian of Bavaria during the Bohemian campaign, and initially offered Upper Austria as their guarantee. He could now recompense him with the Upper Palatinate and, in a secret deal in September 1621, Maximilian was also given the Electoral title. The balance of forces among the Electors was changed for good, and without any consultation of those Electors. When the Palatine councillor Ludwig Camerarius published the secret letters, making it impossible to deny what had been agreed, it was the papacy which demanded that the arrangement be publicly ratified. It also asked for the uniquely rich Heidelberg library to be transferred to Rome in recompense for its support. Following a limited assembly of Catholic princes which stopped short of being a Diet, at Regensburg (February 1623), the emperor reluctantly agreed to the transfer of the library, Maximilian ensuring that a Bavarian *ex libris* was inscribed in each book before it was transhipped to Rome. The formal annexation of the Upper Palatinate to Duke Maximilian was confirmed in 1628. Wittelsbach

Bavaria was no longer a rival of the Austrian Habsburgs but a military and strategic partner whose alliance with the Spanish Habsburgs was based on congruent Catholic interests.

The re-Catholicization of the Upper Palatinate followed immediately thereafter. Protestant schools and churches were closed and transferred to Catholic authorities. The Jesuits organized mass burnings of Protestant books. Confession certificates were introduced as tests of compliance, especially among the nobility. Those failing to attend Mass, or who ate meat on Fridays, were liable to a fine and the threat of expulsion. By 1630, ninety noble families in the Upper Palatinate had converted and more than that number took up exile. As in Bohemia and Upper Austria, the changes offered the opportunity to refashion the élite around those who either had been, or would be, loyal to the Bavarian duke.

The prospects for a peaceful resolution, launched by Duke Wilhelm IV of Saxony-Weimar around the notion of a German Peace League in 1623, were non-existent. The propositions that the Elector Palatine should be allowed back into his territories, that exiles should return and that a peace accord could be built around a reconstructed Peace of Augsburg were unrealistic. Besides, Count Tilly's Catholic League army now moved from the Palatine into Westphalia in pursuit of Christian of Brunswick's forces in the summer of 1623, blocking their escape into the Netherlands and routing them at Stadtlohn on 6 August. The theatre of conflict moved northwards into the heartland of the Protestant princes and territories.

The logic for that shift of emphasis lay in the briefly coinciding interests of Munich, Vienna and Madrid. Although their diplomats and advisers shared a common Catholic outlook on politics and the world, Protestant contemporaries wrongly interpreted that as a Catholic conspiracy or a resurgent myth of Habsburg world monarchy. In reality it depended on a realization that for the moment they had more to gain from standing together than apart. There was solidarity for Spain when it used military force to intervene in the Grisons to secure the Valtelline in 1620, a heavy-handed repression of a largely Protestant population. Support from Munich and Vienna became clearer during the renewed Spanish conflict with the Dutch in the Low Countries in the 1620s. With the expiry of the truce in 1621, Spínola's re-equipped Flanders Army of 70,000 men launched an assault on Bergen-op-Zoom in 1622. Two years later, Spínola invested the nearby fortress town of Breda. The siege lasted nine months and resulted in the deaths of 13,000 inhabitants and defending soldiers before the city surrendered in June 1625. That success was because so many Dutch troops were pinned down by Count Tilly's forces in garrisons along the Rhine, Ems and Lippe.

A more ambitious joint strategy against the Dutch (one not requiring such a large army stationed in the Netherlands) involved crippling the enemy's economic infrastructure. Spain commissioned the construction of twenty purpose-built corsairs at Dunkirk and requisitioned sixty or so other ships for war purposes. The Dunkirkers menaced Dutch and English shipping in the Channel in the 1620s. Whereas over 1,000 Dutch vessels were recorded going to and fro up the Channel in the years 1614–20, only fifty-two risked that passage in the years from 1621 to 1627. The English lost 390 ships (a fifth of its merchant marine) between 1624 and 1628. The economic disruption had a significant impact in both the Netherlands and England. The Anglo-Dutch counter-attack of 1625 was limited to a failed raid on Cádiz and a disastrous expedition to help French Protestants. In the same year a Franco-Savoyard attack on Genoa was successfully repulsed, and the Dutch were expelled from Bahia in Brazil.

In the light of that success, Spain began establishing agents, responsible to a court in Seville, known as the 'Admiralty of the North', or *Almirantazgo de los Países Septentrionales*. The task of the court was to certify the place of origin of goods imported into Spain from northern lands. The objective was to stamp out Dutch goods being smuggled in as French or German. A further measure initiated in 1625 involved constructing a canal linking the Rhine south of Wesel with the Maas at Venlo (the *Fossa Eugeniana*) to deflect commerce away from the republic. Then discussions began between Madrid and Vienna on developing a Habsburg anti-Dutch maritime capacity in the North Sea and the Baltic. Madrid's aim was to complete its economic blockade of the Netherlands; Vienna's aims were to develop the ports in East Frisia and on the Elbe, generate a permanent revenue for the imperial treasury and impose an imperial-led Catholic solution upon the ecclesiastical territories in the Reich and the future of its institutions.

With the spoils from Bohemia and the prospect of permanent revenues from the empire, Ferdinand decided to sponsor a further army. Albrecht von Wallenstein was appointed its commander and ordered to raise 24,000 men in Lower Saxony in April 1625. Wallenstein was a minor Bohemian noble who had risen through service to Emperor Matthias, converted to Catholicism and acquired military experience. Profiting from imperial expropriations and currency debasement in Bohemia, he became the largest landowner in the region and was one of the richest men in the empire. He raised regiments on his own credit. The Flemish Calvinist Hans de Witte was a partner in the consortium which profited from the Bohemian debasement, and his confidence in Wallenstein's assets in Bohemia and elsewhere was at the basis of his willingness to mobilize credit lines with other Calvinist financiers, as well as manage the armaments, munitions and food supply contracts essential to Wallenstein's military effort. With de Witte, Wallenstein advanced sums to the emperor. In return, his estates in Friedland were elevated to a dukedom, thereby making him an imperial prince. Wallenstein's army was, like those of his contemporaries only on a grander scale, a speculative operation.

DENMARK AND THE DESTINY OF THE EMPIRE

The impact of this congruence of Catholic state interests in the empire was profound. In Protestant courts, exiled nobles recounted stories of religious oppression, presenting themselves as the precursors of what would happen elsewhere. Those who stood aside from the conflict (such as Brandenburg and Saxony), having received guarantees from the emperor, began to wonder what would become of the Reich. Even Catholic Electors shared their nervousness, complaining about Spanish troops on their estates and concerned about being dragged into the Hispano-Dutch conflict. Duke Maximilian of Bavaria was outraged to learn of a secret agreement between Emperor Ferdinand and General Wallenstein at Bruck (November 1626) giving Wallenstein permission to occupy lands in the Reich and exact contributions from them to support his forces. The convergence of Catholic state interests faded as imperial intentions became more menacing.

The developments in the empire particularly affected Denmark. The Danish Oldenburg dynasty had emerged in 1536 from an interregnum and civil war to take advantage of the Reformation, consolidate its authority over Denmark, Norway and Iceland and become a significant regional power. Collaboration with its aristocracy was one of the secrets of its success; another was its strategic dominance of the entrance to the

Baltic. As the latter's maritime commerce grew so Danish temptations to turn it into a closed sea (*mare clausum*) became greater. It first exercised its right to do so in 1565 and then levied tolls (2 per cent of the value of the cargo from 1567) on vessels passing through the Skagerrak. Ships were compelled to put into Elsinore, the royal castle at Kronborg, rebuilt in 1585 and a symbol of the power of the Danish monarchy into whose coffers toll-receipts directly went.

Christian IV, crowned king in Denmark in 1596, was the heir to a healthy treasury. Educated to rule, he entered into the task with hyperactive enthusiasm. He launched ambitious projects – creating new towns, founding new industries and sponsoring exploration to Greenland and the Far East. The Danish navy became a serious force in the Baltic, but its dominance was not uncontested. Since the 1560s Sweden, Russia and Poland vied for the eastern Baltic littoral. The relationship between Sweden and Poland became hostile. And Denmark's relationship with Sweden was fraught because Christian IV refused to surrender his dynastic claims to the Swedish crown, and because Danish territories circled Sweden's frontiers to the south and west. Danish-Swedish antagonisms also involved contested claims to Norwegian lands in the Arctic Circle, where both monarchs claimed to be king of the Lapps, rivals to control shipping through the Barents Sea to Archangel. In the Kalmar War (1611–13) Denmark took Älvsborg after a siege of only eighteen days, Sweden's only North Sea port. At the Peace of Knäred (January 1613) Danish pre-eminence in the Baltic and northern Norway was reinforced. Sweden recovered Älvsborg with a ransom of a million *riksdalers* or the equivalent of ten barrels of gold. Free of concerns about his Baltic neighbour, Christian IV could concentrate upon problems in the empire.

The Danish king was a Reich prince (through being duke of Holstein). He had dynastic involvements in the bishoprics of Bremen, Verden and Osnabrück which would be threatened by any change of status imposed by the emperor in secularized ecclesiastical territories. Bremen and Verden controlled the Weser and Elbe estuaries, where Christian IV had mercantilist ambitions. When the imperial court ruled in 1618 that Hamburg was a 'free city', Christian decided to construct a new town (Glückstadt) to constrict Hamburg's maritime traffic. The Habsburg programme of a North Sea-Baltic economic campaign against Dutch commerce directly affected Denmark.

Christian IV's alarm at the emperor's growing military presence in northern Germany was not shared by his Council of State, which regarded involvement in German affairs as a diversion that Sweden would exploit. So when he declared war on the emperor in 1625 it was not as a Danish invasion but as duke of Holstein lending support to the local defence alliance of the Lower Saxon Circle. Things did not begin well for Christian. He and his horse fell from the city wall at Hameln in July 1625. He was unconscious for a couple of days, with rumours of his death giving Tilly hopes of overcoming the opposition quickly. Christian recovered to lead the Lower Saxon campaign the following year against the combined armies of Tilly and Wallenstein, but his allies abroad (the Dutch and England) let him down and his campaign faltered. A counter-offensive failed and, in full retreat, he made a stand at Lutter am Barenberge in the foothills of the Harz Mountains, where he was routed. Half his army was killed, captured or wounded, his senior officers died, and the king himself only narrowly escaped capture. The collapse of the Lower Saxon opposition followed. Wallenstein's and Tilly's forces invaded Holstein in September 1627 and then moved into Denmark itself. Wallenstein became duke of Mecklenburg, a principality with which he could underwrite his debts and support his now mammoth army, numbering (on paper) 130,000 men.

The emperor's pre-eminence in the Reich became a realistic prospect. The plans for a Habsburg North Sea and Baltic anti-Dutch commercial tourniquet were now feasible. Wallenstein was given the titles 'Generalissimo' and 'General of the Ocean and Baltic Seas'. He started work on a canal across the neck of the Jutland peninsula so that ships could bypass the tolls on shipping exacted by Denmark at the Sound. The Mecklenburg port of Wismar was chosen as his naval base, and work began to build a fleet. Before it was ready, the small Pomeranian Baltic sea-port of Stralsund refused to accept a garrison of Wallenstein's troops, and he ordered its bombardment in May 1628. He perhaps had not appreciated its strategically excellent defensive position and, four months later, Wallenstein's forces withdrew as Swedish and Danish reinforcements came to the town's rescue. Emboldened by that reversal and with the Danish fleet intact, Christian mounted a naval counter-offensive. Hoping to make use of those ships in the imperial cause in due course, imperial strategists made an honourable peace with the

Danish king at Lübeck, restoring all his patrimony except the secularized bishoprics without a penny in costs.

The secularized ecclesiastical territories in the empire were the subject of Ferdinand's Edict of Restitution (March 1629). His Jesuit confessor, Wilhelm Lamormaini, assured him that it was a solution which carried divine blessing: 'God promises us the victory shortly. His cause drives us on.' The imperial vice-chancellor, Peter Heinrich von Stralendorf, drafted the text. Superficially, it was nothing more than an interpretation of the Peace of Augsburg. In reality, it was a legislative act without precedence, pronounced as law in the empire without being endorsed by any imperial Diet. It enforced a Catholic interpretation of the Ecclesiastical Reservation – the requirement that ecclesiastical princes in the empire should forfeit Church lands if they converted to Lutheranism after 1552. Such secularizations had occurred on a large scale but they had become sanctioned by time and legalized in princely successions and land transfers. However, the military successes of the 1620s favoured the restitution of such lands in the Rhineland, and secular Catholic rulers had already begun to take advantage of that fact. The edict offered a way for the emperor to bridle a process already in motion and, by emphasizing his own role as arbiter, to reassert imperial authority.

The edict threatened the (Protestant) possessors of fifteen bishoprics in northern Germany as well as the occupants of 500 wealthy monasteries across northern and central Germany – large areas and populations, with substantial revenues. By the end of 1630, five bishoprics and 120 monasteries were restored by imperial commissioners, backed up by Wallenstein's troops. In Magdeburg, where monastic restitution had begun under his authority in 1628, the city rebelled. Representatives from Lübeck and Hamburg, the most important independent Hanse cities, told Wallenstein that the measure compromised their mercantile cooperation with him: 'The edict cannot be sustained ... one cannot simply scrap the religious peace.' Writing back to Rombaldo Collalto, president of the imperial War Council, in November 1629, Wallenstein bluntly told him that the edict had 'turned all the non-Catholics against us'. Three months later, he added: 'their embitterment is so great that they are all saying that if only the Swede [i.e. Gustav Adolf] would come they would gladly die for him'.

The implications of the edict for the empire were huge. The scope for Habsburg ecclesiastical patronage with which to cajole princes and territories to do the emperor's bidding was immense. The power of that patronage was already evident. Saxony had been given Lusatia for its loyalty in the Bohemian rising. Brandenburg's Calvinist Elector's policy was in the hand of his favourite, Count Adam von Schwarzenberg. The latter exploited his contacts in Vienna to assure the duke's succession in Pomerania and his security of tenure in Magdeburg and Cleves. Wallenstein maintained 12,000 troops in garrisons across northern Germany, while despatching 15,000 more into Poland to keep Gustav Adolf tied down in his Polish campaign. A further 17,000 were sent to the Netherlands to reinforce the Spanish, whose army threatened mutiny after the Dutch captured the Spanish silver fleet in 1628. Partly with that windfall, the Dutch began the siege of 's-Hertogenbosch in April 1629, building a 40-mile dyke around its canals and sluices. The resulting polder was then drained, allowing the Dutch to advance and force the surrender of a key stronghold in Spain's frontier fortresses.

With the imperial hold on northern Germany fragile and the continuing risk of a Hungarian attack from Bethlen Gábor, Wallenstein wanted no further commitments. Yet the emperor and the imperial War Council in Vienna demanded he find 14,000 troops for a proposed campaign in northern Italy. On Christmas Day 1627 Duke Vincenzo II Gonzaga of Mantua and Montferrat died. His territories were technically fiefs of the empire, and he was childless. Aware of his ill-health, he had willed his inheritance to his niece, Maria Gonzaga, whom he married to his cousin Charles de Gonzaga, duke of Nevers, to keep the possessions in the family. The marriage took place at Mantua, the day that he died. The duke of Nevers was a resident of the French court and his succession to Mantua and Montferrat threatened Spain's position in northern Italy, especially in contiguous Milan.

The Spanish Habsburgs procured an alternative claimant, declared Nevers's occupation illegal and despatched forces to seize the fortress of Casale in the spring of 1628. What was intended as a short campaign turned into a protracted siege lasting over a year. Braving Alpine snow, French regiments relieved the fortress in February 1629, but the Spanish renewed their attack on it in the summer, asking the emperor for assistance. Ferdinand assented and an imperial army left to besiege Casale in September, despite Wallenstein's opposition, directed by Rombaldo, count of Collalto. Not until July of the following year did the imperial regiments enter Mantua and expel the duke of Nevers. By then, opposition to Wallenstein's extraordinary power, as well as his regiments' garrisons and their exactions in northern Germany, had been expressed by the Catholic Electors of the empire meeting at Regensburg in June 1630. They demanded Wallenstein's dismissal and the reduction of his forces to under a third of their strength. Ferdinand II complied, dispensing with his commander-in-chief in August. Wallenstein's own disillusionment with the direction of imperial affairs made him accept the turn of events with equanimity. Not so Hans de Witte, his banker, who committed suicide. Gustav Adolf had landed with a Swedish expeditionary force at Stralsund just over a month previously.

THE DEMISE OF THE FRENCH PROTESTANT PARTY

In the aftermath of Henry IV's assassination, a Protestant delegation accompanied the pastor André Rivet to present their loyal address to Louis XIII and his mother Marie de Médicis. Among them was the soldier-poet Agrippa d'Aubigné, who recounts how he scandalized the queen and courtiers by refusing to go down on bended knee before his sovereign. His gesture so frightened Rivet that he could hardly deliver his speech for shaking with fear. D'Aubigné explained that he meant no disrespect to his king. Especially in the circumstances of the recent assassination, he owed his sovereign 'reverence'. His point was that (Protestant) nobles owed 'natural' obedience to their ruler, unconstrained by (Catholic) fawning. The Huguenot 'party' fostered attitudes to power that were redolent of the Christian commonwealth. Now that peace had been secured, its general assemblies existed (according to Philippe Duplessis-Mornay) to advance the 'common good' of Protestant Churches. He saw no contradiction between that and the 'common good' of the realm as a whole. He argued that the assemblies were essential to the maintenance of the peace, the electing of deputies to represent their interests at the French court, and the integration of French Protestants into civil society. These were the grounds on which Regent Queen Mother Marie reluctantly assented to calling an assembly to Duplessis's stronghold town of Saumur in 1611.

French politics were moving, however, in another direction. Two royal assassinations in succession created a unique public mood which royal publicists and Gallican magistrates exploited. Henry IV became a Bourbon hero who had sacrificed his life for his kingdom. At the Estates General of 1614–15, summoned to forestall a noble rebellion led by the prince of the blood (Henri, prince of Condé), the demands from the third estate opened with a 'fundamental law' that no authority on earth but that of the king of France existed in his realm. The rest of the *cahier* of demands went on to elaborate reforms which were politely put to one side when the queen mother dismissed the delegates to this, its last convocation before 1789. Marie de Médicis's court excluded Protestant grandees who had enjoyed high favour in the previous regime, and they were inclined to side with other malcontent nobles. Louis XIII's marriage to Anne of Austria, Philip III's daughter (November 1615), convinced Protestants that France had joined the Spanish Habsburg orbit.

The Protestant party was divided between those who believed the best way of protecting it was through negotiation (dismissed as *politiques*) and those who thought that confrontation was the best defence (hard-liners – *fermes, acharnés*). Denied a formal protector, the party's grandees (the duke of Bouillon in the northeast; the duke of Lesdiguières in Dauphiné; the duke of La Force in the southwest, and others) used their regional influence to rival one another to lead it. Some of them found royal pensions and a place at Louis XIII's court more congenial, and in due course converted. In 1620, a royal expedition to integrate Béarn into the rest of the kingdom forced the issue. The Pyrenean viscountcy was part of Henry of Navarre's ancestral lands. Its Reformation was an act of state, directed by his mother, Jeanne d'Albret, after a failed rebellion and invasion in 1569. A Protestant oligarchy ran its affairs through Estates, which preserved its language and traditions as a place where the Salic law did not apply and its princes could be held to account.

Integrating Béarn into France meant disavowing those traditions and reducing the privileged position of its Protestants. Louis XIII's entry into its capital (Pau) in October 1620 was a Catholic victory parade. Béarn's frightened Protestant oligarchs called on their French co-religionists to help. The latter interpreted what was happening as linked to events in Germany and the Rhineland. Aware of their own divisions and military unpreparedness but feeling desperate, they took up arms, led by the militarily resourceful Henri, duke of Rohan, and his less capable younger brother, Benjamin, duke of Soubise. It took five royal campaigns and a decade to crush the military strength of the Huguenots, but the essence of the task was achieved in the first two years during a campaign to the south of France in 1621–2, which removed many Protestant strongholds, leaving La Rochelle, Montauban and Montpellier as exposed relics of its former strength, internally divided and desperate. La Rochelle was the object of a remorseless siege, masterminded by Armand du Plessis, Cardinal Richelieu, in 1628. He ordered the construction of 7.5 miles of siege-works and twenty-nine fortifications. To prevent the city receiving aid from English or Dutch co-religionists, 4,000 workers built a 1,500-yard wall on sunken vessels, filled with rubble. After fourteen months and a failed Anglo-Dutch relief expedition, it surrendered in October 1628.

Montauban and Montpellier were handed over to Louis XIII by the duke of Rohan at the Peace of Alais in June 1629, sacrificing the Huguenot political and military party in return for a renewed guarantee of the religious privileges which the peace at Nantes had accorded them. The fall of La Rochelle was the focus for an orgy of celebrations in Paris, culminating in a victory procession through twelve triumphal arches on 23 December. The frontispiece to the official programme depicts the magistrates of Paris on their knees before the seated king, surrounded by the dukes of Orléans and Soissons. Through the windows in the background are depicted the smouldering relics of La Rochelle. Four of the magistrates look directly at the reader, reminding him that absolute obedience is his duty too.

The duke of Rohan escaped to exile in Venice, taking with him four crates of books. In his enforced leisure, he wrote about politics. His library included Machiavelli and Guicciardini as well as Cicero, Tacitus and the neo-Stoic classics. His lifestyle and outlook were not those of a strict Calvinist, and his loyalty to the Huguenot cause, while not in doubt, had not uniquely inspired his rebellion. He rationalized the latter as a visceral hatred for Spain, whose 'interest is to persecute Protestants in order to aggrandize themselves on the spoils', France's 'interest' being to understand 'the poison which results from that'. His military campaigns were ruthless, reflecting the desperate situation in which the divided French Protestant movement found itself, and about which he had no illusions. Criticized for appealing to King James for outside aid in 1620–21, he said that he would surely have been censured afterwards had he not done so. He understood that politics and war were spheres where Christian morality played no part, that he was living in a world of political and military 'revolutions' for which there were no 'rules'. His heroes were rebels – Alcibiades, Caesar, even the Catholic duke of Guise – to be criticized only when they failed to follow the logic of their own actions. Rejecting the virtues of clemency, he wrote: 'It is the vice of irresolution and a weakness of courage that holds us back, rather than true compassion for the sufferings of others . . . it is thus that we often try to cover our vices with the meanest virtue [pity].' An iron century bred iron in the soul.

18. War at Large

UNINTENDED CONSEQUENCES

In the years 1627–30 military sieges took place hundreds of miles apart and in different theatres of war. At Stralsund (May–Aug. 1628), Casale (spring 1628–March 1629), La Rochelle (Sep. 1627–Oct. 1628), 's-Hertogenbosch (April–Sep. 1629), Casale again (Sep. 1629–Oct. 1630) and Mantua (Nov. 1629–July 1630), they were part of the attritional war taking place across Europe. Their course was as unpredictable as the political and strategic consequences of their outcomes were imponderable.

By negotiating an end to the siege of Stralsund, Wallenstein wanted to avoid 'the inevitable bloodbath' (as he put it) of storming it, damaging relations with Hamburg and Lübeck and compromising imperialist plans. That allowed the city to sign a twenty-year alliance with Gustav Adolf, creating the Swedish bridgehead into North Germany two years later. As Cardinal Richelieu's siege of La Rochelle ended, the aggrieved lieutenant who had assassinated Charles I's favourite, the duke of Buckingham, was executed at Tyburn. Owed £80 in back-pay, wounded in the failed English expedition to the Île de Ré to succour French Protestants in 1626, John Felton had carried out the deed in Portsmouth on 23 August 1628, declaring (in a letter sewn into his hat, one version of which read): 'that man is cowardly base and deserveth not the name of gentleman and soldier that is not willing to sacrifice his life for the honour of his God, his King and his country'. The public outbreak of rejoicing at Buckingham's death and the distrust which lay behind it wrecked Charles's hopes of negotiating with the English Parliament of 1628. The Anglo-French war (1627–9), with its two failed attempts to relieve the La Rochelle siege, came ignominiously to a close. England adopted benevolent neutrality in the Thirty Years War – which meant closet support for the Spanish, the last thing Richelieu wanted. The siege equally strained France's alliance with the Dutch (Treaty of Compiègne, 1624) strengthening fears in the Netherlands that the French were unreliable allies.

The Dutch capture of 's-Hertogenbosch ended peace-feelers between Spain and the Netherlands. In addition to the fortress, the city was the seat of the bishopric in North Brabant and the gateway to the Maas. The population of mainly Catholic Meierij from the surrounding region were now Dutch. From that moment on (even more so when the Dutch took Maastricht in 1632) the Dutch Republic had a fringe Catholic minority whose religion and interests the Spanish were determined to protect. Madrid argued that the region's civil jurisdiction still lay in Brussels. Catholic spiritual jurisdiction was not theirs to assign to someone else. And whatever happened to Church property would have to be discussed alongside the ecclesiastical territories in the Reich. The fall of 's-Hertogenbosch pushed peace further away.

The failed sieges in northern Italy also complicated the European chequerboard. Olivares recognized that Spain's Mantuan war was a gamble: 1627, he wrote, 'will decide the fate of this Monarchy'. The emperor had secured North Germany. Spain had seized the offensive in the Netherlands. France was in open war with its Protestants and had made peace with Spain (Treaty of Monzón, 5 March 1626), ending their differences in the Valtelline. By 1630, however, the pieces were stacked against Spain. The withdrawal of troops from General Spínola's army to northern Italy crippled the anti-Dutch offensive. Dutch capture of the Spanish treasure fleet in 1628 caused fears of another Spanish bankruptcy. Casale and Mantua diverted imperial forces from northern Germany, enabling the Swedes to secure their bridgehead in 1630. The French intervention in northern Italy rendered war between France and both the Spanish and Austrian Habsburgs all but inevitable. Attritional warfare depended for its success on one side acquiring a strategic advantage such that the other would be forced to sue for peace. Its logic, however, was defeated by the war of unintended consequences.

These dominated the period from 1630 to 1648, the year negotiations in Westphalia ended war in Germany and the Netherlands. Sweden's military intervention with French financial and diplomatic backing in

Germany in July 1630 complicated one set of diplomatic, military and political equations. France's declaration of war on the Spanish Habsburgs in May 1635 – followed by a similar declaration against the Austrian Habsburgs a year later – aggravated another. In Sweden's case, the issues were how to secure stable allies among North German territories and in Europe at large such that they could impose their will upon the emperor and secure a peace in which the liberties of the empire were restored but Sweden had 'satisfaction' for the debts which its intervention generated. France was forced to fight attritional warfare on several fronts at once, making common cause with anti-Habsburg sentiments wherever they surfaced. French diplomats took over from the Swedes the notion of a new international order in which the liberties of individual states in Germany would be preserved by a self-sustaining state system. Cardinal Richelieu's difficulty (and Mazarin's after him) was to persuade others that the objective of this new order was not to dismantle Habsburg hegemony and replace it with a French one.

A decade of warfare in central Europe created an army of exiled and dispossessed, mostly Protestants and dispersed in northern Germany, southern Poland and the Netherlands. The reassignment of their assets to others stacked up contrary and disputed interests among various parties. The scale of military operations created armaments, munitions and equipment suppliers with a stake in the continuing conflict. Enterprisers built up regiments of seasoned soldiers with credit- and supply-lines which would all need to be satisfied in any final reckoning. Military machines whose operations depended principally on living off their enemies had the problem of keeping their operations at a scale that was appropriate to the demands of attritional warfare without exceeding the resources to keep them in the field, while guaranteeing that their interests would be met in any final settlement. Military machines whose resource-chains led back to the states in whose name they operated created logistic and fiscal pressures which generated revolt and revolution back home. The costs of war in central Europe kept rising in the 1630s and 40s.

The more complex the political, military and diplomatic equations became, the less the conflicts were about any one issue. The political impasse created by the Edict of Restitution in the empire, the naked pursuit of Habsburg imperial and Spanish interests, then France's bid for hegemony, and the accumulating material destruction, all gave the lie to its being about the survival of Christendom. Spanish commentators openly despised France for its cynicism. The French king was in the clutches of wicked cardinals who wanted to ally him with the Ottomans, the Dutch, the Swiss, 'the enemies of Faith, of Christian people, of kings and the Catholic Church'. Its mooted new international order ignored the significance of the 'German nation' and masked French expansionism. When, after 1640, France supported the Catalan and Portuguese rebellions, the propagandist Francesco Quevedo lamented that France was waging unjust war 'on the whole of Christendom . . . by sowing discord'. Philip IV declared Mazarin to be the 'author of the calamities of Christendom'.

A confessional outlook resurfaced in the international politics of the 1620s but it did not last. By the 1630s it was difficult to interpret the conflicts as between two versions of Christianity. The divisions among Protestants were clear, many Lutherans being just as suspicious of Calvinist activists as they were of more interventionist Catholics. The emperor had relied on the neutrality (even active support) of Protestant princes such as the Landgrave of Hesse-Darmstadt, the Elector of Brandenburg and the Elector of Saxony. Equally, not all Catholics were committed to a struggle against Protestantism. Duke Maximilian of Bavaria pursued his own dynastic and territorial imperatives, which converged in the 1620s with the emperor's, only to diverge again in the 40s. The Jesuits, whom Protestant propaganda epitomized as a secret but united force working for their overthrow, were as divided as the world they ministered to.

The successors to the princely confessors in Munich and Vienna who advised Emperor Ferdinand and Duke Maximilian (Wilhelm Lamormaini and Adam Contzen respectively) advocated accommodation with the Protestants and the abandonment of any sense of providential destiny. Even Emperor Ferdinand II (whose letters sometimes imply that he was fighting a Crusade in the empire) urged his Generalissimo Wallenstein to use the 'pretext of religion' (*praetextum der Religion*) in his public pronouncements just as his enemies did. In 1632, Axel Oxenstierna reminded the Swedish Council of State that their involvement in the war had been 'not so much a matter of religion, but rather of saving the public state [*status publicus*] wherein religion is also comprehended'. Jesuits Johannes Gans in Vienna and Johannes Vervaux in Munich had, along with their Superior General, Muzio Vitelleschi, learned the lessons of what happened when the order became too closely identified with a particular prince's policies, or critical of them. Jean Suffren and Nicolas Caussin, Jesuits in Paris, were left in no doubt by Richelieu that they were there to support the policies of the government, while Olivares's confessor (Francisco Aguado) regarded Spain's war as a spiritual test in which French Catholics were as much the tempters as Dutch Protestants. The military machines on both sides were sustained by credit- and supply-lines that crossed religious boundaries. Religion had become a reason of state, used in public declarations, emphasized in propaganda, legitimizing conflict but increasingly problematic.

The international political equations as well as the complex interests of the parties made it more difficult to imagine how peace was going to be negotiated, and in what forum. Christendom's international order no longer existed. The mediation of the papacy was rejected by the Dutch and other Protestant powers. The Reich's Diet was in desuetude along with its other institutions. The emperor was disinclined to bring the parties of the empire together. At the Regensburg assembly of Catholic Electors in June 1630, the first item on the agenda was 'general peace' but it was never discussed. In 1632, Antoine Wolfath, bishop of Vienna and imperial councillor, suggested that all Catholic states send delegates to a congress to be convened in a neutral town. The emperor was lukewarm, preferring to pursue the option of separate 'compositions' with individual powers in the empire. In the early months of 1635, Richelieu announced Louis XIII's intention of appointing French envoys for the negotiations so long as Philip IV participated too. But France's declaration of war on Spain was only months away and the proposal made no headway. In 1636, the papacy offered to mediate between the parties in Cologne but it never happened. The strategic calculations led each side to think they could gain more from continuing the war.

Only when the balance changed and when the internal pressures created by attritional warfare became too strong to be ignored, did imperial, Swedish and French diplomats agree on the framework of a peace conference. The Treaty of Hamburg of December 1641 laid down its parameters. It was to be held in Catholic Münster and denominationally mixed Osnabrück, with the papacy and Venice providing the convenors. The two cities and their connecting roads were to be made neutral – both being formally exempt from their oath of allegiance to the emperor for the duration of the talks. Food supplies were protected, security arrangements put in place and the imperial postal service extended to cover both locations. Everyone understood that it would be a long process, and it was. Almost seven years later, the Peace of Westphalia was signed in September 1648.

GOVERNED BY OPINION

In 1641, the Bohemian engraver Wenceslaus Hollar illustrated the broadsheet entitled *The World is Ruled & Governed by Opinion*. He depicted a conversation between 'Opinion' (a fickle woman, seated in a tree with a tower of Babel on her head and a globe in her lap) and 'Viator', a cavalier. A travelling jester pours ink on the roots of the tree, which is ripe with broadsheets that fall like leaves all around. It was a satire on the destabilizing impact of news-sheets and pamphlets in the febrile atmosphere of the eve of the English Civil War, when the Stationers' Company monopoly and royal oversight of publications were breaking down. Newsprint magnified, polarized and distorted Europe's conflicts. One of the reasons why it was harder to disentangle the motives and achievements of those involved was because they were obliged to engage in wars of words as well as weapons, opening up the gap between what it was expedient to present as motives for actions and the underlying reality. Blaise Pascal, whose anti-Jesuit controversy made him an aficionado of polemic, had an answer to Hollar's work: 'Power,' he wrote in his *Pensées*, 'rules the world, not opinion, but it is opinion that exploits power.'

That exploitation was augmented by the appearance of regular printed gazettes in the early seventeenth century. They already existed in Strasbourg, Frankfurt and several other cities by 1618. The Thirty Years War expanded their circulation so that, by 1648, there were thirty weekly papers in Europe with an estimated overall distribution of 15,000 copies. They mostly consisted of digests of diplomatic, military and political events, filtering out the strange portents and prodigies which were the pamphleteers' stock-in-trade. Newspapers sold on their capacity to provide up-to-the-minute news across a European spectrum to a reading public who needed to make sense of complex events occurring around them. Generals supplemented their own private sources of information with what the gazettes told them. Ambassadors compiled digests of what they reported. The more newspapers spread, the more they syndicated the information which they published, enabling their coverage to be greater. Contemporaries were able to understand events in a broader context. War was at large in the newspapers; so too was the emerging sense of a general European paroxysm in the 1640s as the news of uprisings and rebellions filled their columns.

It was impossible to distinguish, however, between gazettes and other 'libels' and 'pamphlets'. Newspapers were complemented by newsletters, the latter often produced by the same editors. *Zeitung*, *Aviso* and *Relation* were titles indicating the nature of a publication without distinguishing it from regular newspapers. The *Theatrum Europaeum*, produced by the Strasbourg publisher Johann Philipp Abelin for the first time in 1633 published an overview of events which went back to the Edict of Restitution of 1629. A news encyclopaedia, it was marketed on a subscription basis with engravings by Matthäus Merian. The events of the Thirty Years War created endless possibilities for traditional pamphleteers. Nobles lost their heads and their lands. Heroes were defeated. The unexpected occurred. Armies devastated territories and cities were destroyed. All this was saleable news and, with a crisis in the scholarly market, pamphlets provided complementary publishing opportunities which merged with the demands for political propaganda. Over 200 pamphlets describing the sack of Magdeburg in 1631 inscribed it in collective memory. At their most effective, pamphlet broadsheets contributed to the war-effort by undermining the credibility of an opponent. Advisers and generals (Spínola, Wallenstein and others) were the targets of criticism, not the rulers themselves – the vilification of Frederick V, once he had been expelled from the Palatinate and no longer a prince, being the exception which proved the rule.

As Pascal implied, those in power exploited the press. Rulers swallowed their distaste at placing the secrets of state at the disposal of a wider public while their opponents lost no opportunity to publicize their own declarations. The Bohemian Confederate *Apologia* was printed and circulated to an international audience in 1618. Gustav Adolf's 1630 *Manifesto* appeared in twenty-three editions in five languages. Marie de Médicis had a devoted retinue of publicists to advertise her grievances against her son Louis XIII. She put them to work especially after the 'Day of Dupes' (November 1630) when, attempting to reassert her authority over her son, she demanded (and believed for twenty-four hours that she had achieved) Cardinal Richelieu's disgrace. Aristocrats and princes of the blood (among them Montmorency and Gaston d'Orléans) made sure that their reasons for revolting against Richelieu's regime were well advertised, just as Richelieu himself employed talented publicists to articulate the reasons of state justifying his ministry. Théophraste Renaudot, who owed his monopoly on newspaper production in Paris to the cardinal, proclaimed the *Gazette de France* an independent voice. In reality, materials from the cardinal and the king himself appeared in its pages. The *Gazette* became essential reading to members of literary *salons*. Provincial nobles scanned its pages to find the regiments of their offspring mentioned in its pages. By the end of the Thirty Years War, newspapers had an established place in public life. Twenty-two thousand titles of printed sermons, pamphlets and newspaper issues survive from England for the period of the Civil Wars, 5,000 'Mazarinades' from the Frondes (1648–52), each side using the press as an instrument not of opinion but of action.

THE LION OF THE NORTH

The military intervention of Gustav II Adolf in Germany broadened and intensified the theatre of war and created a complex legacy. Sweden's resource base was tiny (a population of no more than 1.25 million in 1620), as was its administration (Stockholm had a population of 6,000) and its nobility (400 individuals). Its neighbours were either larger or strategically better placed in the Baltic. Denmark held the Sound and presented Sweden's most immediate threat. Across the Baltic lay Poland-Lithuania, six times its size, its riverine ports grown rich on the expanded trade in grain. Both Poland and Sweden laid claims to the Baltic provinces of Estonia and Livonia – the ports of Riga and Reval (Talinn) being summer entrepôts for Muscovy. The deposition in 1599 of the Catholic Sigismund Vasa (elected king of Poland in 1587) and the resulting political turmoil and recriminations in Sweden and Poland created an enmity which was at once mercantile, dynastic, confessional and territorial. Hostilities between Sweden and Poland broke out in 1617–18, and then again in 1621–5. In 1626, Sweden largely overran Livonia, and its armies moved to attack Polish Prussia at the mouth of the Vistula. Wallenstein's despatch of 12,000 troops to Prussia in 1629 demonstrated the threat which the imperial presence on the Baltic coast posed to Swedish security at a time when a broken Denmark could no longer menace its interests.

The resources of the Swedish state were limited and it had few allies abroad. It mobilized a significant proportion of its adult male population through conscription, their registration (*utskrivning*) providing a force which was not very proficient but which (unlike mercenaries) did not require money up-front to raise and then to be paid off at the end. Equally these men had to be coaxed to serve outside Sweden and that persuasion came from the top. King Gustav rebuilt a consensus among the political class and made its financial and judicial administration fit for purpose. The latter was overseen by Count Axel Oxenstierna, whose qualities as an administrator and strategist Gustav had the good sense to recognize. When Oxenstierna was installed as Governor-General of Riga in 1622, he appropriated its port dues to fill Swedish coffers. In 1626, it was the turn of Prussia, Oxenstierna again being installed as the Swedish man in charge at Elbing. In September 1628, it was he who, on the basis of these revenues, raised mercenaries (many of them Scots) to defend Stralsund. Gustav Adolf's objectives were vague, but he won the support of the Swedish Estates for his campaign and all sides understood that the operations would be financed from Germany itself.

The expeditionary force which arrived in Pomerania on 6 July 1630 was modest (14,000 men). Gustav's manifesto, written by Johan Salvius and published in Stralsund, played to German jurists, specialists in the public law of the empire. The Swedish king had come to recover the 'liberties' of the empire, threatened by the Edict of Restitution. He sought Sweden's 'security'. The protection of Protestantism was put to one aside. In a broadsheet, printed shortly after the landing, the king was depicted in armour on horseback between allegorical figures of Justice and True Religion, under the heading: 'The Swedish Joshua'. The accompanying poem contained the earliest references to Gustav as 'The Lion of the North', a Paracelsian prophecy based on the Book of Jeremiah.

Gustav's objectives and ambitions grew alongside his military success. His forces overran Pomerania, forcing its duke by the Treaty of Stettin (20 July 1630) into an 'eternal' alliance which put the province's resources at Swedish disposal. Gustav's search for other allies in northern Germany proved initially illusory. Only Bremen and the city of Magdeburg, threatened by imperial troops, offered their support. By the end of 1630, the Swedes established their headquarters at Bärwalde, which is where they signed a five-year alliance in January 1631 with the French which offered them 400,000 *thalers* to underwrite an army of 36,000 men whose objective was to 'restore the suppressed Estates of the Reich'. In return, Gustav agreed to protect Catholic worship. Saxony and Brandenburg met other Protestant princes at Leipzig in February and declared their neutrality from the Swedish campaign. Maximilian of Bavaria regarded the Swedish arrival with alarm and, distancing himself from the emperor, negotiated a secret treaty (Fontainebleau, May 1631) with France that guaranteed his Electoral title and his territorial integrity in the event of any Swedish aggression.

The scale and pace of the military campaigns escalated. The initial focus was Magdeburg, the Protestant Saxon city besieged since November 1630 by imperial forces under Count Pappenheim, Wallenstein's successor. Gustav promised to protect it and, until April 1631, he counted on diversionary tactics to achieve that objective. Then Count Tilly's Catholic League forces arrived to reinforce Pappenheim's brigades and the city fell on 20 May 1631. Its assault was succeeded by a disastrous fire, the destruction of all but 200 of its buildings and (following its sack) the death of about 20,000 people. The census in February 1632 recorded 449 inhabitants. The disaster obliged Gustav to seize the initiative. Faced with an invasion of Saxony by Count Tilly's troops, its Elector joined the Swedish camp on 12 September 1631. Swedish and Saxon troops met up three days later, just north of Leipzig, which was occupied that same day by Tilly. On 17 September, their two forces gave battle at Breitenfeld: 24,000 Swedes and 18,000 Saxons versus 35,000 imperialists. After five hours of fighting, the Saxons fled but Gustav overwhelmed the imperialists, who suffered about 20,000 casualties, a further 3,000 being captured. Swedish losses amounted to only about 2,100. The victory was celebrated across Protestant Europe. In the broadsheets for the year 1632, more than half focused on Gustav, an exemplary Christian warrior and liberator.

At the end of September 1631, Gustav's forces were once more on the march, this time across Thuringia and Franconia to the Rhineland, a fertile supply region with good communications. Swedish forces entered Frankfurt am Main on 27 November; Mainz capitulated on

22 December. Oxenstierna arrived there the following month to set up Sweden's administrative and supply headquarters. Gustav styled himself 'duke of Franconia' and treated areas under Swedish control as occupied territory. Supplies were requisitioned arbitrarily and places were taxed for military purposes. Church lands were confiscated and handed over to officials and commanders as compensation. Libraries and art collections were plundered and taken back to Sweden. The Swedes acquired more German allies than before, but many of them were forced into agreements to provide zones in which the Swedes could requisition supplies. Those who joined of their own accord were either dispossessed princes (Frederick V of the Palatinate) or minor Franconian princes and Rhineland cities hoping for protection. Richelieu looked on with barely concealed alarm at burgeoning Swedish fortunes, now closer to France's own spheres of influence.

For the Austrian and Spanish Habsburgs Sweden's advance was a catastrophe. Philip IV's garrisons in the Palatinate were eliminated and the Spanish Road broken. Worse followed when Count Tilly's counter-attack on the Swedes at Bamberg in March 1632 failed, giving Gustav the excuse to advance on Bavaria. The League army was crushed, Tilly mortally wounded in the battle of Lech (15 April 1632), and Gustav and Frederick V entered Munich in triumph on 17 May. With Saxon forces invading Bohemia and Maximilian in exile in Salzburg, Emperor Ferdinand considered fleeing to Italy, but instead took the advice of his counsellors and recalled Wallenstein. The precise terms of the agreement which Ferdinand reached with Wallenstein at Göllersdorf in April 1632 will never be known, but they probably granted his Generalissimo the right to sign peace treaties in his name and to confiscate lands he conquered or pardon their rulers. In return, Wallenstein raised a new army of 65,000 men and besieged Gustav's forces at Nuremberg. The city's population was already swollen by refugees and Gustav had to fight his way out with heavy losses. He then engaged with Wallenstein's forces to the southwest of Leipzig at Lützen (16 November 1632). The Swedes emerged victorious and Wallenstein withdrew to Bohemia, but Gustav Adolf had been killed in battle.

Chancellor Oxenstierna took over the direction of affairs in Germany, while a Regency Council was installed in Stockholm to advise Gustav's daughter and heir, Christina. Confronted with a collapse in confidence, Oxenstierna was forced to make generous offers. German counties and bishoprics were off-loaded to colonels as 'donations' to reward them for what they were owed. How to satisfy the financial demands of the military entrepreneurs who kept the Swedish military machine going became the major concern of its strategists through to the end of the war. Oxenstierna hoped to lessen Sweden's burdens by spreading the obligations among German allies, but the Heilbronn League, signed in April 1633, never fulfilled his expectations. The outstanding debts could not always be verified; and, where they could, they were so enormous that they absorbed all and more of the French and Dutch subsidies which the Swedes put at the League's disposal. Worse, France reduced its subsidies and moved to limit Sweden's impact west of the Rhine. In August 1633, French troops invaded Lorraine and, by the end of the following year, they controlled a large stretch of territory in the Reich from Basel up to Lorraine, with garrisons in Speyer, Philippsburg, Mannheim and Trier. Above all, Oxenstierna lost the support of Brandenburg and Saxony. The former could not be reconciled to Sweden's insistence on Pomerania as a territorial guarantee in any eventual peace negotiations. The latter was unwilling to be a junior partner in a Swedish-dominated alliance, especially one led by that 'pen-pusher' (*Plackscheisser*) Oxenstierna. When the Saxon Elector learned the full extent of Sweden's demands for compensation in July 1634, he made overtures to the emperor.

The possibility of luring Saxony back into the imperial fold is one explanation for Wallenstein's failure to exploit the military advantage which he enjoyed in 1633. Exactly what the imperial Generalissimo was negotiating – with Sweden as well as Saxony – constitutes the essence of Wallenstein's enigma. His diplomatic manoeuvres, coupled with his failure to come to the aid of Bavaria, gave ammunition to the growing number of critics in Vienna, orchestrated by the emperor's Jesuit confessor Lamormaini. The Spanish were preparing to send a relief army to the empire and contested Wallenstein's claims to be in charge of all Catholic troops in the Reich. His enemies seized on news that (aware of the plots circulating against him) he demanded his colonels swear an oath of personal loyalty at Pilsen on 12 January 1634. Ferdinand ordered his arrest, alive or dead. Wallenstein was assassinated by members of the garrison at Eger on 25 February 1634, the place to which he fled, apparently en route to the Saxons. The Swedes highlighted the news as one more sign to their wavering German allies that the emperor was not to be trusted.

THE PEACE OF PRAGUE

Ferdinand II now gave the command of imperial forces to his son (later Emperor Ferdinand III). In September 1634, they joined the Spanish relief army, led by the Cardinal Infante, and together defeated the Swedish army and its Protestant allies at the battle of Nördlingen (5–6 September 1634). The forces of the League of Heilbronn, led by Bernard of Saxe-Weimar, were diminished and much of the Swedish army annihilated. Within months, its allies having deserted, Sweden's military position in Germany collapsed. In August 1635, Oxenstierna was taken prisoner in Magdeburg by troops and officers from his own army demanding to be paid. Swedish regiments retreated to Mecklenburg and Pomerania, provinces already devastated by previous campaigns. Johann Georg, Elector of Saxony, concluded a preliminary treaty with the emperor's negotiators at Pirna in November 1634 which laid the basis for the Peace of Prague (30 May 1635).

The strategic context for the peace was set by an imperial treaty with Spain (Ebersdorf, 31 October 1634) renewing Austrian-Habsburg co-operation and committing the emperor to assist Spain against its enemies. The most immediate of the latter were the Dutch, who signed an offensive alliance with the French (8 February 1635). But Duke Charles of Lorraine mounted an invasion in April–May to recover his duchy, taken by the French in 1633. And the Elector of Trier, France's only Electoral ally, was arrested in his own city, possibly on orders from Brussels. France's decision to declare war on Spain was taken on 5 April. With a major campaign on the Rhine in preparation, the emperor was ready to concede some ground on the Edict of Restitution in return for broadening imperial support in the Reich.

The peace began as a bilateral accord with Elector Johann Georg which was extended through pacts with other Electors and ecclesiastical princes. It was never discussed or ratified by the Estates, which Ferdinand claimed could not be held because of the risk of French interference. Its terms implied that, despite compromise, it was a licence for imperial influence in the empire, which is why the French and Swedes argued that they would fight on for 'German liberties' against the emperor. Bogislav Philipp Chemnitz, the leading German publicist for the Swedish cause, attacked the Saxon Elector for having sullied Gustav Adolf's sacred memory and compromised his German roots. Duke Maximilian of Bavaria's support for the accord was secured with some concessions, enough to make him accept that the Catholic League army be dissolved and reconstituted into a separate corps under the emperor's command.

The accord involved a selective amnesty for those who had taken up arms against the emperor. It excluded the Elector Palatine, Württemberg, Hesse-Kassel, other Rhineland counts, and all the Bohemian exiles, as well as those from the ancestral lands. The exclusion of Hesse-Kassel was of key significance since Landgrave Wilhelm V was a Calvinist, the spokesman for his co-religionists, who had his own army. The peace failed because it did not embrace a sufficiently broad constituency of the concerned parties in the empire. It could not do so without compromising what the now elderly and sick Emperor Ferdinand regarded as essential to maintaining imperial authority.

As it was, the proposed concessions required the acquiescence of a committee of twenty-four theologians in Vienna. Lamormaini and eight Jesuits, supported by the papal legate, were overruled by a majority, sustained by the Spanish envoy, who argued that compromise was the lesser of two evils. Those embraced by the amnesty were granted a forty-year suspension of the Edict of Restitution. In its place, an armistice date was agreed (12 November 1627) which would become the normative year (*Normaljahr*) for determining all contested disputes about Church lands and expropriated property. The parties would continue to discuss their differences over these properties but the accord reached would remain in place if they failed to achieve an agreement. In effect, the Edict of Restitution was permanently suspended and the emperor lost the ecclesiastical patronage potential which had been the edict's key to reshaping the empire as a Habsburg monarchy.

Elector Johann Georg of Saxony became the spokesman for the peace in the empire. He was allowed to retain his own army as a separate corps but under the emperor's overall command. His task was not an easy one because of the accumulated claims and counter-claims among the parties in the empire. The attempt to win over key players (such as Duke Georg of Lüneburg) alienated others (for instance, Elector Ferdinand of Cologne), fuelling the opposition to the peace which the Swedes and French fomented. The French secured at Stuhmsdorf (12 September 1635) a continuation of the Polish-Swedish truce, concluded at Altmark in 1629, and made a new alliance with the Swedes (Treaty of Wismar,

March 1636), promising to pay the arrears from the subsidy which had been terminated at the death of Gustav and continue their support. When Emperor Ferdinand III succeeded his father in February 1637, he inherited a faltering peace with parts of the empire annexed by foreign states, in alliance with one another and with discontented elements within the Reich. The younger Ferdinand's decision to summon the Estates of the empire to Regensburg in September 1640 was an acceptance that a new framework for peace had to be worked out.

SUSTAINING ATTRITIONAL WAR

The military operations of Gustav Adolf and Albrecht von Wallenstein mobilized the largest armies yet seen in Europe. Wallenstein had well over 100,000 troops under his command in 1628–9; Gustav Adolf had perhaps 150,000 men in his armies by late 1631. At Breitenfeld, over 30,000 imperial and 40,000 Swedish and Saxon forces were in combat. The underlying strategy for maintaining such massive military concentrations was to coordinate as far as possible the supply and resourcing organizations in order to occupy and defend the key parts of central and North German territory, Bohemia, Silesia and Moravia. The logistical key to the operation was the rivers. The resource portfolio was secured by war taxes (contributions), collected in goods or cash from as wide an area of productive territory as possible. Wallenstein's strategy revolved around the Elbe and Oder, with the supply-chains fed from Moravia, Silesia and Bohemia. Gustav Adolf's relied on the Rhine and its tributaries until he moved from Bavaria into Franconia. The Swedish débâcle at Nuremberg (between the Main and the Danube) was in part attributable to its weakened supply-chains.

After the Peace of Prague, the numbers of troops deployed by belligerents in Germany declined. The War Council in Vienna estimated that it had 73,000 troops mobilized in early 1638, but only 59,000 in 1639. Under Gustav Adolf, the Swedes maintained five campaign armies. By the early 1640s, this had been reduced to just two. The last important battles of the war involved armies considerably smaller than those which had fought in the early 1630s. At Jankau (5 March 1645) in southern Bohemia, 16,000 imperial forces clashed with a similar number of Swedes. At the second battle of Nördlingen (Allerheim,

3 August 1645) 16,000 Bavarian and imperial troops confronted 17,000 French and Hessian combatants. The resulting smaller armies were more resilient and battle-hardened. The ambitions of colonels to over-extend their entrepreneurial operations were curbed. Commanders were better able to manage their supply-chains and the arrears of pay were more controllable. They used their operational freedom of man-oeuvre to protect their field armies, avoid sieges and concentrate on securing or maintaining strategic advantages.

The Swedish army, for example, was gradually rebuilt after the defeat at Nördlingen. From its supply-base in Pomerania and Mecklen-burg, and supported by Baltic toll-revenues and French subsidies, Field-Marshal Johan Banér led campaigns in 1636–7, 1639–40 and 1641 into Silesia, Moravia and Bohemia with an army composed largely of German and Scottish veterans. With a force that rarely exceeded 20,000, he was able to prevent the imperial armies from eliminating the Swedish presence in Germany. His successor, Field-Marshal Lennart Torstensson, continued this strategy, his expedition in 1642 culminating in a crushing defeat of imperialist forces at the second battle of Breiten-feld (23 October 1642). His campaign in 1643 was curtailed by operations in Denmark, but that of the following year into the German heartland wiped out the imperial army commanded by Matthias Gallas at the battle of Jüterbog (23 November). Leading a force of 12,000 infan-try and 4,000 cavalry into the fray, Gallas (the 'army wrecker') retired to Bohemia with only about 2,000 foot and a few hundred cavalry left. He was relieved of his command, and after imperial defeats at Jankau and Allerheim the following year, Vienna reluctantly contemplated concessions at Westphalia.

The trend towards smaller, more professional armies was driven by the practical and political limits of what armies could extract from German territories and a changing relationship between military entre-preneurs and their state sponsors. Ransoms for senior officers tended to become the responsibility of the state and not part of war opera-tions. The imperial-Bavarian and imperial-Saxon armies were no longer financed by contributions extorted by troops from occupied ter-ritories but paid for through regular taxes. The Electors and Estates at the Diet of Regensburg (1641) regularized other payments, at least for troops in garrisons, so that they were, to some extent, financed less arbitrarily.

The cumulative impact of the Thirty Years War on the civilian population in Germany has never been possible to estimate accurately. Although there were deliberate scorched-earth tactics (in Lorraine in the 1630s, Swedish troops in Bavaria in 1632 and 1646), the biggest impact was undoubtedly through scarcities of food, loss of plough-teams and the spread of disease. Although smaller towns were sacked, especially when garrisons refused to surrender, larger towns rarely saw any major military contingents within their walls. The catastrophe at Magdeburg was an exception. The worst devastation took place in the 1630s and early 40s. Grain prices rose to record levels as agricultural production was affected by warfare, climatic instability and the temporary migration of country folk to the towns to escape troops. The resentments towards military exactions appeared in peasant ambushes and resistance. The Sundgau peasantry rose against the Swedes in 1633; peasants in Westphalia joined nobles and imperial cavalry against the Hessian army. There were certainly some places where population levels sank by over 30 per cent as disruptions to family and community resulted in collapsing birth-rates.

Although walled towns were, to a degree, protected, the wealth of patrician élites was eroded by war contributions and unpaid interest on loans and bonds. Contemporary eye-witness testimonies furnish graphic accounts of individual experiences. The diary of Peter Hagendorf, a Catholic soldier, described in matter-of-fact terms his role in the sack of a town in Bavaria in 1634: 'Here I got a pretty girl as my booty, and 12 thalers in cash, some clothes and a lot of linen.' A few weeks later, he recorded the same in another location 'and here again I got a young girl out of it'. The alabaster sculpture by the brilliant miniaturist sculptor from Hall, Leonard Kern, of a Swedish soldier abducting a young naked woman, her hands tied, about to be raped, is a reminder of the brutal encounters which imprinted themselves on the generation which survived.

These form the bedrock to a collective consciousness of an all-destructive war which was evoked afterwards in the classic 1668 German picaresque novel by Hans Jakob Christoffel von Grimmelshausen. *The Adventurous Simplicissimus* recounts the life of a vagrant, Melchior Sternfels von Fuchsheim, who joins the army, changes sides, enjoys a high and low life, ends up in Russia and finally returns to become a hermit. The experiences were not autobiographical but they were read as having been so. They implicitly pointed the finger at the public authorities in the empire who had failed to protect their subjects. It is not surprising that, in Saxony and elsewhere, rulers did not summon the Estates for fear of what they would hear. In those places where they did meet – Hesse-Kassel and the principality of Jülich-Cleves-Berg, for example – there was a crescendo of rage at princely failure. Different confessions and social orders united in saying that they were the state which princely misrule had ruined.

The question of how to sustain attritional warfare was also fundamental to the Spanish and French monarchies. Neither had effective mechanisms for distributing fairly the burdens that warfare on this scale generated. Spain had for so long borne the costs of major military commitments in Europe that it was next to impossible for it to change the means by which it distributed that load. France avoided major external military commitments until the mid-1630s. Its entry into the Thirty Years War was principally to dismantle Spanish Habsburg hegemony in Europe and replace it with its own. To achieve that objective required military campaigns on several fronts at once and the rallying of allies to achieve consonant objectives. The Thirty Years War was transformed into a global struggle which brought Spain and France to the brink of collapse.

HALL OF REALMS

In 1634, decorators worked on Philip IV's new palace, the Buen Retiro outside Madrid. That the Spanish monarchy should have commissioned it in the midst of a war to determine the fate of its empire is surprising. From the outside, the building was unremarkable. The interior decorations were spectacular and none more so than the Hall of Realms, a long room which inspired Versailles's Hall of Mirrors. Both throne room and public gallery, it was Philip IV's theatre of power, conceived by his impresario the Count-Duke Olivares. The scenario magnified Philip's 'authority' and 'reputation', key-terms in Olivares's political lexicon. Authority at home meant firm government and a shake-up. Reputation abroad meant the projection of Spain's power. 'I have always desired . . .' Olivares wrote in 1625, 'to see Your Majesty enjoying a reputation in the world equal to your greatness and qualities.' In the ceiling recesses above each window were the escutcheons of the Spanish monarchy's twenty-four kingdoms. At either end of the hall were those of the Spanish peninsula itself. In the design, this multiplicity was interlocking – a reference to Olivares's centrepiece reform proposal of 1625, the 'Good, Perpetual and Inseparable Union of Arms'.

Spain's problem was how to spread the empire's military costs around its dominions. Olivares's solution was to change its constitution. Each province of the empire – from Peru to Flanders – would contribute to defence in accordance with its economic strength, providing an army of 140,000 which could be deployed when any one of the kingdoms was attacked. The burden would no longer be borne disproportionately by Castile. Rather, Castile's exclusive sense of Spain's destiny would belong to everyone. As his Great Memorial of 1624 said, Philip should no longer be merely 'King of Portugal, Aragon and Valencia and Count of Barcelona', he would be 'King of Spain'. Sardinia and Mallorca reluctantly signed up to the measure while negotiating military and administrative posts for the local nobility. Valencia and Aragon bought themselves out with a cash payment but no ongoing commitments. Catalonia, Portugal and Naples prevaricated. Olivares's cousin Diego Mexia, marquis of Leganés, persuaded Flanders and Brabant to provide an extra half a million *escudos* a year plus 12,000 men for the army in Flanders. This was a considerable commitment, especially when the Dutch offensive of 1629–33 damaged morale. In 1632, the second in command of the Flanders Army, Hendrik van den Bergh, William the Silent's nephew, defected to the Dutch, exploiting resentments at the Spanish exactions, which he compared with the Tenth Penny. The death of Archduchess Isabella in 1633 created an interregnum in which the Estates General was convened. It was the first sign of the provincial unrest which would overwhelm the Spanish monarchy but which, in this instance, was diplomatically resolved.

Around the walls of Buen Retiro ran paintings of Hercules by Francisco de Zurbarán. Superhuman power fitted absolute monarchy, as Henry IV's myth-makers had shown. The Herculean portrayals could be read in various ways: as virtue conjoined with strength, apotheosis, the conqueror of discord, the mastery of passions and the champion of reform. Interspersed were twelve Herculean labours, paintings depicting the monarchy's recent victories. Five occurred in 1625: Breda surrendered to Spínola, a joint Spanish-Portuguese naval expedition drove the Dutch from Bahia in Brazil, an English expeditionary force against Cádiz was humiliated, the Dutch were expelled from Puerto

Rico and the republic of Genoa was rescued. 'God is Spanish and fights for our nation these days,' wrote an exultant Olivares.

The message of the 'victory' paintings was a multiple one. The Spanish empire's military and administrative experience was second to no one else's. Military power protected Spain's reputation better than a phoney peace. 'To get a good general peace, we must first have a good and honourable war,' Philip IV wrote in June 1629. Olivares was the architect of those victories and the room celebrated his statesmanship, confounded his critics and tightened his grip on the king's favour. In the *Surrender of Breda*, painted by Diego Velázquez for Buen Retiro, General Spínola accepts the surrender of Justin of Nassau. Dismounted, Spínola holds out his hand to restrain Nassau from going on bended knee. A magnanimous prince offered clemency. Spain did not expect to reconquer the Netherlands but it sought an honourable peace, which is what France frustrated.

So Spain needed a Herculean effort on all fronts. Olivares came to power as a reformer, sweeping away the duke of Lerma and the taint of the 'favourite'. Olivares always referred to himself as 'minister'. He controlled things through his clan (*parentela*), installed ultra-loyal creatures at court and in administration, and undermined the conciliar mechanisms of the Spanish state by ad hoc committees (*juntas*). In 1621, he set up a *Junta de Reformación* to begin social and moral regeneration in Castile. Its report (1623) was a mixed bag, a sign that 'reformation' had been oversold as Spain's answer to decline. There were measures to slash the number of municipal officials, close brothels and rein in court extravagance. Grammar school places were cut – too much money was being spent in over-educating young people. Censorship was stepped up because novels and plays corrupted society and criticized the regime. Re-militarizing Spanish society was a leitmotif, though it was naval as well as army service, since Olivares accorded greater priority to the former. The Great Memorial offered a solution to uncontrolled government debt. Then, with mounting pressures to fund military campaigns in Flanders and the empire in the 1620s, Olivares abandoned structural reform in favour of quick-fix solutions – bankruptcy (1627), renegotiated credit lines with Portuguese-Jewish merchant bankers, government-sponsored deflation of the near-worthless copper coinage (1628), and a desperate search for new revenue streams to keep pace with the demands of total war.

Olivares justified the latter through the evocation of a titanic struggle in which dynasty, religion and culture were worth any sacrifice in the *causa universal*. Churches were encouraged to pray for forthcoming battles and to celebrate a *Te Deum* of thanksgiving for victories. Stage-plays commemorated great successes. Olivares's publicists became involved in a battle of wills, reaching for reason of state arguments against a rising tide of criticism which regarded the favourite's regime as little short of tyrannical. Institutions that might express opposition were hobbled. Some of the forty delegates of the Cortes were given a percent-age cut in the amounts collected from the taxes which they granted as well as generous expenses and rewards, the latter compromising the revenues which were granted. No social group was exempt from being asked to make donations to the war-effort. Town officials were told to contribute their salaries as forced loans. Members of the royal house-hold sacrificed theirs. The Spanish Church was bullied into surrendering its fiscal privileges. The aristocracy, whose falling rent-rolls made gran-dees dependent on royal pensions, were asked to serve the king with their wallets as well as in his wars. Divided and compromised, they had no choice but to contribute. Olivares's methods became increasingly arbitrary as rebellions increased his paranoia. He then made extraor-dinary demands on the privileged classes, their positive response being proof of their loyalty. Looking back after Olivares's disgrace, Francisco de Miranda drew up a memorandum on the future conduct of affairs. The count-duke's intentions may have been praiseworthy, he conceded, but 'because of his endless demands and fiscal expedients his govern-ment turned into what can only be called a tyranny'.

In 1636, Philip IV confessed that Spain faced 'a general war greater and more furious than any other there has ever been ... our enemies intend to encompass the destruction of my whole Monarchy'. The thea-tres of war ranged from Flanders and northern Germany, northwestern Atlantic waters, Brazil, the Caribbean, the East Indies, North Italy and the Valtelline, Southwest Germany, Alsace, Lorraine, Roussillon and the western Pyrenees. No region of the Spanish empire escaped involve-ment. Throughout the decade, Spain maintained a large army in Flanders as well as an Atlantic naval construction programme. By the late 1630s, it had 150 front-line warships as well as squadrons of Dunkirk priva-teers. Olivares sent regular subsidies to the emperor. He encouraged the French king's brother, Gaston d'Orléans, and other discontented elements from the French court to join the Spanish cause. Although the battle for Mantua was lost, the Spanish retained Milan and the ability to intervene in North Italian politics.

The fall of Maastricht to the Dutch on 22 August 1632 was the first sign that Spanish hegemony was crumbling. It cut the supply-lines between the Spanish garrisons in North-Rhine-Westphalia and Flanders. Faced with the defection of a high-ranking general (den Bergh), the government in Brussels made peace overtures to the Dutch. But Richelieu undermined the peace talks and invaded the duchy of Lorraine. The Spanish increased their subsidy to the emperor (a million florins per annum) and despatched a relief army (24,000 men) to Flanders in 1633 under the duke of Feria (commander in Milan), accompanied by the Cardinal Infante Don Fernando, Philip IV's younger brother and heir designate of Archduchess Isabella. That force met with disaster in the upper Rhine, and yet another relief army (12,000 men) was assembled in 1634, the last Spanish army to pass through the Valtelline before the end of the war.

Spain's military expenditures for 1635 were estimated at over 11 million ducats. In the Hall of Realms, Olivares's painters included four victories from 1633 to underscore the message to his critics that the sacrifices his policies required would achieve results. In late July 1635, a Spanish contingent succeeded in taking the Dutch fortress on the lower Rhine at Schenckenschans (or Schenck's Sconce), overlooking the major route into Gelderland from the east. But the triumph was shortlived. The Spanish garrison surrendered after sustained bombardment on 30 April 1636. Olivares saw the opportunity for bringing the Dutch to the peace table slip away once more. The Spanish invasion of Corbie in France that summer generated panic in Paris, but it was a military diversion to help the strategists in Vienna and was left unexploited.

Spain's overall strategic position then weakened still further as France opened up more fronts against it. The duchy of Milan – whose population was reduced by a third in the years between 1627 and 1633 from famine, war and disease – was threatened from 1635 by a war in which the French joined with Savoy, Mantua and Parma (the League of Rivoli). Spain counter-attacked in Provence and Lombardy and fomented a civil war in Savoy which lasted through to 1642. Bernard of Saxe-Weimar's army, which joined the French in 1635, invaded Upper Alsace in August that year. It then tried over-ambitiously to cross the Rhine and cut

Spanish communications with Flanders. The effort failed, but this became the preoccupation of French strategists in 1638–9. In the second of two confrontations at Rheinfelden (28 February, 3 March 1638), Bernard captured leading imperial generals and went on to besiege Freiburg, which fell easily (10 April 1638) and Breisach on the Rhine, whose siege lasted six months (June–December 1638). Its collapse opened up the rest of Alsace west of the Rhine to French forces and cut Spanish land communications with Flanders.

Back in 1626–7, Catalonia had not committed itself to the Union of Arms scheme. Olivares returned with Philip IV to the Catalonian Estates (*Corts*) and Barcelona municipality in 1632 to negotiate their portion. Catalonia was not the only Spanish province to have customs (*fueros*), but they were more extensive and, with a history of tension between Madrid and Barcelona, more readily appealed to. Barcelona's governing Council of 100 saw no reason to surrender to Madrid's demands. The scheme was to raise forces for an army against France, and Catalonia was dependent on Languedoc and Provence for its commercial vitality and food supplies. The Estates refused royal demands, humiliated the king and compromised Olivares. In 1633, Olivares placed the military headquarters (*plaza de armas*) for the forthcoming war with France in Catalonia. The decision was logical (the target for Spain's counter-attack on France was planned for the Midi) but a deliberate provocation as well since an expeditionary force could also serve as an army of occupation. What transpired was the worst of all worlds. The new army barely materialized and the opportunity to use it never occurred. Castilian *tercios* conducted a diversionary campaign into Guyenne (1636) and then repulsed a French invasion in Guipúzcoa (1638). The only expedition across the eastern Pyrenees border (against the French fortress at Leucate in 1637) did not include a single Catalan contingent. Worse, the Catalans stood back and let the French take the fortress of Salses-le-Château in Roussillon, which surrendered on 19 July 1639.

Philip IV and Olivares were bemused. While Fuenterrabía on the western side of the Pyrenees had withstood a French assault in 1638, Salses had given way with hardly a fight. They resolved to recapture it with an army of 24,000, half of which would be conscripted in Catalonia. But the French refortified the stronghold and the siege dragged on. The garrison finally surrendered on 6 January 1640. Spain now had an 'established war' (*guerra asentada*) within its own borders. Olivares fulminated against the Catalans while recognizing that it was only one of the many setbacks he confronted. There were 'so many calamities everywhere', he wrote, and 'bad news flies'. After the fall of Salses, Castilian and Italian regiments foraged at will, oblivious to the Catalan insistence that their *fueros* allowed no foreign troops to be billeted on their soil.

The Catalan revolt began as a peasants' uprising against these military exactions. Beneath the surface, it was an organized rebellion in which armed gangs, urged on by priests, drove the remaining contingents of the army into the mountains, clearing the way for an insurrection in Barcelona in June 1640. Labourers from outside the city murdered the viceroy and members of his household, forcing the municipal government to head up an armed rebellion. A compromise might have been reached and the situation defused, but Olivares despatched an army of reconquest. The 'invasion' of Catalonia in late 1640 by Castilians under Pedro Zúñiga y Requesens, marquis of Los Vélez, was repulsed at the battle of Montjuïc (January 1641) outside Barcelona by Catalans with French support. In the following year, Catalonia transferred its allegiance to Louis XIII, and a French army and viceroy entered what they now regarded as a French province. Spain had no means of response because another revolt had broken out in December 1640 in Portugal.

From Madrid's perspective, the Portuguese revolt paralleled that in Catalonia. In reality, they were different. Portugal, three times the size and population of Catalonia, was assessed at the same rate as Catalonia under the Union of Arms scheme. The demand for a subsidy of 200,000 *cruzados* (over six years) in 1628 was largely for Portugal's (and its colonies') defence and it agreed to pay. But it coincided with other fiscal measures emerging from the Mantuan war (notably a tax on salt), which provoked protests in Lisbon and other fishing ports in 1628–30. This was the beginning of a decline in relations between Madrid and Lisbon which had been, up to that point, harmonious. The Spanish had observed the concessions negotiated with Philip II by the Cortes of Tomar in return for accepting his rule, back in 1581. In 1624, Olivares told the English envoy Anthony Shirley that the Portuguese were 'essentially faithful and the discontent they display is from pure love of their kings'.

By the early 1630s, however, the mood was changing. A Flemish Jesuit reported in 1633 that 'The Portuguese hold the English in higher regard than any other nation, and the Castilians they hate worse than the very devil . . . they still wait for the arrival of their king Dom Sebastian who is supposed to free them from the Spaniards this very year . . . There have been more rumours of his coming lately than in all the many years since his death.' This was when Olivares's efforts to create a truly Spanish monarchy directly infringed Portuguese *foros*. A succession of viceroys introduced new sales taxes and annoyed the Portuguese nobility. The suspicion took hold that Madrid's demands were insatiable. Through gossip and handbills, a populist hysteria against the Portuguese New Christian financiers spread. Olivares and the king were presented as the puppets of crypto-Jews, allies of rabbinical and Calvinist synods in northern Europe whose ambition was to undermine the wealth and purity of Portugal.

Portugal's rebellion, unlike Catalonia's, had a sovereign leader. John, duke of Braganza, was essential to any uprising because he had the best claim to be the legitimate heir to the Portuguese crown and because the Braganza estates and influence were preponderant. The duke behaved cautiously but Olivares's suspicions during the Catalonian crisis drove him to demand Braganza's immediate presence in Madrid. King Philip wept over the reports of growing unrest in Portugal and rightly feared the worst from Braganza's silence. The latter led the revolt, launched on 1 December 1640, which was successful beyond anyone's expectations. The palace guard, almost the only Castilian military force in the country, was overwhelmed. Miguel de Vasconcelos, the Castilian secretary of state to the Vicereine Marguerite of Savoy, was murdered.

By early the following year, Portuguese armed bands began raiding into Galicia and Extremadura. The new regime signed alliances with France (June 1641) and Sweden (August 1641), and John IV (John of Braganza) was crowned king of a restored nation in December 1641, the previous regime now referred to as *el tirano*. The new king swore that, if ever Dom Sebastian should reappear, he and his heirs would give up the crown to him. That such an event should occur was almost more plausible than that Spain would recover its grip on Portugal. Olivares's hopes of a counter-coup were dashed when his plans were leaked and his Lisbon supporters rooted out. As Olivares contemplated other options, his namesake and long-time opponent Gaspar de Guzmán, duke of Medina Sidonia, grandee of Andalusia, fell under the influence of his cousin, the marquis of Ayamonte. Inspired by the ease of the

Portuguese revolt, Ayamonte proposed a similar uprising in Andalusia. He had the backing of the Dutch, whose naval squadron appeared off the coast in September 1641 as Olivares's informants in The Hague broke the news of what was planned. Ayamonte was arrested and imprisoned and Medina Sidonia sent into exile in Old Castile.

The contagion of revolt unleashed in Catalonia and Portugal offered further opportunities for France and its allies to weaken the Spanish monarchy. The chain-reaction took place in a grim demographic, economic and climatic context in both the Spanish and Italian peninsulas. Madrid, Lisbon, Barcelona and other major cities searched further and further afield for their food supplies in the bad years (1630–31, 1635–6, 1639–40). In the spring of 1641, a prolonged drought once more threatened the harvests of Castile. The years 1640–43 witnessed the highest rainfall ever recorded for Andalusia. Meanwhile, in Italy, a quarter of the population at least succumbed to famine and plague in Lombardy in the years 1628–31, and the disaster was followed with renewed harvest failures and food shortages in Italian cities in the 1640s. Castile's loyalty was assured by its destiny being linked to that of the monarchy; but no one knew for how long that would continue in the face of the rising fiscal, material and human demands from Olivares's government. Philip IV recognized in the summer of 1642 that he had to take control of affairs lest Castile take control of him. Calling Olivares's bluff, he left court to command his defeated Catalonian army, then in Aragon. Seven months later, Olivares was relieved of his responsibilities. In retirement and suffering from mental disturbance, the count-duke had a moment of lucidity when he wrote to his secretary in 1644: 'there were we, trying to achieve miracles and reduce the world to what it cannot be . . . the more we turn this over in our minds, the madder we become'.

The war against the French in Aragon and Catalonia became a campaign of sieges in mountainous terrain. Philip IV assembled an army of 15,000 to recapture the stronghold at Lérida in western Catalonia. The French and Catalonians failed to relieve it and the stronghold fell on 30 July 1644. North of the Pyrenees, however, disaster struck the Flanders Army in 1643. The Governor-General of Flanders set out from Namur with a field army of 27,000 to launch a diversionary offensive through the Ardennes against the French. They besieged the fortress at Rocroi which guarded the Oise, unaware that there was a French army in the vicinity, commanded by Louis de Bourbon, prince of Condé ('le grand Condé', known until his father's death in 1646 as the duke of Enghien). The latter forced a battle (19 May 1643) before the Spanish had time to call in reinforcements. The struggle stood in the balance for much of the day since French infantry were initially no match for the Spanish *tercios*. Spanish cavalry also withstood a French cavalry assault and counter-attacked. But then Enghien led the French cavalry to encircle the Spanish before bombarding the Spanish infantry squares until the German and Walloon contingents gave up and fled. The remaining Spanish were offered surrender terms, but 12,000 of them had been killed. It was not the end of Spanish military power north of the Pyrenees but in Brussels it greatly weakened the resolve to continue the war. Three years later, the French captured Dunkirk and with it the naval base with which Spain dominated the Channel. With a Parliamentary victory in the English Civil War that same year, the Spanish could no longer secure their Channel supply route to Flanders.

Although Spanish publicists continued to regard the Dutch as heretics and rebels, they were forced to confront the reality that they had rebels on their doorstep in Portugal and Catalonia who were not heretics, and who (with the backing of France) were waging an unjust war on the 'whole of Christendom in this Monarchy'. Spain was prepared to do a deal with the Dutch – for it had done so already in 1609 – and acknowledged that 'many foreign powers, kings, princes and republics, even the great Turk himself', held the Dutch in high esteem. Spain was not, however, willing to enter into negotiations with the Portuguese or Catalans, and resisted French attempts to include their representatives at Westphalia.

In Spanish Italy, the fiscal and material demands of Spain's monarchy also resulted in major revolt. Naples was the most populous kingdom after Castile in the Spanish realms. With no established customs (*fueros*) for protection, it was the recruiting ground for the Spanish armies. In the five years to 1635, 50,000 conscripts left southern Italy to fight in Germany and Flanders. With them went large quantities of grain and meat to feed them and relieve shortages in the Spanish peninsula. The kingdom of Naples also faced mounting demands for extraordinary financial contributions (*asistencias de guerra*), which the resident viceroy satisfied by subcontracting their collection to the Neapolitan entrepreneur Bartolomeo D'Aquino. Through patronage and special deals, he established a parallel administration to the viceroy's, which attracted the hostility of the nobility and threatened to engulf Spanish rule.

In neighbouring Sicily, a protest against two years of food shortages took place in the early months of 1647, though it petered out after bloody rioting in the summer. More serious was the uprising that began in Naples on 7 July 1647 following the government's attempt to impose a new tax on fruit. The viceroy had almost no troops to hand and barricaded himself in the Castelnuovo as the crowd gathered around a fishmonger (Tommaso Aniello, known as Masaniello). The reign of 'King' Masaniello was brief – he was murdered ten days later amid suspicions that he was negotiating with the Spanish for his own advancement. But the revolt continued, organized by clandestine groups based on the municipal militia originally raised to defend Naples against the French. It spread inland with other cities falling to the rebels, and acquired an anti-noble dimension. The insurgents seceded from the Spanish monarchy and offered the crown to Louis XIV.

It took the arrival of a Spanish fleet and a large contingent of *tercios*, diverted from the Catalonian campaign, coupled with the nobility whose fear of social revolution overcame their opposition to Spanish rule, to suppress the revolt in the spring of 1648. The French pretender to the throne, the duke of Guise, arrived in Naples (against Mazarin's instructions) to make good his claim, and fell into Spanish hands. With the restoration of Spanish rule, D'Aquino's regime of legitimated financial extortion was swept aside. With popular insurrections also occurring in Andalusia (January 1647), Valencia (October 1647) and Granada (March 1648), the Spanish monarchy seemed on the eve of extinction. Its ministers reserved their greatest scorn, however, for the French, the enemies of a Christendom which Spain believed it had been its destiny to preserve, but which was now no more.

POLITICAL WILL

For an age which took state secrets seriously, it is remarkable how many of them were openly discussed under the guise of 'maxims', 'reasons of state' and 'memoirs' of politicians. None of these documents is more problematic than the *Political Testament* of Armand du Plessis, Cardinal Richelieu. It was published by Louis XIV's Dutch enemies later in the century, who took it as proof of the cardinal's Machiavellian and absolutist motives. Like Olivares, Richelieu saw himself as making history – imposing his view of contemporary events over those of others. Richelieu had an even bigger library than Olivares, a research collection to which members of his 'cabinet' had privileged access. They included his secretaries, physicians and clerics and had connections with two parallel cabinets. One consisted of secretaries of state (his *créatures*) and intendants, through whom Richelieu administered the army and navy and kept an eye on the country. The other was his group of informers and diplomatic agents, the latter including the Capuchin François Leclerc de Tremblay ('Père Joseph'), and Jules, Cardinal Mazarin. They worked towards Richelieu, his secretaries copying his handwriting and signature, others filing and cross-referencing documents, a repertory of political precedents which were the basis for his 'authorized' history, known as Richelieu's *Memoirs*. From that documentation Richelieu's cabinet compiled the *Political Testament*, part résumé, part history, part legacy for Louis XIII.

To the cardinal, divinity meant applying the reason which God has given us to understand the ways of the world. 'God's kingdom is the principle for governing states' begins a key chapter. Richelieu rarely used the term 'reason of state', aware of the Machiavellian baggage that it carried, but 'reason' is on almost every page, justifying the public good, order and obedience. The work looked forward to a time when France would be at peace: 'To ruin the Huguenot party, trim the pride of the grandees, and wage a great war against powerful enemies' was the logic it attributed to Richelieu's ministry, but the objective was to 'arrive at a good peace with assured future repose'. Like Olivares, Richelieu was a reformer. The *Testament* laid out a programme, compiled from memoranda drafted in the 1620s. Unlike Olivares, he reckoned it could be activated only once peace had returned. Richelieu's state was bigger than any one individual (even the king), a vehicle of God's providential will. The French monarchy was a sacral enterprise whose glory was an end in itself. Richelieu camouflaged his partisan politics by appeals to the state. For contemporaries who fell foul of him, it was the attenuation of clemency and the coldness of his calculations which struck fear into their hearts.

There was nothing foreordained about Richelieu's rise to power. He hitched his fortunes to Henry IV's widow, Marie de Médicis, who soon faced opposition from the most powerful men in France, beginning in

1614 when the dukes of Condé, Nevers, Mayenne, Longueville, Vendôme and Bouillon left court, raised troops and declared their opposition to her regency government. Aristocrat-led opposition would be the hallmark of French politics through to the mid-century Fronde. Richelieu condemned and repressed the lightweight and cynical manoeuvrings of the grandees, but their rationale was more considerable than he gave them credit for. Their target became the war ministry of the cardinal-ministers, which they rightly saw as a threat to their position in the state. They sensed that it operated according to values that were different from their own inherited conceptions of loyalty, fidelity and friendship. They believed that, once the cardinal-ministers had been disposed of, an honourable peace with Spain could be achieved.

Richelieu's opponents were within the royal family itself. Marie de Médicis tried to unseat him when he was at his most vulnerable during the Mantuan war. For twenty-four hours in the 'Day of Dupes' (10–11 November 1630) even Richelieu himself believed she had succeeded. But Louis XIII stayed loyal to the cardinal and the king's mother was placed under house-arrest before she escaped to Brussels (1631) and then Amsterdam (1638), a linchpin to the plots against Richelieu until her death in 1642. Gaston de Bourbon, duke of Orléans, was the king's younger brother and heir ('Monsieur') to the French throne until Louis XIV's birth in 1638. Political intrigue against both Richelieu and Louis XIII (to whose throne he periodically aspired) preoccupied him from 1632, when he led an unsuccessful revolt with Spanish support, and took refuge in Flanders with his mother. In 1636, and then again in 1642, he was behind attempts to assassinate Richelieu. Though he was reconciled to the regime from time to time, his loyalty was never to be relied on. Louis de Bourbon, count of Soissons, was Gaston's and Louis XIII's cousin and from the most senior cadet line of the Bourbon house. A party to the 1636 assassination plot, he took up refuge with the duke of Bouillon, Frédéric Maurice de La Tour d'Auvergne, in his principality at Sedan from where they jointly planned Richelieu's downfall and resisted a French invasion in 1641. César de Bourbon, duke of Vendôme, was Louis XIII and Gaston's half-brother. He had been involved in an early conspiracy against the cardinal in 1626 (the 'Chalais Conspiracy'). Implicated in the revolt of 1632, he took up exile in Holland, and then England, continuing to conspire with his son, the duke of Beaufort.

Richelieu's war ministry was never secure. More princes of the blood were in exile in the late 1630s than were resident at the French court. Richelieu relied on nipping assassinations and conspiracies in the bud, and on dividing and weakening his opponents. Several of the latter seized the moment of Louis XIII's death (14 May 1643) to stage a coup. Louis XIII did not trust his wife, Anne of Austria (who was Philip IV's sister), with the regency on her own, fearing that she would become beholden to her brother. But, with the help of the chancellor Pierre Séguier she succeeded in having the council established in her husband's will set aside. Reacting to their once more being excluded from the state, some grandees staged the *Cabale des Importants* (27 May 1643) to achieve what they had failed to accomplish in his father's lifetime. Their failure cemented the hold of Cardinal Mazarin on the loyalties of the regent and the politics of total war against the Habsburgs which he inherited from Richelieu.

The growing dislike for all things Spanish among France's political classes, fomented by the cardinal-ministers, served as a justification for total war. The words 'glory'/'glorious' appear over thirty times in the *Political Testament*, always in a military and diplomatic context. In 1643, Jean Desmarets de St-Sorlin put together a 'heroic comedy' with accompanying ballet entitled *Europe*. Desmarets was at the heart of the French war-effort being Controller General for War and Secretary General of the Navy. He wrote it for performance before Louis XIII and Richelieu in the theatre of the cardinal's palace (now the Palais Royal) in Paris. Innocent 'Europe' is seduced by the Spanish maiden ('Ibère'), who is two-timing him with 'Amérique'. Fortunately a king ('Francion') declares war on the fickle Ibère, liberates Europe and becomes his protector. 'Glory is my sole aim, it alone inspires me,' says Francion. 'Glory awaits you; set forth to aid us in the belief that the Gods are on your side,' replies Europe. The text reveals something of the widespread French conviction that Spain had tried to make itself master of Europe and that France's destiny was to prevent it doing so.

France's armies were not a good advertisement for the military revolution. With the experience of the sixteenth-century civil wars deeply ingrained and the propensity of its aristocracy to lead rebellion against the monarchy, France mostly eschewed subcontracting its military effort to enterprisers. That meant, however, that campaigns were planned from Paris, its armies fed and paid by intendants responsible to the council of state. Its campaigns in 1635 and 1636 were lacklustre. The

Franco-Dutch invasion of Flanders ground to a halt amid divisions in the French high command. The two armies committed to the Eastern Front, whose objective was to defeat the duke of Lorraine while holding the imperialists at bay, failed after supply problems. The campaign in North Italy was starved of resources. Only in the Valtelline did the French secure an unqualified success.

In 1636, the French armies were late into the field. Their key objective was to overrun Franche-Comté and cut the Spanish Road. Resources were devoted to the siege of Dôle (begun in early June), which became the obsession of ministers in Paris. That permitted the Spanish troops in Flanders to take Corbie (15 August) and cross the Somme. Richelieu and the king feared an invasion of the capital and withdrew from Franche-Comté, leaving the imperialists to overrun it and threaten Burgundy. Aristocratic plots and financial shortfalls dogged the 1637 campaigns. The prestige sieges of Landrecies and La Capelle in Flanders were of limited strategic value and only the Languedoc campaign turned in a victory with the capture of Leucate. In 1638, a siege (St-Omer) once more dominated the preoccupations of the French war-effort, though the one foreign enterpriser whom the French were prepared to underwrite (Bernard of Saxe-Weimar) achieved a victory at Rheinfelden on 3 March which opened up the possibility of cutting Spanish supply-lines in the upper Rhine.

The French war-effort began to show results in 1639 as Spain's strategic positions crumbled. The campaign in northern Italy tied down Spanish forces. Salses was captured in Roussillon, forcing the Spanish into a Catalonian campaign. Saxe-Weimar overran Breisach and occupied Franche-Comté. Hesdin in Flanders was captured after a showpiece siege. The basis was laid for slow-won French success in the 1640s. French ministers softened their attitude to military enterprisers, granting Henri de La Tour d'Auvergne, Viscount Turenne, greater autonomy over the German army and the freedom to run it as a strategic and supply unit like other armies in the field. In 1648, Turenne linked up with the Swedes to inflict a terrible defeat upon the imperialists at Zusmarshausen, near Augsburg (17 May), opening the road to the Bavarian capital, Munich. Vienna's reluctance to conclude peace at Westphalia finally evaporated.

Henri de Lorraine-Harcourt relieved Casale and successfully besieged Turin in 1640. Mazarin, skilled in Italian politics, made more allies, and

France intervened in Sardinia and Elba, gaining naval bases from which to harass Spanish shipping in the western Mediterranean. Charles, duke of Lorraine, defected to the French on 28 July 1641 in a further desperate effort to recover his duchy, strengthening the French position towards the middle Rhine, though the 1641 campaign against Sedan was a fiasco. In Catalonia and Roussillon, the French sustained provincial revolt in the Spanish peninsula. The victory at Rocroi was not the decisive strategic encounter against the Spanish that the French hoped for (a major part of the Flanders Army remained intact). But gradually the Spanish position in Flanders weakened. Dunkirk fell to the French in 1646. Ypres and Gravelines followed, and then Lens in 1647, further stimulating the Dutch and Spanish to conclude their peace agreement at Münster on 30 January 1648 (ratified 15 May 1648).

These victories formed the backdrop to the outbreak of the Fronde in Paris. A *fronde* was a catapult. It was used to throw mud and stones at the carriages of grandees in Paris. The word was adopted in pamphlets and songs to designate those who were against the war ministry and Cardinal Mazarin (whose carriage was often attacked). Those who led the opposition in 1648 were the highest-placed magistrates in the kingdom, members of the sovereign courts in Paris, especially the Parlement and the Chamber of Accounts. They had become politicized as a result of a string of fiscal measures, proposed by the Controller General of Finance from 1643, Michel Particelli d'Emery. D'Emery's objective was to find ways to tap into urban wealth – protected by privileges – to fund the war-effort. His proposals directly affected the wealth of senior magistrates, culminating in new fiscal edicts imposed on the Parlement in a formal registration session on 15 January 1648. The judges responded by going on strike. Then, in April, the renewal of the Paulette (the tax which office-holders paid for the right to hand on their office) fell due. Mazarin hoped to be able to divide the magistrates by offering different groups favourable terms, but the judges decided to collaborate and the Parlement declared the Edict of Union (*Arrêt d'Union*) on 13 May.

The edict's twenty-seven articles aimed to undo what the magistrates saw as the illegality of the war ministry. The powers of intendants were unilaterally revoked. The farming of taxes was made illegal and the activities of tax-farmers (*traitants*) curtailed. The level of the *tailles* was reduced by 25 per cent, the amount which it was presumed had been creamed off by the financiers, and payments of arrears cancelled. New office-creations were restricted. The use of *lettres de cachet* (direct orders from the king, not subject to legal redress) to arrest individuals arbitrarily was terminated. When the government attempted to quash the edict, the Parlement called on the other sovereign court judges to join them in common session in the Chambre St Louis in the Parlement on 15 June.

The Chambre meetings had the feel of an alternative government in the making, but the magistrates were aware of the delicacy of their position. Law-givers, they were not natural law-breakers. They wanted to undo the illegality of the war ministry and nudge Mazarin and Anne of Austria into making peace, but they had no diplomatic status and could not will the war to end. They had been most concerned for their own privileges and investments, but they wanted to appeal to a broader constituency, aware that they could readily be presented as self-interested. Magistrates could not ignore the popular resentments which the war ministry had created ('Come *fronder* [i.e revolt] with the Duke of Beaufort' was on the *billets* handed to a leading magistrate at the height of the political crisis), but they did not conceive of their role as tribunes of the people. As dukes and peers, the princes of the blood were members of the Parlement as of right. They had been excluded from the regency government by the judges' own decision in 1643. The magistrates could hardly reverse that in 1648, but the princes used their contacts and influence among the magistrates, as well as in published declarations, to advance their own position, and attack the Mazarinistes.

A powerful speech from the advocate general, Omer Talon, at the *lit de justice* of 15 January 1648 laid out what would become the judges' best defence for their legal opposition: that they were protecting Louis XIV from the illegality which Mazarin and the regent were perpetrating in his name. For Talon, eloquence was the soul of the Parlement, yet its power lay in its impact beyond the law courts. In a speech against fiscal edicts, Talon declared that the Parlement was 'at the head of the people with the character of sovereignty, to manage their interests and represent their needs and that, in this capacity, it could oppose the will of kings – not through provoking their wrath through violent opposition, but through imploring justice through remonstrance'. Yet that part of the speech he specifically asked not to be recorded in the official register of the court. The power of the councillor-judge Pierre Broussel, a leading figure in the events of 1648, and again in 1652, lay precisely in his ability to articulate what ordinary people thought – that 'there was no State necessity' which obliged financiers to suck the life-blood out of poor people; that the Parlement was the embodiment of the king's justice; that the judges were incorruptible figures of probity against those who pretended that they were *grands politiques* but whose 'sole aim was money'.

So, despite their united façade, the judges were divided on how to proceed. Mazarin and Anne of Austria were also unsure about how to handle an opposition whose solidarity they had not anticipated. They initially gave way. Particelli d'Emery was disgraced in July. The financiers, whose interests he had championed, finding that their activities had been declared illegal and that a general peace was likely in the near future, refused to lend any more money. The French government unilaterally cancelled all loans and contracts into which it had entered. The king's uncle, Gaston d'Orléans, appeared in the Parlement, setting himself up as mediator with the regent and Mazarin, persuading them to accept most of the terms of the Edict of Union.

Then, in August, the context changed. As the implications of decisions already taken in the Chambre St Louis sank in, Gaston d'Orléans tried in vain to terminate it. When news of Condé's victory at Lens (20 August) arrived in Paris, Mazarin sensed it was the moment for a *coup de théâtre*. As the *Te Deum* at Notre-Dame celebrating the victory took place on 26 August, three judges (including Broussel) were arrested. The result was a spontaneous erection of barricades by a Paris population which had also become politicized by the swelling mass of pamphlets. The court withdrew for its safety from Paris to Rueil, and the princes of the blood (Condé and Conti) acted as intermediaries in conferences in which a reconciliation of sorts was achieved. On 22 October 1648, the court accepted fifteen articles, agreed with the judges in the Chambre St Louis, the same day France formally signed peace with the emperor at Westphalia.

With that reconciliation, Mazarin was seeking to buy time. He had plans to conduct an economic blockade of Paris and, with the peace, he could redeploy troops to that effect. The Parlement responded by banishing him in January 1649. But the blockade had its impact (grain prices in the capital rose to four times their usual winter levels), while Mazarin and Anne of Austria were perturbed by the execution of Charles I on the 30th of that month and Spain took advantage of French divisions to launch an invasion of Picardy. Further reconciliations followed (the Peace of Rueil, 11 March; St-Germain-en-Laye, 1 April 1649) and the court re-entered

Paris the following August. By then, however, the Fronde had acquired other dimensions. Dissension in Rouen, Bordeaux and Aix-en-Provence, coupled with noble-led oppositional movements, meant that France remained divided and its continuing war against Spain hobbled.

France was not exempt either from the meteorological and economic catastrophes that took place elsewhere in Europe in this period. In the region around Beauvais, the years from 1647 to 1651 were marked by disastrous harvests as a result of bad weather, by terrible poverty and mortality. The population fell by about a fifth and did not recover again before the eighteenth century. Contemporaries represented the scale of the crisis in apocalyptic terms. 'If ever one had to believe in the Last Judgment,' wrote a pamphleteer in 1652, 'I believe it is now.' Marie-Angélique Arnauld ('Mère Angélique'), abbess of the Jansenist retreat at Port-Royal, just south of Paris, took the sufferings around her as a call to prayer, for 'a third of the world has died'. The risk of a more popular and radical Fronde, which had been real and present in 1648, resurfaced in 1651, and was always in the background until Louis XIV's coronation on 7 June 1654.

REPUBLIC AT WAR

In 1639, Amsterdam's aldermen decided upon a new town hall. It was eventually commissioned as the ink dried on the Peace of Westphalia in 1648. Seven years later, and after over 13,000 wooden piles had been sunk into the soggy subsoil and 8.5 million guilders into the project, it was completed – the largest administrative building anywhere in Europe at the time. Set into the marble upper floor were two maps of the world, each depicting a celestial hemisphere. These highlighted the presence of the Dutch East India Company, and made the point which would have been obvious by looking over to the docks from the cupola: the Dutch were a world power. Rembrandt was commissioned to produce eight canvases around the theme of the revolt of Claudius Civilis, the one-eyed Batavian whose conspiracy and rebellion were documented by Tacitus. In the end, only one of them materialized, depicting the agreement Claudius and his co-rebels swore to, not by the kiss of peace but by the touching of swords – a reminder that this federated republic was an aggressive military power.

The political divisions over the truce were, for a time, buried by the republic's commitments to the renewed anti-Spanish struggle. On land, that meant maintaining at least 30,000 men in the forts which, by 1621, protected its southerly and easterly flanks. Those forces left a margin of offensive capacity for Stadholder Mauritz and his successor, Frederik Hendrik. But the costs to the republic grew rapidly and the impact of Spain's economic blockade dislocated its mercantile economy. Abortive peace talks coincided with the period (1627–1631) when the army of the States General was, for the first time in the eighty years' conflict, larger than that of the Spanish (over 70,000). With significant land victories, Frederik Hendrik was prepared to negotiate from strength, and the Spanish were willing to listen. But the maritime war continued apace. The blockade of Flanders was tightened; Piet Hein ransacked the shipping in Bahia harbour and then captured the Mexican silver fleet in Cuba. His ships returned to Holland in January 1629 with goods and treasure worth over 11 million guilders, or two thirds the annual cost of the Dutch army. The public debate about the peace talks became intense, dividing provinces and towns of the republic and paralysing its affairs.

The land campaign was mostly a stalemate through the 1630s and 40s, the Stadholder increasingly convinced that he could not work with the States of Holland, who would neither support his army adequately nor make peace. The economic war continued, but with less success for the Dutch. The levels of Dutch losses to the Dunkirk privateers rose while its own blockade of the Flanders economy faltered. Portuguese sugar planters staged an insurrection against Dutch Brazil in 1645, and since sugar was (along with the Guinea trade) the Dutch West India Company's staple, its shareholders became less enthusiastic for continuing the war. The revolts of Portugal and Catalonia opened the door to renewed Dutch trading with the Spanish peninsula, removing another blockage on negotiations with Spain, with whom the Dutch concluded a truce in January 1647.

Three months later, Stadholder Frederik Hendrik died (14 March 1647), succeeded by Willem II, who did his best to frustrate the peace at Münster and oppose its implementation. He opened independent negotiations with France and resisted reductions in the size of the Dutch army proposed at the Estates of Holland in May 1650. On 30 June, he ordered the arrest of six of their leaders (including Jakob de Witt, father of Johan de Witt, the future Grand Pensionary) and launched surprise military assaults on Dordrecht and Amsterdam in July. That on Dordrecht was foiled by dense fog. The attack on Amsterdam involved 10,000 troops under Willem's cousin, Willem Frederik, prince of Nassau. Although the city prepared to defend itself, there were internal divisions and it chose to parley, accepting the Stadholder's terms that the Dutch army would not be disbanded, and reinforcing his position in Holland. For a few weeks, the possibility of a civil war in the Dutch Republic was real, but within months Willem Frederik succumbed to smallpox. His son Willem (later William III) was born a week after his death, and the internal crisis provoked by the signing of the Peace of Westphalia was resolved by two decades of Stadholder-less rule dominated by the Holland Regents.

THE PEACE OF WESTPHALIA

With many preliminaries, diplomatic delegations arrived in 1643 in the two towns which had been agreed. Thirty miles apart from each other, Münster had been a Catholic city since shortly after the collapse of the Anabaptist rising, while Osnabrück was a bi-confessional town with two Lutheran and two Catholic churches, and a majority Lutheran town council. Both cities carried the scars of the war, but Osnabrück suffered worse, subjected to the troops of the Catholic League (1628–32) and a forcible Catholicization, and then Swedish war contributions. Catholic plenipotentiaries gathered in Münster, with the papal nuncio from Cologne (Chigi) and an ambassador from Venice (Contarini) as convenors. The Swedes acted as convenors for the Protestant delegations in Osnabrück. German states attended either, depending on their religion, trying to act as best they could as though they were two halves of a common Diet – the French and Swedes had demanded that they have seats at the negotiating table from the beginning. Negotiators never met in plenary session, so everything was conducted bilaterally. Their discussions had no precise beginning or ending. The number of participants provides a clue to the attendant complexities. At various stages, 176 plenipotentiaries represented 196 rulers. Only England, Poland, Russia and Turkey were absent.

Most of the important discussions took place after November 1645. That was when Maximilian von Trauttmansdorff, imperial Lord

Steward and President of the Privy Council in Vienna arrived in Münster with instructions to make far-reaching concessions – especially to Sweden. He had it in his power to offer 1618 as the normalized year for ecclesiastical territories and properties in the empire (though not in Habsburg ancestral lands). The duchy of Pomerania could be granted to Sweden as satisfaction for its war costs, along with Rostock, Wismar and parts of the bishopric of Bremen. Habsburg possessions in Alsace could be ceded to France – although Trauttmansdorff and the Spanish plenipotentiary, Gaspar de Bracamonte y Guzmán, count of Peñaranda, had differing instructions and views about what concessions could be made, a discrepancy which French diplomats sought to exploit. In 1646, Mazarin proposed a marriage between the Spanish infanta, María Teresa, and Louis XIV, in which the Spanish Netherlands (or perhaps some of the latter and Franche-Comté) would be the dowry. But then the Spanish crown prince, Baltasar Carlos, died on 9 October 1646 and the prospects of Louis XIV as heir presumptive of the Spanish crown became too great. When Mazarin's proposals were leaked to the Dutch plenipotentiaries by the Spanish, their distaste for the potential French presence on their border led them to sign a truce with Spain in January 1647.

France and Sweden's hopes of laying the foundations of a new international order at Westphalia were frustrated. The instructions to the French envoys at Münster (Abel Servien, marquis de Sablé, and Claude de Mesmes, count d'Avaux) of September 1643 laid out two federations of individual princes, one in Germany and the other in Italy, both functioning under French protection. That in Germany would replace the laws and institutions of the empire and reduce the emperor to a Doge. At the same time, France demanded control over Alsace, and then later (in 1645) Lorraine, retaining key fortresses (Breisach, Philippsburg, Ehrenbreitstein) beyond the Rhine. German princes and territories recognized that it was hardly in their interests to emasculate the empire and replace it with overlordship by Sweden and France. Trauttmansdorff made common cause with them and rejected the demands for any radical reframing of the empire. Sweden was content with any proposals which guaranteed its position in North Germany. The eventual terms of the Peace of Westphalia contained no collective security of the kind the French envisaged beyond a vague clause of mutual guarantee. The Westphalian accord was not the precursor of balance of power politics among Europe's states. Rather, it was an attempt to reinstate the notion of prescriptive rights and established customs through the mechanism of a revived empire, in which the powers of the emperor were restricted by the clause requiring all major political decisions to be taken in future with the consent of the imperial Diet.

Above all, the Peace of Westphalia sought to settle the religious conflicts in German lands on a permanent basis. The normative year was eventually agreed as 1624, before the major re-Catholicization of ecclesiastical territory in northern Germany had begun but after the conquest of the Palatinate. All confessional disputes were henceforth to be solved in the imperial Estates not on the basis of majority decision but by negotiation between the Catholic and Protestant Estates in the Diet. Religious minorities who had enjoyed the right to practise their religion freely in 1624 would continue to do so. The Habsburg ancestral lands were exempt from these clauses, but it was evident to all parties that the principal casualty of the Westphalian accords was the emperor's attempt to re-Catholicize the empire. The Peace of Westphalia brought the age of politico-religious contentions in Germany to an end and, with it, fundamental disputes over the nature of the imperial constitution. Its failure was that it was not a truly European peace accord. France's war with Spain continued. The treaty provided no solution for containing the French monarchy. On the contrary, the clauses about the future status of the Spanish dominions in the Low Countries and Franche-Comté, and the uncertain status accorded northern Alsace and Lorraine (and the French dependencies of Metz, Toul and Verdun), provided opportunities for Louis XIV to exploit its terms at the expense of his neighbours later in the century.

19. Times of Troubles to the East and West

'THE WHOLE WORLD IS SHAKING ...'

The Thirty Years War was Europe's central preoccupation in the years before the mid-seventeenth century. Its impact – considerable on all those parties directly engaged – was only part of a broader tumult which afflicted Europe in the mid-century, a tumult felt beyond Europe in the wider world as well. '. . . There is great shaking and the people are troubled.' This was the reaction of an inhabitant of Moscow in June 1648 to the momentous events that were then convulsing the Russian capital. During the 'Salt Riot' (or 'Moscow Uprising') crowds of angry insurgents, abetted by the tsar's sharp-shooters (*streltsy*) who had been sent to disperse them, invaded the Kremlin and ransacked the quarters of leading ministers, murdering several of them. That triggered other riots and rebellions. Over a hundred merchant and noble houses in Moscow were set alight and, within hours, half the capital (according to the horrified Swedish ambassador) had been burned down. Other uprisings broke out in sympathy, especially in the fortress towns on the steppe frontier in the Ukraine. With fears of a return of Russia's 'Time of Troubles' (*smuta*) – the twenty years of war, devastation and famine in the early seventeenth century – the Romanov dynasty's rule was openly thrown into doubt. Only with widespread concessions, coupled with hard-line repression, did the tsar and his adherents gradually over the following five years recover their authority.

Meanwhile, seismic events were occurring in another capital to Europe's east. In June 1648, an earthquake struck Constantinople, demolishing the aqueduct which supplied the city with its water, severely damaging the Hagia Sophia and other mosques and killing several thousands of worshippers at Friday prayers. A Venetian source reported that preachers blamed the natural disaster on the failure of the Ottoman state to follow the teachings of the Prophet. Two months later, at the beginning of August, the return of a janissary officer from the war front in Crete to demand reinforcements sparked off a palace revolution. Conspirators strangled the chief minister (Ahmed Pasha), whose body was thrown into the street, where it was dismembered by the crowd – hence his nickname 'Thousand Pieces', *Hezarpare*. In the subsequent janissary revolt, Sultan Ibrahim was deposed. Following a sentence of doom (*fatwā*) from the Chief Mufti, pronounced on 18 August, he was strangled by the public executioner. His eldest son, the seven-year-old Mehmed, was proclaimed sultan in his place and his grandmother, Kösem Sultan, manipulated power in his name. Widespread rioting broke out in the capital and protesters gathered in the Hippodrome to make their voice heard. But the janissaries surrounded and killed them in their thousands, in cold blood. As in Moscow, the events in Constantinople called into question the sultan's rule, and the regime struggled over the next decade to recover its stability.

Much in the individual backgrounds of these events explains why they occurred: in Muscovy, the emerging tsarist autocracy following the Time of Troubles; in the Ottoman empire, its geo-strategic problems, coupled with its structures of rule. But there were common elements too, which reinforce the conclusion that the contemporaneous mid-century turbulence in Europe was neither coincidental, nor limited to Europe alone. Both Moscow and Constantinople were capitals of large composite empires, ruling diverse regions. Each political system felt the competitive demands of war, and the need to modernize and finance the state. Each responded in ways which made it seem more out of touch with its subjects.

In addition, extreme climatic events rendered already vulnerable sections of the population even more fragile. Severe drought afflicted the usually fertile steppe-lands of the Ukraine in 1639, 1640 and 1645. There were exceptionally early frosts, followed by poor summers and harvests in 1647 and 1648. Population levels, said government commissioners in 1645–6, had shrunk from two decades previously. Similar droughts, coupled with early frosts, ruined the harvests of upland Anatolia and in the Balkans, while the Nile floodwaters (which irrigated its huge delta, feeding much of the Ottoman empire) were at their lowest ebb for the century in 1641–3, and again in 1650. Taking place in a grim climatic, economic and social context, the upheavals in Russia and the Ottoman empire destabilized Europe's steppe frontier, and especially the Polish-Lithuanian Commonwealth.

POLAND-LITHUANIA: BEFORE THE DELUGE

By the early seventeenth century, the Polish-Lithuanian Commonwealth was a huge landmass. In 1618, troops under the command of the Polish Crown Prince Władysław Vasa stood before the gates of Moscow and tried to seize the city. Faced with no choice after the Time of Troubles, Michael Romanov (acclaimed tsar in 1613) ceded all the lands conquered over the preceding decade by the Commonwealth. Smolensk, the heavily fortified city on the Dnieper, only 200 miles from Moscow, fell, despite its newly constructed stone kremlin, to the Polish-Lithuanian forces, in 1611. Although this success made the Commonwealth over twice the size of France, it also increased the vulnerability of its frontiers. The Muscovites launched an assault on Smolensk in 1632, but failed to recapture it. Meanwhile, although the Commonwealth did not become directly involved in the Thirty Years War to the west, it was influenced by it.

Its bruising encounters with Sweden (1600–11, 1617–18, 1621–5, 1626–9) resulted from dynastic conflict, religious division and commercial-strategic rivalries. In the last phase, Gustav Adolf launched an amphibious invasion of Polish Prussia in May 1626, overrunning it with passive support from its mainly Protestant urban populations and threatening the port of Gdańsk. Polish forces, their cavalry among the best in Europe but their infantry and artillery no match for the Swedes, held on with detachments from Wallenstein's army in 1629. The resulting truce at Altmark (26 October 1629) gave the Swedes control of most of Livonia and the port of Riga, and the right to tax Polish trade through its cities on the Baltic. The Poles held on to Gdańsk and prevented themselves being dragged into the escalating German conflict. The Commonwealth concentrated on its other vulnerable frontiers to the east and south, but its weaknesses were exposed.

Those internal problems were the result of a composite monarchy, whose union was superficial and whose asymmetry created dilemmas which could not be resolved. It prided itself on being a Christian commonwealth whose political heart lay in its three Estates: king, Senate and Chamber of Envoys (Sejm). In the latter, Poles, Lithuanians, Livonians and Prussians all had a voice. The Senate (150 members) included Catholic senior clergy, Palatine nobles, appointees to castellans and government ministers. The kingship was elective and, ever since the death in 1572 of King Sigismund Augustus, and in answer to demands from the lower and middle nobility, it had been agreed that not just the Diet but the whole nobility enjoyed the right to participate in royal elections. Nobles would turn up in their thousands to the Wola Field outside Warsaw where the Convocation Diet organized elections. The Diet also negotiated the new monarch's electoral agreement (*Pacta Conventa*) to which he was obliged to swear before being crowned.

In addition, every Polish king was required to bind himself to the eighteen Henrician Articles (*Articuli Henriciani*), which had first been adopted at the election of King Sigismund's successor, Henry de Valois, in 1573. They guaranteed the elective and non-hereditary nature of the Polish monarchy. The king's marriage had to be approved by the Senate. The monarch was required to summon a Diet once every two years for six weeks, and its approval was required for all new taxes. Between meetings of the Diet, sixteen resident senators were elected to serve in rotation on a royal council. Kings could not declare war or summon the *levée en masse* (*pospolite ruszenie* – levies of nobles) without the Diet's approval. Monarchs swore to abide by the Warsaw Confederation's guarantees of religious freedoms. Finally, if the Polish king infringed the laws and privileges of the nobility, the Articles authorized the right to disobey, legitimating noble confederations against the king (*Rokosz*). Every Polish king from 1573 onwards swore that 'if anything has been done by us against laws, liberties, privileges or customs, we declare all the inhabitants of the kingdom freed from obedience to us'.

Among the Christian commonwealths of the later sixteenth century such restrictions did not seem extraordinary. Polish contemporaries did not think that their monarchy was weak. They had differing views about the merits of mixed government, but many of them would have subscribed to the ideals expressed by Łukasz Opaliński on the eve of the Deluge that a strong state was not inimical to virtuous Poles protecting their liberties. On the contrary, they understood that their kings had considerable latitude for initiative. Ordinary Diets only lasted six weeks every two years. The king set the agenda. Most of the time was spent on petitions and local issues. Polish monarchs manipulated the Senate council such that ordinary nobles came to suspect that it was acting in magnate or monarchical interests rather than their own. Their mistrust of their kings was increased by the election of Jagiellon-descended foreign dynasts to the throne – a reflection of the prevailing dignity of royal blood and a reluctance to elevate a native magnate family over its peers. Foreigners were suspected of pursuing their own interests at the expense of the Polish Commonwealth.

This was particularly so in the case of the Polish Vasa kings (Sigismund III, Władysław IV and John II Casimir), who maintained their claim to the Swedish throne. Equally Sigismund III's pro-Austrian affiliations and the influence of Jesuits at the Polish court figured largely in the Sandomierz Rebellion (the Zebrzydowski *Rokosz*, 1606–9) with its demands that Jesuits be expelled from the Commonwealth, royal office-holders elected and King Sigismund deposed. There was a negative sentiment that the best way to protect the Commonwealth was to block initiatives, and especially foreign adventures. 'Our happiness is remaining within our borders, guaranteeing health and wellbeing,' wrote the bishop of Płock in 1634.

What Opaliński called 'non-government' (*nierząd*) became a hostage to fortune, however, towards the middle of the seventeenth century. The Polish fiscal-state was weak and unreformed, its revenue base inadequate and undermined by monetary instability. The efforts to raise taxes through trade tariffs and exploiting domain revenues merely increased noble suspicions of its intentions. Its military state depended on magnate levies which had no regular training. Fiscal weakness meant that fortresses were limited and poorly maintained. The nobility refused to pay for military forces contracted outside the Commonwealth. The Polish-Lithuanian state was the more dangerously exposed for not having responded to changes in European warfare – as Prince Władysław Vasa appreciated during his European tour of 1626–7 which took in visits to the Flanders Army as well as the Venetian dockyards. In his *Pacta Conventa* he pledged to build a military academy for the Commonwealth, found a navy, and reform its infantry and artillery. Yet by 1647 the Polish royal guards totalled 1,200 and just 4,200 troops garrisoned the Ukraine.

The one military component which the Commonwealth could deploy was the Cossack host. Originally adventurers and freebooters, the Cossacks of the Zaporozhian Sich (along the lower Dnieper river) had become a substantial military force. But they were independent and difficult to manage. King Stefan Batory attempted to do so by registering those – mainly in the frontier towns of the Ukraine – whom they regarded as capable of bearing arms for the Commonwealth. The numbers of those registered increased in wartime, but declined in the subsequent peace; and there were always far more unregistered Cossacks who felt aggrieved that they had been excluded. In 1630, they rebelled and appealed to the clergy and laity of the Orthodox Church. The Commonwealth appeased the rebels by increasing the number of registered Cossacks to 8,000. Meanwhile, however, Polish settlers continued to flood into the Dnieper valley and, in 1635, the federal Diet unilaterally reduced the number of registered Cossacks to 7,000, and instigated the building of a new fort at Kodak on the lower Dnieper, garrisoned with contingents from the federal army. These measures provoked another uprising by the Cossacks, who sacked Kodak, murdered the new garrison and appealed to the Orthodox faithful. As a contemporary chronicle from Lvov said, the Cossacks 'treated the Poles contemptuously, killed the Germans like flies, burned towns, and slaughtered the Jews like chickens'. Adam Kysil, a government commissioner sent to negotiate with the rebels, conceded that whatever was agreed could only be a truce since the Cossack problem was a 'boil endlessly on the verge of bursting'.

Cossack brutality succeeded in the short term in alienating its own supporters. A Polish show of force coaxed the Cossack Sich into an agreement in 1638. They agreed a reduction in the number of registered Cossacks to 6,000, promised not to attack the Tatars (or Ottomans) without royal permission and agreed to take their orders from federal agents, appointed by the crown. Those agents, however, quickly became yet another avenue for Polish-Lithuanian settlements and land-grants in the Ukraine, the stationing of Polish troops in the major towns and the fostering of further unrest. Far from a truce, the result was another major uprising (the Ostrzanin Uprising, after its leader Hetman Yakiv Ostrzanin), in which ordinary Cossacks, outraged by a decision of the federal Diet making them the equivalent of peasants and therefore subject to enserfment, spread their grievances by leaflets, distributed by

Orthodox monks, Cossack elders and sympathizers across the Ukraine. Although this was suppressed by the magnates, it was a symptom of a wider simmering social and religious malaise in the region.

Polish Ukraine – the lands on the left bank of the river Dnieper – had originally been part of the grand duchy of Lithuania. With the formation of the Commonwealth it fell under Polish hegemony – Polish law, officers and Catholic faith. The under-populated region attracted immigrants from all quarters, who settled in new towns or expanded the old ones, a frontier society which lacked the social solidarities of old-settled lands. To compensate for that, and to provide for frontier defences and reward its servants, the Polish crown made massive grants of land in the Ukraine to a small number of magnates of Polish origins. Their estates grew spectacularly as Polish landowners exploited the black-earth riches of the steppe with serf-based domains. Their estate managers tended to come from just one group of immigrants – the expanding Jewish population which, by 1648, numbered at least 45,000. By 1640, some 10 per cent of the Ukraine's landowners controlled two thirds of its population and landmass. The 1638 uprising was suppressed by two of them: Jeremi Wiśniowiecki and Mikołaj ('Bearpaw') Potocki. Wiśniowiecki's estates were made up of some 616 Ukrainian settlements in 1630. By 1640 that figure had risen to 7,600. In 1645, it was 38,000 and he had over 200,000 subjects. Potocki had similarly large holdings which were further increased as a reward for his loyalty in 1638. As their estates grew, so did their influence over the indigenous middle nobility and largely Orthodox non-Polish population, both groups disaffected, alienated and resentful.

The election of King Władysław IV in 1632 brought to the throne a reformer with international ambitions. He forged alliances with the emperor (marrying the sister of the future Ferdinand III in 1637), Spain and Denmark and made enemies among the nobility for promoting fiscal and military change. Then, making capital from the Cretan War and with backing from Rome, Venice and Muscovy, he planned a military intervention against the Ottomans in 1646, hoping to consolidate an unstable frontier and solve Cossack unrest by launching a campaign in which they had a stake. He recruited Cossacks, only to have the federal Diet demand he dismiss them. In 1647 and in poor health, he resurrected the plan under the auspices of a 25,000-strong army organized privately by Wiśniowiecki. But he died in May 1648 just as the Khmelnytsky Cossack rebellion gathered force.

Bohdan Khmelnytsky, the leader of the uprising, was the son of a middle-ranking Ukraine nobleman. He was educated by the Jesuits (though he remained Orthodox), read and spoke several languages, and knew the wider world. Entering service as a registered Cossack, he served in the Polish war of 1619 against Moldavia and, captured by the Turks, spent two years in Constantinople. In the 1630s, he led Cossack contingents against the Ottomans in naval assignments in the Black Sea and acted as a negotiator on behalf of the Cossack Sich on the eve of the 1638 revolt. His own experience of magnate oppression occurred in 1645 when his estates were seized without redress by Aleksander Koniecpolski. When Khmelnytsky failed to win satisfaction from the king, he took his cause around Cossack regiments, and then to the Sich. At the end of January 1648, he was elected Cossack Hetman, issued demands which amounted to an independent Ukraine, made common cause with the Crimean Tatars, and then inflicted two crushing defeats on the Polish forces (Zhovti Vody, 16 May 1648; Korsun, 26 May 1648). Entering Kiev at the head of a large Cossack army at the end of 1648, he declared his objective as to 'liberate all Ruthenians from Polish misery . . . to fight for the Orthodox faith'. The people (by which he meant the Rus) are 'our right hand'. 'The main reason for the war between us and the Cossacks is the difference over the Ruthenian religion,' wrote the Polish Parliament-man Andrzej Fredro. The Commonwealth faced a civil war with social, religious and ethnic overtones.

The latter were particularly evident in the victims of Cossack rage. A 'Victory March' sung by the rebels celebrated how 'Crook-Nose', a Cossack captain, 'chops the soldiers' heads off their shoulders', leaving 'Polacks, hanging like a black cloud/Now Polish glory's sore and shattered'. They also massacred Jews in their thousands. Rabbi Nathan Nata Hannover described the slaughter in his *The Abyss of Despair*, a chronicle of the rising. At Nemyriv in June 1648, the local populace abetted the Cossacks to enter the stronghold where the Jews had taken refuge. They slaughtered everyone they could in the next two days (6,000, according to his estimate). Women jumped over the walls and drowned rather than be molested or murdered. At least 10,000 Jews (a quarter of their overall number) were probably killed, with perhaps

8,000 more taking up refuge elsewhere and 3,000 being sold to the Tatars as slaves.

Behind the migrations southwards, and the rage and despair of the rebellion itself, lay the unpredictable weather patterns which had prevailed in the region since the later 1630s. Cold summers accompanied by late spring heavy snow and frosts disrupted the short growing seasons and harvests in 1641–3 and 1646. Plagues of locusts attacked the crops in 1645–6, and the horrible winter of 1646–7 was followed by torrential rains and flooding in the autumn and winter of 1647. As the uprising began, it was unseasonably hot and dry, with locusts again destroying the harvest. An inscription in the church of St John the Baptist at Sambir from that year read simply: 'There was great hunger throughout the Christian world.'

Khmelnytsky claimed that he had King Władysław's authorization for the revolt, although the letter has never been found, and was probably forged. Nevertheless it was one of the ways by which, over the following three years, Khmelnytsky made good his ambitions to rally the Ukraine and Belarus against the Polish Commonwealth. He placed armies in the field as large as those which fought in the Thirty Years War and looked for allies abroad. The Crimean Tatars played a decisive role in an increasingly bloody conflict. In return for their participation they were granted licence to raid in the Ukraine and seize Catholic Christians and Jews for sale as slaves in Ottoman markets – Orthodox Catholics treating both (even Uniates) as legitimate targets. At the battle of Berestechko (on the Styr river, 28–30 June 1651) over 60,000 Polish troops confronted a Cossack and Tatar host of over 100,000 and eventually overwhelmed them. The Tatars withdrew, taking Khmelnytsky with them as a hostage. He managed to negotiate his release, making further promises to reward them for their services, and reassembled a Cossack host, confronting the Poles once more, this time successfully, at the battle of Bila Tserkva (24–5 September 1651), leading to a truce which was not ratified by the Sejm.

As Khmelnytsky marched towards Moldavia in the early summer of 1652 in order to cement his alliance with its rulers against the Poles, the Polish crown's forces, mostly magnate levies, gave battle at Batih (1–2 June 1652) on the river Boh. Khmelnytsky commanded at least 40,000 Cossacks and Tatars. The Polish army was not more than 15,000 strong, but it was well entrenched in a defensive camp. Internal divisions in the Polish forces enabled Khmelnytsky to overcome them, and 8,000 Polish soldiers were captured and slaughtered. The treaty which Khmelnytsky signed with Muscovy in January 1654 established (in Muscovy's eyes) its hegemony over the Kievan Rus and became the prelude to its, and Sweden's, invasion of Poland, which the Commonwealth was, by then, in no position to repulse.

THE 'FALLING OUT IN THESE THREE KINGDOMS'

In 1662, James Heath published his *Brief Chronicle of all the Chief Actions so fatally Falling Out in these Three Kingdoms* emphasizing the interrelatedness of what remained distinctive struggles in the British Isles – the Bishops' War (1639–40) and following Scottish Civil Wars (1644–5), the Irish Confederate Wars (1641–53) and the English Civil Wars (1642–6, 1648–9 and 1650–51). Superficially, there are parallels to be drawn between how things transpired in the east and in the west in the years approaching the mid-century. Like Poland-Lithuania, the British Isles had been only tangentially involved in the Thirty Years War. Its disengagement occurred after token support for the Palatinate in 1621–2, a disastrous Anglo-Dutch naval expedition to Cádiz (November 1625), a failed Anglo-Dutch coalition with Denmark in support of its intervention in the empire, and a dismal effort to relieve French Protestants (1627–9).

Like Poland's, British commerce suffered from the severe economic dislocation in the Baltic, the Channel and across central Europe. Contingents of Polish volunteers – as their Scottish equivalents in the Swedish armies – served in European armies, just as Protestant exiles from Bohemia and Germany turned up in Poland and London. London merchants and English gentry reassured themselves that, in comparison with Germany, they were living 'halcyon days' ('What though the German drum/ Bellow for freedom and revenge? The noise/ Concerns us not, nor should divert our joys' ran an English elegy). The times of troubles in the British Isles happened as the Thirty Years War and its aftermath preoccupied others.

The British state, like the Polish Commonwealth, was a composite monarchy whose union was superficial, and whose asymmetries created dilemmas which could not be resolved. The dominant group in England, as in Poland, was a middling nobility ('gentry', *szlachta*), which felt itself alienated from the magnate class whose wealth and power could be manipulated by monarchs, and could in turn divide the nobility as well. The gentry's preoccupation became that their kings' concerns were different from theirs, and that their rulers were not to be trusted because they threatened the laws, traditions and liberties of the commonwealth. As in Poland, the union in the British Isles involved an asymmetry in which one element (Scotland) became the neglected junior partner. In addition, the English fiscal-state was weak, with powers of granting taxation vested in Parliaments whose willingness to do so grew less the more their monarchs exploited prerogative sources of revenue for objectives which were alien to their own. In the British Isles, too, there was a third element (Ireland) where the problems involved a toxic mix of discontented resident landlordism, ethnicity and religion which resulted in uprisings of singular brutality.

In England and Scotland, the Churches were by law established. Debates about their uniformity, structure, ceremonies and worship reflected and fed into wider divisions, especially when the drive for uniformity in the Church came from the monarchy. The Puritans in England and the Presbyterians in Scotland were implanted within lay and clerical society north and south of the border. Both were convinced that they stood for the fundamental laws and liberties of their country as embodied in Church and state, and which were imperilled by the Stuarts. But the problems emerged first in Scotland, where the Covenanting movement took root among those who refused to conform to the Perth Articles (1618). Charles I's more extensive plans for accomplishing a uniformity of worship, in line with those spearheaded by William Laud south of the border, were highlighted in the year of Laud's inauguration as archbishop of Canterbury (1633), when Charles went north of the border for the first time, and a proposal for a new Scottish liturgy was placed before the Scottish Parliament. Bishops were required to wear their vestments and clergy their surplices while ministering holy communion. New Church Canons (1636) tightened the conformity of Scottish Presbyterians to Protestant practices south of the border and were silent about the Kirk, its general assemblies, Sessions and Presbyteries. The following year a new Prayer Book was imposed by royal authority, a guide to worship to be followed by every parish in the Kirk, and the standard by which nonconformity would be judged.

By announcing its intentions the government allowed time for the Kirk to mobilize and its organization furnished the means to do so. On 23 July 1637, a premeditated protest against the new book occurred at St Giles in Edinburgh. As the unrest spread, the authority of the bishops and the Privy Council north of the border was paralysed by an organized opposition ('the Supplicants'). Their cause married opposition to religious innovations with a defence of vernacular laws and customs. It enjoyed the support of the nobility and the Estates ('Tables') of the Scottish Parliament. The fifth Table, coordinating the nobility and representatives of the other three Estates became a Directorate of Operations through which a National Covenant was distributed for signature. Drafted by a Presbyterian minister, Alexander Henderson, and a Scottish lawyer, Archibald Johnston of Wariston, it was signed by individuals from almost every part of the country. Royal efforts to overawe the Covenanters were outmanoeuvred and Charles decided to put the revolt down by military force, using a combined English and Irish army but resourced on prerogative revenues, without calling an English Parliament.

That initiative came apart in 1639. Charles's efforts to rally a minority of Scottish opponents to the Covenanters under George Gordon, marquess of Huntly, petered out. So did the attempt to raise a force in Ireland. The levying of militia in English counties on prerogative powers was bitterly contested, not least because the Covenanting cause mirrored widespread English grievances against Laudian innovations in their Church. One man in Newcastle stood up for the Covenanters because they 'did but defend themselves against those that would have brought in Popery and idolatry'. He refused to fight, 'for unless his conscience moved him to it, he would not fight for any prince in Christendom'. When the king reviewed the troops at his disposal at York in April 1639, two peers refused to take the oath of service – William Fiennes, Viscount Say and Sele, and Robert Greville, Lord Brooke, both members of the Providence Island Company and backers of the Hampden case. Before the year was out, the conflict was already known as the 'Bishops' War'. But with his army too feeble to risk a fight, Charles negotiated in order to buy time. He summoned an English Parliament to do the job properly in 1640.

The Short Parliament, meeting on 13 April 1640, sat for only three weeks. Unlike the Polish Sejm, the English Parliament had the possibility of elections in two-member county constituencies where freeholders (whose numbers had grown as inflation and a diffusion of wealth lowered the threshold) had the right to vote. An unprecedented number of MPs in the Short Parliament took their seats after contested elections. As far as the king was concerned, it had only one piece of business to transact: the granting of supply to put down a revolt. To MPs, the redress of grievances took precedence, and their list (after eleven years without a Session) was long. Harbottle Grimston, MP for Essex, put it bluntly: the dangers at home were as great as those 'abroad' (that is, in Scotland). 'The Commonwealth has been miserably torn and massacred and all property and liberty shaken, the Church distracted, the gospel and professors of it persecuted and the whole nation is overrun with multitudes and swarms of projecting cankerworms and caterpillars, the worst of all the Egyptian plagues.' Grimston was among a minority of veterans from the fractious Parliaments of the 1620s. So too was John Pym, MP for Tavistock, a Providence Island Company member and trusted operator for Lord Brooke, Lord Saye and John Hampden. On 17 April 1640, Pym delivered a speech that turned specific grievances into a common cause without making it sound like an attack on the king. Charles, out of time and patience, dissolved the Parliament without gaining resources or answering grievances, and with a war still to fight.

Military mobilization in English counties in the aftermath of the Short Parliament was even more sluggish than the previous year, while the payment of Ship Money collapsed. The English state was a pediment whose pillars rested on subcontracted power to self-governing local entities. If the latter voted with their feet, there were limits to what the Privy Council, Lords Lieutenants or judges on Assize could do to command their obedience. The efforts to force men to serve in the army were resented, especially when it was for a cause that many of those impressed did not believe in. The Covenanting army, aided by contingents of Scots who had seen service in the Thirty Years War, seized the initiative and moved across the Tweed from Berwick, bearing a Bible 'with a mourning cover', its drummers beating a funeral march to indicate that their cause was God's truth. When the English forces gave battle at Newburn on 28 August 1640 to stop the advance, they lost, and the Scots entered Newcastle unopposed. Charles agreed a ceasefire which involved monthly payments to the Covenanter forces for its duration. The only way that the king could persuade the City of London to release a loan with which to pay for the truce was to hold another Parliament. This, the Long Parliament, met in November 1640 after new

elections (even more contested than those of its predecessor). It convened in an atmosphere of national crisis in the aftermath of a Parliament
which had been summarily dismissed, its grievances unheard, to pay for
a war which the king had lost, and for a cause which the majority of the
Commons did not believe in, and which they associated with a king and
regime in which they had no trust.

MPs queued up in the opening sessions to present petitions that
voiced their accumulated resentments against the Personal Rule and
those most identified with it. They emphasized their fears of Catholic
influence at court – epitomized by Charles I's French wife, Queen Henrietta Maria. Popular demonstrations accompanied the release of three
prominent victims of opposition to Laudianism. William Prynne, a Puritan lawyer and virulent anti-episcopal polemicist lost his fortune, his
freedom and his ears in two separate proceedings against him in Star
Chamber (1634, 1637). His companions in the second proceedings
were Henry Burton, a Puritan preacher, and John Bastwick, a physician.
Burton's attack on Laudian bishops was unrelenting, culminating in sermons which accused their innovations of amounting to a popish plot.
For his part, Bastwick accused them of being the tail of the Beast. Like
Prynne, Burton and Bastwick were fined, mutilated and imprisoned
after a hearing at Star Chamber. Freed in November 1640, they were
escorted in triumphal London processions as martyrs to the cause.

Initially, the Long Parliament had difficulty determining what that
cause was. Burton, Bastwick and Prynne stood for virulent opposition to
Archbishop Laud, popery, episcopacy and Personal Rule. Those were
different issues, one of them (episcopacy) more divisive than the rest. But
initially those potential divisions were subsumed into attacks upon William Laud and Thomas Wentworth, earl of Strafford, and those most
associated with Charles's rule. Laud was impeached on a charge of high
treason, and imprisoned in the Tower of London on 1 March 1641 to
await trial. John Finch, the chief justice who had presided over Hampden's Ship Money case, was also impeached and fled abroad. In April
1641, the case for Strafford's impeachment failed and the Commons
resorted to a Bill of Attainder, which was passed although the majority
of MPs abstained from the vote. The king reluctantly signed the warrant
for his execution on 10 May after threats from a London mob and an
unpaid army. Under pressure from his London creditors he also agreed
to the Triennial Act (February 1641), which required the summoning of

a Parliament every three years and outlawed the raising of prerogative revenues like Ship Money without Parliament's consent.

The Westminster Court of Star Chamber, the strong arm of the Privy Council, which had sentenced Burton, Bastwick and Prynne, was abolished. So too was the Court of High Commission, its equivalent in the Church, a familiar target of Puritan rage. Behind the scenes, the leading lights in the Long Parliament (the informal 'Junto') had their work cut out to keep the Commons and Lords in step, and to focus MPs on what most expected would be a resolution of the crisis. John Pym – his ability to mobilize a common cause with a veneer of moderation once more in evidence – emerged as a key player in negotiations with a minority of Puritan-minded peers to marginalize the potential divisiveness of what was to happen in the Church in favour of a deal with the king which he could not wriggle out of.

A CONFUSION OF TONGUES

'When will you agree among yourselves? it seems you are erecting the Babel you so much talk of.' That was how the prelate and Stoic Joseph Hall criticized the 'Protestation', Pym's equivalent of an English National Covenant in May 1641. The Protestation required MPs, and then the whole country, to sign up to an oath to uphold the 'doctrine' of the Church, the 'honour and estate' of the king, the 'power and privilege of Parliament', and the 'lawful rights and liberties of subjects'. It was an effort to secure national unity around a moderate solution to the fundamental differences in the nation. But, though it sought to defend the Church from popery, it had nothing to say about the governance, worship and destiny of the English Church. That failure opened the door to a coalescence of royalist opinion around the defence of the Prayer Book and Church. On the other side, radical doubts emerged about the trustworthiness of the king, with the possibility of equally radical changes in the Church in the offing.

Those disagreements were hidden by general opposition to the imprisoned William Laud. His critics described him as an Arminian, an exponent of the Dutch theologian's critique of Calvinist views of grace and salvation. Arminius's views had already demonstrated their capacity to divide the Dutch Republic, where they became associated with those willing to conclude a truce with the Spanish. That Arminianism had become an English issue was evident from the religious conference held at York House, the London residence of the king's favourite, the duke of Buckingham, at the beginning of Charles I's reign in 1625. The subject of the debate was the writings of the English prelate and Arminian promoter, Richard Montagu, bishop of Chichester. Both sides claimed they had the better of the arguments. In reality, the anti-Calvinists won where it mattered, in the heart and mind of Charles I. His Church and court increasingly favoured Arminians. Their critics, excluded from both, were forced to consider other ways of protecting what they held dear: to contemplate emigration, to go to law, to publish and to make a nuisance of themselves

Laudianism, however, was not centrally about Arminianism. William Laud preached the opening sermon at the Parliament in February 1626. His text was 'Jerusalem is builded as a citie that is at unitie in itself' (Psalm 122). His point was that the king's governance and that of the Church were as one: 'So the *Church*, and the *Commonwealth*, *Gods* house, the Temple, and the *Kings* house, the house of *David*, are met in my text.' His aim was to link the Church in England to the Universal Church, whose historic roots lay in sacred Hebraic antiquity. The Temple was its model. To depart from that was to put what was left of the unity of Christendom in jeopardy. For Laud, that unity relied on its priests. Episcopal government guaranteed stability in Church and kingdom, just as patterns of worship which acknowledged and taught respect for sacral power reflected how one should behave towards divinely ordained royal power. His almost paranoid obsession with Puritan subversion was already evident: 'They, whoever they be, that would overthrow *sedes Ecclesiae*, the seats of ecclesiastical government, will not spare, if they ever get power, to have a pluck at the throne of David. And there is not a man that is for parity – all fellows in the Church – but he is not for monarchy in the state.'

Laud was determined to unify the Church in opposition to the Puritans whom he saw as attacking the remnants of Christendom at its core. It inspired his efforts to rebuild St Paul's in London, insert senior clergy into the Privy Council and local commissions of the peace, change the position of the communion table to be an altar, enforce the injunctions on bowing and kneeling before it, and limit lay influence over the appointment of ministers. Such innovations, introduced without Parliamentary approval, involved ordinary people in parishes. They divided them and, since the English Church was, like its state, dependent on local self-government, that blunted their implementation and increased the controversy surrounding them. At the heart of local opposition to Laudianism was the belief that it was closet popery.

Anti-popery tapped into the wellsprings of the English Reformation and the anxieties concerning its survival. It united Laud's critics, playing a disproportionate role in the avalanche of pamphlets from 1641. Popish plots became the preferred instrument for Pym and the Junto to focus political loyalties and mobilize suspicions about the king's objectives. Unity was all the more important because it was lacking in the Commons debates over the future governance, rituals and worship in the Church. On 11 December 1640, the 'Root and Branch' petition – it attracted thousands of signatures – was presented at the Commons by radical London parishioners. The text attacked the bishops, claiming that they undermined preaching and encouraged 'lewd and dissolute, ignorant and erroneous men in the ministry, which swarm like the locusts of Egypt over the whole kingdom'. As a result, 'only Papists, Jesuits, priests and such others as propagate Popery or Arminianism had prospered'.

The issues the petition raised were divisive. The English Reformation had been enacted in Parliament. So too had the powers of its Church, which Laudianism had perverted. What Parliament had created, Parliament could change. But should those changes be (as Scottish Presbyterians and radical English Puritans argued) in the direction of a Church without bishops, devoted to a godly reformation of the social order, established according to the Word of God and the example of the earliest Christian Churches? If not, what sort of Church should replace the collapsing episcopal authority (after Laud's imprisonment and the abolition of High Commission)? The answers to these questions were, as Hall said, confused.

As the Long Parliament reconvened on 20 October 1641 after its harvest recess, populist anti-popery and Puritan anti-episcopal populism were evenly balanced. There was a drift of opinion to the king, especially in the House of Lords, where the legal status of the bishops in their midst was an immediate and pressing issue. That direction was reversed, however, on 1 November, when privy councillors announced to the Commons 'certain intelligences ... of a great treason, and general rebellion, of the Irish Papists'. Less than two months later, the anxieties which this raised in England set a course irreversibly towards armed conflict. On the one hand, Charles wanted to raise an army to repress the Irish rebellion. On the other, Parliament-men feared that such a force would be deployed against them.

Increasingly politics was taking place outside Westminster – in the London Guildhall and on the capital's streets, and in provincial towns and communities where the rumours of papal plots multiplied, and in the corridors of Charles I's attenuated court, where royalists sought a *mise en scène* which would break the deadlock. The Grand Remonstrance (8 November 1641), presented by Pym from the 'committee on the state of the kingdom', put forward the case for Charles I's government being a long-running plot to subvert religion and liberty. The remonstrance passed through the Commons with a narrow margin, and then was printed and distributed. Meanwhile, a municipal revolution took place in the City of London which swept away the royalist-orientated aldermen and replaced them with their opponents, whose first action was (in concert with the Parliament-men) to elect a Committee of Safety and put themselves in charge of the London militia. Fearing a loss of control in the city, Charles I entered Parliament on 4 January with a posse of soldiers to arrest five members of the Commons and one peer, ringleaders of the opposition. But they had been tipped off and were nowhere to be found. The king's *mise en scène* turned into a *mise en catastrophe* which proved that he was as incompetently untrustworthy as he was painted. In March 1642, Parliament published an ordinance, taking over the country's trained bands of militia. In July, it voted to raise an army and put the earl of Essex in command of it. With the king also raising forces in counties loyal to him, and despite local attempts to avoid taking sides, the Civil War gradually took shape.

IRISH REBELLION AND THE CONFEDERATE CAUSE

On 22 October 1641, the native Irish of Ulster under the leadership of Sir Phelim O'Neill set out to capture the country from the representatives of the king in alliance with the Old English settlers of the Pale. Their motives were mixed, powerful and opportunistic. The Ulster conspirators resented their exclusion from royal service, especially under the government of Charles I's Lord Deputy in Ireland from 1632, Thomas Wentworth (later the earl of Strafford). Wentworth had learned his politics in a tough school, serving as president of the Council of the North. His correspondence talked of being 'thorough', by which he meant restoring the fortunes of King and Church (and advancing his own). His general idea was that the fractiousness of the 1620s (in which he had played his part) needed time to subside. After a decade or so of a firm royal touch, with reformed finances and Church, Charles I could then summon an English Parliament whose loyalties he could command. Ireland became the experiment for that approach.

Wentworth went out of his way to be ruthless, and not merely with the native Irish Catholics who were the usual targets of English neo-colonialism and who had been disenfranchised, their lands confiscated, their last stronghold (in Ulster) overrun with Scottish and English settlers, and their principal leaders in exile. He played off the 'Old English' (the main landholders of the kingdom, mostly Catholic, excluded from office by successive English governments, but retaining a powerful influence in the Irish Parliament) against the 'New English' (more recent Protestant settlers, including the Scottish Presbyterian planters in Ulster, their interests aggressively pursued by law and force). Manipulating the 1634 Irish Parliament, he achieved a lavish grant of subsidies and the power to vet titles to property. Due legal process was bent by 'a little violence and extraordinary means' (as he put it) to uphold the crown's claims to determine landed titles and recover former Church lands which had been incorporated into the estates of the Old English landowners. Wentworth's support for the pursuit of Laudianism in Ireland was a way of countering the growth of Scottish Presbyterianism in Ulster through its planters. But it was dangerous because it divided the narrowly based English governing ascendancy at its weakest point – the Irish Protestant Church, shorn of resources and enfeebled in its mission to the Catholic majority population.

Wentworth's recall to England in September 1639 left an administration in Ireland internally divided and leaderless, a vacuum which allowed the native Irish, particularly in Ulster, an opportunity to regain their fortunes. Like the Old English, they reacted with alarm to the triumph of Presbyterian Covenanters in Scotland and the shrill anti-papal tone of the politics in Westminster. As Charles's basis for support in

England ebbed, so he looked elsewhere in his kingdoms for those whose loyalties he could count on. They included the Old English, who were led to believe (through the prospect of concessions) that they had royal acquiescence in resistance to the new Protestant settlers and Ulster planters, even royal blessing for a revolt which, in its timing, was the very reverse of a blessing for Charles I in England.

The October 1641 revolt failed to take the seat of English administration in Ireland at Dublin. Instead, it acquired the loyalties of all those who, over the generations, had suffered at its hands. Initially they concentrated on theft and property, but then the insurgents and their supporters turned to more murderous extremes. Thousands of English colonists were massacred, many deliberately assassinated. Thousands more were chased from their homes, despoiled of their belongings and clothes, and forced to take refuge wherever they might. On 20 December 1641, Charles I nominated commissioners to collect testimonies from English refugees sheltering in Dublin. Other affidavits were collected from those at Cork. Their accounts – over 19,000 pages of depositions under oath from witnesses who were far from unbiased – provide a picture of what happened in the early months of the Irish rebellion that was very different from that which was reported in England and on the continent thereafter.

In the over 300 surviving pamphlets from English presses the events were described as a pogrom of Protestants, a 'barbarous butchery', depicted in terms which evoked the reported 'savagery' of American Indians, and the massacre of St Bartholomew. One Irish minister was reported at the end of 1641 to have declared that 154,000 Protestants had been massacred in Ulster alone. That became the official figure, referred to in the Commons during debates and multiplied fourfold by John Milton among other pamphleteers from 1646 onwards. The depositions, however, reflect the more complex and varied reality of Irish grievances. In Ulster, victims told of armed insurgents bent on vengeance against the brutal colonialism of English planters, supported by troops. In Connaught and Clare, by contrast, the dislike of plantations was clear, but ethnic divisions were less in evidence. In Leinster, to the south, where there were no plantations, the uprising took the form of a peasant revolt. In Munster to the southwest, there were fewer massacres because the Old English nobility rapidly had things in hand.

The rebels established their sway over the middle and west of the island. They framed an oath, like the Scottish Covenant, pledging their loyalty to the English monarchy, to Ireland and to the Catholic faith. Faced with an English Parliament which, on 19 March, forced the king to sign the Adventurers Act, pledging Irish land in return for loans in order to send forces to Ireland, and prohibiting the king from issuing pardons to the rebels, they formed their own provisional government. The latter was conjured into existence through the organization of Catholic bishops, and steered by Ulick Bourke, earl of Clanricarde, a leading Catholic lord from County Galway. Based on a General Assembly (to strengthen their loyalist credentials it was never termed a Parliament) and an executive (called the Supreme Council), the Catholic Confederates ran most of Ireland from 1642 until they were defeated by Oliver Cromwell in 1649. They had agents in European capitals and raised their own finances and military forces.

The Confederates successfully opposed the English Parliament and Scots Covenanters, an independent government in all but name. While proclaiming their loyalty to Charles I, they negotiated with him, demanding that any agreement be ratified by a post-war Irish Parliament. Their aims were to achieve full rights of worship and participation in government of Irish Catholics and self-government. More radical Confederates wanted plantations in Ulster and elsewhere reversed, the establishment of Catholicism as the state religion in Ireland, and an alliance with Spain or France (who had supported them with modest subsidies from the beginning) in pursuit of their objectives.

Such demands placed Charles I on the horns of a dilemma. Horrified by the massacres of 1641, he had committed himself to seeking redress for Protestants who had suffered in the uprising and made other promises. Yet, as his military position in England weakened in 1643, so he became more willing to entertain concessions to the Confederate cause, ones which sought to tempt them into helping him without compromising him with English Protestant royalists. In September 1643, the Confederates negotiated a ceasefire with James Butler, duke of Ormonde and commander of the royalist army in Ireland. In 1644, a beleaguered Charles despatched Edward Somerset, earl of Glamorgan, with secret orders to agree to the Confederate demands in return for Irish Catholic armies to fight for him in England and Scotland. A copy of Glamorgan's secret orders fell into the hands of the Long Parliament, for whom they were a propaganda coup – further proof of the king's perfidy.

Faced with embarrassing questions from his own supporters, Charles was compelled to proclaim Glamorgan a traitor. To deter any effort to use Confederate soldiers in England the Long Parliament passed the 'Ordinance of No Quarter' in October 1644, giving localities *carte blanche* to ill-treat Irish (and, increasingly, any suspect royalists). In the end, the only military effort Charles extracted from the Confederates was a small force sent to Scotland under James Gordon, marquess of Montrose, enough to start another civil war there in 1644 by exploiting the Catholic loyalties among Highland clans and their hatred of the Covenanting duke of Argyll. In England, however, the Confederates, increasingly under the hard-line influence of the papal envoy Giovanni Battista Rinuccini, who had arrived in early 1645, merely encouraged Charles I to entertain false hopes of help from across the Irish Sea and to imagine that he could manoeuvre himself out of his increasingly hopeless position by manipulating all sides in whatever way seemed most convenient to him, compromising him with his own supporters and those with whom he would eventually have to negotiate a peace.

'THIS BLOODY AND UNNATURAL WAR'

Charles I could have won the English Civil War. Loyalty to a legitimate king counted for a great deal. Twice as many peers fought for the king as for Parliament, recognition of the significance of the hierarchy of order, inherited privilege and obedience. They had their retainers in local society, even though many aristocrats had become courtiers, rendering their local networks remote. Their wealth gave Charles the initial resources with which to pay his troops. The earl of Worcester reportedly contributed over £300,000 to the king's coffers. Charles I was the crowned head of the monarchy in the British Isles, with whom foreign princes expected to do business. Through his wife he had privileged access to the French court and was entitled to think that it would help him in return for promises of support in the future. He also had supplies of cavalry and horses through his princely relatives in the Netherlands and a corps of officers, many of whom had recent experience of service on the continent. He could draw on thirteen years of governing the kingdom. Most people feared the prospect of open conflict and shied away from committing themselves until they were forced to do so. His concern to remain true to his principles – a rejection of the mischievous propaganda against him and a projection of a defence of the Church and the obedience due 'unto the natural person of the prince' – emphasized the unity of his cause. His opponents could readily be presented as opportunistic and divided.

Yet, despite the superficial unity of a monarchical cause, competitive honour and wounded pride often set cavaliers against each other. The royalist heartland – in the West Midlands and Welsh marches – was threatened by Parliamentarian raids, exposing their supply-lines and administrative base. The latter was weakened by a failure to regulate the relations between royalist commanders and local authorities – leading to a sense of arbitrary exactions upon people. The result was that the royalist cause eventually became vulnerable to reprisals from local populations and divided from within between those who were prepared to consider a negotiated settlement (and therefore concessions) with the Parliament, and others (especially around Queen Henrietta Maria and Prince Rupert) who saw a fight to the finish as the only possible outcome. Charles I's access to credit in support of his campaign was limited to the confiscation of plate and valuables from royalist towns, the mortgaging of assets (principally his wife's) and promises.

The Parliamentarians gained control of the fleet (vital in securing the neutrality of other European powers) and some coastal garrisons, and could count on the City of London and loyalties in the wealthy Home Counties. Yet Parliament's divisions over episcopacy, which had barely been patched over in 1641–2, resurfaced over other issues: the prosecution of the war as a defensive or offensive campaign; if the latter, how it was to be supplied and paid for; in what way a peace could be negotiated with (or forced on) the king. These issues, taken separately and together, raised questions about the legality of Parliamentary actions and the divisive social consequences of what they were about.

The Parliamentary way of doing business was hardly conducive to running a war. Even after the defection of royalists from the Parliament, attendance was still not far short of 200 MPs (with about thirty peers in the Lords). The predilection for establishing committees to handle specific business multiplied delays and opportunities for division. But, unwieldy though it undoubtedly was, Parliament also provided an avenue for the local grievances created by the prosecution of the war. Had that not existed, it is difficult to imagine that (even in extreme necessity and with all the persuasive skills of Pym and leading Parliament-men) they would have succeeded in gaining consent for extraordinary fiscal impositions and military impressments. The transformations in the Parliamentary war-effort in 1643 were the key to its eventual success.

The greatest chance of a royalist victory occurred early in the war. In the first major battle (Edgehill, 23 October 1642) the earl of Essex's Parliamentary forces, barely managing a draw, beat a hasty retreat towards London to protect the capital. Prince Rupert pressed home the advantage and, on 12 November, attacked Brentford. The possibility of a royalist encirclement of the city was real. But Essex rallied the London militia and faced down the royalists at Turnham Green. Then, as royalists consolidated their grip on northeast England, captured Bristol (July 1643), made gains in the southwest and pressed on through Lincolnshire into East Anglia, they sought to exploit Parliamentary divisions with offers of negotiation. Pym used the emerging sense of desperation to gain assent for compulsory assessments across all Parliamentary territory, the introduction of an excise (farmed out to professional tax-collectors) and compulsory impressments of soldiers. In the autumn of 1643 the Parliamentarians held on to Gloucester and concluded a treaty with the Scots for a 20,000-strong Covenanter army to re-enter the northern shires which they had vacated two years earlier.

The Covenanter intervention changed the balance of forces. At the same time, the treaty with the Scots opened up simmering divisions in Westminster between the wavering bands of Parliament-men who sought a peace, and those who wanted to prosecute the war with greater determination. The Covenanters were prepared to intervene because Charles planned to use Irish Confederate forces to invade the west coast of Scotland. But they wanted commitments from the Westminster Parliament to a Presbyterian Church order to rebuild the now shattered foundations of the English Church. On 12 June 1643, the Westminster Assembly was established: 120 hand-picked Calvinist-minded English ministers with thirty lay assessors from both Houses of Parliament and eight Scottish commissioners. Their brief was to provide a blueprint for a new English Church – which turned out to be a Presbyterian one.

Henceforth, those in Westminster seeking peace began to coalesce with those opposed to the Scots and dismissive of their scriptural claims to Presbyterianism being a divinely sanctioned form of Church government.

John Pym died on 8 December 1643 – the state funeral readily accorded him by MPs a testimony to his contribution to their cause. Before the end of the year important Parliamentary defections were rebuffed by Charles and the news of his understanding with the Irish Confederates held other waverers to the Parliamentary cause. In 1644, Parliament's military victories turned the tide of the war – especially that at Marston Moor (2 July 1644) in North Yorkshire, weakening the royalist grip on the north and setting the scene for a gradual collapse of royalist positions more generally. The king was eventually forced to surrender to the Covenanter army at Southwell, Nottinghamshire on 5 May 1646.

The victors at Marston Moor included the MP and commander Ferdinando Fairfax, the Major-General of the Eastern Counties Parliamentary Association, Edward Montagu, earl of Manchester, and his second-in-command, Oliver Cromwell. As Westminster tensions grew, they spread to the City of London, the Parliamentary army and more broadly. In London, nonconformist congregations took advantage of the collapse of Church authority to establish their presence and to voice their opposition to a Presbyterian Church settlement. Called 'Independents' by their critics, they found an echo among those fighting in the armies on the Parliamentary side.

Both royalists and Parliamentarians had taken to grouping shires together into associations for military purposes. The Parliamentary Eastern Association, faced with persistent royalist attacks into Lincolnshire, reformed its forces into what became known as the 'New Model Army'. Cromwell, in particular, was content to accept, and promote up the ranks, those whose religious views were nonconformist and who, socially speaking, came from below the upper crust. The division between those in the Parliamentary army who were anxious for a settlement and those who wanted to go on and win the war at whatever cost was laid bare. It resulted in the Self-denying Ordinance (eventually agreed to by Parliament on 3 April 1645), which was a thinly disguised purge of Parliament's senior officers and the emergence of Independents in the army as well. By the time of the king's surrender, the divisions in the country after 'this bloody and unnatural war' were as much within the Parliamentary cause as between Cavaliers and Roundheads.

As elsewhere in Europe, climate irregularities contributed to the perception of uniquely harsh years during the 1640s in the British Isles. The Irish rebellion of 1641 had coincided with a hard winter (with heavy snowfalls and severe frosts) resulting in deaths attributed by observers to cold and starvation, especially among those trying to flee the massacres. Later that same decade (as also in Ireland) failed harvests and an epidemic of plague brought famine in Scotland 'the lyke of which had never beine seine in this kingdome heretofor, since it was a natione'.

Meanwhile, the material destruction from the first Civil War in England was colossal. To fund its armies, the Parliamentary administration raised over £30 million in taxes and penalties, although still more was requisitioned locally. That unprecedented burden became still heavier in the aftermath of the king's surrender. Disastrous weather ruined the grain and hay harvests for the next six years in a row. The Essex clergyman Ralph Josselin noted in his diary in May 1648: 'such terrible frosts that the ear [on rye] was frozen and died', followed (in June) by the report: 'corn laid, pulled down with weeds; we never had the like in my memory'. That same year James Howell, one-time clerk to the Privy Council, told a correspondent from London that a 'famine doth insensibly creep upon us'. ''Tis true,' he added, 'we have had many such black days in England in former ages, but those paralleled to the present are as the shadow of a mountain compared to the eclipse of the moon.'

THE EXECUTION OF A KING

In such worsening economic circumstances, winning the war changed nothing. A peace still had to be negotiated with the king on terms that would protect the Parliamentarians and yet preserve the monarchy. The Covenanters had to be rewarded for their intervention, and they expected the Presbyterian Church government proposed by the Westminster Assembly to be implemented. The Parliamentary army had done the fighting but it had not been paid. The costs of its arrears amounted to £3 million. Parliamentary exactions, especially in the circumstances of the terrible harvests of 1647–9, caused widespread grievances against politicians whose legitimacy rested on elections which went back to November 1640. When by-elections were held from 1645 onwards, those returned to the Long Parliament were Independents, committed to further radical reforms of the judiciary and against the fragile and readily contested Presbyterian leading lights among its MPs and in the City of London. Presbyterian hopes rested on a negotiation with the king and the disbandment of the army with promises of arrears of pay based on realizing episcopal assets.

Meanwhile, as the prospects of being rewarded with what they saw as their just deserts receded in the spring of 1647, the rank and file of the Parliamentary army became restive, appointing 'agitators' to present their case to their commanding officers and commissioners from the Parliament. On 3 June 1647, they seized the king, transferring him to army custody as a bargaining counter. Two days later, regiments signed up at a general rendezvous to the Solemn Engagement of the army, a declaration that they were not a 'mercenary army' but a force raised to fight for the rights of 'freeborn Englishmen'. Those rights were equated with liberty of conscience, fixed-term Parliaments and hostility to arbitrary rule. The latter now included that of a Parliament whose financial apparatus and membership were accused of corruption and wanting to preserve its authority for ever. The inspiration for this programme came from London Independents and radicals, called 'Levellers' by Presbyterians, who believed that they were a threat to property and order. The Presbyterian minister Thomas Edwards's *Gangraena* (1646) offered a 'Catalogue and Discovery' of 'Errours, Heresies, Blasphemies and pernicious Practices of the sectaries of this time'. Calling on others to report the threats to the established order from the pullulating profusion of sects, he collated the evidence into a laborious exposition which revealed the widespread fears of the equivalent of a disease in the social body.

In 1648, there were risings in the name of the king in Wales and Cornwall, a revolt against the Presbyterian-dominated Parliament in Kent, Essex and Lincolnshire, and a defection of part of the navy from Parliamentary control. With the Confederates in Ireland, Stuart loyalists active in the west of Scotland, and open divisions among and between the Parliamentary army, Parliament and the City of London, it is not surprising that Charles I felt that he could yet recover what he had lost in military defeat. He refused to discuss abdication and let it be known that he was prepared to be a martyr in defence of sacred royal authority – a power he demonstrated by healing people with scrofula (the 'Royal Touch') when given the opportunity.

The paradox at the heart of the execution of Charles Stuart on 30 January 1649 was that the majority of the fifty-nine signatories to the death warrant were not republicans. A minority of convinced anti-monarchists had surfaced in the wake of the Civil Wars, especially among army radicals and in the press, but they played almost no role either in the king's death or in the subsequent establishment of the Commonwealth. The central arguments for the regicide came from the Bible, texts instrumentalized by events to prove that the king was a 'man of blood', an inveterate violator of the public peace, whose crimes against his people could not go unpunished. In the *Theatre of God's Judgments* (its fourth edition appearing in 1648), Cromwell's teacher Thomas Beard explained (in relation to the massacre of St Bartholomew) that mass murderers could not escape retribution. In a sermon preached before Parliament in the aftermath of the battle of Marston Moor, Henry Scudder called, on the basis of Old Testament texts, for those who had spilled so much blood to be brought to book. In *The Just Man's Justification* (1647) the Leveller John Lilburne called for Charles I to pay the price with his blood for that which he had caused to be shed by others. Those arguments were deployed in the debates of the House of Commons and at the Council of the Army between October 1647 and 6 December 1648. Cromwell was among those who were convinced that Charles I was indeed a 'man of blood', his guilt evident from his devious actions and from the judgements of divine providence in battle against him. But he was not sure that he, or others in the army, had the authority from God to intervene. In similar circumstances, King David had refused to punish Joab for the murder of Abner. Other solutions lay to hand – perhaps a legal trial, leading to Charles's replacement by one of his two sons.

But then a crisis occurred which overwhelmed Cromwell's caution and that of the army council in general. On 6 December, a military coup, organized by Colonel Pride, commander of the regiment which guarded the capital, purged the Long Parliament of those whom they suspected of being Presbyterians and favourable to a peace deal with the king: forty-five MPs were arrested, 186 were excluded and eighty-six others refused to take part in any further proceedings as a protest. Seventy MPs were left as a 'Rump' Parliament. For Cromwell, Fairfax and the leading figures in the army, this complicated the question of their legitimacy. It called into doubt their capacity to launch the legal trial against the king in the High Court of Parliament. They now faced concentrated and vocal opposition from Presbyterian preachers in London and the remaining members of the House of Lords, who accused the army of acting as an instrument of tyranny. Then, on 18 December, the generals received intelligence that the Dutch States General had signed an agreement with the Irish Confederates. The possibility of a naval blockade of London was real, as was the launching of a royalist-inspired invasion of England from Ireland in the spring of 1649. Charles I's rejection of the army's eleventh-hour attempt to reach a negotiated settlement with him sealed the metamorphosis of Charles Stuart from 'man of blood' to public enemy, charged with 'traitorously and maliciously' levying 'war against the present Parliament and the people therein represented', the principal accusation which he faced in the sham trial (albeit one which preserved the formalities of a real one) which took place in the week of 20–27 January 1649.

Charles's path to the scaffold, erected against the north wall of the Banqueting Hall in the palace of Whitehall, took him past the paintings which he had commissioned from Peter Paul Rubens in 1635 to commemorate his father, James I. The latter was depicted as King Solomon. The Hall was turned into Solomon's Temple. The king was shown in majesty, distributing equitable justice; bringing peace and prosperity to the land; and obliging war and rebellion to go on bended knee before him. The day of his execution, a printing press in London distributed the first copies of the retrospective apotheosis of his monarchy, the *Eikon Basilike (The Royal Portrait)*. The image of the frontispiece, the portrait referred to in the title, depicted the king on bended knee in prayer, his eyes fixed upon an eternal crown, in his hand a crown of thorns and at his feet a terrestrial crown, inscribed with the word 'vanity'. The 'man of blood' became, on the day of his death, transfigured into a martyr, a man of suffering, and the basis for a restored royalism.

The results of the troubles in the west were therefore very different from those in the east. The levels of material destruction may even have been greater in England than in many parts of the European continent. A quarter of a million men and women are estimated to have died in the Civil Wars – 7 per cent of the population (as compared with less than 2 per cent in the First World War). The political fallout was also entirely distinct because the Parliamentarians had won the military battle decisively. It was Charles I's unwillingness to understand the consequences of defeat, his persistence in playing off the different struggles to his advantage and seeking outside help, which lost him his head.

The king's execution unleashed a revolution. It was followed by the abolition of the monarchy (17 March 1649), the House of Lords

(19 March) and the Privy Council. The Act Declaring England to be a Commonwealth (19 May 1649) constituted England 'a Commonwealth and Free State ... by the supreme authority of this nation', its affairs vested in the officers of a Council of State. The office of bishop had already been abolished by Parliamentary ordinance (9 October 1646) and many clergy purged and ejected. Royalist aristocrats took up exile, their wealth confiscated. The English Republic consolidated the transformations in the English fiscal and military state which the Civil Wars had instigated. But, with the resurgence of Protestant sects and radical groups in the Parliamentary New Model Army in the wake of the Civil Wars, there was no agreement about how Parliaments should be elected, about what should happen to Church lands and tithes and other fundamental issues in the Church, and about turning the Republic into a Puritan 'godly commonwealth'. Those divisions, coupled with a persistent royalism and a monarch in exile to which it could turn, set a term to the English revolution.

In the meantime, the revolution was exported to other parts of the British Isles, rewriting the union which the Stuarts had instigated. Cromwell conquered Ireland (1649–53), defeating the Confederate-Royalist coalition and occupying the country. Penal laws against Catholics provided the basis for the confiscation of large amounts of land and its assignment to army veterans who were owed back-pay, and Protestant adventurers. The latter were those merchants and Anglo-Irish speculators who under the Adventurers Act (March 1642) agreed to lend money to Parliament for the subjugation of the Irish rebellion. The Scottish Covenanters, despite their conflicts with the Scottish royalists, signed a treaty with the exiled Charles II Stuart at Breda (1 May 1650). With nothing to lose, Charles agreed to everything they asked for – most significantly an independent Presbyterian Scotland, free from English interference. Cromwell hastily left the remains of the Irish campaign in the hands of lieutenants and arrived in Scotland in July 1650 with an army which defeated the Scots at the battle of Dunbar (3 September 1650). When the Scottish Covenanters and royalists joined forces and regrouped against the English, a further army (under General John Lambert) crossed the Firth of Forth and defeated the Scots at the battle of Inverkeithing (20 July 1651). The remnants of the Scottish army went south of the border to link up with the English royalist rearguard, to be finally defeated in 1653. By the Tender of Union

('Declaration ... concerning the Settlement of Scotland', 28 October 1651) the English Parliament proposed that Scotland be 'incorporated into, and become one Common-wealth with this England'. The Scottish Parliament was dissolved and Scotland was given thirty seats in the Westminster Parliament. Although several acts and ordinances for the 'incorporating' and 'uniting' of Scotland and England were put forward, it was finally approved only in 1657. So, although the union was a *de facto* reality, persistent royalist insurgency in the Highlands and the delay in legitimating what both sides regarded with suspicion compromised its implementation. That, in turn, placed the survival of the English revolution further in jeopardy.

Conclusion: Europe's Paroxysm

There are many myths about the Middle Ages. Most of them began life in the sixteenth and early seventeenth centuries, which is when the conception of a 'middle age' first took root. Christendom was not one of them. On the contrary, it was a myth which the Middle Ages had created about itself. It described the project (and accompanying intellectual and institutional apparatus) which united western Christianity. The period following the Protestant Reformation witnessed the progressive and eventually comprehensive disintegration of that project, and the myth which lay behind it. By 1650, Christendom lay devastated and drained, broken in pieces. There was nothing left beyond the yearning for a vanished unity, a 'Paradise lost'. 'Europe', which is increasingly how what had once been Christendom was now conceived, was not a project but a geographical projection, a map on which its divisions could be represented, a way of delineating its political, economic and social fragmentation.

With more fluid and pluralist forms of information diffusion in different media by the mid-seventeenth century, contemporaries assembled these various fragmentations into a chronology of enveloping crisis. Gallus Zembroth, a wine-grower and notable from Allensbach (a village near Konstanz), looked back to the 'indisputable omens' of 1618 (a reference to the great comet of that year), 'assuredly a harbinger of the thirty-year war which followed', according to the later Strasbourg chronicler Johann Walther. Hans Herberle, a cobbler from Neenstetten (a village north of Ulm), writing in about 1630, tried his best to encapsulate what had happened since 1618: '... war, rebellion, and much spilling of Christian blood ... in Bohemia ... in Brunswick, Mecklenburg, Lüneburg, Friesland, Brandenburg ... and indeed almost the whole of Germany'. But then his abilities to make sense of things gave up: 'I cannot relate and describe all this.' From being a '15-Years' War' (in 1633) it became a '20-Years' War' (in 1638) until, by the time Sebastian Wendell, another wine-grower, looked forward in his diary in 1647 to the negotiations at Münster and Osnabrück, it became a 'thirty years war'. Wendell did not live to see the peace, but Jeremias Ullmann, a chronicler from Silesia, did. He noted: 'On 24 October – God be thanked for it – (after the war has lasted full 30 years and carried off hundreds of thousands of souls, swallowed up hundreds of millions of *Gulden*, and produced nothing but afflicted people and desolate towns and villages) the noble, golden, and long-desired peace has been concluded.' Only gradually did the notion of the Thirty Years War consolidate as a way of understanding that part of the paroxysm, and how it had disrupted people's lives.

Europe's channels of communication acted like an echo-chamber in which, as events unfolded, they reverberated to an ambient anxiety. Contemporaries put together in their minds explanations for the disordered world around. In 1635, Hans Conrad Lang, a clothier from Konstanz, thought that what was occurring was such that 'has never been heard in human history'. 'The world is in complete revolt,' wrote a Catalan in 1640. In a sermon for a day of fast during the Long Parliament on 23 January 1643, the English preacher Jeremiah Whitaker declared (reflecting his biblical text): 'these days are shaking, and the shaking is *universal*: the Palatinate, Bohemia, Germania, Catalonia, Portugal, Ireland, England'. A year or so later, the Swedish diplomat at the Peace of Westphalia, Johan Salvius, reported: 'we hear of revolts by the people against their rulers everywhere in the world'. He made sense of it as some kind of 'great miracle', wondering whether 'this can be explained by some general configuration of the stars in the sky'.

When the Landgrave of Hesse published his *Meteorological History* in 1652, he suggested that the disordered weather over the previous twenty-four years might be explained by the planets. In 1645, the Welsh clergyman James Howell drew on his belief in a Providentialist universe to explain the congruence of general disorder: 'God Almighty has a quarrel lately with all mankind, and given the reins to the ill spirit to compass the whole earth; for within these twelve years the strangest revolutions and horridest things have happened, not only in Europe but all the world over, that have befallen mankind, I dare boldly say, since

Adam fell, in so short a revolution of time.' In Scotland, a pamphlet describing the monstrous birth of conjoined twins, a boy and girl, in September 1647, interpreted the event within the Protestant parameters of God's warning to the world: 'nature seemed to be disquieted and troubled; in so much that the heavens proclaimed its entrance into the world with a loud peal of thunder'. As the storm reached its climax, the monster announced with a 'hoarse but loud voice . . . I am thus deformed for the sins of my parents'. That same year, John Taylor's *The World Turn'd upside down* was republished (it had first appeared in 1642), offering a 'brief description . . . of these distracted times', a prelude (he thought) to a coming Millennium. A Paris magistrate, writing in 1652 as the troops of the prince of Condé massacred citizens in a public meeting, mused: 'If one ever had to believe in the Last Judgment, I believe it is happening right now.'

Historians have been inclined to link together these anxieties, and the various revolts and disorders of the period of the later Thirty Years War, into a 'general crisis' – the first in what was now widely perceived of as 'Europe'. Perhaps contemporaries were correct to interpret it as a global crisis as well. There is certainly evidence to suggest that meteorological disturbances had a disruptive impact on settled civilizations across the planet towards the middle of the seventeenth century. It is possible – probable, even – that this, in turn, jolted the emerging patterns of world commerce, affecting (notably) the flows of precious metals to Europe. The various economic regions of the globalized world were like, says one economic historian, ponds of different depths, connected one to another by channels. Those channels easily dried up, or became blocked by war and other disruptions. Those whose livelihoods depended on the economic activity from one region to another were left to complain about the destructive impact of the failure of their markets, and (in particular) their inability to sell goods.

That inability was directly related to interruptions to the flows of silver and other commodities. Those flows were, as the London merchant Thomas Mun outlined in his *England's Treasure by Foreign Trade* (written around 1630), the 'rule of our Treasure'. That treasure seemed increasingly to be dividing Europe as well. 'My grandmother used to say' (reported Sancho Panza, Cervantes's stoical squire in *Don Quixote*) 'that there are only two families in the world: the haves and the have-nots.' The 'have-nots' were much more precarious by 1650, risking death from malnutrition, cold and disease. They were especially at risk in the extraordinary meteorological and associated economic conditions of the mid-century. There is no doubt that Europe's weakening social and cultural cohesion, the growing divisions between its urban and rural worlds, greater economic divergences between north and south, not to mention the weakening intellectual consensus, contributed to the intensity of contemporary perceptions of anxiety. But it was the proximity and scale of war, and the way in which revolt and disorder invited participation from those outside the political élites which lay at the heart of contemporary experiences of a world turning upside down.

When examined in closer detail, the various revolts and uprisings of the later 1640s become more contingent, symptomatic of Europe's fundamental divisions, less evidently based around a common set of grievances or capable of being interpreted within an overall schema. That said, they shared three commonalities which help to make sense of the profound changes which had taken place in Europe over the previous century and a half. The first is that they occurred on a regional and national scale which indicated that the nature of Europe's localism was reconfigured into something broader, mobilized by media and social forces which were new. The second was that they were mostly led by conservative figures, moved to preserve what they regarded as vernacular senses of law, tradition and sometimes religion, against forces which they saw as alien (the state), ungodly or simply untrustworthy. They disliked being 'cajoled' (the word was a new importation into the political vocabulary of the period). But they understood that they could as easily be discomforted by populist forces (which they distrusted and resented) as by 'innovators' in Church and state. So there were limits to the degree to which they were willing to countenance political change. Thirdly, profound anxiety created paralysis, but also dynamic creativity and change, hyperactivity as well as passivity. These elements were all in play in Europe in the late 1640s among the shapers of the new age.

To regard the mid-seventeenth century as a general crisis implies that the history of what came after it was a resolution of that crisis through transition to a world that was very different from what had gone before. That was not, however, the case. Europe did not fundamentally change. Even in the British Isles, where there was a revolution, it did not last. Poland-Lithuania, overwhelmed for a time, survived.

There was no new international order. Instead, European states confronted the uncomfortable reality of French hegemony. And, in answer to mid-century revolts and disorder, rulers arrived at social compacts – implicit understandings with their élites to make sure that the latter shared in the benefits of rule in return for their support. Those compacts were secured with varying degrees of ease and complicity. Religion, however, retained its capacity to disturb and divide European polities and international relations through to the end of the century. The impact of the Protestant Reformation did not suddenly cease in 1650. Europe's social cohesion also remained fractured. It was not until the beginning of the eighteenth century that something resembling an intellectual consensus would emerge. Global cooling, too, was reversed only in the next century. 'Paroxysm' (a violent spasm in an organism) is a better analogy than 'crisis' since its prognosis is a return to the status quo.

The disintegration of Christendom did not mean the collapse of Christianity. On the contrary, Europe's paroxysm was accompanied in religion by the same mixtures of passivity and activity that characterized its political sphere. Enormous energies were still deployed towards establishing a global Catholic Christianity. Protestant and Catholic Churches intensified their enforcement of orthodoxies based around people subscribing to beliefs encompassed in creeds. Committed clerics and well-meaning notables still sought to build godly commonwealths around patterns of social behaviour and conformity. A small English nonconformist congregation which moved to Leiden in the 1600s to escape the intrusive demands of the Church in England negotiated a land patent from the London Virginia Company in 1619 to settle in 'New England' – the Pilgrim Fathers. Among their motives were the 'hard life' which they had in the Netherlands and the vulnerability of their congregation, but also the opportunity that a new life elsewhere gave them for their children not to be 'drawn away by evil examples' and 'the great hope for the propagating and advancing of the gospel of the kingdom of Christ in those remote parts of the world'. For others, dreams of a new life away from Europe's divisions remained unrealized. Among Samuel Hartlib's correspondents seeking to escape the Thirty Years War were those who wanted to establish utopian Christian communities (that of 'Antilia' was planned for an island in the Baltic). The duke of Rohan investigated the possibility of purchasing Cyprus in the 1630s and turning it into a model Protestant godly commonwealth.

Alongside such activist Christian responses in the face of a divided, hostile and alien Europe lay others which were more inward-looking. The philosopher and pansophic visionary Jan Amos Komenský (Comenius) experienced the paroxysm at first hand. Exiled from Bohemia in 1621 with the loss of his property and manuscripts, he spent his life in restless wanderings which took him to England on the eve of the Civil War, Sweden at the end of the Thirty Years War and Transylvania. In 1670, a work emanating from his collection of curious millennial dreams was published as *A Generall Table of Europe*. Its preface laid out the continent's political and religious divisions in a world context before summarizing the 'late grand Revolutions' as the essential context for interpreting the dreams. In one of his earliest works (*The Labyrinth of the World and the Paradise of the Heart*, composed *c.* 1623), Comenius imagined a pilgrim being taking to the top of a mountain in order to look over the 'labyrinth' of the city beneath him. He took in all its divisions, and especially its intellectual and religious contentions. It was like being shown a map of Europe. In the end the pilgrim realized that true unity (a harmony of God-given wisdom) lay only in the panacea of the soul within.

At 10.30 p.m. on Monday 23 November 1654, the French philosopher and *dévot* Blaise Pascal had a moment of spiritual ecstasy that marked him for the rest of his life. He could not properly describe it but on the piece of parchment which was found sewn into his waistcoat after his death, he evoked it in staccato phrases: 'Certainty, certainty, heartfelt joy, peace ... Joy, joy, joy, tears of joy'. He found his paradise of the heart in a 'hidden God' (*Deus absconditus*: Isaiah 45:15) who lets those who seek find him. Christendom was dissolved, but conscientious Christianity had found its voice.

Acknowledgements

This book was written in four places, each of them contributing to its final form. I have incurred debts of gratitude in each of them. It was begun in Sheffield (UK), where I had the good fortune to work for my professional career with the most supportive and stimulating colleagues and students that one could wish for. Mike Braddick, the late Patrick Collinson, Karen Harvey, Linda Kirk, Tom Leng, Bob (R. I.) Moore, Anthony Milton, Gary Rivett, James Shaw and Bob Shoemaker have no doubt influenced these pages. It was mainly written, however, in one of the world's great libraries, the Bibliothèque Nationale in Paris. While I was in post at the University of Paris-1, Nicole Lemaitre, Thierry Amalou, Isabelle Brian, Wolfgang Kaiser and Jean-Marie Le Gall opened up my mind to perspectives and possibilities which found their way into this book. It was completed in first draft at the FRIAS School of History at the Albert-Ludwigs Universität Freiburg, where the text benefited from its magnificent university library and the distinctively stimulating environment of FRIAS, for which I owe a debt of gratitude to its directors. It profited from conversations with Freiburg colleagues and friends, notably Ronald Asch and the other members of his research seminar, as well as Leonhard Horowski, Christian Wieland, Lucy Riall, Till Van Rahden, Gia Caglioti, Isabelle Deflers and Jakob Tanner. My research assistant in Freiburg, Adrian Steinert, not only kindly fetched and carried books from the library but also read all the chapters, picking up errors and suggesting things I should have read. Textual revisions took place in the Charles E. Young Library at the University of California, Los Angeles. There, I was fortunate to enjoy the stimulating company of Teo Ruiz and Russell Jacoby. The text reflects engagements and discussion with students, most especially in Sheffield, but also latterly in Paris, Freiburg and Warwick. Without the fun of working with them, it would not have been worth writing.

ACKNOWLEDGEMENTS

The format of the series precludes precise references to those upon whose work the book is based. They will recognize their contributions in its pages. Specific colleagues kindly answered queries, and I am very grateful to them for their help: Judith Pollmann (Leiden), Alastair Duke (Southampton) and Philip Benedict (Geneva). Anyone who has written a book such as this about Europe will know how dependent one is on an ocean of scholarship in different languages, and how one can present only a cupful of it. Jonathan Dewald, Robert Schneider, Joe Bergin, Pat Hunt, Phil McCluskey and Scott Dixon kindly read part or all of the manuscript and gave me the benefit of their critique – above and beyond what one should expect of colleagues and friends. My father Philip acted as first reader of the early draft, and helped me find the work's 'voice'. The series editor David Cannadine put me on my mettle to reshape and sharpen the argument, and crucially proposed what became its eventual theme. Simon Winder at Penguin was the editor of whom every author dreams: shrewd, patient and uncompromising where it matters. The copy-editor, Bela Cunha, ironed out many factual and grammatical wrinkles. Cecilia Mackay handled illustrations research expertly. John Hillman, a valued friend, told me where the text left him confused or cold. The person who matters most, however, is the one who shared its ups and downs: my wife Emily. With the slightest of arm gestures she would indicate that the Penguin's wings were flapping. The work is dedicated to her. More importantly, so is the time which its completion releases, with the promise to explore together more of the Europe in its pages.

Freiburg
January 2013

Further Reading

This book has been written by an intellectual jackdaw, let loose in large libraries. The debts to the scholarship of others are immense, but the format of the series precluded the attributions to those whose work it draws on. The following does nothing to acknowledge them either. It is a pointer towards some accessible material – exclusively recent monographs – in English that I think will be useful in following up the themes of this book. Statistical tables and appendices, not included in this publication because of their bulk, may be consulted at the author's website: http://www.markgreengrass.co.uk. The dates of birth and death of those people mentioned in the text, with regnal dates where appropriate, are to be found in the index.

Arnade, Peter, *Beggars, Iconoclasts, and Civic Patriots: The Political Culture of the Dutch Revolt* (Ithaca, 2008)

Asch, Ronald G. and Birke, A. M. (eds.), *Princes, Patronage and the Nobility. The Court at the Beginning of the Modern Age, c. 1450–1650* (London and Oxford, 1991)

— (eds.), *The Thirty Years War: The Holy Roman Empire and Europe, 1618–1648* (Basingstoke, 2002)

Baena, Laura Manzano, *Conflicting Words. The Peace Treaty of Münster (1648) and the Political Culture of the Dutch Republic and the Spanish Monarchy* (Ithaca, 2011)

Behringer, Wolfgang, *Witchcraft Persecutions in Bavaria: Popular Magic, Religious Zealotry and Reason of State in Early-Modern Europe* (Cambridge, 2004)

Beik, William, *Urban Protest in Seventeenth-Century France: The Culture of Retribution* (Cambridge, 1997)

Benedict, Philip, *Christ's Churches Purely Reformed. A Social History of Calvinism* (New Haven and London, 2002)

— and Gutman, Myron P. (eds.), *Early Modern Europe. From Crisis to Stability* (Newark, 2005)

Bercé, Yves-Marie, *Revolt and Revolution in Early Modern Europe: An Essay on the History of Political Violence* (Manchester, 1987)

Bethencourt, Francisco and Egmond, Florike (eds.), *Correspondence and Cultural Exchange in Europe, 1400–1700* (Cambridge, 2007)

Blair, Ann, *Too Much to Know. Managing Scholarly Information before the Modern Age* (New Haven and London, 2010)

Bonney, Richard J., *Political Change in France under Richelieu and Mazarin, 1624–1661* (Oxford, 1978)

—, *The European Dynastic States, 1494–1660* (Oxford, 1991)

— (ed.), *Economic Systems and State Finance* (Oxford, 1995)

— (ed.), *The Rise of the Fiscal State in Europe, c. 1200–1815* (Oxford, 1999)

Bossy, John, *Christianity in the West, 1400–1700* (Oxford, 1985)

Boxer, Charles, *The Dutch Seaborne Empire, 1600–1800* (London, 1965)

—, *The Portuguese Seaborne Empire, 1415–1825* (London, 1969)

Braddick, Michael, *God's Fury, England's Fire* (London, 2008)

Brady, Thomas A., Oberman, Heiko A. and Tracy, James D. (eds.), *Handbook of European History 1400–1600. Late Middle Ages, Renaissance and Reformation* (2 vols., Leiden, 1995)

Braudel, Fernand, *Civilization and Capitalism, 15th–18th Centuries* (3 vols., London, 1985)

—, *The Mediterranean and the Mediterranean World in the Age of Philip II* (2 vols., Los Angeles, 1995)

Brook, Timothy, *Vermeer's Hat: The Seventeenth Century and the Dawn of the Global World* (London, 2008)

Brown, Jonathan and Elliott, J. H., *A Palace for a King: The Buen Retiro and the Court of Philip IV* (New Haven and London, 1980)

Brown, Keith M., *Kingdom or Province? Scotland and the Regal Union, 1603–1707* (Basingstoke, 1992)

Burke, U. Peter, *Popular Culture in Early Modern Europe* (London, 1978)

—, *Languages and Communities in Early Modern Europe* (Cambridge, 2004)

Bushkovitch, Paul, *The Merchants of Moscow, 1580–1650* (Cambridge, 1980)

Bussmann, Klaus and Schilling, Heinz (eds.), *1648. War and Peace in Europe* (Münster and Osnabrück, 1998)

Calabi, Donatella and Christensen, Stephen Turk (eds.), *Cities and Cultural Exchange in Europe, 1400–1700* (Cambridge, 2007)

Cameron, Euan, *The European Reformation* (Oxford, 1991)

—, *Enchanted Europe. Superstition, Reason, & Religion, 1250–1750* (Oxford, 2010)

Canny, Nicholas and Pagden, Anthony (eds.), *Colonial Identity in the Atlantic World* (Princeton, 1987)

Clark, Stuart, *Thinking with Demons. The Idea of Witchcraft in Early-Modern Europe* (Oxford, 1997)

—, *Vanities of the Eye: Vision in Early Modern European Culture* (Oxford, 2007)

Collinson, Patrick, *The Reformation* (London, 2003)

Cook, Harold J., *Matters of Exchange. Commerce, Medicine, and Science in the Dutch Golden Age* (New Haven and London, 2007)

Cressy, David, *Birth, Marriage and Death. Ritual, Religion and the Life-Cycle in Tudor and Stuart England* (Oxford, 2000)

Crosby, Alfred W., *The Columbian Exchange: Biological and Cultural Consequences of 1492* (Westport, CT, 1972)

—, *Ecological Imperialism: The Biological Expansion of Europe, 900–1900* (Cambridge, 1996)

Dandelet, Thomas James, *Spanish Rome, 1500–1700* (New Haven and London, 2001)

Daston, Lorraine and Park, Katharine, *Wonders and the Order of Nature, 1150–1750* (New York, 1998)

Davis, Natalie Zemon, *Society and Culture in Early Modern France* (Stanford, 1975)

—, *The Return of Martin Guerre* (Cambridge, MA, 1983)

Dewald, Jonathan, *The European Nobility, 1400–1800* (Cambridge, 1996)

—, 'Crisis, Chronology, and the Shape of European Social History', *American Historical Review*, 113 (2008), 1031–52

Dickens, A. G. (ed.), *The Courts of Europe. Politics, Patronage and Royalty, 1400–1800* (London, 1977)

Dixon, C. Scott, *The Reformation in Germany* (Oxford, 2002)

—, *Protestants. A History from Wittenberg to Pennsylvania, 1517–1740* (Oxford, 2010)

— [with Freist, D. and Greengrass, M.] (eds.), *Living with Religious Diversity in Early Modern Europe* (Aldershot, 2009)

Dooley, Brendan and Baron, Sabrina A. (eds.), *The Politics of Information in Early-Modern Europe* (London and New York, 2001)

Duke, A., *Reformation and Revolt in the Low Countries* (London, 1991)

Eire, Carlos M. N., *War against the Idols: The Reformation of Worship from Erasmus to Calvin* (Cambridge, 1986)

Elliott, J. H., *The Old World and the New, 1492–1650* (Cambridge, 1970)

—, *Richelieu and Olivares* (Cambridge, 1984)

— (ed.), *Spain and its World, 1500–1700* (New Haven and London, 1989)

— and Brockliss, Laurence W. B. (eds.), *The World of the Favourite* (New Haven and London, 1999)

Evans, Robert J. W., *The Making of the Habsburg Monarchy, 1550–1700. An Interpretation* (Oxford, 1979)

Findlen, Paula, *Possessing Nature. Museums, Collecting and Scientific Culture in Early Modern Italy* (Berkeley, 1994)

Fox, Adam, *Oral and Literate Culture in England, 1500–1700* (Oxford, 2000)

Freedberg, David, *The Eye of the Lynx. Galileo, his Friends, and the Beginnings of Modern Natural History* (Chicago, 2002)

Freist, Dagmar, *Governed by Opinion: Politics, Religion and the Dynamics of Communication in Stuart London, 1637–1645* (London, 1997)

Friedrich, Karin, *The Other Prussia: Royal Prussia, Poland and Liberty, 1569–1772* (Cambridge, 2000)

Frost, Robert, *The Northern Wars: War, State and Society in North-eastern Europe, 1558–1721* (Harlow, 2001)

Ginzburg, Carlo, *Night Battles: Witchcraft and Agrarian Cults in the Sixteenth and Seventeenth Centuries* (Baltimore, 1983)

—, *The Cheese and the Worms: The Cosmos of a Sixteenth-century Miller* (Baltimore, 1992)

Glete, Jan, *Warfare at Sea, 1500–1650. Maritime Conflicts and the Transformation of Europe* (London, 2001)

—, *War and the State in Early Modern Europe. Spain, the Dutch Republic and Sweden as Fiscal-Military States, 1500–1660* (London and New York, 2002)

Goffman, Daniel, *The Ottoman Empire and Early Modern Europe* (Cambridge, 2002)

Gordon, Bruce, *The Swiss Reformation* (Manchester, 1998)

—, *Calvin* (New Haven and London, 2009)

Grafton, Anthony, *Cardano's Cosmos: The Worlds and Works of a Renaissance Astrologer* (Cambridge, MA, 1999)

Greenblatt, Stephen, *Marvellous Possessions. The Wonder of the New World* (Chicago, 1991)

Greengrass, Mark, *The Longman Companion to the European Reformation, c. 1500–1618* (London, 1998)

Gregory, Brad S., *Salvation at Stake. Christian Martyrdom in Early Modern Europe* (Cambridge, MA, 1999)

Grell, Ole Peter and Scribner, Robert W. (eds.), *Tolerance and Intolerance in the European Reformation* (Cambridge, 1996)

't Hart, Marjolein C., *The Making of a Bourgeois State. War, Politics and Finance during the Dutch Revolt* (Manchester, 1993)

Headley, John M., *Church, Empire, and World: The Quest for Universal Order, 1520–1640* (Aldershot, 1997)

— and Tomaro, John B. (eds.), *San Carlo Borromeo: Catholic Reform and Ecclesiastical Politics in the Second Half of the Sixteenth Century* (Washington, 1988)

Henderson, John, *The Renaissance Hospital Healing the Body and Healing the Soul* (Oxford, 2006)

Hillerbrand, Hans (ed.), *The Oxford Encyclopedia of the Reformation* (4 vols.) (New York and Oxford, 1996)

Hoffman, Philip T., *Growth in a Traditional Society: The French Countryside, 1450–1815* (Princeton, 1996)

Hsia, R. Po-chia, *Social Discipline in the Reformation: Central Europe 1550–1750* (London, 1989)

—, *The World of Catholic Renewal 1540–1770* (Cambridge, 1998)

— (ed.), *A Companion to the Reformation World* (Oxford, 2006)

— (ed.), *The Cambridge History of Christianity*, vol. 6. *Reform and Expansion: 1500–1660* (Cambridge, 2007)

— and Nierop, Henk van (eds.), *Calvinism and Religious Toleration in the Dutch Golden Age* (Cambridge, 2002)

Hufton, Olwen, *The Prospect Before Her: A History of Women in Western Europe*, vol. 1 *(1500–1800)* (London, 1995)

Israel, Jonathan I., *The Dutch Republic and the Hispanic World, 1606–1661* (Oxford, 1982)

—, *The Dutch Republic. Its Rise, Greatness and Fall, 1477–1806* (Oxford, 1995)

—, *Conflicts of Empires. Spain, the Low Countries and the Struggle for World Supremacy, 1585–1713* (London, 1997)

Jütte, Robert, *Poverty and Deviance in Early Modern Europe* (Cambridge, 1994)

Kamen, Henry, *Philip of Spain* (New Haven and London, 1997)

—, *Empire. How Spain Became a World Power (1492–1763)* (London, 2002)

Kaplan, Benjamin J., *Divided by Faith. Religious Conflict and the Practice of Toleration in Early Modern Europe* (Cambridge, MA, 2007)

Khodarkovsky, Michael, *Russia's Steppe Frontier: The Making of a Colonial Empire, 1500–1800* (Bloomington, 2002)

Kivelson, Valerie, *Cartographies of Tsardom: The Land and its Meanings in Seventeenth-century Russia* (Ithaca and New York, 2006)

Knecht, R. J., *Renaissance Warrior and Patron: The Reign of Francis I* (Cambridge, 1994)

—, *The Rise and Fall of Renaissance France, 1483–1610* (2nd edn, Oxford, 2001)

—, *The French Renaissance Court, 1483–1589* (New Haven and London, 2008)

Le Roy Ladurie, Emmanuel, *The French Peasantry, 1450–1660* (Aldershot, 1987)

—, *The French Royal State, 1460–1610*, trans. Juliet Vale (Oxford, 1994)

Lestringant, Frank, *Mapping the Renaissance World: The Geographical Imagination in the Age of Discovery* (Los Angeles and London, 1994)

Lloyd, Howell, Burgess, Glenn and Hodson, Simon (eds.), *European Political Thought, 1450–1700: Religion, Law and Philosophy* (New Haven and London, 2008)

Lockhart, P. D., *Denmark in the Thirty Years' War, 1618–1648: King Christian IV and the Decline of the Oldenburg State* (Selinsgrove, 1996)

—, *Denmark, 1513–1660: The Rise and Decline of a Renaissance Monarchy* (Oxford and New York, 2007)

MacCulloch, Diarmaid, *The Later Reformation in England, 1547–1603* (Houndmills, 1990)

—, *Reformation: Europe's House Divided 1490–1700* (London, 2003)

Maclean, Ian, *Logic, Signs and Nature. The Case of Learned Medicine* (Cambridge, 2007)

Mayr, Otto, *Authority, Liberty and Automatic Machinery in Early Modern Europe* (Baltimore and London, 1986)

Monod, Paul Kléber, *The Power of Kings. Monarchy and Religion in Europe,* *1589–1715* (New Haven and London, 1999)

Monter, William, *Calvin's Geneva* (New York, 1967)

—, *Ritual, Myth and Magic in Early Modern Europe* (Brighton, 1983)

—, *Judging the French Reformation. Heresy Trials by Sixteenth-Century Parlements* (Cambridge, MA, 1999)

—, *The Rise of Female Kings in Europe, 1300–1800* (New Haven and London, 2012)

Mortimer, Geoff, *Eyewitness Accounts of the Thirty Years War 1618–48* (Basingstoke, 2002)

—, *Wallenstein. The Enigma of the Thirty Years War* (Basingstoke, 2010)

Murdock, Graeme, *Calvinism on the Frontier, 1600–1800: International Calvinism and the Reformed Church in Hungary and Transylvania* (Oxford, 2000)

Nierop, Henk van, *Treason in the Northern Quarter: War, Terror, and the Rule of Law in the Dutch Revolt* (Princeton, 2009)

Oberman, Heiko A., *Luther: Man between God and the Devil* (London, 1993)

Ogilvie, Brian W., *The Science of Describing. Natural History in Renaissance Europe* (Chicago, 2006)

O'Malley, John W., *The First Jesuits* (Cambridge, MA, 1994)

—, *Trent and All That. Renaming Catholicism in the Early-Modern Era* (Cambridge, MA, 2000)

— and Bailey, Gauvin Alexander (eds.), *The Jesuits and the Arts, 1540–1773* (Philadelphia, 2003)

Ó Siochrú, Micheál, *Confederate Ireland, 1642–1649. A Constitutional and Political Analysis* (Dublin, 1999)

Pagden, Anthony, *The Fall of Natural Man: The American Indian and the Origins of Comparative Ethnology* (Cambridge, 1982)

—, *European Encounters with the New World* (New Haven and London, 1993)

—, *Lords of All the World: Ideologies of Empire in Spain, Britain and France, c. 1500–c. 1800* (New Haven and London, 1995)

Pálffy, Géza, *The Kingdom of Hungary and the Habsburg Monarchy in the Sixteenth Century* (New York, 2009)

Park, Katharine and Daston, Lorraine (eds.), *The Cambridge History of Science,* vol. 3 *(Early Modern Science)* (Cambridge, 2006)

Parker, Geoffrey, *The Army of Flanders and the Spanish Road 1567–1659: The Logistics of Spanish Victory and Defeat in the Low Countries' Wars* (Cambridge, 1972)

—, *The Dutch Revolt* (London, 1977)

—, *Spain and the Netherlands, 1559–1569* (London, 1979)

—, *The Military Revolution: Military Innovation and the Rise of the West 1500–1800* (Cambridge, 1988)

—, *The Grand Strategy of Philip II* (New Haven and London, 1998)

—, *Philip II* (Chicago, 2002)

—, *Global Crisis: War, Climate Change & Catastrophe in the Seventeenth Century* (New Haven, 2013)

— (ed.), *The Thirty Years' War* (London, 1984)

—, *Success is Never Final. Empire, War and Faith in Early Modern Europe* (London, 2002)

Parrott, David, *Richelieu's Army. War, Government and Society in France, 1624–1642* (Cambridge, 2001)

—, *The Business of War. Military Enterprise and Military Revolution in Early Modern Europe* (Cambridge, 2011)

Pettegree, Andrew (ed.), *The Early Reformation in Europe* (Cambridge, 1992)

—, *Reformation and the Culture of Persuasion* (Cambridge, 2005)

—, *The Book in the Renaissance* (New Haven and London, 2010)

— (ed.), *The Reformation World* (London, 2000)

Prestwich, Menna (ed.), *International Calvinism, 1541–1715* (Oxford, 1985)

Pullan, Brian, *Rich and Poor in Renaissance Venice: The Social Institutions of a Catholic State, to 1620* (Cambridge, MA, 1971)

Rabb, Theodore K., *The Struggle for Stability in Early Modern Europe* (Oxford, 1976)

Ranum, Orest, *Paris in the Age of Absolutism: An Essay* (New York, 1968)

—, *The Fronde. A French Revolution, 1648–1652* (New York, 1993)

Roodenburg, Herman (ed.), *Forging European Identities, 1400–1700* (Cambridge, 2007)

Roper, Lyndal, *The Holy Household: Religion, Morals and Order in Reformation Augsburg* (Oxford, 1989)

Rothman, E. Natalie, *Brokering Empire. Trans-imperial Subjects between Venice and Istanbul* (Ithaca, 2011)

Ruggiero, Guido (ed.), *A Companion to the Worlds of the Renaissance* (Oxford, 2002)

Schilling, Heinz and Tóth, István György (eds.), *Religion and Cultural Exchange in Europe, 1400–1700* (Cambridge, 2006)

Scott, Tom and Scribner, R. W. (eds.), *The German Peasants' War. A History in Documents* (Atlantic Highlands, NJ, 1991)

— (ed.), *The Peasantries of Europe: From the Fourteenth to the Eighteenth Centuries* (New York, 1998)

Scribner, R. W., *For the Sake of Simple Folk. Popular Propaganda for the German Reformation* (Cambridge, 1981)

—, *Popular Culture and Popular Movements in Reformation Germany* (London, 1987)

—, Porter, Roy and Teich, Mikuláš (eds.), *The Reformation in National Context* (Cambridge, 1994)

Seed, Patricia, *Ceremonies of Possession in Europe's Conquest of the New World, 1492–1640* (Cambridge, 1995)

Sharpe, Kevin, *The Personal Rule of Charles I* (New Haven and London, 1992)

Skinner, Quentin, *The Foundations of Modern Political Thought* (2 vols., Cambridge, 1978)

Slack, Paul, *Poverty and Policy in Tudor and Stuart England* (London and New York, 1988)

—, *The Impact of Plague in Tudor and Stuart England* (Oxford, 1990)

Soly, Hugo (ed.), *Charles V, 1500–1558, and His Time* (Antwerp, 1999)

Stein, Stanley J. and Stein, Barbara H., *Silver, Trade, and War. Spain and America in the Making of Early Modern Europe* (Baltimore and London, 2000)

Stone, Daniel, *The Polish-Lithuanian State, 1386–1795* (Seattle, 2003)

Stradling, R. A., *Philip IV and the Government of Spain, 1621–1665* (Cambridge, 1981)

—, *The Armada of Flanders: Spanish Maritime Policy and European War, 1568–1665* (Cambridge, 1992)

—, *Spain's Struggle for Europe, 1598–1668* (London, 1994)

Thompson, I. A. A. and Bartolomé Yun Casalilla (eds.), *The Castilian Crisis of the Seventeenth Century: New Perspectives on the Economic and Social History of Seventeenth-Century Spain* (Cambridge, 1994)

Tomlinson, Howard (ed.), *Before the English Civil War. Essays on Early Stuart Politics and Government* (London, 1983)

Tóth, István György, *Literacy and Written Culture in Early Modern Central Europe* (Budapest, 2000)

Tracy, James D. (ed.), *The Rise of Merchant Empires. Long-distance Trade in the Early Modern World, 1350–1750* (Cambridge, 1990)

—, *The Political Economy of Merchant Empires. State Power and World Trade (1350–1750)* (Cambridge, 1997)

—, *Emperor Charles V. Impresario of War. Campaign Strategy, International Finance, and Domestic Politics* (Cambridge, 2002)

Trevor-Roper, Hugh, *Religion, the Reformation, and Social Change* (London, 1967)

—, *Renaissance Essays* (London, 1985)

Tuck, Richard, *Philosophy and Government, 1572–1651* (Cambridge, 1993)

Vivo, Filippo di, *Information and Communication in Venice: Rethinking Early Modern Politics* (Oxford, 2007)

Vries, Jan de, *The Economy of Europe in an Age of Crisis, 1600–1750* (Cambridge, 1976)

— and van der Woude, Ad, *The First Modern Economy: Success, Failure, and Perseverance of the Dutch Economy, 1500–1815* (Cambridge, 1997)

Walsham, Alexandra, *Charitable Hatred. Tolerance and Intolerance in England, 1500–1700* (Manchester, 2005)

Walter, John and Schofield, Roger (eds.), *Famine, Disease and the Social Order in Early Modern Society* (Cambridge, 1989)

Warde, Paul, *Ecology, Economy and State Formation in Early Modern Germany* (Cambridge, 2006)

Webster, Charles, *From Paracelsus to Newton. Magic and the Making of Modern Science* (Cambridge, 1982)

Weiss, Gillian, *Captives and Corsairs: France and Slavery in the Early Modern Mediterranean* (Stanford, 2012)

Whaley, Joachim, *Germany and the Holy Roman Empire*, vol. 1: *Maximilian I to the Peace of Westphalia, 1493–1648* (Oxford, 2012)

Wieczynski, J. A., *The Russian Frontier: The Impact of Borderlands upon the Course of Early Russian History* (Charlottesville, VA, 1976)

Wiesner-Hanks, Merry E., *Women and Gender in Early Modern Europe* (Cambridge, 2008)

Wilson, Peter H., *Europe's Tragedy. A History of the Thirty Years War* (London, 2009)

Wormald, Jenny, *Court, Kirk, and Community. Scotland, 1470–1625* (London, 1981)

Yates, Frances A., *The Rosicrucian Enlightenment* (London, 1972)

—, *Astraea. The Imperial Theme in the Sixteenth Century* (London, 1975)

Index

(*r.* = regnal dates of leading rulers)

(*r.* 1603–25), 9, 59, 134, 138, 146,
215–16, 305, 457, 527, 536, 540, 565,
573–4, 576, 589, 602
Jamestown, 156
Jankau, Battle of (1645), 559, 618
Janssens (Jansenius), Corneille, 486
Japan, 467–8, 490
Jarnac, Battle of (1569), 405, 420
Java, 164
Jeanne d'Albret, queen of Navarre
(*r.* 1556–72), 402, 405–6, 427, 601
Jerez, Francisco, 180
Jerusalem, 9, 12, 29, 124, 301, 479
Jesuits, 8, 162, 191, 220, 230, 453, 477,
462, 479–81, 528, 582–3, 593, 607,
648, 651
and Christian missions, 255, 466
and education, 212, 214, 246
Jews, xxvii, 81, 116, 328, 351, 381, 454,
501, 628, 651
anti-Semitism, 328
Ashkenazim, 449
Karaite, 449
Sephardic, 142
Joachim of Fiore, 500
Joachimstal, 105, 381
Joanna, queen of Castile and León
(*r.* 1504–55) and Aragon (1516–55),
264, 267, 278, 280
Johann Casimir, count palatine of
Simmern, 447
Johann Frederick, elector of Saxony
(*r.* 1532–47), 383
Johann Georg, elector of Saxony
(*r.* 1611–56), 617
Johann Mauritz, prince of Nassau-Siegen,
169, 192
Johann VI, count of Nassau, 446
John II Casimir, king of Poland
(*r.* 1648–68), 648
John III, king of Portugal
(*r.* 1521–57), 305
John the Constant, elector of Saxony
(*r.* 1525–32), 345, 350
John Zápolya, voivode of Transylvania
(*r.* 1511–40) and king of Hungary
(*r.* 1526–40), 264, 299, 302–3

John Sigismund Zápolya, voivode of
Transylvania (*r.* 1556–71) and king of
Hungary (*r.* 1556/9–71), 498
Johnston, Archibald, 655
John-William, duke of Cleves, Jülich and
Berg, 580
Joinville, 425
Jonson, Ben, 536
Josselin, Ralph, 669
Jost
Lienhard, 372
Ursula, 372
Jud, Leo, 339
Jülich-Cleves succession dispute, 566,
581, 586
Julius II, Pope (*r.* 1503–13), 103, 269, 275,
283, 503
Julius, duke of Brunswick-Wolfenbüttel,
205
Junta de Reformación, 623
Jüterbog, Battle of (1643), 619

Kabbalah, 195, 199–200, 328
Kappel am Albis, 339
Kappel wars, 440
Karl II of Austria, Archduke, 444, 581–2
Kassel, 207
Kelley, Edward. *See* Talbot, Edward
Kent, 71
Kepler, Johannes, 199–200, 219,
223–4, 566
Kern, Leonhard, 620
Kežmarok, 381
Khlesl, Melchior, 584, 586
Khmelnytsky, Bohdan, 23, 651–3
Kiev, 175
Kildare rebellion, 92
Kipper-und Wipperzeit, 120
Kircher, Athanasius, 192
Kirkby Malham, 132
Klis, 263
Knäred, Peace of (1613), 566, 596
Knights of Malta (of St John of Jerusalem),
301
Knipperdollinck, Berndt, 377
Knox, John, 306, 432, 455
Köbel, Jacob, 44